REX'S RX

IT'S A WONDERFUL LIFE: "Frank Capra's durable c⬛⬛⬛ ⬛⬛⬛ an inspiration for g⬛⬛ ⬛⬛⬛ new magic with e⬛⬛ ⬛⬛⬛rized.' I deplore this ⬛⬛⬛ ⬛⬛⬛ith Christmas trees, ⬛⬛⬛ *⬛⬛erful Life* is one of the rare ⬛⬛⬛ enhanced by color. It's a movie to treasure."

THE SILENCE OF THE LAMBS: "It's the scariest American movie since *Psycho*. The first time I saw *The Silence of the Lambs* I sat next to a teenage girl who spent most of the film with her head buried in my raincoat. The second time, I sat next to a sophisticated critic who covered her face with her notebook, pleading 'Tell me when it's safe to look.' The finale is unforgettable, and so is the film—black, hair-frying, a masterwork of unbearable maximum anxiety and tension that will leave you limp as a dead butterfly's wing."

LOVE STORY: "Computer-programmed emotionalism. . . . *Love Story* shines only through the radiant performances of Ryan O'Neal and Ali MacGraw, who hold the whole mess together admirably without benefit of helpful direction, camera work, or dialogue. It is their charm and sincerity—helping to make the audience forget it's being had—that turns *Love Story* into a life story."

BLUE VELVET: "In the brain-damaged garbage department, *Blue Velvet* gives pretentiousness new meaning. It should score high with the kind of sickos who like to smell dirty socks and pull wings off butterflies, but there's nothing here for sane audiences.

"Critics are something else. Some of them like kinkiness and incoherence. One is quoted with this doozie: 'You've never seen anything like it in your life!' That's true. And I never want to see anything like it again."

1992-1993 Edition

Rex Reed's Guide to Movies on TV & Video

A DOVE BOOK

WARNER BOOKS

A Time Warner Company

WARNER BOOKS EDITION

Cover design by Anne Twomey
Cover photograph by Peter Cunningham

Warner Books, Inc.
1271 Avenue of the Americas
New York, NY 10020

Ⓦ A Time Warner Company

Printed in the United States of America

First Printing: November, 1992

10 9 8 7 6 5 4 3 2 1

To the faceless millions of moviegoers who share my passion for life on the screen . . . who grew up, like me, shaped and moved by countless hours in the dark . . . who loved the movies then, still do, and always will . . .

This book is for you.

REX REED

Rex Reed's Guide to Movies on TV & Video

ABSENCE OF MALICE (1981)

★ ★ ★ ½ Directed and produced by Sydney Pollack. Screenplay by Kurt Luedtke. With Paul Newman, Sally Field, Bob Balaban, Melinda Dillon, Wilford Brimley, and John Harkins.

In a plastic world of packaged formulas, when movies dealing with issues and ideas are as rare as one of grandma's home-baked pie crusts made from scratch, it is indeed a pleasure to be able to say something positive for a change about something coming out of Hollywood. *Absence of Malice* is a film worthy of praise. It is timely, provocative, brilliantly written, acted, and directed—and it will stick to your ribs the way few movies do these days.

Sally Field plays a Miami reporter who has been working for the city's leading paper three years. She needs a scoop. Nothing much is happening, so she decides to check into the latest developments on a case involving the mysterious disappearance of a local union boss. (Unsolved police cases are always good for a few columns of page 3 copy.) Overhearing some gossip about a local liquor wholesaler whose name is being mentioned in the case as a possible suspect in the case, she decides to print the rumor. Paul Newman plays the innocent man who suddenly reads his name in the paper involved with a scandal that could possibly lead to a murder rap. Before he can establish an alibi or plead not guilty, his business is ruined by the longshoreman's union, his reputation is smeared, and his best friend commits suicide.

"Do you think this is right?" he asks. "I'm never sure what's right," says the reporter. "I just print the truth and let someone else figure out what's right." Reporters can obviously never be trusted with a confidence, but this movie probes even deeper than that into the issues facing the press today. The question "Does the press overstep its power?" is only part of the complex problem.

You get an honest, unvarnished close-up of journalism and how it works as *Absence of Malice* takes you into the makeup department, smoke-filled city room, and even the microfilm lab of a big-city newspaper. (Interiors were actually filmed inside the *Miami Herald*.) You get the dilemma reporters face when torn between human instinct and doing their jobs. And you get the hopeless frustration, confusion, and rage of the people who see their whole lives spread naked in banner headlines and gossip columns.

It's a tangled web that a lot of people are reexamining as more and more journalists get called to task for misrepresenting facts, making up stories, printing misleading information, and ruining lives in the process. Even if your feelings are ambivalent on the subject, you'll find *Absence of Malice* a spellbinding, compelling, lacerating film that will make you search your own conscience and ask yourself questions about the press in the way *Prince of the City* made you rethink everything you ever felt about cops.

Sally Field is not a villain. She's a good reporter. Her big mistake is her eagerness to make a name for herself in a profession where the printed word can make byline celebrities out of faceless reporters at the expense of innocent bystanders. She's a patsy, too, since her information has been planted by corrupt politicians to pacify an anxiety-ridden public. Her ambition leads her to front-page glory even though she didn't check her facts or do her homework.

Her problems increase when she falls in love with the man she's trying to expose. Paul Newman's problem is clearing his name without destroying her credibility and her career. Everybody gets hurt, nobody walks off into a Technicolor rainbow with the loose ends neatly tied together. But in the end you'll learn something fascinating and vital about your own society and how it works. Journalists do have power—deservedly so—but they are part of the system we all live by, too. They're human beings. They're not above the law any more than the President is, but are subject to individual judgments under the same laws as everyone else.

Newman reclaims his kingpin status as the screen's greatest leading man—strong, vulnerable, concerned, intelligent, durable. Sally Field delivers another of her appealing three-dimensional portraits of young contemporary American women—aggressive, smart, little-girl tough. Under Sydney Pollack's resourceful direction, they form the most magnetic team of decent people trapped by the system the screen has presented in years.

Absence of Malice is a film that not only finds them at the top of their artistic form, but gives them something meaty and meaningful to shake us out of our complacency. It works splendidly on many levels—as an exposé of political corruption and greed, as a forum for different opinions on press abuse, and as a compassionate love story. It will shock and disturb you, but you'll come away thinking.

THE ACCIDENTAL TOURIST (1988)

★ ★ ★ ★ Directed by Lawrence Kasdan. Screenplay by Frank Galati and Kasdan. Produced by Kasdan, Charles Okun, and Michael Grillo. With William Hurt, Kathleen Turner, Geena Davis, Amy Wright, Bill Pullman, Robert Gorman, David Ogden Stiers, and Ed Begley, Jr.

The Accidental Tourist is a lovely, quirky movie so unique it manages to be intelligent, funny, deeply moving, and a work of art all at the same time. Lawrence Kasdan's brilliant and faithful rendering of the Anne Tyler novel is for viewers who demand a bit more from a movie than special effects and noise. The offbeat hero is a glum travel writer who wanders the globe without feeling any connection to the places or people he encounters. In a sensational performance, William Hurt is Macon Leary from Boston, a writer of guidebooks for weary business travelers, or "accidental tourists." He's tired and drawn, with a sickly pallor and dead eyes—deeply

traumatized by the death of his son, trapped in his own dreary prison of remorse. Even his dog is neurotic. Geena Davis won a Supporting Oscar as the space cadet dog trainer who teaches this man how to live again, and Kathleen Turner, in a small but rewarding role, is the wife who learns to appreciate him only after she's lost him.

The Accidental Tourist is about the dark recesses of the human heart and the unpredictable nature of relationships. It's a moment-to-moment movie, full of small insights and big feelings—with another miraculous performance by William Hurt that proves why he's this generation's most consummate screen actor. Offbeat, distinguished, and unforgettable.

THE ACCUSED (1988)

★ ★ ★ ½ Directed by Jonathan Kaplan. Screenplay by Tom Topor. Produced by Stanley R. Jaffe and Sherry Lansing. With Jodie Foster, Kelly McGillis, Bernie Coulson, Leo Rossi, Ann Hearn, Carmen Argenziano, Steve Antin, Tom O'Brien, and Peter Van Norden.

Based on the true story of a woman who was gang-raped in a bar while the patrons watched and cheered, The Accused is a scalding look at both the dehumanizing consequences of rape and the judicial system itself.

This time the victim, beautifully acted by Jodie Foster, is a feisty tart with a salty tongue who refuses to be floated through the criminal courts like a statistic. Her honesty touches a chord in the heartstrings of the assistant district attorney (Kelly McGillis), prompting her to press on with the investigation after the case is closed. The second half of the film is a precedent-setting trial in which McGillis prosecutes the witnesses to determine if onlookers who encourage a felony are as criminally responsible as the perpetrators. Braving the community and McGillis's superiors, these two women open up new ways to look at the treatment of rape victims as second-class citizens in a so-called civilized society.

The Accused is not for children; the rape scene is particularly brutal and ugly. But it holds the attention of a mature audience on several levels. I admired the way Tom Topor's script avoided sanitizing the Jodie Foster character to make her more sympathetic. And Jodie Foster's mesmerizing performance makes her trashy, tough, and sexually precocious. But is that any justification for violence? You may not like her, but you'll be rooting for her right to justice. *The Accused* is also about friendship between two people from opposite sides of the law and society, and the two stars play their polarization with a humanity that connects in a surprising way. This is a powerful film that sweeps you up in its tension and excitement, and makes you think about the world you live in and the people who share it with you.

AFTER HOURS (1985)
★ 1/2 Directed by Martin Scorsese. Screenplay by Joseph Minion. Produced by Amy Robinson. *With Griffin Dunne, Rosanna Arquette, Verna Bloom, Cheech Marin and Thomas Chong, Linda Fiorentino, Teri Garr, John Heard, Catherine O'Hara, Dick Miller, Will Patton, and Robert Plunket.*

Do you have days when nothing goes right, when you feel disoriented, when everything around you is strange and you seem to be living in a nightmare from which you can't wake up? If you live in New York, these feelings come with the territory, and that's the subject of *After Hours*, a black comedy by Martin Scorsese that is so bizarre and loopy it defies ordinary description.

After Hours is the ultimate New York nightmare of the eighties. I guess you could call it a black comedy. It is very black indeed, though rarely funny. Mostly it's interesting because it signals a radical departure for director Scorsese, who usually puts his fist where his camera should be. This is not a recommendation, unless you're the kind of person who enjoys watching freaks twitching on the IRT and calls it subway art.

It's an exaggerated study of what happens when an uptown New Yorker finds himself in the wrong downtown neighborhood on a rainy night with only 97 cents in his pocket and can't get home. For Paul Hackett, a dull yuppie nerd who teaches people in offices how to use word processors, the trip from East 91st Street to the bowels of Soho turns into a voyage to an alien planet inhabited by the kind of people the rest of us only read about in publications like *Details*.

Paul's nightmare adventure begins, like many things do in New York on rainy nights, with a chance encounter in a coffee shop. Paul is sitting there, reading Henry Miller, when he meets a pretty wacko who tells him where he can buy a far-out plaster of paris bagel-and-cream cheese paperweight. Like most yuppie squares, Paul's got nothing better to do,

so he follows this peculiar Alice down the rabbit hole to a loft in Soho. Instead of a nice sexy adventure in a new environment, the gullible dope finds himself trapped in a hostile element of all-night decadence, surrounded by weirdos who make the Mad Hatter's tea party look like a needlepoint lecture at the Rhode Island School of Design.

First there's Rosanna Arquette as the neurotic girl who lures Paul to the hell that lies below Houston Street. After describing a six-hour rape, she confides that she broke off her marriage because her husband yelled "Surrender, Dorothy!" every time they had sex. This girl collects first-aid manuals for burn victims. Then there's her kinky roommate (Linda Fiorentino), who sculpts nude men out of paste and real twenty-dollar bills, wanders around the loft topless, and collects sadists who tie her to the furniture, bound and gagged like her own sculptures.

This is the wrong kind of encounter session, even for a displaced person like Paul, but every time he tries to haul it back uptown to the safety of bag ladies and Charivari boutiques, the film turns into another vignette that delays action and pads out the running time.

Before the nightmare ends, Paul has culture-clashed with two burglars (Cheech and Chong), a morose bartender (John Heard) whose girl has just committed suicide, a demented waitress (Teri Garr) who invites him up for a TV dinner, a lonely homosexual (Robert Plunket) who chooses Paul for his first gay experience, and a mob of murderous punk vigilantes wearing Mohawk haircuts whose gang leader is a girl who drives an ice cream truck. Why Paul doesn't call a friend with his 97 cents to come downtown and rescue him is a blazing question that plagued me throughout, but common sense is not one of the strong points in a Martin Scorsese film. Maybe the point he's making is that yuppies have no friends. Just wondering.

This is not a movie. It's a series of classroom exercises from a zoned-out acting school that specializes in surrealism for fun and profit. The plot is similar to *Desperately Seeking Susan*, but it has no attitude. Scorsese's sledgehammer style robs the oddball material, written by Joseph Minion, of any real humor. The pivotal role of Paul is nicely played by Griffin Dunne, a gifted young actor with an expression of perpetual confusion, but since he has been directed to react instead of act, there isn't much in the performance a sane audience can identify with.

The result is too queer to be boring, but if I'm ever asked to repeat the experience, I think I'll call in sick.

AGNES OF GOD (1985)
★ ★ ★ ½ Directed by Norman Jewison. Screenplay by John Pielmeier, based on his stage play. Produced by Patrick Palmer and Jewison. *With Jane Fonda, Anne Bancroft, Meg Tilly.*

On stage, *Agnes of God* was a powerful, persuasive drama about faith and miracles, among other things, that provided three fine actresses (Elizabeth Ashley, Geraldine Page, and Amanda Plummer) with an emotionally charged vehicle for their secular talents. The result was theatrical fireworks.

The movie version of *Agnes of God* reduces some of the sizzling fireworks to soggy firecrackers, but it's still a three-woman show in which the stars sparkle longer than the wet fuses they ignite.

Based on a true incident, *Agnes of God* tells of the tragic events surrounding the birth of a baby in a Catholic convent of cloistered nuns. The mother is Sister Agnes, a young novice who has murdered the infant at birth by strangling it with the umbilical cord, then concealed her crime by stuffing the baby's corpse into a trash basket. Innocent, unworldly, uneducated, Sister Agnes has never read a book or seen a TV show. She didn't even know she was pregnant. Now she doesn't remember the delivery, much less the conception, of the dead baby.

Jane Fonda is the court-appointed psychiatrist assigned to determine whether the young nun is sane enough to stand trial for murder. Anne Bancroft is the mother superior—watchful, protective, and enraged by this intrusion from the outside world. Meg Tilly is the haunted, suffering novitiate. All three are riveting.

Norman Jewison has opened up the play from its original set of an office with two chairs and an ashtray to create the strange, antiseptic environment of a cloistered Quebec convent, leading the movie audience on a guided tour from the bell tower to the basement. Then he contrasts the Spartan serenity of the convent with the bustle of downtown Montreal, to point up the sharp and dramatic differences between religious and secular society.

Sven Nykvist's gloomy but delicate cinematography wraps the whole thing in an ethereal glow of Canadian winter through which no sun filters. From the eerily beautiful voices of nuns singing through vespers to soul-searching close-ups of the actresses' faces, everything possible has been done to transform *Agnes of God* into a film of substance. It never quite makes it.

Despite the artistry on display, the central problem that plagued the play remains. John Pielmeier, who has adapted his own drama for the screen, has written a mystery story in which the mystery is never satisfactorily solved. Where did the baby come from? Who was the father? Was it God? Is Sister Agnes a murderer?

There are no answers to these vital questions, and to make matters more confusing, the film mixes in a lot of mystical allusions to the dark forces in religion and psychoanalysis that don't quite jell, either.

The comparisons to *Equus* are obvious. The young nun says the baby was divinely inspired. The mother superior pleads with the doctor to keep an open mind about immaculate conceptions. The shrink, rooted in the soil of logic, not only knows there's no such thing as a virgin birth but is herself a lapsed Catholic who can never bear children because of an abortion, making it difficult for her to show objectivity. With the tortured, half-mad young nun at the center of the triangle, we get the older nun fighting for her spiritual health and the hard-edged doctor fighting for her mental health. Anne Bancroft represents the mysteries of God, as Jane Fonda represents the cynicism of logic and reason, while Meg Tilly, as Sister Agnes, revives the possibility of miracles in us all.

I find myself on the doctor's side. I can't buy the miracle. But settling back to watch three dynamic actresses going at each other like cats attacking a sparerib, I had a fine time. The chemistry between Fonda and Bancroft fairly explodes with kinetic energy. It's odd to see a health and physical fitness freak like Fonda chain-smoking (not to disillusion followers of her Jane Fonda workout books and videos, Jane announced that the cigarettes are fakes) but gratifying to see how thoroughly she throws herself into the role. In her desperate need to comprehend the strangeness of the cloistered convent world around her and find her own salvation in the process, Fonda works furiously to snap free from the worldly knowledge that chains her to reality, attack and upheaval simmering beneath the surface of her cool,

classical career-girl veneer. She is really an amazing technician, and Bancroft and Tilly swirl around her with their own confined passion untilthe screen fills with dramatic intensity.

Even if *Agnes of God* leaves you restless and troubled, you won't be bored by the acting. The film is to these three superb ladies what a jam session is to jazz musicians. I don't know how many reasons you need to see a movie these days, but here are three good ones.

AIRPLANE! (1980)
★ 1/2 Directed and written by Jim Abrahams, David Zucker, and Jerry Zucker. Produced by Howard W. Koch. With *Robert Hays, Julie Hagerty, Lloyd Bridges, Peter Graves, Leslie Nielsen, Robert Stack, Kareem Abdul-Jabbar, Barbara Billingsley, and Ethel Merman.*

Real comedy is in short supply these days, and *Airplane!* does nothing to relieve the gloom. This spoof of all those corny *Airport* movies starts out funny (the tail of the plane sifts through dark clouds like a shark's fin churning through the moonlit surf in *Jaws*) and ends up assaulting the senses with sick jokes ad nauseam. Bereft of ideas, it just steals everybody else's until it's the audience that gets mugged.

Trans-American's Flight 209 leaves the ground from Los Angeles to Chicago with more nuts on board than you'll find in a pecan pie. The voice for the white-zone parking has a fight with the voice for the red-zone parking and the idea is funny.

But once all the loonies board the plane and everyone establishes a character identity through some kind of sophomoric sight gag, there isn't much left but to wonder which old movie the next cliché will come from. There's a singing nun, a girl who needs a heart transplant in six hours, a gay pilot with a hunger for the little boys who visit his cockpit, some religious zealots, a doctor whose nose grows like Pinocchio's when he lies, and other assorted fraternity-house inventions that come off like rejected ideas from the Harvard *Lampoon*.

When they all get food poisoning from the fish course and a terrible storm appears, it's up to the stewardess to fly the plane in the noble Karen Black tradition, with the aid of her boyfriend, an ex-fighter pilot who is now afraid of planes.

Back in the control tower, a similar group of zanies are calling the shots by radio, led by Robert Stack, who removes his sunglasses to reveal . . . a smaller pair of sunglasses underneath.

While the air controllers play computer basketball on radar screens, Dr. Leslie Nielsen takes a look at his dying passengers and sighs: "Haven't seen anything like this since the Anita Bryant concert."

In flashback, we see substitute pilot Robert Hays so rattled by the shell-shocked officer in his hospital ward who thinks he's Ethel Merman (the officer rises up in bed to sing "Everything's Coming Up Roses" and it's Ethel Merman herself in drag) that he gives up flying and hosts Tupperware parties for the natives in Africa.

A group of press photographers moves into the chaotic control tower back in Chicago. "Okay, boys, let's take some pictures!" says one of the cameramen, and the others take the pictures from the wall and leave. "We're running out of time!" yells the stewardess, and the movie runs out of gas before the airplane does.

Airplane! is the brainchild of three comedy writers from Milwaukee who began their careers with a cretinous mess called *The Kentucky Fried Movie*, and have graduated to the sophomoric level of *Naked Gun* and *Naked Gun 2½* In *Airplane!* they assembled some Abbott &

Costello routines that some-times make you laugh out of pure silliness, but when some-body says the you-know-what will hit the fan and there's a close-up of you-know-what hit-ting the fan, then it's time for a barf bag.

The satire lacks sharp focus, the gags misfire badly, and *Air-plane!* needs to go back to the hangar for an overhaul.

ALICE IN WONDERLAND (1951/ Rerelease 1981)

★ ★ ★ ★ Directed by Clyde Geronimi, Hamilton Luske, Wilfred Jackson. Screenplay by a staff of thirteen Disney writers. Produced by Walt Disney. With the voices of Kathryn Beaumont, Ed Wynn, Sterling Holloway, Verna Felton, Richard Haydn, Jerry Colonna, and Bill Thompson.

It took me only thirty years to catch up with *Alice in Won-derland.* What a fool I was to wait so long. The dreamy, beautifully animated Walt Dis-ney canvas of fairy tale whimsy is well worth the wait.

You can't fool the kids to-day. They've seen *Roger Rab-bit* and been exposed to so much brutality, violence, sex, and condescending cartoon fare on TV that they will not sit still for anything second-rate. I in-vited a group of youngsters to watch *Alice* with me, not know-ing what to expect and fearing the worst from them and from myself. What a happy surprise we had. I loved the movie and they were enchanted. The only sounds from the peanut gallery were oohs, aahs and giggles of rapture and occasional ap-plause. They were riveted to the screen and they didn't even need popcorn.

Not many children's movies hold up that well. Not even all of Disney's hold up that well. *Alice in Wonderland* is some-thing very special, indeed.

It started more than a century ago when a girl named Alice Pleasance Liddell asked Lewis Carroll to tell her a story with a bit of nonsense in it. The result made literary history and, with all due respect to the other film and theatrical versions of the past decades, the Disney ani-mated cartoon version made history, too. More than a mil-lion drawings were made for the film and a production staff of 750 artists worked three years to complete it.

The result is not the homely little Victorian girl from Sir John Tenniel's illustrations for the Lewis Carroll books, but a golden-haired second cousin to Cinderella and all the other Dis-ney princesses. And the musi-cal sentiments she expresses, in the lovely songs and through the dulcet tones of Kathryn Beaumont's off-screen voice, run more to "Bluebirds, friendly how-de-do birds" than the dour philosophy set forth in the "Alice" stories. So Disney took liberties. So who's complaining?

The rest of the goofy characters follow Alice and make tuneful, ginger-peachy contributions.

Following the White Rabbit down the rabbit hole, Alice discovers a world that would captivate even Lewis Carroll. There's a doorknob with a nose. There's Tweedledum and Tweedledee, with heliotrope cravats, and the Walrus and the Carpenter luring that poor family of dopey oysters with their talk of cabbages and kings and sealing wax.

I loved the bread-and-butterflies, and especially the Mome Raths, honking and scooting about like car horns gone berserk in Tulgey Woods.

The fabulous Mad Hatter, a marvelous goofy lunatic, cavorts about in the unmistakable voice of the late, lamented Ed Wynn, while the Cheshire Cat, with its accordion teeth, its removable head, its pink nose, and its annoying way of confusing Alice just when she needs him most, is Sterling Holloway.

Nor will I soon forget Richard Haydn's snooty, conceited Caterpillar, an adroitly complicated snob who perches on his leaf, smokes his hookah, and blows superior letters at Alice like "OOO . . . RRR . . . UUU?" These were the days when the Disney studios were really cooking, and if you can't tell the difference between the creations of real art they were turning out then as compared with the dull, movable line drawings they're offering now, then you just flunked Technique Appreciation.

How we've changed since the good old days. Potheads, dopers, and cynical social commentators now find all sorts of rude things lurking behind the nursery school charm and innocence of *Alice in Wonderland*. Some folks even insist it's the first great "head" movie, and wouldn't think of seeing it again without being stoned. When the flowers snub Alice because they think she's a weed from some alien garden, some folks insist the story is a mask for racial intolerance and bigotry. Others point to references to drugs, such as hallucinatory mushrooms and hashish.

Children, who sometimes display more imagination and wisdom than adults, will have a grand time letting Disney's imagery wash over them. And even if your tastes are more demanding, you'll still appreciate the immaculate cinematography, the dandy songs, the luscious Technicolor, and the friendly pacing. Don't wait thirty years to experience *Alice in Wonderland*. See it now— and if possible, see it with some young friends. They might teach you things you never knew. They know everything that goes on through the looking glass, and they don't know a thing about Freud.

ALIENS (1986)

★ ★ ½ Directed and written by James Cameron. Produced by Gale Anne Hurd. With Sigourney Weaver, Michael Biehn, Carrie Henn, Paul Reiser, Lance Henriksen, and Jenette Goldstein.

The sensational response to 1979's *Alien* was due to the oozing, snapping, reptilian creature that ripped its way out of John Hurt's chest.

Well, hold on to something sturdy. In *Aliens*, the inevitable sequel, it happens to just about everybody.

Aliens, another futuristic horror movie in outer space, is even more horrible than you might imagine. In the original, a group of astronauts poked around too long on an obviously treacherous planet, got zapped by pulsating pods, and ended up with indigestion, screaming bloody murder as their bodies exploded with creatures the size of Jackie Gleason.

Sigourney Weaver, the only survivor, now emerges from a thermal sleep after fifty-seven years. Her headaches and nightmares are completely understandable, but what I find baffling is that after fifty-seven years, she still hasn't kicked the smoking habit.

Never mind. Writer-director James Cameron has to get the story moving somehow, so he devises the ominous plot to get poor, hysterical Sigourney back to LV-426, the hideous planet where the horrors began. No way, José, says Weaver. But in the fifty-seven years she's been playing Rip Van Winkle, the planet has been colonized. Now the people have mysteriously disappeared and Sigourney is dispatched to check it out.

Object: Locate and destroy acid-spewing, flesh-eating mutations before they multiply.

Equipped with high-tech artillery, tanks, lasers, and the latest in intergalactic combat weapons, Weaver and the space marines take a full forty-five minutes to reach the deserted space station. The only survivor, a little girl who has been living in the underground pipes, leads them to horrors the mind cannot fathom, and the rest of this two-hour-and-fifteen-minute wallow in stomach churning special effects piles on the gore with unsparing disregard for the audience's digestive system.

Will the spaceship be able to leave before the power blows everyone to pieces? Will Sigourney rescue the child from the queen of the monsters, a cross between Grace Jones and a five-hundred-ton praying mantis? Whatever it is laying the eggs that produce these slimy creatures is what you wait for, and when you finally see it, nothing in movie history that I can recall will fully prepare you for the shock. Any way you slice it, *Aliens* is not for the fainthearted.

Everyone bleeds, vomits, spews blood, and agonizes unspeakably until the audience becomes desensitized to the violence and carnage.

Aliens is sometimes visually captivating, but much more often murky and oppressive. James Cameron directs with a penchant for strobe lights and prolonged stalking. The visual effects are fantastic, but the story gets lost in a feverish effort to score mountainous effects with molehill material.

It is clear from the start that Sigourney Weaver needs her pals from *Ghostbusters* along for the ride. In any case, do not see it after a meal. Or before one, either.

ALTERED STATES (1980)

★ ★ ★ ½ Directed by Ken Russell. Screenplay by Sidney Aaron (Paddy Chayevsky). Produced by Howard Gottfried. With William Hurt, Blair Brown, Bob Balaban, Charles Haid, Thaao Penghlis, and Miguel Godreau.

Altered States is a powerful, terrifying, suspenseful, mind-blowing movie that provides the great actor William Hurt with a memorable vehicle for his formidable debut and gives the audience a jolt of electricity they won't soon forget.

Based on the novel by Paddy Chayevsky and directed by the usually uncontrollable Ken Russell, *Altered States* shows what can happen when a young medical student, for scientific reasons, submerges himself—under the influence of mind-altering drugs—in a tank filled with lukewarm water. At first he sees sex as a mystical experience, then imagines himself crucified on a cross, then emerges in a state of rapture. Years later, in Boston, he's married to a fellow student (Blair Brown) and is the father of two kids. He's still crazy and, between teaching classes at Harvard Medical School, he's still determined to follow in the footsteps of such early experimenters with drugs as Timothy Leary, Aldous Huxley, and Dr. John Lilly to see just how far a man can go in altered states of consciousness to bridge the gap between genetic chemistry and total madness.

Believing that everyone is searching for his or her own true "self" in order to find God and the meaning of life, Hurt, as Dr. Eddie Jessup, sacrifices his marriage, his children, and almost sacrifices his own sanity by eating hallucinogenic mushrooms, regressing in the water tank to a simian state, then to that of an anthropoid, and then to that of a caveman.

In the last transfer, he reverts to the womb and achieves an embryonic state that unravels the clues to evolution—and he almost loses his life in the process. What Chayevsky has written (the screenplay is also by him, but a pseudonym appears in the credits for reasons only his agent understands) is a contemporary *Dr. Jekyll and Mr. Hyde* mixed with the Faust legend and flavored with a bit of the Incredible Hulk. The result will fry your hair.

It is the subject matter, of course, that gives the flamboyant Ken Russell a perfect opportunity to impose his wild imagination in cinematic terms, and the special effects are the best since *2001: A Space Odyssey*.

Always believable, likable, and fascinating, Hurt alternates between guilty mortal and mad scientist with minimal pain to the terrified audience. He is a most gifted actor and this film was the beginning of a major career.

To the lay mind, a lot of scientific dialogue seems clinical and confusing, but even when the film turns wilder than an Aztec slumber party it is magnificently documented and based on real scientific experiments that are continuing— with a great deal of alarm to the scientific community.

When Hurt discovers no absolute truth and that life is transitory, the message seems disappointing to sci-fi fans and to freaks who expected more, but the "only-love-is-real" point of the ending is just what most of the survivors of the sixties will tell you, too.

Hurt learns that, for all of his harrowing experiences, love is the only reality worth having. In this sense, *Altered States* is a highly moral film that makes a profound statement about the horror it puts its audience through.

It is far and away one of Ken Russell's best films—ambitious, frightening, visually exciting—absorbing without overreaching or overstating. This time he found the perfect formula for blending all the right elements of social drama, fantasy, science fiction, melodrama, and horror in a single film with a language of its own. A devastating movie!

ALWAYS (1989)

★ ★ ½ Directed by Steven Spielberg. Screenplay by Jerry Belson. Produced by Spielberg, Kathleen Kennedy, and Frank Marshall. With Richard Dreyfuss, Holly Hunter, John Goodman, and Audrey Hepburn.

Always is the pale and sappy remake of Steven Spielberg's favorite love story, *A Guy Named Joe*, the classic with Spencer Tracy and Irene Dunne. Richard Dreyfuss and Holly Hunter can't fill their shoes, but hey, it's got aerial action, forest fires, and Audrey Hepburn. What's so terrible? And if you believe true love is for always—lasting even after death—this romantic fable will give you something affirmative to think about. There's enough depressing stuff around. This one will make you feel good.

AMADEUS (1984)

★ ★ ½ Directed by Milos Forman. Screenplay by Peter Shaffer. Produced by Saul Zaentz. With F. Murray Abraham, Tom Hulce, Elizabeth Berridge, Simon Callow, Roy Dotrice, Christine Ebersole, and Jeffrey Jones.

Wolfgang Amadeus Mozart died mysteriously in 1791. Thirty-two years later a mediocre, forgotten composer named Antonio Salieri attempted suicide and was dragged off to an insane asylum claiming to be the man who murdered him.

How much is truth and how much is fantasy? What really happened? These are the questions Milos Forman addresses in *Amadeus*, the big, expensive, but ultimately exhausting film Peter Shaffer has adapted from his London and Broadway stage successes.

The questions don't matter. In *Amadeus*, the lavish style in which they're posed steals the show. Filmed at gargantuan expense in Prague, the film drips with opulence in its recreation of eighteenth-century Vienna.

From the howling madhouse where Salieri tells the story in flashback to a visiting priest, to the masked balls of the royal court, *Amadeus* spares no cost in filling the screen with flashy sets, glittering costumes, and what seems like more extras than there were subjects in the Austrian Empire. If it's majesty you're after, *Amadeus* is a visual treat.

Why, then, is it often such a big yawn? Hard to say. The story is interesting enough. As the past unravels across the gnarled creases of Salieri's mind, we see the parallel lives: Mozart, a rich, privileged fop and self-pronounced child prodigy who wrote his first symphony at seven, destined to be celebrated forever, and Salieri, the poor boy who never achieved the same level of fame, fortune, or immortality and is now forgotten except for the Shaffer play.

We see the powdered, giggling Mozart, a ridiculous mess, work his way up to a cherished position in the court, while Salieri watches his own position as official court composer usurped by the arrogant young visitor from Salzburg. As Salieri is ridiculed by the obnoxious brat Mozart in front of his own king, the first seeds of hate are sown almost from the two composers' introduction. Missing no opportunity to wreck his rival's career and ruin his health, Salieri simultaneously worships him as a musical genius. Thus we have the tragedy of a mediocre talent surpassed by a great talent who was a mediocre person.

Salieri constructs the ultimate revenge against Mozart's God-given talent. He anonymously commissions the brilliant composer to write a requiem mass, then plans to murder him and unveil the mass at Mozart's funeral, claiming the work as his own.

How the plan goes awry is part of the film's ironic finale. Ultimately, Forman and Shaffer present us not only the story but the dual themes of mediocrity vs. genius and man vs. God. Whew! There's enough high-mindedness here to fill three movies, and there are times when that's exactly what *Amadeus* is.

With all the pomp and pageantry, there are painfully dull stretches, especially the midsection of the film, which includes some clumsy stagings of the Mozart operas themselves. Extraneous subplots are introduced and abandoned. We really don't need to know how Mozart's father got worked into his operas, or how Mrs. Mozart balanced the books. And there's entirely too much music.

A film is not a concert hall. There is so much Mozart, played endlessly and without relevance, that after the film's premiere, at a disco party for attending luminaries, I overheard one actor remark: "I never thought I'd be so glad to hear some good old rock and roll!"

The actors are a mixed bag. F. Murray Abraham won the Oscar but turns the plum role of the tortured, perverse Salieri into much less of a centerpiece than it was when the overwhelmingly talented Ian McKellen played it on Broadway. It is not his fault. He works hard, breathing so much credibility into Salieri's mixture of loathing and hero worship that he often resembles a crafty, pockmarked reptile. But it's a quiet, studied performance, and Tom Hulce's Mozart is a one-man fireworks display that overpowers everything else in the film that even smacks of subtlety.

Hulce makes you see how a vulgar little snob with such a piercing Henry Aldrich giggle like Mozart could produce works of such beauty and perfection. It's a dazzling virtuoso turn, and it's not all pyrotechnics, either. Hulce strips away the pretentiousness and shows the human heart underneath as well.

Elizabeth Berridge, who plays Constanze, Mozart's wife, is a total disaster. With her pinched, metallic voice and her community theater artistry,

it doesn't matter how much she pinches her bodice into one of the low-cut Viennese gowns. She still looks and sounds and acts like a preppie schoolgirl who got lost on her way to a Michael Jackson concert.

There is nothing wrong with *Amadeus* that a good pair of scissors couldn't fix. It's massive and often impressive. But it runs two hours and thirty-eight minutes, and the result often seems more like two weeks and thirty-eight hours.

AMERICAN GIGOLO (1980)

★ ★ Directed and written by Paul Schrader. Produced by Jerry Bruckheimer. With Richard Gere, Lauren Hutton, Hector Elizondo, Nina Van Pallandt, Bill Duke, Brian Davies, and Frances Bergen.

John Travolta may be smarter than you think. When he dropped out of *American Gigolo* everyone said he was ruining his career. He had already made one flop, *Moment by Moment*, in which he played a California hustler in love with a married society matron. *American Gigolo* was a similar version of the same story.

So Travolta took a walk and Richard Gere stepped into his Georgio Armani suits. Travolta made the right decision. Everyone should have walked off the set and kept right on going.

The gigolo in Europe is a paid escort who provides a tuxedoed arm for lonely women for a negotiable fee. The gigolo in *American Gigolo* is a somewhat lower form of primate, a smarmy and immoral male prostitute with cool talk, swinging hips, and tiny brains who exercises his pectorals even while talking on the phone.

You can hire him for anything at a stiff price. He'll translate foreign languages, act as a tour guide in the Hollywood discos, or beat you black and blue for sexual kicks. He's got a snazzy sports car and a closet full of tight pants and a tax-free income that is completely illegal. But he doesn't have a heart.

Richard Gere plays the part like a soda jerk auditioning for porno flicks. Lauren Hutton plays the bored wife of a California politician who humiliates and trashes herself for one night in his hormone heaven.

"Tell me everything about you," she says after meeting him in a hotel bar. "We just made love, didn't we?" he says with a smirk. "Then you know everything there is." He's right. And that doesn't make for a very interesting movie.

Gere poses in full frontal nudity, like a Playboy bunny, and there are X-rated love scenes

accompanied by the filthiest dialogue this side of a Navy cargo ship marooned at sea. None of it exists for any necessary purpose except to titillate the Richard Gere Fan Club.

Paul Schrader, who wrote and directed *American Gigolo*, is obsessed with lurid sex. He also wrote *Taxi Driver* and served as writer-director on *Hardcore*.

All three films seem to be a kind of masturbation trilogy, created by an uptight puritan trying to break away from a strict Calvinist upbringing but still shackled to his old-fashioned belief that behind every midnight perversion hangs a paper moon with a silver lining.

Schrader's films are oddly hypnotic as long as he concentrates on the steamy, neon seductiveness of the underworld. They grow stale when he works weak plots into their violent ambience and they totally collapse when he tacks on happy endings.

American Gigolo is well photographed, with the womblike darkness of Gere's world always threatened by the blinding sunshine of the Hollywood sewer that waits behind the drawn venetian blinds. It works up a heat rash of frenzy when it centers on the hustler bars, taco stands, and tenderloin movie houses of Hollywood Boulevard. But it falls apart when the gigolo gets out of bed, finds himself framed for a violent sex murder he didn't commit, and seeks revenge on the black homosexual pimp who is trying to send him to the electric chair. As a routine murder mystery, it's too routine.

Finally, the movie turns ludicrous when the Beverly Hills socialite races to his rescue and in a series of out-of-place dissolves stolen from the visual style of *Chinatown*, we see a hardened criminal with no regard for human life learning the meaning of honesty, integrity and humanity through the love of a good woman. If you buy that one, then you'll also buy the rumor that Bergdorf's is selling genuine mink coats for a buck ninety-five.

Richard Gere is a capable actor, but if he's going to play tough guys with hearts of gold, he'd better have a look at some old John Garfield movies. He's so arrogant in *American Gigolo* that he seems to be snubbing his own movie. Lauren Hutton has the fashionable look of a society girl, the right boutique clothes from Rodeo Drive, and a deep, throaty voice to match. She's the new Lizabeth Scott. It's also nice to see Hector Elizondo again as a savvy vice cop who

secretly envies Gere while he's booking him. And it's always pleasant to see Candice Bergen's mother, the soigné Frances Bergen, this time as a ritzy matron who enjoys the gigolo's company on special occasions. To all of them, I say "Better luck next time," and check with John Travolta first.

AN AFFAIR TO REMEMBER (1957)

★ ★ ½ Directed by Leo McCarey. Screenplay by Leo McCarey and Delmer Daves. Produced by Jerry Wald. *With Cary Grant, Deborah Kerr, Richard Denning and Cathleen Nesbitt.*

One of the most requested titles in the video vaults, this soapy sob story seems corny and dated, but I'll wager audiences will still weep as much as they did in 1957. Cary Grant and Deborah Kerr are the stars, and their performances are romantic as ever. The story is the familiar one about two strangers who meet on an ocean liner, fall in love although they are engaged to others, and make a bargain to marry after a six-month separation if they both feel the same way. In the meantime, she gets hit by a car and crippled for life, he thinks he's been stood up, and the rest is for you and the Kleenex to share.

ANATOMY OF A MURDER (1959)

★ ★ ★ ★ Directed and produced by Otto Preminger. Screenplay by Wendell Mayes. With James Stewart, Lee Remick, Ben Gazzara, Eve Arden, Arthur O'Connell, George C. Scott, Orson Bean, Kathryn Grant, Murray Hamilton, and Joseph N. Welch.

This Otto Preminger classic may be the best courtroom drama ever filmed. James Stewart, in one of his most brilliant performances, plays a small-town Michigan defense attorney hired to defend a moody Army lieutenant (Ben Gazzara) accused of murdering a man who may or may not have raped his wife. Suspecting the lieutenant of foul play and his pretty, seductive wife of hiding secrets of her own, Stewart takes the case to court and unravels the mystery in an exciting climax. Lee Remick as the lieutenant's trampy wife, George C. Scott as the prosecuting attorney, Eve Arden as the loyal secretary, and real-life lawyer Joseph N. Welch as the shrewd judge all turn in convincing portrayals. A flawless picture of an American court at work, and a real nerve-grabber.

ANCHORS AWEIGH (1945)

★ ★ 1/2 Directed by George Sidney. Screenplay by Isobel Lennart. Produced by Joe Pasternak. With Gene Kelly, Kathryn Grayson, Frank Sinatra, Billy Gilbert, Jose Iturbi, and Dean Stockwell.

Anchors Aweigh teams Gene Kelly with Frank Sinatra as two sailors on the loose in Hollywood romancing would-be opera singer Kathryn Grayson. The plot sags with schmaltz, but dance enthusiasts will thrill to the famous sequence that combines live action with animation as Kelly dances through a fairy-tale set with the characters from the Tom and Jerry cartoons. This is one of the great dance numbers of all time. The rest of the film is pedestrian stuff.

ANGELO, MY LOVE (1983)

★ ★ 1/2 Directed and written by Robert Duvall. Produced by Gail Young. With Angelo Evans, Michael Evans, Steve Tsigonoff, and Millie Tsigonoff.

The budget on Angelo, My Love, a movie about Gypsies directed by actor Robert Duvall, wouldn't pay the ginger ale bill on Dino DeLaurentiis's mega-flop King of the Gypsies, yet it accomplishes twice as much for a fraction of the cost. Where King of the Gypsies featured such famous Gypsies as Shelley Winters and Brooke Shields covered with Polynesian pancake makeup, *Angelo, My Love* focuses on the real thing. The Gypsies aren't played by Mexicans or dark-skinned Methodists, but by authentic New York Gypsies appearing as themselves. The result represents six years of love and sweat that distills the complicated essence of Gypsy life into a vital and entertaining movie. If you have any natural curiosity about modern Gypsies, it will enlighten you considerably.

Angelo is a Gypsy street kid whose mother is a fortune-teller. The film takes place mostly in the New York locales where it is still being lived daily by Angelo and his family, but there is the impression that the Gypsies move around so much that he hasn't progressed beyond a second-grade education.

What Angelo lacks in formal book sense, he makes up in horse sense. He's a lively, humorous kid with a fresh mouth. He can also con you out of your own identity if you don't watch out. The film follows Angelo to a disastrous encounter with normal schoolkids in an alien classroom where he clearly does not belong, sorts out his problems with family superiors

and competitive siblings, and lifts the veil on the strange world Angelo inhabits.

If all you know about Gypsies begins and ends with Marlene Dietrich in *Golden Earrings*, this movie is practically an education in subculture sociology.

The Gypsies obviously trusted Duvall completely, for they allowed him to invade their secrecy, explode their myths, and reveal their strange ways like no other outsider has ever done. We see their vendettas, their passions, their marital taboos, their fear of ghosts, and their own peculiar brand of tribal justice called "kris." When they lapse into their own musical language, subtitles are provided. Mostly we just learn that Gypsies will steal your heart, along with your wallet, and they can be a lot of fun while doing it.

What little plot there is can be written on the head of a pin. When Angelo accuses an older Gypsy of stealing a family ring, the boy and his brothers chase the thief to Canada. Angelo wants the ring for his "gajo" girlfriend Patricia, and almost disgraces the family to get it back. (A "gajo" is to Gypsies want a "shiksa" is to Jews.) Oddly, while Angelo is plotting his childlike revenge, Duvall's camera concentrates on the thieves—a wonderful drunk named Patalay, and his dopey, peroxided, horse-faced sister, Millie. Stealing chickens in broad daylight and dreaming of making a movie called *The Invisible Gypsy*, in which they would never get caught, these colorful villains play themselves and you couldn't find anyone better at Central Casting.

I found myself much more interested in these hirsute, bear-like Gypsies with noses like bicycle horns than in little Angelo and his family honor. It is one of the film's great charms that each character, large or small, emerges with equal stature.

Duvall has a quick, vibrant energy and an eye for comic detail that does not miss a thing. The film is half written, half improvised, although he has tried to make it all look spontaneous and natural.

Sometimes the result is a mumbling sound track with everyone talking and shouting at the same time, but most of the time it is just like life.

ANNA (1987)

★ ★ ★ Directed by Yurek Bogayevicz. Screenplay by Agnieszka Holland. Produced by Zanne Divine and Bogayevicz. With Sally Kirkland, Paulina Porizkova, Robert Fields, Ruth Maleczech, Stefan Schnabel, and Larry Pine.

Mercurial Sally Kirkland won an Oscar nomination and emerged a star in this compelling story of an aging Czech film star trying to eke out a meager living in Manhattan. Cover girl/model Paulina Porizkova is the adoring peasant girl who comes to America in search of her screen idol, driving the older woman to madness. It's a quirky, touching film—sort of like *All About Eve* with kielbasa—but, like Meryl Streep in *Sophie's Choice*, Kirkland seizes a difficult assignment and turns it into a rampaging tour de force. With a hair-raisingly authentic Slavic accent and a range of emotions from pathetic to passionate, she devours the film like raw steak. Positively smashing.

ANNA KARENINA (1935)

★ ★ ★ ½ Directed by Clarence Brown. Screenplay by Clemence Dane and Salka Viertel. Produced by David O. Selznick. With Greta Garbo, Fredric March, Basil Rathbone, Reginald Owen, Maureen O'Sullivan, May Robson, and Freddie Bartholomew.

Greta Garbo gives one of her most enduring performances in the memorable 1935 classic *Anna Karenina*. A lush, elaborate tale of doomed love during the reign of Czar Nicholas I of Russia, this Tolstoy saga was given first-rate production values by MGM and is enriched by opulent sets and museum-quality costumes, as well as the supporting performances of Fredric March, Freddie Bartholomew, Maureen O'Sullivan, and Basil Rathbone. But it is Garbo—tragic, noble, valiant, and luminous—who keeps the magic going after more than half a century.

ANOTHER COUNTRY (1984)
★ ★ ★ ½ Directed by Marek Kanievska. Screenplay by Julian Mitchell. Produced by Alan Marshall. With Rupert Everett, Colin Firth, Michael Jenn, Robert Addie, Cary Elwes, Anna Massey, and Betsy Brantley.

Not every schoolboy at Eton becomes a Russian spy like Guy Burgess. Why, then, did this celebrated defector turn against his crown and country to seal himself from everything he knew and live the rest of his life in exile?

Another Country, the probing, disturbing film by Julian Mitchell adapted for the screen from his smash-hit London play, attempts to explain. For jaded filmgoers looking for something different, it's well worth investigating.

No reference is made to Guy Burgess by name, but the implications are obvious. The film begins in 1983 in Moscow, where a journalist is interviewing the now elderly, placid man called Guy Bennett (brilliantly played by the astonishing young British actor Rupert Everett, who recreates his stage success). In the course of the interview, Bennett tells the story of his 1932 school days, and how a young man of class and breeding became an outlaw figure in the school establishment.

These were the days when being "different," or a nonconformist of any kind—whether homosexual or political—was to elect derision and social ostracism over popularity and acceptance.

The film, beautifully photographed by Peter Biziou and capably directed by Marek Kanievska, English-born of Polish parentage, takes a chilling look at the way England's public schools (i.e., what Americans call private or prep schools) distort and adversely shape the lives of the upper classes at a very early age.

The hallowed halls where the seeds of treason are sown are a hellish hotbed of paranoia and fear. We never see the classrooms or the teachers. Order is imposed on the weaker boys by the older and most ruthless students. To qualify for rank and privilege, boys must succumb to bullying, beating, and the petty tyrannies of an adolescent society in which homosexuality plays a carefully circumscribed role.

Young Bennett (or Burgess, as the case may be) is in the catbird seat until his passion for a younger boy subjects him to so much pain, hypocrisy, and emotional blackmail that he surrenders to the Marxist philosophy of his only chum and supporter, a brilliant fellow student convincingly played by Colin Firth.

The point is that the road to Moscow is already paved with English hypocrisy and public-school vice—a case made very persuasive by the intelligent script, the stifling atmosphere, and the excellent ensemble work of a faultless cast. Everett is properly arrogant and sardonic without being fey, Firth is outstanding as the token leftist, handling a mouthful of Marxist propaganda with vigor and assurance, and Cary Elwes, as Everett's young lover, makes a confused adolescent forced into an emotional situation beyond his years both human and attractive.

There are problems. For a film in which passion plays such a vital part, there is precious little of it. The best scene in the film is the one that shows the two boys getting tenderly drunk together in a posh restaurant off campus and half confessing their mutual affection. The rest of the time we must sympathize only because of what the characters say. We never actually see how they feel. To make problems worse, the boys aren't really very likable in the first place. They all grasp ruthlessly, self-servingly, for power.

These reservations aside, *Another Country* gives an extraordinarily informed view of how "playing the game" is required of the British upper classes, both at school and in life, and how covering one's true feelings is really "doing the decent thing." It has fire and inspiration and it smacks of the truth.

ANOTHER WOMAN (1988)

★ ★ ★ ½ Directed and written by Woody Allen. Produced by Robert Greenhut. With Gena Rowlands, Philip Bosco, Betty Buckley, Blythe Danner, Sandy Dennis, Mia Farrow, Gene Hackman, Ian Holm, John Houseman, Martha Plimpton, David Ogden Stiers, and Harris Yulin.

Another titanic performance by the luminous Gena Rowlands is the emotional center-piece of this quirky, enigmatic, but tender and ironic examination of a woman in a midlife crisis. Rowlands is a brilliant, accomplished, confident philosophy professor who seems to have everything but really has nothing because she's lost the ability to trust her own feelings. Anguished and lost, analyzing everything intellectually without dealing with her emotions, she begins to see herself as others see her, doubting her friendships, questioning her values, and dissecting her marriage. Gene Hackman, Sandy Dennis, Blythe Danner, Ian Holm, John Houseman, Mia Farrow, and Betty Buckley head the distinguished cast that wanders in and out of her barren line of vision like shadows in a dream—all delivering cameos that illuminate the dark recesses of her confused and guarded life. The film is a stylized homage to Ingmar Bergman, with a style that is fragmented and an ending that left me edgy, dissatisfied, and perplexed. But this is one of Woody Allen's most mature films and possibly the great Gena Rowlands's finest performance. Woody Allen without laughs is like a bun without a burger, but *Another Woman* is so elegant, hypnotic, and thoughtful you won't miss the gags at all.

APOCALYPSE NOW (1979)
★ ★ ½ Directed and produced by Francis Ford Coppola. Screenplay by John Milius and Coppola. *With Martin Sheen, Robert Duvall, Marlon Brando, Frederic Forrest, Albert Hall, Sam Bottoms, Larry Fishburne, Harrison Ford, Scott Glenn, and Dennis Hopper.*

Apocalypse Now has enough moments of greatness to remind us that a real cinematic talent is at work, but like all geniuses who think they are Orson Welles, Coppola needed desperately to stand back and take an objective view of what all those years, all that money, and all that sweat turned into before the film was finally released.

After so much initial flap in the press, Coppola really didn't do much of anything to change or improve the final print, and the *Apocalypse Now* he gave us is a sour, sad muddle; a ridiculously overpublicized (not to mention insanely overpriced) blending of Joseph Conrad's uncinematic *Heart of Darkness* and Vietnam in a gumbo of pretentious twaddle. The battle scenes are arresting, if you're into battle scenes. But oh, the dreary philosophy that wrecks the final thirty minutes of the film (not to mention one of the most inept, self-serving, mumbo-jumbo performances in screen history by Marlon Brando, who sounds like he's being amplified through the bottom of a vat of fudge).

The problem with *Apocalypse Now* is that it has no apocalypse. Coppola was in over his head and didn't know how to get out, so the movie ends in an incoherent haze of smoke and darkness when it should have ended with fireworks.

There is very little plot: A cold-blooded Army captain (Martin Sheen) is dispatched to the darkest jungles to terminate the command of a highly decorated, widely respected colonel (Marlon Brando) who has gone mad, set up his own pagan civilization, and started executing Vietnamese on his own, playing God while dreaming of a snail crawling along the edge of a straight razor.

Sheen starts on a physical voyage and ends up on a spiritual voyage. It would've been better for the structure of the film if it ended with the completion of the physical voyage, because there is so much action between his departure for Cambodia and his arrival at Brando's jungle paradise that

the film looks like the Götterdämmerung of war movies.

Unfortunately, the whole thing ends up in a psychological mess—an artfully camouflaged mess, but a mess all the same—and we're left with the tired message that in war, as in life, there are opposing forces—rational and irrational, good and bad, moral and immoral—and sometimes the dark side of the heart triumphs.

Meanwhile, there are great things in it, like a helicopter raid led by a demented officer (Robert Duvall) in a Boy Scout uniform who sends men to their deaths to capture a beach so he can go surfing. Shouting "I love the smell of napalm in the morning," he plays Wagnerian opera from loudspeakers during attacks, then flies in T-bones and Budweiser for a barbecue in the ruins of a burning village.

In these scenes the horror, cruelty, and stupidity that was Vietnam comes shining through. But when Sheen reaches his jungle destination, the grit and realism Coppola has established turns into something out of an old Val Lewton Saturday matinee creeper with Lon Chaney.

And there is Brando, bald as an acorn squash, crawling around in a mud cave, mumbling gibberish in the dark to conceal his paunch, while the natives get restless around their bonfires chanting a lot of hugga-mugga like extras from *Macumba Love*.

ARACHNOPHOBIA (1990)

★ ★ ★ Directed by Frank Marshall. Screenplay by Don Jakoby and Wesley Strick. Produced by Kathleen Kennedy and Richard Vane. With Jeff Daniels and John Goodman

The dictionary defines the word as a paralyzing fear of spiders. Be warned. If you don't have it before seeing this movie, you'll have it when it's over. The first victims are entomologists exploring prehistoric ruins in Venezuela who find horror below the earth on a canyon floor filled with hairy critters. From webs the size of circus tents, the monsters big as gorilla paws hitch a ride back to America in a coffin and set up housekeeping in the barn of country doctor Jeff Daniels. First the crickets start dying. Then the neighbors. The real thrills start when the whole town goes on a spider hunt, finding terror lurking inside every teacup and toilet bowl. Daniels is a fine, naturalistic actor who makes every minute believable because he's so honest and unaffected. John Goodman provides the laughs as a local exterminator. But it is really the humongous queen spider laying eggs in the wine cellar played by the Bela Lugosi of the spider world that turns *Arachnophobia* into a real hair-pulling, hand-wringing throat clutcher. I may never go into my basement again, even with the lights on.

ARTHUR (1981)

★ ★ ★ Directed and written by Steve Gordon. Produced by Robert Greenhut. With Dudley Moore, Liza Minnelli, John Gielgud, Geraldine Fitzgerald, Jill Eikenberry, Stephen Elliott, Tod Ross, and Barney Martin.

Arthur is about a weak, spineless, noisy little creep named Arthur, who also happens to be a midget millionaire, an alcoholic who cannot be trusted to cross the street without the aid of his butler-babysitter-best friend, Hobson.

The only hope for Arthur, his family insists, is to marry a rich girl and go to work in her father's business. Arthur would rather die, but what choice has he got? It's either knuckle under or surrender a three-quarters-of-a-billion-dollar inheritance.

One day Arthur meets Linda, a working-class kook from Queens, while she's shoplifting at Bergdorf's. The rest of this amiable, but thoroughly untidy little comedy devotes itself to the ways in which (1) Linda nabs Arthur, (2) Arthur gets to keep the girl and the inheritance, and (3) Hobson gives Arthur courage to take control of his life before the butler drops dead of cancer.

There are a few tiny smiles, but nothing that ever threatens to break into a guffaw, despite the stylish, energetic playing of Dudley Moore as the hairy, obnoxious Arthur, Liza Minnelli as the practical and thoroughly befuddled Linda, and Geraldine Fitzgerald as Arthur's ruthlessly eccentric old grandmother. If the plot were any more than wafer thin, the entire movie would melt in the middle of a bite.

Still, it is well worth seeing for a smashing performance by Sir John Gielgud, who steals the film as the grouchy, wonderful old snob of a butler. It is entirely possible Sir John has been frittering away his time in all those heavily embroidered classics. He's a wildly wicked first-rate comedian, and this film proves it. This time he's given the bird to the Bard, and the result is a character of the most curmudgeonly charm since Clifton Webb dumped oatmeal on that spoiled brat in *Sitting Pretty*.

THE ASPHALT JUNGLE (1950)

★ ★ ★ ½ Directed by John Huston. Screenplay by Huston and Ben Maddow. Produced by Arthur Hornblow, Jr. *With Louis Calhern, Marilyn Monroe, Sterling Hayden, Jean Hagen, James Whitmore, and Sam Jaffe.*

The Asphalt Jungle is John Huston's penultimate film noir, a crime picture that drags the stunned and uneasy viewer down a manhole into the sewer inhabited by big-city rats of every description—safecrackers, petty hoodlums, silky and deadly blondes, double-crossing cops, greasy bookmakers, sleazy ex-cons—with muscle and grit that is rare even for gangster movies. The style is brilliantly naturalistic, the black-and-white camerawork has the clarity of stainless steel, the plot is intriguing. The viewer is actually asked to participate in a jewel robbery; the safecracking we're in on is the final word in suspense. And the most evil characters in the film are so well etched that by the time it's over, they seem like old comrades. Louis Calhern, Marilyn Monroe, Sterling Hayden, Jean Hagen, James Whitmore, and Sam Jaffe head an impressive cast. A microscopic study in corruption that is unforgettable!

ATLANTIC CITY (1981)

★ ★ ★ ★ Directed by Louis Malle. Screenplay by John Guare. Produced by Denis Heroux. With Burt Lancaster, Susan Sarandon, Kate Reid, Michel Piccoli, Hollis McLaren, Robert Joy, and Al Waxman.

Louis Malle, who once turned the sewers of Calcutta into images of stark and arresting beauty, has trained the eyes of his cameras on Atlantic City, that decaying bastion of human waste on the Jersey shore where you can smell the rot before you reach the boardwalk. And in the ruins he's found a metaphor for hope among the doomed and deserted flotsam of American life.

Atlantic City is an odd, perceptive, moody, vigorous, and completely original experience that challenges description. Like the sleazy town itself, it's a Coney Island of the mind.

In contrasting styles of farce, realism and gangster melodrama, this unique and satisfying movie shifts gears so often that you have to stay on your toes to keep up with it. In the shadows of gaudy casinos and rotting transient hotels marked for demolition, a Whitman's sampler of assorted screwballs is brought together by fate. Susan Sarandon is Sally, a dumb but spirited run-away from Saskatchewan who works in an oyster bar to pay for croupier lessons. Her dream is to end up dealing blackjack in some remote but glamorous place like Monte Carlo.

In the same shabby rooming house, there is Lou (Burt Lancaster), a battered old man who runs small errands for the underworld and dreams of being a big shot like his old idol Bugsy Siegel. There is also Grace (Kate Reid), a bawdy recluse with arthritis who dreams of someday recapturing the lost beauty that first brought her to Atlantic City years earlier as a contestant in a Betty Grable look-alike contest.

Into their gauzy, crummy world of escape comes Sally's flaky hippie husband, with her pregnant sister and a stolen cache of cocaine in tow. The drugs are stashed in the old man's room while the proper buyer can be contacted, and suddenly Lou sees the opportunity to make a killing of his own, be a big man on the boardwalk, and treat the ladies to a taste of the good old days. In an atmosphere of dreams gone sour, three misfits roll the dice and learn the meaning of survival.

This is a richly textured film filled with startling images: Lancaster watching Sarandon through venetian blinds as she rubs her arms and breasts with lemon juice to remove the stink of fish while a cassette tape recorder plays Bellini's *Norma*, the shame on Lancaster's face as he walks Grace's mangy poodle past the saltwater taffy stands that are crumbling beneath the weight of the wrecker's ball, the sounds of hammers and drills as progress records the renewal of a dream to the strains of "On the Boardwalk in Atlantic City," a song from an old June Haver movie.

There is irony everywhere as old dreams are replaced by new, yet everything seems to be dying, even Resorts International star Robert Goulet. Thugs, celebrities, drug pushers, housewives, pimps, and construction workers move together in a sonorous rhythm to the jingle of cash registers as the losers keep an eye on the dealers who keep an eye on the money. The images burst with life even when they're at odds with the thematic content. There is always something to watch and absorb in *Atlantic City*.

The performances are of the highest caliber. Sarandon is hysterical, harassed, desperate, funny, endearing; Kate Reid is like a blond bulldog barking at the stub where its tail used to

be; Lancaster gives one of his most polished and sincere portrayals as an absurdly touching bon vivant whose athletic prowess and eroded pride spring to life when he finally kills someone just like in the movies.

In films like *The Leopard*, *Conversation Piece*, and *1900* Lancaster has repeatedly demonstrated the lyrical poetry of the aging process. *Atlantic City* provides him with an even richer role that suits his age and persona the way his newly acquired white walking suit fits his still-rugged physique under all that snowy hair. In its sense of time warp, its innocent belief that crime does pay, and its complex, contrasting moods, *Atlantic City* finds a fresh new way to examine the ugliness of American life and still come up with the belief that it's a country where anything can happen, all dreams are possible, and nothing is ever as simple as it seems.

A marvelous film with a landscape of its own comes as quite a relief from most of the uninspired formula movies we so often see, and much of the credit should go not only to Louis Malle but to John Guare, whose bizarre roller coaster screenplay accomplishes what only great movies can. It takes us out of ourselves and shows us things we've never seen or heard before. To everyone concerned, the applause from this corner is loud and sincere.

AT CLOSE RANGE (1986)
★ Directed by James Foley. Screenplay by Nicholas Kazan. Produced by Elliott Lewitt and Don Guest. *With Christopher Walken, Sean Penn, Christopher Penn, Mary Stuart Masterson, Millie Perkins, and Eileen Ryan.*

There are so many things wrong with *At Close Range* that I could never recommend it to any but the most hardened film buffs, yet I was both fascinated and repelled by it. It's about as vile and mean-spirited an American family as you'd ever want to meet in an alley or a cornfield after dark. I didn't feel too comfortable in a movie theater, either.

At Close Range is *Life with Father* with rape, murder, crime, and all manner of human atrocities thrown in.

Father in this instance is Christopher Walken, the personification of paternal evil, who, as a murderous thug named simply Brad, Sr., heads a gang of thieves and killers who hide out in a barn in the middle of remote rural farm country.

He has two sons, Brad, Jr., and Tommy, played by the brothers Sean and Christopher Penn. The kids are bored, tough, pill-popping teenage dropouts who are living refuse waiting for a garbage dump.

Kicked out of his home for being a good-for-nothing lout, Brad, Jr., goes to live with his father. Dad's the kind of all-around provider whose idea of giving his kid a present is to hand him a loaded gun and dare him to pull the trigger. The kid wastes no time willingly and eagerly getting initiated into a life of crime, and recruits his younger brother and other buddies to steal tractors, appliances, museum relics, even cop cars.

They're a pack of wild hooligans, without supervision, guidance, or ambition. It takes a real murder to convince Brad Jr. this might not be as much fun as the movies.

Too bad. Dad won't let him go. The kids have witnessed too much. Dad rapes his son's bride-to-be, the kid turns state's evidence against his own father, and the carnage that results is stomach-churning.

At Close Range, supposedly based on a true story, is like being in a dark room with a poisonous snake. You never know where it will strike next. It isn't much of a social document, because there is no aspect of society depicted in it that any sane or normal person can identify with. It has no message. It is simply a violent action film in which the violence is almost pornographic. It has no point of view and no resolute morality of good guys vs. villains. Everyone is contemptible.

Worse still, a great deal of the acting is so incoherently self-indulgent that the film could use subtitles. Sean Penn is too old to play a mixed-up teenager, and his sour snarl doesn't help. I am also confused as to why he goes through three-quarters of the film with peroxided curly hair and appears in the end with a dark brown crewcut.

Mary Stuart Masterson, as his girlfriend, is a Molly Ringwald clone who is somewhat less repugnant.

But it is really Christopher Walken who reduces his dialogue to incomprehensible gibberish. Walken gets weirder and weirder with every appearance. Bug-eyed and dissipated, he looks wasted, like burned dough. He also gives one of the oddest performances, with one of the most peculiar accents, on record. Mumbling, jerking, and sucking his tongue, he doesn't seem mean so much as submental.

Still, there is something riveting about this film. It's a macabre curiosity. Everyone weeps and bleeds a lot, and I can think of better ways to spend my time than watching Sean Penn give himself a pedicure by chewing his toenails off with his teeth.

Yet the screenplay by Nicholas Kazan is taut, and director James Foley makes uncanny use of the camera: With the same economy, he knows when to tighten a shot for maximum effect, when to track, and how to invest each scene with searing immediacy. Even the most gruesome of violent occurrences—from the vicious cock fight to blowing a girl's brains out at close range—seem vividly real.

At Close Range is not my particular cup of poison. It is not, to be truthful, a movie for anyone with a weak stomach. I can't imagine anyone caring about any of the horrible maniacs who occupy the premises,but if you're interested in violence as art or the American lower classes as fodder for melodrama, James Foley emerges when the smoke clears as a young director with talent.

THE AWFUL TRUTH (1937)

★ ★ ★ ★ Directed and produced by Leo McCarey. Screenplay by Vina Delmar. With Cary Grant, Irene Dunne, and Ralph Bellamy.

What a pleasure to have for home viewing one of my all-time favorite screwball comedies, *The Awful Truth*. Leo McCarey won a 1937 Oscar for Best Director for this wacky and sophisticated charmer, and you'll know why when you see how he handles Cary Grant and Irene Dunne and their beloved fox terrier, "Mr. Smith" (played by Asta of the *Thin Man* pictures). Cary and Irene are getting a divorce. He wants her back after he discovers her engagement to a wealthy Oklahoma oil baron (Ralph Bellamy). The antic ways he tries to win her over a second time lead to a lot of laughs. When they say "They don't make Hollywood comedies like they used to in the good old days," they're talking about movies like this one.

BABETTE'S FEAST (1987)

★ ★ ★ ½ Directed and written by Gabriel Axel. Produced by Just Betzer and Bo Christensen. With Stephane Audran, Jean-Phillipe Lafont, Gudmar Wivesson, Jarl Kulle, Bibi Andersson, Brigitte Federspiel, and Bodil Kjer.

Gabriel Axel's Danish film and 1987's Oscar winner for Best Foreign Film is an Isak Dinesen tale about a French servant (beautifully, stoically played by Stephane Audran) in a strict Lutheran household in Denmark. To repay her hard, deprived hosts for their kindness, she spends her entire lottery winnings doing the one thing she knows how to do best—she cooks an elaborate, exotic, eponymous meal filled with game and liquors and desserts they've never experienced before. The meticulous preparation, serving, and devouring of this feast changes the lives of everyone involved, enhancing the true meaning of friendship. Impeccably acted, and suffused with charm and delicacy, this is one film that's a meal in itself.

BABY BOOM (1987)

★ ★ ★ ½ Directed by Charles Shyer. Screenplay by Shyer and Nancy Myers. Produced by Nancy Myers. With Diane Keaton, Harold Ramis, Sam Shepard, Sam Wanamaker, James Spader, Pat Hingle, Britt Leach, Mary Gross, and Victoria Jackson.

Diane Keaton is J. C. Wiatt, the quintessential *Ms*. magazine career girl—married to her job, working twelve hours a day, making six figures a year, with no time for human emotions. Even her lovemaking with roommate-boyfriend Harold Ramis is timed to never take up more than four minutes of her valuable time. Then the bottom falls out. The brainy executive inherits a baby from a distant relative she hasn't seen since 1954 and she finds herself up to her stock market reports in baby food, baby diapers, and baby thermometers, trying to find what she calls "quality time" to pop a Valium and wash it down with a baby bottle. Her boss says "You can't have it all" but the rest of this delectable comedy says you can, as the frustrated J.C. hangs up the corporate ladder and moves to a two-hundred-year-old farm in Vermont where she's as out of place as Goldie Hawn in *Private Benjamin*.

The first half of *Baby Boom* is about the struggles of a lady yuppie to scratch her way to the executive washroom. The second half is about the struggles of a displaced city mouse scheming to get back to town. Broke, despondent, and hysterical, all she's got is a cupboard full of applesauce from a hard winter. The way she turns her predicament into a commercial bonanza by marketing designer baby products out of her own mail-order kitchen makes this one of the wittiest, most intelligent, and most endearing comedies in years. Diane Keaton gives the richest, funniest performance of her life in a tour de force of neurotic, frazzled timing that proves why she's a real star. A sophisticated screwball comedy that's a work of art.

BABY DOLL (1956)
★ ★ ★ Directed and produced by Elia Kazan. Screenplay by Tennessee Williams. *With Carroll Baker, Karl Malden, Eli Wallach, Mildred Dunnock, and Lonny Chapman.*

One of the best of Tennessee Williams's steamy southern dramas about mendacity under the magnolias, this rare, seldom-revived movie classic is a welcome treasure. The great Elia Kazan directed, and this gem launched the career of luscious Carroll Baker as a Lolita-like Mississippi child bride who drives men wild with frustrated lust. Karl Malden is magnificent as her mad husband, Eli Wallach gives one of the greatest performances of his illustrious career as a lecherous cotton baron, and Mildred Dunnock is merely sensational as Baby Doll's retarded Aunt Rose Comfort. When it was first released, this film was denounced by the Catholic Church, condemned by the

Legion of Decency, and the center of a storm of censorship controversy. Now it's regarded as a high-water mark in cinema. It's sexy, but also howlingly funny — a real home-video find!

BACKDRAFT (1991)
★ Directed by Ron Howard. Screenplay by Gregory Widen. Produced by Richard B. Lewis, Brian Grazer, Pen Desham, John Watson. With Kurt Russell, William Baldwin, Scott Glenn, Jennifer Jason Leigh, Donald Sutherland, Rebecca De Mornay, and Robert De Niro.

They start a lot of fires in *Backdraft*, none of them under the right people. Conceived as an expensive look at the lives of firefighters, something burned up in the process between script and final cut. In the ashes, all that remain are the fires. Almost two and a half hours of nothing but fires. Anything resembling plot, character development, acting, coherence, or real people was extinguished in the lab.

Kurt Russell and William Baldwin are handsome sibling rivals who learn to love each other in the flames. Jennifer Jason Leigh, as a political activist at City Hall, and Robert De Niro, as a beleaguered fire chief, are reduced to walk-ons.

(She has one sex scene with Mr. Baldwin, but since she doesn't end up with him in the end, what's the point?) Donald Sutherland makes a worthless guest appearance as a demented arsonist behind bars (director Ron Howard's homage to Dr. Hannibal Lecter in *Silence of the Lambs*, no doubt). There are lots of red herrings, falling pipes, and exploding windowpanes, a minor mystery about the true identity of the wacko who is setting all the fires and burning down Chicago. (It is not Mrs. O'Leary's cow.) And when the firemen stop inhaling smoke fumes, they light cigarettes and say "Fire is a living thing. It breathes, it eats, and it hates. Only way to beat it is to love it a little." It's been ages since I've seen so many decent actors or so much money wasted on such pretentious drivel.

This is not a movie about real people. It's a movie about uncorking the valves on fire hydrants. The term *backdraft* is explained three times and I still don't know what it means. Pyromaniacs may love it, but the only real audience for this bomb is the dogs who chase fire trucks.

THE BAD AND THE BEAUTIFUL (1952)

★ ★ ★ Directed by Vincente Minnelli. Screenplay by Charles Schnee. Produced by John Houseman. With Kirk Douglas, Lana Turner, Dick Powell, Walter Pidgeon, Barry Sullivan, Gloria Grahame, and Gilbert Roland.

They say Hollywood has never turned out a truthful movie about itself, but *The Bad and the Beautiful* is a powerful and provocative exception. Magnificent performances by an all-star cast, a sharply biting script by Charles Schnee that won an Oscar, exquisite direction by the great Vincente Minnelli, and brilliant sets and cinematography combine to authentically capture the look and flavor of Hollywood's gloomy, dusty mansions, movie lots, sets, and studio production offices to give a marvelous reflection of the Hollywood that no longer exists. *The Bad and the Beautiful* ranks right up there with *Sunset Boulevard* and the George Cukor–Judy Garland remake of *A Star Is Born* as one of the quintessential movies on movies.

Kirk Douglas gives, in my opinion, his greatest performance as a complex, creative, and totally ruthless heel of a producer who rises from B-thrillers to box-office hits by riding on the talents of a movie star (Lana Turner), a screenwriter (Dick Powell), and a director (Barry Sullivan), all three of whom he used, abused, and double-crossed, but all three of whom rose, with his help, to positions of wealth and power in the industry. Walter Pidgeon, the head of the studio, calls the three greats for a conference and asks them to join forces for one last picture to reestablish the failed producer's career. They hate him, and as each begins to tell his or her story, you find out why. But this is the picture business, and in the end, the lure of yet another great vehicle draws them to the phone to listen to the producer's transatlantic call describing the project. Minnelli leaves the audience suspended, with a lady-or-the-tiger finish, and everything in between will keep you riveted.

Lana Turner also gives her finest performance as the down-and-out alcoholic daughter of a dead silent-screen star. Gloria Grahame, as Powell's flirtatious southern belle wife, won a Supporting Actress Oscar. Many of the actual behind-the-scenes wardrobe and makeup personnel at MGM play themselves, lending an even eerier believability. From start to finish *The Bad and the Beautiful* is a serious, scalding, and captivating classic.

BAD DAY AT BLACK ROCK (1955)

★ ★ ★ Directed by John Sturges. Screenplay by Millard Kaufman, based on Howard Breslin's story "Bad Time at Hondo." Produced by Dore Schary. With Spencer Tracy, Robert Ryan, Lee Marvin, Ernest Borgnine, Anne Francis, Dean Jagger, Walter Brennan, and John Ericson.

A 1955 blockbuster from MGM, *Bad Day at Black Rock* stars Spencer Tracy in his most offbeat role: a one-armed World War II veteran who travels to a burned-out town in the desert to deliver a medal to a Japanese-American war hero who saved his life in combat, only to discover that the war hero has been murdered by a gang of psychopaths headed by Robert Ryan and Lee Marvin. Tracy is marked for death, and the judo display with which the one-armed man defends himself against the entire town is the most exciting showdown since *High Noon*. Ernest Borgnine, Anne Francis, Walter Brennan, and John Ericson head a superb supporting cast under John Sturges's rocket-fire direction in a thriller that leaves you reaching for smelling salts.

THE BAD SEED (1956)

★ ★ ★ Directed and produced by Mervyn LeRoy. Screenplay by John Lee Mahin. With Nancy Kelly, Patty McCormack, Eileen Heckart, Evelyn Varden, William Hopper, and Henry Jones.

The Bad Seed is a flawed but compellingly acted little thriller about a darling, pigtailed eight-year-old named Rhoda Penmark who curtsies and smiles sweetly as she brutally assaults and drowns a fellow schoolmate, pushes an old lady down a flight of stairs, and burns the janitor to death in a locked shed. Maxwell Anderson's shocking Broadway play was an enormous hit because of its shattering climax, where Rhoda survived to plan more havoc. The movie, directed by Mervyn LeRoy, adheres to the now outmoded censorship code that insisted all villains had to pay for their crimes. The finale is a letdown. But the acting is mesmerizing and the film was nominated for four Oscars. Little Patty McCormack is a terrifying forerunner to the menacing kids who came later in *The Omen* and *The Exorcist*; Nancy Kelly is wonderful and touching as her mother; Evelyn Varden, Eileen Heckart, and Henry Jones fuse the tension with naturalism. *The Bad Seed* is still a classic that demands and holds attention thirty-five years later.

BALL OF FIRE (1941)

★ ★ ★ ★ Directed by Howard Hawks. Screenplay by Billy Wilder and Charles Brackett. Produced by Samuel Goldwyn. *With Barbara Stanwyck, Gary Cooper, Oscar Homolka, Dana Andrews, Dan Duryea, S. Z. Sakall, Richard Haydn, Henry Travers, Tully Marshall, and Gene Krupa.*

If you've never seen this comedy gem with Gary Cooper as an egghead professor working on a new encyclopedia and Barbara Stanwyck as a nightclub floozie who teaches him a new "slanguage," then run — don't walk — to the nearest VCR and get to know what great Hollywood filmmaking in the Fabulous Forties was all about. Billy Wilder wrote it, Howard Hawks directed, and it's an all-time treasure.

LA BAMBA (1987)

★ ★ ★ Directed and written by Luis Valdez. Produced by Taylor Hackford and Bill Borden. *With Lou Diamond Phillips, Esai Morales, Rosana DeSoto, Danielle von Zerneck, Elizabeth Pena, and Joe Pantoliano.*

The story of Ritchie Valens, *La Bamba* is about the teenage cult hero of the 1950s who died in the same tragic plane crash that claimed the life of Buddy Holly. Richly textured, sincerely acted by a dedicated cast, sensitively written and compassionately directed by Luis Valdez, *La Bamba* chronicles Ritchie's meteoric rise from a life of poverty among California's Mexican fruit pickers to a privileged seat in the rock and roll hall of fame. The road was full of potholes. Sick of racial prejudice, tortillas, and hardships, Ritchie's dream was rock and roll, and his guitar was the key to his escape. Part Chicano, part Yaqui Indian, he had nothing to start out with in life but his own raw talent—and the support of a mother who even paid for his first gig in an American Legion hall with her own rent money. Ritchie wanted more. He longed to perform the Mexican folk song "La Bamba" in his own rocking style. The rest is history.

Newcomer Lou Diamond Phillips is outstanding as Ritchie, even though the songs on the soundtrack are performed by Los Lobos. Rosana DeSoto, as Ritchie's mother, is wonderful, too, as is Danielle von Zerneck, as his waspy high school sweetheart Donna, a girl from a higher social status who inspired his first hit single. But it is really Esai Morales who steals the film as older brother

Bob—a desperate, raging, ethnically traumatized bull of a man torn between personal failure and the success of a younger brother he both loves and resents. It's not the songs—or the period—but the human relationships that sustain the interest here. The material is so simple it almost writes itself. That mindless teenage world of bubble gum and Dick Clark seems tame and tepid now. But some real kids with passion and soul, like Ritchie Valens, wrote the pages of that chapter in rock history. And now that it's over, "La Bamba" is one of the songs—and one of the movies—most likely to be remembered.

THE BARKLEYS OF BROADWAY (1949)

★ ★ ★ Directed by Charles Walters. Screenplay by Betty Comden and Adolph Green. Produced by Arthur Freed. *With Fred Astaire, Ginger Rogers, Oscar Levant, Billie Burke, Jacques François, George Zucco, and Grace Robbins.*

This is the musical that reunited Fred Astaire and Ginger Rogers after a ten-year screen absence. It's their final film together and the only one they ever made in Technicolor. They play a husband-and-wife dance team who go their separate ways when she decides she'd prefer to be a dramatic actress instead of a musical comedy star. After many comic detours, they are reunited at the end, of course, to George and Ira Gershwin's "They Can't Take That Away From Me." In between there are many highlights, including Fred's memorable and imaginative "Shoes with Wings On," in which he plays a cobbler with magic shoes that dance on their own. Oscar Levant is on hand, performing a Tchaikovsky piano concerto between wisecracks, and Ginger has a fine, funny turn playing Sarah Bernhardt between tap numbers.

BATAAN (1943)

★ ★ ★ ½ Directed by Tay Garnett. Screenplay by Robert Andrews. Produced by Irving Starr. *With Robert Taylor, George Murphy, Robert Walker, Thomas Mitchell, Lloyd Nolan, Desi Arnaz, Lee Bowman, Barry Nelson, and Phillip Terry.*

The grim story of the heroic defense of Bataan in World War II is told in true and ugly detail in this harrowing but monumental war picture. The admiration inspired by the brave American soldiers hanging on in the face of disaster shines through in this story of the last days on that battle-scarred peninsula: Thirteen battered fighters struggle to hold a rear point while the U.S. and Filipino armies fall back on Corregidor. Robert Taylor, in one of his finest performances, is the hard-boiled sergeant who inherits the abandoned commando unit when an Air Force lieutenant (George Murphy) relinquishes control. Robert Walker is the kid who ponders the meaning of life while facing death. Thomas Mitchell, Lee Bowman, Lloyd Nolan, Desi Arnaz, and Barry Nelson lend sturdy support as the American heroes who keep the Japanese back on the edge of their own self-dug graves. Suspense, tears, and genuine reality make *Bataan* worth remembering.

BATMAN (1989)

★ ★ ★ ½ Directed by Tim Burton. Screenplay by Sam Hamm and Warren Skaaren. Produced by Jon Peters and Peter Gruber. *With Michael Keaton, Jack Nicholson, Kim Basinger, Pat Hingle, Billy Dee Williams, and Jack Palance.*

If everyone presumably has already seen the highest-grossing motion picture of all time, will anyone want to see it twice? I hope the answer is yes, and I'm one of them. Forget about that silly 1960's TV series with Batman and Robin, his wimpy sidekick, in their K mart

jerseys. Tim Burton, former Disney animator and director of *Beetlejuice*, turns the adventures of the mortal caped crusader into a stormy, breathtaking roller-coaster ride through comic-book hell. This is no campy cartoon, no Saturday matinee serial with dialogue like "Pow!" and "Shazam!" This *Batman* is serious stuff. The streets of crime-riddled Gotham City are dark, wet, and crowded with underworld killers. The sets are like lavish tributes to expressionistic German horror flicks. Gone are dum-dums like swishy Robin, the idiotic Cat Woman, and moronic Penguin. Instead, we get real stars—Michael Keaton as charming millionaire playboy Bruce Wayne by day and Batman by night; gorgeous Kim Basinger as ace photographer Vicki Vale; and, most important, the great Jack Nicholson as the most fiendish psycho since Adolph Hitler. With his face frozen into a hideous grin, green hair, purple suits, orange shirts, and an evil giggle that rises from the corridors of Hades, he's a singing, prancing Jack the Ripper.

Holy Combustion! Batman's got an indestructible Batmobile, a voice-activated car James Bond would kill for. It can crash through anything, shield itself from bullets and bombs, and it needs no fuel. In the air, there's the Batwing, and on the ground he's a one-man army, but any way you slice it, this Batman is no Superman clone. In fact, both hero and villain seem to need a psychiatrist. With crashing music, songs by Prince, spectacular sets by Anton Furst (the genius behind the Bond films) and dizzying camera angles, *Batman* is a flamboyant essay in motion and fantasy as funny as it is terrifying. The excitement, artistry, and humor make this an original and inspired entertainment.

BEAT THE DEVIL (1954)

★ ★ ★ Directed and produced by John Huston. Screenplay by Truman Capote. *With Humphrey Bogart, Jennifer Jones, Gina Lollobrigida, Robert Morley, and Peter Lorre.*

Try to imagine Truman Capote writing a movie for Humphrey Bogart. Give up? So did Capote, who, from all reports, made up the script each day, reading it aloud to the cast as they went along. The result was a commercial disaster, but this offbeat, bizarre, absurdly arrogant crime spoof has now become a cult classic among movie buffs, who insist it is one of director John Huston's best films. The wild plot involves a shipwrecked boat on its way to Africa carrying among its passengers a bewildered Bogart and his wife Gina Lollobrigida, a gang of uranium swindlers including Robert Morley and Peter Lorre, and a wacky liar, played by a surprisingly funny Jennifer Jones in a blonde wig. Masterpiece or mess? You be the judge, but don't miss one of the queerest thrillers ever made.

BEAUTY AND THE BEAST (1991)

★ ★ ★ ½ Directed by Gary Trousdale and Kirk Wise. Written by Linda Woolverton. Produced by Howard Ashman, Alan Menken and Don Hahn. *Featuring the voices of Angela Lansbury, Robby Benson, Paige O'Hara, Jerry Orbach, Richard White, David Ogden Stiers, and others.*

This is one of the most accomplished films ever created by the animators at Walt Disney. Yes, the Jean Cocteau film from France still enthralls, but the fairy tale seems more magical and festive with the Disney touch. The art has a three-dimensional quality, as though the settings are cardboard cutouts. When the camera moves in and out of the haunted woods leading to the castle where the prince had been imprisoned as a beast waiting for the true love of a beautiful maiden to make him human again, you forget you are watching a cartoon. Actual zoom lenses home in from vast landscapes to close-ups of Belle's frightened face the way they do in live-action features. The songs, by Howard Ashman and Alan Menken, are cleverly interwoven between narrative action and production numbers better than in most movie musicals, and a fine cast of performers have a ball with the voices. Paige O'Hara makes a sturdy Belle, the pretty bookworm, while Robby Benson will surprise you as the gentle Beast. Best of all is Angela Lansbury as a singing teapot, who leads the castle in a dazzling Busby Berkeley spectacular of cork-popping champagne bottles and dancing kitchen utensils. A real knockout, for every age imaginable.

THE BEDROOM WINDOW (1987)

★ ★ ★ ½ Directed and written by Curtis Hanson. Produced by Robert Towne. With Steve Guttenberg, Elizabeth McGovern, Isabelle Huppert, and Wallace Shawn.

The Bedroom Window was a box office disappointment, and I can't understand why. It's a genuinely pulse-quickening romantic thriller for grown-ups in the Hitchcock tradition, and it looks even better on a small screen. It's an imaginative and entertaining murder mystery in which Steve Guttenberg plays a Baltimore architect engaged in a casual affair with his boss's wife (French actress Isabelle Huppert). One rainy night from his bedroom window she witnesses a brutal attack on a young woman by a homicidal maniac. In a romantic gesture of chauvinism, he calls the cops and pretends to be the witness so she won't have to become involved. This innocent act of good citizenship turns out to be everyone's downfall. He's forced to lie under oath at the psycho's trial, and becomes a hunted man by both the cops and the maniac. The only one who can catch the killer and save Guttenberg is the killer's original target, played by Elizabeth McGovern. Add romance, steamy sex, and more plot curves than a Coney Island Cyclone, and you've got a nifty little suspense thriller that will fry your nerves. Guttenberg, in his first dramatic role, is likable and solid as Sears. And McGovern, as the spunky cocktail waitress who turns the tables on everybody, does her best work on film to date. Lovers of crossword puzzles will have a ball.

BEING THERE (1979)

★ ★ ★ ★ Directed by Hal Ashby. Screenplay by Jerzy Kosinski. Produced by Andrew Braunsberg. *With Peter Sellers, Shirley MacLaine, Melvyn Douglas, Jack Warden, Richard Dysart, and Richard Basehart.*

Being There is a remarkable film that makes you think while it's making you laugh, arousing and instructing you on all kinds of levels, including a few you might not even be aware of. It is certainly the best thing Peter Sellers ever did, and totally unlike anything else he ever did before or after.

Jerzy Kosinski, the brilliant writer of black and biting fables, has adapted the screenplay from his own critically acclaimed novel, giving the film a sparse but vital feeling of his own prose that no other scenarist could provide. It was a stroke of genius on director Hal Ashby's part to give Kosinski this assignment, and even though it was, to my knowledge, his first experience in writing for the cinema, he did not let anyone down.

Without a single gag or punch line, the film is hilarious. Some of the funniest moments in *Being There* occur when nobody is saying anything at all. This is an accomplishment every comedy writer in Holly-

wood should be forced to study. Oh, what they could learn from this picture! And oh, what some morons could learn about playing comedy from watching Sellers! By playing it absolutely straight, with no funny faces or pratfalls or custard pies, Sellers achieves a classic comedy impersonation.

The best lesson to be learned from comedy is that it is only funny when it is dead-on serious. Judy Holliday knew the secret; the imbeciles in films like *Animal House* didn't.

Sellers plays a mentally retarded gardener named Chance, raised and protected by a rich old eccentric who dies and leaves him bewildered and homeless. Chance can't read or write and everything he knows is what he has learned from watching TV.

Wandering the streets of Washington, D.C., he gets hit by a limousine carrying the wife (Shirley MacLaine) of a dying billionaire financier (Melvyn Douglas) who is also one of the chief advisers to the President of the United States. Shirley takes his home to heal and because his stoic blankness convinces everyone he's deep and wise, Douglas wants to make him head of a new institution to distribute financial assistance to businessmen. The President

(Jack Warden) wants to make him a personal assistant in a White House advisory capacity. Shirley just wants to make *him*.

Before Chance can get his thoughts organized to the point of telling them he needs a job as a gardener, the financial editor of the *Washington Post* is calling him for quotes, the TV talk shows are making him a celebrity, and the computers, the CIA, and the research morgues at the newspapers are all baffled. He has no identification, no Social Security number, no driver's license, and the "man of mystery" ends up the front runner in the political chess game.

All he wants is food, a nice bed, and a TV set that shows Big Bird, *Hollywood Squares*, and commercials for Posturepedic mattresses. Instead, there is a good chance he'll be the perfect closed-mouthed candidate for the next election. *Being There* uses this illiterate Candide as a metaphor for a whole nation of illiterates who are slowly surrendering their brains to a TV fixation. Kosinski is obviously concerned with the pervasive influence of television and the way in which its impact is felt from the living room to the Oval Office.

But his vitriolic pén, dipped in the acid of comic parable, takes on other targets: sex, politics, critical perception, and, ultimately, the human condition itself. Ashby's direction is lean but filled with innuendo and there are magnificent performances by everyone. Still, it is Sellers who gives the film its center and its balance. He is the talisman that proves the American fascination with the unknown.

When we don't understand something, we embrace it. When it refuses to be explained, we run it for office. A brilliant film, provocative and different, and howlingly funny.

THE BELLE OF NEW YORK (1951)
★ ★ ½ Directed by Charles Walters. Screenplay by Robert O'Brien and Irving Elinson. Produced by Arthur Freed. With Fred Astaire, Vera-Ellen, Marjorie Main, Keenan Wynn, and Alice Pearce.

Dazzling special effects highlight this charming turn-of-the-century foolishness, with Fred Astaire as a playboy who has stranded five brides at the altar and Vera-Ellen as the prim Salvation Army belle who finally snares him. Marjorie Main is hilarious as Fred's rich aunt, and the songs by Johnny Mercer and Harry Warren provide imaginative settings for

Fred to do wonders with trick photography. "Seeing Is Believing" has the two stars literally dancing off rooftops into the clouds above New York City, and "Currier and Ives" takes them on a tour of the seasons against lush backdrops inspired by famous Currier and Ives prints. But the pièce de résistance is Fred's lively solo "I Wanna Be a Dancing Man," a number that so inspired Bob Fosse the great choreographer-director worked an entire section around it in the Broadway musical *Dancin'*.

BEST FOOT FORWARD (1943)

★ ★ ★   Directed by Eddie Buzzell. Screenplay by Irving Brecher and Fred Finkelhoffe. Produced by Arthur Freed. *With Lucille Ball, William Gaxton, Tommy Dix, June Allyson, Nancy Walker, Gloria DeHaven, and Virginia Wiedler.*

An MGM musical bubble rescued from the dusty vaults for home viewing, this 1943 Technicolor romp has nothing on its simple mind but pleasure. Lucille Ball plays a movie star who gives her fading career a boost by invading an all-male military school as a publicity stunt, causing trouble for the cadets and their girls. There are gags galore, people popping out of closets, close encounters with the dean, dazzling musical numbers, and the classic drill-field song "Buckle Down, Winsocki!" to keep the action moving. June Allyson, Gloria DeHaven, and poker-faced Nancy Walker — three nubile young MGM starlets who later became big stars themselves — share the fun, and Harry James and his orchestra always mysteriously show up to provide swing music when you least expect them. Light and sparkling, *Best Foot Forward* is guaranteed to put a smile on the grouchiest face.

BEST FRIENDS (1982)

★ ★ ★   Directed by Norman Jewison. Screenplay by Barry Levinson and Valerie Curtin. Produced by Joe Wizan. *With Burt Reynolds, Goldie Hawn, Jessica Tandy, Barnard Hughes, Audra Lindley, Keenan Wynn, Ron Silver, Carol Locatell, and Richard Libertini.*

Will *his* fans, asking only for the good-old-boy image, mistake his best and most serious work for laziness?

Will *her* fans, content with her silly dingbat image, accept her deeper, more complicated growth as an actress of substance?

These are the questions faced by Burt Reynolds and Goldie Hawn and posed by *Best*

Friends, an understated film which went down in the books as a box office failure but deserves a second look.

In *Best Friends* Burt and Goldie play Hollywood screenwriters who have, for five years, been an unbeatable team as writers, lovers, and roommates.

It's such a perfect arrangement. Why spoil it by getting married? he insists. She's afraid she'll lose her identity. Finally they compromise, sneaking off secretly to a chapel in the Spanish section of Los Angeles — giving scriptwriters Valerie Curtin and Barry Levinson a chance to milk a few feeble laughs from a José Jimenez preacher. So far, this movie is a nonmusical parody of *They're Playing Our Song* and going nowhere fast.

But it's on the honeymoon that the real relationship begins and the movie starts cracking. In the blizzards of Buffalo, her parents (Jessica Tandy and Barnard Hughes) turn out to be nutty old eccentrics who never stop babbling, while in the cornball vulgarity of a Virginia condominium, his parents (Keenan Wynn and Audra Lindley) live with eighteen thousand other people in nitwit suburban catatonia.

Each is driven bananas by the other one's parents. He almost freezes to death from open windows; she almost dies from an overdose of Valium. Clearly the real honeymoon was the five years of sin, while their billion-dollar relationship as friends is now devalued to the equivalent of a slot-machine slug as man and wife.

What a pleasure it is to see Reynolds doing what's right for the script's subtleties instead of going for easy laughs. He doesn't drop his pants, roll his eyes, or drive a truck into the scenery. He actually seems inspired by Goldie, who gives her most beautifully modulated performance since *Sugarland Express*.

The mature, complex risks they take in *Best Friends* result in a warm romantic comedy that is funny and painful, like life. It isn't ha-ha funny, like most of their films, but it is endearingly, realistically, exasperatingly funny the way it catalogues real human situations everyone can identify with.

Meanwhile, director Norman Jewison cleverly juxtaposes the Hollywood they live in—with its scrambled brains running studios, its movie lingo, and its plastic luxury—with the worlds they both come from, their middle-class chaos and cornball plastic reality.

What they ultimately learn is the key to real success; how to be the best of lovers *and* the best of friends. Okay, it's corn. But the charisma and emotional directness of the two stars make the corn human, viable, uplifting.

BETRAYAL (1983)

★ ★ ★ ½ **Directed by David Jones. Screenplay by Harold Pinter. Produced by Sam Spiegel. With Ben Kingsley, Patricia Hodge, and Jeremy Irons.**

Articulate dialogue, sophisticated emotions, and intelligent restraint are rare commodities in movies. *Betrayal*, the elegant film of Harold Pinter's play, has plenty of all three.

I am amazed to find myself admitting this, because when the play opened on Broadway in 1980, I considered it preposterously tiresome. It just proves, once again, how much more persuasive and intimately revealing the film medium can be. In a finely honed, vastly improved movie version, a pretentious theatrical bore has been brought to life with impressive brio.

One of the things I hated about *Betrayal* was the fact that it was written backward. This conceit didn't work on stage, but it has an oddly realistic impact on screen. You may think

it's odd to see an entire movie backward, but that's the way we see life, from an experienced view. The time warp works.

In the very first scene, a husband and wife are cleaning up after a party. An argument ensues. They hit each other. A child enters and begins to cry. Feelings are raw; there is sadness, anger, and pain. We are witnessing the end of something, and we are watching it in silence, since it's all taking place through a window. *Betrayal* begins where most marriages (or love affairs) end—then travels in reverse, until the last scene in the film is really the first scene in anyone else's film.

The viewer must adjust his own sense of cinematic proportion, work his way into the stubborn structure the film imposes. *Betrayal* demands a commitment, but once you get over the jet lag, the results are rewarding.

Betrayal is about three people—Robert, Emma and Jerry. Robert (Ben Kingsley) is married to Emma (Patricia Hodge). Jerry (Jeremy Irons) is having an affair with Emma. Robert and Jerry have been best friends for years. Robert knows what's going on. Jerry doesn't think Robert knows what's going on.

Emma knows that Robert knows, but hasn't told Jerry that Robert knows. Robert, meanwhile, has been betraying them both with someone else. It takes seven years to reveal all.

The movie seems less arch, less claustrophobic, than the play—mainly because David Jones does a masterful job of directing. His camera does a lot to enhance style, isolate moments of conflict, and emphasize feelings that the stage can only hint at.

He's also cleaned up the famous Pinter pauses and underscored the dramatic interactions, so the adultery theme sounds and looks more like it's being lived by real people instead of blank icons.

Best of all, there are central performers who balance the triangular equation with crisp aplomb. Most distinguished is Kingsley, who doesn't vaguely resemble the way he looked in *Gandhi*. As a dry vermouth of a man more concerned with his squash game than his crumbling marriage, he emerges, in this about-face, as a real artist of stunning versatility and lasting stature. It's good to have him back, but we're twice blessed to have him in a movie as rich and satisfying as *Betrayal*.

BETSY'S WEDDING (1989)

★ ★ ½ Directed and written by Alan Alda. Produced by Martin Bregman and Louis A. Stroller. With Alan Alda, Madeline Kahn, Molly Ringwald, Ally Sheedy, Joe Pesci, Joey Bishop, Catherine O'Hara, and Anthony La Paglia.

In *Betsy's Wedding*, Alan Alda shows off and gives daughter Molly Ringwald a fabulous formal wedding. What happens next is every bride's nightmare. This is not a new idea. It was done before—and better—in the Spencer Tracy-Elizabeth Taylor classic, *Father of the Bride*, from which writer-director-star Alda steals whole scenes shamelessly. But the idea still works and by the time the big evening arrives, the Jewish side of the family screams, "It's escalating—like the arms race!" The Italian side of the family is up to their ears in debt and the mob. Mom (hilarious Madeline Kahn) wants a rabbi. Pop wants a priest. Betsy's parents are losing their house. Her older sister (Ally Sheedy) is in love with a gangster. The wedding lands on the rainiest day of the year and the tent leaks. It's silly, but never dull. The ethnic differences make for a lot of humor about religion. Betsy is a fashion student who designs freaked-out clothes for astro-zombies, which makes for a lot of funny comments on fashion victims. Alda's script is crisp, his pacing lively. And the actors all play it for real instead of for guffaws, which makes everything twice as amusing.

BEVERLY HILLS COP (1984)

★ ★ ★ Directed by Martin Brest. Screenplay by Daniel Petrie, Jr. Story by Danilo Bach and Petrie. Produced by Don Simpson and Jerry Bruckheimer. With Eddie Murphy, Judge Reinhold, John Ashton, Lisa Eilbacher, Ronny Cox, and Steven Berkoff.

Eddie Murphy's rise from street urchin to megamillionaire was swift, and with a few raunchy exceptions, welcome. It wasn't long before they were writing specially tailored vehicles for him, the way they used to order up scripts for Gable, Bogart, and the Marx Brothers. *Beverly Hills Cop* is a custom-made comedy from the Eddie Murphy fitting room. Chock-full of noise, rhythm, and smart-ass dialogue, *Beverly Hills Cop* fits the cool, freshmouthed, jiveass hipness of Murphy's screen persona like a crash helmet. It begins with a series of car crunches as the finger-popping comedian busts a slimy gang of cigarette hijackers in Detroit, and ends with another blast of gunfire and violence (much of it tongue-in-cheek instead of the usual bloody gore) as he outwits a slimy gang of drug smugglers in posh Beverly Hills. The property damage in between is inestimable.

Murphy plays Axel Foley, the Lou Costello of the Detroit Police Department. Always in hot water, he just can't play by the rules. When an old childhood pal is murdered, he ignores the warning by his own superiors to stay out of the case and heads for Beverly Hills to find the killers.

In jeans and sneakers, he checks into the swankiest hotel by posing as a *Rolling Stone* reporter who's doing a piece on Michael Jackson, and before you can say "Which way to the Polo Lounge?" he's up to his cauliflower ears in trouble.

This movie went down like lye in Los Angeles, where the favorite pastime is self-inflicted character assassination, because it makes the Beverly Hills cops, with their three-piece Johnny Carson suits and their charge accounts at Spago, look like snide, aging preppy jokes. Square, conservative, and clean-cut, they get outsmarted every time by the Detroit punk with the *Saturday Night Live* charisma.

Much of the humor in *Bev-*

erly Hills Cop is distilled from Axel's head-on collision with both the sterile state-of-the-art mentality of the Beverly Hills Police Force and the almost laughably unreal foreign planet ozone layer of La-La Land culture in general. Finding the killers and exposing a cocaine racket inside the California art world becomes secondary to the humorous clash between Murphy and everything that personifies Hollywood's favorite word, *trendy*.

Along the way, an oddball friendship develops between the Detroit skull-buster and two Beverly Hills detectives, as Axel teaches the cloak-and-suitors a few things and the nerds with their computers, sophisticated electronic police methods, and rule books end up saving his life.

The overweight, square detective and the young, naive, refined detective are played with restraint and humor by John Ashton and Judge Reinhold, respectively. Lisa Eilbacher lends stylish support as another of Axel's childhood friends who bails him out of jail and offers him a snazzy red sports car to drive and a pretty shoulder to lean on.

But center stage belongs to Murphy. Script and direction are unimportant. Everything else is a supporting act.

It's refreshing to see a performer who is essentially nothing more than a kid with moxie stand there and do the most astonishing double-takes and get away with it.

Every third word still begins with *F*, but Murphy's wild and daring roadhouse personality has a winning nature. Here, for the first time, he gets a chance to demonstrate his vulnerability, too. His laugh, his stance, his bulldozer self-confidence make you want him to confide in you. You want to know this guy. You want him on your team.

When this movie came out in 1984, I figured Eddie Murphy would, like his partners in mayhem on *Saturday Night Live*, be a star for fifteen minutes. I was wrong. His clock is still ticking.

BIG (1988)
★ ★ ★ ½ Directed by Penny Marshall. Written and produced by Gary Ross and Anne Spielberg. With Tom Hanks, Elizabeth Perkins, John Heard, Jared Rushton, and Robert Loggia.

Tom Hanks reveals new heights of his comic technique by creating an adolescent body language as funny as it is accurate. He's a thirteen-year-old boy who wishes to be "big" and—shazam!—magically wakes up in the body of . . . Tom Hanks! The laughs start rolling immediately, as Hanks swings his hairy legs over the edge of a bunk several sizes too small, crashes to the floor, and painfully tries to fit into a thirteen-year-old's jeans. Somehow he ends up in a corporation where he becomes a big star testing toys and the movie introduces a romance with career woman Elizabeth Perkins, who doesn't know she's seducing a thirteen-year-old virgin. The movie finally runs out of steam, jokes and sight gags, but at least two-thirds of *Big* provide one of the brightest entertainments of the 1980s.

THE BIG CHILL (1983)

★ ★ ★ 1/2 Directed by Lawrence Kasdan. Screenplay by Kasdan and Barbara Benedek. Produced by Michael Shamberg. With Glenn Close, Kevin Kline, JoBeth Williams, Jeff Goldblum, Tom Berenger, William Hurt, Mary Kay Place, and Meg Tilly.

The Big Chill is one of many films, plays, and books created by sixties radicals who grew up to be eighties capitalists, each of them asking the same question: "Where did we all go wrong?" Somewhere along the way, they gave up their ideals

and settled for success. Now they feel guilty about it.

No contemporary writer-director of films seems better qualified to hang a SOLD OUT sign on his soul than Lawrence Kasdan, who may have started his career with art in mind but ended up writing popcorn movies like *Raiders of the Lost Ark*, *The Empire Strikes Back*, and *Return of the Jedi*, as well as writing and directing the sexy film noir *Body Heat*.

Like John Sayles's *Return of the Secaucus Seven*, Kasdan's film is a "reunion" movie, set in that dusty emotional landscape between idealism's postnatal depression and midlife crisis. It is intelligently written, intensely personal, and very, very funny.

The opening introductory passages are memorable and sharp: The seven people we're about to meet are all shown getting the news that Alex, one of their best college chums from fifteen years ago, has committed suicide. The eighth person, seen only from the point of view of his socks, ties, and cufflinks, turns out to be the corpse.

Descending on a small town in South Carolina for Alex's funeral, the old friends hear the minister ask in the eulogy "Where did Alex's hope go?"

and for the rest of the picture they find themselves asking the same thing of each other. They all started out so fresh, so full of lofty plans for saving the world. Now the yard is littered with Porsches, Cadillacs, and Mercedes, the kitchen is filled with electric marvels, the dining table is groaning under the weight of a feast. But is anybody happy?

There are the hosts, Sarah (Glenn Close) and Harold (Kevin Kline). Sarah's a doctor whose practice doesn't amount to much, so she had an affair with Alex, the friend who just killed himself; Harold's the rich owner of a company that sells jogging shoes and he's about to become even richer when he sells out to a conglomerate for a colossal profit margin.

Their weekend guests are Michael (Jeff Goldblum), who gave up a promising career as a rabble-rousing investigative journalist to write slick crap for *People* magazine; Sam (Tom Berenger), who went from campus revolutionary to TV star; and Karen (JoBeth Williams), who gave up a writing career and settled for being the suburban wife of a dull button-down advertising executive who remains faithful to her not out of love but out of fear of

getting herpes from somebody else.

There is also Nick (William Hurt), who came back from Vietnam with an injury that rendered him impotent and a cynicism that drove him to drugs; and Meg (Mary Kay Place), who sold out her law career and now wants one of the guys to father her baby. The "outsider" is Chloe (Meg Tilly), the dead friend's girl, who never heard of Woodstock. She reminds them all of what they were like at her age, back at the University of Michigan.

When *The Big Chill* opened at the Toronto Film Festival, a Canadian critic wrote "The people are essentially the same person—they all sound like they'll go back to Hollywood and write *Return of the Jedi*." This is basically true: In the course of the weekend, they define themselves by what they say and do instead of by what they feel and think, and in the end there isn't much point except that there's nothing wrong with good intentions, but there's nothing wrong with baking cranberry-nut bread, either.

Yet in the process, there's a terrifically entertaining movie here that throbs with great dialogue and great acting.

The ensemble work by the supremely gifted cast is so

natural, so real, so skillfully integrated, that you know everything about their relationships just by the way they look at each other. Each has an individuality, but their precision playing contributes to part of a communal fabric that redefines the complexities and perimeters of friendship.

The writing is hip, witty, full of irony, and the direction pushes things along stylishly. Kasdan isn't above throwing in a little comedy, a little soap opera, a little nostalgia, and more than a little sentimentality. The old friends rehash old unfulfilled passions, frustrations, and competitiveness and explore new longings. It could get gummy with reflection, but not the way Kasdan keeps things crisp. He knows the value of pace, tempo and structure.

Ultimately, *The Big Chill* comes up with the same answer as all of the other movies and plays by guilty sixties survivors: If you don't end up with what you always wanted in life, it's because you didn't have a very clear picture of what it was you wanted in the first place. It's hardly big news, but everyone responsible for this rich, sincerely intentioned movie is talented enough to make everything old look new again.

THE BIG COUNTRY (1958)

★ ★ ★ ½ Directed by William Wyler. Screenplay by James Webb and Sy Bartlett. Produced by William Wyler and Gregory Peck. *With Gregory Peck, Jean Simmons, Charlton Heston, Carroll Baker, Charles Bickford, Burl Ives and Chuck Connors.*

A big, brawling blockbuster Western on the grandest of scales, this William Wyler classic from 1958 is every bit as exciting and eye-filling now as it was more than thirty years ago. Gregory Peck turns in one of his most solid performances as a pacifist who innocently finds himself caught up in a war between two evil cattle barons having a long and bloody feud over water. The adjacent ranch is owned by gorgeous, exquisitely underrated Jean Simmons. Charlton Heston is a burly ranch foreman who slugs it out with Peck toe to toe, six guns blazing. The bloodthirsty barons are Charles Bickford and Burl Ives, and Carroll Baker is Bickford's cupcake daughter. Violent battles, range wars, cattle stampedes, and turbulent romance ignite the screen in this classic sagebrush saga. It's long, but there is never a dull moment.

THE BIG EASY (1987)

★ ★ ★ Directed by Jim McBride. Screenplay by Daniel Petrie, Jr. Produced by Stephen Friedman. With Dennis Quaid, Ellen Barkin, Ned Beatty, John Goodman, Ebbe Roe Smith, Lisa Jane Persky, and Charles Ludlam.

Maybe you think cop movies are a dime a dozen, but *The Big Easy* is different. It's about a series of grisly homicides and it's about police corruption among the cops who are supposed to be investigating. It's colorful, it's fresh, it's full of spicy dialogue, it's sexy, and it's set in New Orleans, a city of carnival-like sounds, smells, and colors that have never been so vividly captured on film. Dennis Quaid is a Cajun detective who bends the rules. He's on the take in little ways, like every other cop in the French Quarter. Ellen Barkin is a member of the district attorney's office who believes in obeying rules, playing by the book. When he gets framed on a corruption charge for accepting a bribe, she's the one who has to prosecute the guy she loves. They're a dynamic screen duo. In every scene, the sexual tension builds to a crackling chemistry, and even their dialogue is a mixture of antagonism and seductiveness. Add voodoo, warehouses full of Mardi Gras

floats where danger waits, a flotilla of corpses, hot New Orleans jazz, and a heroin war, and you've got a tabasco sauce cocktail. *The Big Easy* is what they call New Orleans. "The Big Surprise" is what I call this movie. It moves with energy. It never slows down. It's got the heated authenticity of a hot night on Bourbon Street, and both Quaid and Barkin fuse their roles with personality. Best of all, this is a movie that shows you things you've never seen before. A thoroughly engrossing thriller.

BILOXI BLUES (1988)

★ ★ ★ Directed by Mike Nichols. Screenplay by Neil Simon. Produced by Ray Stark. With Matthew Broderick, Christopher Walken, Matt Mulhern, Corey Parker, Casey Siemaszko, Markus Flanagan, Michael Dolan, Penelope Ann Miller, and Park Overall.

The further adventures of Eugene Jerome, the precocious, bewildered teenager from *Brighton Beach Memoirs*, after he's drafted and sent to boot camp in Mississippi. This is Mike Nichols's funny adaptation of Neil Simon's cockeyed view of army life, so expect the entire platoon of likable meatheads headed by Matthew Broderick to assault you with wry humor instead of jokey one-liners. You may not scream with laughter, but this one is guaranteed to put a smile on your face and keep it there.

BIRD (1988)
★ ★ ★ ★ Directed and produced by Clint Eastwood. Screenplay by Joel Oliansky. *With Forest Whitaker, Diane Venora, Michael Zelniker, Samuel E. Wright, Keith David, Michael McGuire, and James Handy.*

If you only think of Clint Eastwood as two-fisted Dirty Harry, you have a major discovery in store for you. Pianist, jazz buff and first-rate director, Big Clint has made the ultimate movie about jazz and about his idol, Charlie "Yardbird" Parker. There has never been a musician like him and there has never been a movie like *Bird*. It distills the essence of the greatest alto saxophone player of all time into a passionate and truthful look at both the man and his music. With a history of nervous breakdowns, suicide attempts, drug addiction, and bleeding ulcers, Bird was a self-destructive genius, but his music revolutionized jazz. When he died in 1955, at the age of thirty-four, the coroner thought he was twenty years older. It's not a pretty story, but Eastwood has captured every conflicting nuance with a passion that borders on obsession, and in a fabulous tour de force, Forest Whitaker brings Bird to life with throbbing vitality. Whitaker doesn't just play Bird. He *is* Bird. His performance seems haunted. Half focusing his eyes like broken shutters, absorbing all and missing nothing, he is mesmerizing. Diane Venora is also marvelous as the white wife who tried to save him, then help him, then bury him. Eastwood recaptures not only the essence of the man himself, using all the original Charlie Parker recordings on the soundtrack, but the entire swing era. The movie captures Bird and his music with the driving tempo of a jam session. This is a dynamic, powerful tribute not only to a stormy legend but to the whole jazz era that gave him life. It's the best film I've ever seen about jazz, establishing Eastwood as one of America's most accomplished filmmakers. But better than that, it proves with the pain and the passion of his music that Bird lives on!

BIRDY (1984)
★ ★ ★ Directed by Alan Parker. Screenplay by Sandy Kroopf and Jack Behr. Produced by Alan Marshall. *With Nicolas Cage and Matthew Modine.*

Once in a blue moon a film comes along that is so unusual, so different, so full of risks and surprises that it defies description.

Such a film is *Birdy*. In a crazy, offbeat kind of way, it is an amazing accomplishment, a brilliant and precocious feat of filmmaking, and as skillful as anything you are ever likely to see. It is also a failure, but more about that later.

Birdy is a kind of love story between two teenagers who grow up to be soldiers. It is also a strange gossamer fantasy about a boy who wants to be a bird. Everything I am telling you is enough to send most filmgoers racing to the nearest Pia Zadora movie. But *Birdy* is asking for it. It's a movie that makes its own rules, and breaks a lot of others, and dares to be different.

Two friends who grew up together in the Philadelphia slums are now war veterans. Vietnam has destroyed them both. Al (Nicholas Cage) has survived, but his face is scarred beyond recognition, partially restored by plastic surgery, swathed in bandages. Al is summoned by Army doctors to visit his childhood buddy, a guy named Birdy (Matthew Modine). He is now in a psycho ward, where he lies naked on the floor, catatonic,

staring at the sky outside the bars on his window.

Birdy has spent his life in a world of birds, catching and taming pigeons, dressing up in bird feathers, studying the mating and reproductive patterns of birds, imitating them, trying to fly. Ironically, it is now Birdy who ends up in a cage, just like his pigeons and canaries.

Through flashbacks, we see the boys growing up, testing each other's loyalty, sharing weird experiences. A strange story emerges about a boy who doesn't fit in anywhere except in the world of birds and a friend who loves him in spite of his eccentricity.

For a while *Birdy* seems to be an impossible dream, poking fun at ornithology. Then the mood changes, the style turns surrealistic. The story evolves not through external plot mechanics, but through the thoughts inside Birdy's head. Obsession turns to madness.

The hatching of an egg becomes a slow-speed miracle of trick photography. The camera becomes a bird, swooping across rooftops, soaring above clotheslines, landing on windowsills.

Compared to the freedom of flying, normal experiences like the high school prom become unreal to Birdy. He loses all interest in life and becomes a bird in his mind. It's a movie that cannot easily be—no pun intended—pigeonholed.

Alan Parker proves, with each successive film, that he isn't interested in formulas. Audiences expect—and get— something new and surprising with each of his films. From *Midnight Express* to *Fame*, from *Shoot the Moon* to *Pink Floyd—The Wall*, his films are daring, gutsy, controversial.

Some of the best scenes in *Birdy* involve animals. There's a harrowing encounter with a cat, photographed from a birds-eye point of view, that is as suspenseful and gripping as anything ever filmed.

And the film comes closer to actually teaching us what it feels like to fly than anything in *Superman*. The two central performances by Nicholas Cage and Matthew Modine are measures of skill and craft that should be role models for young actors. The cinematography by Michael Seresin is revolutionary and beautiful.

Still, *Birdy*, for all its virtuosity, is a disappointment. Parker works us up over two lovable nuts, finds the center of their truth, then doesn't have the vaguest idea how to get them out of their predicament. The movie has no ending. It just

stops. *Shoot the Moon* was a great film, wrecked by an enigmatic, unsatisfying finale. So is *Birdy*. It left me feeling angry and cheated.

For movie buffs tired of the same old predictable pablum, *Birdy* offers an exhilarating challenge. But the ending is strictly for the birds.

THE BLACK CAULDRON (1985)

★ ★ ★   Directed by Ted Berman and Richard Rich. Screenplay by David Jonas, Vance Gerry, Ted Berman, Richard Rich, Al Wilson, and Roy Morita. Produced by Joe Hale.

Most children's cartoons either insult the intelligence of the young audiences they are made for, or scare the living daylights out of them. *The Black Cauldron* is not guilty of the first sin. It has some scary sequences, but as kiddie films go, it's pretty sophisticated stuff.

The Black Cauldron is a spectacular fairy tale about a young farm boy named Taran, who for mysterious reasons is assigned to guard a sweet, goofy-looking pig called Hen Wen from the evil clutches of a monster called the Horned King.

Hen Wen is no ordinary pig. This little porker has clairvoyant talents and is the only creature that knows the hiding place of the Black Cauldron, a strange vessel that contains the power to rule the world.

On the way to a hidden cottage in the forbidden forest, Hen Wen is attacked by flying dragon birds with heads like snapping Dobermans, and dragged off to the Horned King's castle of horrors.

In his quest to save the pig and the world, little Taran meets up with an enchanting new group of Disney characters: a princess in distress, a traveling minstrel musician named Fflewddur Fflam, and a furry creature called Gurgi, who looks like Jackie Gleason in a teddy-bear costume.

The search for the black cauldron leads this merry band of courageous heroes through the torture dungeons of the black-hearted Horned King, an underground hole inhabited by twinkling fairies, and the swamps of a dreaded place called Morva.

There's a lot of adventure here, plus enough scary stuff to satisfy the most demanding of children. More than ten years in the making and budgeted at $25 million, *The Black Cauldron* is probably the most ambitious Disney project since *Pinocchio*. The story line is often ponderous, but the film is rich with color, imagination, and entertainment value.

The animation doesn't look flat, like comic-book pages, but instead has a three-dimensional quality with images that jump right off the screen at you. Picture deep whirlpools, the reflection of a lighted candle shimmering in water, or a wine cellar in which the vats of wine are punctured, sending jets of wine pouring in a variety of directions.

The result is a film of great charm, energy, and imagination that should delight audiences young and old. *The Black Cauldron* is one Disney feature even Uncle Walt might have been proud of.

THE BLACK HOLE (1979)

★ ★ Directed by Gary Nelson. Screenplay by Jeb Rosebrook and Gerry Day. Produced by Ron Miller. *With Maximilian Schell, Yvette Mimieux, Anthony Perkins, Ernest Borgnine, Joseph Bottoms, Robert Forster and the voice of Roddy McDowall.*

The Black Hole is disheartening evidence of how little creativity was left at the Disney studios after the old man died. Thing got better later, with *Roger Rabbit* and *Beauty and the Beast*, but this one had a $20 million budget and not even 10 cents worth of imagination. These guys weren't content to steal ideas from every other sci-fi movie ever made; they even ripped off a few Disney clones along the way.

It's 20,000 leagues *above* the sea, with the same ending as *Fantasia*. Maximilian Schell is Captain Nemo, doing his mad scientist bit, and the black hole is a rotating galaxy of bottomless gravity, pulling anything that wanders too close into its eternal pit. There is no story, merely improbable situations serving to drag an audience bored out of its mind from one special effect to the next, and we've seen them all before in better movies than this. The result is unintentionally laughable.

Ernest Borgnine gives his worst performance since *McHale's Navy*. His fellow crew members are Joseph Bottoms, Yvette Mimieux, and Anthony Perkins. With them is a floating robot with cute eyes, built like the Pillsbury Doughboy. I liked him better as R2D2 in *Star Wars*. For all his well-timed quips, the robot fails to provide the comic relief he was designed for.

When the good guys land on the mammoth Death Ship anchored just out of reach of the black hole, they meet Maximilian Schell doing his James Mason imitation from *20,000 Leagues Under the Sea*. His right-hand man is an evil-looking robot with four arms and rotating switchblades for hands, which quickly slice Tony Perkins's midsection into scaloppine. Yvette Mimieux has ESP. When all other communication systems fail, everyone turns to her and asks her what's happening.

Later, Yvette finds herself wrapped in tinfoil on a lazy Susan, heading under the ray gun designed to zap her brain. She wards off laser beams by arching her eyebrows like Marjorie Main. But the biggest letdown comes when they actually travel through the black hole, after Schell and his mad schemes go up in sparks. First it looks like they tried to film an LSD trip, then changed their minds and decided on Dante's Inferno, a fiery pit with the evil robot standing on a rock like Lucifer.

I liked it better when Mickey Mouse spent "A Night on Bald Mountain." For all the crescendos in the energetic sound track (every theme stolen from John Williams's score for *Star Wars*), it is impossible to care whether any of these characters make it or not. The robots in this one float through the air, but you can see the strings without even looking. *The Black Hole* is merely the pits.

THE BLACK STALLION (1979)

★ ★ Directed by Carroll Ballard. Screenplay by Melissa Mathison, Jeanne Rosenberg, and William D. Wittliff. Produced by Francis Ford Coppola, Fred Roos, and Tom Sternberg. With Mickey Rooney, Kelly Reno, Teri Garr, Clarence Muse, Hoyt Axton, Michael Higgins, and Cass-ole as the Black Stallion.

Having performed the chore for a prepubescent Elizabeth Taylor in *National Velvet*, Mickey Rooney is well versed in the art of teaching children to love horses, a job he repeats in *The Black Stallion*, a bizarre little children's film.

The differences in cinematic styles that have developed in the years between are self-evident. Personally, I'll take *National Velvet*. They knew how to tell stories in 1944. *National Velvet* was a movie about people and love and nature and the indestructibility of the human spirit. *The Black Stallion* is a movie about camera angles.

For reasons unexplained, a small boy is shipwrecked off the coast of North Africa in 1946 and washed ashore with a wild Arabian stallion. On a desert island, the sole survivor of a horrible, mind-altering accident, this boy would in real life die of sunburn, starvation, or grief.

But the movie child, in typical boy's book fairy tale splendor, is in no time at all making fires (was he a Boy Scout?), spearing fish, dining on kelp and seaweed, taming the wild horse through endless shots of slow-motion waves, and doing underwater Esther Williams ballets on horseback in cutoff pajama bottoms. Finally rescued by fishermen and hauled back to civilization with a horse in tow, the boy meets Rooney, a has-been trainer whose farm provides a spare barn for the desert stallion.

After an interminable amount of arty cinematography showing people's faces through haylofts and rain-drenched windshields, the boy and the horse race to glory in the American equivalent of Taylor's *National Velvet* finale, with grizzled old Rooney rooting from the sidelines.

There's nothing new here, except a lot of filters, zoom lenses and stop-frame camera wizardry that substitutes drearily for plot, theme and character development. There's so little dialogue in *The Black Stallion* that I often felt like I was watching a silent movie. More scenes of people communicating with each other and less pretentious sitar music by Carmine

Coppola would have helped enormously.

It's always a pleasure to watch an old pro like Rooney, and the kid, played by a freckle-faced dumpling with a speech impediment named Kelly Reno, works with a nice, appealing ease. But after the terrifying shipwreck that washes his father overboard and the stunningly photographed encounter with a vicious cobra, nothing much happens to the boy or the audience. Director Carroll Ballard is content to wash his film imagery with a minimum of explanation. The result is that I went away knowing nothing about the kid, the horse, the kid's weirdo mother or anything else—least of all where the whole thing is supposed to be taking place.

Ballard manages to make an all-American town seem as comfortably familiar as a tribal village in Pakistan. All of it is camouflage for what is really just another boy-meets-horse story; in its back-breaking dedication to avoiding clichés *The Black Stallion* creates new clichés of its own. This is one kid's movie that tries to be so different it just might end up boring the kids to death.

BLACK WIDOW (1986)
★ ★ ★ Directed by Bob Rafelson. Screenplay by Ron Base. Produced by Laurence Mark and Harold Schneider. *With Debra Winger, Theresa Russell, Dennis Hopper, Sami Frey, and Nicol Williamson.*

Alluring Theresa Russell plays a cunning, evil sex kitten who marries and poisons a series of wealthy husbands with the deadly sting of a black widow spider, and feisty Debra Winger plays the sleuth from the Justice Department who tracks her down in this slick, satiny thriller. Things get tense when Winger falls for the villainous killer's next victim, and the cat-and-mouse game builds to a pulsating climax, with a few real surprises along the way. Craftily directed by Bob Rafelson, beautifully photographed, and featuring some fine performances—especially by Theresa Russell, who is a cross between Kathleen Turner and a Siamese cat.

BLADE RUNNER (1982)
★ ½ Directed by Ridley Scott. Screenplay by Hampton Fancher and David Peoples. Produced by Michael Deeley. *With Harrison Ford, Rutger Hauer, Sean Young, Edward James Olmos, M. Emmet Walsh, and Darryl Hannah.*

Ridley Scott, director of *Alien*, has this time stolen his ideas from old Humphrey Bogart–Alan Ladd film noirs and transposed the action to science fiction. The conceit doesn't work because the acting is deadly and the script is six feet under, but a chilling atmosphere is evoked that might keep less discerning viewers awake between lethal punchouts. Set in the twenty-first century, the thin plot line involves a group of man-made robots called "replicants," used for slave labor in the colonization of other planets but declared illegal on earth. Now a group of these replicants have somehow managed to return to earth in search of answers to their mortality. Special "blade runner" units are employed to track them down and execute (or "retire") them on sight before they get out of hand.

Harrison Ford is the tough cop in the Alan Ladd trenchcoat assigned to the job. He's the kind of racist cop who, in the old days, would have called black men "niggers." He calls the robots "skin jobs." His biggest risk is retiring other humans by mistake, and his job is even further complicated when he falls in love with one of the robots, named Rachel, raised as a human experiment and therefore capable of human feelings. The narrative dialogue is sci-fi Dashiell Hammett and Ford, in his dug-up zombie voice, makes it all sound even sillier than it was intended. "I had a bellyful of killing, but I'd rather be a killer than a victim," he drones, like a twanging, adenoidal John Wayne. Using his only two expressions—wide-eyed and open-mouthed—Ford creeps through smoky interiors and streets drenched with fog and rain in what looks like an interplanetary Chinatown, saying demented things such as "Rachel was special—no termination date. I don't know how long we'd have together. Who does?" He, in turn, is stalked by Rutger Hauer, as the Apollo of the robots—a genetic juggernaut whose batteries are going dead. The replicants, see, eventually run out of gas, like seltzer bottles, and Hauer is looking for petrol. By the time he expires, like Margaret Hamilton in *The Wizard of Oz*, he has broken Ford's fingers and smashed his face.

Exotic sets that look like the inside of a can of red kidney beans are part of the film's extravagance of mood and wacko atmosphere. The extraordinary music is by Vangelis, who caused a sensation with his score for *Chariots of Fire*, but there is entirely too much of it and it is used badly throughout. Instead of enhancing or underscoring a scene, it often seems to take the place of the scene itself. The whole thing ends up empty and peculiar, and, like all movies about artillery and hardware and nothing much else, ultimately boring.

BLAZE (1989)

★ ★ ★ Directed and written by Ron Shelton. Produced by Gil Friesen and Dale Pollack. *With Paul Newman and Lolita Davidovich.*

Scandal, corruption and sexual hijinks form the backdrop for this wild and wacky chapter in backwoods Louisiana politics about legendary Governor Earl K. Long and his turbulent backstreet romance with stripper Blaze Starr. If the sixty-five-year-old three-time governor with a talent for graft and a weakness for sluts and the twenty-eight-year-old Bourbon Street burlesque queen looked like Paul Newman and newcomer Lolita Davidovich, it's easy to see why guns and G-strings clicked from the first introduction. Newman has never been less inhibited. Horny and often horizontal, battling the state legislature or bedding a bimbo, he's the kind of bayou bonehead who always leaves his boots on. Sexy Miss Davidovich combines innocence and sensuality in a dazzling debut. Ron (*Bull Durham*) Shelton wrote and directed with humor, energy, and enough raunchy facts to keep you entertained. Believe it or not, the story is true. Politics makes strange bedfellows and *Blaze* proves it. Pop open a Coors and let this one stomp through the room like a rodeo bull.

BLOOD ON THE SUN (1945)

★ ★ ★ Directed by Frank Lloyd. Screenplay by Lester Cole. Produced by William Cagney. *With James Cagney, Sylvia Sidney, Wallace Ford, and Rosemary DeCamp.*

The robust spy drama *Blood on the Sun* written by blacklisted screenwriter Lester Cole, pits James Cagney against a sinister Japanese underworld mob, as an American newspaperman in Tokyo who undercovers secret plans for World War II. A very entertaining adventure in the Cagney tradition—tough, hard-hitting, and agile as an angry mongoose in a nest of vipers.

BLOOD SIMPLE (1985)

★ ★ ★ Directed by Joel Coen. Screenplay by Ethan and Joel Coen. Produced by Ethan Coen. *With John Getz, Frances*

McDormand, Dan Hedaya, and M. Emmet Walsh.

Bold, tricky, stylish thriller about a two-timing wife, a jealous husband, a double-crossing private eye, and a corpse that won't stay buried. Made in Texas on a remarkably tight budget, this film noir sleeper was the big hit on the film festival circuit, and it works just as well on the small screen. Not for the faint hearted, it ends in a gruesome splatter of gore, blood, and violence, with practically the entire cast of newcomers slashed and shot to death. But if mystery, mayhem, and plot twists are your brand of parlor guessing game, you'll love *Blood Simple*.

BLOSSOMS IN THE DUST (1941)
★ ★ ★ *Directed by Mervyn LeRoy. Screenplay by Anita Loos. Produced by Irving Asher. With Greer Garson, Walter Pidgeon, Felix Bressart, Marsha Hunt, Fay Holden, and Samuel S. Hinds.*

Greer Garson, the flame-haired ruling queen of MGM in 1941, touched millions of hearts with *Blossoms in the Dust*, the inspiring true story of Texan Edna Gladney, whose love gave a home to countless orphans and changed the adoption laws forever. Beautiful as she was in Technicolor, Greer Garson was so noble the wags in Hollywood started calling her "Lassie with Dimples." (They also called Lassie "Greer Garson with fur.") Still, she commands attention in an affecting story that earned respect. She is a vision of loveliness and when she bravely faces the legislature to have the word *illegitimate* removed from birth records in the state of Texas, I doubt if there will be a dry eye in your living room. Bring Kleenex.

BLOWING WILD (1953)
★ ★ ½ *Directed by Hugo Fregonese. Screenplay by Philip Yordan. Produced by Milton Sperling. With Gary Cooper, Barbara Stanwyck, Anthony Quinn, Ruth Roman, and Ward Bond.*

In *Blowing Wild*, Gary Cooper plays a two-fisted prospector, stranded in the Mexican oil fields, who tries to save old pal Anthony Quinn and his no-good wife Barbara Stanwyck from bandits. The explosions are terrific when the desperadoes attack and dynamite the oil wells, and Cooper and Stanwyck set off some erotic fireworks of their own. Stanwyck is at her trashy, eyebrow-flashing best when she pushes Quinn into a burning oil well with lip-smacking relish. The theme by Dimitri Tiomkin, performed with cracking whips by the offstage voice of Frankie Laine, is a direct steal from "High Noon."

THE BLUE LAGOON (1980)

★ Directed and produced by Randal Kleiser. Screenplay by Douglas Day Stewart. *With Brooke Shields, Christopher Atkins, and Leo McKern.*

The Blue Lagoon is a dopey idyll about two shipwrecked children who learn to spear their dinner, build a house out of bamboo, and live the island life. They don't know the Lord's Prayer from the Pledge of Allegiance, but they know about four thousand ways to serve bananas. Years pass. Their bodies grow from children to adults, and pretty soon, watching her eating coconuts for two, he's saying, "How did your tummy grow like that?" and *The Blue Lagoon* begins to look less like a film about two kids surviving in the wilderness and more like a film about two surfers on a wild weekend at Malibu. Brooke Shields and Christopher Atkins prance around naked like two guppies in heat, there is portentous music by the Australian Symphony, and gorgeous underwater cinematography by the brilliant Nestor Almendros.

The rest is food for the porpoises.

BLUE VELVET (1986)

No ★ Directed and written by David Lynch. Produced by Richard Roth. *With Kyle MacLachlan, Laura Dern, Isabella Rossellini, Dennis Hopper, Hope Lange, Dean Stockwell, Jack Nance, Brad Dourif, and George Dickerson.*

Blue Velvet, one of the sickest films ever made, opens with shots of small-town America. Roses blow in the breeze wafting through a graveyard. A man watering his lawn has a stroke. The earth rumbles. Black creatures rise from the soil. They are never seen again. This is not a science fiction movie. Or maybe it is. Nothing in it has any resemblance to anything on this planet.

A boy walking in the woods finds a human ear. Strange sounds of crashing surf and howling winds come from the ear. The boy is Jeffrey Beaumont, played by Kyle MacLachlan, a pallid young actor who had the misfortune to star in the ill-fated *Dune* and TV's *Twin Peaks*, which were also directed by David Lynch. Here is surely a young actor who needs to choose his friends and employers more wisely.

Jeffrey is home from college to help out in his father's hardware store. He takes the ear to the cops, who are understandably baffled. Jeffrey enlists the aid of a local cop's daughter, Sandy (Laura Dern), to solve the mystery.

Playing amateur sleuths, they uncover a sinister plot involving a sleazy nightclub singer (Isabella Rossellini) whose husband and baby have been kidnapped by a hopped-up, psyched-out wacko, played by king of the wackos, Dennis Hopper.

From this point on, nothing in *Blue Velvet* makes one shred of sense. "It's a strange world," says the ossified Jeffrey. It's an even stranger movie.

Imagine a town in North Carolina which looks like both Tobacco Road and Rodeo Drive in Beverly Hills. Picture the one saloon in town where a weird woman in a bizarre wig mounts the bandstand every night and sings only one song—the old Bobby Vinton hit "Blue Velvet."

Then shudder while you watch the entire town being terrorized by a demented maniac. He charges into the singer's apartment after she's stripped the boy to his birthday suit and forced him to do things he's only heard about in porno movies. While the boy hides in the closet, the lunatic Hopper pulls out an oxygen mask, inhales large doses of something

George Bush has only heard of in White House drug reports, slams his fist into one of Isabella's orifices that is not her ear, and stuffs her bathrobe down her throat before sexually mutilating her.

Apparently the whole town is being terrorized by this slimy butcher. The local police chief is found tortured and electrocuted, riddled with bullets, and sitting upright in an easy chair. The trail leads to a suburban apartment where stoned businessmen and peroxided matrons are running some kind of combination brothel–crack den ruled by a grotesque drag queen who wears forty pounds of strawberry lipstick and sings country and western songs, played by former child star Dean Stockwell.

Violence, graphic sex and nudity, sado-masochism and every perversion known to man follow in bountiful supply, accompanied by plenty of lurid camp, eye-rolling acting, idiot dialogue and off-key choruses of "Blue Velvet."

Lynch packs the film with gratuitous torture tableaux, sacrificing coherence for sensationalism. He's such an inept director that although I believe he directed such trash wallows as *Eraserhead* and *Dune*, I no longer believe he could have possibly helmed a great film like *The Elephant Man*. Surely Mel Brooks, who produced that one, must have rolled up his sleeves and taken over.

I haven't the vaguest idea what *Blue Velvet* is about, except the desecration of a pop tune I danced to the night of my senior prom. It is a shock and a disgrace to see otherwise respectable people like Laura Dern, Hope Lange, Dean Stockwell, and the handsome but dissipated Kyle MacLachlan in a piece of tripe like this.

Dennis Hopper finally goes as berserk as his reputation indicates offscreen. He holds the record in this one for saying the most F-words in movie history. As for the lovely but misguided Isabella Rossellini, all I can say is that her mother, Ingrid Bergman, must be turning in her grave. If she had lived to see her daughter wobbling naked across somebody's front lawn covered with teeth marks and cigarette burns, she would have probably made a citizen's arrest.

In the brain-damaged garbage department, *Blue Velvet* gives pretentiousness new meaning. It should score high with the kind of sickos who like to smell dirty socks and pull wings off butterflies, but there's nothing here for sane audiences.

Critics are something else. Some of them like kinkiness and incoherence. One is quoted with this doozie: "You've never seen anything like it in your life!" That's true. And I never want to see anything like it again.

BODY DOUBLE (1984)

★ Directed and produced by Brian De Palma. Screenplay by Robert J. Avrech and De Palma. Story by Brian De Palma. *With Craig Wasson, Melanie Griffith, Gregg Henry, Deborah Shelton, Guy Boyd, and Dennis Franz.*

Everyone wondered how Columbia Pictures, a company owned by Coca-Cola, could make an unmitigated piece of garbage like *Body Double*. The answer is simple. After you see it, you need a Coca-Cola just to settle your stomach.

This turgid, brainless claptrap is about a schleppy, toad-faced, oversexed voyeur actor with claustrophobia who gets fired from his role as a vampire in a sleazo horror-porno flick because he goes berserk every time they close the coffin lid on his face. They should have closed a coffin lid on the whole picture, but director Brian De Palma is just beginning.

Through plot manipulations

so demented they defy description, the actor (played with maximum wimpiness by the indigestible Craig Wasson) finds a free Hollywood sublet in a bizarre mountaintop house that looks like a spaceship, complete with rotating beds and a telescopic view of a sexy neighbor. There's never a dull moment in this chick's pad. Every night she's invaded by thieves or masked psychos or she's putting on an erotic show.

In an insulting parody of Hitchcock's *Rear Window* De Palma has the nerd actor getting vicariously involved in the sexy neighbor's activities through the lens of his telescope. When he retrieves her purse from a maniac at the beach, the whole thing turns into a send-up of *Vertigo*. The actor gets dizzy spells. The sexy nympho starts writhing in lust. "Yes." "No." "Yes!" Is De Palma serious? You begin to think the whole movie is a spoof. No movie can be this awful on *purpose*!

But no. De Palma is just a bad director who makes Michael Cimino and Andy Warhol look like Cecil B. DeMille.

Through more plot twists than a scenic railway, the Peeping Tom pervert turns out to be a patsy. The friend who found him the spaceship sublet is a homicidal killer disguised as a Navajo Indian who sneaks into his ex-wife's condo and grinds her through the floor with an electric drill. As blood pours through the floorboards of the bedroom above, a vicious dog is busily tearing out the actor's throat in the room below. The neighbor who bumps and grinds turns out to be a peroxide, gum-chewing punk-rock porno star, played by Melanie Griffith with staggering ineptitude.

They all end up back on the set of the vampire movie, where the dumb porno star climbs out of her grave and says, "Am I missing something?" I knew exactly how she felt.

Totally lacking in structure, style, coherence, and talent, it is one of the most disgraceful abuses of money that has ever been trashed upon the screen. *Body Double* should be reviewed with a machine gun, since it seems to have been made with one.

The script, by De Palma and Bob Avrech, is a compost of moronic ideas loosely strung like hippie beads from Teepee Town, the direction like a term project for Career Self-Destruction 101, the acting an abysmal collection of amateurish, self-indulgent ego massages.

There might be an audience of college kids and immature

bird brains who find this kind of swill amusing, but pollution experts are advised to alert their demolition squads. This is a job for the Sanitation Department, pest-control division.

BORN ON THE FOURTH OF JULY (1989)

★ ★ ★ ★ Directed by Oliver Stone. Screenplay by Stone and Ron Kovic. Produced by A. Kitman Ho and Stone. *With Tom Cruise, Kyra Sedgwick, Raymond J. Barry, Jerry Levine, Frank Whaley, Caroline Kava, and Willem Dafoe.*

Get ready to be stunned. Oliver Stone, director of *Platoon*, picks up where that shocker left off. *Platoon* showed what happened in the frontline trenches of Vietnam. *Born on the Fourth of July* is a devastating look at what happened to the survivors of that hell, and a blistering indictment of the people who sent them there. Tom Cruise stars as Ron Kovic, the all-American Marine from Long Island who went in a man and came back a paraplegic. Fed the lies of heroism from childhood, Kovic was drilled to be number one at everything. But in the disorganized chaos of war, he killed a fellow soldier accidentally, witnessed the brutality no hero would inflict on a fellow human, and ended up a near-fatal casualty, paralyzed, abused,

and abandoned in an understaffed, underfunded veteran's hospital. In the long and tormented years that followed, he survived to write the book upon which this staggering film is based, but the psychological damage took longer to heal. The rats, squalor, drug abuse, and apathy in the V.A. hospital are harrowing to watch. In fact, this is a grim, powerful film, hard to take on many levels, but is brutally real. It makes you think—and it makes you angry. Tom Cruise is galvanizing. But depressing as it is, every American with a conscience should consider it an obligation—even a top priority—to see *Born on the Fourth of July*.

BRAZIL (1985)

★ ★ Directed by Terry Gilliam. Screenplay by Gilliam, Tom Stoppard, and Charles McKeown. Produced by Amon Milchan. *With Jonathan Pryce, Ian Holm, Michael Palin, Katherine Helmond, Bob Hoskins, and Robert De Niro.*

Brazil is a surrealistic British science fiction comedy from demented Monty Python director Terry Gilliam, set in a computerized, futuristic Nazi government where everything is collapsing under the weight of bureaucratic red tape.

A tribute to excess and bad taste, it has nothing to do with

Brazil or any other place in the world atlas, although the popular song "Brazil" from the 1930s does blast constantly from the soundtrack, for no apparent reason.

Jonathan Pryce, as a space-age Walter Mitty, is a civil service puppet who works for the Ministry of Information. He has a domineering mother who has been turned into a plastic gargoyle through cosmetic surgery, and he's in love with a lady truck driver who may or may not be a terrorist.

The incomprehensible plot has something to do with a computer error that results in the wrongful arrest of a Mr. Tuttle instead of a Mr. Buttle, but the real focus is on hardware, sets, and violent comic routines that mix up George Orwell's *1984* with Alvin Toffler's *Future Shock*, with some Woody Allen, Franz Kafka, and *Alice in Wonderland* thrown in. It's a mess.

Some of the jokes are imaginative—meals, ordered by menu number, are all scoops of the same indigestible pureed mush in designer colors. If your air conditioner breaks down, a pair of sadistic government plumbers like Tweedledum and Tweedledee rip your apartment to shreds, exposing every pipe and leaving your home hanging in rubber entrails that look like elephant intestines.

If your life is in danger from the continual terrorist bombings, you get a recorded message at Central Services. Even the travel posters advertise "Fun Without Fear, Luxury Without Suspicion," and any survivors of the Hitlerian government interrogators who withstand torture too long jeopardize their credit ratings.

Brazil is a warning about the nightmare that awaits us in a future society when the computers go berserk. The consequences are ugly beyond description, the camera work and visual designs are arresting, and there is a funny guest appearance by Robert De Niro as a gun-carrying repairman who scales buildings like a human fly and looks like Sid Caesar.

Despite the presence of such great British actors as Jonathan Pryce, Ian Holm, Michael Palin, and Bob Hoskins, I'd still rather see the real Brazil. I'm sure getting there would seem like half the time it takes to watch the movie.

BREAKER MORANT (1980)
★ ★ ★ ★ Directed by Bruce Beresford. Screenplay by Jonathan Hardy, Bruce Beresford, and David Stevens. Produced by Matthew Carroll. *With Edward*

Woodward, Bryan Brown, and Jack Thompson.

There is greatness in *Breaker Morant*. No longer an infant in swaddling clothes where world cinema is concerned, Australia had already established itself as a country of energy and talent, but with this drama of epic dimensions about a military court-martial that turned into a kangaroo court in the Boer War, the film industry of the land down under made a bit of screen history all its own.

In a desert outpost in South Africa, three dashing officers of the Australian Bushveldt Carbineers are accused of murdering prisoners and missionaries, then tried and convicted of war crimes they insisted were carried out under orders from British high commander Lord Kitchener himself. The facts do point a finger at the accused as guilty. Captured men were shot in acts of impulsive cruelty, and their captors indulged on the excuse of personal revenge for the barbarous mutilation of the body of the Carbineers' wounded CO.

But director Bruce Beresford does not settle for a war story. He uncovers the ironies and ambiguities which lie behind this bare confrontation. After a thrilling action sequence, when Boer commandos storm the camp and the three prisoners display exemplary courage in fighting them off, Beresford begins to explore the characters of the accused in Ibsenite fashion.

A new dimension is introduced when they are assigned a defense lawyer who has never tried a case before but who develops courtroom skills as the trial proceeds, punching holes in the prosecution witnesses and revealing insufficient evidence. Ignored by Lord Kitchener himself, who fled the country rather than testify, they become unwilling and innocent pawns in England's attempts to make peaceful amends toward its German allies.

In introducing an even deeper theme that asks the question "How can a trio of junior officers be condemned for any crime when the whole Boer War was patently criminal?" the parallels with Vietnam become unmistakable. This was a war against an enemy without uniforms whose women, children and missionaries were also spies and saboteurs, while the British turned a blind eye to their own troops burning villages and herding noncombatants into concentration camps. Trapped in a war it could not win, England needed scapegoats to impress international opinion about their "good intentions" in withdrawing from South Africa, and the Australians were easy sacrifices. Doomed from the outset to face the firing squad, these martyrs have since become legends in Australian military archives and Commander Morant (called "Breaker" because he broke in wild horses as a civilian) has become a folk hero because he was the Englishman who chose to die like an Aussie.

Whether the accused and convicted soldiers were villains or heroes is not the point of this fascinating story. The real question is whether the atrocities of war are committed by madmen or by normal men turned mad by circumstances. A wasteful miscarriage of justice, the story of *Breaker Morant* is a devastating example of England's military hypocrisy that riles the Aussies to this day. I know nothing about the Boer War and am usually bored stiff by courtroom dramas, but I was mesmerized by Beresford's muscular direction, by the characterizing of ideas rare to the screen, by the beautiful camera work, and by the brilliant script that intercuts all of the heel bashing and saluting of army ritual with penetrating insights into the characters of the men on trial.

And finally, it is a triumph of acting skills. Edward Woodward as the accused Morant conveys the spirit of a man lost to two worlds, and the marvelous Jack Thompson, as the inexperienced defense counsel who unravels the truth and remains powerless to save his clients, emerges as an Australian Paul Newman.

BREAKING AWAY (1979)
★ ★ ★ ★ Directed and produced by Peter Yates. Screenplay by Steve Tesich. *With Dennis Christopher, Dennis Quaid, Daniel Stern, Jackie Earl Haley, Paul Dooley, Barbara Barrie, and Robyn Douglass.*

Feel like trading in your favorite movie for something new and better? *Breaking Away* is a safe bet. It's an absolutely wonderful, poignant film about being young and relentlessly hopeful, about running your sweetest dreams headlong into the brick wall of adult skepticism and then finding a way to pick up the pieces again.

Four kids are stuck in Bloomington, Indiana. They didn't make it to college and can't ever dodge the reminders of what they're missing—the Indiana University campus, the pretty coeds, the convertibles with out-of-town plates, and the rich-looking, sneering jocks.

But for these boys, there's no

fitting into life in Bloomington, either. Here the streets are lined with small frame houses, the parents feel cheated by life and hold their kids back, the lawns are decorated with white plastic swans—an atmosphere so palpably conveyed, you can sense these imaginative kids gasping in the stagnant air of the suburbs.

For Dave Stoller, the main character, the outlet is simple. He's obsessed with the idea of being an Italian bike racer. He adopts an Italian accent, plasters his walls with maps and posters of Italy, renames the family cat Fellini, and even feeds him "nice-a meatballs" from a Cinzano ashtray.

There's a visible method in his madness. An only child, he reminds people that Italian families are big and stick together. The son of a carping, crabapple father, he says, "We Italians are poor, but we are happy." Being Italian is his escape, his chance to be somebody, and Dennis Christopher is the stringbean actor who carries it off sweetly and brilliantly. He's actually a blond, gangly-limbed kid with a crooked grin and a Hoosier walk, but on his bike he's Nureyev dancing—sailing through a dreary town with a "Ciao!" for everyone in sight.

He convinces a pretty coed that he's an exchange student, watches his buddies get clobbered in the student lounge, and loses everything when the real Italian bike team comes to town. Illusions shattered, he eventually gets to show what kind of pasta the real Dave is made of in one of the most suspenseful action races ever filmed.

The father, formerly a stonecutter—locals are called "cutters" instead of "townies"—is reduced to selling used cars to smart-aleck campus punks. A man sealed off by his bitterness, he has had it up to here with a son who shaves his legs, and sick to death of "Eye-talian *ini*" food—lingu*ini* tortell*ini* fettuc*ini*—and would give anything for a plate of greasy french fries. The Caruso records are driving him out of his tiny mind, and he can't stand being called "Papa," either. He is nevertheless somewhat resuscitated when his son suffers a shattered fantasy. Paul Dooley is the father who starts out as a funny caricature like Dagwood Bumstead and ends up one of the film's strongest characters.

The way all of this freshness and originality is pulled off is inspiring. Peter Yates produced and directed, from a beautiful script by Steve Tesich that combines elements of Booth Tarkington, Carson McCullers, and J. D. Salinger. There are subtle touches throughout, minor themes that are aptly picked up at the right time but never allowed to linger too long, and dialogue that reveals character in subtle brush strokes while it makes you laugh.

Some of the shots of Dave riding his bike are especially beautiful and elegant, such as the one on the highway of him pedaling behind a Cinzano truck through cornfields and perfectly still, hazy midwestern air. The bike becomes his balloon to Oz, and it gives the film a symbolic flying-carpet breeze of detachment and freedom that lifts the heart and spirit.

The supporting players are uniformly rich in character and nuance, with excellent work by Dennis Quaid, the redneck who dreams of Wyoming and hates the smugness of the college Ivy Leaguers; Daniel Stern, the sharp-witted basketball player who could have gone to college; and Jackie Earl Haley, the peewee with bad skin who plans on getting married and won't take any kidding about it.

The mother, played by Barbara Barrie, provides so much long-suffering patience for both son and husband that you'll want to hug her. *Breaking Away* is about the summer they all grow up together and learn compassion, and is an exemplary film to cherish and savor. It's so life-affirming and infectious that I walked right out and yelled "Ciao!" to the first bike rider I saw.

BRIGHT LIGHTS, BIG CITY (1988)
★ ★ ★ Directed by James Bridges. Screenplay by Jay McInerney. Produced by Mark Rosenberg and Sydney Pollack. *With Michael J. Fox, Kiefer Sutherland, Phoebe Cates, Swoosie Kurtz, Frances Sternhagen, Tracy Pollan, John Houseman, Dianne Wiest, Jason Robards, and William Hickey.*

Michael J. Fox comes of age in this grim but fascinating descent into yuppie hell. As a nice country boy hypnotized by the glitter of the Big Apple, he experiences life in the fast lane, sweats bullets, falls in with the cocaine crowd, and almost self-destructs. While his life falls apart, Kiefer Sutherland, as his coke-sniffing pal, Dianne Wiest, as his dying mother, and Jason Robards, as his pickled boss, all lend excellent support, but it's a new, polished, mature Mr. Fox who makes this movie seem like Oz photographed through the bottom of a double vodka martini. As he disintegrates, he makes you care. Fine film, fine performance.

BRIGHTON BEACH MEMOIRS (1986)

★ ★ ★ Directed by Gene Saks. Screenplay by Neil Simon, from his play. Produced by Ray Stark. With Blythe Danner, Bob Dishy, Jonathan Silverman and Judith Ivey.

Discontent with being the most successful comedy writer in America, Neil Simon took to dredging up the autobiographical material in his own life, doubling his fame and fortune in the process. *Brighton Beach Memoirs*, the first of these plays about his life to reach the screen, tells us a lot about who Neil Simon is. It's his own personalized holiday greeting card, and it fits every occasion. Simon calls himself Eugene Jerome. The year is 1937. The place is Brooklyn during the Depression, where fifteen-year-old Eugene finds it hard to grow up funny. His principal function in life, it seems, is running errands and interference for the other occupants of his overcrowded household—his widowed Aunt Blanche and her two daughters, his eighteen-year-old brother Stanley, and his long-suffering parents—as well as enduring tortuous meals of liver and cabbage and spaghetti and ketchup prepared by his badgering, kvetching mother. It's rare when Eugene gets a free moment to face the camera and confide to the audience his two secret desires—to become either a pitcher for the Yankees or a great writer of plays and movies. Since we know how he turned out, the longing and self doubt are twice as touching.

This is not funny ha-ha Neil Simon. His lucid, cockeyed sense of humor is here, but it's laced with compassion, too. We really get to know these people. Pop, wonderfully played by Bob Dishy, has to worry about his bankrupt business and how to keep a roof over the heads of seven people. Aunt Blanche (Judith Ivey) has to worry about getting married again and two daughters with growing pains. And at the center of it all is the enchanting Blythe Danner, as Eugene's mother, whose unpleasant job is to keep everyone together as the maternal backbone of the family. Danner is miscast. She's about as Jewish as Maureen O'Hara. But she's such a great actress that she has the power to convince you she's the quintessential Jewish mother.

Young Jonathan Silverman makes you feel every ounce of pain and confusion, as well as the heartburn of growing up sensitive in a family of hard-boiled realists. From Gene Saks's warm direction to the nostalgic thirties music by Michael Small, *Brighton Beach Memoirs* is like a swell family reunion, with all its joy, laughter, and tears. The family may not be yours or mine, but they'll make you feel welcome all the same—and glad to be there.

BROADCAST NEWS (1987)
★ ★ ★ 1/2 Directed, written and produced by James L. Brooks. With William Hurt, Holly Hunter, Albert Brooks, Robert Prosky, Lois Chiles, Joan Cusack, Peter Hackes, and Jack Nicholson.

Broadcast News is one of the most intelligent, heartwarming romantic comedies in years. It's also funny, entertaining, and as timely as the six o'clock news. The setting is the Washington news bureau of a major TV network; the focus is on three aspiring journalists climbing the ladder to national success. William Hurt is the glamorous moron who brings us the news without knowing anything about it. Naturally the network grooms his pretty face for stardom as an anchor. Albert Brooks, as a talented and dedicated reporter, can't get to first base because he's ethnic and lacks star charisma. And the incandescent Holly Hunter is the crackerjack

workaholic producer who can't balance integrity in her work ethics with a good sex life, but loves both guys. With Brooks, she's maternal. With Hurt, she compromises her standards, but what the hell? Sometimes, she says, great sex with a shallow fake is better than no sex at all.

Broadcast News creates these memorable characters and fills the roles with marvelous actors. You'll even like Jack Nicholson's delicious cameo as the veteran network star who seems oilier on camera than Geraldo Rivera. Following everyone's triumphs and failures through on-camera crises and off-camera heartbreaks, you'll regard them all as old friends long before the final sign-off. Exposing the hypocrisy that goes on behind the scenes in TV news, the competitive jockeying for position among anchormen, the tribulations of being a smart woman in a man's world, the fight for standards, and the incompetence that rules the airwaves, director-writer James (*Terms of Endearment*) Brooks leaves the audience laughing but uncomfortable in the knowledge that the news has nothing to do with news at all—it's show business. After *Broadcast News*, you may never be able to watch Tom Brokaw, Dan Rather or Peter

Jennings again without wondering who they really are—and you just might not want to know the answer.

BROADWAY DANNY ROSE
(1984)

★ ★ ★ ½ Written and directed by Woody Allen. Produced by Robert Greenhut and Charles H. Joffe. With Woody Allen, Mia Farrow, and Nick Apollo Forte.

Regardless of their personal problems, Woody Allen's professional relationship with Mia Farrow enhanced her career, stretched her previously thin talents, forced her to break down inhibitions, and shocked audiences into looking at this once-mousy, pinched-faced little girl with renewed strength and admiration. She's very funny in *Broadway Danny Rose*, and funny is money.

Broadway Danny Rose is not a great movie by anyone's standards, least of all Woody Allen's—from the man who gave us *Zelig* it is even something of a letdown—but in a period of severe comedy drought it quenches the thirst for laughter with zest and sweetness. Photographed in black and white by Gordon Willis, the genius who gave *Zelig* its period flavor, this film also has a texture and patina that evokes the tacky Broadway atmosphere of the fifties, a time when Woody himself was starting his career as a Jewish stand-up comic. (Somehow the Stage Deli, the Waldorf lobby, and Staten Island look better in black and white.) This is the world *Broadway Danny Rose* lives in, and Woody, in the title role, captures it brilliantly.

Danny Rose is a fast-talking agent-manager of second-rate vaudeville acts. There are lots of stories about his colorful, crazy schemes, and the comics and show-biz locals sit around the Stage Deli and repeat them like Catskills routines.

In flashback, we get the longest and perhaps funniest (the humor, frankly, comes and goes) anecdote. This is the one about the time Danny Rose got involved with a gum-chewing floozie named Tina Vitale, who was already involved with Danny's star client, a fat, finger-snapping Italian egomaniac singer named Lou Canova, and all of them got chased by gangsters and almost ended up in the Hudson in a cement canoe.

The story is of such lightweight froth it falls flat before Woody can get it into the oven. But the style, imagination and observance of detail give the film a lift that will leave you giddy with admiration.

Tacky is the key word here.

It permeates everything, from Woody's terrible print shirts and Times Square sports jackets to the sandwich named after him at the Stage Deli—cream cheese on a bagel with marinara sauce.

There's one hilarious scene in which Woody serves a pathetic Thanksgiving dinner to his clients out of cardboard cups. The room is filled with the kind of show business you don't even get in lounge acts in Atlantic City: a penguin on roller skates dressed like a rabbi, a one-legged tap dancer, a talking parrot, a blind xylophonist, and a tiny bird named Pee Wee that pecks out "September Song" on piano keys.

We see Woody talking Milton Berle into using his star performer on an NBC special. We visit an actual taping of—are you ready?—the *Joe Franklin Show*. We get the scruffy, seedy promoters, hucksters, groupies, fall guys, and gun-toting tootsies that made up the world of Lindy's and Toots Shor's thirty years ago.

Best of all, we get Mia Farrow.

Mia is the reincarnation of Barbara Nichols—the gum cracking, teased-beehive, stiletto-heeled tomato who wants to, you know, like, be somebody.

She's in and out of a lot of mob limos, but what she does legitimately—if you get the picture—is sort of decorate rooms in gold wallpaper, purple pillows, and jungle motifs with lots of striped zebra and bamboo. ("My problem," she says, chewing her Juicy Fruit furiously, "is I look at my work and I think it's ugly.")

Wearing ten pounds of cotton candy on her head and talking through what sounds like a deviated septum, she is merely marvelous.

Broadway Danny Rose is a one-joke movie like *Zelig*, but it lacks the quality of great comedies (of which *Zelig* is one of the greatest) because its simplicity does not leave you with any questions about the condition of man.

When you recover from the intermittent laughter of *Broadway Danny Rose*, you will not be left with a trail of reflections about truth and human nature. It's merely an entertainment, which is perfectly fine and, in Woody's hands, even better than fine.

The beauty of the joke is the form Woody gives it. The entire film is presented, almost poker-faced, as a parody of Damon Runyon, with Woody and Mia as an updated Nathan Detroit and Miss Adelaide. It may not be Woody's best work, but Woody Allen on an off day is better than everybody else on Sunday.

BRUBAKER (1980)
★ ★ ½ Directed by Stuart Rosenberg. Screenplay by W. D. Richter. Produced by Ron Silverman. With Robert Redford, Jane Alexander, Yaphet Kotto, Murray Hamilton, David Keith, Morgan Freeman, M. Emmet Walsh, Matt Clark, Richard Ward, Albert Salmi, and Wilford Brimley.

Brubaker is an honest, well-meaning, desperately sincere attempt to examine the evils and injustices in the prison system and it deserves to be seen by conscientious audiences everywhere.

Where did it go wrong? Maybe because it carves a hunk of roast beefcake too predictably. Robert Redford is so predictably reliable in it that the film holds no excitement, no thrill of new discovery.

In *Brubaker*, Redford is so damned self-righteous, so determined, and so unyieldingly heroic that there's nothing left in his performance for the viewer to discover. His jaw is so set you can almost hear the bones crack.

Brubaker is based on the real-life experiences of Tom Murton, who worked as a warden in a primitive Arkansas prison in 1968, improving conditions and irritating the corrupt prison officials until his discovery of three bodies buried on prison property led to his dismissal. He hasn't worked in the prison system since, and it took him almost eleven years to get his story to the screen. It's a harrowing story, made even more grim and terrifying by the filmmaker's poetic license, and the first hour or so—during which Redford pretends to be a prisoner, to get a firsthand glimpse of prison life—is as shattering as anything you're likely to see in a movie.

Sleeping in filthy beds that become available only when someone dies in them, sitting on floors of mud and cold water, kept awake by homosexual rapes all around him, forced to watch the worst beating since slavery was outlawed, Brubaker witnesses enough cruel and beastly punishments to make the Black Hole of Calcutta look like Disneyland and *Fortune and Men's Eyes* look like an episode from Baby Snooks.

After Redford admits his true identity, he shaves, dons a plaid shirt and clean jeans, and becomes the same Redford who could just as well be lecturing at

Yale, campaigning for ecology, or running for political office.

Redford, or Brubaker (it becomes impossible to distinguish between the two, which is a credit to the actor but ends up backfiring on the movie itself) encounters as much graft, corruption, and hostility on the outside as he does in the barracks. The guards hoard the food supply, reselling it to the inmates for a price. Even the state police are on the take, the trustees are sabotaging the prison crops, the local businessmen are ripping off the prison, the prison board members are making a profit.

Brubaker makes the prisoners feel like human beings, but he won't play the politician's crooked games, so he loses because he won't compromise his principles. It's a perfect role for Redford—the brave, noble hero fighting the system—but although his cry for penal reform is well taken, the film is more interesting when the cry is maimed and horrible and more like a scream.

Stuart Rosenberg has done a fine job of documenting the details, there is authenticity in W. D. Richter's screenplay (even though some of the events have been manufactured), and the actual Ohio prison locales lend an almost documentary realism to the grisly events.

Fine, concerned performances abound—by Redford, Jane Alexander as a state government employee with high connections, Yaphet Kotto as a tough prisoner who is the last to come around to Brubaker's ideas, and Murray Hamilton as a slimy politician.

Brubaker is a "worthy" picture with all of the responsibility the word implies, but it leaves the viewer feeling hopeless and dissatisfied.

BUGSY (1991)

★ ★ ★ ★ Directed by Barry Levinson. Screenplay by James Toback. Produced by Mark Johnson, Barry Levinson, and Warren Beatty. *With Warren Beatty, Annette Bening, Harvey Keitel, Ben Kingsley, and Joe Mantegna.*

Bugsy is no ordinary hood-makes-good flick. Ben "Bugsy" Siegel was a renaissance mobster, and the mesmerizing movie Barry Levinson has distilled from the psychological complexities of his flamboyant personality is no conventional crime-wave thriller. It's big and beautiful and glamorous and completely enthralling.

I don't know if the real Bugsy (you called him by his nickname at your own peril; sometimes it cost you your life) was as charismatic in reality as he is played by Warren Beatty, but who cares? Beatty gives his best performance in years, probably because he wisely left the direction in someone else's hands; he's charming, unpredictable, reckless, and romantic, not the sort of oily thug you get in Martin Scorsese movies. And Annette Bening, full of passion and wiseguy wisecracks, plays gun moll Virginia Hill with such energy and spunk the chemistry is apparent and juicy. (Their love scenes don't look like acting.) The fact that you like them both and dread the inevitable finale, where Bugsy keeps his date with a machine gun, is the film's greatest triumph, and perhaps its greatest flaw. (Mobsters aren't supposed to be *sympathetic*, God knows, but what can you do with Mr. Beatty? He's got more appeal than Cagney.) Purists and historians may argue that Bugsy was not that glamorous in real life, but in a movie this elegant and stylish you find yourself acting out your primal lust for power. He's the dark side of the American Dream. Yes, I found myself *admiring* Bugsy, and the world he lived in.

Mr. Levinson has done a terrific job of bringing that world to life. Unlike Mickey Cohen, Lucky Luciano, and Meyer Lansky, who form a Greek chorus around the star, Bugsy was a magnetic, quixotic individual with two wild dreams—to kill Mussolini and open a lavish hotel in Vegas. From the time he leaves his wife and two daughters home in Scarsdale and heads for California on the Super Chief to seize control of the West Coast rackets, it is clear he is destined to become a legend. He was an actor looking for a starring role (he even made a screen test) who invented himself. Immersed in mudpacks, cucumber slices on the eyes, and hair nets, he was vain, violent, arrogant, irrational, intemperate, and sometimes quite mad. Naturally, he found himself right at home in Hollywood. The film has buckets of insights into his manipulative and dangerous charm; the movie industry craved and feared him from the start. I loved the scene where he walks up to opera star Lawrence Tibett's house and knocks on the door, lingering long enough to charm the man out of his own home while his best friend George Raft (cunningly played by Joe Mantegna) waits in the limo in disbelief. But he could be tender, too. I also liked the scene where he tries to give a birthday party for his daughter, decorating the cake himself with chocolate frosting and pink candles, while setting up the building of the Flamingo Hotel with the mob assembled in the living room. When he finds a strange guy in his underwear in Virginia's living room, he knocks him through a plateglass window, not realizing he's her baby brother, then buys the victim a red Cadillac convertible. He even takes a moment while beating a rival thug to bloody steak tartare to check his reflection in the mirror, carefully adjusting his cowlick. In jail, his meals are prepared by a private chef and served on the best china and crystal. When Virginia smashes a glass ashtray in his face, he yells: "For chrissakes, that's Baccarat!" I mean, you have to like a scumbag with that kind of taste.

James Toback's brilliant screenplay gives Bugsy the stature and appeal of a president or a great humanitarian, and although you can't make a gangster film without some blood and gore, Mr. Levinson keeps the violence to a minimum. Stylistically, it's a remarkable effort—with a continuous sense of gliding motion, photographed slickly through rain and smoke and steam, under-

scored by Jo Stafford, Johnny Mercer, and Peggy Lee records. The music, clothes, and cinematography are elegant and meticulously breathless. And the historic facts that lead to Bugsy's downfall (selling four hundred percent of the Flamingo stock to the Mafia and opening on Christmas Day in the middle of a blinding rainstorm and a power failure) are rivetingly relayed while the screenplay cracks and pops. Says tough starlet Virginia Hill on their first meeting: "You got nothing to offer but some dialogue—dialogue comes cheap in Hollywood. Why don't you go outside and jerk yourself a soda?" This is the best gangster picture since *The Godfather*—brutal, lush, hypnotic, and inspired. I never checked my watch, and it left me wanting more.

BULL DURHAM (1988)

★ ★ ★ Directed and written by Ron Shelton. Produced by Thom Mount and Mark Burg. *With Kevin Costner, Susan Sarandon, Tim Robbins, Trey Wilson, Robert Wuhl, Jenny Robertson, and Max Patkin.*

They used to say baseball movies never make money, but this one changed that jinx. It's about not one—but *two*—of the great American pastimes—baseball and sex. The Bulls are a minor league team from Durham. Tim Robbins is Nuke, a bumpkin pitcher with a big talent and a brain the size of a melting M&M. Kevin Costner is Crash, a veteran catcher with super intelligence but no future. He joins the Bulls to teach the kid the ropes. Salivating, undulating, and bedding them both from the bleachers, there's Susan Sarandon, in the best and sexiest role of her career—as a baseball groupie who sleeps with a new recruit each season. What a movie. What a team. The pitcher's wearing women's garters. The Jesus freak is marrying the local slut on the field in the second inning. And the first baseman's got a voodoo curse on his mitt. *Bull Durham* has hot love scenes, wonderful characters, home run performances, and some of the best comic writing in years. This is one baseball movie that wins the pennant—even if you don't like baseball.

THE BURNING BED (TV, 1984)
★ ★ ★ Directed by Robert Greenwald. Screenplay by Leiman Goldemberg, based on a book by Faith McNulty. Produced by Carol Schrader. *With Farrah Fawcett, Paul LeMat, Richard Masur, Grace Zabriskie, Penelope Milford, and James Callahan.*

Doubting Thomases who still regard Farrah Fawcett as one of Charlie's sexy but inept Angels will eat crow with relish when they see this surprisingly mature actress stripped of glamour in the harrowing true-life story of Francine Hughes, a Michigan mother of three—and a battered wife. Driven mad with cruelty and abuse, desperate to protect her children and save her own life, she was driven, on the night of March 9, 1977, to light a match to the gasoline-soaked bedroom where her ex-husband was sleeping and end her nightmare. This highly acclaimed TV movie spans twelve years in the life of an unsophisticated woman who fell victim to a rising national epidemic of wife abuse. Shattered, her future in doubt and her past a holocaust of bitter memories, Francine survives the ordeal to become a heroine in the field of women's rights. Fawcett, as the centerpiece of this sobering drama, gives the unpleasant catalogue of true events a personal passion and honesty that is haunting and definitely not for the squeamish.

CABIN IN THE SKY (1943)
★ ★ ★ ½ Directed by Vincente Minnelli. Screenplay by Joseph Schrank. Produced by Arthur Freed. *With Ethel Waters, Eddie*

"Rochester" Anderson, Lena Horne, Rex Ingram, Kenneth Spencer, Oscar Polk, Butterfly McQueen, Duke Ellington and Louis Armstrong.

Vincente Minnelli battled the cynics who ruled MGM in 1943 and came up with this all-black musical fantasy that has become a movie classic. The legendary Ethel Waters made movie history singing Harold Arlen's "Happiness Is Just a Thing Called Joe," and Lena Horne, Eddie "Rochester" Anderson, Duke Ellington, and Louis Armstrong make stunning contributions. A genuine delight.

CALAMITY JANE (1953)

★ ★ ★ ½ Directed by David Butler. Screenplay by James O'Hanlon. Produced by William Jacobs. *With Doris Day, Howard Keel, Allyn Ann McLerie, Philip Carey, Gale Robbins, and Dick Wesson.*

Doris Day, at the height of her career as America's singing sweetheart, galloped through this perky, tuneful spoof of the Old West in 1953 and scored one of her biggest movie hits. Doris is the tomboy desperado of the title (reminiscent of Betty Hutton in *Annie Get Your Gun*) and Howard Keel costars as Wild Bill Hickok. The rich score includes one of Doris's

most colossal hit songs, the ever-popular "Secret Love." Doris didn't sing it to her leading man. She sang it to a horse.

CALIGULA (1980)

No ★s Directed by Tinto Brass. Screenplay adapted (by Bob Guccione) from the original by Gore Vidal. Produced by Bob Guccione. *With Malcolm McDowell, Teresa Ann Savoy, Helen Mirren, Sir John Gielgud, Peter O'Toole, and Guido Mannari.*

Caligula was a demented Roman emperor who ruled the pagans from A.D. 37 to 41. His reign was short and so was his popularity, but by the time he was murdered at the age of twenty-nine he had already been around too long.

Caligula, the abominable $17 million trough of rotten swill a group of hard-core pornographers masquerading as Penthouse Films International, Ltd. have pieced together about his life, also seems to last twenty-nine years, although it wears itself out much faster.

Gore Vidal, who wrote the original screenplay, sued to have his name removed. Considering the idiotic dialogue that belches dumbly from the screen, I don't blame him. Why he wanted to trash up his name by getting involved with this pile of junk in the first place is a mystery. I guess he figures somebody might compare him with Albert Camus.

The credits now read "Adapted from an original screenplay by Gore Vidal." I assume the "adapting" was done by Bob Guccione. One thing is obvious. Guccione has less talent for filmmaking than a four-year-old.

Actors, unfortunately, are not as lucky as Gore Vidal. Once their faces appear on the screen, they're stuck. John Gielgud has the good taste to slash his wrists and disappear from the film after the first ten minutes of agony.

Helen Mirren, a fine actress from England's National Theater, plays Caesonia, the wife of Caligula, as though she knows exactly what the film is about even when nobody else does. Peter O'Toole, toothless and covered with sores, is also wise enough to do his ham acting and exit early. He plays Caligula's grandfather, the emperor Tiberius, who had already murdered his family and half of Rome before the film begins. It's nice to see him grab his paycheck and run.

But that leaves poor, pitiable Malcolm McDowell in the title role, playing incest, homosexuality, necrophilia and rape as though they were cocktail sports in Brighton. In the first scene, when McDowell is romping half-naked (the real nudity comes later) through the forest with his sister-lover Drusilla, he is already crazier than three drunken billy goats.

He comes out of the starting gate so high with insanity that his performance has nowhere to go from there. The sister is played by Teresa Ann Savoy, a dim-witted actress who looks like a Poor Pitiful Pearl doll.

Hands are shoved into fires. Freaks are tortured and mutilated. Babies' heads are smashed against marble walls. The most graphic sexual aberrations flourish in close-ups that would be banned on 42nd Street. Torsos are dismembered, while blood and viscera splatter the camera lens.

There are vulgar sets, tacky costumes, and dopey lines like "The priestesses of Isis are meeting at my house tonight!" And in between howlers like that one, a screen full of naked Penthouse centerfolds fondle each other, crawl around on all fours like asylum inmates, roll their tongues, and do the most imaginative things with spikes.

Meanwhile, Caligula throws orgies, mocks gods, overthrows the government, and insults the best families in Rome while a thunderous orchestra plays music that sounds like "Stormy Weather."

In an interview, Bob Guccione stated that he expected *Caligula* to be the most controversial film since Howard Hughes made *The Outlaw*. Hughes is no longer here to defend himself, but Jane Russell should have sued. In closing, Guccione boasted: "I feel this film will attract from ten to fifteen imitators in its first year and I don't think films will ever be the same." He's wrong about the first part (what imitator in his right mind would *want* to make the *second* worst film ever?) but right about the last part. Movies won't be the same. They can't sink any lower than *Caligula*.

THE CANNONBALL RUN (1981)
1/2★ Directed by Hal Needham. Screenplay by Brock Yates. Produced by Albert S. Ruddy. With Burt Reynolds, Dom DeLuise, Farrah Fawcett, Jack Elam, Adrienne Barbeau, Roger Moore, Dean Martin, Sammy Davis, Jr., Molly Picon, Peter Fonda, and Bianca Jagger.

Burt Reynolds has made rotten movies before—strung end to end his movie flops would, in fact, form a highway of rotting celluloid trash from here to the Chinese border.

But never in his misguided career was there ever a Burt Reynolds film rottener than *The Cannonball Run*. A mindless stupidity perpetrated by mental midgets, this swill has been described by critic Jeffrey Lyons as "making *Smokey and the Bandit* look like *Richard III*."

Compared to what I think of this abomination, that's practically an endorsement. Plotless and without a shred of imagination or creativity, *The Cannonball Run* is a home movie made by Big Burt and his brainless buddies with a Polaroid somebody gave them.

It pretends to be about a cross-country race on the highways, but all it does is give a lot of outrageous fakes an opportunity to waste a lot of money mugging in scrambled vignettes that would embarrass a high school camera class. Burt and his obese sidekick Dom DeLuise are racing in an ambulance with the kidnaped Farrah Fawcett tied to a stretcher with a junkie proctologist (Jack Elam) who does disgusting things to her with fingers and hypodermic needles.

Dean Martin, bloated and unsteady, and Sammy Davis, Jr., emaciated and high as a kite, dress like priests in a red Ferrari. Bert Convy is on a motorcycle. Roger Moore is Seymour Goldfarb, an egomaniac heir to a girdle fortune who thinks he's James Bond, in a Rolls.

Adrienne Barbeau is a slut who bribes the highway patrol out of speeding tickets by unzipping her purple satin combat fatigues. Molly Picon, Bianca Jagger, and Peter Fonda are a few of the "guest stars" unfortunate enough to be desperate enough for exposure to do anything for a day's pay.

Hal Needham, who directed *Smokey and the Bandit* and *Smokey and the Bandit II*, is an ex-stuntman dedicated to destroying property, insulting the intelligence of mankind, and giving a finger to the law. He couldn't direct traffic in the Mojave Desert at midnight. One of the most dismaying things about today's self-indulgent and self-destructive movie industry is the way cocky, no-talent jerks like these get the money to litter the screen with garbage.

Described as "the automotive equivalent of the Bay of Pigs," *The Cannonball Run* has only one philosophy: "There's not one state in the union that has the death penalty for speeding." It would be a service to society if there was a death penalty for making mind atrophying garbage like *The Cannonball Run*.

THE CANTERVILLE GHOST (1944)
★ ★ ★   Directed by Jules Dassin. Screenplay by Edwin Blum. Produced by Arthur Field. *With Charles Laughton, Robert Young, Margaret O'Brien, William Gargan, Rags Ragland, Una O'Connor, Elizabeth Risdon, Reginald Owen, and Peter Lawford.*

Oscar Wilde's *The Canterville Ghost* is a whimsical tale that has delighted children for decades, but MGM's 1944 rendition made this charming fable more delicious than ever. The incomparable Margaret O'Brien is the aristocratic moppet whose stately castle in England is invaded by American GIs to the dissatisfaction of the family ghost, a pompous, chickenhearted coward played with abandon by the great Charles Laughton. This old ghost has been haunting the manor since 1604, and his soul can only be freed by a brave descendant who turns out to be Robert Young, one of the raucous Yanks. Fanciful and funny, *The Canterville Ghost* is a timeless treat in which pintsized Margaret even dances the jitterbug.

CAN'T STOP THE MUSIC (1980)

★ ★ ★ Directed by Nancy Walker. Screenplay by Allan Carr and Bronte Woodard. Produced by Carr. *With The Village People, Steve Guttenberg, Valerie Perrine, Bruce Jenner, Tammy Grimes, Barbara Rush, June Havoc, Paul Sand, Jack Weston, and Leigh Taylor-Young.*

Can't Stop the Music was made by Allan Carr, who was responsible for the abominable *Grease*, so naturally I expected the worst. The big surprise is that although *Can't Stop the Music* is certainly one of the silliest movies ever made, it is also a vibrant and uplifting musical whose energy succeeded in both confusing and entertaining me so completely that I'm not sure I can even begin to assess it rationally. All I can tell you is that it is worth seeing twice, and from me that is rare praise indeed.

Probably the longest and most expensive television commercial ever made, its sole purpose was to promote, publicize, and cash in on the puzzling success of that campy singing group the Village People. These glorified chorus boys, dressed in costumes that tease and illuminate the sexual fantasies of the Gay Liberation Movement, rose from an inside joke in the dunes and discos of Fire Island to international stardom, filling empty record industry coffers from Timbuktu to Tin Pan Alley.

Idolized and applauded by children and adults of every age, language and cultural background without the vaguest idea what the Village People were singing about in homosexual send-up songs like "YMCA," the group cleverly fingered the pulse of a chaotic society enmeshed in rapidly changing values and made it dance along to a disco beat. Because they cashed in early and swan-dived into oblivion, their trendy appeal now seems, in retrospect, deservedly short-lived (one can scarcely imagine a whole string of movies starring the Village People). Therefore, *Can't Stop the Music* is out of date before it even begins. (I have visions of stunned movie audiences in the year 3000 watching this movie in some museum retrospective on the planet Venus and wondering what the hell the excitement was all about back in 1980.)

But on the other hand, the people who made it cleverly incorporated many of the production values of the old MGM musicals and brought them up to date in a glittering package for the rock and disco demands of a contemporary society, and the result is a revolutionary kind of musical that explodes on the screen like Roman candles. Whatever else you think of it, you won't be bored by the musical numbers.

The problem is that *Can't Stop the Music* does stop the music for occasional stretches of plot and dialogue (also conceived by Allan Carr and Bronte Woodard, who wrote *Grease*) that are so dopey they have to be seen to be believed. If you can suspend belief long enough to treat this entire movie as a total camp, you'll have a romp.

The Village People can't act, but they are in excellent company, since nobody else bothers to do much acting, either. Valerie Perrine is in hot water the minute she tries to make something out of her role as a retired fashion model who plays den mother to the good-natured lunatics in her Greenwich Village neighborhood. Steve Guttenberg is her appealing house-sitting roommate who writes rock songs, the Village People are assorted characters recruited from various street corners to audition his songs for record mogul Paul Sand, and Bruce Jenner is a stuffy tax lawyer who gets involved in the madness when he delivers a cake.

Wafting in and out of all the imbecilic confusion are such grand old pros as Tammy Grimes, as an aggressive agent in the Eileen Ford mold who gets her false fingernails caught in the dials of phone booths trying to talk Valerie into a milk commercial; June Havoc, as Guttenberg's mother, who uses her training as a former chorus girl to outsmart record moguls in contractual negotiations, and Barbara Rush, as a rich society matron whose enthusiasm for the kinky kids provides them with a launching pad to stardom in the form of a charity show in San Francisco.

Look closely and in cameos you'll even spot Portia Nelson, Sammy Davis's wife Altovise, comic Marilyn Sokol, Jack Weston, Leigh Taylor-Young, Chicago columnist Aaron Gold, and Muriel Slatkin, owner of the Beverly Hills Hotel. The movie contains so much "inside" show-business information that I'm not sure the kids it's aimed at will understand it at all.

There are references to Judy Garland at Carnegie Hall, Fruit of the Loom jockey shorts, Rod Stewart, Neil Bogart of Casablanca Records (the record company pursuing the Village People in the movie is called "Marrakesh Records"), Marvin Hamlisch, and Celebrity Service.

The kids who reveled in the gyrations of the Village People didn't seem to get the homosexual implications in everything the group (and the movie) stood for. They responded to the Village People the way they responded to Pee Wee Herman—as grownups who dress up in their fantasies the way children do at birthday parties. I don't think they ever had a clue what the big spectacular "YMCA" number was all about, with its quick shots of complete male frontal nudity as Valerie Perrine dances through the showers. Every gay centerfold from *Blueboy* and *Playgirl* seems to have been recruited for this number, and on the day it was filmed every gay bar on Santa Monica Boulevard must have been empty.

Will the kids understand what's happening when Bruce Jenner attacks Valerie Perrine for hanging out with guys who are "weird," and she counters with "There's not a person alive without peculiarities and as long as they don't hurt anybody, it's none of my business"? Maybe not. And later, when Jenner discards his three-piece Barney's suit and dances down Christopher Street in cutoffs to symbolize his own liberation, nine-year-olds still squeal with glee.

Frankly, none of this matters if you can break down your own uptight defenses the way Jenner does and let *Can't Stop the Music* wash over you like a warm surf. It doesn't matter how hip you are to the gay scene to get the implicit humor in the Village People's dressing room when the leather man gets an attack of nerves and says "Leather men don't cry" and the cowboy, in an aside to the audience says, "Oh, yes they *do*!"

It doesn't much matter, either, if you don't know the Steve Guttenberg character is based on Paul Jabara, or the Paul Sand character is a combination of David Geffen and Neil Bogart. It's the spirit that counts, and *Can't Stop the Music* is loaded with it.

From the wonderful opening number (David London singing "The Sound of the City") to the star-spangled finale, the music lifts you off your feet and keeps you moving. The choreography, by Arlene Phillips, is hot, the costumes sizzle, the photography by Bill Butler is eye-poppingly lush, the direction by Nancy Walker is as corny and awful and perfectly suited to the film's dopiness as all the stuff she learned in the old MGM days. What she's done is feed all the juices from her creative past into a cinematic Cuisinart. The yield is a puree of Technicolor musicals that combines the best of Busby Berkeley with the best of contemporary musical ideas. Perpetual motion is what *Can't Stop the Music* is all about. It's a glorious mess, but its feet never stop dancing.

When I tape MGM musicals from TV late shows for my personal library of video cassettes, I often edit out the dialogue between numbers, so the idiocy of *Can't Stop the Music*'s freaked-out plot didn't bother me. The people are all so naturally high on vitamins (and other things) that they mean no harm and everybody ends up happy, dispensing such joy, sweetness, and goodwill to men that the movie's exuberance is contagious. No serious critic could praise it without embarrassment, yet if you can believe it, the movie is so bad it's good.

CAPE FEAR (1991)
★ Directed by Martin Scorsese. Written by Wesley Strick. Produced by Barbara de Fina. With Robert De Niro, Jessica Lange, Nick Nolte, Joe Baker, Juliette Lewis, Martin Balsam, and special guest appearances by Gregory Peck and Robert Mitchum.

I'd like to nominate Martin Scorsese's *Cape Fear* as one of the top ten comedies of 1991. The laughs may be unintentional, but they sure kept me from fidgeting. *Cape Fear* is the latest unnecessary, unsolicited, and unsuccessful remake of a classic that was better the first time around. Mr. Scorsese, who prides himself on originality, should have better sense than to tamper with the tried and true. In this case, he has not only failed to enhance the original, he's darn near trashed it. His interpretation of the 1962 black-and-white thriller about a man protecting his family from a maniac is, in the words of the film's producer Barbara de Fina (better known as Mrs. Scorsese), "a revisionist version of a very specific genre." The word *revisionist* must explain the pretentious camera work that keeps turning from color to black-and-white at the oddest moments. For the first half hour, everyone walks into the camera, turning the screen to a blank dissolve. Later, people get washed into X rays. Sometimes the film is out of focus. So much for revisionist art for auteurs. The rest of the movie is pretty lousy, too.

In one of his goofiest screwball performances, Robert De Niro eats so much scenery he should be tested for asbestos poisoning. In the role originally played (with oh so much more clarity) by Robert Mitchum, De Niro is now a tattooed, weight-lifting, cigar-smoking psycho who rapes, mutilates, and cannibalizes his victims while drawling like a revue skit parody of Tennessee Williams. The family he terrorizes is almost equally wacky. The husband, originally played with valor and courage by Gregory Peck, is now Nick Nolte, a lawyer who has no ethics, and is something of a guilt-ridden, two-timing, bespectacled wimp as well. The wife (where is Polly Bergen, now that we need some class and balance?) is Jessica Lange, a tough, angry, miserable cynic who seems to hate everybody in sight, including her own teenage daughter. Not that I blame her. This pouting, oversexed, and unfocused brat is the best defense I can think of for having your tubes tied. Played by the dreadful Juliette Lewis, she's a repulsive, retarded little jerk, too. Why they live in a sleepy hamlet in the Carolinas called New Essex is anybody's guess and how the insane De Niro finds them is equally baffling.

But ready or not, here he comes—poisoning the dog, raping and mutilating Mr.

Nolte's new office girlfriend, slipping the daughter marijuana in the high-school drama department and Henry Miller's *Sexus* under the geranium pot. Of course, the cops, the lawyers, the judges, and all the king's men of New Essex sit back and do nothing. After the maid and the private detective they hire end up in small lakes of blood on the kitchen floor, Nolte & Co. flee to the family houseboat in Cape Fear and get labeled "fugitives from the law" for their pain.

The movie gets sillier. De Niro hangs along for the ride by strapping himself under the family Cherokee for the long trip to the cape, where the most peaceful lagoon in South Carolina turns into a raging sea not even Moses could part with the aid of Cecil B. DeMille. The bloody, nauseating finale is a gross-out. Since when does "revisionist" art turn an unbeatable suspense genre rooted in reality into another endless installment of *Nightmare on Elm Street*?

Gruesome and violent as it is, *Cape Fear* is funnier than it is scary. The new script, by Wesley Strick, is an elongated sick joke. After the delirious daughter, who can't make up her mind whether she's sexually aroused or morally disgusted by De Niro, finally decides to throw a pot of boiling water in his face, he says, "Are you offering me something hot?" Are these the same guys who made *Taxi Driver*? Mr. Scorsese even uses Bernard Herrman's original film score, which only serves as a reminder of how much better movies sounded in the old days. Campily, he even drags in poor old Robert Mitchum and Gregory Peck as a cracker-barrel lawyer (complete with his backwoods drawl and white ice-cream suit from *To Kill a Mockingbird*)—for no artistic purpose at all other than to embarrass them both. By attempting to define his new American family in vague psychological spasms of nineties alienation and distrust, Mr. Scorsese only coarsens them and makes their every response to attack suspect. This does a disservice to the actors, who get bruised and knocked around excessively for their art with no payoff. Watching De-Niro out of control like a berserk clown in horror makeup, they all seem to feel obligated to match his overacting. Mr. Nolte becomes dysfunctional in the process, while Ms. Lange just seems mean and hysterical. The Carolinas are played by Florida, the lake that turns into a storm at sea is played by a ninety-foot water tank, the suspense and tension turn phony, and they could have achieved just as much impact in Brooklyn Heights.

CAREFUL, HE MIGHT HEAR YOU (1984)

★ ★ ★ ★ Directed by Carl Schultz. Screenplay by Michael Jenkins, based on the novel by Sumner Locke Elliott. Produced by Jill Robb. With Wendy Hughes, Robyn Nevin, Nicholas Gledhill, John Hargreaves, and Geraldine Turner.

The pain and confusion of childhood is one of the most heartbreaking experiences to survive in life and one of the most difficult subjects to tackle in motion pictures. Thanks to the genuine, heartfelt honesty and dedication of a superlative company of artists and technical craftsmen, the subject has been enriched and informed by *Careful, He Might Hear You*.

Careful, He Might Hear You is, in my opinion, the most beautiful, touching, and eerily haunting Australian film since *Breaker Morant*.

Based on the lyrically moving cult novel by Sumner Locke Elliot, *Careful, He Might Hear You* is the heart-tugging story of a bright, impressionable and completely disoriented boy who finds himself innocently drawn into a custody battle between two aunts who hate each other.

Six-year-old P.S. (a nickname inherited from his bohemian mother, who died in childbirth) has been left in the care of his Aunt Lila, who has raised him from a baby and who has given him as normal an upbringing as her limited financial station and poor health will allow. Shuttled between warm, down-to-earth Lila and his glamorous, precise, and formal Aunt Vanessa, P.S. finds himself a pawn in a deadly game of mismatched egos.

At Aunt Lila's, he plays baseball with other kids, gets his face smudged, and eats jam sandwiches. At Aunt Vanessa's, he's subjected to humiliating exercises in table etiquette, piano lessons, and dancing classes, and sent to a snobbish private school where the other children torture him and make him feel inferior. Vanessa wants full guardianship to ease her frustrations over a long-lost affair she had with P.S.'s charming but irresponsible father, who abandoned him to work in the gold mines. Lila and her husband George want to adopt him, but she's an asthmatic and he's unemployed.

Inadvertently, the boy becomes a wedge between the two sisters—one poor but proud, the other rich but neurotic and willful. The court turns P.S. over to the aunt who gave him all of the advantages, but the story does not end there.

P.S. has learned from experts how adults manipulate each other. Imitating the grownups with his own form of childish cruelty, he reduces the rich aunt to tears and nervous hysteria, and like the story of Moses in the bulrushes, *Careful, He Might Hear You* presents, with tragic consequences for everybody, another example of how the person who loves most sacrifices more. In the end, it is P.S. who demands his own identity and grows up, but the price he pays will obviously haunt him the rest of his life.

Not since the baffling, piercing things witnessed and felt by Frankie Addams in *The Member of the Wedding* or Rufus in *All the Way Home* has the world loomed so large in the eyes of a child on film.

Major directors the world over have tried for years to turn this complex story into a movie, and every star from Angela Lansbury to Jean Simmons has been announced at one time or another for the meaty roles of the two bitterly opposed aunts locked in combat over the soul of a child. But it took Australian director Carl Schultz to get it made and he's done a brilliant job indeed.

Schultz's focus is a child's gradually changing perception of the grown ups around him. At first he's enthralled by the way Vanessa introduces him to Peter Pan and Winnie the Pooh. As he grows, he realizes a darker side to her character and matches it with his own. This flawed image builds up the pressure on them both as her idealization inaudibly but irrevocably snaps.

Attention is arrested not by plot development but by the way Schultz invests significant things—a toy soldier in an empty nursery, a cemetery overgrown with buttercups, washed white in the summer heat—with a mysterious, luminous life of their own. It's a majestic American debut that establishes him as a major director of power and sensitivity.

Sumptuously mounted and gorgeously photographed by the great Australian cinematographer John Seale, the film is made with enormous care and precision.

Wendy Hughes conjures memories of a young Vivien Leigh in the role of Vanessa—flighty, edgy, her inner turbulence constantly checked by a dazzling outer sweetness and a radiant smile. Robyn Nevin, as Lila, is starchy, pragmatic, and perfectly frumpy, providing the exact counterpart to her sister's worldly demeanor the film demands. John Hargreaves, as P.S.'s good-for-nothing but dashing rogue of a father, manages the impossible feat of showing both how wild and sensitive a wandering man of that nature can be. But it is really little Nicholas Gledhill who steals the picture. With saffron hair and voluminous, all-seeing eyes clear as swimming pools, he is the camera through which the landscape of life passes. Here is a child who is simultaneously pitiful and adorable, vulnerable and tough, innocent and dangerous. His work is small but exquisite, and I should not be at all surprised if he grows up to be the Australian Montgomery Clift.

In the way it explores the vast dimensions of love, examines the magic and the loss of children forced to mature before their time, and demonstrates how all the advantages in the world cannot make up for a barren heart, *Careful, He Might Hear You* is a rare and exemplary film. It's memorable and enchanting, and it puts Australia back where it belongs as a leading satellite in the world of movies.

CAROUSEL (1956)

★ ★ ½ Directed by Henry King. Screenplay by Phoebe and Henry Ephron. Produced by Henry Ephron. With Gordon MacRae, Shirley Jones, Cameron Mitchell, Barbara Ruick, Robert Rounseville, Gene Lockhart, and Claramae Turner.

Carousel is the lyrical Rodgers and Hammerstein hit about a New England merry-go-round barker (Gordon MacRae) and his golden girl (Shirley Jones), who remains faithful in love even after death. The festive clambake, the surging "Soliloquy" in which the hero sings about the coming birth of his first child, and the beauty of Claramae Turner singing "You'll Never Walk Alone" are some of the highlights. The Heaven sequences and the angels' return to earth in time for the high-school graduation are too stagey and stiff for the screen, but the score still enthralls.

CASUALTIES OF WAR (1987)

★ ★ ★ ½ Directed by Brian DePalma. Screenplay by David Rabe. Produced by Art Linson. With Michael J. Fox and Sean Penn.

Overshadowed by Oliver Stone's Platoon and Born on the Fourth of July, Brian DePalma's Casualties of War did disappointing business at the box office. I hope it will find a wider audience on home video. The setting is Vietnam again, but this is no ordinary war flick. It's the true and terrifying tragedy of a squad of combat soldiers so dehumanized by a war they didn't understand that they lost all reason—abducted, raped, and murdered a young Vietnamese civilian with the excuse that "in war anything is possible." Michael J. Fox is wonderful as the one grunt with a conscience, torn from his family before he had time to become a man. Sean Penn is a hard, street-tough, foul-mouthed sergeant, scarcely more than a boy himself, so enraged by the destruction around him that he goads his squad into dragging an innocent girl along on a combat mission. The psychological tension in Casualties of War is as shattering as the battle footage. Fox is forced to watch the rape at knife-point, and then, when mob insanity grips the squad, to helplessly witness the vicious and pointless murder. But after the ordeal ends, his is just beginning. The army ignores the facts. Now he has the revenge of his own men to face. For a pint-sized shrimp, Fox has a hammerlock grip on the role. David Rabe's taut script is no Platoon revisited. DePalma's tough, terrific direction shows both the carnage of a war with no leaders and the psychological damage it did to heroes and heels alike. Movingly, it illuminates the stark tragedy that results from a conflict of human values where one boy hangs on to his ethics and everyone else follows the rules even though there are none. A masterful, lacerating, and deeply disturbing cinematic achievement.

THE CATERED AFFAIR (1956)
★ ★ ★ ½ Directed by Richard Brooks. Produced by Sam Zimbalist. Screenplay by Gore Vidal. With Bette Davis, Ernest Borgnine, Debbie Reynolds, Barry Fitzgerald, Dorothy Stickney, and Rod Taylor.

With this film adaptation of Paddy Chayefsky's hit TV play, Bette Davis found her best director, Richard Brooks, and the finest role of her post-*All About Eve* career. In fact, *The Catered Affair* became one of her favorite films of all time. It's a poignant, naturalistic, often deeply touching little gem of a movie that deserves a fresh look.

Critics and fans had a hard time accepting Bette as a working-class Bronx housewife, frying eggs and shopping the fish market, fat and dowdy in rubber padding and off-the-rack dresses. But once you recover

from the sound of her Irish Catholic accent and the visual shock of her flabby appearance, you begin to see what heights of acting this often hammy star was capable of. As an abused, neglected, hardworking woman, she becomes obsessed with the marriage of her only daughter (surprisingly played without a trace of glamour by Debbie Reynolds), determined to give her the wedding with all the trimmings she never had herself, even though it costs her poor husband (Ernest Borgnine, in his finest performance since *Marty*) his life savings. The trials and tribulations of the wedding are as beautifully detailed in Gore Vidal's impeccable screenplay as the development of the characters themselves. Before this charming, funny, moving film ends, you will feel like you're a member of the family. (And you'll want to adopt the cantankerous uncle, Barry Fitzgerald, and accompany him for a canasta game at the Green Grass Bar and Grill.)

Richard Brooks, a great director with a special feel for actors, brings the story to vivid life. The marvelous music by Andre Previn, the flawless cast, and the perfect writing and atmosphere add up to a kind of blue-collar *Father of the Bride* with fish and chips. A rare and unforgettable experience, but for maximum effect, skip the awful colorized version and stick to black and white.

CHAPTER TWO (1979)

★ ★ ★ Directed by Robert Moore. Screenplay by Neil Simon (adapted from his play). Produced by Ray Stark. With Marsha Mason, James Caan, Valerie Harper, and Joseph Bologna.

A warm and embracing sugarplum comedy—subtle, intelligent, uplifting, and really about something.

I have come unhinged by Marsha Mason, and it's a genuine pleasure to see her in a role that emphasizes and showcases all of her natural talents so wisely. She should be good as a divorced actress who meets a recently widowed writer, marries him after a whirlwind courtship, and then settles down to the psychological adjustments of a new life with a man still haunted by his first wife. It happened to her in real life when she married Neil Simon so fast that the gossip columnists didn't even know she knew him.

So the film is really a valentine to her humanity, humor, and courage. But James Caan matches her, scene for scene,

and hangs in there with her with verve and valor. It's by far the best work either of them has ever done on screen. Simon has pruned away some of the gags, sharpened the insights in the play and carved from what was already a fine piece of writing the finest screenplay he had written to date.

What a treat it is to hear real people saying real things to each other in a mature (though perhaps too often glib) manner. The heart and the wisdom shine through and the happy ending is not one of those Hollywood rainbows painted on with Technicolor.

Valerie Harper looks underfed, undernourished, and underpar as Mason's flaky friend Faye (another Valerie named Perrine would have been a more suitable choice for the assignment), but both she and Joe Bologna, as Caan's annoying but concerned brother Leo, are excellent second bananas.

Robert Moore directed with uncanny sensitivity. (The fifth star of *Chapter Two* is Simon's old friend the telephone, which rings insistently, incessantly, and often. The telephone is murder in films, but it performs with purpose and distinction here.) This movie is very funny, but instead of forgetting what you laughed at, you'll take home the humor because it creates a warm glow in the heart that can't be shaken off later.

CHARIOTS OF FIRE (1981)

★ ★ ★ ★ Directed by Hugh Hudson. Screenplay by Colin Welland. Produced by David Puttnam. With Ben Cross, Ian Charleson, Ian Holm, Nigel Havers, Sir John Gielgud, Brad Davis, Dennis Christopher, Lindsay Anderson, David Yelland, and Nicholas Farrell.

Chariots of Fire is a fresh, original film that parallels the lives of Harold Abrahams and Eric Liddell, two of England's most cherished sports heroes who won gold medals for track in the Paris Olympics in 1924. It is one of the finest films about sports I've ever seen, but it is also about sentiments considered old-fashioned by today's standards—love of country, fear of God, loyalty to the team, pursuit of honor, learning humility in victory. It masterfully reconstructs a time and a sensibility when people like its two central heroes competed without show, fuss, subsidy, commercial gain or the kind of narcissistic public preening we get from today's athletes. The film is absolutely true and Colin Welland's vivid, intelligent screenplay not only holds a magnifying glass to historical facts but illumines the era in which they took place.

The film begins in 1919, when Liddell, the devout Christian son of Scottish missionaries, discovers his talent for running on the rugby field. For him, winning a race is a religious experience and the Olympic medal becomes a prize he wants to win for God. Meanwhile, at Cambridge, Abrahams discovers running as a way of working out his aggression and anger in the subtly prejudiced world of upperclass anti-Semitism. The son of a Lithuanian immigrant determined to make an Englishman of his son in an Anglo-Saxon world, Harold uses his ability to run like the wind as both a weapon and a defense against bigotry.

When Eric and Harold compete for the first time in 1923, the Scot wins. Harold enrages the academic hierarchy (starchily played by Sir John Gielgud and director-turned-actor Lindsay Anderson) by hiring a professional coach who, even worse, is half Arab. The film follows their struggles and defeats, examines their private lives, and reveals without sentimentality the growing compassion in their relationship with other teammates as they find themselves united by king and country and their respective gods at the Paris Olympics in 1924.

It doesn't matter if you can't hobble as far as the nearest bus stop. The film's overwhelming impact will touch and affect you as it catches you up in the collective experience and transports you mentally and physically into the athlete's world. Ben Cross and Ian Charleson are magnificent as Abrahams and Liddell, and there are sterling contributions by an exemplary supporting cast, from Brad Davis and Dennis Christopher as the American challengers, to Ian Holm, as the Jewish runner's coach. The quiet scene in which he learns of his student's win as the national anthem rises from the Olympic Stadium and drifts through his hotel room is one of the emotional highlights in a film crowded with home-hitting truths. Hugh Hudson holds atmosphere, period detail, thrilling sports action, and subtler issues and attitudes so firmly in balance that I can scarcely believe this is his first feature film as a director.

The standing ovation of cheering, tear-drenched admirers at the film's premiere at the Cannes Film Festival was demonstrable proof that with *Chariots of Fire* a director of

major importance had arrived to justifiable applause. Its Best Picture Oscar ratified it. Oddly, his subsequent films have not lived up to Hugh Hudson's promise, leading me to concur with Frank Capra's assessment of movie directors: "The movie makes the man, not the other way around."

CHATTAHOOCHEE (1989)
★ ★ ★ ½ Directed by Mick Jackson. Screenplay by James Hicks. Produced by Fay and Aaron Schwab. *With Gary Oldman, Dennis Hopper, Frances McDormand, Pamela Reed*

Chattahoochee is the true story of one man's descent into the harrowing hell of a state mental hospital and the courage with which he survived to change things. The man was Emmett Foley, a Korean War hero who cracked under the strain of civilian life in 1955 and got locked away in a Florida loony bin at Chattahoochee—a primitive, filthy, inhuman snake pit. The atrocities he endured are grimly catalogued and not for the fainthearted. But Gary Oldman, as Emmett, gives the film such a spirit of dignity, courage and humanity that he even becomes a hero to his fellow patients—especially Dennis Hopper, as another victim of the system with no hope of getting well or getting out. Frances McDormand, as the dopey wife who forgets him and moves on, and the marvelous Pamela Reed, as the sister who brings Emmett a Bible in which he kept records of the hospital abuses, are also excellent. Miraculously, Emmett did survive and his records led to 137 reforms that restructured the face of mental health care in America today. Gripping and shocking, *Chattahoochee* means to horrify and provoke, but it is also inspiring as it demonstrates once again how ordinary people can do extraordinary things in the war against injustice. It's powerful stuff that makes you cheer for the human race.

CHEYENNE AUTUMN (1964)
★ ★ ★ ★ Directed by John Ford. Screenplay by James Webb. Produced by Bernard Smith. *With James Stewart, Richard Widmark, Edward G. Robinson, Carroll Baker, Karl Malden, Dolores Del Rio, Sal Mineo, Ricardo Montalban, Arthur Kennedy, Gilbert Roland, John Carradine, and Victor Jory.*

If you're a cavalry-and-Indians buff, you can't overlook this John Ford masterpiece—an epic frontier Western about the cruel mistreatment of the Cheyenne Indians who, sick and starving, started a brave, painful fifteen-hundred-mile trek back to their homeland in 1878. But the master of Westerns makes the film more than just an annotated footnote to American history. He fills the screen with breathtaking scenery, epic battles, and heartrending human drama. Richard Widmark, Edward G. Robinson, Jimmy Stewart, Karl Malden, Carroll Baker, Dolores Del Rio, Ricardo Montalban, Sal Mineo, and a cast of thousands give this wrenching human story heart and passion. One of the greatest Westerns ever made, *Cheyenne Autumn* is the film that inspired *Dances with Wolves*.

CHILDREN OF A LESSER GOD (1986)
★ ★ ½ Directed by Randa Haines. Screenplay by Hesper Anderson and Mark Medoff, based on Medoff's play. Produced by Burt Sugarman and Patrick Palmer. *With William Hurt, Marlee Matlin, Piper Laurie, Philip Bosco, Alison Gompf, John F. Cleary, and John Basinger.*

William Hurt is a sympathetic and talented speech therapist in a school for the deaf; newcomer Marlee Matlin is his most difficult pupil—barricaded emotionally against the silent world that has hurt her—who refuses help but becomes his lover. Matlin, who is hearing impaired in real life, makes the sentimental, conventional story glow with life and energy. Her pride, egotism, and angry humor give Hurt something real to play against. The result is an emotional tug-of-war that is mesmerizing. My main problem with this film is that it is basically a two-character play in which only one character does all the talking. But its sensitivity and heart are undeniable.

THE CHILDREN'S HOUR (1961)
★ ★ ★ Directed and produced by William Wyler. Screenplay by Lillian Hellman and John Michael Hayes. *With Audrey Hepburn, Shirley MacLaine, James Garner, Fay Bainter, Miriam Hopkins, and Veronica Cartwright.*

This is William Wyler's moving dramatization of Lillian Hellman's blistering Broadway hit starring Oscar winners Shirley MacLaine and Audrey Hepburn as idealistic, unmarried teachers whose lives are destroyed by the vicious lie that they are lesbians. The great Fay Bainter is sensational as the dowager who spreads the accusation, Miriam Hopkins (who starred with Merle Oberon and Joel McCrea in *These Three*, Wyler's much tamer 1936 version of the same play) is prop-

erly thorny and irrational in the unsympathetic role of MacLaine's addled aunt who only worsens the situation, and James Garner is unusually gentle as the tortured fiancé of Miss Hepburn. Homosexuality was a taboo subject on the screen when Wyler made the first version of the Hellman play in 1936. Hollywood still shuddered in 1961, although most critics consider the second version equally wimpy. But the texture of this film and the integrity of the performances still captivate me. By today's standards, it's pretty tame stuff.

THE CHINA SYNDROME (1979)
★ ★ ★ ½ Directed by James Bridges. Screenplay by Bridges, Mike Gray, and T. S. Cook. Produced by Michael Douglas. *With Jane Fonda, Jack Lemmon, Michael Douglas, Scott Brady, James Hampton, Peter Donat, and Wilford Brimley.*

Jane Fonda, who always wanted to play Brenda Starr, gets her chance in *The China Syndrome*. It's both a thriller and a complex human document about people who are brave, complicated, intelligent, and ready to fight for the survival of their values at great personal risk. A monster movie with modern technology as the villain, *China Syndrome* is a perfect vehicle for Jane, who plays a TV reporter for a Los Angeles station, thirsty for a break in hard news, but relegated to feature coverage of such pablum as whale migrations, hot-air balloons, and birthday parties at the San Diego Zoo. The film opens with Fonda, coiffed and color coordinated, doing a live "remote" on singing telegrams. It looks like a send-up of the six o'clock news. But this is a Jane Fonda movie, so even if it were a comedy, the suspicion is that there's something more sardonic in store than a put-down of some local Barbara Walters. Just wait. What happens next will curl your hair.

On a trip to a nuclear power plant to cover a routine "soft news" story on nuclear energy, Jane witnesses an accident that could affect the lives of everyone in Southern California. Something about uranium pellets being used to conserve energy in steam turbines. Her radical cameraman (Michael Douglas) secretly films the accident, but returning to the station they discover that nuclear plants fall under top government security, unauthorized photography is a felony, and the station manager won't telecast the "scoop," for fear of a massive lawsuit. Douglas won't ac-

cept this cover-up, so he steals the film from the vault, calls in some nuclear physicists and uncovers a scandal that could lead to the deaths of thousands of people by radiation poisoning. How Jane's ethics jeopardize both her job and the life of her confidential news source (Jack Lemmon), how she races the clock against the murderous government-protected scientists to bring her story to the public's attention, and the eventual tragedy that results form the basis for this taut, tightly coiled suspense thriller.

"China Syndrome" is scientific jargon for nuclear destruction by which enough radioactive waste escapes to destroy an area the size of Pennsylvania before you can blink an eye, not to mention the cancer that can show up later. With so many ultramodern nuclear plants in existence and no proof that radioactive wastes can be disposed of adequately and safely, the film raises serious questions about how much the nuclear power industry controls our lives and our future health. There is so much scientific mumbo-jumbo in the script by James Bridges, who also directed with nail-biting tension, that you'd have to be an expert on energy conservation, a physicist, or a cosmic scientist to understand it all. But worry not. The great thing about *China Syndrome* is that Jane Fonda doesn't understand all of the talk about faulty relays in the generator circuits, either. We never know any more than she does, and vice versa, but we're with her all the way. Bridges, a fine director whose previous films *The Paper Chase* and *September 30, 1955* were lauded by critics and overlooked by the public, demonstrates a rare ability to elicit natural performances from actors, and he gets superb work from Fonda, Douglas and especially Lemmon, in the pivotal role of a plant supervisor with a conscience. As a writer, he has a strong sensitivity and a genuine feeling for people and the way they talk and live and relate to each other. *China Syndrome* reveals the elaborate machinery of the news media in its daily processes as well as the behind-closed-doors atmosphere of the energy resources industry, and packs a wallop as a first-rate detective story along the way. No wonder the utilities companies sent disclaimers to critics when this film was released, warning them to ignore its cynicism. I prefer to ignore the anonymous monopolies that send me bills, and send everyone responsible for *The China Syndrome* roses instead.

A CHORUS LINE (1985)
★ ★ Directed by Richard Attenborough. Screenplay by Arnold Schulman. Produced by Cy Feuer and Ernest Martin. *With Michael Douglas, Alyson Reed, Vicki Frederick, Gregg Burge, and Nicole Fosse.*

Since it first opened its heart to New Yorkers down at Joe Papp's Public Theater on Lafayette Street, *A Chorus Line* won nine Tony awards and a Pulitzer Prize, established the longest running record on Broadway, and became everybody's favorite musical. Leave it to the movies to ruin a perfect friendship.

The movie, directed by Richard Attenborough, was a long time coming. Among the giants who tackled it and threw in the towel in defeat were Mike Nichols and the show's creator, Michael Bennett. They said it couldn't be done. They were right.

The unbeatable concept remains: a darkened theater, a spotlit stage, a voice in the shadows shouting directions through a microphone, and seventeen desperate, worried Broadway gypsy dancers competing for jobs in a chorus line.

The theme is survival. The

human elements are hope, fear, need, frustration, ambition, and dreams. Attenborough, clear-headed about the goals, has tried to serve the original material faithfully. The camera has changed it for him. Instead of enhancing a great work of art, the movie version only ends up truncating it.

"Step, push, turn, touch, kick!" The cattle call brings jobless hoofers into the empty Mark Hellinger Theater in thundering herds. Hundreds of hopefuls are called, few are chosen. To toil in the background, for little pay and no glory, a dancer must have the grace of Astaire, the coordination of Bob Fosse, the athletic prowess and physical stamina of Gene Kelly, the extensions of Baryshnikov.

The final eliminations will leave jobs for only eight people.

In the theater *A Chorus Line* was a collective, communal experience. The audience was auditioning, too. We shared the tension, the sweat, the nerves, and the anxiety at the same time the dancers went through the motions of getting that job. Their rejection was our pain. Their success was our joy. The man in the dark who held their fates in his hands controlled us, too.

Through his tough, probing interviews he—and the audience—got to know his dancers. We were all in it together.

The movie separates us. Attenborough works up disciplined energy, and the sparks fly when the seventeen semifinalists leap and tap and soar and grind their way through the dance routines. But the film cuts away too often from the gypsies to the reactions of Zach, the choreographer (played by Michael Douglas, the last person on the face of the earth to play a Michael Bennett—styled choreographer-taskmaster).

We get flashbacks to his love affair with Cassie, a retired dancer now trying to make a comeback, that doesn't lead to any cinematic payoff. We get flashcuts to Cassie's early career, her arguments and conflicts with Zach, her search for an apartment to sublet, the traffic jam that prevents her from making the audition on time.

These irritating interruptions narrow the thrust and slow the pace. You end up feeling the movie is dull and flat and you don't know why.

Songs have been cut for no reason. New routines have been added (also for no reason). The obnoxious "opening up" process every play goes through on its way to the screen robs the chorus line of necessary dramatic presence by taking the audience on an unnecessary tour of the backstage dressing rooms and even the street outside the theater.

This leaves the aspiring dancers precious little time to do their stuff, hold our attention, and draw us into their lives.

Lord knows they try. From spectacular Vicki Frederick, who masks Sheila's aging vulnerability as an over-the-hill dancer behind brittle wisecracks, to libidinous Gregg Burge and fragile, porcelain-glazed Nicole Fosse (daughter of Gwen Verdon and the great Bob Fosse), the dancers have individuality, charisma, and talent galore.

But they're at the mercy of the medium and Arnold Schulman's fragmented script.

The one sour casting note is a dismaying performance by Alyson Reed, a performer I've always admired, as Cassie. As spectacular as she was in the title role of Broadway's ill-fated *Marilyn*, she displays no magic to the cruel movie camera.

She doesn't sing, dance, or do much of anything else of importance for the first ninety minutes. In the final half hour of this two-hour stretch, she finally climbs the stairs, victimized by a series of arty, pretentious camera tricks, and sings "What I Did For Love." She is as alarmingly off-key and atonal as a fingernail on a blackboard.

If. If you never saw *A Chorus Line*. If you saw it and hated it. If you never felt the pulsating excitement or moving pathos. If you've been brain-dead for the last ten years. If you fall into any of these "if" categories—then maybe you'll warm to the watered-down, sluggish movie more than I did.

But if you are among the legions of *Chorus Line* fans, you can't escape the fact that this is a sorry disappointment, a well-intentioned but poor substitute for the real thing, a stand-in for a star.

CHRISTIANE F. (1981)

★ ★ ★ Directed by Ulrich Edel. Produced by Bernd Eichinger and Hans Weth. With Natja Brunkhorst, Thomas Haustein, Jens Kuphal, and Reiner Wolk.

Within a year of its release, *Christiane F.* was the most popular film in German history, outgrossing every movie ever made in that country. It's the violently realistic account of a 13-year-old girl who became a prostitute in the Zoo railway station in Berlin to finance her heroin addiction, told in harrowing details taken directly from the sensational autobiography that began as a series of investigative articles in the German magazine *Stern* and ended in a best-selling book that was later translated into English. The film was made by Ulrich Edel, a graduate of a Munich film school, and like the book, developed something of a cult following among teenagers as a warning against drug addiction. European adolescents lined up to see it again and again, and German audiences labelled it "today's *Rebel Without a Cause.*"

This might be overselling the product, for *Christiane F.*, in my opinion, stands a chance of encouraging drug abuse because of the attractiveness of its two young stars and its pot-smoking opiatic haze of David Bowie music just as much as it pretends to reduce drug use by the terrifying portrait it draws of heroin. Either way, it is a hair-raising voyeuristic descent into the bowels of hell for people of all drug persuasions. It certainly is not boring.

Christiane F. begins smoking pot and popping pills at age 12 in a church youth club. At 13 she takes to the needle to gain peer acceptance after a David Bowie concert. She speedily finds her life falling to pieces.

Sex with her boyfriend, who sidelines as a homosexual prostitute, not only lacks charm—it ceases to exist. After school, she hits the streets as a child prostitute to pay for their growing habits. Trying to cure each other by locking themselves in a dark room, they explode with vomit all over the walls, the sheets and each other.

Things get worse when she's injecting her veins in a public toilet and another junkie bursts out of an adjacent urinal to wrestle the syringe from her hands. The movie drags on and on, with endless closeups of hypodermics being jammed into tongues and jugular veins until only the strongest stomachs are likely to survive its absurdly inflated length.

The film deals almost exclusively with the effects of drugs, not the causes. And there are never any adults around to help or care.

Christiane (realistically played by a courageous child named Natja Brunkhorst, who became such a big star she was forced to leave Germany in order to continue her schooling in peace) luckily manages to cure herself and survive, but there are still an estimated 50,000 teenage addicts left behind who are fighting for their lives in filthy toilets and bedrooms.

The film offers no solution for their predicament. Nor does it mention the fact that at the time this film was made, West Germany's increasing drug problem was closely related to the large number of American military bases nearby.

A CHRISTMAS CAROL (1951)

★ ★ ★ ★ Directed and produced by Brian Desmond-Hurst. Screenplay by Noel Langley. *With Alistair Sim, Jack Warner, Kathleen Harrison, Mervyn Johns, and Hermione Baddeley.*

Among the many versions of this immortal Charles Dickens fable, the 1951 treatment with Alistair Sim as Scrooge is the most trenchant and powerful. Instead of the traditional candy floss and artificial cheer, director Brian Desmond-Hurst goes for the real moral Dickens intended, and illuminates the agony of Scrooge's tortured soul. The result is an inspired and shining tribute to Dickens, as well as to peace and goodwill toward men.

CHRISTMAS IN CONNECTICUT (1945)

★ ★ ★ ★ Directed by Peter Godfrey. Screenplay by Lionel Houser and Adele Comandini from an original story by Aileen Hamilton. Produced by William Jacobs. *With Barbara Stanwyck, Dennis Morgan, Sydney Greenstreet, S. Z. Sakall, Robert Shayne, Reginald Gardiner, and Una O'Conner.*

One of the greatest Hollywood comedies ever made, this 1945 classic is often shown on TV in truncated form, but on video you get the whole thing, complete with Barbara Stanwyck's famous flapjack scene. (Wherever she flaps them, they stick to the ceiling.) Stanwyck is magnificent as a tough career girl-journalist who hits pay dirt with a phony magazine column called "Diary of a Housewife" in which she pretends to be America's foremost authority on country living, sewing, cooking, marriage, and babies. In truth, she's a single girl in a cold-water New York flat who can't boil an egg. When her pompous publisher (the great Sydney Greenstreet) dreams up a feature about Christmas on her country farm, the fast-thinking Barbara goes berserk tying to find a farm, a cook, a surrogate husband, and a baby by Christmas Eve! The results will put a warm glow in your heart and the sound of merry laughter will stick with you for days. Dennis Morgan co-stars in this holiday treat, one of my all-time favorites.

CHRISTMAS IN JULY (1940)

★ ★ ★ Directed and written by Preston Sturges. Produced by Paul Jones. *With Dick Powell, Ellen Drew, William Demarest, Raymond Walburn, Ernest Truex, and Franklin Pangborn.*

It's the middle of summer, but when a $20-a-week coffee company clerk is mistakenly informed he's won $25,000 in a slogan contest, he and his wife go on a marathon Christmas shopping spree, turning a premature holiday into a slapstick riot only the great Preston Sturges could dream up. Dick Powell, Ellen Drew, William Demarest and a whole Christmas stocking full of 1940 Hollywood character actors turn this timeless satire on greed and American consumerism into a gift-wrapped delight for all seasons.

CINDERELLA (1950)

★ ★ ★ ★ Directed by Wilfred Jackson, Hamilton Luske, and Clyde Geronimi. Produced by Walt Disney. *With the voices of: Ilene Woods, William Phipps, Eleanor Audley, Rhoda Williams, Lucille Bliss, and Verna Felton.*

Walt Disney's labor of love, often reported as his own personal favorite, is now available on home video. Don't even think of passing it by. The hundreds of artists who created this animated classic have brilliantly splashed upon the screen a flowery, three-dimensional, and rather glamorous rendition of the fairy tale about the scullery maid, the wicked stepsisters, the glass slipper, and Prince Charming in extravagant storybook terms with lushly romantic images and a musical score that sparkles. Cinderella, Prince Charming, the loyal mice people, the pumpkin coach, the hideous stepmother, and an assortment of barnyard creatures come alive like real friends you'll want to make a home for. And that love song "A Dream Is a Wish Your Heart Makes"—not to mention the cunning "Bibbidi-Bobbidi-Boo"—are songs to treasure. It's sugary and fanciful, but *Cinderella* is also an enduring, timeless work of art.

CINDERELLA LIBERTY (1973)

★ ★ Directed and produced by Mark Rydell. Screenplay by Darryl Ponicsan, from his novel. *With Marsha Mason, James Caan, and Eli Wallach.*

Cinderella Liberty is the depressing study of a pleasant but neurotic Seattle prostitute (Marsha Mason) and the good-natured sailor (James Caan) who meets her on a Navy pass, beats her at a game of pool, enters her life, marries her, becomes a surrogate father to her mulatto son, even goes AWOL to provide her with a decent and honest life. Pretty grim stuff, despite the ribald comedy scenes, but well worth seeing for the charismatic, compassionate, and warm-hearted performances of Marsha Mason (nominated for a 1973 Oscar) and James Caan.

CITY HEAT (1984)
★ ★ ½ Directed by Richard Benjamin. Screenplay by Sam O. Brown (Blake Edwards) and Joseph C. Stinson. Produced by Fritz Manes. *With Clint Eastwood, Burt Reynolds, Jane Alexander, Madeline Kahn, Rip Torn, Irene Cara, Richard Roundtree, and Tony Lobianco.*

Today's bankable male stars fall into two categories: the character actors with Broadway training (Hoffman, De Niro, Pacino, Redford, et al.) and the manufactured personalities who can't do much more than play themselves (Eddie Murphy, Bill Murray, Dan Aykroyd, et al.).

For this latter group, which includes Burt Reynolds and Clint Eastwood, special vehicles must be processed and marketed to fit their limited talents, please their fans, and keep the money pouring in at the box office. Microwave movies.

City Heat is an empty-headed gangster-movie spoof in which Reynolds and Eastwood send up both the old trenchcoat flicks of the thirties and each other.

Nobody in his right mind expects much from a computerized vehicle like this, so nobody gets much. The stars try to do for *City Heat* what Newman and Redford did for *The Sting* but the macho combustion only fizzles. *City Heat* never heats up; it just rains on their parade.

Set in 1933, *City Heat* teams the torrid twosome as a poker-faced odd couple, trading insults and cracking jokes between machine-gun attacks.

Clint is a stoic Kansas City cop. Burt is his former chum, an ex-cop who has turned in his badge to operate a seedy private eye business that is on the skids. Jane Alexander is the nice girl in both their lives — Burt's underpaid, long-suffering secretary, who has the hots for Clint on the side.

City Heat not only fritters away the abilities of the three leads to sustain movies of their own, but wastes the considerable talents of a fine supporting cast, too. Richard Roundtree is Burt's crooked partner, who gets dusted early by leering rival mobsters (Rip Torn and Tony Lobianco), forcing Burt and Clint to team up in the fight for law and order. They hate each other, but the way they wink at each other and flirt outrageously, you know they love their paychecks.

The film has plenty of vintage Caddys, period pop songs, Prohibition speakeasys, and bathtub gin — all photographed in the color of bronzed baby shoes. It also has Madeline Kahn, doing a Judy Holliday impression as a dumb-like-a-fox bubblebrain socialite who beats her kidnappers at poker, and Irene Cara, as a doomed Billie Holiday—styled saloon singer.

For dialogue, you get one-line gags written by Blake Edwards under the pseudonym Sam O. Brown, like ''Snotballs play hard'' and ''Cross me and you're snail food.'' The script seems to have been written with crayons.

Mostly you just get endless takes of Clint and Burt smirking and mugging and marking time until lunch. Burt stages a one-man pageant of self-love in which there are no contestants. Clint remains aloof, crunching his lower jaw and sneering from the sidelines unless some bozo spills his coffee or breaks his windshield. Then he gets mad. His eyes begin to twitch and all hell breaks loose. The rest is just noise and panic.

Richard Benjamin tries to keep the bedlam from getting out of hand, but he's no match for these diabolical egos. It's fun watching them upstage each other, but then they don't seem to know how to end the jest.

Couldn't somebody find a writer with the comic punch to provide a final tag? Instead, the two battered icons face each other in a Kansas City street drenched with rain (it is always raining in this picture) and glare at each other, muttering flatly while the credits roll. The rain drizzles, while the movie fizzles.

Star solidarity is a harmless thing, but this is one detente that needs renegotiating.

CLEAN AND SOBER (1988)

★ ★ ★ Directed by Glenn Gordon Caron. Screenplay by Tod Carroll. Produced by Tony Ganz and Deborah Blum. With Michael Keaton, Kathy Baker, Morgan Freeman, M. Emmet Walsh, Tate Donovan, Henry Judd Baker, Luca Bercovici, Claudia Christian, Pat Quinn, and Ben Piazza.

Clean and Sober is another harrowing case history about the evils of substance abuse, informed and elevated beyond the status of a recruiting film for Alcoholics Anonymous by the splendid and shockingly honest central performance of Michael

Keaton. Capturing all of the ugliness of a drunk and a coke addict, he also reveals the inner torment and degradation of a respectable man who faces his own weakness and shame. Bloated, balding, and bugeyed, he's nobody's idea of a movie star. But in a brave, courageous, and daring stretch for a comic, he's raw and powerful. This is not a comedy. It's not for the squeamish, either. But *Clean and Sober* does establish Michael Keaton as a serious dramatic actor of range and substance in a film that is morbidly fascinating.

THE CLOCK (1944)
★ ★ ★ 1/2 Directed by Vincente Minnelli. Produced by Arthur Freed. Screenplay by Robert Nathan and Joseph Schrank. *With Judy Garland and Robert Walker.*

Long overdue on home video, this MGM classic was hailed upon its release by the toughest of film critics, James Agee, as "emotionally perceptive, with more ability, life, resource, and achievement in it than in any fiction film I have seen for a long time." Charmingly and beautifully told, it's a tender and refreshingly simple love story about a frightened soldier and a lonely girl who meet, fall in love, and marry during a forty-eight-hour furlough in New York City.

Judy Garland—young, healthy, and in peak form—is the wistful secretary from a small town, and Robert Walker—shy, awkward, and all-American—is the sweet, lost boy in uniform she meets accidentally on a Sunday under the clock at Penn Station. Together they spend the afternoon falling for each other and the overwhelming city—wandering from the Central Park Zoo to the Metropolitan Museum to dinner in one of those candlelit cellars that no longer exist in Greenwich Village. A milkman (the great character actor James Gleason) gives them a lift that turns into an all-night ride. His wife gives them breakfast and advice. They lose each other in a subway jam without knowing each other's last names. When they finally find each other again under that clock, they know they are going to spend the rest of their lives together. Then they spend a frantic Monday battling the cruel bureaucracy of the city, marrying in an ugly civil ceremony drowned out by the roar of elevated trains. Dreams turn sour, and the rest of this achingly enchanting film shows how they put the pieces back together in the light of love.

Throughout, ace director Vincente Minnelli invades their courtship with appealing characters and turns *The Clock* into a rich image of a great and bustling city whose pulse beats have never been recorded with more accuracy. Judy Garland proved, with this film, she could handle every adult emotion thrown her way, and Robert Walker proved why he was every American girl's dream of the boy they'd most like to wait for on the home front during World War II. *The Clock* is not just an indelible love story but a film of great mood, insight, and emotional maturity. Cynics might find it dated and corny, but it still holds me spellbound. It's the kind of movie that makes you feel good about the human race and long for the perfection with which great films by great directors like Minnelli used to be made.

COAL MINER'S DAUGHTER (1980)

★ ★ ★ ★   Directed by Michael Apted. Screenplay by Tom Rickman. Produced by Bernard Schwartz. With Sissy Spacek, Tommy Lee Jones, Beverly D'Angelo, Levon Helm, Phyllis Boyens, and Ernest Tubb.

Coal Miner's Daughter, a spirited, honest, and life-affirming film, is the story of Loretta Lynn, who started out in the dirt-poor surroundings of a tarpaper shack in Butcher Hollow, Kentucky—a backwoods junction where you were either a coal miner, a moonshiner, or you left town.

Today she's a multimillion-dollar one-woman business with a traveling eleven-man band, platinum hit records, a clothing franchise, and a five-thousand-acre ranch in Tennessee. She's the queen of country and western music. This is the story of how she got there. It's a heartwarming story all the way.

The early scenes of Loretta, played with ferocious sincerity by Sissy Spacek, have a wonderful ring of authenticity. There she is, slopping the hogs, feeding her five brothers and sisters in her hillbilly cabin with newspapers glued to the walls and poverty all around. "She's gettin' to be a woman," says her pa—"she's goin' on fourteen."

One day nineteen-year-old Doolittle Lynn hits town, smart and cocky and just out of the Army. He falls for Loretta at a pie supper even though she knows so little about cooking that she fills her apple pie with salt instead of sugar.

Ignorant, with no sex education, Loretta marries the guy, spends a disastrous wedding night in a freezing cold motel, and returns home pregnant while her husband heads for Washington state to pick fruit.

This off-again, on-again romance provides *Coal Miner's Daughter* with some of its funniest scenes. All Loretta wants is a wedding ring; Doolittle keeps giving her a guitar and urging her to sing, despite the fact that she's so shy she throws up in front of strangers.

She doesn't know what key she sings in (with country and western music, does it matter?) and only plays three chords on the guitar, yet he pushes her into a career. This girl is so unpretentious that her first publicity photos were taken in front of a bedspread hung on the wall.

From a homemade career driving around the South in a beat-up Chevy, visiting radio stations, and living on baloney sandwiches in the backseat, Loretta makes it to the Grand Ole Opry in Nashville, and the rest is music history.

If I loved this movie, you can take my word for its value, because I hate country and western music and after growing up in Texas towns where Roy Acuff was a bigger star than Clark Gable and all of my shirts ended up as patchwork quilts, I'm not exactly knocked out by down-home rural charm, either.

But this movie gets under your skin with its energy and focus and completely unpretentious sweetness. If it's as pure and likable as the real Loretta Lynn appears to be on TV talk shows, much of the credit must go to Sissy Spacek, who justifiably won an Oscar for it.

This flowering peony of an actress is not only mesmerizing as Loretta Lynn, but also does all of her own singing, revealing a voice rich and full and genuinely rustic as a gingham bonnet.

With the spray net, the forty pounds of hair, the cowboy boots, and the perfect sowbelly accent, she lights up the screen as well as the amplifiers in Nashville.

And she is matched every step of the way by Tommy Lee Jones, who goes from ambitious "good ol' boy" to lonely, middle-aged backstage husband as he creates Loretta's stardom, then tries to exist like a man in the shadows behind her pin spots.

Beverly D'Angelo is also wonderful as country star Patsy Cline, and there are guest appearances by Ernest Tubb, Minnie Pearl, and other Grand Ole Opry pioneers.

This delectable film has been beautifully directed by Michael Apted on real locations instead of phony Hollywood sets. Even the house at the end where Loretta and Doolittle fight over the extra bedroom is Loretta Lynn's own estate in Hurricane Mills, Tennessee,

There isn't a false note or artificial scene in the movie. Even if you think country music sounds like frogs stoned on Wild Turkey, you'll love this movie and the people in it, not only because it's true from start to finish, but because they're worth caring about. *Coal Miner's Daughter* is an entertaining, energetic grass roots "movie movie," as all-American as a cherry cobbler and a total joy from beginning to end.

COBRA (1986)
1/2★ Directed by George P. Cosmatos. Screenplay by Sylvester Stallone. Produced by Menachem Golan and Yoram Globus. *With Sylvester Stallone, Brigitte Nielsen, and Reni Santoni.*

Cobra, yet another Sylvester Stallone ego trip, is "Rambo Goes to Hollywood." It is ninety minutes of unrelievedly nauseous, imbecilic swill, custom-tailored for the star's pecs, and cheaply packaged to appeal to the lowest animal instincts of an audience that gives me the shudders just to think about.

The movie starts and the kind of audiences this movie attracts yell: "Rambo!" A serial killer slaughters innocent shoppers in a supermarket. The cops call Cobra, a mysterious renegade cop from the "zombie squad" with a special talent for annihilating night slashers. "I'll blow this place up!" smiles the maniac. "Go ahead—I don't shop here," snarls Stallone, sipping a Coors. "Kill, Rambo, kill!" screams his audience.

As the movie roars on in a blaze of machine-gun fire, Stallone the Cobra turns Los Angeles into a battlefield. He drives a weird car with a license plate that reads AWSOME 50. I don't know if the "50" refers to his age or I.Q.

Cobra, whose real name is Marion, has this philosophy, see: Kill off the hoods and rats before the courts and judges can get hold of them and set them free. He douses one thug with gasoline and sets him on fire. He hangs another creep on an industrial hook in a steel factory and drops him into a flaming furnace. "Well done!" yells the audience.

There's a minuscule plot about a pretty, tough model,

played by Brigitte Nielsen, who talks with a strange accent like Arnold Schwarzenegger in drag. The model has seen one of the killers from a secret society called the New Order, who are slaughtering half of Los Angeles for no apparent reason. It's up to Cobra to save her, in and out of the sack.

But the actors are of no importance. The real stars of *Cobra* are the guns, knives, torture devices, and hand grenades.

Cobra features several car crashes, explosions, the obligatory destruction of human lives and public property, and the consumption of a horrifying amount of junk food. "This thing is so out of control I don't know where to begin!" shouts the police commissioner. Blood splashes the camera lens.

When the violence and the rock and roll soundtrack subside briefly, the girl rubs Stallone's deltoids and coos, "Where will you go when this is all done?"

"The bank!" screams the audience.

THE COLOR OF MONEY (1986)
★ ★ ★   Directed by Martin Scorsese. Screenplay by Richard Price. Produced by Irving Axelrad and Barbara De Fina. With Paul Newman, Tom Cruise, Mary Elizabeth Mastrantonio, Helen Shaver, John Turturro, and Bill Cobbs.

Twenty-five years after he made movie history in *The Hustler* Paul Newman won an Oscar recreating his original role as pool-hall con man Fast Eddie Felson in *The Color of Money*. He's now bored, cynical, and rich—a Chicago liquor salesman looking for a new young hustler to sponsor. He finds him in Tom Cruise, a likable, tough airhead with a doo wop hairdo and a mean-spirited, low-life girlfriend (brilliantly played by Mary Elizabeth Mastrantonio). As Newman orchestrates the kid's career, the film moves along with grit and exhilarating power. The dialogue is smart and flip, and Martin Scorsese's direction is fluid and volatile. Newman's change from heel to hero in the end is something worth applauding, and he masters every nuance of the role with precision and authority. He's like aged bourbon, and he seems to inspire everyone around him. As his protégé, Tom Cruise delivered his most winning screen performance up to 1986. This is a movie that moves at a brisk pace, with a ball in every side pocket. Newman gets better with age and this time he emerged a winner in more ways than one.

THE COLOR PURPLE (1985)

★ ★ ★ ★ Directed by Steven Spielberg. Screenplay by Menno Meyjes (from the novel by Alice Walker). Produced by Spielberg, Kathleen Kennedy, Frank Marshall, and Quincy Jones. *With Whoopi Goldberg, Oprah Winfrey, Margaret Avery, Danny Glover, Rae Dawn Chong, and Adolph Caesar.*

Spoilsports who believe Steven Spielberg incapable of anything but adventure sagas for the teenage consumer are cordially invited — along with people who still believe in movies of substance and artistry — to *The Color Purple*.

Based on the Pulitzer Prize-winning novel by Alice Walker, *The Color Purple* is a noble, compelling, powerfully acted, magnificently photographed, richly textured film of heartrending impact that spans four decades in the lives of a black family in the South and traces the heroic growth of one woman from the chains of early-twentieth-century slavery to fully realized independence. It is Spielberg's finest film.

It also marks the film debut of Whoopi Goldberg, former Broadway comedienne and short-sketch artist, who demonstrates the skill with which she can tackle the demands of a complex character with sus-

taining force. As the centerpiece of this epic story, the character of Celie is one of the screen's most unforgettable heroines.

She first appears at fourteen, in 1909 an unloved child who has given birth to two babies by her own father, both torn from her arms and given away to strangers. When her mother dies, her father marries a girl Celie's age.

"Spoiled, ugly, but no stranger to hard work," Celie is married off to a cruel widower called "Mister" (Danny Glover). Abused as a surrogate mother for his own kids, a workhorse, and a sexual object, Celie is forced through ignorance and bigotry to surrender her own youth and accept adult responsibilities before she's old enough to know anything about life, a child-woman so imprisoned by her own servitude that a rural mailbox on a road near the edge of a dusty cornfield becomes her only link to the outside world. And even that is forbidden to her.

From her lonely heart, Celie talks to God, then to her sister Nettie, who has taught her to read and write. "I don't know how to fight — I only know how to stay alive," says Celie. *The Color Purple* is the valiant story of how she survives, blossoms like the purple flowers that exude beauty even in the ugliest environment of her childhood, and finds her own inner strength and self-value.

Playing different ages as well as a thousand different moods and emotions, Whoopi Goldberg is magnificent. From a dull-eyed pacifist who takes her beatings the way most people take their morning coffee, to a proud cane rod of a woman, brittle with age but wise with inner spirit, she communicates her knowledge of how injustice burns. She is three-dimensional, restrained, dignified, and finally justifiably proud of the way her life turns out. It's a mesmerizing performance.

Also buzzing around her like dazed butterflies are supporting players of great depth and magnitude. By 1916, Mister brings home a fancy woman named Shug Avery (beautifully acted by the gorgeous actress–blues singer Margaret Avery, a young version of Dorothy Dandridge and twice as galvanizing), who becomes a source of inspiration and eventual liberation to the other black women around her.

By 1922, Celie's stepson Harpo (Willard Pugh) opens a backroads juke joint and introduces to the family a combustible wife named Sofia, played with robust force by Oprah

Winfrey, the popular Chicago talk-show hostess, who makes a stunning acting debut. Sofia is a tough, rotund, zestful black lady who takes no scrapes from any man, black or white. As the story progresses, her own spirit and pride bring her to a sad downfall, and we see how little control black women had over their own lives in the changing South.

Rae Dawn Chong, as a younger-generation black girl sniffing the winds of change, plays Harpo's second wife. Adolph Caesar is grand and plucky as Mister's dandy, bantam-rooster father, always dispensing the wrong advice. Akosua Busia makes a memorable contribution as Celie's beloved, long-lost sister Nettie.

All of them move like the pages of a novel turning. Seasons pass, relationships grow and change. Celie is always the camera, recording everything as it passes across the landscapes and reflects in the retinas of her eyes.

Black, dirt-poor, with no skills and no education, Celie ultimately learns through the restorative power of love to stand up and be counted. When she announces her declaration of independence, it's a red-letter day in movies. If your eyes are dry at the end of *The Color Purple*,

I advise you to consult a good doctor. Maybe your heart has atrophied.

Written with strength and sensitivity by Menno Meyjes, *The Color Purple* has been touched and informed by love from opening frame to closing fadeout by a newly recharged Steven Spielberg. Not since *The Sugarland Express* has he demonstrated such care and humanity for real people, and he's sprinkled a big picture with so many luminous small touches that it has a poetic vision unique to big-scale American films.

Images dance before the eyes: black children hopscotching through a field of buttercups, a man playing a honkytonk piano on a river raft, a beautiful hussy belting the blues on Saturday night, followed by the music of a Sunday morning . fire-and-brimstone gospel meeting. The plantations and the ramshackle cabins, the general stores, and first automobiles, the rocking chairs silhouetted against the orange-hot sunsets in the cotton fields — every image necessary to transport the audience to Georgia in the infancy of this century is artfully, rapturously recreated with beauty and awe.

Out of the pain and sadness, Spielberg and Goldberg awaken Celie and her audience to renewed hope, and *The Color Purple* becomes a life-affirming experience, that rarefied film that revives faith — in movies and mankind.

THE COMPETITION (1980)
★ ★ **Directed and written by Joel Oliansky. Produced by William Sackheim.** *With Richard Dreyfuss, Amy Irving, Lee Remick and Sam Wanamaker.*

The Competition is a pretentious movie that takes itself seriously and ends up being often unintentionally hilarious, and that's even worse. The idea — two young concert pianists fall in love while competing for an international music prize — is sound enough, but good intentions go regrettably haywire thanks to writer-director Joel Oliansky's ludicrous dialogue and some baffling pacing that has musicians spouting lines like ''I wanted you so much I couldn't make a fist!'' between excerpted concertos by Beethoven, Prokofiev, Liszt, Chopin, Brahms, and Saint-Saëns. Quite a bizarre and unsatisfactory experience, if you ask me.

Movies about baseball players, jazz musicians, and ballet dancers have always been high-risk factors, but a movie about rival concert pianists is a new one on me. There are six pianists in *The Competition*: an edgy thirty-year-old who has always been a runner-up and never a winner, a brilliant schoolgirl who studies under the tutelage of a famous man-hating has-been, a sixteen-year-old Russian who becomes hysterical when her tutor/chaperon defects, a black eccentric who performs concertos in the nude while scandalizing room service, a ghetto New York Italian lover boy whose ambition is to play Las Vegas and make more money than Liberace, and a stone-faced craftsman called "Steel Fingers."

In giving us fleeting glimpses of these six finalists, the film begins as a kind of high-minded *Fame,* with none of the energy or vitality of that exciting film. Then it switches in midstream to a subplot about the girl (Amy Irving) and her browbeating, emasculating, frigid instructor (Lee Remick). There are shades of *The Seventh Veil* here, with Remick playing James Mason to Irving's Ann Todd, but even the faint suggestion of a lesbian jealousy is quickly abandoned by the confused script, and poor Lee Remick is left to say insincere lines like "It costs extra to carve schmuck on a tombstone but you'd definitely be worth the expense" to symphony conductor Sam Wanamaker. This leaves some pretty music and a totally unbelievable romance between Amy Irving and Richard Dreyfuss that made me wince with embarrassment.

Dreyfuss is arrogant, rude, and unfriendly, often swallowing his lines in an inaudible mutter. He has a nervous, dehydrated look, as though his face had been dried out in a microwave oven. Amy Irving is wooden as ever, and Lee Remick is hopelessly miscast as the sixth generation in a line of direct descendance from Beethoven.

All of these people know a lot about eighteenth-century music, but they don't know a thing about real life and they don't say a word that sounds like the way real people talk. The result is a strange, muted film about sensitive, detached people who do nothing to involve the viewer's interest or sympathy. For all of its technical talk about music and all of its attempts to make a statement about love and rivalry, *The Competition* comes off like sour notes played on a piano that needs tuning badly. There should really be a reward for the audience that sits through it.

COMPROMISING POSITIONS (1985)

★ ★ ★ Directed by Frank Perry. Screenplay by Susan Isaacs. *With Susan Sarandon, Raul Julia, Edward Herrmann, Judith Ivey, Mary Beth Hurt, Joe Mantegna, Ann DeSalvo, and Josh Mostel.*

Compromising Positions is a sophisticated comedy, a murder mystery, and a wise and convincing commentary on feminism all rolled into one funny and vibrant entertainment. Susan Sarandon is spunky and appealing as a Long Island housewife who plays amateur sleuth after her dentist is murdered, and finds herself marked as the killer's next victim. Crisp direction by Frank Perry, a witty script by Susan Isaacs, and excellent supporting performances by Raul Julia, Judith Ivey, Edward Herrmann, and Mary Beth Hurt all add up to superior filmmaking.

CONAN THE DESTROYER (1984)

★ Directed by Richard Fleischer. Screenplay by Stanley Mann. Produced by Dino De Laurentiis. *With Arnold Schwarzenegger, Grace Jones, Wilt Chamberlain, Mako, Tracey Douglas, and Sarah Walter.*

Conan, the Stone Age Charles Atlas, is back and Arnold Schwarzenegger is again laughing his way to a bank near you. *Conan the Destroyer*, the sequel to *Conan the Barbarian*, is neither a variation nor a continuation of the first unintentional 1982 laugh riot. It's just more of the same and twice as stupid.

After creating Neanderthal meatheads and Conan for pulp magazines in 1932, writer Robert E. Howard committed suicide. He must have foreseen the movies to come. In this one, Conan models more yak-fur jock straps and searches for a lost jewel in an island castle guarded by an evil wizard. So much for plot.

To drag the plotless prehistoric pastiche to its numbing conclusion, director Richard Fleischer and producer Dino De Laurentiis have teamed Schwarzenegger with a scruffy band of zombies that includes disco queen Grace Jones and athlete Wilt Chamberlain. They swim through underwater caverns, stop the sacrifice of a virgin princess, and survive boring catastrophes in papier-mâché tunnels, caves, and fortresses.

For an adventure fantasy on even the most simple minded level, *Conan the Destroyer* doesn't contain one shred of imagination, energy, tension or excitement. As far as the Mexican locations are concerned, the whole thing looks so phony it might as well have been filmed on the Universal backlot.

The dialogue goes something like this: "I need you." "I'm yours." Later, when Conan rests a moment between skull-crushings, the nubile virgin princess oozes up to him and coos: "I suppose nothing hurts you." Conan blinks in his best duh-what's-up-Doc? expression, and says, "Only pain." While the rest of the world grapples with economic recession, there are oafs sitting around the pool at the Beverly Hills Hotel actually getting paid for writing this kind of dopey drivel.

It's a blessing for the actors in *Conan the Destroyer* that the dialogue is so moronic because there isn't a performer in the movie who is capable of handling more than one syllable at a time without getting a hernia. The acting is so bad it often sounds dubbed in from another soundtrack.

Grace Jones is handy with a medieval bat (a talent developed from fighting off fans at rock concerts, no doubt) but is called upon to do nothing more strenuous in the acting department than hiss like a radiator. She wears a crew cut and a raccoon tail and as little else as the censors will tolerate. Most of the time she appears to be in

great pain, as though some part of her anatomy is on fire. It is doubtful that Chamberlain could say "Dinner is served" with much conviction.

As for Schwarzenegger, the human bulldozer, it is clear that nothing much comes out of the Nautilus School of Dramatic Art except thighs the size of lawn mowers. Since the first Conan movie, he's added three inches to his biceps, but only one expression to his acting repertoire—the look of total disgust.

COOKIE (1989)

★ ★ ★ Directed by Susan Seidelman. Screenplay by Nora Ephron and Alice Arlen. With Peter Falk, Emily Lloyd, and Dianne Wiest.

Created by Nora Ephron, Cookie (Emily Lloyd) is a spunky, streetwise Brooklyn teenager headed for the same kind of trouble that landed her father Dino (Peter Falk) in the slammer for thirteen years for labor racketeering. Dino never married Cookie's mother (Dianne Wiest), a bubble-brained dingbat, but that doesn't faze her. Dino's coming home and all she thinks about is reuniting father and daughter and being a "normal" family. Of course there's nothing normal here, and for Cookie and Dino it's hate at first sight. The big surprise comes when Cookie turns out to be smarter at outsmarting crooks than her dad and they both take over the Mafia, turning the East Coast underworld upside down. This is a quirky *Godfather* with laughs, told from a precocious teenager's point of view—fresh, different, and fun. *Cookie* will steal your bankroll—and your heart—in a comedy that never crumbles.

THE COTTON CLUB (1984)

★ Directed by Francis Ford Coppola. Screenplay by William Kennedy and Coppola. Produced by Robert Evans. With Richard Gere, Gregory Hines, Maurice Hines, Lonette McKee, Diane Lane, Bob Hoskins, James Remar, Gwen Verdon, Honi Coles, and Fred Gwynne.

All my life I've been hearing about the Cotton Club, that Harlem bastion of glamour, sequins, and jazz that characterized the Roaring Twenties in New York night life. And for a great deal of my life, it seems, I've been hearing about the movie Francis Ford Coppola was making about it. Well, here's the movie. But where is the Cotton Club? Somewhere on the cutting-room floor. *The Cotton Club* is a disaster. It's really *two* disasters. It's a gangster movie and a musical.

Coppola proved with the *Godfather* films that he knows about the gangsters. He proved with *Finian's Rainbow* that he knows about musicals. This one succeeds as neither.

The musical got slashed to celluloid shreds in the editing lab, and the gangster movie that took over is a turgid farrago of worn-out clichés, botched ideas, and wasted money. At no point in this lumbering ego trip is the widely publicized $58 million budget evident onscreen.

Two dull plots are unraveled simultaneously to no avail. The gangster movie is about two brothers. The good brother (Richard Gere) is a cornet player who can't get into the Cotton Club band because he's white. So he saves the life of mobster Dutch Schultz (James Remar), falls in love with the thug's bubble-brained teenage gun moll (Diane Lane), and becomes a Hollywood star overnight. The bad brother (Coppola's nephew, Nicolas Cage) turns into a crazy killer and gets his guts blown away.

The musical movie is about two brothers—black hoofers played and danced by Gregory and Maurice Hines. The ambitious brother shafts his sibling, goes solo, and becomes a Cotton Club star. The other ends up playing in a smaller speakeasy, where he is occasionally joined by the successful brother, who goes everywhere with his tap shoes on. The girl in the story is the gorgeous Lonette McKee, who tries to pass for white to become a big-time torch singer. Everyone ends up miserable.

Does anybody care? The characters are so one-dimensional, the script so sophomoric, and the cutting so frantic that nobody ever amounts to anything more than a cardboard cereal-box cutout.

Every time, the story line threatens to come alive, Coppola shaves months and even years off everybody's life and you don't know who anybody is. As a result, there are no performances worth noting, only bewildered actors doing impersonations of live people.

Bob Hoskins, the great British actor, works without a trace of his usual cockney accent and gives the film its only punch as Owney Madden, owner of the Cotton Club, who wants to get out of the rackets and retire while he's still in one piece.

The other gangsters all wear tuxedos, go to nightclubs every night, and swear at each other. You wonder what this dull lot would have done after the invention of television.

All you ever learn about the Cotton Club is that it headlined black performers for white patrons, exploiting both. Otherwise, it's a pretty tepid place with a second-rate chorus line.

The musical sequences are rather shoddy, except for a number where Honi Coles leads a gang of elderly tap dancers in a rousing tap routine at the Hoofers Club and a brief bit where the Hines boys work up some steam on a chorus of "Crazy Rhythm."

But even when the dancers take over, Coppola is so busy cutting away from their feet in a dizzying series of camera tricks that you are rarely conscious of any movement. A dance number without feet is like a picnic without food. Wandering around in the confusion is the great dancer Gwen Verdon, who doesn't dance at all.

When Lonette McKee raises her smoky, sad voice to the sky on Harold Arlen's haunting "Ill Wind," you get the mood and the pathos of what it was like to be black, brilliant, and betrayed in a white man's world in 1928, but this marvelous performer is wasted. Even the song serves as a backdrop for building violence, not for singing the blues.

You learn more about the Cotton Club and the people who made it famous just by listening to old records by Lena Horne, Cab Calloway, and Ethel Waters. All you learn from *The Cotton Club* is how to throw away $58 million on a bad movie. It's a pompous stinker.

COUSINS (1989)

★ ★ ★ Directed by Joel Schumacher. Screenplay by Stephen Metcalfe. Produced by William Allyn. *With Ted Danson, Isabella Rossellini, Norma Aleandro, Lloyd Bridges, Sean Young, and William Petersen.*

Cousins is a colorful and exceptionally winning American version of the 1975 French classic *Cousin, Cousine.* It was a box-office disappointment, but in the warmth of your own living room, you'll find it a charming way to spend a cozy evening. It begins and ends with weddings—and all of the events in between bring together two families so earthy, so noisy, and so alive you may want to adopt them for your own. When the great Norma Aleandro, playing the matriarch of the Costellos, marries Lloyd Bridges, the patriarch of the Kozinskis, about four hundred people are suddenly related by marriage, and when they get together it sounds like a Rolling Stones concert. Isabella Rossellini is the bride's daughter Maria, a legal secretary with a family of her own. Ted Danson is the groom's nephew Larry, an aging hippie who teaches ballroom dancing. Maria and Larry suspect his wife Tish (Sean Young) has been sleeping with her husband Tom (William Petersen), an unfaithful heel who sells BMWs. So the two new cousins get together to talk about it and find in each other a friendship they never found at home. When all of these people learn what "kissing cousins" really means, friendships turn to love and eventually change both marriages. But no one gets seriously hurt, and the audience goes away feeling a lot of joy. Meanwhile, several other generations of cousins—not to mention parents, aunts, uncles, nieces, and stepchildren—all catch spring fever, too. *Cousins* is like a big family reunion full of relatives you've never met before—one of those lusty events where so many things are going on at the same time you can't describe them all. You just have to be there. Rich, romantic, and greatly welcome.

THE CRACKER FACTORY (TV, 1979)

★ ★ ★ Directed by Burt Brinckerhoff. Screenplay by Richard Shapiro. *With Natalie Wood, Perry King, Peter Haskell, Vivian Blaine, Juliet Mills, Marian Mercer, and Shelley Long.*

Natalie Wood rarely ventured into the world of TV, but this unusual and touching 1979 television movie displays the abundant charisma and talent of the late star to glowing effect. In a disturbing drama with comedy undertones, Natalie plays a distraught housewife who suffers a nervous breakdown in a supermarket and finds herself committed to a mental institution. Using her charm, wit, and sense of humor, she befriends the inmates and staff to avoid both psychotherapy and medical treatment but finds the road back to sanity long and perilous. An odd, compelling, and extremely winning star vehicle for an actress who was much more sensitive and multifaceted than a lot of critics realized.

CRIMES AND MISDEMEANORS (1989)

★ ★ ★ ★ Directed and written by Woody Allen. Produced by Robert Greenhut. With Caroline Aaron, Alan Alda, Woody Allen, Claire Bloom, Mia Farrow, Joanna Gleason, Anjelica Huston, Martin Landau, Jenny Nichols, Jerry Orbach, and Sam Waterston.

Woody Allen is back, pricking the conscience and tickling the funny bone. But what makes this his most unusual film—and one of the best—is the profound mixture of zany humor and piercing tragedy he uses to do it. Woody's favorite subject—guilt—is explored through the eyes of a diverse group of neurotic New Yorkers with varying degrees of conscious morality. Woody plays a documentary filmmaker with no success and a miserable marriage to Joanna Gleason. He resents her money and her two brothers, too—one is Alan Alda, a TV producer into limos, bimbos, and Emmy Awards. The other is Sam Waterston, a rabbi who is going blind. The rabbi is a patient of Martin Landau, a world famous ophthalmologist, married to wonderful Claire Bloom, and who is a father and philanthropist, but he's having a secret affair with a vindictive, emotionally unstable flight attendant (Anjelica Huston) who threatens to destroy his reputation. How all of these characters come together in a tapestry of complex human relationships is one of the film's most fascinating achievements. There's a lot going on here and it requires serious attention, but as the powerful and ruthless man destroys a life to save his own while the innocent nerd loses everything, Woody shows the moral choices people make in life and the price they pay. With a work that is stylish, intelligent and often hilarious,

Woody once again has made a great movie that holds a mirror to us all.

CRIMES OF PASSION (1984)
★ ★ ★ ½ Directed by Ken Russell. Written and produced by Barry Sandler. With Kathleen Turner, Bruce Davison, John Laughlin, Anthony Perkins, and Annie Potts

Forget Dracula and Frankenstein. Ken Russell's *Crimes of Passion* is a *real* horror film, about horrors of the human mind that drive people to the depths of degradation before they can find the true nature of their own humanity. It is shocking, brutal, repellent, sexually graphic.

But it's like being in the same room with a poisonous snake. You can't bear to look, but you wouldn't dare close your eyes for a single second. You're afraid of what it might do next. *Crimes of Passion* was slaughtered by most critics and dismissed by many filmgoers as just another slice of raunch and sleaze. Some bypassed it as just another Tony Perkins psycho flick. It's all those things, but a great deal more. It made me ill, but at the same time I found it profound and thoughtful.

It's not a great film, and sometimes it's even a mess. But I haven't been able to shake it off. As a frank and scalding exposé of the dark side of human nature, *Crimes of Passion* is unlike anything I've experienced, and at the heart of it is a titanic performance by Kathleen Turner that is positively staggering.

What is it all about? This is the hard part. On the surface, it seems conventional enough. An attractive sportswear designer by day, Joanna Crane (Kathleen Turner) is a stylish, chic, compulsive, ambitious career girl. By night, she's China Blue, a gaudy, peroxide-wigged, kewpie doll prostitute—a human garbage receptacle for all the problems and sicknesses of a neurotic world.

"How low can you get?" asks one of her slimy clients. "As low as you can afford," she snaps, chewing on a "beat me, eat me" licorice whip.

Through plot contrivances too irrelevant to go into, Joanna's double life is observed by Bobby Grady (John Laughlin), an unhappy square married to a drudge of a wife, and the Reverend Shayne (Tony Perkins), a mad religious street corner zealot who makes her his own personal target for execution in order to cleanse his soul of sin.

Distraught over his own loveless marriage and desperate for the kind of sexual relationship he's never known, Bobby plunges into a world of Quaaludes, kinky fantasies, and sex toys, while the preacher goes berserk.

It's the killer-stalks-prostitute subplot that turns *Crimes of Passion* into *Psycho Goes to Church* and eventually reduces the movie to the level of a conventional thriller. But it would be a sorry mistake to pass it by on that basis. *Crimes of Passion* has a lot more on its mind. Here is a girl who submerges herself in a midnight world of self deprecation because she can't find fulfillment or trust or compassion in the reality of a normal life.

Here is a man who has been living a lie, thinking his marital relations were safe and satisfying, who finds the sexual happiness he lacks in a girl who deals in fantasy. How these two people find love by stripping away their protective veneers and doing something with and for each other instead of *to* each other in bed—this is the part of the film that moved me.

No other film in my memory has dealt so honestly with the effect of pornography and sexual permissiveness on society. Why are we drowning in pornography on every street corner? Why are more housewives becoming part-time prostitutes?

Why are singles bars so popular? Why are child abuse and kiddie porn the leading news topics of the day? Why are more kids turning to drugs?

For the answers, you must face some unpleasant facts about the lives we live today in a frenetic society that often seems to be going insane all around us. The people who made this film must have known going in that it would never appeal to a broad or universal audience. In that respect, it is courageous and destined for controversy. It's not the kind of picture you can recommend easily or even discuss at polite dinner parties. But it's an amazing film. In many ways, it's revolutionary, too, forcing us to face repellent facts about sex the way *A Clockwork Orange* forced us to face our own feelings about violence.

The actors are first-rate, but I'll always remember Kathleen Turner. I don't know any other actress with the range, ability, and emotional depth to carry it off.

At Kathleen's toughest, a loving wife pays her $100 to bring one last bit of satisfaction to her sick and crippled husband, who is dying of cancer. The poor man collapses in the prostitute's arms in tears, and the mixture of human suffering, compassion and terror in her face is something I cannot forget. She's gorgeous, vulnerable, funny, both dream girl and slut of sluts—often all at the same time.

To defend *Crimes of Passion* is to invite ridicule, but I'm glad I saw it. Its powerful message—that it's all right to be afraid if you can learn to share your fears with someone else instead of losing yourself in fantasy—is one to applaud. Despite the wacko subplot and Ken Russell's hysterical direction (subtlety is not his strength and never has been), it's a movie that, for all its flaws, is about the way we live now.

To avoid it just because you've got a weak stomach is like avoiding the six o'clock news because you might hear something nasty.

CRIMES OF THE HEART (1986)

★ ★ ★ Directed by Bruce Beresford. Screenplay by Beth Henley. Produced by Freddie Fields. *With Diane Keaton, Jessica Lange, Sissy Spacek, Tess Harper, Sam Shepard, David Carpenter, and Hurd Hatfield.*

Sissy Spacek, Jessica Lange, and Diane Keaton give performances that are truly inspired in this deliciously daffy tale of three sisters—modern-day Scarlett O'Haras—havin' a tryin' day in Mississippi. Sissy, the baby of the family, has just shot her husband. Lange has just returned from a singing career that got sidetracked by drugs and insanity. And Keaton, who stayed home takin' care of their dyin' granddaddy, only has one ovary. Move over, Tennessee Williams. Offbeat, original, and thoroughly captivating.

CRIMINAL LAW (1989)

★ ★ ★ Directed by Martin Campbell. Screenplay by Mark Kasdan. Produced by Robert MacLean and Hilary Heath. *With Gary Oldman, Kevin Bacon, Joe Don Baker, and Karen Young.*

Two fine actors at the peak of their versatility make this one of the most gripping and original suspense thrillers in years. Gary Oldman, who usually plays freaks and wackos, is this time a brilliant defense attorney and Kevin Bacon, the clean-cut actor with the all-American face who usually plays preppies, is the psycho—a cold-blooded killer who rapes and butchers his victims. Acquitted and freed, he goes on another homicidal rampage and the lawyer is hired to defend him again. This time the lawyer decides to trap the client, and to do it he's got to break the law himself—a risk that leads him into some dark and dangerous situations. Tightly written and crisply directed, with an edgy tension in every scene, *Criminal Law* has more chills than any horror movie in recent memory. In their battle of wits, the two stars are terrific, and the terror is so genuine, it might make you scream out loud. A thinking man's *Psycho*.

CROCODILE DUNDEE (1986)

★ ★ ★ Directed by Peter Faiman. Screenplay by Ken Shadie, John Cornell, and Paul Hogan. Produced by John Cornell. With Paul Hogan, Linda Kozlowski, John Mellion, and David Gulpilil.

The big box-office surprise of 1986 turns out to be even more fun the second time around. Paul Hogan, the charismatic comic book hero from Down Under, is the Australian crocodile hunter who finds himself battling monsters of a Manhattan variety in this cross between *The African Queen* and *Tarzan's New York Adventure*. Pleasant but mindless fun.

CROSS CREEK (1983)

★ ★ ★ ★ Directed by Martin Ritt. Screenplay by Dalene Young. Produced by Robert Radnitz. With Mary Steenburgen, Rip Torn, Peter Coyote, Dana Hill, Alfre Woodard, Joanna Miles, Ike Eisenmann, Cary Guffey, and Malcolm McDowell.

The hardships faced by an early feminist struggling to become a writer in a man's world form the backbone of Martin Ritt's beautiful film *Cross Creek*.

If the fledgling writer depicted here was half the writer Marjorie Kinnan Rawlings turned out to be, then *Cross Creek* would only be half the movie it is.

Fortunately, we are blessed with a study in female determination in the tradition of *My Brilliant Career*, but with twice the artistic achievement and three times the heart.

The picture is an unpretentious, truthful, implicitly feminist biography that focuses on the early career hurdles scaled by the soft-spoken novelist who later won a Pulitzer Prize for her historic novel *The Yearling*.

It begins in 1928, when most women Marjorie's age were dancing the Charleston and drinking bathtub gin. Married to a newspaperman named Charles Rawlings, she was different.

Getting nowhere as a reporter in a city room full of cigar-chomping men, frustrated in her attempts to write Gothic romance novels on the side, Marjorie made a brave decision to change her life. With a stipend from her father's will, she invested in an orange grove in the hammock of Florida's "cracker country" and moved to the hick town called Cross Creek.

Divorced, alone, frightened, generally derided for her strong determination at a time when most women were clinging vines, Marjorie found upon her arrival that her plantation was nothing more than a tarpaper shack in the middle of an alligator-infested swamp, her orange grove a derelict ruin in the middle of the wilderness.

Superbly directed by Martin Ritt with a performance of quiet strength and lyrical sweetness by Mary Steenburgen, *Cross Creek* tells a surprisingly warm and often inspiring story of backwoods people who ended up as characters in her books and stories, and Marjorie herself, who learned to love the rustic new environment and find the center of her soul in the people and nature around her.

Building a dam to save her orange crop, working side by side with the men in devastating heat, trying to get her black maid's boyfriend out of prison, watching her assets evaporate, observing the hard-knock lives of sharecropper neighbors, she remains spirited and tenacious. Encouraged by famous literary editor Maxwell Perkins (Malcolm McDowell), she eventually learns that her real strength lies in the description of life around her. The heartbreaking desolation of a neighboring girl whose pet fawn is killed by her strange, tortured father becomes the fodder from which *The Yearling* grew. (Rip Torn is wild and thrilling as the hard-drinking tormented man Gregory Peck later played in the movie version.)

The severity and austerity of Cross Creek eventually pay off in Marjorie's writing, and in time she even finds love, with a kind, gentle, patient local hotelkeeper, Norton Baskin (played with great presence and charm by Peter Coyote).

Best of all, Marjorie found the courage to stand on her own two feet, never let anyone take advantage of her, treat others fairly, and seize control of her life. She died in 1953, and her numerous books are read, published, and taught in twentieth-century novel courses to this day. She will endure.

Cross Creek provides Mary Steenburgen with a role that is sensitive and feisty. Martin Ritt's films have often centered on strong, independent women learning how to express themselves—*Hud* won an Oscar for

Patricia Neal and *Norma Rae* did the same thing for Sally Field.

Contrasted to the rugged, masculine swamp, Steenburgen's Marjorie seems delicate as a ripe persimmon, but she works with such honesty and conviction that she literally transforms herself right before your eyes into a resolute, fully functional, and extraordinarily self-fulfilled human being.

Also worth saluting is John Alonzo's cinematography, which captures the desolate but picturesque landscape of the Florida backwoods brilliantly.

Some critics have expressed indifference—even hostility—toward this sweetly textured little film—probably because it makes too much sense, it has narrative structure, and because it contains no sex, guts, violence, or politics. For me, it's comforting to know at a time of flaky, stomach-souring, brain-atrophying junk movies, somebody still has the sensitivity and self-assurance to make a lovely, splendid film with a heart as big as Texas and virtues that last. And thank God, it doesn't have a computer or a rock song in sight.

The audience for *Cross Creek* may be small, but it will, in the final analysis, also be privileged—and grateful.

CROSSFIRE (1947)

★ ★ ★ Directed by Edward Dmytryk. Screenplay by John Paxton, based on Richard Brooks's novel *The Brick Foxhole*. Produced by Adrian Scott. With Robert Young, Robert Mitchum, Robert Ryan, Gloria Grahame, Paul Kelly, Richard Benedict, and Sam Levene.

Richard Brooks's gritty right hook to the prissy jaw of anti-Semitism was a controversial blockbuster in 1947. It holds up smartly. Robert Ryan is the Army bully who kills a Jew, Robert Young is the detective who hounds him, and Robert Mitchum is the sergeant in the middle. With sultry Gloria Grahame as the tough nightclub hostess with a heart of gold. A lot of pop psychology and "message" mongering, but still very powerful filmmaking.

CRUISING (1980)

No ★ Directed and written by William Friedkin. Produced by Jerry Weintraub. With Al Pacino, Karen Allen, Paul Sorvino, Richard Cox and Don Scardino.

It sickened me to sit through *Cruising*, but after the public outcry at its premiere, how can it be ignored on home video? A depraved and mindless junk movie that should never have been made, it exploits homosexuals as both ignorant Stepin

Fetchit types *and* villainous enemies of contemporary society, the way old Westerns used Indians as savages. Some gay activists rightfully feared it would legitimize violence and give the public the impression that the gay community is totally insane. Others insisted the film would incite lunatics to an epidemic of "fag bashing," maybe even murder. This is nonsense. (To my knowledge, Diane Keaton is still alive after *Looking for Mr. Goodbar*.) In the final analysis, it is doubtful that any of these issues will be of the slightest concern. And why should they? Critics and public should worry not about the gay politics originally clouding the film in a haze of chaos, but whether the damned thing is any good or not.

It is here that *Cruising* cuts its own throat. The sad truth is that it is a terrible film, trashy and malicious and almost totally incoherent.

There's a gay Jack the Ripper on the prowl in the S&M leather bars and frypan-faced Al Pacino is the cop recruited to sniff him out among freaks with pierced ears, hair faces, and Nazi stormtrooper drag, with an appalling lack of psychological motivation. Friedkin drools over the pain, danger, and kinkiness of this tiny aspect of the gay world without ever attempting to explain or understand it.

Since the film is not a documentary, it should have some point of view. There isn't the slightest indication that the director knows what he's doing or what *Cruising* is about. Even on the level of a dumb detective flick, it is illogical and stupid. As far as I can tell, the message in *Cruising* is that homosexuality is like heroin addiction. If you hang around it too long, you'll get hooked. The notion that Pacino's cop character ends up slaughtering gays out of his own sexually disturbed schizophrenia is the film's biggest joke of all.

I knew nothing more about either Pacino or the gay killer he caught his mental disorder from at the end of the movie than I did going in, and even less is revealed about their victims. The film is morally reprehensible because it makes no enlightening point about its subterranean trip through the slimy sewers of the gay underground.

It exists for titillation and cheap thrills alone. It has no energy or life. It reveals no interesting images, characters or insights. It is poorly written, hideously photographed and badly acted. And it depicts the heterosexual lovemaking between Pacino and his girlfriend (Karen Allen) with just as much ugliness and brutality as the casual, impersonal sex it shows in the gay underworld. Despite their muscles, the gays in the film are gray and terminal washouts. Friedkin doesn't seem to like anybody.

Maybe *Cruising* would be worth recommending if only for a superstar performance by Al Pacino, but the fact is he's almost laughable. With his Toni home permanent, his green complexion, and his lumpy body, he hits the gay bars in his paunchy chains-and-leather drag looking like a hairy avocado.

He gets no help from Friedkin, who has written and directed him as a sad, schlocky stereotype. Pacino looks sick to his stomach throughout, as though he is understandably in culture shock. Never is there any clue to what he's actually feeling about his sexual confusion, and when he drags in wearing his menacing costume from the New York toilets, his girlfriend treats the pain he heaps on her as though he is making her late for a manicure.

Cruising is full of lies, distortions, and ambiguities that are likely to offend just about everybody. When it isn't lingering luridly over crowd scenes full of gay psychopaths kissing, handcuffed hands on each other's nipples, snorting cocaine and sucking amyl nitrates, it's cross-cutting to closeups of steak knives slicing through bloody sirloins.

Friedkin's corny symbolism is as obvious as the homophobic violence he pretends to investigate. Except for his right to make any movie he chooses, he can't be defended on any other level.

The important issues of gay rights and the violence perpetrated against homosexuals in an apathetic society are more important than *Cruising*, but they are subjects that remain unexplored by William Friedkin.

CRUSOE (1989)
★ ★ ★ ½ Directed by Caleb Deschanel. Screenplay by Walon Green. Produced by Andrew Braunsberg. *With Aidan Quinn*

Crusoe is a literary classic for all ages with a visual splendor that only enhances the book. This time Robinson Crusoe is a Virginia slave trader from the early 1800s who, as sole survivor of a shipwreck, finds himself on a tropical island where the tables turn, and the roles of master and slave are terrifyingly reversed. Directed by the great cinematographer Caleb

Deschanel, the film is breathtaking to look at and the shipwreck sequence is spectacular. The story has been altered. Crusoe is now a man alone, without Friday as a companion, who must learn to re-examine his own values under punishing circumstances. It's a morality tale in addition to an adventure, and practically a one-man show for the gifted actor Aidan Quinn. He shows the resourcefulness, humor, loneliness, intelligence and frustration of a man who must learn to survive in an alien world. The film has a minimum of dialogue, but it brings great literature to life in an astonishing way, appealing to the child in us all.

CRY FREEDOM (1987)

★ ★ ★ Directed by Richard Attenborough. Screenplay by John Briley, based on books by Donald Woods. Produced by Norman Spencer and John Briley. With Kevin Kline, Penelope Wilton, and Denzel Washington.

Richard Attenborough's *Cry Freedom* is in the same league as his award-winning *Gandhi*—a rare, uplifting film that manages to thrill and excite its audience, gluing you to your seat and teaching you something at the same time about the world you live in. It's the true story of Steve Biko (Denzel Washington), leader of the oppressed black nations in South Africa, who was imprisoned without trial and tortured to death in police custody in 1977. It's also the harrowing story of Donald Woods (Kevin Kline), a white newspaper editor brave and honest enough to risk his life to ferret out the truth.

With an ugly racist state as the backdrop, the friendship that developed between these two opposing forces changed their lives. Biko showed Woods how black men live under the horror of apartheid—banned, segregated, little more than slaves—and as Biko educated Woods, Attenborough educates us all. South Africa comes alive. The smells, the music, the sounds invade our senses while the vast canvas of life under dictatorship invades our consciences. After Biko's death, Woods was branded a traitor. Under house arrest, he and his wife found out what it was really like to be black in their own society of white supremacy. Woods's job was terminated, his children were almost killed. All he had left was his family and the book he planned to publish about the truth and he had to get them all out of the country. The latter part of the film is about his daring escape, manuscript in hand, disguised as a priest. It has every element of a suspense thriller, but it's doubly exciting because it's true.

Kevin Kline gives the finest performance of his career as Woods—a man dedicated to education and freedom. Denzel Washington is inspired as the black martyr. And everything—from the brilliant John Briley script to Attenborough's rich, detailed, meticulous direction—brings the complex issues together on a human level that transcends conventional moviemaking.

A CRY IN THE DARK (1988)
★ ★ ★ Directed by Fred Schepisi. Screenplay by Robert Caswell and Schepisi. Produced by Verity Lambert. With Meryl Streep, Sam Neill, Bruce Myles, Charles Tingwell, Nick Tate, Neil Fitzpatrick, Maurie Fields, and Lewis Fitzgerald.

Meryl Streep's galvanizing performance as an Australian housewife convicted in 1982 of murdering her baby daughter is the centerpiece of this otherwise depressing drama. The story is true, and Streep, at her bold and fearless best, is uncompromising in playing a difficult and not very sympathetic character. (She was finally exonerated four years later.) The horrible death, the unfair trial, the public outrage, and the woman's private grief are explored with restraint and conviction. But it is still the work of a committed actress that makes the movie worth watching. With an Aussie accent and one of Cher's old Cleopatra wigs, she gives it all she's got.

DAMN YANKEES (1958)
★ ★ ★ Directed and produced by George Abbott and Stanley Donen. Screenplay by George Abbott. With Gwen Verdon, Tab Hunter, Ray Walston, Shannon Bolin, and Jean Stapleton.

Damn Yankees followed *Pajama Game* as the second movie version of the two Broadway smash hits by the short-lived team of Richard Adler and Jerry Ross. It brought sizzling Gwen Verdon to the screen in her original starring role as Lola, the femme fatale from baseball hell who tries to tempt "Shoeless Joe from Hannibal, Mo." (Tab Hunter) into throwing the World Series. Great songs, dazzling Bob Fosse choreography, and most of the Broadway cast members hit a musical home run. Singing "Whatever Lola Wants," the great Gwen Verdon is as sinuous and beguiling as Eve, but the real surprise is Tab Hunter—clean-cut, naive, and clumsily appealing in the boogie-woogie ballet "Two Lost Souls," performed with Gwen Verdon in a smoky, soft-lit nightclub. It's the dandiest number in the whole film.

DANCE WITH A STRANGER (1985)

★ ★ ★ Directed by Mike Newell. Screenplay by Shelagh Delaney. Produced by Roger Randall Cutler. With Miranda Richardson, Rupert Everett, Ian Holm, Matthew Carroll.

Dance with a Stranger is the mesmerizing, unforgettable dramatization of a celebrated British murder case that moodily creates a time and period of the sleazy fifties. Ruth Ellis, a peroxide blond nightclub hostess, shot her rich playboy lover to death on a London street and became the last woman in England to be hanged for a crime of passion. Miranda Richardson is quite eerily effective in the leading role, a cross between Marilyn Monroe and Madonna. A murky and disturbing experience, filmed and acted with great flair.

DANCES WITH WOLVES (1990)

★ ★ ★ ★ Directed and produced by Kevin Costner. Screenplay by Michael Blake. With Kevin Costner, Graham Greene, and Mary McDonnell.

Any movie that runs three hours is an hour too long, I don't care how good it is. Any movie in which half of the dialogue takes place in the Sioux Indian language is additionally questionable. Both of these problems plague Dances With Wolves, the Oscar-winning Western directed by, produced by, and starring Kevin Costner, so it is with much surprise that I found myself thoroughly mesmerized by the entire experience. This is the best film about the plight of the American Indians since Cheyenne Autumn. It's a big, blistering, leisurely, and completely riveting saga in the John Ford tradition. Both spectacular and moving, its impact is awesome.

Costner plays a Civil War soldier in 1863 waiting to have his leg crudely amputated without anesthesia on the front lines. The doctors are so tired they go for coffee, he escapes, and that's the only thing that saves him. Attempting suicide, he gets mistaken for a hero and sent to the western frontier, away from the front lines, where he serves the U.S. Cavalry in a different way, assigned to a mysterious, deserted fort where everyone seems to have been killed in an Indian raid. With nothing but loyalty as a soldier to guide him, he waits dutifully for help and rations that never arrive, his only friends a horse and a curious wolf. Thus begins a strange and lonely truce with the surrounding Sioux that leads to friendship, every detail of which is recorded in a diary from which the narration moves the plot along from one encounter to the next. From the meeting with a white woman raised by the Sioux who has almost forgotten English, to the discovery of a herd of slaughtered buffalo, he gets to know these strange people as one of them. They are simple, confused people, destined to become as endangered a species as their beloved buffalo. Family-oriented, dedicated to bravery and harmony, the Sioux are nothing at all like the predatory monsters the white man feared. Here, the film takes on a contemporary metaphor about how we fear and kill what we understand least. (Shades of Bensonhurst.) Costner is not making an entertainment full of bugle calls and cavalry attacks and Indian raids, although there is plenty of that to keep you awake. He's more fascinated by the depiction of a vanishing frontier. The film ends thirteen years before the last Sioux chiefs surrendered, signifying the end of the American West.

I was deeply moved by the plight of the Indians as well as the relationships that develop between Costner, a sensitive man with more guts than brains, and the Indians. The subplot involving the white woman who becomes his wife is very much like a continuation of *The Searchers* and what might have become of the Natalie Wood character had she not been rescued by John Wayne. Gorgeously photographed, with peppermint skies and incredible sunsets, *Dances With Wolves* (which is an Indian nickname for Costner's character) never bores, and it contains a wealth of period information. But maybe there's such a thing as too much reverence. This movie, good as it is, as sensitive to detail and observance, is still too long. It needs cutting and there are many places where a pair of scissors could be easily applied. Still, it's a noble, sumptuous tapestry of frontier life, showing the devastating impact of history on an entire people. And Kevin Costner, as both actor and director, emerges as a great deal more than just another pretty face.

DANCING LADY (1933)

★ ★ Directed by Robert Z. Leonard, with songs by Richard Rodgers and Lorenz Hart. Screenplay by Allen Rivkin and P. J. Wolfson. Produced by David O. Selznick. *With Joan Crawford, Clark Gable, Franchot Tone, May Robson, Robert Benchley, Nelson Eddy, the Three Stooges, and Fred Astaire.*

Joan Crawford, in one of her rare musicals, sang and danced her way from burlesque to Broadway in this curio. Joan's tap shoes often land on the MGM soundstage with the thud of hippo hooves. But the real historic value of this 1933 oddity is the movie debut of a fey, balding, skinny hoofer whose film career nobody had much hope for five decades ago. His name? Fred Astaire. After Crawford dragged him around the floor, you'll understand why he switched to Ginger Rogers for the next ten years. Also starring Clark Gable, Nelson Eddy, and the Three Stooges.

DANGEROUS LIAISONS (1988)

★ ★ ★ 1/2 Directed by Stephen Frears. Screenplay by Christopher Hampton. Produced by Norma Hyman and Hank Moonjean. *With Glenn Close, John Malkovich, Michelle Pfeiffer, Uma Thurman, and Keanu Reeves.*

In *Dangerous Liaisons*, the visual splendor and moral decadence of eighteenth-century France come vividly alive. It's sophisticated, witty, and as close to a movie masterpiece as you're likely to find in the 1980s. First a shocking French novel, then a torrid movie with Jeanne Moreau, and most recently a Broadway play, it finds new life under the ferocious, inventive, nasty, and inspired direction of Stephen Frears. The theme is the abuse of sexual power among the lacy, frilly, and malicious aristocrats of 1782. Glenn Close and John Malkovich are the vain, corrupt generals who manipulate their conquests in the bedroom like soldiers on the battlefield, and Michelle Pfeiffer, delicate as a rose, is the virtuous victim of their deadly game of seduction. Of course, what these villains don't count on is falling in love themselves, and when they do, they orchestrate their own destruction.

Glenn Close plays her meanest role since *Fatal Attraction* and although she does look like one of those American Revolution paintings of George Washington, hers is a chilling portrait of evil, cold as marble. John Malkovich is the one jarring mistake. With his wimpy, droning voice and clammy, snake-like body movements, he's all wrong as a powerful and persuasive lady-killer. If this is the master seducer of Paris, I'm Yogi Berra. Sumptuous sets, lavish costumes, and lush camerawork add to the stylish decadence until *Dangerous Liaisons* becomes one epic that dazzles the eye while it grips the emotions.

DANGEROUS WHEN WET (1953)

★ ★ ★ Directed by Charles Walters. Produced by George Wells. Screenplay by Dorothy Kingsley. *With Esther Williams, Fernando Lamas, Denise Darcel, Jack Carson, Charlotte Greenwood, William Demarest, and Barbara Whiting.*

As a kid, my favorite movie star was Esther Williams. Okay, so I had no critical perception. I admit it. But soaking wet or draped in Helen Rose chiffon, MGM's swimming sweetheart is still one of the quintessential visions of all-American beauty who ever graced a Technicolor musical, and this is one of her all-time best. Esther plays a farmer's daughter whose entire family is about twenty years ahead of the health and physical fitness craze. Every one of them de-

cides to swim the English Channel, from Ma (played by high-kicking Charlotte Greenwood) to Pop (William Demarest) to kid sister (Barbara Whiting). Fernando Lamas (who met his future wife on this picture) plays a French lothario, glamorous Denise Darcel is the fly in the suntan oil, and Jack Carson is Esther's crotchety, cantankerous coach. The delightful score is by Johnny Mercer and Arthur Schwartz, and for Esther's big underwater ballet with Tom & Jerry, the MGM cartoon department invented a new technique combining live action and animation so the star seems to be swimming with an entire cast of comic-strip crustaceans. Jacques Cousteau and Mrs. Paul will love it.

THE DARK PAST (1948)

★ ★ ½ Directed by Rudolph Maté. Screenplay by Philip MacDonald. Produced by Buddy Adler. *With William Holden, Lee J. Cobb, Nina Foch, Adele Jergens, and Stephen Dunne.*

Neat psychological thriller from 1948 with William Holden as a ruthless outlaw tortured by recurring nightmares, Lee J. Cobb as a shrink who attempts to outwit the gangster while he and his houseguests are being held captive, and wonderful Nina Foch as a gun moll who learns her man is suffering from an Oedipus complex. Taut, suspenseful, and a neat forties black-and-white "B" programmer.

DARK VICTORY (1939)
★ ★ ★ Directed by Edmund Goulding. Produced by David Lewis. Screenplay by Casey Robinson. With Bette Davis, George Brent, Geraldine Fitzgerald, Humphrey Bogart, and Ronald Reagan.

Dark Victory is Bette Davis's most unforgettable tearjerker. Rolling those eggs Benedict eyes as a vain society girl who learns she has only a year to live, bombastic Bette pulls out the stops in a timeless high watermark in movie soap operas. Cynics dismiss it as a Camille without camellias, but there is no compromise in Bette's star turn in a great role—rangy, emotional, eloquent, tender, gay, irresponsible, and finally responsible, mature, and sincere. She turns a battle with a brain tumor into a gallant, tragic, romantic adventure in bravery—pretending time is standing still and knowing deep inside that time is running out. George Brent, as the surgeon who loves her too late to save her, gives one of his most poignant performances and Geraldine Fitzgerald adds some beautifully crafted strokes of her own in the role of Bette's loyal, despondent friend. It is generally agreed that Davis's 1938 Oscar for the spotty *Jezebel* was premature; she should have won for *Dark Victory* (and later, for *All About Eve*) and she went to her deathbed telling everybody the same thing.

DARLING (1965)
★ ★ ★ Directed by John Schlesinger. Produced by Joseph Janni and Victor Lyndon. Screenplay by Frederic Raphael. With Julie Christie, Laurence Harvey, Dirk Bogarde, and Roland Curram.

Julie Christie won an Oscar in 1965 for her corrosive portrayal of a pretty, amoral tramp on the climb in high society. At the time, England was going through its mod "swinging London" phase, and this scalding satire by John Schlesinger remains the apex of the whole genre of movies about that period. Impulsive, restless, selfish, self-absorbed, Julie Christie perfectly embodies the heartless heroine who uses men like Kleenex on her way to the top, and Dirk Bogarde, Laurence Harvey, and Roland Curram are three of the distinguished actors who provide bed and breakfast along the way.

THE DAY OF THE DOLPHIN (1973)

★ ★ ½ Directed by Mike Nichols. Screenplay by Buck Henry. Produced by Robert E. Relyea. *With George C. Scott, Trish Van Devere, Paul Sorvino, Fritz Weaver, Jon Korkes, Edward Herrmann, and John Dehner.*

Lassie Come Home for fish. My apologies. Dolphins are not fish. They're mammals. The only thing fishy is the story. The plot—sentimental, English-speaking dolphins whose love for George C. Scott keeps them from assassinating the President of the United States—is so absurdly unbelievable that if it had been directed by anyone less gifted than Mike Nichols it would be hooted off the screen. But this is serious corn, sweetly buttered by people with gallant intentions, and somehow it miraculously works. Part gentle nature study, part tense mystery, it's got everything—murder, blackmail, family entertainment, dolphin-napping, and a thrill a minute, with a few tears for the whole family along the way. Scott, as the government marine biologist, is partic-

ularly good, but the dolphins, named Alpha and Beta, are even better.

DEAD POETS SOCIETY (1989)

★ ★ ★ ★ Directed by Peter Weir. Screenplay by Tom Schulman. Produced by Steven Hoyt, Paul Junger Witt, and Tony Thomas. *With Robin Williams, Robert Sean Leonard, Ethan Hawke, Josh Charles, Gale Hansen, Dylan Kussman, Allelon Ruggiero, James Waterston, Norman Lloyd, and Kurtwood Smith.*

That fragile, undeveloped time in life when a teenage boy makes the transition from youth to maturity, standing tenuously on the threshold of manhood, is hard to get right on film. I've never seen this coming of age more sensitively or intelligently captured than it is in *Dead Poets Society.* The year is 1959, the setting a strict, stuffy New England prep school where students are taught to work hard, obey orders, follow rules, and turn into hard little clones of their uptight parents. This is the year it changes. Why? Because Robin Williams invades these halls of ivy and turns tradition upside down. He plays John Keating, a former student recruited to teach English lit. The cold, conservative faculty—and his eager, gullible students—have never seen anything like him. He's crazy, eccentric, and a rebel with a cause, whose teaching methods are so unorthodox, he even instructs the kids to tear up their own textbooks.

Williams is no sentimental Mr. Chips. He has a passion for teaching, encouraging the students to respect words and ideas, think for themselves, and stand up and be counted in life. Ultimately, an innocent act of self-expression leads to tragedy for one boy and the teacher becomes the scapegoat. So the film is really about the high cost of nonconformity. But Peter Weir's direction has a nice leisurely pace that allows the actors to develop characters instead of caricatures. From the lyrical cinematography to the sensitive, dedicated performances by the boys and especially Robin Williams's mesmerizing three-dimensional centerpiece, *Dead Poets Society* is a warm, human film of immense feeling and insight. "Seize the day!" is the professor's watchcry. Seize the chance, and see this movie!

DESERT BLOOM (1986)

★ ★ ★ Directed by Eugene Corr. Screenplay by Corr and Linda Remy. Produced by Michael Hausman. *With Jon Voight, JoBeth Williams, Ellen Barkin, Annabeth Gish, Allen Garfield, and Jay D. Underwood.*

A sensitively written, beautifully acted coming-of-age film told through the eyes and memories of a thirteen-year-old girl who survived environmental danger and family turmoil while growing up in the Nevada desert during the A-bomb tests in the 1950s. Looking more like luscious Susan Hayward every day, JoBeth Williams is appealing as the maternal anchor in the family; Jon Voight is memorable as the shell-shocked, violent stepfather; and Ellen Barkin is spirited as the visiting aunt with a tarnished reputation. So realistic you can smell the perfume, taste the beer, and hear the foreboding rumble of atomic blasts in the background as the domestic tensions unravel. If you find yourself drowning in a muddle of cinematic junk, *Desert Bloom* will revive your faith in the movies. It's original and satisfying.

DESK SET (1957)

★ ★ ★ Directed by Walter Lang. Screenplay by Phoebe and Henry Ephron. Produced by Henry Ephron. *With Spencer Tracy, Katharine Hepburn, Joan Blondell, Gig Young, Dina Merrill, and Neva Patterson.*

Desk Set teams the incomparable Spencer Tracy and Katharine Hepburn in a hip, cheerful, and thoughtful charade from 1957 that inadvertently predicted the dawn of the computer age. She's a reference librarian in a broadcasting company whose crackerjack brain stores the facts and figures that run the company. He's the efficiency expert who wants to replace her with machines. When they lock horns, the results are sophisticated and delightful. Kate is great standing up to Tracy's wry quizzes with accuracy and wit, making a monkey out of him and his blasted computer, and even after he installs the mechanical monster in the name of progress, she looks at it with wilting Hepburn *hauteur*. They can tote phone books on their heads or balance feathers on their chins and be amusing—even in a trifling omelette like this. He's masculine and stubborn, she's feminine and glib. The rest of it is no match for their amiable intelligence, including the computer.

DESPERATELY SEEKING SUSAN (1985)

★ ★ ★ Directed by Susan Seidelman. Screenplay by Leora Barish. Produced by Sarah Pillsbury and Midge Sanford. *With Rosanna Arquette, Madonna, Aidan Quinn, Mark Blum, Robert Joy, and Laurie Metcalf.*

Preston Sturges meets the New Wave. That's an apt description of *Desperately Seeking Susan*, a breezy, fresh, and completely captivating little "sleeper" that made me dizzy with joy.

Roberta Glass is a bored housewife from Fort Lee, New Jersey, married to a yuppie dork who sells bathroom appliances. Like many affluent housewives who live a more glamorous life by escaping into a world of TV soap opera, Susan gets romantic kicks by reading the personal ads in the tabloids. For some time, she's been intrigued by secret messages from a guy named Jim who is "desperately seeking" a girl named Susan.

Suffocating in a shopping-mall world of plastic values and mediocre materialism, Roberta decides to investigate by answering the ad herself. Following the real Susan, vicariously living her wild Holly Golightly life, and pretending she's part of a kinkier world for a few harmless hours, Roberta gets more than she bargains for.

Susan (played by Madonna) is junk-shop couture, punk-rock idealism, and Day-Glo glitter. Roberta (played by the marvelously charismatic Rosanna Arquette) is suburban sensible, with a smart pageboy, a shoulder-strap Lois Lane handbag, and a wardrobe from Bamberger's.

The housewife's conversion to Madonna's hands-on lifestyle is miraculously tacky.

Then Roberta knocks herself out and gets amnesia and the real fun begins. Now she's wearing more than Susan's clothes. She's got her problems, too.

Susan's boyfriend Jim (Robert Joy), a rock singer, assigns his pal Des (Aidan Quinn), a projectionist at the Bleecker Street Cinema, to protect her. Des falls in love with Roberta, thinking she's Susan. To complicate things, Roberta, who doesn't know *who* she is, becomes Divina, Queen of the Night, in a magic show.

Pursued down filthy alleys in a purple tutu with a shopping bag in one hand and a cage full of doves in the other, arrested by the cops for soliciting, and stalked by a homicidal maniac, Roberta sinks deeper into an acute identity confusion.

As the plot gets crazier, the movie grows more fascinating. Now everybody's desperately seeking Roberta—including her square husband Gary—and the only clue poor Roberta has to unlock the mystery is a key to a locker at the Port Authority Bus Terminal.

It's a hip, neurotic, updated, third-stream Hitchcock movie, and without question a most entertaining one.

Susan Seidelman is a wunderkind. She blends the farcical elements of mistaken identity, role confusion, and Marx Brothers madness with the lyrical innocence of a modern fairy tale.

And she does it all with a backdrop of New York that is exquisitely high-tech contemporary: Mohawk cuts, surreal discos, spaced-out punk extras, the iridescently lit world of midnight neon where Roberta ends up in Susan's spike heels.

If anything, what she's created is an up-to-the-minute *Alice in Wonderland*, with Roberta slipping down the rabbit hole into 1985 Manhattan.

To serve that purpose, Seidelman has cast the film impeccably. As rotten a singer as Madonna is, she's a kooky, swinging actress in a role that fits her like a sequin G-string. (Unlike her later work in *Dick*

Tracy, she makes a statement here without even trying.)

The guys are good, too, but the film's real miracle is Rosanna Arquette, who radiates star quality from the first reel to fadeout. The girl has just enough wisdom, mixed with just enough soul, to be sexy, adventurous, wacky, and sane all at the same time. She's a cross between Edie Sedgewick and Betty Crocker.

DICK TRACY (1990)

★ Directed and produced by Warren Beatty. Screenplay by Jim Cash and Jack Epps, Jr. With Warren Beatty, Al Pacino, Madonna, Glenne Headly, Charles Durning, Mandy Patinkin, Dustin Hoffman, James Caan, Paul Sorvino, James Tolkan, William Forsythe, R. G. Armstrong, and Dick Van Dyke.

A comic strip ghost walks the screen. Maybe *walks* is the wrong word. *Struts* is more like it. Rather in the manner of an arrogant king, treating people like annoying intruders with quizzical contempt, behaving with smiling disregard for the feelings of others, and mowing down everything in sight at whatever cost to credibility and coherence. The character is called Dick Tracy and looks remarkably like an aging Warren Beatty, but when the hype fades and the smoke clears, this boring fiasco is really nothing more than Batman in a yellow Burberry.

Dick Tracy boasts a budget in the neighborhood of $30 million, eighty speaking roles and three hundred technical credits, not to mention a mediocre score by Stephen Sondheim and an incredible array of pop-art sets by Richard Sylbert that look like the pop-up centerfolds in Hallmark cards. I don't know what I expected from all the publicity, but the dreary outcome of this ambitious *Dick Tracy* with its tired caricatures of cartoon thugs and gum-chewing floozies has an incoherent structure that does not remotely justify such a lavish waste of money and talent. It's like being invited to Tiffany's for breakfast and being served a soggy bagel.

I was never a childhood fan of the Chester Gould characters who populated *Dick Tracy*. Unlike Billy Batson, the crippled newsboy who turned into Captain Marvel, Jr., or Clark Kent, the mild-mannered wimp who changed into Superman in *Daily Planet* phone booths, Dick Tracy, with his silly two-way wristwatches and his lemon-Jell-O Alan Ladd trenchcoats just seemed like an ordinary G-man to me. Fearless, square-jawed and incorruptible, he was always admirable but overshadowed by the colorful hoods, molls, and assorted goons he chased to deliver law and order to an innocent public. Warren Beatty, who produced and directed the film, has left out the most endearing characters (Gravel Gertie and Sparkle Plenty are nowhere to be found, although I fear they may turn up in—God forbid—Part 2) and enlisted an all-star cast for the rest.

Numbers, Pruneface, Flattop, The Rodent, Little Face, Itchy, and others are back, with James Caan, Paul Sorvino, James Tolkan, William Forsythe, and R. G. Armstrong appearing briefly and unrecognizably behind tons of latex like ghouls on their way to a Halloween party on Bleecker Street. In the comic strip, it was funny trying to read the jabberwocky in the voice blurbs for Mumbles, who invariably said things like "Mmaarbbboddkcj-ckwy" and "Gallumifropryg." Dustin Hoffman is Mumbles, and what comes out of his mouth really is "Amfofoyg-arrup" but it isn't funny. He sounds just like Mickey Rourke. Charles Durning, as the bewildered police chief, Dick Van Dyke as the crooked D.A., and

especially Al Pacino as (Crack! Pow! Bam!) Big Boy, the vicious underworld kingpin who leaves a string of cracked walnuts behind as clues, are wasted in cameos, as is Mandy Patinkin, as 88 Keys, the moronic piano player who masterminds the plot to frame, disgrace, and jail Dick Tracy so Big Boy and his rackets can flourish while the detective is behind bars. The role amounts to little more than a few maniacal high-pitched giggles and an aborted duet with Madonna which falls mostly on the cutting-room floor.

The women in the film don't fare much better. To my dying day I will never understand the trashy phenomenon called Madonna. Her vulgar, raunchy undulations, her execrable music, her white zombie makeup all add up to the specter of an anguished and rather pitifully sexless corpse selling necrophilia wholesale. In a role Marilyn Monroe was born to play, she turns Tracy's sexual Lorelei called Breathless Mahoney into a series of lurid and ridiculous come-ons that seem pointless. I always get the uneasy feeling that Madonna needs a bath. I am convinced her armpits smell like Bloody Marys. She can't sing the second-rate songs Stephen Sondheim has written for her, which is probably why Mr. Beatty cuts away from the musical numbers with jarring constancy, and she doesn't even try to act; she just scratches the roots of her peroxide straw hair and licks the gummy residue of hr purple lipstick like a lost hooker blinded by headlights at three in the morning. Worse still, there is Glenne Headly as Tracy's long-suffering girlfriend, Tess Trueheart. Madonna may lack Marilyn's genuine sexiness and vulnerability, but Miss Headly lacks even the remotest claim to charisma. She is not one of those actresses the camera loves to flatter. With her dour face and hideous cranberry wig, she looks desperately in need of a blood transfusion.

If the casting throughout is disastrous, at least Richard Sylbert deserves praise for his imaginative sets. The wet streets, blue buildings, and yellow cabs look polyurethaned. The kelly-green cobalt-blue and fire-engine red cars brighten the crime-riddled gang world Tracy moves in like racing jelly beans. The dazzling garish sets and rubber makeup exude the kind of punch we expect from the Sunday comics, but it's the script that lacks both energy and style. And at the heart of this misguided collision of uncertain attitudes, there is always the sullen petulance of Warren Beatty, who acts with the deadly earnestness of a suburban file clerk playing King Lear. He squints his eyes and grits his teeth and rubs the muscle in his jaw to look like a tough guy, but displays for the camera the same humorless ego reserved for Barbara Walters on TV interviews. Under his own direction, he lumbers clumsily and uncomfortably, like a man wearing aluminum foil jockey shorts. *Dick Tracy* is a bad joke that backfires, but Warren Beatty is the only one who doesn't get the punch line.

DIE HARD (1988)
★ ★ ★ Directed by John McTiernan. Screenplay by Jeb Stuart and Steven E. de Souza, based on *Nothing Lasts Forever* by Roderick Thorp. Produced by Lawrence Gordon and Joel Silver. With Bruce Willis, Alan Rickman, Bonnie Bedelia, Alexander Godunov, Reginald Veljohnson, Paul Gleason, De'voreaux White, William Atherton, Hart Bochner, and James Shigeta.

Bruce Willis is flexing and stretching and *Die Hard* is his gym. Before this action-packed suspense thriller ends, he gets quite a workout—and so does the audience. Willis plays a New York cop who arrives in

L.A. on Christmas Eve to patch up his marriage to Bonnie Bedelia. While he's in the bathroom of his wife's office freshening up, the entire highrise building is invaded, seized, and sealed off by terrorists, and the poor guy spends the rest of the movie scaling elevator shafts, crawling through heating ducts, and crashing through glass doors to save the hostages. This can get pretty explosive—especially when a guy's shirtless and wearing no shoes. Bruce Willis meets the demands of high-octane action with both brawn and humor. He's exasperating, pigheaded, ready with a quip even when he faces his own mortality, seemingly indestructible, yet always human. It's a role for Stallone or Schwarzenegger, but they couldn't act it. Willis not only acts it, he lives it, turning *Die Hard* into one of the hottest hits of 1988.

DIRTY DANCING (1987)

★ ★ ½ Directed by Emil Ardolino. Screenplay by Eleanor Bergstein. Produced by Linda Gottlieb and Eleanor Bergstein. With Patrick Swayze, Jennifer Grey, Jerry Orbach, Cynthia Rhodes, Kelly Bishop, Jack Weston, Jane Brucker, Lonny Price, Charles "Honi" Coles, and Bruce Morrow.

Sounds juicy. Prurient. Lurid, even. It's not. It's just a sweet nostalgia romp set in 1963, the time of Kennedy, moon rockets, and the Beverly Hillbillies—a time when anything faster than a fox-trot was considered by the scandalized parents of pre-Beatles teenagers as "dirty dancing." The setting is a summer resort in the Catskills where seventeen-year-old Frances Houseman (Jennifer Grey) is vacationing with her parents. Everybody calls her Baby, but this is a summer when Baby nixes the badminton tournaments and clean-cut waiters from Ivy League colleges and learns to be a woman. Her teacher is a dance instructor with the charisma of Valentino, a dark horse named Johnny Castle (Patrick Swayze). Back in the staff quarters after hours, Johnny teaches Baby the twist and the mashed potato, and after her inhibitions break down she becomes a big star in the mambo contest. He's a streetsmart wise guy from the wrong side of the tracks who learned dancing in a hurry from Arthur Murray. She's a nice, pampered, naive Jewish princess. Their love affair seems doomed from the start, but the sweetness that carries the movie beyond the dance floor is the way Baby brings out the dignity and self-respect Johnny's never had and Johnny brings out the womanly wisdom Baby's never experienced. In one of the corniest finales on film, even Baby's square, uptight parents see the light and fall for "dirty dancing." Jennifer Grey is too bland to give the movie much zip, making it easy for the dynamic, charismatic Patrick Swayze to steal every scene and every dance number. It's a harmless dandelion fuzz movie, but it has dippy appeal and manages to turn Swayze into the kind of major screen presence marquees light up for.

THE DOGS OF WAR (1981)

★ ★ ½ Directed by John Irvin. Screenplay by Gary Devore and George Malko. Produced by Larry DeWaay. With Christopher Walken, Tom Berenger, Colin Blakely, and Maggie Scott.

In the old days, when life was simpler and the world was sane, you could call somebody like Dolly Levi and get your problems solved for a modest fee. Today, nobody wants a wedding catered, a courtship arranged, or a cake baked. They want kings deposed, planes hijacked, governments overthrown, and buildings bombed, so they call a mercenary.

The Dogs of War, from the book by Frederick Forsyth, is a movie about mercenaries—who they are, where they go, what they do, and why. It's violent, bloody, inhumane, and not my kind of movie at all. But if you're curious about mercenaries, you're not likely to find a more thrilling movie on the subject.

The chief soldier of fortune here is Jamie Shannon, who roams the globe, selling his services to the highest bidder, never questioning the morality of each assignment, only the fee. He is played by Christopher Walken, who seems too frail, skinny, and pallid for the role, but whose own bizarre features and frozen, dead eyes add a certain ruthlessness to the monster he's playing that probably would be missing in a more conventional-looking actor.

Anyway, he's tough. You know that right away because he keeps a gun in the fridge next to the pickles. And he's had concussions, fractures, tropical diseases, and every physical punishment known to man and doctor as a result of his dangerous job. When the film begins, he's just returned from blowing up half of South America, but before he can sit down to a beer and a *Kojak* rerun, another mysterious "employer" arrives, offering him more bills for his Swiss account if he'll travel to an African dictatorship called Zangaro to "check it out."

Posing as a nature photographer interested in local birds, Shannon snaps photos of the military installations and gets himself whipped and beaten into quince jelly by the local thugs, barely escaping alive. By the time he gets back to an American hospital in a state of collapse that resembles the creature from the Black Lagoon, you can certainly sympathize with his decision to retire from guerrilla warfare and take up something more comfortable, like ranching.

He even tries to settle down with an old flame, move to Colorado, and get his life together. Nothing works out, and there's a brand-new $100,000 offer from the same mysterious business conglomerate that wants him to return to Zangaro and blow the dictatorship to feathers for reasons that never become entirely clear (something about inserting a new dictator in exchange for mineral and mining rights).

The rest of the movie shows how mercenaries prepare for combat, negotiate munitions purchases, and hire their crews, always following the philosophy that no man is indispensable and all men are expendable. Things get confus-

ing when they flit from New York to London, Paris, Belgium, and Spain without clueing the audience in to their locations, and when they finally arrive in Africa for the big shootout, the resulting fireworks are exciting but somewhat less than credible. (The first time Shannon arrives in Zangaro, he can't even leave his hotel room after dark without finding a rifle in his ear, but the second time he arrives with an entire battalion of mercenaries, the whole group walks through the streets without being noticed by a living soul. It could only happen in the movies.)

I guess I must be living in a dream world, but I don't pretend to understand mercenaries, revolutions, and guns for hire. Nor do I understand movies about them. Still, there's taut direction by Norman Jewison, and two fine performances—by Colin Blakely, as an English reporter who pays a supreme price for trying to relate the world of mercenaries to the real world the rest of us live in, and by the charismatic Tom Berenger, as a mercenary with both personality and heart.

THE DOLLMAKER (1984)
★ ★ ★ ½ Directed by Daniel
Petrie. Screenplay by Susan
Cooper and Hume Cronyn, after
the novel by Harriette Arnow.
Produced by Bill Finnegan. *With
Jane Fonda, Levon Helm, Amanda
Plummer, Susan Kingsley, and
Geraldine Page.*

Jane Fonda, the aerobics
queen, returns to her distinguished mantle as Jane Fonda,
the honest, sensitive, and
deeply committed actress, in an
Emmy award-winning role as
Gertie Nevels, a woman of rugged pioneer stock from the
green Kentucky hills who in
1944 finds herself uprooted
from the simple country life she
loves and transported to Detroit. Uneducated but resourceful, she uses the only skill she's
got—whittling ax handles into
dolls—to keep her family warm
and safe in the freezing city
winter. This is an arresting portrait in courage and true grit, a
tribute to the indomitable spirit
of a remarkable woman, and a
towering triumph for Jane
Fonda. Stripped of all makeup,
using a staggeringly accurate
backwoods accent, and swad-
dled in clothes that look like the
hair shirts on Biblical lepers,
Fonda does everything within
her range and power to make
you forget her public image and
accept her as a plain, determined woman living in poverty
and deprivation. A marvelous
film.

DOMINICK AND EUGENE (1988)
★ ★ ★ Directed by Robert M.
Young. Screenplay by Alvin
Sargent and Corey Blechman.
Produced by Marvin Minoff and
Mike Farrell. *With Tom Hulce, Ray
Liotta, Jamie Lee Curtis, and
Robert Levine.*

Tenderhearted, beautifully
acted, and genuinely touching,
this sleeper is about twin brothers, twenty-six years old, living
on the wrong side of the tracks
in the tough working-class section of Pittsburgh. Nicky,
played by the marvelous, versatile Tom Hulce, is twelve minutes older than Eugene, but a
childhood accident left him
slow-witted, a little kid trapped
in a man's body. Eugene (Ray
Liotta) is the lucky brother, a
brilliant medical student with a
great future, doing his hospital
residency in California. The
bonds of brotherly love are hard
to sever, especially since
Nicky's job on a garbage truck
has paid for Eugene's education. But Gene wants his own
life, free of his brother's depen-
dence, and marriage to Jamie
Lee Curtis. Nicky's childlike
world is shattered and there's
violence and tears before the
final resolution that will keep

you riveted. Saved from soap opera suds by two brilliant young character actors who never make a false move, *Dominick and Eugene* is a small, unheralded gem with big feelings. Ray Liotta, memorable as the psychopath in *Something Wild* and the ambitious hood in *Goodfellas*, is intensely moving as the frustrated Eugene. Tom Hulce, I am convinced, can play anything. This is a far cry from his giggling Mozart in *Amadeus*, but in his expressions of innocence, sweetness, and terror he shows how sensitive and intelligent a mentally handicapped person can be. This movie made me laugh and cry and feel good about people. More than that, I cannot wish you. You'll be grateful you discovered this one.

DOWN AND OUT IN BEVERLY HILLS (1986)

★ ★ ★   Directed and produced by Paul Mazursky. Screenplay by Mazursky and Leon Capetanos. *With Richard Dreyfuss, Bette Midler, Nick Nolte, Tracy Nelson, Evan Richards, Elizabeth Pena, Little Richard, and Mike the dog.*

Bette Midler and Richard Dreyfuss are the Maggie and Jiggs of Beverly Hills. As the Whitemans, they've made a fortune manufacturing clothes hangers, moved from Brooklyn to a pink house filled with neurotic servants, neurotic friends, a neurotic son who can't decide whether he wants to be Steven Spielberg or Boy George, a neurotic daughter who is anorexic, and a neurotic dog named Matisse.

The Whitemans have it made, but they're suffering from the torment of affluence. Even their gardener has a condo in Hawaii.

Enter Nick Nolte. As a Skid Row derelict named Jerry Baskin, he wanders into the Whitemans' sculptured lawn and throws his filthy body into their azure-blue swimming pool. Shallow and self-absorbed, the Whitemans find this bum a new cause. They save him from drowning, determine to rehabilitate him, and extend the milk of human charity by remolding him in their image. The results are hilarious.

In this zeitgeist of nouveau-riche vulgarity in a world of pointless West Coast mobiles, designer toothbrushes, and trendy neuroses, the Whitemans are Gold Card victims and the bum isn't buying. He repays their generosity by criticizing their Thanksgiving dinner, disrupting the household, and seducing the Whiteman wife, daughter, and maid.

By the time he's sent packing, the daughter is eating again, the Mexican maid is staging her own political revolution in the laundry room, and Mrs. Whiteman learns to release her stress and tension long enough to experience her first orgasm in a decade. He's changed the whole family and the family has changed him. In his new designer casuals from Rodeo Drive, garbage can fare will never taste the same after dining on caviar from Jurgensen's.

Paul Mazursky, the director of this amiable silliness, has based *Down and Out in Beverly Hills* on a 1932 Jean Renoir film, *Boudu Saved from Drowning*. The original was about a tramp pulled from the Seine by a bookseller who tries to make him over in his own bourgeois image. The tramp just wants to be left alone. That he always manages to resist respectability, doing in his savior in the process, gives Renoir's little classic its haughty strength and freshness. Mazursky's bum resists, too, but in the end he returns to the luxury and comfort of the Whitemans' middle class tackiness. This weakens the premise and leaves the audience unsettled.

Mazursky, himself a transplanted New Yorker who has bitten the apple of Hollywood

success, can't seem to make up his mind as to how he feels about his characters. He likes them all. His film has savvy, but no real attitude. By failing to define his characters more closely—especially the derelict intruder—he seems to be biting into a satire without teeth. He's gumming it.

Still, there are wonderful satirical touches here that are worth investigating. Nolte gives a humorous performance as the crafty creep who goes from suicide to being approached in trendy sushi bars by exotic girls soliciting story ideas for MGM.

Dreyfuss is a perfect amalgam of sweating, Rolexed nervousness and good intentions, and Bette Midler is a major surprise. Even in her towel turbans and Carmen Miranda heels with orange hair that makes her look like a lead in *La Cage aux Folles*, she is subdued, soft, the ultimate victim of charge-account tackiness, and genuinely touching.

It isn't easy to satirize Beverly Hills, a place that sends itself up by just existing. But there's one scene, in which the neurotic dog is coaxed by a highly paid dog psychiatrist to eat from a pink porcelain bowl by pretending the dog food is imported pâté, that squeezes new comic juice out of even a wacko place like La-La Land.

Inspired lunacy.

DRAGON SEED (1944)

★ ★ ½ Directed by Jack Conway and Harold S. Bucquet. Screenplay by Jane Murfin and Marguerite Roberts, based on the novel by Pearl S. Buck. Produced by Pandro S. Berman. With Katharine Hepburn, Walter Huston, Aline MacMahon, Akim Tamiroff, Turhan Bey, Hurd Hatfield, J. Carroll Naish, Agnes Moorehead, Henry Travers, Frances Rafferty, and Jacqueline de Wit.

Katharine Hepburn as an idealistic Chinese patriot fighting the invading Japanese is something that has got to be seen. Even then you might not believe it! With her eyes pinned back and her coolie hat, she looks fetching in silk and Peck & Peck pajamas, and you just know the rice comes from the nearest Szechuan take-out. But this rarity is almost never shown anywhere, and as one of the most lavish MGM spectacles, it has a certain curiosity value. The saga of a lumbering nation stabbed and humiliated by vicious little enemies and a specific family of honest farmers uprooted emotionally and geographically during a reign of terror, *Dragon Seed* catalogues

atrocities, famine, guerrilla warfare, locust plagues, and a massive fire that burns an entire farm community into scorched ashes. Unfortunately, it fails to produce a unified set of characterizations as strong or as faithful to Pearl Buck's novel as the physical production. You have to supply a lot of illusion to buy Kate Hepburn as a Chinese farm girl. She sounds like a Vassar sophomore ordering dim sum, while the other members of her family seem to hail from Liverpool, Heidelberg, and Gary, Indiana.

DRAGONSLAYER (1981)

★ ½ Directed by Matthew Robbins. Screenplay by Hal Barwood and Robbins. Produced by Hal Barwood. With Peter MacNicol, Caitlin Clarke, Sir Ralph Richardson, John Hallam, Peter Eyre, and Albert Salmi.

Dragonslayer uses crashing music and tumultuous horror movie effects to little avail as its dim-witted fairy-tale plot develops, employing amateur night contestants instead of seasoned actors to carry the load of badly needed professionals.

Ralph Richardson, the last sorcerer in the Dark Ages who knows how to dispose of dragons, dies early, leaving his sorcerer's apprentice, a callow youth with more brio than brains, to lead a pack of scruffy peasants on a slaying expedition. Twice a year, the medieval king sacrifices virgins to the dragon, who leaves the villages and farms unburned as his part of the bargain. The victims are selected by lottery, and when the courageous princess discovers her name has been omitted from the drawing, she volunteers like a good princess should.

The dialogue is full of howlers like "That princess what's her name, she sure surprised me!" The dragon is a great scaly behemoth with dripping fangs and breath that can reduce a mountain to shrubbery faster than a plague of gypsy moths.

But crudely filmed and badly acted, *Dragonslayer* has none of the boy's-book splendor of other escapist adventures like *Raiders of the Lost Ark* or *Superman II*.

THE DREAM TEAM (1989)

★ ★ ★ Directed by Howard Zieff. Screenplay by Jon Connelly and David Loucha. Produced by Christopher W. Knight. *With Michael Keaton, Christopher Lloyd, Peter Boyle, Stephen Furst, Dennis Boutsikaris, Lorraine Bracco, Milo O'Shea, Philip Bosco, and James Remar.*

The Dream Team gives Michael Keaton, one of the screen's most charming and versatile comics, a dynamite workout. He's the ringleader of a therapy group of wackos in a psychiatric clinic in Trenton, New Jersey, who are on their way to a baseball game in New York City when their doctor-chaperon accidentally witnesses a murder, gets mugged by the killers, and is dragged off to a hospital, leaving the four loonies unattended and broke to fend for themselves in the jungle of Manhattan. The more they try to save their shrink before he becomes the killers' next victim, the deeper they sink into trouble. As the pace quickens, so does the pulse. This is a zany comedy that never stoops to the level of idiot farce. You'll laugh like the whole world has gone crazy, but the laughs are straight from the heart.

DRESSED TO KILL (1980)

★ ½ Directed and written by Brian De Palma. Produced by George Litto. *With Michael Caine, Angie Dickinson, Nancy Allen, Keith Gordon, Dennis Franz, and David Margulies.*

Dressed to Kill is not as stupid as Brian De Palma's *The Fury*, not as dopey and campy as his *Carrie*, and not as stylish as his *Obsession*. It lies somewhere in the middle, violent and slobbering and smutty.

The opening shows Angie Dickinson in the shower, licking her lips and having a pornographic fantasy. The face is Angie's, but the rest of the body belongs to some poor girl who needed the money. The hands rubbing the soap all over the body, doing things with fingernails and Camay that Hitchcock would never have gotten away with, look like Angie's hands. One critic has suggested that Angie stood behind the naked girl and rubbed her hands all over her stand-in's body, but as sick as this movie is, my mind isn't warped enough to buy it.

Anyway, while her husband shaves with a straight razor, a maniac slips into the shower and rapes our Angie from behind. It's a fantasy, of course, and the women in this movie spend most of their time having sexual nightmares that would curl even Nancy Friday's hair. After her workout in the shower, Angie goes to the Metropolitan Museum, where she has another fantasy involving a man on the bench beside her.

Aroused to a frenzy, she follows him through the galleries while De Palma's camera apes Hitchcock's *Vertigo* to the point of laughable parody. It's a long, silent scene, with heavy music playing against suspense and long camera pans past mocking canvases. Outside, the stranger scoops her into a waiting taxi, performs a bit of fast oral sex to the cab driver's own lusty delight, and when she wakes up, she discovers she's got a venereal disease. But that's a piece of cake compared to the maniac in the Marilyn Monroe wig wanting to slice her into raw hamburger in the elevator. Angie has her *Psycho* scene early in the shower, then like Janet Leigh, disappears from the movie forever. When she goes, so does the movie.

The rest of it involves Michael Caine, a weirdo psychiatrist who knows the identity of the killer, and Nancy Allen, a spunky prostitute who has witnessed the murder and whose own life is in danger.

Now we have a demented killer who needs a sex operation, a nice woman looking for cheap sex, and a hooker who invests in the stock market—all of them used for laughs in a sniggering sophomoric way that tells more about De Palma's own sexual hang-ups than it does about the characters he's unable to develop.

Nice women with sex fantasies and whores who get paid

for theirs on the job are treated with the same cartoonish attitudes—equally bad, perverse, and easily erasable if there's a straight razor around. (Nobody in this movie uses anything but a straight razor, which leads me to believe this kind of thing could never happen anyway if people would only use a Gillette Trac II.)

There's one harrowing subway scene in which the hooker tries to escape the razor-happy killer by snuggling up to a gang of black hoodlums for protection. The poor girl enrages them with her advances and winds up chased into the dark labyrinth of the subway, the thugs on one side and the killer on the other.

De Palma seems to be saying that women are foolish sex objects and men are animals who exist for the purpose of knocking them around for even crazier sex kicks. Women will be understandably outraged by this trashy sendup of everything they've worked so hard to improve about locker-room opinions, but anyone with sensitivity and intelligence should also find plenty of reasons to be insulted. De Palma has the same kind of teenage dirty-doings-behind-the-barn mentality as Paul Schrader. Both of them are knee-deep in porno magazines and don't know how to

get out. Most of the time, I found myself laughing, not out of fear or nerves, but out of disbelief that a grown man could pass off horror and carnage and pornography as phony art.

De Palma has obviously been so influenced by Hitchcock that his work is impotent. He doesn't borrow from his master anymore; he just rips him off until there's no joke, no parody, no fun in even spotting the parallels.

Dressed to Kill debases a lot of human values in a style that is lurid and psychologically unhinged. There's something to offend just about everybody here.

DRIVING MISS DAISY (1989)
★ ★ ★ ★ Directed by Bruce Beresford. Screenplay by Alfred Uhry. Produced by Richard D. Zanuck and Lili Fini Zanuck. *With Jessica Tandy, Morgan Freeman, Dan Aykroyd, Patti Lupone, and Esther Rolle.*

If you don't already know why Jessica Tandy won the Oscar for Best Actress of 1989, in the Best Film of the year, experience both triumphs with *Driving Miss Daisy*. It's that rare treat that blows in as infrequently as a migration of blue butterflies—a perfect motion picture! Alfred Uhry has adapted his Pulitzer Prize-winning play for the screen like a needlepoint canvas without a stitch out of place, and Miss Tandy and Morgan Freeman illuminate the sensitive roles of an elderly Jewish dowager in Atlanta and her proud black chauffeur with a dignity that turns acting into art.

What begins as a tense, crotchety, and distrustful relationship in 1948 endures for twenty-five years, exploring the uneasy perimeters of friendship while mirroring two decades of social change in the growing South. Through shared experiences, both wrenching and humorous, a deep-rooted mutual respect builds and a moving portrait of two displaced minority figures reaching out to each other is etched into the viewer's conscience without ever being phony or manipulative. When the two victims of different prejudices witness the bombing of an Atlanta synagogue, and when Miss Daisy comes *that close* to asking her driver to join her at a fund-raising dinner for Martin Luther King, the simple story becomes a metaphor for the uneasy bridge between white and black cultures in the evolution of the South. Morgan Freeman finds the heartstrings in his gentle, compassionate character and plays them like chords in a sonata, while the incandescent Jessica Tandy—stubborn, proud, feisty, and independent—is as beautiful, indestructible, and awesome as the dogwoods and magnolias on her lawn. She's a national treasure and *Driving Miss Daisy* is an American masterpiece.

DR. JEKYLL AND MR. HYDE (1941)

★ ★ ★ ½ Directed and produced by Victor Fleming. Screenplay by John Lee Mahin. *With Spencer Tracy, Ingrid Bergman, Lana Turner, Donald Crisp, Ian Hunter, and C. Aubrey Smith.*

Spencer Tracy, Ingrid Bergman, and Lana Turner add artistry and glamour to this 1941 version of Robert Louis Stevenson's often-filmed thriller. This is probably the first drug flick and the best of the mad monster movies, and Tracy gives the aristocratic doctor-fiend added dimension as well as thrills. When he drinks that bubbling potion and grows fangs, you just know nobody on the MGM lot was safe for days.

A DRY WHITE SEASON (1989)

★ ★ ★ Directed by Euzhan Palcy. Screenplay by Colin Welland and Palcy. Produced by Paula Weinstein. *With Donald Sutherland, Susan Sarandon,*

Janet Suzman, Jurgen Prochnow, and Marlon Brando.

This powerful anti-apartheid movie from South Africa stars Donald Sutherland as an affluent white man shocked out of his complacency when the horror stories about beatings, racism, and the massacre of innocent black children hit home. Once his consciousness is sufficiently raised, he risks his family, friends, job, and even his life. In his struggle a painful story is told—not only about one man's courage to expose the truth but also about a country where human rights have no meaning and murder is legal. Valid contributions are made by a sincere cast—Susan Sarandon as a crusading reporter, Janet Suzman as Sutherland's smug and superior wife, and Jurgen Prochnow as a smooth-talking police agent who is little more than a fascist in a business suit. But it's really Marlon Brando, in one of his rare appearances as a defense attorney, who proves there are no small roles when they're played by big actors. He's big as Orson Welles and twice as hammy, but he steals the picture.

DUBARRY WAS A LADY (1943)
★ ★ Directed by Roy Del Ruth. Screenplay by Irving Brecher. Produced by Arthur Freed. *With Lucille Ball, Red Skelton, Gene Kelly, Virginia O'Brien, Douglass Dumbrille, Donald Meek, Rags Ragland, and Zero Mostel.*

Cole Porter's 1939 Broadway hit, filmed by MGM in 1943, is an obscure but frothy and fun-filled Technicolor musical with Red Skelton and Lucille Ball, the screen's two hottest redheads of the day, re-creating the roles played by Bert Lahr and Ethel Merman onstage. Red's a nightclub hatcheck boy who swallows a Mickey Finn and dreams he's Louis XV, and Lucy is the club singer who ends up wrecking the French court as historic *femme fatale* Madame Du-Barry. Gene Kelly, Virginia O'Brien, Dick Haymes, Jo Stafford, and the Tommy Dorsey orchestra are also on hand to make the songs and dances and elaborate dream sequences come alive. A silly concoction with nothing on its mind but entertainment. Unfortunately, only three Cole Porter songs made it to the screen from the original score because Lucy couldn't sing.

DUEL IN THE SUN (1947)

★ ★ Directed by King Vidor. Written and produced by David O. Selznick. *With Gregory Peck, Jennifer Jones, Joseph Cotten, Lionel Barrymore, Lillian Gish, Herbert Marshall, Walter Huston, Charles Bickford, Harry Carey, Tilly Losch, and Butterfly McQueen.*

The "artiest" Western ever made, this David O. Selznick classic is a kind of *Gone with the Wind* in saddlebags, with Gregory Peck and Joseph Cotten as two hot-blooded brothers fighting to the death for the love of a beautiful half-breed Indian girl (Jennifer Jones) who lives on the ranch owned by their father, a Texas land baron played by Lionel Barrymore. Passionate, over-wrought, and overproduced, this 1947 extravaganza is nevertheless a must-see for movie buffs. There has never been anything quite like it, and when you see the star-crossed lovers plug each other with bullets, then climb an interminable ant-hill to die in each other's arms, you'll be glad there hasn't been.

AN EARLY FROST (TV, 1985)

★ ★ ★ ★ Directed by John Erman. Screenplay by Ron Cowen and Daniel Lipman. Produced by Perry Lafferty. *With Aidan Quinn, Ben Gazzara, Gena Rowlands, D.* *W. Moffet, Sylvia Sidney, John Glover, and Sidney Walsh.*

The powerful, heartbreaking 1985 TV movie about AIDS caused controversy and excitement on the living-room screen, but even though the world is now better educated, neither time nor media exposure can dilute the original impact of this honest, stirring, and deeply touching Emmy Award-winning drama. Aidan Quinn is superb as the young attorney who must tell his family that he's not only gay but also dying of a disease they cannot understand. Ben Gazzara and Gena Rowlands are decent and moving as his devastated parents. D. W. Moffet is the tragic, confused lover, and Sylvia Sidney is marvelous as the compassionate grandmother. The study of how each member of an American family comes to terms with the most terrifying epidemic of our time makes for riveting, electrifying viewing. An absolute must for anyone with a heart, a soul, a conscience.

THE EGG AND I (1947)

★ ★ ★ ½ Directed by Chester Erskine. Screenplay by Erskine and Fred F. Finklehoffe, based on Betty MacDonald's bestseller. Produced by Erskine and Finklehoffe. *With Claudette Colbert, Fred MacMurray, Marjorie Main, Percy*

Kilbride, Louise Allbritton, Richard Long, and Donald MacBride.

The best movie ever made about city slickers battling the great outdoors. Claudette Colbert and Fred MacMurray buy a run-down chicken farm and tackle forest fires, collapsing barns, county fairs, Indians, and a lady wolf in a station wagon who uses a newfangled milking machine instead of Chanel No. 5 to wreck a marriage. This is the first film to introduce Marjorie Main and Percy Kilbride as Ma and Pa Kettle. The characters were so popular they spawned an entire series of successful films on their own. Fresh, funny, and thoroughly entertaining, and you haven't lived until you've seen the sophisticated Claudette fall smack on her fanny in a pigpen, wrestling a sow named Cleopatra.

84 CHARING CROSS ROAD (1987)

★ ★ ★ ½ Directed by David Jones. Screenplay by Hugh Whitemore and Helene Hanff. Produced by Geoffrey Helman. With Anne Bancroft, Anthony Hopkins, Judi Dench, Jean De Baer, Maurice Denham, Eleanor David, Mercedes Ruehl, and Daniel Gerroll.

Literacy is a disappearing commodity on the screen today, but I'm happy to say it can be found in abundance in *84 Char-ing Cross Road*, an intelligent, sophisticated, and soothing film that enriches the soul and warms the heart. It's a true story in which Anne Bancroft and Anthony Hopkins give distinguished performances of sincerity and perception as two strangers on opposite sides of the Atlantic whose lives are linked through a series of letters spanning more than twenty years. She's Helene Hanff—a salty, opinionated New York spinster with a passion for rare books. He's Frank Doel—a dull, repressed married clerk in a London bookstore, one of those quaint old British shops right out of Dickens. Their friendship begins in 1949 with an ad in the *Saturday Review*. A correspondence begins between the book lover and the bookseller, and as the letters continue, Helene sends postwar tins of Christmas hams and nylons, bringing joy and generosity into the lives of her overseas friends she's never met. Though they never do meet, Helene's letters from Frank finally spiral her, years later, and after his death, to the London she loves —and one last chance to see the shop before it's torn down.

What distinguishes this film is its feeling for character: the Americans sending bundles of supplies to their deprived friends in Britain, and for the proud but impoverished British sending in return the only things they've got—the sense of history and civilization they've preserved through books. In short, it offers insights into human nature, with an appreciation of each person's strengths and frailties —elements rarely present in today's escapist Hollywood action epics. Never a box-office blockbuster, but well worth the investment of time and attention a serious filmgoer is willing to make, *84 Charing Cross Road* clings like the scent of tobacco in a trenchcoat pocket.

END OF THE LINE (1987)

★ ★ ★ Directed by Jay Russell. Screenplay by Jay Russell and John Wholbruck. Produced by Mary Steenburgen, Lewis Allen, and Peter Newman. *With Wilford Brimley, Levon Helm, Mary Steenburgen, Barbara Barrie, Kevin Bacon, Holly Hunter, Bob Balaban, Clint Howard, Rita Jenrette, Howard Morris, Bruce McGill, and Trey Wilson.*

End of the Line, a low-budget film produced by Mary Steenburgen, is funny and endearing and loaded with charm. It's got a heart as big as the state of Arkansas, where it was filmed, and contains a message about the dignity of the grassroots American heartland. Wilford Brimley and singer Levon Helm (he was marvelous as Jane Fonda's Depression-hit husband in *The Dollmaker* on TV) are two old codgers who have worked all their lives in a burned-out railroad whistlestop called Clifford, Arkansas. Now the big corporation in Chicago that owns the depot is shifting to air freight and the whole town is going out of business. So the two old geezers tell their wives they're going bird hunting and, equipped with a change of Sunday clothes and a box of beer and lunch meat, they steal a locomotive and head for Chicago on a mission from God: to tell their fancy chairman of the board a thing or two, man-to-man, and see their country from the train along the way. The results are heartwarming, scary, adventurous, and symbolic of the American way of life. Mary Steenburgen, Kevin Bacon, Holly Hunter, Barbara Barrie, and Bob Balaban are just a few of the supporting stars who contributed their time and talent to a project they believed in, but it's the two old guys who own the picture — wonderful character actors who don't look or talk like movie stars, but like real people. They're like the old steam engine, displaced by progress, and this is their time to stand up and be counted. This is a little movie full of life and love that proves the little guy can still fight back and beat the system.

ELENI (1985)

★ ★ ½ Directed by Peter Yates. Screenplay by Steve Tesich. Produced by Nick Vanoff, Mark Pick, and Nicholas Gage. With Kate Nelligan, John Malkovich, Linda Hunt, Oliver Cotton, Ronald Pickup, Rosalie Crutchley, and Dimitra Arliss.

Thirty years after his mother was tortured and murdered by Communist guerrillas in the Greek Civil War, reporter Nicholas Gage returned to Greece to track down her killers and avenge her death. The result was a widely acclaimed best-seller, *Eleni*, which was distilled by director Peter Yates and screenwriter Steve Tesich into a grim, well-intentioned, but seriously flawed movie.

You need a course in Greek politics to understand *Eleni*. Then you need a lot of Christian charity to forgive the disastrous casting of John Malkovich, a vastly overrated actor with a lot of sloppy mannerisms and a voice like a dial tone. Throughout Gage's book you get the impression that he was a man of steel, haunted and driven by rage and passion. He must be

shocked to see himself played by a monotonous wimp.

There are other problems. The film doesn't explain the Greek Civil War well enough for the audience to differentiate between the Communists, the peasants, and the royalists. As far as I know, the Greeks are still fighting among themselves, and they can't explain it, either.

This is tough on an audience, because we need to know why the terrible things that happened to Eleni were a result of such complex political subterfuge.

Eleni was apolitical. She was a kind, compassionate, courageous woman who found herself caught up in the conflict in which twenty-eight thousand Greek children were sent to Soviet labor camps. Miraculously, she orchestrated an escape for Nick and his three sisters through the land mines surrounding their village, and faced a firing squad on a trumped-up charge of treason, paying with her life for saving the lives of her children.

This is strong stuff, with all the elements for gripping filmmaking. But *Eleni* is really two movies.

One is the story of how an innocent peasant woman caught up in the horrors of war prays for a miracle that will reunite her family with their father, who has already emigrated to America.

The other is the story of how her son returns to Athens as bureau chief of the *New York Times*, revisits the ruins of his old village, walks the paths where he last saw his mother alive, and tries to find the people responsible for his mother's execution. The flashbacks, flash forwards, and rapid-cut juxtapositions of time and mood are first irritating, then just plain boring.

The flashbacks to the 1940s are more interesting than the present-day crusade of Nicholas Gage. The Greek peasants are marvelous characters, and there are some harrowing experiences.

A great Greek actress like Melina Mercouri, or even Irene Papas, could tear your heart out and win an Oscar for the role of Eleni. Where did they get the dismaying notion to cast Kate Nelligan?

Totally miscast, not even the right nationality, with an accent that belongs in the Royal Shakespeare Company, she works hard but just seems to be going through the motions. With her black shawls and painted eyebrows, she looks about as Greek as Shirley MacLaine.

But it is really John Malkovich who destroys credibility and saps *Eleni* of the driving energy it needs. He mumbles. He moans. He drawls in a voice so soft and limp you can barely hear him.

In the end, when he faces the monster who betrayed and killed his mother, Malkovich finally comes to life. Beautifully directed by Peter Yates, this scene has real tension and power. But it comes too late. *Eleni* has already died of tedium.

THE ELEPHANT MAN (1980)

★ ★ ★ ½ **Directed by David Lynch. Screenplay by Christopher DeVore, Eric Bergren, and David Lynch. Produced by Jonathan Sanger and Mel Brooks. *With John Hurt, Anthony Hopkins, Anne Bancroft, Freddie Jones, Wendy Hiller, and Sir John Gielgud.***

One of the most interesting theatrical conceits in the Broadway production of *The Elephant Man* was the way Philip Anglim (later David Bowie and others) played the pathetically deformed John Merrick. Horrifying photos of the real "elephant man" were projected at the beginning of the play, demonstrating all of the patient's grotesqueries. From then on, his pain and deformity were all suggested by the actor, who did more with body language than even the most imaginative horror-movie makeup.

When Mel Brooks announced his plans to make a film version of this moving play, everyone was up in arms with visions of cheap thrills, Hollywood horror, and Lon Chaney masks from *Phantom of the Opera*. The good news is that the movie is carefully, soundly, and artistically conceived, with magnificent actors and a film reality complete with horror makeup that does not diminish its theatrical impact, but truly enhances it.

Purists will argue that the story worked better without the special effects, but that's comparing apples to alligator pears. The film would be utterly ridiculous without exposing the true aberrational nature of the "elephant man." How could you accurately re-create Victorian London in every grisly detail and then show the "elephant man" as a normal actor, walking around with a limp?

The film, directed by David Lynch, is a solemn, courageous, and extremely hypnotic experience that does not pretend to be based on the play, but on the published reminiscences of Sir Frederick Treves, the doctor who treated John Merrick, and the book *The Ele-*

phant Man: A Study in Human Dignity by Ashley Montagu. It is a fine, admirable, and very exciting film and certainly a most noble and artistic cinematic achievement.

At the beginning, elephants sway across the screen to a drumbeat, blowing their trumpets and swaying their trunks while a woman writhes in horror and pain, apparently giving birth to a monster. We are thus prepared for the Victorian Gothic that follows. The play only suggested that world, but the film opens it up, with its crude medical laboratories, smelly wharfs, and filthy slums.

This was the time of Sweeney Todd and Jack the Ripper murders and the flavor, fever, and ferment of those times are beautifully reflected in the somber black-and-white cinematography by Freddie Francis, as well as the Stuart Craig sets and the Patricia Norris costumes.

When first discovered, the "elephant man" is a freak in a sideshow on the streets of Whitechapel. Monstrously disfigured, "reeking of deplorable stench," and covered with growths and scales, the man, whose real name was John Merrick, was suffering from a then-unknown disorder at first believed to be elephantiasis but later thought to be more directly related to abnormal bone development.

A victim of ignorance and brutality, he was an object of ridicule as a carnival freak when Treves moved him to London Hospital and spent four years "civilizing" him. The film (and the play) raised the moral question of whether Merrick was really helped by this humanizing process or indeed was exploited on yet another higher level as a martyr of society.

In the eyes of all who helped him, he became a mirror to their own vanity. Merrick found the affection, compassion, and tenderness he needed, and when the governing committee of the hospital tried to turn him out as "incurable," even Queen Victoria and Princess Alexandra of Wales intervened on his behalf, until in the end, Merrick had found his soul in the samaritanism of others whose own motives remain questionable.

It's the *Hunchback of Notre Dame* theme, philosophically expanded, imaginatively rendered.

The film has perhaps less eloquence than the play. There's more emphasis on the lurid aspects of Merrick's life—especially his masochistic relationship with the evil Bytes, the lowlife who exploited him (wonderfully acted by Freddie Jones, who creates the slimiest villain since Robert Newton's Bill Sykes in David Lean's *Oliver Twist*).

Anthony Hopkins is marvelous as the always questioning doctor; the great Wendy Hiller etches an unforgettable portrait of the starchy head nurse whose initial disgust changes in time to human sympathy and kindness; John Gielgud lends strong support as the head of the hospital; and Anne Bancroft is superb as the respected stage actress whose initial curiosity about the elephant man leads to a compassion that surpasses charity. Their relationship has less of a sexual undertone in the film and is much more believable than the play, and there is one excellent scene in which Merrick attends his first play and the audience gives him a standing ovation that tears your heart out.

It is here and throughout that John Hurt's genius elevates the film to heights of artistry. Once you get used to the ghastly makeup, he makes the human being underneath hugely real and three dimensional. This is a bravura performance by a dazzling young actor who communicates more with his voice than most actors ever learn. Much craft and caution and dedication have gone into *The Elephant Man*, turning a repellant and somewhat heart-wrenching story into a richly satisfying film that will leave you devastated.

THE EMERALD FOREST (1985)

★ ★ ★ ½ Directed and produced by John Boorman. Screenplay by Rospo Pallenberg. With Powers Boothe, Charley Boorman, Meg Foster, Dira Paes, and Rui Polonah.

The seven-year-old son of an American construction engineer is playing on a dam site at the edge of the Brazilian rain forest. When his parents turn around, he's vanished. This opening scene grabs you by the throat, and for most of the film that follows, the suspense assumes an almost physical force. A true story, *The Emerald Forest* tells what happens to the lost child. Kidnapped and raised by a tribe of Stone Age Indians, the boy grows up to hunt with a bow and arrow, speak a strange language, and learn the rites of manhood in trials of great physical stamina and courage. For ten years, his father searches the primitive Amazon jungles. When their parallel stories cross a decade later, the boy, now seventeen, saves his own father from death but refuses to return to the civilized world of computers and Egg McMuffins. John Boorman has done a marvelous, backbreaking job of unraveling the mysteries of an uncharted corner of the universe, and the leading role is played by his own son Charley. Powers Boothe and Meg Foster are fine as his distraught parents, but it is young Charley, as a kind of space-age Bomba the Jungle Boy, who steals the picture. *The Emerald Forest* is a bizarre, exotic, compelling, and mystical movie experience.

EMPIRE OF THE SUN (1987)

★ ★ ★ ★ Directed by Steven Spielberg. Screenplay by Tom Stoppard, based on the novel by J. G. Ballard. Produced by Steven Spielberg, Kathleen Kennedy, and Frank Marshall. With John Malkovich, Miranda Richardson, Nigel Havers, and Christian Bale.

Empire of the Sun was my favorite film of 1987, but the Academy of Motion Picture Arts and Sciences didn't even nominate it for best picture. Oh, well. Nobody ever accused Oscar voters of good taste. Now, on home video, *Empire of the Sun* more than lives up to my initial praise. It may sound like one of Spielberg's adventures à la *Raiders of the Lost Ark* but the only thing it has in common is its epic size. For this is a deeply touching drama of human dimensions about an eleven-year-old English boy trapped by the Japanese invasion of Shanghai during World War II. Young James (Christian Bale) is separated from his parents during the evacuation when he lets go of his mother's hand to retrieve his toy airplane, and in the chaos and horror that follow, he grows old before his time in a concentration camp. Scavenging for survival, the bright boy with a privileged background turns into a savage; his only link with civilization is his friendship with an American thief (John Malkovich) who teaches him to steal food from the dying and shoes from the dead.

The theme here is what wrongs war does to children. It's a film of awesome faces and images—and scenes, like the evacuation of Shanghai, that fill the screen with phenomenal scope and grandeur. The shot of the boy, dressed for a party as an Arab prince, innocently stumbling upon an abandoned Japanese fighter plane in an empty field has the kind of breathtaking energy and imagination that separates great filmmakers from hacks. Every scene is orchestrated and photographed for maximum impact, yet it all seems to be happening without effort. Young Mr.

Bale, who plays James through four years of torture, beatings, disease, and death, is something of a miracle among child actors—a kid who never makes a phony move. A few scenes manipulate the audience's emotions shamelessly, but in a film of such magnitude, why nit-pick? *Empire of the Sun* confirms Spielberg as one of the most accomplished film directors of the 1980s.

THE EMPIRE STRIKES BACK (1980)

★ ★ ★ ★ Directed by Irvin Kershner. Story by George Lucas. Screenplay by Leigh Brackett and Lawrence Kasdan. Produced by Gary Kurtz. With Mark Hamill, Carrie Fisher, Harrison Ford, Billy Dee Williams, Anthony Daniels, David Prowse, Peter Mayhew, Kenny Baker, Frank Oz, Alec Guinness, and the voice of James Earl Jones.

The Empire Strikes Back opens with a fantastic battle between the Defenders of the Force (the good guys) and Darth Vader's monsters in which Our Side's rocket ships zip around armored juggernauts resembling five-hundred-foot-tall camels on hydraulic legs with death-spitting tongues.

The action never lags after that, and this sequel to *Star Wars* is more fun, more human, and more dazzling than the original. A menagerie of wonderful mutants has joined R2D2 and Chewbacca, Princess Leia's troops leap to battle across the polar ice cap on Arctic kangaroos, and young Luke Skywalker gets kidnapped by Abominable Snow Creatures.

But the best thing in this comic book marvel of the space serial to end them all is the adorable scene-stealing Yoda—a green goblin twenty-six inches high with pointy ears, sad eyes, and a Hobbitlike demeanor, brought to life by Frank Oz, creator of the Muppets. He gives Luke a crash course on how to take on Darth Vader through positive thinking and metaphysics, giving the film more life, heart, poetry, and psychological depth than its predecessor.

The excitement is without pause and the twists and bizarre characters are blends of the best technology the screen can offer, with the simplest and most gratifying kind of fairy-tale storytelling.

Irvin Kershner directed all of the artillery and hardware with great panache, John Williams orchestrated it with sonorous glee, and if original *Star Wars* creator George Lucas wants to go on imitating on the largest possible scale the Saturday afternoon serials of his youth, I would be the last person on earth to stop him.

ENDLESS LOVE (1981)
★ ½ Directed by Franco Zeffirelli. Screenplay by Judith Rascoe. Produced by Dyson Lovell. *With Brooke Shields, Martin Hewitt, Don Murray, Shirley Knight, Beatrice Straight, Richard Kiley, and Penelope Milford.*

In the good old days, when Elizabeth Taylor was growing up, they made movies with teenage girls flipping out over horses, chipmunks, and senior proms. Today, we get teenage girls driven to madness by lust.

Endless Love is about the consuming passion of puppy love, burning so deeply into the teenage mind that there is no recovery, no cure, and the prognosis is negative.

Brooke Shields is Jade, a fifteen-year-old whose parents (Don Murray and Shirley Knight) are aging hippies. Their bohemian permissiveness attracts all the kids in suburban Chicago. The movie is so awash with dopey dialogue that is it no wonder fine artists like Shirley Knight, Richard Kiley, Don Murray and Beatrice Straight have to fight for their lives to emerge with their integrity intact. The screenplay, by Judith Rascoe, is unspeakable.

Add to all of this a cloying pop song by Diana Ross, cinematography that makes the people look photographed through grape juice, and heavy-handed direction by Franco Zeffirelli that cuts away to open windows every time the kids have a go at each other between the sheets, and you have what adds up to one of the most accidentally hilarious pictures you've ever seen.

Brooke Shields plays the love-shredded fifteen-year-old with all the passion and commitment that goes into the making of a tunafish salad. Martin Hewitt, as her seventeen-year-old swain, makes a formidable debut with ten times the emotional maturity of his co-star. Beatrice Straight, with her flaming red hair, is supposed to be the boy's poor socialist mother, a Jewish intellectual with left-wing obsessions. She's about as Jewish as Doris Day. Everyone else is as hopelessly miscast.

The big problem here is that we never get a chance to see or feel what these kids are going through because the film is too busy doing all of our thinking for us. Lugubrious music drowns the movie in schmaltz. The talk is soap opera talk. Everything is a fake, from the air-conditioned look of the suburbs to the seedy hotel room where David and Jade meet after years of forced separation.

Zeffirelli manipulates us as though we were all teenagers, which is the precise audience he anticipated to fall for all the bloated sentimentality that oozes from the screen. (Behind the plastic palms of Hollywood stockholders meetings at the time, *Endless Love* was known as "Endless Money.") What a surprise when the picture flopped dismally.

My advice is for everyone to go back and have a good, hard look at *Splendor in the Grass*. Same theme, but in the hands of Elia Kazan and William Inge, the story of an overwhelming first love became a film for posterity. *Endless Love* is just another film for Brooke Shields's posterior. The filmmakers probably don't know it, but there is a difference.

ENEMIES, A LOVE STORY (1989)
★ ★ ★ 1/2 Directed, written, and produced by Paul Mazursky. With Ron Silver, Anjelica Huston, Lena Olin, and Margaret Sophie Stein.

Farce and tragedy meet with unexpected freshness in Paul Mazursky's offbeat film about Holocaust survivors in New York who find themselves confused and out of place in 1949. Ron Silver is Herman, a Polish Jew in Coney Island who is married to three women at the same time—and the absurdity of his escapades is often very amusing stuff in the middle of a serious subject. He survived the war but can't escape the ghosts or the nightmares. Now in Brooklyn, he's married to Margaret Sophie Stein, as the former maid who saved him from the Nazis. But over in the Bronx, he's got a second wife—gorgeous Lena Olin, a fiery, voluptuous Auschwitz survivor. Herman's life is already a mess, but suddenly the wife he thought was dead (Anjelica Huston) shows up in Manhattan. Poor Herman is so confused. He loves them all for different reasons, uses them, betrays them, and leaves them all in pain. Ironically, it's the wives who end up sticking together. This is an unusual, demanding film full of great performances and period details—from the cabbage smells to the Forties cars. It's exasperating, exciting, funny and the best movie about bigamy since *The Captain's Paradise*.

E.T.: THE EXTRA-TERRESTRIAL (1982)

★ ★ ★ ★ Directed by Steven Spielberg. Screenplay by Melissa Mathison. Produced by Spielberg and Kathleen Kennedy. *With Henry Thomas, Robert MacNaughton,* *Drew Barrymore, Dee Wallace, and Peter Coyote.*

E.T.—Steven Spielberg's masterpiece that shows how real movies are made—is a simple story, but a major achievement in the complex feelings and emotions it communicates. It's the detailed, inspired account of an alien who lands in a pine forest on the California coast and gets separated from his people when their spaceship is forced to make a sudden departure.

Frightened, alone, and three million light-years from home, the small creature wanders into the home of a suburban divorcee with three young children who lure him into the house with Reese's Pieces, then secretly take on the responsibility for his safety. The children are first terrified of the creature, who looks like a walking toadstool with large myopic eyes, but in time they learn to share their toys and show the creepy but lovable little one, whom they call "E.T.," where he is on their globe. Always there is the looming threat of man, with his Geiger counters and disturbing flashlights, but in the innocent, unquestioning world of children E.T. finds warmth and friendship.

There is one wonderful, classic scene in which the kids dress their new friend in a sheet and take him out on Halloween. The audience roars when E.T., passing a child trick-or-treating who is dressed like Yoda from *Star Wars*, almost loses his sheet in an attempt to communicate with what he thinks is another alien. E.T.'s near-death and eventual rescue by a network of children on bicycles who help him get back home are among the most heartwrenching sequences modern cinema can offer. Designed by Carlo Ramaldi, who manufactured King Kong, E.T. was destined to become an international household word.

Melissa Mathison, who collaborated on the screenplay of *The Black Stallion*, wrote the film. John Williams, who scored both *Star Wars* and *Close Encounters*, has composed music that is stunning and beautiful.

The children are played with a wisdom and brilliance far beyond their years by Henry Thomas, Robert McNaughton, and Drew Barrymore (granddaughter of the late John Barrymore). They are splendid, but young Henry Thomas, who broke my heart as Sissy Spacek's son in *Raggedy Man*, is something of a miracle. It is clear that special effects play an important part in *E.T.*, but this

is no easily categorized sci-fi adventure. Spielberg calls it "a science fiction fable, a fairy tale for the 1980s," but it is, more important, about human values, the understanding people have toward one another. It's about compassion and friendship—a love story between a young boy and an 880-year-old extra-terrestrial from an unknown planet somewhere in the uncharted universe that leaves all who see it with a warm and radiant glow of optimism and joy. Here is unimpeachable proof that great movies are still possible and, when they happen, they speak a universal language of cinema.

EVIL UNDER THE SUN (1982)
★ ★ ½ Directed by Guy Hamilton. Screenplay by Anthony Shaffer. Produced by Richard Goodwin and John Brabourne. *With Peter Ustinov, Colin Blakely, Jane Birkin, Nicholas Clay, Maggie Smith, Roddy McDowall, Sylvia Miles, and James Mason.*

Agatha Christie and Cole Porter meet for the first time in *Evil Under the Sun*; the introduction is less harmonious than it should be. This trifle is another entry in a series of starstudded bores produced by Richard Goodwin and John Brabourne, proving all over again how much better Dame Agatha fares on paper than she does on film. The modest pleasures enjoyed by armchair sleuths in the Christie murder mysteries are so bloated beyond recognition in these fancy film masquerade parties that the films look like horse shows in which the horses think they're unicorns.

In the tradition of *Murder on the Orient Express*, *Death on the Nile*, and *The Mirror Crack'd*, this overbudgeted extravaganza takes a glamorous location (this time a swank seaside hotel in Spain), stuffs it with oddball characters and period costumes, and complicates the plot with one corpse (Diana Rigg, a gold-digging musical comedy vamp who gets strangled on the beach) and eight movie star suspects, all to the tune of a cornucopia of Cole Porter songs from the 1930s. Guy Hamilton is once again the director, and if you thought he dragged things out too sluggishly in *The Mirror Crack'd*, you'll be unhappy to learn that *Evil Under the Sun* makes that disappointing Miss Marple movie seem like a photo finish at Belmont Park.

Rotund supersleuth Hercule Poirot, once again played by Peter Ustinov, is up to his dewlaps in clues, alibis, motives, and suspects, but since there is only one murder, you only get a fraction of the usual thrills. Among the suspicious hotel guests are James Mason and Sylvia Miles, about as mismatched a couple as you are likely to find on a movie screen, as Broadway producers who are desperate to sign the murdered woman even though she bankrupted them with her last show; Roddy McDowall, as an obnoxious writer who has dug up some filth about his subject she doesn't want printed; Jane Birkin, as the dowdy wife of a young man (Nicholas Clay) who has fallen for the temptress' lethal charms; and Colin Blakely, as a millionaire who wants to reclaim a precious jewel.

It comes as no surprise that the most delicious performance comes from Maggie Smith, as the hotel proprietress who turns out to be an ex-chorine, *bona fide* tart, and a lifelong enemy of the murder victim.

Everyone sails, swims, and flirts to Cole Porter's greatest hits while doing their best to bring some life to the dull lines written by Anthony Shaffer, who also wrote *Sleuth*. Best scene: Diana Rigg, before her untimely demise, singing "You're the Top" while Maggie Smith tries to upstage her by harmonizing off-key in her shrill, Daisy Duck contralto.

The cast works so hard to disguise the emptiness in one of Dame Agatha's most conventional and unexciting stories that you can almost see the perspiration. "With Hercule Poirot," says Ustinov in his drollest Belgian accent, "mysteries never last long." *Evil Under the Sun* proves him wrong.

EXECUTIVE SUITE (1954)

★ ★ ★ ½ Directed by Robert Wise. Screenplay by Ernest Lehman. Produced by John Houseman. *With Barbara Stanwyck, William Holden, June Allyson, Frederic March, Paul Douglas, Shelley Winters, Louis Calhern, and an all-star cast.*

If you liked *Wall Street*, you'll love this star-studded MGM blockbuster about how greed and power corrupt big business. After the sudden death of its president, a giant furniture manufacturing company's seven top board members become locked in a suspenseful struggle for corporate control. In the boardroom battle that ensues, you get a devastating look at the prototypes who grapple for power and money, how management works, and how executives jockey for position behind closed doors, stopping at nothing to reach the top, including blackmail. Barbara Stanwyck is tough as marble as the major stockholder whose vote will decide the company's future. Frederic March, William Holden, Paul Douglas, June Allyson, Shelley Winters, Louis Calhern, Nina Foch, Walter Pidgeon, and Dean Jagger lend incredibly polished support. Robert (*Sound of Music*) Wise is the director, and John Houseman the producer of this brilliant study of ruthlessness on the executive level. The subject matter might seem stuffy, but trust me. For a movie that takes place mostly in conference rooms, there isn't a dull or wasted moment in *Executive Suite*.

EYEWITNESS (1981)

★ ★ ★ Directed and produced by Peter Yates. Screenplay by Steve Tesich. *With William Hurt, Sigourney Weaver, James Woods, Pamela Reed, Kenneth McMillan, Christopher Plummer, Irene Worth, and Albert Paulsen.*

William Hurt is a movie star without any of the conventional requisites for the job. He's no hero in the classic sense of the word, he has none of the mystery and darkness of recent idols, none of the muscular awe of yesteryear, and he doesn't even photograph particularly well (he has a square, clumsy chin and watery eyes and usually wears glasses). But he's built a loyal following because he's so damned sure of himself, with a pride that never borders on arrogance. His audience follows him because they trust him.

In Peter Yates's film *Eyewitness* he plays Daryll Deever, a quiet, introspective Vietnam veteran who works as a night janitor in a New York office building where a murder is committed. Every night in the wee small hours, when his job is finished, Daryll goes home to the lonely little flat he shares with a vicious watchdog companion, flicks on his VCR, and watches reruns of the night's Eyewitness News, centering particular attention on the show's cool, statuesque reporter Tony Sokolow (Sigourney Weaver).

Having developed a huge crush on her from afar, he is delighted to discover that she's been assigned to cover the murder, and by pretending to know more than he does in order to get closer to her, he endangers both of their lives and leads them into a vortex of mayhem, espionage, and international intrigue.

In *Eyewitness* he has the same touching vulnerability he had in *Altered States*, but he also radiates a kind of "Geewillikers" innocence that is corny but seductive. He's the working-class WASP out to conquer a Jewish princess who doesn't know she's been outclassed. When he glumly admits to her in bed that rich girls always marry rich guys, he's smiling inside and so are we. After all, she's in his bed, not her fiancé's, and I doubt that there will be anyone who isn't rooting for her to stay there.

Eyewitness was written by Steve Tesich, who collaborated with director Yates on the fresh, innovative *Breaking Away*, and in embroidering a contemporary romantic thriller they come up with another sparkling original—a tense, taut suspense yarn in which the characters do not create the mystery but are created by it. Again, it is the witty, charming human observation that gives the film its unique appeal, and although *Eyewitness* means to be a murder mystery, it is also a social comedy that dissolves class barriers in an appealing way.

Since the murder victim is a Vietnamese businessman, both Daryll, a decorated marine who deplores the Vietnam experience, and his eccentric buddy

Aldo (James Woods), who was court-martialed for cowardice, are immediate suspects. Aldo has big dreams of starting a business but spends more time worrying that the former mayor of Saigon is now running a pizza parlor in the United States. Woven throughout are Aldo's sister Linda (Pamela Reed), who has had a dull, indifferent affair with Daryll to please her brother, and Daryll's tortured, loudmouthed father (Kenneth McMillan), a wheelchair-imprisoned cripple whose wife no longer loves him.

On the upper register of the equation, there is the reporter, who has turned her back on a career as a classical pianist to dabble in broadcast journalism, disappointing her intellectual Russian-Jewish parents (Irene Worth and Albert Paulsen) and her fiance (Christopher Plummer), a rich Israeli diplomat dedicated to smuggling Jewish immigrants out of Russia.

These complicated neurotic social studies are beautifully realized, but they are more expertly drawn than the rather baffling and unconvincing mystery plot that surrounds them. Keen observers and amateur sleuths weaned on Hitchcock movies are likely to abandon their logic early.

Why, for instance, does Dar-

yll's man-eating dog always threaten to tear every visitor to pieces except the one character who punches him out in the kitchen? When Aldo arrives and physically attacks Daryll, the dog doesn't seem to be at home.

And when Plummer turns out to be not only a distinguished Zionist humanitarian but a mercenary who will stop at nothing, the two opposing forces in his underdeveloped character do not satisfactorily jell. There are so many red herrings here that the film begins to smell.

In lesser hands, *Eyewitness* might be a letdown. But Tesich writes fresh, crunchy dialogue and Yates knows his way around the mystery genre so well that he not only opens up the personalities of his characters but illuminates the atmosphere around them, too.

There is some music, to build and heighten suspense, but the high intensity texture of the film is based on sounds of life—traffic, TV sets, janitors' carts rolling across marble halls at midnight, the hiss of steam, and the angry machinery of trash compactors. There's enough action to keep you scared—that ferocious dog, motorcycle chases, and a shootout in the riding stables on West 89th Street—and enough crisp style for more than one political thriller. Above all, there is the thrill of watching a major actor shine through the material like the morning sun. William Hurt gives an already gratifying mystery a compelling mystery all his own.

THE FABULOUS BAKER BOYS (1989)

★ ★ ★ ★ Directed and written by Steve Kloves. Produced by Paula Weinstein and Mark Rosenberg. With Jeff Bridges, Beau Bridges, and Michelle Pfeiffer.

The Fabulous Baker Boys has everything you could hope for. It's one of the best movies ever made about jazz musicians. It has the best original jazz score—by composer Dave Grusin—since *Sweet Smell of Success*. It has sensible, mature dialogue and crackerjack direction—both by the gifted young Steve Kloves. And the three stars are nothing short of sensational.

Jeff and Beau Bridges are a stroke of casting genius as the Baker Boys—a second-rate lounge act slugging away at two pianos in cheesy cocktail bars and seedy nightclubs, and Oscar-nominated Michelle Pfeiffer is the girl singer who changes their act and their lives. Jeff is Jack, the cold, chain-smoking loner, in a rage with life because he's got the talent but not the courage to cut out on his own. Beau is older brother Frank—the act's morale booster and business manager, a dull, pear-shaped family man with two kids and no illusions.

The act is going nowhere until the boys hire a chick singer to add some color. She's Susie—an ex-hooker who chews gum, shows up late, and has no sense of responsibility. But she can sing like Julie London and what she does on top of a grand piano crooning "Makin' Whoopee" will melt your ice cubes. Tensions build and all three end up facing truths about each other in surprising and unconventional ways.

Among the thrills are Pfeiffer's voice and Beau's sensitive, honest acting. Pudgy, balding, and frustrated, he makes the unrewarding after-dark world of second-rate show business really come alive. There is nothing second-rate, however, about *The Fabulous Baker Boys*.

A FACE IN THE CROWD (1957)

★ ★ ★ Directed by Elia Kazan. Screenplay by Budd Schulberg. With Andy Griffith, Patricia Neal, Walter Matthau, Lee Remick, Anthony Franciosa, and Kay Medford.

A Face in the Crowd is an obscure triumph by Elia Kazan, written by Budd Schulberg, about the abuse of media power. Similar in theme to *Network*, it tells the hypnotic, electrically charged story of a backwoods hillbilly singer (played with terrifying honesty and authority by Andy Griffith) whose rise to fame via the hypnotic medium of TV poisons his mind and sets him on a course of self-serving greed and evil that eventually misshapes the lives and consciences of millions of his gullible fans. Patricia Neal, Anthony Franciosa, and Walter Matthau lend miraculous support, and in the role of the sensual, childlike bimbo cheerleader who marries the country and western zealot, Lee Remick catapulted to stardom.

FAHRENHEIT 451 (1967)

★ ★ ★ ½ Directed and written by Francois Truffaut. Produced by Lewis M. Allen. *With Julie Christie, Oskar Werner, Cyril Cusack, Anton Diffring, Jeremy Spenser, Bee Duffell, Alex Scott, and Mark Lester.*

Ray Bradbury's science fiction oddity about a horrifying futuristic police state in which books are banned has been fired with imagination and passion by the late, great Francois Truffaut to give an apocalyptic view of classic dimension. In a world where childbearing is illegal, sex is taboo, men read comic strips with no words, people live in numbered cell blocks watching red lights flash on TV screens, individuality is forbidden, and nonconformity is out, Oskar Werner plays a fireman who is the last of the free thinkers, and Julie Christie in a dual role plays both his emotionless wife and a young teacher with a cache of the world's great literature hidden in her uncle's house. The film contains many arresting, beautifully photographed scenes, including a fire that destroys the greatest books of the centuries while the screen turns orange. The final scene is heartbreaking and unforgettable: the last book people left in the world wander through a snowfall reciting pages of Dickens, Jane Austen, and *Alice in Wonderland* like wounded madmen, speaking aloud the last remainders of a once-literate civilization. A powerful, scary, magical work by one of the world's greatest directors.

FANNY AND ALEXANDER (1983)

★ ★ ★ ★ Directed and written by Ingmar Bergman. Produced by Jorn Donner. *With Pernilla Allwin, Bertil Guve, Jan Malmsjo, Erland*

Josephson, Kabi Laretei, Gunn Wallgren, Ewa Froling, and Gunnar Bjornstrand.

In a time of culture schlock in which most movies resemble video manuals typed on IBM computers, *Fanny and Alexander* is something of a miracle.

It is not about thermonuclear technology, the end of the world, or teddy bears from outer space. It is, instead, lush, lavish, romantic, deeply satisfying, sometimes terrifying, and ultimately enchanting. Miracle, hell; *Fanny and Alexander* is a masterpiece.

Ingmar Bergman, the great Swedish director, spent years writing, polishing, and filming this rich tapestry of life in turn-of-the-century Stockholm.

The result is a great film that provides a vast and sweeping view of paradise found, lost, and recovered, as it explores the lives of the Ekdahl family—a large, lusty theatrical clan with insatiable passions and grand emotions. Far from the dark, brooding Bergman films of the past, it is gorgeous, joyful, and optimistic; like a riveting, bountiful novel, it overflows with dramatic characters and literary insights, and its story carries you along in a trance.

The year is 1907. From the waxed woods and burnished lamps to the wine-red drapes and regal carpets, the Ekdahl house prepares for a family reunion on Christmas Eve. One by one, the happy faces of this theater-owning family are reflected in the candlelight, from the matriarchal grandmother who controls the money and the lives of her three sons, down to Fanny and Alexander themselves—angel-faced children who will inherit the Ekdahl legacy in the troubling years to come.

Rich and privileged, the children have been raised in the exciting, protective make-believe of their grandparents' theater. Their mother, Emilie, is a beautiful and talented actress; their father, Oscar, is a bad actor but good business manager. Floating through their lives are chattering maids, family retainers, the uncles with their financial problems and their long-suffering wives, and even Isak, the old Jewish junk dealer who has seen all the wars, mendacity, and cold weather he cares to see and is a comfort to Grandmother in her old age.

From their safe, candlelit world, Fanny and Alexander are plunged into a grim and horrifying abyss. While mourning the sudden death of their father, they are further traumatized when their mother renounces her career and marries a stern, sadistic Protestant bishop. Life under his cruel domination turns into a Spartan existence of austerity, deprivation, and sacrifice.

The vast and colorful canvas of their lives forms a landscape that passes across the retinas of their clear adolescent eyes like scenes from a train window. The odyssey that takes Fanny and Alexander from dappled nurseries to the terrors of hellfire and damnation and back again into the life-affirming world of the Ekdahls is accompanied by Bergman's usual myths, illusions, and dreams.

The film contains some ponderous symbols, confusing magic, and overripe melodramatics, as is the master's trademark, but overriding the occasional lapse into self-consciousness is his overwhelming artistic vision. Sven Nykvist's opulent cinematography is like early twentieth century oil paintings brought to life, and the performances by Bergman's talented repertory company are indelible.

Throughout, the Bergman themes of truth and reality vs. lies and illusion permeate the sentimental spirit and pepper an old-fashioned feast with arresting and sometimes alarming images and emotions. The cumulative effect is as thrilling as anything the movies are likely to achieve.

FATAL ATTRACTION (1987)
★ ★ ½ Directed by Adrian Lyne. Screenplay by James Dearden. Produced by Stanley Jaffe and Sherry Lansing. *With Michael Douglas, Glenn Close, Anne Archer, Ellen Hamilton Latzen, Stuart Pankin, Ellen Foley, Fred Gwynne, and Meg Mundy.*

Fatal Attraction is the movie that forced husbands back into the movie houses, dragged there by their wives. Half morality lesson about the dangers of casual sex, half slasher flick, this slick, suspenseful and always professional domestic thriller suffered from a "How do we end this thing?" finale that never rang true. But Glenn Close, as the one-night stand who turned into a scheming wacko, and Michael Douglas, as the straying husband whose affair turned into a nightmare, are terrific. A big box-office blockbuster that loses a bit of punch on home video, but worth a look just to see what got everybody excited in 1987, and why.

FATHER OF THE BRIDE (1950)
★ ★ ★ ★ Directed by Vincente Minnelli. Screenplay by Frances Goodrich and Albert Hackett. Produced by Pandro S. Berman.

With Spencer Tracy, Elizabeth Taylor, Joan Bennett, Russ Tamblyn, Don Taylor, Billie Burke, and Leo G. Carroll.

I don't usually associate great performances of an almost historic importance with comedy, but in this MGM jewel, director Vincente Minnelli extracted from the legendary Spencer Tracy one of the all-time classic tour de force portraits of American fatherhood. Frustrated, affectionate, trying to hold on to his sanity in a household berserk with wedding fever, Tracy is lovable and irascible at the same time. Elizabeth Taylor, more breathtaking in her youthful perfection that at any other time in her long and impressive career, is superb as the daughter Tracy is about to reluctantly sacrifice, and Joan Bennett got the best plum of her own career as the wife and overenthusiastic mother of the bride. Tracy and family bounce from one crisis to another, and we follow them hilariously through rehearsal, wedding gifts, and the nightmarish big day when the caterers wreck their house, like old friends and relatives. This is truly a family flick that is perfect in every detail, and it hasn't aged one day in forty years. An absolute must for anyone who really loves the movies.

FATHER OF THE BRIDE (1991)
★ ★ ★ Directed by Charles Shyer. Produced by Nancy Meyers, Carol Baum, and Howard Rosenman. Written by Frances Goodrich and Albert Hackett, with new dialogue by Nancy Meyers and Charles Shyer. *With Steve Martin, Diane Keaton, Martin Short, Kimberly Williams, Kieran Culkin, B. D. Wong, Peter Michael Goetz, and George Newbern.*

Father of the Bride was a flawless MGM classic which cannot be improved (see preceding review), so I approached the Disney remake (MGM no longer had the money to do the job itself, which is as sad a comment on the state of cinema in 1991 as I could conjure in a nightmare) with alarm and dread. I was right about one thing—it makes no improvement on the original at all, and doesn't even try. I was wrong about another—the story can be told again, with humor and reverence, without trashing any memories. No, it's not a masterpiece. But it's no disgrace, either.

To get basic prejudices out of the way at the top, Steve Martin is no Spencer Tracy, Diane Keaton is no Joan Bennett, and Kimberly Williams, as the daughter, couldn't hold up Elizabeth Taylor's eyebrow pencil. Charles (*Baby Boom*) Shyer, the director, is not in the same league with Vincente Minnelli, either, but at least he has the good sense to copy that great director's concept right up to and including the same camera angles. The result is a decent if unnecessary Xerox of a timeless jewel that chronicles the financial waste, pretentious snobbery, and material vulgarity of American weddings with only an occasional foray into sitcom parody. The occasional attempts to update the material, such as Dad telling his future son-in-law "Drive safely and don't forget to fasten your condom—er, seat belt!" only evoke cheap laughs at the expense of humanism. Dumb neurotic tics and corny sight gags are Mr. Martin's forte, while Ms. Keaton eats her hair and giggles in a manner that suggests they'd rather be playing the ingenues instead of the grown-ups. But for the most part, this is a decent and pleasantly respectful reincarnation that doesn't bastardize the 1950 classic.

The premise is the same: weddings are inventions of the devil whose sole purpose seems to be finding new ways to bankrupt the middle-class. Martin Short makes a funny, incomprehensible appearance as a flamboyant caterer who turns a lovely American home into a shambles—drilling holes in the ceiling, removing the furniture, ensconsing swans in the tulip beds, and charging $250 a head for a cake nobody eats. Then it snows for the first time in thirty-six years, freezing the swans and killing the tulips, while the heaters melt the ice sculptures. Pretty funny, until Dad goes berserk over hot dog buns in the supermarket and ends up in jail. This is where the film reaches its absolute nadir. Most of the time, however, the good news is the film remains faithful. Mr. Shyer and his wife, co-writer Nancy Meyers, even share screenplay credits with the original (and far superior) writing team of Frances Goodrich and Albert Hackett. Some of their memorable scenes remain intact, such as the trip up the stairs to fling open the bride's door on her wedding day, revealing to her Dad the beauty of his grown-up little girl in a three-way mirror, and the scene following the aftermath of the chaos, in which the parents dance romantically through the confetti and debris, recapturing the essence of their own enduring marriage. Scenes like these are a welcome indication that some young filmmakers still admire the great artistry of their predecessors.

Steve Martin never manages to capture Spencer Tracy's conflicting emotions of frustration, good-natured curmudgeonliness, and commitment to family values. He just goes through the hysteria index. And, oddly, the film looked crisper in the original black and white. But this is not a *Father of the Bride* to scoff at. It has spontaneity and resonance enough to keep Louis B. Mayer from turning over in his grave with apoplexy.

FERRIS BUELLER'S DAY OFF (1986)

★ ★ Written and directed by John Hughes. Produced by John Hughes and Tom Jacobson. *With Matthew Broderick, Alan Ruck, Mia Sara, Jeffrey Jones, Jennifer Grey, Cindy Pickett, and Lyman Ward.*

John Hughes, the resident industry shrink to Hollywood's brat packers, teeny-boppers, and space cadets, turns out teenage movies faster than gerbils procreate.

Ferris Bueller's Day Off is about one day in the alleged life of an allegedly bright seventeen-year-old high school senior who knocks his brains out playing hooky.

The theme inspires universal compassion (who has not cut school at least once, no matter what era?), but the way it is executed could not possibly hold the interest of anyone old enough to own a driver's license.

Ferris Bueller (Matthew Broderick) is a born con artist. When he's not talking a mile a minute to his girlfriend Sloan (Mia Sara) and his best friend Cameron (Alan Ruck), he's stepping aside, facing the camera and addressing all the rest of us in the audience, an annoying conceit that interrupts the action and wreaks havoc on the film's already lazy tempo.

In his dedication to the joy of loafing, Ferris audaciously convinces his parents he's ill, the student body starts raising money to save his life with a kidney transplant, and the dean of students thinks all sorts of people are dying.

But Ferris isn't dying. He's just lying, and it's the ninth time in the same semester.

A large part of this tedious film is devoted to the elaborate schemes writer-director Hughes dreams up to keep three kids out of school and on the lam.

Answering machines are fixed. A fake body run by strings attached to a doorknob rolls around in Ferris's bed to fool concerned and nosy parents. A sickbed message is recorded through a loudspeaker to answer the doorbell and deter inquisitive truant officers.

Some of this subterfuge is ingenious, but it soon wears thin.

While the kids are bulldozing their way into an expensive restaurant, catching a ball game at Wrigley Field, and staging their own musical production number from *Grease* in the middle of a mysterious parade (if it's a holiday, with floats and fife-and-drum corps and 10,000 extras, why does anyone need to play hooky from school in the first place?), the principal, determined to catch Ferris red-handed, slinks around like a CIA agent on secret maneuvers.

Ferris and his friends are like the Marx Brothers. The poor principal is Margaret Dumont. While the kids manage to fake out parents, teachers, and snooty headwaiters with the most preposterous antics, the principal gets chased, his car ticketed and towed away, his wallet lost, his clothes shredded by a vicious dog, and his dignity demolished.

Like all John Hughes movies, *Ferris Bueller's Day Off* has no more relation to real kids, living or dead, than the latest reports on nuclear waste relates to Eskimos. The kids are all eccentric, mischievous, and foul-mouthed. The adults are all gullible and stupid. Nobody over forty ever seems to be within shouting distance.

Matthew Broderick is too long in the tooth to play precocious teenage nerds, and it is a genuine shame to see a fine actor like Jeffrey Jones, trained in Shakespeare and electrifying as Emperor Joseph II in *Amadeus* reduced to the farcical buffoon status of Leon Erroll. As the harassed and tattered school principal reduced to mud-splattered hysterics, he looks as if he could kill somebody.

Ferris Bueller's Day Off is light-years ahead of its lousy predecessors *Sixteen Candles*, *The Breakfast Club*, and *Pretty in Pink*, but it is also light-years away from anything acceptable. If it has any virtue at all, it is that you can at least be thankful Molly Ringwald isn't in it.

FIREFOX (1982)

★ Directed and produced by Clint Eastwood. Screenplay by Alex Lasker and Wendell Wellman. With Clint Eastwood, Freddie Jones, David Huffman, Warren Clarke, Ronald Lacey, Kenneth Colley, and Stefan Schnabel.

It took years for me to join the Clint Eastwood Fan Club (see *White Hunter, Black Heart* and *Bird* reviews elsewhere in this book). My conversation began in 1990. I still don't think much of his early films, and

Firefox was certainly one of the worst.

In this one, Big Clint was clearly exhausted. It's not easy keeping all that macho goonery going full tilt when even tailored scripts no longer made any sense. In *Firefox* he plays a role even his fans won't believe. Are you ready for Clint Eastwood as a Jewish pilot who speaks Russian and has periodic epileptic seizures? If you are, then there's this film company called Warner Brothers you can pick up cheap with a VISA card. Anyway, this shell-shocked pilot is drafted by unidentified secret agents to steal a sophisticated MIG-31 aircraft from Russia and deliver it to NATO. The plane can do everything but make stroganoff. It is even equipped with an anti-radar device that is invisible, and can enable the pilot to zero in on a bomb target without even pressing a button, feeding info into a computer bank that bombs the city or continent below through brain waves in the pilot's flight helmet. The code name for this superstar missile is Firefox. That's about all you need to know. The plot never advances beyond outline stage, although the film that follows is interminable.

Practically the entire film is composed of expositional dialogue accompanied and illustrated by graphs, maps and charts. Clint Eastwood speaking Russian is so unintentionally hilarious that he sounds like one of the cavemen in *Quest for Fire* learning pig Latin.

The rest of the cast is mostly British, faking it incoherently with Russian accents. Get Eastwood attempting Russian with a flat, dead cowboy drawl and Shakespearean linguists mumbling English with tongue-swallowing Russian dialects, and subtitles are needed throughout. Not only is *Firefox* one of the most unintelligible conglomerates of gibberish ever made, but the dialogue is mostly spoken in pitch-black darkness, so you don't even have the added advantage of being able to read the lips. The result is one of the dullest spy movies ever made—and one of the least audible.

The last half hour ends up just another cockpit movie, with the Russians in hot pursuit of the stolen plane (more graphs, maps and charts) while Big Clint delivers a muttered dialogue beneath his breath to his control panel. If you cut out two hours and left only enough for a short subject, you wouldn't get enough footage to keep anyone awake. It's an outrage that any movie could be this bad.

It leaves you in a stupor, too groggy and anesthetized to react, the way you wake in the middle of the night in front of a TV test pattern.

FIRST BLOOD (1982)

½★ Directed by Ted Kotcheff. Screenplay by Michael Kozoll, William Sackheim, and Q. Moonblood. Produced by Buzz Feltshans. With Sylvester Stallone, Richard Crenna, Brian Dennehy, David Caruso.

Curdled hatred and hysterical vengeance are the result of ignorance, and never has the theme been more unnervingly pictured as in Sylvester Stallone's violent *First Blood*, the first of the *Rambo* pictures (the sequel was called *Rambo: First Blood Part II*).

Scruffy, unshaven, long-haired, and smelling like a used jockstrap, Stallone is a Vietnam veteran who drifts through the snow-capped grandeur of the great American Northwest, to a dumb hick town to visit a war buddy, who has died of cancer. Shaken by the discovery, he is on his way out of town when the local redneck sheriff (bullishly played with hateful meanness by Brian Dennehy) throws him in jail for vagrancy. When the local cops bully and beat him for no reason, the experience reminds Sly of his experiences in Nam. He freaks out, busts up the jail, and escapes on a motorcycle, with police cars, helicopters, and vicious Dobermans in hot pursuit. Protected only by the rugged terrain and aided only by crude survival skills picked up in the Army, Sly wages a one-man war against his hostile oppressors, accidentally killing one of them in self-defense.

It is some time before we discover via shortwave radio that he's a Green Beret highly skilled in guerrilla warfare, and a hero with a Congressional Medal of Honor. None of it matters to the sheriff, who has nothing but contempt for returning soldiers or anyone else who resists his local authority. And so we are treated to a nihilistic exercise in contemporary fascism, in which another innocent man is persecuted because he refuses to conform. The twist, of course, is that the deeper into the forest primeval the cops wander, the more helpless they become. Sly has seen the enemy, and it is the guy next door. The hunted becomes the hunter. The rest is all chases, explosions, car crashes, and gallons of blood spurting all over the camera as Sly wreaks havoc on the town for revenge.

None of this is very original; it's a mere variation on every macho script from *The Most Dangerous Game* to *Southern Comfort* with no new surprises. (The title is a war term referring to the side of the aggressor that shoots first in any armed dispute.)

The trouble with *First Blood* (aside from its nauseating carnage) is not that the premise is unbelievable (backwoods cops are probably as violent and incompetent on most local levels as they are depicted here) but that the cards are stacked on both sides of a no-win war with so many clichés.

The civilians are so stupid, gross, and inhuman. Stallone is such an innocent and noble hero. And Richard Crenna, as the Pentagon colonel who trained him, is so wise and philosophical. Finally, you begin to wonder if they haven't all seen the same John Wayne movies.

Still, it's a perfect movie for Stallone because it calls for lots of brawn and almost no dialogue. This is as it should be, for as likable and sincere as he is, when it gets around to acting the big final scene, you can't understand a word he says. As he throws himself into a kindly colonel's arms, crying like a baby, the tumultuous babble that pours forth sounds alarmingly like a stroke victim practicing his ABCs. Simply awful.

A FISH CALLED WANDA (1988)
★ ★ ★ ½ Directed by Charles Crichton. Screenplay by John Cleese. Produced by Michael Shamberg. *With Jamie Lee Curtis, Kevin Kline, John Cleese, and Michael Palin.*

A Fish Called Wanda is a screwball comedy with nothing on its mind but laughs, a throwback to *The Lavender Hill Mob*. In fact, the director is the same Charles Crichton. The writer and star is John Cleese, one of the zany Monty Python gang. The result will make you scream for mercy. Four hopeless misfits pull off a diamond robbery in London. The female member of the gang is an American gun moll named Wanda (Jamie Lee Curtis). The other Wanda is a fish owned by Cockney crook Michael Palin, a s-s-stooge who s-s-stutters. Then comes the double-cross: Wanda is in love with Otto (Kevin Kline), who pretends to be her brother. Wanda and Otto turn in the Cockney crook, who has hidden the key to the vault where the diamonds are hidden in Wanda's fish food. Wanda has to seduce the Cockney's lawyer, an uptight, inhibited clod. This is where John Cleese comes in. He's hysterical. He does a seduction scene in Italian, and even gets a nude scene.

These are the maddest crooks since that gang that couldn't shoot straight. Maddest of all is the versatile Kevin Kline, who is so stupid he thinks the Gettysburg Address is the place where Lincoln lived. The actors all have individual moments of comic brilliance. It's Monty Python Meets Charlie the Tuna.

THE FLAMINGO KID (1984)
★ ★ ½ Directed by Garry Marshall. Screenplay by Neal and Garry Marshall. Produced by Michael Phillips. With Matt Dillon, Hector Elizondo, Molly McCarthy, Richard Crenna, and Jessica Walter.

There's a gentle charm about this nostalgic look at the early sixties that's easy to take. Matt Dillon plays a Brooklyn teenager in 1963 who takes a summer job parking cars in a posh beach club, gets a taste of the good life, and learns a painful lesson in phony values. Garry Marshall's direction is solid, the support from such veterans as Richard Crenna and Jessica Walter is winning, and *The Flamingo Kid* turns out to be the first Matt Dillon movie that does not require subtitles.

FLASH GORDON (1980)
½★ Directed by Mike Hodges. Screenplay by Lorenzo Semple, Jr. Produced by Dino De Laurentiis. With Sam J. Jones, Melody Anderson, Topol, Max von Sydow, Ornella Muti, Timothy Dalton, Brian Blessed, and Mariangela Melato.

Flash Gordon is idiotic swill designed to appeal to the folks who lined up for *Superman* and *Star Wars*. But those movies proved how entertaining comic book fantasies can be in the hands of artists with skill, talent and imagination. *Flash Gordon* just proves how dumb and trashy this genre can be in the hands of fools and hacks. *Superman* appealed to the fantasy level in all of us. *Flash Gordon* is 42nd Street flotsam, designed for freaks and low IQs.

"Hi, my name's Flash!" says the quarterback for the New York Jets to his new girlfriend Dale, a dim-witted travel agent who does somersaults in outer space. Inexplicably, they get locked up in the rocket ship of a nutty scientist named Dr. Hans Zarkov, who yells, "We'll go up and counterattack them!" when he gets pelted with moon rocks. "Them" are the decadent denizens of a distant planet ruled by the evil Emperor Ming (Max von Sydow, from the Ingmar Bergman films). He takes one look at Dale and starts to drool while making preparations for her virgin sacrifice.

Fortunately for Flash, who looks like a lifeguard at the Beverly Hills Hotel, the demented Ming has a nymphomaniac daughter who takes one look at his peroxided head and black chest hairs and decides she'd like to see more. "I like you a lot!" she purrs as Flash slips out of leather hot pants left over from the costume budget of a gay porno flick. Don't underestimate Ming. He's so slimy he'd even torture his own daughter. "Bring me the bore worms!" he orders, while the nymphet writhes in agony. "Oh, no!" screams the princess in the best Maria Montez tradition, "Not the bore worms!"

But the sadomasochism is just beginning. As Flash is being bullwhipped on a revolving LP with sharp spikes in the floor, Dale coos, "I love you, Flash, but we've only got fourteen hours to save the earth!" Somehow Flash survives swamp creatures, quicksand, zap guns, X-ray rifles, flying soldiers from The Wizard of Oz, and other unspeakable tortures to save the day in his jet-propelled dune buggy while the audience moans with disbelief.

Sam J. Jones, who sort of wrestles with the role of Flash Gordon like a Malibu surfer attacking a giant octopus, has hair like garden mulch. They bleached it to weeds but forgot the roots. Melody Anderson, as Dale Arden, sounds like a Barbie doll gone berserk.

Hopeless as they are, in and out of their clothes, they haven't been helped much by the tacky sets, fake rear-screen projection, cornball disco music by a rock group called Queen, or amateurish chroma-key visuals that give them blue lines around their heads like old Godzilla movies made on the cheap in Japan. The intergalactic cities look like rooms full of Jell-O molds drenched in Day-Glo glitter. Five minutes of all that orange, pink, and chartreuse has a psychedelic effect that should make Flash Gordon a big winner with dope fiends. But after a few minutes your eyes begin to water, your ears begin to melt, and you feel like you just might throw up.

Sad to see Max von Sydow, Topol, and that wonderful Italian actress Mariangela Melato mixed up in this nauseating bilge, along with hordes of Playboy bunnies, hawk men, moon girls, and unemployed circus dwarfs. Just proves, I guess, that people will do anything for money.

FLETCH (1985)
½★ Directed by Michael
Ritchie. Screenplay by Andrew
Bergman, based on the novel by
George McDonald. Produced by
Alan Greisman and Peter Douglas.
With Chevy Chase, Joe Don Baker,
Dana Wheeler-Nicholson, Richard
Libertini, Tim Matheson, M. Emmet
Walsh, George Wendt, Kenneth
Mars, and Geena Davis.

Fletch is the kind of sophomoric sludge Jerry Lewis used
to turn out in his sleep. Here we
have Chevy Chase instead. The
improvement is hardly noticeable.

Chevy Chase is a star. Not
much of a star, but the kind who
still gets dumb movies fi-
nanced.

In *Fletch* he plays an investigative reporter for a Los
Angeles newspaper who uses a
series of undercover disguises
to get his stories. It's a conceit
that provides him with enough
costume changes and enough
comic situations to move the invisible plot from one skit to the
next without much interference
from the script.

The result is a scissors-and-
glue job that seems to have been
made up on the set.

Disguised as a doctor, Chevy
is forced to remove a patient's
spleen. Posing as a hippie guru,
he roller skates on the beach.
Running from the cops, he dons

a waiter's uniform, invades a
convention banquet, grabs the
speaker's mike, and leads the
congregation—and the pursuing cops—in a chorus of "The
Star Spangled Banner."

He wears novelty teeth, seer-
sucker suits, and baseball caps.
He calls himself Don Corleone,
Gordon Liddy, and Igor Stra-
vinsky. These are the jokes, but
the comedy is so benign it
would make the Three Stooges
yawn.

It is impossible to believe the
director is the same Michael
Ritchie who once brought such
a sardonic touch to *The Candidate* and *Smile*. There isn't a
shred of wit within three thousand miles of *Fletch*.

Maybe it's not the director's
fault. Who could direct dialogue like the poker-faced
drivel in Andrew Bergman's
screenplay? A girl opens the
door in a towel. Chase says,
"Could I borrow your towel?
My car just hit a water buffalo!" Is that a laugh riot, or
what?

Another character throws up
his hands and yells: "Jesus H.
Christ on a popsicle stick!" Do
people actually get paid to write
this kind of stuff out in La-La
Land? Or do they just phone it
in from the nearest Taco Bell?

It takes a special kind of desperation to speak like this, and

Chevy Chase meets all the requirements. Whether he's trading insults with a brutal chief of police (Joe Don Baker), seducing the bubble-headed wife (Dana Wheeler-Nicholson) of a murderous, dope-dealing bigamist (Tim Matheson), or just standing in the middle of the screen grinning stupidly at his own profile, Chevy Chase is always the same.

He's such a boring actor he doesn't have the flair or energy to bring any of the disjointed sketches in *Fletch* to life. Whatever the emotion, he delivers it with numbing similarity—sardonic and smug.

Fletch was rumored to contain wisecracks galore. It isn't wise, and all you see are the cracks.

THE FLY (1986)

★ Directed by David Cronenberg. Screenplay by Charles Edward Pogue and David Cronenberg, from the story by George Langelaan. Produced by Stuart Cornfeld. With Jeff Goldblum, Geena Davis, John Getz, Joy Boushel, Les Carlson, and George Chuvalo.

There is nothing wrong with *The Fly* that a gigantic, five-hundred-pound fly swatter can't cure.

This sick, unnecessary remake of the campy 1958 cult classic with Vincent Price is the goofy story of a scientist who accidently switches heads with a pesky housefly and is doomed to spend the rest of his days flitting from sugar bowl to toilet bowl, yelping "Help me!" You know the rest. The original still pops up on late-night creature features on TV.

What you don't know is the maniacal, shlocky way Canada's freaky B-movie director David Cronenberg has brought the story up to date.

This version has sex, nudity, home computers, laser beams, and slimy effects borrowed from *Aliens* to gross you out. It's not as genuinely terrifying as *Aliens* since it's really a movie about Day-Glo makeup. In fact, it's pretty funny.

The fly is played by Jeff Goldblum, a bug-eyed actor who looks like an insect already. Some might call this perfect casting.

Trouble is, Goldblum looks more like a fly *before* his experiment goes awry. Covered with spores and hives, flitting across the room and landing on the walls while vomiting white hydrochloric acid from his mandibles, he doesn't much look like a human fly. He looks like a melted peanut-butter cup.

The first forty minutes of *The Fly* is science fiction small talk about teleportation, laser transfers, and molecular fusion. This is strictly formula Frankenstein lab filler, created to pass time until the really disgusting stuff happens.

Finally the mad doctor enters his homemade teleport pod that looks like a psychedelic phone booth, and pulls the switch, not realizing there's a fly in there with him.

Goldblum attacks the sugar. Coarse hair grows on his back. The strength of an army buzzes through his wings. He looks bad. He smells bad. His ears fall off. He drips ooze all over the kitchen sink. Always a joker, he says: "I've been mated with a fly and we haven't even been introduced!"

Is this scary? Or just plain laughable? *The Fly* is supposed to be a horror flick about metamorphosis, but it turns out silly and, eventually, just plain revolting. The people around me were giggling uncontrollably in all the wrong places and covering their eyes at the same time.

In the 1958 original, there was something oddly moving about the plight of a man doomed to watch his wife ignore him in her flower garden. Goldblum doesn't diminish in size; he turns into a hoary monster like a mutation who knows the heartbreak of psoriasis.

And he tries to take his girlfriend with him. As a sickening subplot, there's Geena Davis, as a reporter impregnated by fly sperm.

This is all quite grim, with much vomiting, bleeding, and carrying on in the process. But frankly, I've had worse scares from the bugs at backyard barbecues.

The Fly is guaranteed to nauseate kids of all ages. Quick, Mom, grab the insect repellent.

FOOTLOOSE (1984)
★ ★ ★ Directed by Herbert Ross. Screenplay by Dean Pitchford. Produced by Lewis J. Rachmil and Craig Zadan. With Kevin Bacon, Lori Singer, John Lithgow, Dianne Wiest, John Laughlin, and Christopher Penn.

The best things in life are seldom free, but the best things in the movies are often the most unexpected. Being told that something with as unappealing a title as *Footloose* was about kids, rock music, and flashdancing, I dreaded it like root canal. Narrowminded and patronizing, I went to *Footloose* in the line of duty, ready for pain. Today I'm gorging myself on humble pie, and the taste isn't bad at all.

Footloose, to my everlasting

amazement, is a film of such spirit, optimism, and human values that it sent me dancing down the street, the way old Fred Astaire musicals used to do.

It is the first musical about youth, dancing, and rock music that is exciting, contemporary, and clean-cut all at the same time. It leaps. It soars. It never falters. It's a real movie musical that breaks new ground while honoring the artistry and time-tested traditions of movie musicals in their salad days. I think much of the credit for making *Footloose* crisper, fresher, and more entertaining than its basic material warrants must go to its director, Herbert Ross.

Think of it as a hip moral fable. Certainly there is something not quite literal about the midwestern hick town that serves as its setting. In this repressed Bible Belt backwash of town meetings and toll house cookies, the local kids are miserable. Dancing is against the law. There hasn't even been a school prom for the past five years. This is Jerry Falwell country, and the local preacher rants against the pestilence of crime, immorality, and rock and roll.

Suddenly there's a new kid in town. Ren (Kevin Bacon) brings from Chicago a big-city knowledge of discos, astro-music, strobe lights, and the newest tapes by groups like Police and Men at Work. Ren shakes up the preacher, the school, the cops, and especially the preacher's bored, rebellious daughter, Ariel (Lori Singer). Harassed and blamed for everything, he lets off steam by dancing.

It isn't long before the whole school dances with him, and by the time Ren stands courageously alone before the preacher and the town council to plead for the right to have a school dance, I doubt if there will be a member of the audience who isn't cheering him on.

In a touching revelation of his belief that dancing celebrates life, Ren even finds a biblical passage from Ecclesiastes to prove his point. From this scene on, the movie isn't quite sure what to do with itself, so it just explodes in a frenzy of pyrotechnic dancing, ending the fable with more innocence than coherence.

Who's quarreling? A movie this entertaining has a right to be naive. Herbert Ross knows what he's doing. He's the only director left in Hollywood who really knows how to make a musical. He runs old dance numbers in his head. He knows choreography and how to photograph it. That's why *Foot-loose* has an energy that is unique.

Ross gives the material a tone and beat that goes beyond the music. Instead of *Flashdance* it reminds me more of an MTV version of *Good News*. The best dance sequence in the movie, when Ren is teaching his awkward but good-hearted friend Willard how to dance, is like the "Be a Ladies Man" number in *Good News* when Peter Lawford taught his pals how to be campus lotharios.

And the scenes of the kids decorating a dirty old flour mill for their prom, then adjusting their bowties and party dresses—as well as the final great let-'er-rip dance number—is all reminiscent of the "Varsity Drag" finale in *Good News*. The music is today, but the artistry is not improvised.

The actors are superb. Kevin Bacon as Ren is a smashingly creative, charming, and magnetic actor with an enormous range. As Ariel, Lori Singer is lovely to look at and completely believable.

There are wonderful contributions from John Lithgow as the strict but inherently decent preacher and Dianne Wiest, who radiates an inner wisdom and sweetness as the compassionate wife of a man of God—

loyal and supportive but able to see both sides of the issues.

Beautifully photographed, with a real feel for atmosphere and detail, *Footloose* has a genuine regard for the intelligence of teenagers instead of degrading them with the usual sick and one-dimensional clichés we've been getting from Hollywood lately. It kicks up its heels and howls at the moon with a joyful noise, and the happiness is contagious.

FOR THE BOYS (1991)

★ ★ ★ ★   Directed by Mark Rydell. Screenplay by Marshall Brickman, Neal Jimenez and Lindy Laub. Produced by Bette Midler, Bonnie Bruckheimer, and Margaret South. *With Bette Midler, James Caan, George Segal, Patrick O'Neal, Christopher Rydell, Rosemary Murphy, Norman Fell, Bud Yorkin, Dori Brenner, and Melissa Manchester.*

Bette Midler has skinned her pretty kneecaps in some of her movies, but she's on solid ground again in *For the Boys*. That's solid as in a jive beat with a reet pleat, because it describes not only Bette's dazzling performance but a lot of the music, too. She is Dixie Leonard, a singing comedienne of legendary stature who has survived three wars, devastating personal losses, and a cornerstone in the history of early television, and *For the Boys* is the glittering, heartrending saga of a career that spans half a century. It is also the story of her partner, Eddie Sparks (played to the hilt by James Caan), who fought with her, fist to schnozz, every step of the way. This is a show business saga as gripping and spectacular as any splashy MGM biopic, but with a fat heart, a witty, intelligent script, exemplary production values, and a refreshing reluctance to slide into we've-been-here-before clichés.

From the first few bars of a big-band Dave Grusin arrangement of the great Johnny Mercer evergreen "I Remember You" (which serves as Eddie Sparks's theme song throughout the movie), we're off and running. A limo is dispatched to transport the aging Dixie Leonard to a TV special in her honor where she will be presented with the National Medal of the Arts (something like the Kennedy Center honors) by none other than the President of the United States. Covered with wrinkles and liver spots, Bette looks like an old Shirley Booth, but is probably not as nice and decidedly more vulgar. Explaining to the coltish young production assistant why she will never appear on the same

stage with Eddie Sparks, her story cuts to 1942 when her career began on a USO tour in World War II. She was a chick singer with a wacky sense of humor, married to a combat photographer stationed in North Africa, and the mother of a four-year-old son, and Sparks was already a big star and America's premiere singing, dancing funny man. It's hate at first sight, but even in a blackout she's such a smash hit singing "P.S. I Love You" that the boys in uniform catapult her to stardom. Eddie's fatuous offstage ego and Dixie's dirty mouth and undeniable talent trigger a series of personality collisions that span five decades, while they become the biggest thing since Hope and Crosby, playing airfields, camps, and hospitals from Piccadilly to the Sahara.

Radio gives way to television and by the 1950s they're still trading insults in every living room in America while the widowed Dixie goes through the growing pains of her kid, whom Eddie spoils with poker games and sex education while Dixie's uncle and head writer (George Segal) gets fired for his left-wing politics. Sixteen years after that blowup, they've been through the cold war in Korea, and Dixie swallows her pride with a Valium to team up one more time for Vietnam. Through the years, Dixie and Eddie experience private heartbreak and tragedy while the world cheers them publicly and a story emerges of love and loss and change. By the time Dixie relents one last time for today's celebration of "one of the legendary comedy teams in show business history," *For the Boys* has become a testament to the invincibility of the human spirit. If you're not crying and cheering and feeling invincible yourself by the time the orchestra plays "I'll Remember You" in the glorious finale to this buoyant film, you'd better get your pulse checked.

Directed by Mark Rydell, *For the Boys* gives each decade a distinct look and feel, from the romantic nostalgia of the 1940s to the ugly, depressing realities of Vietnam. The actors change with the periods, which give Ms. Midler a wide range of costumes and vocal styles to show off. As good as she is in the early big band jitterbug stuff, with her snoods and wedgies, she is equally effective in battle fatigues singing a tearful John Lennon song in Nam on Christmas Day, 1969. Mr. Caan matches her every step of the way with mischievous humor and self-serving

cornball grandiloquence. Both stars get chewy roles.

Nobody goes away hungry. From the songs to the combat scenes to the laughter and tears of soldiers under fire, there is something memorable going on in every frame of this epic musical, yet it mixes basic human emotions with world-class entertainment. There's only one word for so much value and the word is fabulous. *For the Boys* is for the boys, the girls, and everyone else with a heartbeat.

FORT APACHE, THE BRONX (1981)

★ ★ ★ **Directed by Dan Petrie. Screenplay by Heywood Gould. Produced by Martin Richards and Tom Fiorello. With Paul Newman, Ken Wahl, Edward Asner, Danny Aiello, Rachel Ticotin, Pam Grier, and Kathleen Beller.**

If your brain has been starved for a two-fisted police drama in the Humphrey Bogart–George Raft tradition, Paul Newman delivers one in *Fort Apache, the Bronx*. This is the real forty-first precinct in New York City, the toughest beat in town. It's nicknamed Fort Apache because it stands in the middle of that burned-out jungle, the South Bronx, and it's like an armed fort in the middle of a territory full of savages.

This forty-block radius has

the highest crime rate, the worst number of corrupt cops "on the take," the biggest list of disability claims from cops injured on the job, and the largest number of men out on sick leave at any given time on the city payrolls.

No wonder. Nobody wants to go to work at Fort Apache. The brave cops who do get through it alive have to deal with junkies, child abuse, muggings, rapes, street prostitution, vandalism, riots, and other horrors most New Yorkers don't even dream about in nightmares.

Rookie cops are slaughtered in their own squad cars, men in uniform are walking targets for hoods and lunatics, and it's open season on cops at all hours of the day and night. Nobody goes into the battleground without a gun, but as Newman says: "It don't matter how many guns you got—you still only got two hands."

Newman plays that rare bird you hear and read about in sentimental paperbacks—the honest cop. He's from three generations of Irish cops named Murphy. He's dedicated eighteen years to the job, delivered seventeen babies on the beat, and learned to take the poor pay, low prestige and public contempt as part of the breaks.

But he also has compassion for the poverty-stricken inhabitants of this sewer who are tired of being victims of their own environment.

When he sees a fellow cop throw an innocent Puerto Rican kid to his death from the top of a building, he has to wrestle with his own conscience. Should he turn stool pigeon and stop the police brutality and corruption on the force, or let it pass the way the other cops do? Then his own girlfriend, a nurse at the local hospital, dies of a heroin overdose, and he finally cracks. For the first time, he must face his own moral ethics and his own value as a human being. The rest of this galvanizing movie shows what happens when Newman decides to fight injustice his own way, turn his back on the precinct, and clean up Fort Apache. But once a cop, always a cop, and there's a surprise ending that will leave everybody cheering.

This action-packed thriller grabs you by the throat and doesn't let go. The daily routine on Newman's gruesome beat is so realistically detailed by director Dan Petrie that *Fort Apache, the Bronx* sometimes has the quality of a social documentary. To show the urban blight known as the South

Bronx, the movie has been filmed not on Hollywood sets but in the dangerous streets, alleys, garbage, and burned-out buildings that make the real place look like a bombed-out ruin in World War II. The precinct is real, not the figment of the screenwriter's imagination.

The harrowing events are based on the true adventures of former cops Tom Mulhearn and Pete Tessitore, who spent years in the battle zone. The cop jargon, masterfully written by Heywood Gould, is accurate. The conditions are shocking. *Fort Apache, the Bronx* delivers a kidney punch you won't forget, and does it with integrity and intelligence.

It also provides Paul Newman with a meatier role than usual. Crashing through the camera lens as the Newman everybody loves—the Newman from *Hud* and *Cool Hand Luke*—he's rough as cowhide on the outside, but gentle as a soft-boiled egg. Rugged. Sensitive. Funny. Explosive. And Edward Asner is perfect as his foil—the solid, sour-faced precinct captain who takes over Fort Apache and tries to go by the book to straighten out the mess it's in.

There are other splendid performances, too, by Ken Wahl,

as Newman's happy-go-lucky partner who uses humor to ease the tensions of his job; by Danny Aiello, as a crooked cop; and by Pam Grier, who sheds her usual sexy image to play a drug-crazed prostitute who carries a razor blade in her teeth to slash her customers' throats.

The movie does not, of course, tell the whole story of life in the South Bronx. It gives the impression that the place has burned itself off the map of the civilized world, and there isn't one shot of a normal family sending its kids to school or a working mother buying groceries or concerned citizens trying to make a better life for their community.

In defense of the infuriated citizens of the South Bronx who resented the black eye this movie gives their neighborhood, I do agree that I find it odd that the movie was made by people whose only previous exposure to the place has been from the window of a limousine on its way to Kennedy Airport.

Still, it is a powerful, breathlessly exciting look at big city cops, the rotten job they have to do, the people they're sworn to protect, and the lawbreakers on both sides. As a movie, it's a knockout, taut and credible.

FOR YOUR EYES ONLY (1984)
★ ½ Directed by John Glen.
Screenplay by Richard Maibaum
and Michael Wilson. Produced by
Albert R. Broccoli. *With Roger
Moore, Carole Bouquet, Topol,
Julian Glover, Cassandra Harris,
Desmond Llewellyn and Janet
Brown.*

Roger Moore, back again for
another James Bond autopsy,
seems exhausted, distracted, a
visitor on the set in a hurry to
get the whole thing over with.
The army of 007 stuntmen and
stand-ins does the work while
Moore makes dull appearances
behind the wheels of cars, grinning at his dumb dialogue, and
trying not to yawn.

This is the worst Bond movie
ever made and Moore seems to
know it better than anybody.

For Your Eyes Only presents
new perils, new gadgets, the
latest assortment of guns, explosives, cars marked for demolition and an endless
assortment of cartoon cuties (as
scantily clad as possible but
never naked—the title *For
Your Eyes Only* must apply to
the censor).

But we've seen it all before,
so we know we're not missing
anything. This movie is so ob-
tuse and so glued together from
old egg crates and chewing gum
wrappers that I couldn't even
locate the plot. Something

about a transmitter, lost in a
shipwreck, that guides nuclear
missiles by computer which
Bond must retrieve for England
before it falls into the hands of
the Russians. Does anybody
care?

Dangling from a mountain of
solid rock, cracking up cars in
quaint rural villages, hanging
on to the wing of a plane in
midair, or being dragged
through shark-infested waters
as fish bait, the stuntmen earn
their salaries, while Moore
gives everybody his amused
look or his perplexed look or
his "Let's-break-for-tea" look.
The big fight scenes and the underwater escapes with the oxygen hose in shreds look faked
and ordinary.

There's no suspense, no tension, no surprise. Worst of all,
there's no attempt to beef up the
007 character to anything beyond cardboard. He doesn't
even have fun in bed. The
women are around for decora-
tion, and Bond doesn't seem to
notice them. The game is up,
the series has run out of steam,
and it's time to throw in the
towel. Roger Moore must have
agreed, because four years later,
after more than a decade of
playing 007, that's exactly what
he did.

48 HOURS (1982)

★ ★ ★   Directed by Walter Hill.
Screenplay by Roger
Spottiswoode, Walter Hill, Larry
Gross, and Steven E. de Souza.
Produced by Lawrence Gordon
and Joel Silver. With Nick Nolte,
Eddie Murphy, James Remar,
Sonny Landham, and Annette
O'Toole.

48 Hours is a Clint Eastwood
movie without Clint Eastwood.
Instead, it's got Nick Nolte,
looking puffy and out of shape,
as a bedraggled, two-fisted cop
on the trail of two mad-dog killers terrorizing San Francisco.
So far, so bad.

But *48 Hours* also has Eddie
Murphy as a horny, wise-
cracking convict from San
Quentin who teams up with the
cop as his reluctant partner because Nolte thinks Murphy
knows how to find the killers.
The authorities give this odd
couple forty-eight hours to find
the hoods before Murphy has to
go back to the slammer. They
hate each other, but they need
each other—and hereby hangs
what little tale there is.

Meanwhile, *48 Hours* takes
you on a sleazy, breezy tour of
San Francisco, something you
won't get at American Express.

The action is relentless, with
much fashionably filthy macho
dialogue, a lot of electric energy, some rather nasty violence, a few typical women
who get brutalized and left behind in tears, and some fast-
paced smashups in the usual assortment of moving vehicles
that are standard equipment for
San Francisco cop movies.

It adds up to a breathless
tempo that never gives anyone
time to nap on the job, but attempting to achieve flash and
speed, director Walter Hill
leaves little room for nuance.

Nolte learns something about
the underworld he's been fighting from his association with
the black convict; Murphy
learns about the cop mentality
he's always hated by posing as
one. Both get an insider's point
of view of an outsider's world,
and this is the irony we're expected to marvel at. I was too
busy enjoying the humorous elegance with which Eddie Murphy managed to steal the whole
movie in his film debut. There's
a terrific scene in which Murphy takes on hostile redneck
cowboys in a hillbilly bar and
knocks heads together with the
security of the cop's badge for
protection that is a triumph of
comic social revenge.

48 Hours wouldn't have been
half as entertaining or exuberant with Clint.

FOUR FRIENDS (1981)

★ ★ ½ Directed by Arthur Penn. Screenplay by Steven Tesich. Produced by Penn and Gene Lasko. *With Craig Wasson, Jodi Thelen, Jim Metzler, and Michael Huddleston.*

Arthur Penn's quirky, neurotic films are never easy to like, but they are often so polished and so personal that they aren't easy to ignore, either.

He's a hard director to "Penn down" because his films are always so different. One of his biggest flops, *Mickey One*, was one of my favorite movies. One of his biggest successes, *Bonnie and Clyde* took years to grow on me. Two of his other biggest flops, *The Chase* and *The Missouri Breaks*, remain among my least favorite lacerating memories of all time.

What an odd career. Except for *The Miracle Worker* I don't think he's ever made a film everybody agreed on. *Four Friends* has been called both "a disaster" and "one of the year's best." My own rather qualified and somewhat bewildered reaction lies somewhere in between.

Four Friends is the complex story of a Yugoslavian immigrant growing up in East Chicago, an industrial annex of Gary, Indiana, and is based largely on the autobiographical experiences of its author, Steve Tesich, who won an Oscar for his fine film script for *Breaking Away*. Like Danilo Prozor, the idealistic young protagonist of *Four Friends* (played with bruised, optimistic decency by Craig Wasson), Tesich has always been an outsider obsessed with finding the real America and defining what it means.

The film is hugely personal as it follows Danilo through Roosevelt High School to college and five years beyond graduation. The results are sometimes absurd and often corny and melodramatic, but the vision this film telegraphs of what it was like to be young, hopeful, and betrayed by a dream in the turbulent 1960's is unique and riveting.

Since Danilo's refugee parents are already disillusioned and beyond saving, he quickly learns to transfer his need for a molecular family unit to his three best friends: David, a fat Jewish boy whose destiny is to inherit his family's mortuary business; Tom, a good-natured clunk who goes to war; and a silly voluptuary named Georgia who thinks she's possessed by the soul of Isadora Duncan.

America is seen first as a beach blanket bingo movie, as Penn lovingly recreates the sock hops in the gym, the beer parties at the beach, and the bubble-gum rock of the fifties. Later, it turns into a surreal nightmare as Danilo lives through the Kennedy assassination, the civil rights chaos, the hippie movement, and marriage to a rich society debutante with a murderous father (brilliantly played with menacing madness by novelist James Leo Herlihy).

In the end, Danilo is still searching for America, the land of milk and honey that has always eluded him. He hasn't matured, he hasn't learned anything, he's still moon-faced and starry-eyed over the once-exotic, now-battered Georgia.

I no longer cared how it all turned out. I was exhausted waiting for him to grow up. (Things are not helped by the miscasting of Jodi Thelen, an annoying and very mannered actress who never comes close to suggesting what Georgia's allure is all about.) *Four Friends* fails because its audience outgrows its "coming of age" innocence before the movie does. When Danilo lives through so much and gets reduced to drooling dopiness by the sight of Georgia dancing madly under the spray of a New York fire hydrant, I just groaned, "Not *her* again!"

Maybe you have to be one of the immigrants in Jan Troell's *The New Land* or Elia Kazan's *America, America* to fully relate to the pain and disillusionment Danilo goes through. It is the outsiders who have suffered the biggest setbacks in their search for roots. Now it is the outsiders who are making movies about their experiences. *Four Friends* is an interesting, sincere work, but you are likely to go away feeling distanced by its oddness instead of feeling moved by its not believable "golly gee" naïveté.

FRANCES (1982)
★ ★ ½ Directed by Graeme Clifford. Screenplay by Eric Bergren, Christopher Devore, and Nicholas Kazan. Produced by Jonathan Sanger. With Jessica Lange, Sam Shepard, Kim Stanley, and Bart Burns.

As true Hollywood horror stories go, none is more lurid or harrowing than the one about Frances Farmer. This is the one they tried to hush up, the one they still find too depressing and embarrassing to talk about.

Small wonder. A lot of corpses have littered the paths to Forest Lawn since Frances was a star, but she was the original victim who paved the way for Marilyn Monroe, Montgomery Clift, Jean Seberg, and dozens of others who tried to fight the system and got smashed for their rebellion.

Frances tries to chart the meteoric rise and catastrophic fall of the film star who suffered more atrocities in her short, unhappy life than most people dream about in nightmares.

It isn't half as electrifying as *Will There Really be a Morning?*, the autobiography published shortly after her death in 1970, or *Shadowland*, the in-depth reportage by William Arnold that revealed some shocking aspects of her case even Frances didn't know about.

If you want to know the real story, read those two books. If you want the condensed version, see the sincere but undeniably glossy movie Hollywood has made from some of the facts, leaving out others, erasing whole episodes, and generally making a mess of things.

If you know nothing about Frances Farmer, if you've got her confused with the woman who wrote cookbooks and packaged chocolates, then don't miss *Frances*. It features some great acting and manages to impose enough of the incredible story on your nervous system to leave you outraged, stunned, and deeply moved. *Frances* works in spite of itself.

The movie begins when Frances, a golden-haired Seattle sixteen-year-old, wins a prize for writing a passionate essay on the death of God. She was feisty, gorgeous, and smart as blazes, but her mother, Lillian Farmer, was a publicity-seeking anti-Communist crackpot and frustrated nobody who grabbed newspaper space by throwing herself on the ground in hysterics at a railroad station and labeling her daughter an atheist and a "pinko sacrifice."

Poor Frances never had a chance. With her crazy, hatchet-faced mother fanning the flames, Frances made enemies everywhere she turned. When Paramount signed her up for stardom, she alienated the press, the moguls, the fans, and especially Louella Parsons, who did her level best to destroy the independent young starlet. Frances wore pants, smoked cigars, drove a jalopy, cursed like a sailor, and turned up her pretty nose at the superficiality of big box office.

After Hollywood stardom at twenty-three; Broadway stardom in *Golden Boy* at twenty-five; the love affair with Clifford Odets, who used her to make himself famous, then kicked her out of his life; punishment by the studio moguls;

self-punishment with alcohol and amphetamines; railroaded sanity hearings; and incarceration for years in hellhole asylums, subject to electroshock therapy, vats of ice, rats, gang rapes—after all that and a climactic ice pick lobotomy forced upon her by a maniac doctor, it ends with Frances Farmer discharged from this chamber of horrors in 1950 as a glassy-eyed zombie. She died of throat cancer twenty years later, a broken and forgotten symbol of Hollywood's past.

The film is chronological; the threads of her scattered life are held together by a fictional narrator (a corny device) played by Sam Shepard. Much of the nastiness is here, but there are too many directorial conceits that get in the way of the action.

When Frances is freed from the asylum, there's a quick cut to a dream fantasy showing a younger, healthier Frances coming out of a refreshing swimming pool in slow motion. When the head shrink at the first sanitorium refuses to release her although she has never been proved insane, he crushes the shavings from his pencil into a box and slams the lid down tight. The metaphor is almost laughable.

Graeme Clifford, an Austra-lian editor making his directorial debut, is too inexperienced to tackle such a labyrinthian project. He fails to distill the script's confusing components into a cohesive film with any real style. Also, for a story so full of ugliness and violence, *Frances* has a curiously lush texture, as if photographed through hollandaise sauce.

Still, *Frances* is worth seeing—above all else, for the scalding performances by Jessica Lange, whose Frances can only be described as miraculous, and by Kim Stanley, who tells us more about Frances's gargoyle of a mother with one stony silence than anything in the script. Together, they are hypnotic, possessed by ghosts.

Lange offers so much more than the portrait of a lovely martyr; she ferrets out the paradox Frances was in a brilliant, intricately polished piece of work full of irony, pain, and energy.

Kim Stanley, as everyone knows, is simply one of the most distinguished actresses of this era. Twenty years ago she would have been playing Frances herself. Now she uses her bulk and her ravaged, time-scarred face to bring out the sourness at the core of a mother who so desperately wanted to live in the spillover from her daughter's spotlight that she was even willing to sacrifice her to the fires of hell when her own dreams were rejected. There is greatness in Stanley's performance, even if there was no greatness in the miserable monster she plays. It's a hair-raising fireworks display of skill and craft.

So the movie shows what happened, not why. Read the books for the sordid facts. But see the movie for a fascinating final "compromise" in the life of a dream girl who learned the meaning of the word the hard way.

FRANTIC (1988)

★ ★ ★ ½ Directed by Roman Polanski. Screenplay by Polanski and Gerard Brach. Produced by Thom Mount and Tim Hampton. *With Harrison Ford, Betty Buckley, John Mahoney, and Emmanuelle Seigner.*

Roman Polanski's nail-biting suspense thriller is a gem. Instead of cheap chills, it concentrates on the growing anxiety and frustration of ordinary people caught up in a web of harrowing intrigue over which they have no control, gripping the viewer in a vise of mounting terror. Harrison Ford, as the square American cardiologist whose wife disappears in Paris during a medical convention, is the perfect Hitchcockian hero —cool, tough, uncomplicated, but finally driven berserk by circumstances. He's Gary Cooper in torn britches. The great thing about *Frantic* is the way it takes such a calm approach to the maddening events that drive a sane person to rage—and even murder. We never know more than Ford does at any moment, so while he solves the mystery, we're solving it with him. This movie shows every raw and tense moment he goes through as he's driven frantic. It's real. It's sensible. It builds with breathless intensity. It's Polanski's best film since *Chinatown.*

THE FRENCH LIEUTENANT'S WOMAN (1981)

★ ★ Directed by Karel Reisz. Screenplay by Harold Pinter, based on the novel by John Fowles. Produced by Leon Clore. *With Meryl Streep, Jeremy Irons, Hilton McRae, Emily Morgan, Charlotte Mitchell, and Lynsey Baxter.*

Critics go ape over Meryl Streep, and I wish I knew what all the fuss was about. When *Time* magazine calls her "America's greatest actress," it's enough to send any rational person scurrying to the dictionary to see what Mr. Webster has to say about "oversell" and "overkill." The American public, of course, has gotten used to her subsequent films and accents, but her first starring role on film, in *The French Lieutenant's Woman*, doesn't display much of the alleged magic she's reportedly superendowed with. The box-office coffers were not rewarded by this odd, pretentious film adaptation of the John Fowles bestseller.

Fowles used words like *haunting*, *irresistible* and *alluring* to describe his Victorian heroine, the mysterious Sarah Woodruff. Reading about her, standing erect on the raw, rugged British coast while the cruel waves lashed the rocks of the claw-shaped pier beneath her feet as she stared into the bleak Atlantic waiting for the return of the French lieutenant who destroyed her reputation and then deserted her to a life of shame, I saw Vivien Leigh or Gene Tierney in the role. Meryl Streep is more like a Vassar student researching a paper on marine life at the time of *Moby Dick*. Gazing out to sea, she could be looking for a whale. Bony and angular, with milky

skin and enormous, awkward hands and feet, she doesn't exactly light up the screen with charisma. She has the kind of self-aware craftsmanship you learn in acting school, but she doesn't seem to have much humor, and there isn't a shred of what Ann Sheridan used to call "oomph."

Sarah is described in the novel as moody, ambiguous, a total enigma of a woman who drove the respectable young aristocrat Charles Smithson mad with lust. Wouldn't you think a woman thus capable of reducing a man of station in the snobbish Victorian era to the status of an outlaw should be played by an actress with sex appeal? Streep is not only drab to look at, she also seems depressed and exhausted. She's too icy for my taste—a Grace Kelly sculpted by Baskin-Robbins. Scratch her and you get club soda.

The film itself is only slightly more appealing. Karel Reisz and his cameras have invaded the windswept coastal village of Lyme Regis and converted Fowles's actual locations into a visually stunning evocation of 1867. The film has a prosaic elegance that extends from its flourishing period costumes to its authentically researched antique furniture. But Harold Pinter's script only manages to confuse things to the point where a simple love story turns into an elliptical literary pretension.

Fowles wrote two endings to the book. Pinter solves that technical snafu by telling two stories simultaneously. On one hand, we get the one about Sarah, the sullen sensualist who deliberately chose a bad reputation to exempt herself from the oppressive restrictions imposed on other Victorian women, and Charles Smithson, who abandons his career and fiancée for one night of ecstasy in Sarah's arms. On the other hand, we get a second plot about contemporary movie folks who are making a movie of *The French Lieutenant's Woman*, replete with wake-up calls, location shooting, rehearsals, studio cars, a romance between the stars, and thousands of extras in porkpie hats.

In both stories, it's the man who becomes obsessed with the woman who finds her own freedom, but the story on the screen ends happily while the off-screen lovers part sadly. This cross-cutting allows the movie to illustrate ironic contrasts and similarities between the morality of two different eras, but it's

an annoying conceit that destroys the illusion of Fowles's book and makes the audience irritable. What we get is Daphne Du Maurier in hot pants, or *My Cousin Rachel* in Calvin Klein jeans.

Jeremy Irons makes a limpid leading man in both roles, and Meryl Streep is even less convincing as a contemporary actress than she is as a fatalistic Victorian feminist. I admired Pinter's lean dialogue, his ironic asides, and his awesome cheekiness in taking so many liberties with style, content, and continuity, but I was never really in tune with *The French Lieutenant's Woman*. It's studious and stolid when it should've been a lot more fun. There's probably a message, but what is it? God knows there's plenty of style, but who needs it? The book is much more rewarding than the movie.

FRIENDLY PERSUASION (1956)
★ ★ ★ ★ Directed and produced by William Wyler. Screenplay by Michael Wilson, based on the novel by Jessamyn West. With Gary Cooper, Dorothy McGuire, Anthony Perkins, Marjorie Main, Richard Eyer, Robert Middleton, Mark Richman and Walter Catlett.

Gary Cooper, Dorothy McGuire, and Anthony Perkins are magnificent as Indiana Quakers facing a moral and religious crisis during the Civil War. The great William Wyler shines a light on every dark and humorous corner of Quaker life as he examines the hearts and souls of these peace-loving Christians, forced to choose between their pacifist faith and fighting to prevent the destruction of their farm. A beautiful, moving study of decent, good-hearted people caught up in a time of historic American turbulence and violence that transcends all seasons. Acting honors go to the luminous Dorothy McGuire, who abhors violence and runs her family with strict moral values, and to Gary Cooper, who is wonderfully spirited and compassionate as her liberal-minded husband, but Anthony Perkins's chivalrous, awkward, and soul-searching performance as the son on the brink of breaking his parents' faith in the scriptures deserves special credit, too. It's a refreshing change of pace from his eye-rolling psycho roles. Except for a gooey theme song by the unctuous Pat Boone, this is just about as perfect as movies can get.

FULL METAL JACKET (1987)
★ ★ ★ ½ Directed and produced by Stanley Kubrick. Screenplay by Kubrick, Michael Herr, and Gustav Hasford. *With Matthew Modine, Arliss Howard, Vince D'Onofrio, Dorian Harewood, Lee Ermey, Adam Baldwin, Kevyn Major Howard, and Ed O'Ross.*

Maybe you thought you saw it all in *Platoon.* But you haven't seen anything yet. Stanley Kubrick's apocalyptic vision of Vietnam is a rich and terrifying visual tapestry of war from every angle that explores the madness in us all. Seen through the eyes of Matthew Modine as a bright Marine recruit covering the war as a correspondent for *Stars and Stripes,* it begins in a South Carolina boot camp with the dehumanizing process of turning boys into men. Here we watch the pain and humiliation inflicted on a fat, screwed-up mental case by a sadistic drill instructor hell-bent on turning sensitive recruits into lethal killing machines. Then *Full Metal Jacket* moves forward, from the surrealism of combat duty to the full-scale horror of Vietnam itself. We see the soldiers reduced to robots, and the once-dignified Vietnamese people, bartering everything from their dogs to their daughters in desperation to stay alive. The film is scalding, original and unflinching in its madness. As both history and art, it is superior to *Platoon* in every way. One of the most important films of 1987.

GANDHI (1982)

★ ★ ★ ★ Directed and produced by Richard Attenborough. Screenplay by John Briley. *With Ben Kingsley, Candice Bergen, Edward Fox, John Gielgud, Trevor Howard, John Mills, Martin Sheen, Rohini Hattangady, Ian Charleson, and Athol Fugard.*

Gandhi is the kind of massive accomplishment for which ordinary adjectives like *brilliant* or *sweeping* or *magnificent* seem anemic and inadequate. It is simply the best movie of 1982, winning eight Oscars, including Best Picture, Director, Actor and Screenplay.

Richard Attenborough brought this epic about the life of Mahatma Gandhi to the screen after twenty years and $20 million. It is a film that combines eye-popping spectacle with deeply felt and sincerely communicated inner truth and idealism to distill the essence of a complex figure from a less chaotic and more sober era while remaining relevant to the concerns of today.

Attenborough's biggest concern was finding a cinematic way to show the gargantuan accomplishments of Gandhi's life in the space of a regular film that doesn't ramble incoherently, while remaining faithful to his spirit and giving the restless audience a sense of continuing plot and action.

Gandhi achieves all of this without ever boring its audience for a minute, although at over three hours its length might still be excessive to some nervous fidgets.

But stick with it and you will be rewarded with an opulent yet inspired work of rare artistry that manages to explain an enigma of human martyrdom without manipulating the audience through cheap sentimentality.

So many celebrated peace lovers (and warmongers) have made such a killing out of peace (and war), it comes as a revelation and a relief to relive the story of a man who sought neither fame, money, nor power, but devoted his life to uniting millions in the worship of peace through nonviolence, humility, compassion, and truth.

Attenborough's film examines the ideals, hopes, dreams, and disappointments of this legendary guru while providing a rich tapestry of India.

The story begins in January, 1948, in New Delhi—when an assassin's bullet ends the life of a man who changed the course of world history—and works its way back to 1893, when Gandhi was a young, British-trained attorney sent to South Africa to defend Indian immigrants against tyranny and injustice under England's domination.

Without seeking conflict or inviting trouble, he began his odyssey for human rights by seeking equality for Hindus with the philosophy, "Even if you are a minority of one, truth is truth."

Fined, imprisoned, harassed, beaten savagely, Gandhi was physically and financially humiliated, but no one could destroy his dignity or self-respect. "They can have my dead body—but not my obedience," he declared, and millions took notice.

Back in Bombay in 1915, he began to dedicate his life to one goal—uniting all of India, with its filthy, illiterate, overpopulated, sprawling, primitive, poverty-stricken chaos, and giving each person a sense of national pride. Miraculously, he became the first Indian in two hundred years to gain concessions from the British, and

eventually, through peaceful, nonviolent refusal to cooperate with the rulers, he forced them to grant India independence and freedom.

Stopping revolutions through fasting almost to the point of death, then getting arrested all over again by the very British demagogues he had protected from bloodshed, he remained undaunted.

Churchill called him a "half-naked fakir" but we're still talking about him now, more than forty years after his death, and his influence is still being felt wherever there is injustice. All of this is captured in the film, and more: the strange rituals, the odd ways, the uncontrollable masses, the awesome scope, size, and complexity of the nation he tried to civilize.

The film has problems: After the peaceful exit of the British and the establishment of Indian independence, the story is essentially over. The film continues, delving into the split between the Hindus and the Muslims that divided India and Pakistan—all of which is anticlimactic and, frankly, very confusing.

Still you are never burdened with pretentious symbolism. Attenborough has wisely chosen to tell the story according to the facts and resist the temptation to deify Gandhi.

Candice Bergen, as *Life* magazine photographer Margaret Bourke-White; John Mills, as the viceroy who would like to have demolished his foe; Martin Sheen as a reporter who followed the "great soul" through his victories and his defeats and ended up experiencing a spiritual force that cleansed his soul; and other distinguished performers such as John Gielgud, Ian Charleson, Trevor Howard, and Edward Fox—all contribute portraits of inestimable value.

But the real, devastating miracle of *Gandhi* is the overwhelming performance by Ben Kingsley who ironically is half-Indian and is from the same village where Gandhi was born, in the title role. Kingsley impersonates the man with hypnotic physical resemblance, and seems haunted from within. He seems so real, so natural, with the same hesitant voice and strangely poetic walk, that he brings an unshakable moral force to the screen. The punishing demands of the role are very nearly unequaled, but Kingsley's triumphs go beyond makeup, aging, time consumption, or personal research. There's a spiritual glow that ignites whoever is watching.

Kingsley *is* Gandhi. It's not a performance; it's a spiritual rebirth.

Add exotic Ravi Shankar music, a humane and intelligent script by John Briley, and the design mosaic of a film that includes thousands of people and hundreds of authentic locations over a million miles of rugged terrain, and you have a film that staggers the mind and feeds the soul. Such greatness is rare. It's a lesson in history—and a lesson in moviemaking—you will never forget.

GARBO TALKS (1984)
★ ★ ½ Directed by Sidney Lumet. Screenplay by Larry Grusin. Produced by Elliot Kastner. With Ron Silver, Anne Bancroft, Harvey Fierstein, Carrie Fisher, and Howard da Silva.

Crisp, agreeable comedy of manners and foibles about an eccentric old broad dying of cancer whose last wish is to meet Greta Garbo, and her square nerd of a son who becomes obsessed with bringing about the miracle. Anne Bancroft is sadly miscast in a role the late Thelma Ritter was born to play, but Sidney Lumet's direction is warm and sophisticated, and there are wonderful, dotty cameos by Carrie Fisher, Dorothy Loudon, Hermione Gingold, and Harvey Fierstein.

GENTLEMEN PREFER BLONDES (1953)

★ ★ ★ ½ Directed by Howard Hawks. Screenplay by Charles Lederer, based on the musical comedy by Anita Loos. Produced by Sol C. Siegel, with songs by Jule Styne, Leo Robin, and Hoagy Carmichael. *With Marilyn Monroe, Jane Russell, Charles Coburn, Tommy Noonan, Elliot Reid, and George "Foghorn" Winslow.*

In *Gentlemen Prefer Blondes*, the Monroe mannerisms all combine in a very sexy explosion of music, comedy, and romance unequaled in the rest of her career. Marilyn turned Anita Loos's quintessential gold-digger Lorelei Lee into a parfait of dizzy, delectable delight singing "Diamonds Are a Girl's Best Friend," and Jane Russell matched her every move as her brainy brunette roommate Dorothy. Charles Coburn is delightful as Piggy, a horny old millionaire Marilyn sets her sights on ("I just love finding new places to wear diamonds," she gushes while the old man blushes) and six-year-old George Winslow, as a precocious kid who helps Marilyn squeeze her derriere through a ship's porthole, is hilarious. But it's really the genius casting of the two stars, igniting the screen with their particular boffo appeal, and the lavish Jack Cole dance numbers created for them, that made *Gentlemen Prefer Blondes* a smash.

GHOST (1990)

★ ★ ★ Directed by Jerry Zucker. Screenplay by Bruce Joel Rubin. Produced by Lisa Weinstein. *With Patrick Swayze, Demi Moore, and Whoopi Goldberg.*

Ghost is the first movie in which Patrick Swayze proves he can act. As a yuppie stockbroker knifed by a mugger, he returns as a genial ghost to prove to his girl (Demi Moore) he still loves her beyond death and even solves his own murder with the aid of a fake medium (Oscar-winner Whoopi Goldberg). The hunk literally walks through walls while the freaked-out fortune-teller shrieks "No way!" The picture is actually more charming and tolerable than the plot, and the actors rise above the script heroically.

THE GHOST AND MRS. MUIR (1947)

★ ★ ★ Directed by Joseph L Mankiewicz. Screenplay by Philip Dunne, based on the novel by R. A. Dick. Produced by Fred Kohlmar. *With Rex Harrison, Gene Tierney, George Sanders, Natalie Wood, Edna Best, Vanessa Brown, Anna Lee, and Robert Coote.*

A classic from 1947, *The Ghost and Mrs. Muir* is about a salty sea captain who haunts the occupants of a cozy cottage on a bluff overlooking the English Channel, and a romantic widow who not only refuses to be scared away but develops a glowing affection for the saucy ghost in the bargain. One of the most spirited romantic fantasies of the 1940s, with engaging performances by Rex Harrison as the wily ghost, Gene Tierney as the lonely girl, and George Sanders as the prissy suitor who competes with the ghost for her favors. This *Ghost* is gently humorous and sparkling good fun.

GHOSTBUSTERS (1984)
★ ★ ★ ½ Directed and produced by Ivan Reitman. Screenplay by Dan Aykroyd and Harold Ramis. With Bill Murray, Dan Aykroyd, Harold Ramis, Sigourney Weaver, Ernie Hudson, Rick Moranis, Annie Potts, and William Atherton.

Hilarity and horror rarely mix, but *Ghostbusters* is a deliciously daffy exception. Written by Dan Aykroyd and Harold Ramis, it's a happy surprise.

Ghostbusters is a delightful variation on an old theme—the Three Stooges movies, or the Abbott and Costello movies, where dopey dumb-clucks end up in haunted houses fighting off ghosts while boxing each other's ears and slapping each other around in a mélange of merriment and mayhem. But *Ghostbusters* brings the genre up to date, with witty, zonked-out dialogue and sizzling special effects that quicken the pulse while goosing the funnybone.

The Three Stooges are now Bill Murray, as Dr. Peter Venkman, a spacey scientist who specializes in psychic phenomena; and his two lunatic sidekicks, Aykroyd and Ramis, as nutty parapsychologists who talk "telekinetic residue" and "full-torso apparition" like they were reading computer readouts at IBM. ("We actually touched the etheric plane," says Aykroyd, and the others nod goofily, like they understand.)

When the university they work for cancels their money, grants and lab facilities, for wrecking The New York Public Library, they go into business for themselves in an abandoned firehouse where nothing works but the fireman's pole.

With a brand-new motto ("We're ready to relieve you") these corny clowns set about ridding New York of its psychic turbulence—eliminating noises, smells, poltergeists, and "class five full-roaming vapors."

Sigourney Weaver is their first client—a luscious career girl who has a demon in her icebox. In no time, Manhattan finds itself in the grip of an epidemic of supernatural disturbances, and the ghostbusters find themselves up to their geiger counters in exorcisms and horrors from hell as psychic forces from beyond the grave stage a twentieth-century Armageddon from the penthouse of a luxury co-op on Central Park West.

The dazzling special effects come in when New York becomes a psychic battlefield. Skies boil over skyscraper roofs. Streets open up to swallow police cars. Death and destruction comes in the form of a hundred-foot-tall Stay-Puff Marshmallow Man.

Mixed in with the laughs, which are cool instead of cockeyed, are so many eye-popping miracles that boredom is never even remotely possible.

The ghostbusters are marvelously cast: Bill Murray, with his zoned-out eyes and horny hipness, is ably supported by the terminally stupid looks of Aykroyd and Ramis. Rick Moranis, as a jerk accountant who gets possessed by the devil, and William Atherton, as a villain from the Environmental Protection Agency who unleashes the ghosts while inspecting the madcap trio's premises for noxious gases, are an endearing backup team. As usual, the calm, collected, and always sexy Sigourney Weaver makes the thankless role of female foil something special indeed.

Richard Edlund's visuals, which strike just the right balance between the scary and the screwy, and the rich cinematography by Laszlo Kovacs add a special patina to this mad *Saturday Night Live* sketch gone haywire, and the sound, steady direction by Ivan Reitman elevates the whole thing from insanity to satire.

In the technical departments, in the tongue-in-cheek performances, and in the shrewd comic writing, *Ghostbusters* towers above most modern comedies and is miles ahead of any competitors.

GHOST STORY (1981)

★ ★ Directed by John Irvin. Screenplay by Lawrence D. Cohen. Produced by Burt Weissbourd. *With Fred Astaire, Douglas Fairbanks, Jr., John Houseman, Melvyn Douglas, Alice Krige, and Craig Wasson.*

I always thought the plague that hit Hollywood could easily be cured with one enchanting dose of Fred Astaire. Well, in this Grade Z horror called *Ghost Story*, Fred could use some medicine himself. This truly wretched piece of junk wastes the time, energy, and talent of everyone involved. It's a sad example of how to abuse senior citizens. Practically everyone involved in this trashy sleaze looks bewildered, miserable, and ultimately embalmed by a mortician for open-casket viewing.

A terrific cast of seasoned pros has been assembled, all of them are wasted, and the awful truth is that without them this movie would be just another 42nd Street grindhouse potboiler. Maybe the money was great, or maybe they read the superbly eerie novel by Peter Straub the movie is based on. Either way, not a shred of the novel's literary quality remains, most of the atmosphere and plot have been sacrificed for cornball special effects, and nothing remains except close-ups of old stars looking panic-stricken and tortured by the mess they're in. *Ghost Story* is a horror, all right, but it isn't even remotely scary.

In a beautiful picture-postcard village in Vermont (we know it's a beautiful picture-postcard village because every other long shot of the village is a picture postcard) there are four old codgers in dinner jackets who call themselves the "Chowder Society" and who meet to exchange ghost stories in the dark. Fred Astaire, Melvyn Douglas, John Houseman, and Douglas Fairbanks, Jr., are the macabre old crows.

The deep, dark secret they have shared for several decades is that years ago, when they were young and handsome, they buried a poor girl alive inside a car that sank to the bottom of a lake and the poor critter has been trying to get out of her watery grave for half a century. Now her ghost has returned to give everybody the creeps and claim the lives of the old geezers who murdered her. If it sounds familiar, it is. You've seen this corpse-returns-from-beneath-the-swamp-to-seek-revenge idea a thousand times.

Ghost Story has a haunted house, an escaped maniac from an insane asylum, a blizzard, spooky organ music, eerie lighting, terrible nightmares, and portentous predictions of evil things to come, but nothing ever happens. It's a rip-off, a joke on the gullible audience, and a travesty of the talents involved.

The ghost is played by Alice Krige, the English actress who played the Gilbert & Sullivan singer in *Chariots of Fire* with such charm. She is cruelly photographed and hideously misused here. Her best scenes are the ones where the rotting flesh falls from her face like melting Halloween pumpkin wax, which doesn't say much for the way Hollywood uses a promising talent. Lawrence Cohen's script is moronic, and John Irvin, the director, doesn't have a clue how to sustain even the most minimal suspense.

Melvyn Douglas died shortly after the film was completed. He must have seen the answer print.

GIRL CRAZY (1943)
★ ★ ★ Directed by Norman Taurog. Produced by Arthur Freed. Screenplay by Fred Finklehoffe. *With Mickey Rooney, Judy Garland, June Allyson, Nancy Walker, Rags Ragland, Guy Kibbee, Gil Stratton, Robert Strickland, Henry O'Neill, Frances Rafferty and Tommy Dorsey and his orchestra.*

Mickey Rooney is a spoiled brat New York playboy exiled to an all-male college–dude ranch out West, and Judy Garland is the dean's granddaughter, who helps him put on yet another campus fund-raising show—this time a rodeo! The great score by George and Ira Gershwin, the spectacular "I Got Rhythm" finale staged by Busby Berkeley, and the energy and charisma of the two stars made this one of MGM's best 1943 musicals. With peppy June Allyson, pickle-faced Nancy Walker, and Tommy Dorsey and his orchestra.

THE GLENN MILLER STORY (1954)
★ ★ ★ ½ Directed by Anthony Mann. Screenplay by Valentine Davis and Oscar Brodney. Produced by Aaron Rosenberg. *With James Stewart, June Allyson, Charles Drake, George Tobias, Harry Morgan, Louis Armstrong, Frances Langford, and Gene Krupa.*

The Glenn Miller Story is one of the most touching and durable of all Hollywood musical "biopics," thanks to a convincing, three-dimensional performance by Jimmy Stewart as the beloved bandleader whose smoothly swinging style was as much a part of the American fabric during World War II as bobby sox and bacon rations. The intelligent script tells the appealing story of a restless small-town boy who had a consuming ambition to play the trombone in a dance band, to get ahead in the music world, and to develop his own orchestra with a personality and a sound unique in popular music. It follows the no-nonsense pattern of Miller's life without hokum thrown in to jazz up the story, and it ends as his life actually ended with his disappearance in a military plane in 1944.

June Allyson got one of the plum roles of her career as the girl who snagged the guy and married him, and there are marvelous guest appearances by Louis Armstrong, Frances Langford, Gene Krupa and the Modernaires. Dozens of Glenn Miller hits are here, their original arrangements enhanced by newly mastered stereophonic sound. The musical sequences are beautifully and artfully photographed, the direction by Anthony Mann is solid and the entire film has an unpretentious sweetness that throbs with tender sentiments. A fine and timeless little gem indeed.

GLORIA (1980)
★ ★ ★ ½ Directed and written by John Cassavetes. Produced by Sam Shaw. *With Gena Rowlands, Juan Adames, and Buck Henry.*

Gena Rowlands burns a hole through the screen in *Gloria*, a titanic entertainment that will make your hair stand on end

with tension and excitement. I think I've loved her ever since I first saw her on the screen in a low-budget MGM trifle called *The High Cost of Loving*, back in 1958. Why she didn't become one of the handful of truly bankable superstars is a mystery I have yet to unravel, but in the intervening years her beauty and talent grew bigger while the parts grew scarce, and except for occasional TV blockbusters like *Strangers* with Bette Davis and *A Question of Love* with Jane Alexander, her primary exposure in films has been in those made by her late husband, John Cassavetes. The work they've done together—films like *A Woman Under the Influence* and *Opening Night*—has been too esoteric to attract wide audiences, although they both became the darlings of critics and film buffs in the process.

Gloria, their sixth film together, strikes a fine balance between personalized filmmaking and commercial marketing. It is Cassavetes's most accessible and conventionally structured film, and it provides the ravishing star with one of her richest roles.

Gloria is a retired gun moll and ex-showgirl who has given up her glamorous past as well as her old mob connections to live out her days in a seedy but respectable peace. She's got her Ungaro clothes, her tabby cat, some money in the bank, and a tacky but serviceable apartment in a dilapidated building in the Bronx. Her needs are simple, and she's no longer dancing on the lip of anyone's volcano. But Gloria is innocently drawn into big trouble anyway when she throws a raincoat over her pink pajamas one morning and shuffles down the hall to borrow some coffee.

The timing is rotten. It turns out that her mousy-looking neighbor (Buck Henry) has been moonlighting as a mob accountant and giving interviews to the FBI on the side about mob revenue. When Gloria arrives, still half asleep, the whole family is on the verge of being wiped out in a gang-style killing. Desperate, the neighbors shove their seven-year-old son Phil into Gloria's arms along with the mob's account ledger, and in her attempt to get the child out of Manhattan to Pittsburgh, Gloria finds herself plastered all over the newspapers, wanted by both the cops and the mobsters she used to know. She hates kids, but to turn her young charge over to the mob would be cold-blooded murder, and she can't turn to the cops because she's got a police record herself. Sweat breaks out on the peachy half-moons under her eyes, as Gloria takes stock of her options: "Kid, you know what desperate is?" She grits her teeth, pulls up her stockings, adjusts her girdle, and takes on the system, and in the panic, danger, courage, and gunfire that result, Phil finds his manhood and Gloria finds her heart.

Gloria is about desperate people on the lam, but it is also a love story about the most mismatched odd couple since Edward G. Robinson and Margaret O'Brien. Gena Rowlands flames, sizzles, and explodes with energy, vibrancy, and power. Beneath the peroxide and the tough-tootsie talk, there's a three-dimensional woman coming alive, and the kid actor, Juan Adames, keeps up with her all the way. Cassavetes wrote, produced, and directed the film with precision and care, providing fascinating views of the violent underworld of New York as well as the intimate emotional terrain of a woman's soul. The picture seethes with humanity and spirit and the suspense is breathtaking.

THE GODDESS (1958)
★ ★ ★ ★   Directed by John Cromwell. Screenplay by Paddy Chayevsky. Produced by Milton Perlman. *With Kim Stanley, Lloyd*

Bridges, Patty Duke, Betty Lou Holland, Steven Hill, Elizabeth Wilson, Joan Copeland, Burt Brinckerhoff, and Joyce Van Patten.

Great acting—the kind that surpasses mere craft and professionalism—is rare on film, but what I consider the greatest performance ever captured on the movie screen by an actress is now available for home viewing. Kim Stanley in *The Goddess* is that miraculous meld of artist and role that only happens once in a lifetime. Long regarded as the finest actress of her generation by theater people, this legendary performer always eschewed flashy screen roles and easy Hollywood money to toil on the New York stage. The quirky, complex, and Stanislavski-impassioned star of such classics as *Picnic*, *Bus Stop*, and *A Touch of the Poet*, she electrified theater audiences before making her film debut in this searing, emotionally charged screenplay by Paddy Chayevsky. It's the haunting study of the emotional decline of a neglected, unwanted small-town girl from the Maryland slums whose sexual charisma and driving ambition to become a star lead to a life of self-destruction. As she sleeps her way to stardom, trashing the loyal and generous

people who love her along the way, the pinnacle of fame she eventually reaches as a silverscreen goddess leaves her empty, suicidal, lonely, and decimated. It's based on a composite of many actual screen goddesses—from Rita Hayworth to Marilyn Monroe—but the story is not the compelling factor that make *The Goddess* a memorable film. It's Kim Stanley's monumental, keenly observed, painfully realized performance. Patty Duke also made her film debut playing Kim Stanley as a child, and there is amazing support by Lloyd Bridges (TV fans who only think of him as the aging star of *Sea Hunt* or father of Beau and Jeff are in for a major surprise) as a sensitive ex-prizefighter on the way down whose life is shredded by a marriage to the actress on her way up (shades of Joe DiMaggio). This is a powerful, heartbreaking movie about the tragedy loneliness brings, especially in Hollywood. Galvanizing, and an absolute "must" for any serious collector.

THE GODS MUST BE CRAZY (1984)
★ ★ ★ ½ Directed, written and produced by Jamie Uys. *With Nixau, Marius Weyers, Sandra Prinsloo, Louw Verwey, and James Uys.*

What do you mean, you never heard of Botswana? It's an African territory. It's got the Kalahari Desert. It's even got a one-man movie industry named James Uys. Okay. I confess. I never heard of it either. But *The Gods Must Be Crazy*, a sweet, gentle, and completely captivating little comedy, has put Botswana on the map.

This odd little movie was made in 1979 and was already an international success before its premiere in the United States five years later. It became the biggest foreign box office hit in history. If you're looking for something offbeat and disarming, your curiosity will not go unrewarded.

Uys, who wrote, produced, and directed *The Gods Must Be Crazy*, has concocted a mad farce that defies convention. In theme and structure, the movie has a spirit of its own that resists any ordinary attempt to describe it.

It begins as a documentary with dry, straight-faced narration about a peaceful primitive tribe of tiny bushmen who live in a gracious, simple world, digging for roots and foraging for berries, without any knowledge of crime or violence.

Their tranquility is suddenly shattered when somebody throws a Coca-Cola bottle out of an airplane window and it lands kerplop in the middle of their village.

This cursed, troublesome Coke bottle is believed to be a gift from the gods—at first a symbol of beauty and usefulness, later a cause of hate, jealousy, and violence. An artifact of civilization disrupts the loving, placid happiness of these tribal innocents, and one brave young native is dispatched to return the awful thing to the god that sent it in the first place.

The story is interrupted by a flaky microbiologist from a nearby game preserve; a pretty, prim, and very proper girl who is on her way to teach in a mission school in the desert; and a group of murderous revolutionaries who have just bungled an assassination attempt on the president.

How these disparate elements end up in the same place—and what any of this has to do with the offending Coke bottle—is what this wacky comedy is all about.

The poor bushman thinks the white people he encounters are gods and keeps trying to return the evil Coke bottle. They don't want the thing. Confusion reigns, while everyone encounters shoot-outs, a rhino that stamps out campfires, and a jeep that drives backward.

The most delightful thing about *The Gods Must Be Crazy* is the way it undercuts the goofy people it invents with real animals, natives, and nature that surround them. The absurdity of modern life—complete with cars, processed food, and nervous breakdowns—is brilliantly contrasted with the simplicity of the childlike natives. The result is a cross between *National Geographic* and *Mad* magazine.

Uys extracts a rich and sincere set of performances from all his actors, especially a real tribal bushman from the Kalahari named N!xau, and keeps a manic energy going from start to finish. The laughs do not come from slick American-style comic turns, but from a head-on collision with logic that is refreshingly different. *The Gods Must Be Crazy* is a total delight.

GOODBYE, MR. CHIPS (1939)

★ ★ ★ ½ Directed by Sam Wood. Screenplay by R. C. Sherriff, Claudine West, and Eric Maschwitz, based on the novel by James Hilton. Produced by Victor Saville. *With Robert Donat, Greer Garson, Paul Henried, Terry Kilburn, and John Mills.*

This classic 1939 MGM tear-jerker, based on the famous novel by James Hilton, is about a beloved British schoolmaster looking back over the happiness and tragedy of his life while the boys whose lives he changed grow up, become men, and return to haunt him. Robert Donat won the Oscar for his memorable portrayal of one of fiction's greatest characters and Greer Garson made her film debut, lighting up the screen with radiance and beauty as the woman whose love guided the starchy Chips to greatness. A nostalgic wallow that transcends sentimental corn through inspired acting, technical proficiency, and cinematic artistry. (Remade without success in 1969 as a musical, with Peter O'Toole and Petula Clark, neither of whom displayed an ounce of the charm and spontaneity of the originals.)

GOOD MORNING, VIETNAM (1987)

★ ★ ½ Directed by Barry Levinson. Screenplay by Mitch Markowitz. Produced by Mark Johnson and Larry Brezner. *With Robin Williams, Forest Whitaker, Tung Tanh Tran, Chintara Sukapatana, Bruno Kirby, Robert Wuhl, J. T. Walsh, Noble Willingham, and Floyd Vivino.*

Good Morning, Vietnam is a long, rambling and rather pointless vehicle for the multifaceted Robin Williams, but his performance is a one-man tour de force that cannot be forgotten. As a renegade disc jockey tweaking the nose of the military brass, breaking all the rules, and flaunting regulations, Williams brings laughs and lunacy to the troops and keeps them going while risking his own Army future and even his life. A comic genius, Williams goes berserk on the air, imitating everything from helicopter engines to Ethel Merman's singing jamming the Viet Cong radar.

THE GOOD MOTHER (1988)

★ ★ ★ Directed by Leonard Nimoy. Screenplay by Michael Bortman, based on the novel by Sue Miller. Produced by Arnold Gilmcher. With Diane Keaton, Liam Neeson, James Naughton, Jason Robards, Ralph Bellamy, Teresa Wright, Asia Vieria, Joe Morton, Katey Sagal, and Tracy Griffith.

The Good Mother is an affecting look at the plight of a divorcee torn between the future of her child and the man she loves that never sinks to the level of soap opera, thanks to a galvanizing performance by Diane Keaton. She's a good, loyal, compassionate mother who has concentrated her adult life on independence and turned her daughter Molly into a free-spirited individual uninhibited by the conventions that govern the lives of most children. Then she falls for a sculptor named Leo (brilliantly played by sexy newcomer Liam Neeson) who shares her passion for honesty. He opens not only a new window to her sexual frustrations, but a whole door she never knew existed. But when Molly relates an innocent experience she shared with Leo in the bathroom, the wounded pride of the stuffy, jealous ex-husband (James Naughton, handling an unsympathetic role with charisma) threatens to destroy everything Keaton believes in by challenging her in a nasty custody suit. Testing her values even further by blaming it all on Leo, the mother pays an enormous price and so does her lover, the willing scapegoat who takes the rap for her mistakes and then fails to understand her rejection.

The Good Mother gives Diane Keaton a meaty role and she plays it with a whole spectrum of emotional colors—fear, obsession, warmth, rage, and despair. It introduces issues to make you question your own values. This film is so intimate it makes you blush. It's not an entertainment, but it will shatter and touch you with honesty. In an age of "So what?" movies, *The Good Mother* is one you'll take home and think about.

GOOD NEWS (1947)
★ ★ ★ Directed by Charles Walters. Screenplay by Betty Comden and Adolph Green. Produced by Arthur Freed. With June Allyson, Peter Lawford, Mel Tormé, Ray McDonald, and Joan McCracken.

Good News is the ultimate college musical. MGM pulled out all the stops to transport a twenties concoction to the forties for this lavish, gorgeously photographed, tune-filled campus entertainment, and it became one of the box-office triumphs of 1947. Maybe college wasn't this colorful for Mom and Dad, but everyone who sees *Good News* will wish it had been. June Allyson does for bobby sox what Marilyn Monroe did for a sweater. Peter Lawford is the football player she must tutor in French so he can win the big game for Tait College. Libidinous Broadway dancer Joan McCracken breaks things up in the soda shop singing and dancing "Pass That Peace Pipe." Mel Tormé, looking as young and goofy as a newborn calf, heads the crooning campus sidekicks. The old

songs are still full of fragrance: "Just Imagine," "Lucky in Love," "The Best Things in Life Are Free," and a rousing senior prom finale, "The Varsity Drag." Dig out your Yale pennants and your raccoon coats and have yourself a ball. In *Good News* there's something for everybody.

GORILLAS IN THE MIST (1988)
★ ★ ★ Directed by Michael Apted. Screenplay by Anna Hamilton Phelan. Produced by Arnold Glimcher and Terence Clegg. With Sigourney Weaver, Bryan Brown, Julie Harris, John Omirah Miluwi, Iain Cuthbertson, Constantin Alexandrov, and Waigwa Wachira.

The true story of Dian Fossey, the anthropologist who spent twenty years with the rare mountain gorillas of Rwanda, is an exhilarating film that begins in 1966 when she aggressively talked her way into a research job in Africa and ends tragically with her murder in 1985. The murder is still unsolved, but the killer could have been anyone, for in her determined efforts to save the endangered gorillas, she terrorized the natives by pretending to be a white witch, and enraged the animal poachers who were capturing baby gorillas for zoos. Passion turned to obsession, and in the best performance of her career, Sigourney Weaver captures every aspect of this amazing woman from tenderness to rage. The dense jungle slopes and mist-shrouded mountains are exquisitely recorded in the actual locations where Fossey lived, worked, and died, and the scenes with the wild gorillas are more awesome than anything in *Out of Africa*.

GORKY PARK (1983)

★ ★ Directed by Michael Apted. Screenplay by Dennis Potter. Produced by Gene Kirkwood and Howard W. Koch, Jr. *With William Hurt, Lee Marvin, Joanna Pakula, and Brian Dennehy.*

Gorky Park is as cold and cheerless as a Harlem radiator on a subzero morning. It's supposed to be.

Based on the Russian detective thriller by Martin Cruz Smith, its bleak winter setting is supposed to chew its way into your bones like a flu bug as the Soviet bureaucrats plow their way deeper into its mysteries with icy jaws and gray, steely eyes. But this is the movies, not the public library. We need more than landscape and black overcoats. *Gorky Park* never comes to life; it just lies there, like a stiff on ice. Bring cough drops.

Three bodies are found in the snow of Gorky Park in downtown Moscow. Their faces and fingertips have been torn away, their identification papers destroyed. Who are they? Why have they been butchered and frozen in this grisly manner? The investigation is led by Russia's chief cop, Arkady Renko, played by all-American William Hurt, but when dental techniques suggest one of the victims is an American, in comes the KGB.

The chase leads to Lee Marvin, an American businessman who comes to Moscow to buy sable pelts and is rumored to be a messenger for the Kremlin. When the Russian detective is puzzled by the traces of chicken blood on the corpses, a two-fisted American cop (Brian Dennehy) who just happens to be behind the Iron Curtain at the time delivers the film's best and only funny line: "I've been to your wonderful Soviet markets—I've never seen anything fresh enough to bleed." That's as light as the picture gets.

Meanwhile, as the plot thickens into shashlik, we are given a tour of the Russian black market, where a Russian sleazepot (with a curious Cockney accent) can sell you anything from a Sony Betamax to a priceless icon, as well as a demonstration of the inner workings of a Russian forensics lab (close up of worms eating the flesh off a decapitated human head).

Of course, Lee Marvin is more sinister than he appears to be, and there is a complex love triangle between Marvin, Hurt, and a sexy dissident who would like to defect to someplace warm—like Chicago.

What eventually unravels is an intricate plot about smuggling live sables into America that ends up in Stockholm, where a great number of guns go off in the snow before it's over. Even then, it's unclear just who is killing whom—or why. After the pieces to the puzzle are turned over, you may wonder why you ever bothered.

In its favor, *Gorky Park* does achieve a dark and murky ambience, full of tension and edginess. It's hard to believe the director is the same Michael Apted who directed *Coal Miner's Daughter* with such warmth and feeling.

Using Helsinki as a stand-in for Moscow, he manages to build the same gray feeling for Moscow's bleak, empty ugliness, while imparting a sense of the frustration and plodding nothingness that goes with the daily regimentation of Russian police work.

Still, it's hard to believe Russian KGB agents say "Holy Mother!" when taken by surprise, or that they address each other as "Comrade Chief Pathologist" and "Comrade Chief Investigator." And as Renko, William Hurt uses black hair and sallow complexion to look like a downtrodden Soviet bureaucrat, but is so hopelessly miscast that he just comes off like a robot.

You're better off spending two hours in the warmth of the Russian Tea Room.

GRACE QUIGLEY (1985)

No ★'s Directed by Anthony Harvey. Produced by Christopher Pearce. Screenplay by Martin Zweiback. With Katharine Hepburn, Nick Nolte, Elizabeth Wilson, Chip Zien, Kit Le Fever, William Duell, and Walter Abel.

Understandably, there aren't many roles these days for living legends over seventy, but even a spunky septuagenarian like Katharine Hepburn should spare her fans the embarrassment of watching her being reduced to an abomination like *Grace Quigley*.

From all reports, it's her own fault. Twelve years ago, a script was thrown over George Cukor's fence. Hepburn, who was visiting there at the time, and for whom the script was intended, read it and has been trying to film it ever since. There are still quite a few smart people left in Hollywood, contrary to popular opinion, and none of them would touch it.

Finally, the financing was secured from Menachem Golan, head of Cannon Films. The film was completed in 1983. They tried to figure out what to do with it for two years. Unveiled for the first time at the 1984 Cannes Film Festival, *Grace Quigley* turned out to be not only a disaster but one of the festival's major scandals. It has since been reedited, rewritten, and drastically restructured, with a different ending. It is still asinine.

The great Hepburn plays the unlikely title role—a sad, lonely old lady existing in the cruelty and apathy of New York with more than her share of problems. Barely making ends meet on Social Security, she lives in a squalid flat, with a parakeet named Oscar her sole companion. After witnessing the contract killing of her sleazy landlord by a two-bit hit man (Nick Nolte), the penniless but crafty old lady, who is not beyond a little petty larceny herself, takes a motherly interest in this slob, then develops the bright idea of setting him up as a partner in a lucrative business to murder off all the hopeless, despondent, and sick senior citizens she can round up for a hefty fee.

The submental thug begins to think of himself as a good samaritan and the movie turns from a Joe Orton—styled black comedy to a thinly veiled apology for neo-Naziism, as this despicable duo (they even call themselves "angels of death") rounds up all the customers they can find, offering them group rates, like Blue Cross, and special discounts for friends. In one monstrous sequence, Hepburn smiles beatifically while four old people are gassed to death with carbon monoxide as they sing "When Irish Eyes Are Smiling."

Didn't anyone connected with this euthanasia propaganda realize it shares its premise with the same master plan Adolf Hitler used to exterminate six million Jews, pretending it was a "good deed"? He called it his "ultimate solution," and so does Mrs. Quigley. (The original title of the film was *The Ultimate Solution of Mrs. Quigley*.) Either way, it stinks.

Success makes Mrs. Quigley even loopier. Corrupted by the power she has over people, she demands that the killer rub out a rude taxi driver because he stole her shoe, and threatens to turn him over to the district attorney's office. We are meant to laugh at all of this, but there's a nastiness to it that is sickening. Finally, in a desperate attempt to win back the audience and keep the movie on course, screenwriter Martin Zweiback and director Anthony Harvey abandon the plot altogether and resort to farce, with a chase scene through the streets of New York involving an entire funeral full of runaway hearses crashing into buildings and parked cars and Kate Hepburn on a motorcycle.

When I first saw this loathsome and mean-spirited film, the two stars, immersed in situations beyond resolution, walked into the Atlantic Ocean and drowned. Fortunately, that sour finale has been scrapped, but not improved. In the new ending for home video they just laugh idiotically at the camera. I doubt if any sane or rational person will laugh back.

Nick Nolte is in such a state of physical deterioration he looks like a tub of melted margarine. But my concern is Hepburn. It is genuinely mortifying to see this icon and national treasure in *Grace Quigley*, an offense to human decency that is one of the biggest mistakes of her career.

THE GREATEST SHOW ON EARTH (1952)

★ ★ ★ ★ Directed and produced by Cecil B. DeMille. Screenplay by Fredric Frank, Barre Lyndon, and Theodore St. John. *With Charlton Heston, James Stewart, Betty Hutton, Dorothy Lamour, Cornel Wilde, Gloria Grahame, Henry Wilcoxon, Lawrence Tierney, and Emmett Kelly.*

Cecil B. DeMille's spectacular tribute to the circus is a must for any serious collector of home videos. Winner of the Best Picture Oscar in 1952, this timeless classic never ages. Packed with action, lavishly staged production numbers, and heart-stopping adventure, it will thrill and delight audiences of all ages as long as there's magic under the big top and drama in the center ring. The all-star cast is headed by James Stewart, as a fugitive hiding behind the face of a circus clown; Betty Hutton, as the trapeze star in love with Charlton Heston, the "big boss" with sawdust for blood; Cornel Wilde, as the daredevil aerialist who competes for her affections; Gloria Grahame, as the vamp who rides elephants and almost loses her life in the process; and Dorothy Lamour, as the good-hearted showgirl who has circus in her heart. Sprawling across the mammoth canvas, filled with real-life acts and circus people, and glittering in marvelous Technicolor, this great homage to Ringling Bros.—Barnum and Bailey shows the circus in every aspect with almost documentary brilliance and detail. The spectacular train-wreck sequence is a milestone in itself. P. T. Barnum said there's a sucker born every minute, and I'm still a sucker for every gripping and fascinating minute of *The Greatest Show on Earth*.

THE GREAT MUPPET CAPER (1981)

★ ★ ★ ½ Directed by Jim Henson. Screenplay by Tom Patchett, Jay Tarses, Jerry Juhl, and Jack Rose. Produced by Frank Oz. With Jack Warden, Diana Rigg, Charles Grodin, the Muppets (performed by Jim Henson, Frank Oz, Dave Goelz, Jerry Holson, and Richard Hunt), and cameos by Robert Morley and Peter Ustinov.

The second of the talking toys' feature-length excursions into big-screen moviemaking, *The Great Muppet Caper* is even better than *The Muppet Movie*. This time, Fozzie and Kermit are crack reporters for the *Daily Chronicle*, Gonzo is their photographer, Jack Warden their curmudgeonly editor,

and they're all on the trail of a gang of London jewel thieves. Diana Rigg is a famous fashion designer who owns one of the world's biggest gems—the "baseball diamond"—and Charles Grodin is her idiot brother who leads the thieves disguised as fashion models during the day.

Miss Piggy plays the fashion salon receptionist, temporarily surrendering her prom dresses for Chanel suits and demure pearls. This is the kind of liberal society in which frogs get the best tables in posh supper clubs and a truck driver like Peter Ustinov finds a hitchhiking pig more of a femme fatale than any of the cycle sluts in *The Cannonball Run*. How could anyone feel otherwise, when the pig in question is the one and only Miss Piggy? She even gets to do some Ann Miller tapping drenched in ostrich plumes and surrounded by chorus boys in top hats, white ties, and tails. Later, Miss Piggy steals the movie's big fashion show in her sequin bathing suit and even does an MGM underwater production number imitating Esther Williams in a dream ballet.

Hiding under a table at the nightclub with his camera, doing a photographic essay on kneecaps, Gonzo overhears the villains' plans and all the Muppets join together to save Miss Piggy from the slammer and rescue the stolen jewels. The big showdown pits James Bond–style criminals carrying blowtorches, walkie-talkies, and computerized safecracking tools against the Muppets with their Frisbees, yo-yos, and peanut butter. It's a population explosion of Muppets—a cat with an eye patch, tap-dancing mice, a Peter, Paul, and Mary singing trio, some freaked-out musicians that look like aardvarks, and various and assorted singing chickens in an extravaganza of songs (the delightful tunes are by Joe Raposo) and action and endearing romance that blends nursery school imagination and sophisticated technology with beautiful costumes and lavish sets adding immeasurably to the film's happy look and feel. This is a musical in the nicest tradition, with zany and beloved characters who have moved into my heart to stay.

THE GREAT SANTINI (1980)

★ ★ ★ ★ Directed and written by Lewis John Carlino. Based on the novel by Pat Conroy. Produced by Charles A. Pratt. With Robert Duvall, Blythe Danner, Michael O'Keefe, Lisa Jane Persky, Stan Shaw, Theresa Merritt, and Julie Anne Haddock.

A wonderful, offbeat, and immensely gratifying film.

Don't be detoured by that unfortunate title. *The Great Santini* is not a movie about a trapeze act. Robert Duvall plays Bull Meechum, a gung-ho, hell-raising ace Marine fighter pilot so admired by his fellow yahoos in uniform that they nickname him "the great Santini" because of his feats in midair. But if Bull rules the skies, he's a troubled king on domestic turf. He moves his gentle, Southern belle ·wife (rapturously played by the wonderful Blythe Danner) and his four kids around from one military base to another at three A.M. to avoid highway traffic, sets them up in rented houses and new schools, lines them up like a drill squadron, makes them salute official household orders, and expects them to be tough as nails, excel at sports, and tow the line.

There's a special combat at home which is pretty much the way he runs the Marine Corps. "Hack it or pack it!" is Bull's motto, and everything is reduced to an endurance test or a feat of bloodthirsty competition. There's nothing more impotent than a warrior between wars, and the oldest boy, Ben, says: "I was praying we'd go to war so King Kong would have somebody else to fight besides me." Ben is no sissy, but no matter how many basketball games he wins, he can never measure up to his dad's definition of a man's man, and this is one of the central conflicts in a film brimming with radiant human self-discoveries.

A man like Bull wants a son on the threshold of manhood to be a Marine like his dad. It's the American way. The kid is torn between wanting to please his father and a desperate need to taste his own freedom and try his own wings.

There's a tender scene in which Bull wakes up the boy on his eighteenth birthday at four A.M. to bang him in the chest with his birthday gift—a World War II fighter squadron jacket. His mother's present, on the other hand, is a personal letter: "Gentleness is what I've always admired most in men— whatever you do, wherever you go, you will always have my blessing."

The heart-tearing thing about these relationships is that everybody thinks he's doing the right thing. There is love in this family, although it sometimes manifests itself in the form of violence, and without feeling manipulated in any way, the viewer is drawn into the vortex of that love until its complexities are absorbed in subliminal ways that leave you moved and stimulated.

The Great Santini is the story of a macho man afraid of growing old, a boy afraid of growing up, a family unhinged by natural forces, friendships between outcasts (Ben learns to share his real feelings with a crippled black boy who sells honey and teaches Ben more of a lesson about real courage and bravery than he has ever learned from his own father), and a mother who tries to hold all of the elements together.

There's not a false note in it. No element ever reaches the dangerous perimeter of cliché. For every sensitive longing the boy feels, there is a smart-mouthed retort from the precocious sister (Lisa Jane Persky is terrific) who deals with dad in her own defensive way. "You've got to learn how to interpret the signals your father gives off," says Blythe Danner to the girl after she's had a noisy fight with Duvall. "He always gives off the signals of a psychopathic killer," comes the reply, "so what does it matter how you interpret them?"

Lewis John Carlino, who wrote and directed this exemplary film from Pat Conroy's marvelous novel, emerges as one of the screen's finest craftsmen. He has distilled from the actors three-dimensional performances that sing with love and anger and the honest vitality of human exchange. There are real feelings here, spoken and expressed the way people actually think and feel and talk. The location shooting in Beaufort, South Carolina, simply and wisely utilizes the heat and boredom and honeysuckle ambience of the film's perfectly modulated action.

And the actors are really amazing. One of the miracles of *The Great Santini* is how this bullheaded Marine manages to emerge as likable and as understandably human and complex as the other characters he bullies, and a large part of that triumph belongs to Robert Duvall, who strips the character of artificiality and stereotype and leaves him naked.

Blythe Danner, long one of my favorite actresses, soars to the highest ranks of the acting profession as the camellia-skinned, wise, and all-knowing mother, searching every shadowy corner of her character to illuminate hidden insights. Trying to make sense of the pieces in the family puzzle, bring the people she loves together, and bridge the gap between her love for Bull and the kids' fear and resentment of him, she ignites the screen with uncommon maturity and strength. With subtle brush strokes, she paints a portrait of a woman that is left on the canvas of the mind with indelible ink.

And Michael O'Keefe, as the teenage Ben, is just about the best young actor to emerge on the screen from obscurity since Montgomery Clift. All of them have contributed sincerely and lovingly to what I consider a film like *Breaking Away*—a real "sleeper" in need of a public to awake from its slumber and discover it.

People are always asking me, "Don't you ever get tired of movies?" The answer is yes, I'm often exhausted and defeated by junk, the bloated and mindless inanities that are belched forth to insult us all. But then a movie like *The Great Santini* comes along, moves me to tears, knocks me off my feet with its artistry and vision, and somehow I realize all over again that movies do count. They can even be art.

GREEN DOLPHIN STREET (1947)
★ ★ ★ Directed by Victor Saville. Produced by Carey Wilson. Screenplay by Samson Raphaelson. *With Lana Turner, Van Heflin, Donna Reed, Frank*

Morgan, Edmund Gwenn, Gladys Cooper, Dame May Whitty, Reginald Owen, and Richard Hart.

MGM's 1947 epic was the forerunner of the big-budget disaster movies that were all the rage in the late sixties and the seventies. Nothing since has quite equaled it for pure grandeur and excitement. This movie fairly trembles and explodes with cinematic-effects, with gorgeous, hysterical Lana Turner screaming her head off in the wilds of New Zealand as she fights off native uprisings, hurricanes, tidal waves and mammoth earthquakes. It also has murder, intrigue, family conflict, illicit romance, adultery, and Oscar-winning visual and sound effects. Best scene: Donna Reed, trapped in a cave as the tide rises round her, forced to climb the rocks with her bare hands to a convent on top of the cliff. (After this harrowing experience, she naturally becomes a nun.) Fabulous acting by Van Heflin, Gladys Cooper, Dame May Whitty, Frank Morgan, Edmund Gwenn, and the entire MGM stock company.

GREMLINS (1984)

★ ★ Directed by Joe Dante. Screenplay by Chris Columbus. Produced by Michael Finell. Executive producer Steven Spielberg. *With Hoyt Axton, Zach Galligan, Phoebe Cates, Polly Holliday, and Scott Brady.*

Parents planning on showing their kids *Gremlins* for pure escapism should be forewarned: The price of admission is nothing compared to the psychiatrist bills that will pile up after the kids come out screaming and traumatized. After *Gremlins*, a lot of children are going to be frightened to death of their own toys.

Gremlins is part comedy, part horror movie, and part rip-off of *E.T.* In every respect, it is a sorry disappointment.

The idea is that a child's most cuddly and devoted pet can turn vicious and deadly when least expected—an idea that will not appeal to kids and will make adults ask: "So what?"

Either way, *Gremlins* is pretty gimmicky second-rate stuff from director Joe Dante and producer Steven Spielberg, when much more first-rate stuff is expected.

The gremlins in this fable are furry little animals that look like a cross between E.T. and a koala bear, with donkey ears.

When the film begins, a nutty inventor of gadgets that don't work buys a gremlin for $200 in the dark subterranean recesses of an antique shop in Chinatown. The Chinese kid who makes the sale gives the inventor three warnings that sound like fortune cookies: Keep the gremlin away from all bright lights, never drop any water on him, and never feed him after midnight.

The man (Hoyt Axton) goes home to small-town America and gives the gremlin to his son Billy (Zach Galligan) for a Christmas present. The gremlin, now called Gizmo, is a cute little creature. It talks. It sings. It loves Clark Gable movies on TV.

But there is trouble in paradise. When it gets wet, Gizmo goes berserk, a group of furry Ping-Pong balls pop out of its body, and soon there's a whole gang of these chattering little rodents running around the attic and some of them are quite nasty. When they eat after midnight because Billy's electric clock stopped, they grow cocoons and turn into flesh-eating monsters with razor blades for claws and ice picks for teeth.

Nothing can stop a mean-spirited gremlin with homicidal tendencies. One of the best scenes in the movie is when one of the little monsters falls into the YMCA swimming pool and the screen fills with boiling, gurgling water as an entire army of these grotesque horrors begins to multiply.

Soon they are munching through the streets on Christmas Eve, leveling houses with snowplows, causing traffic accidents, setting fires, and eating the local citizens alive in front of their Christmas trees.

Billy's mother (Frances Lee McCain), alone in the house with only a butcher knife for protection, kills some of the gremlins with kitchen appliances and a microwave oven, but in the neighbors' houses, the body count is rising.

The special effects people, along with Chris Walas, who designed the very real, lifelike gremlins, have a field day with the carnage and destruction, but the scriptwriter, Chris Columbus, doesn't know how to get the movie back on course.

Between gremlin attacks we get the usual nonsense about the meanest woman in town (Polly Holliday), a greedy dragon who seems modeled after Margaret Hamilton's wicked witch in *The Wizard of Oz*. We also get a dopey subplot about Billy's romance with a local barmaid named Kate, who hates Christmas because—are you sitting down?—her father died in a chimney dressed like Santa Claus!

When *Gremlins* isn't boring, it's just embarrassingly silly. In the middle of their murderous rampage, the creatures break into a tavern, smoke cigarettes, drink tap beer, play poker, and indulge in a bit of trendy break-dancing. Worse to come, they all end up in a movie house watching *Snow White and the Seven Dwarfs* singing, ''Heigh-ho, Heigh-ho, it's off to work we go,'' like an invasion of demented Muppets.

The ending, when little Gizmo, the good gremlin, helps save the day by using Santa's toys as weapons, is final proof of how unimaginative the filmmakers are. Everything builds up to an *E.T.* homage, with Gizmo saying good bye to his friend Billy. There's a message here somewhere. Something about how the world misuses what it doesn't understand.

The message gets diluted in a lot of noise and gimmicks, and in the final tally it's the *Gremlins* audience that gets misused, not the gremlins.

A GUY NAMED JOE (1943)

★ ★ ★ ½ Directed by Victor Fleming. Screenplay by Dalton Trumbo. Produced by Everett Riskin. *With Spencer Tracy, Irene Dunne, Van Johnson, Lionel Barrymore, James Gleason, Ward Bond, Barry Nelson, and Esther Williams.*

Spencer Tracy starred with Irene Dunne in this World War II tearjerker. Steven Spielberg of all people claims this is one of his all-time favorite movies and remade it in 1990 as *Always*, a poor copy which only served to prove that nobody will ever top Tracy as a pilot killed in combat and sent back to the front by archangel Lionel Barrymore to guide a younger pilot to safety. This mix of fantasy, romance, war action, and comedy could have been a fanciful, fruity fiasco, but the sturdy direction by the great Victor Fleming and the solid script by Dalton Trumbo gave the all-star cast plenty to work with. Van Johnson is wonderful as Tracy's young sidekick, and the pretty young thing making her bow on the dance floor at the soldier's canteen is none other than Esther Williams.

HAIR (1979)

★ ★ ½ Directed by Milos Forman. Screenplay by Michael Weller. Produced by Lester Persky and Michael Butler. *With John Savage, Treat Williams, Beverly D'Angelo, Dorsey Wright, Annie Golden, and Don Dacus.*

Some people will wonder how they could ever make a movie out of *Hair*. Others will ask why. Now that I've seen it, I know how they did it, but I'm still asking why. The 1960s rock musical was an onstage hippie protest against everything from Nixon politics to Ozzie and Harriet. *Hair* the movie, directed by Milos Forman, suffers from the same time warp, glorifying free love, bisexuality, long hair, draft-card burning, LSD, and body odor. With nothing but noisy music and no plot, the people responsible for dragging *Hair* out of its closet had to find a way to contemporize it so it wouldn't seem dated beyond rescue. A lame structure was invented, involving an Oklahoma farm boy who boards a bus to the Big Apple to visit the draft board. In Central Park, he comes across a group of homeless, rootless, mindless mite-brains who are much too old to be hippies, and gets introduced to a new life-style.

Thoroughly stoned, jailed, humiliated, and confused, our hero ends up in an Army training camp in Arizona, with the flower children in hot pursuit. The leader of the pack, a hirsute hobo named Berger, cuts his own hair and exchanges clothes with the soldier so he can sneak off the base for a rendezvous with the gang, and gets mistakenly sent to Vietnam in his straight buddy's place. To my everlasting surprise, none of this is boring, and some of it is

actually endearing. The problem is that all of it is just plain unnecessary.

At a time when yesterday's hippies are either running record companies or working in government jobs in Washington, *Hair* is as tired as a ten-year-old bikini. What it had to say in 1967, to cynics who wanted no part of conventional society, was productive and vital. Kids piled into the defunct nightclub called Cheetah, smoked pot, and made love, not war. Later the message reached the masses on Broadway, and the Ragni-Rado-MacDermot songs like "Aquarius" and "Let the Sunshine In" became hymns for a restless generation with no use for soap, underwear or sixties values. Years have passed and the old words are now old hat. We've heard them too often, and we're on to other pursuits. There is nothing more pathetic than forty-year-olds and up who grow long hair and wear hippie beads, and finding new ways to recycle *Hair* for the masses is like thinking up new ways to cook liver.

To pipe adrenaline into the collapsed arteries, choreographer Twyla Tharp was engaged to give the dances oomph. I have never been able to figure out Twyla Tharp. Her routines look like a cross between make-it-up-as-you-go-along and follow-the-bouncing-ball. Most of the dancers seem to be writhing in agony from athlete's foot. "Opening up" the old numbers doesn't add up to much, either. Instead of Diane Keaton singing "Black Boys" and Melba Moore singing "White Boys" as they did in the Broadway production, we now get a black draft board licking its lips lasciviously over white inductees in their jockey shorts, while uniformed white goons drool over naked black biceps. The rest of it resembles a pagan ritual energized by massive doses of angel dust.

The performers look like Broadway gypsies dressed in Stress-Flex garbage bags and fright wigs. They're too polished and sophisticated to impersonate innocent flower children, and when John Savage, Treat Williams, and the rest shed their clothes and jump into the Central Park lake for some moonlight skinny-dipping, all I could do was wonder how much of the production budget went for tetanus shots.

HANNAH AND HER SISTERS (1986)

★ ★ ★ ★ Written and directed by Woody Allen. Produced by Robert Greenhut. With Woody Allen, Mia Farrow, Michael Caine, Carrie Fisher, Barbara Hershey, Dianne Wiest, Max Von Sydow, Maureen O'Sullivan, Lloyd Nolan, and Daniel Stern.

Hannah and Her Sisters is a Woody Allen valentine—a Tiffany-wrapped billet-doux to the whole neurotic world that is a piece of his own heart.

If you are still in touch with your own heart, or feel the need to share it with people you love, you'd be mad to miss it. *Hannah and Her Sisters* is a masterpiece.

Painfully accurate and richly comic, it is Woody's most complex yet most accessible film. No wonder critics treated it like the second coming; *Hannah* is a work of astonishing wisdom and maturity that embraces life in all its crazy, contradictory emotional contexts, touching, instructing, and uplifting the lives of all who see it. Although I still have personal fondness for *Zelig*, this is, in a broader sense, Woody's greatest film.

What's all the fuss about? It's hard to say, just as all of Woody's films are hard to pinpoint and describe. If Chekov were alive today, an outpatient at Mount Sinai, a Bobby Short fan, and writing for the *New Yorker*, you'd get *Hannah and Her Sisters* in a nutshell. Constructed in short chapters, with a rainbow spectrum of characters taking turns as narrators, *Hannah* needlepoints a canvas of contemporary New York life, exposing sadness and joy and the ritual of self-discovery in every stitch.

The plot spreads over three Thanksgivings at the spacious Central Park West apartment of Hannah (Mia Farrow), with Hannah and her sisters Lee (Barbara Hershey) and Holly (Dianne Wiest) as the centerpieces.

The progeny of Bohemian show-biz parents who spar endlessly and endure their children's crises superficially, the girls are rivals, friends, and catalysts, and in two years of their lives we get a roundelay of survival techniques that could happen nowhere else but a planet unto itself like the isle of Manhattan.

Hannah is an actress who would give up Ibsen in a second to have babies. She's divorced from Mickey (Woody Allen), after having twins by artificial insemination from his ex-writing partner, and now she's married to Elliot (Michael Caine), a successful financial adviser with keen business acumen but not much substance.

Elliot loves Hannah's cool, controlled, slightly flaky but always capable domestic grip on reality, but he lusts after her

beautiful, erotic, unfocused sister, Lee. Lee lives with a brooding, depressed, cynical painter (played by master of gloom Max Von Sydow) who is always threatening suicide.

But the queen of neurosis is Holly (amusingly essayed by Dianne Wiest), a cocaine-sniffing, chain-smoking, anxiety-ridden dilettante who has failed at everything. Holly can't get an acting job, so she opens the Stanislavski Catering Service with her pushy, competitive girlfriend April (Carrie Fisher).

Hannah, who holds everything together with a maternal perfection that infuriates everyone, keeps a place in her heart—and at her Thanksgiving table—for all strays.

Her self-assurance is unnerving, especially to her ex-husband Mickey, an ulcer-ridden hypochondriac who wafts through the streets of New York between *Saturday Night Live* and various hospital testing labs, convinced he's dying.

Mickey tries everything. He converts to Catholicism from Judaism, stocking up on Wonder Bread and Hellman's mayonnaise. He even tries to convert Holly to happiness.

Mickey is so depressed he'd like to kill himself, but his parents would be so devastated he'd have to kill them first to spare them the humiliation. Holly is into ESP, punk rock, and drugs, Mickey is into vitamins and Cole Porter. In one hilarious scene which distills the essence of Woody himself in real life, he takes her to hear Bobby Short at the Carlyle—an experience she endures with all the pleasure of the Nuremberg trials. One of the film's chief delights is a surprise ending which leaves a glow on the heartstrings. "The heart is a very resilient little muscle," says Woody, and in this life-affirming discovery you get the film's philosophy.

Like all Woody Allen movies, *Hannah and Her Sisters* is full of wonderful human characters (each one a short story with a literate structure) who search for the big answer to life's mysteries. This time they learn that the only answer that means anything is that there is no answer. But by keeping their hearts open, they discover the Cracker-Jack-box prize is optimism.

The film is so wise and truthful that I saw myself in every character in it, and that is something that rarely happens at the movies. Woody Allen movies are like Mabel Mercer records—their artistry seems deceptively simple, but they tell the truth about us all.

The cast is like a finely honed repertory company, each contributor uniquely individual yet melting warmly into the overview. To achieve this stunning effect of symmetry and balance, Woody used actual locations as well as truths about his actors.

Mia Farrow's apartment is really her own cocoon on Central Park West. Some of the children in her Mother Goose nursery are her own children—natural, adopted, and surrogate. Her mother, a once-beautiful actress still charged with vitality and charm, is Maureen O'Sullivan, Mia's real-life mother. The sisters are very much derived from Mia's own siblings.

Woody is, well, Woody. But a rejuvenated, all-things-possible Woody, vulnerable and baffled, yet romantic and brave.

Sensitive to the point of agony, Dianne Wiest gives the film's most piercing performance. Her Holly is the tortured, funny, mixed-up Holly Golightly we all know in the New York Cuisinart of life—desperate for a man, but always looking in the wrong places, bouncing from one contemporary thrill to the next and always crashing in self-defeat, finding comfort in the embrace of people she resents the most for giving it, a full-bodied mess everyone wants to save.

The great Italian cinematographer Carlo Di Palma has captured the essence of contemporary New York the way Woody Allen has exposed the frayed capacity for love in his New Yorkers. In *Hannah and Her Sisters*—even in the courageous happy ending—the camera has trapped us all. The experience is hilarious, deeply affecting, and genuinely enchanting.

THE HAPPIEST MILLIONAIRE (1967)

★ ★ Directed by Norman Tokar. Produced by Bill Anderson. Screenplay by A. J. Carothers, based on the play by Kyle Crichton and the book by Cornelia Drexel Biddle. *With Fred MacMurray, Geraldine Page, Greer Garson, Gladys Cooper, Hermione Baddeley, Lesley Ann Warren, John Davidson, and Tommy Steele.*

This is the last live-action film personally supervised by Walt Disney before his death, and despite its flaws it contains some passable family ingredients—lavish sets, perky singing and dancing, and harmless sentimental charm. It's the true (sort of) story of Philadelphia millionaire Anthony Drexel Biddle, an eccentric, strongwilled "Life with Father" character who boxed with Boy Scouts and kept alligators in his conservatory. Fred MacMurray plays the kind of role that made Clifton Webb famous with great relish. And lord, what a cast: Geraldine Page, Greer Garson, Gladys Cooper, John Davidson, Lesley Ann Warren, Tommy Steele. Corny, folksy, often more labored than funny, and a low-brow enterprise by some high-brow talent.

HARDCORE (1979)

★ ★ ½ Directed and written by Paul Schrader. Produced by Buzz Feitshans. *With George C. Scott, Season Hubley, and Peter Boyle.*

This tough, hard-hitting drama about a man searching for a runaway daughter who has gotten sucked up in the porno-movie underworld is like a car door that slams on your hand, leaving a painful memory every time you look at your blackened fingernails.

Hardcore sings the lowdown blues of distraught parents everywhere whose wayward children have disappeared into the underbelly of smut and sex that pollutes big-city police blotters (more than a million, according to FBI files). It is, you will see, a highly original look at an important issue made entertaining by a superlative cast headed by George C. Scott and a gutsy script by Paul (*Taxi Driver*, *Blue Collar*) Schrader, who also directed.

Scott, in one of his most polished and keenly observed characterizations, plays a furniture manufacturer from Grand Rapids whose deeply rooted Dutch Reformation Church background has bridged a rigid gap between his mousy teenage daughter's boredom and the more enticing realities of progressive society. Her first taste of freedom—a Calvinist Youth Convention in California—opens her eyes to an exotic world, forbidden to humble Christian girls, and she disappears from her religious group at Knott's Berry Farm.

The beautifully modulated scenes of Scott's middle-class American home life—Bible readings, saying grace before dinner, strong religious faith in all matters of daily routine—are of little consolation to him now in his rage and grief. His values are shattered and no amount of friendly advice from his fellow churchgoers ("It's hard sometimes for us to understand the Lord's ways"—"He's testing you"—"You have to have faith!") will ease his conscious-stricken moral-

ity. His emotional upheaval as he watches his daughter in a trashy porno film procured by a sleazy private detective (Peter Boyle) is a pure and telling moment. A lot of things happen in this world that Middle America, lobotomized by TV and Sunday school and chicken and dumplings, knows nothing about. *Hardcore* is a movie that shows you some of them.

Scott takes up the hunt, wandering from one gimmicky massage parlor to the next, pretending to be a rich porno-flick producer looking for a tax shelter. From a putrid motel room in Van Nuys, he gets a hard look at the world of kiddie porn, smarmy personal ads in underground newspapers, skin flicks, drugs, and the kind of corruption and horror that feeds on the tenderloins of Los Angeles, San Diego, and San Francisco.

Season Hubley gives an energetic, kinky, and totally mesmerizing performance as a prostitute who leads him to an eventual confrontation with his estranged child, but before the final reunion the audience gets a guided tour of this world of sex for sale, where you can get child prostitutes, rapes, sexual tortures, even murder for a price. It's a bloody eye-opener for everybody and probably a stomach-turner for some. The faint of heart are forewarned.

Schrader, who wrote and directed, comes from a staunch Calvinist background himself, so *Hardcore* is in some ways an obsession of personal vision. He's like a choirboy who has wandered astray, seen the ugliness of the world, and wants to set it straight. He exhibits both bouts of affection and sharp disapproval of his simple Christian characters, but in the end *Hardcore* suffers from the same kind of conventional Hollywood resolution that wrecked *Taxi Driver*. At the end of *Taxi Driver*, the runaway child prostitute, after witnessing the most brutal massacre this side of Wounded Knee, went home to her baffled parents and lived happily ever after. I didn't believe it for a minute, and I don't believe the final frames of *Hardcore* either, when father and daughter stage a tearful homecoming of the heart that went out of style when David Selznick died.

Schrader has tried to have it every way at once, and *Hardcore* ends up being not hard core enough when it matters, then soft around the center like a melting macaroon when it matters even more. He knows alienated men and children the way a shaver knows his morn-ing mirror—and he gets to the roots of the screwed-up floating garbage of this twilight world in incident and dialogue, but he doesn't know how to get out of the unmade bed he's invented and still soothe the jangled nerves of his censors, studio execs, and viewers.

So at the point where we most need to know the terrifying consequences of self-destruction, he lays on the rainbow message: "No matter how low you sink, it'll be okay as long as Daddy comes to get you!" He's given us gangrene, then sent us home with a Band-Aid.

THE HARVEY GIRLS (1945)

★ ★ ★ ½ Directed by George Sidney. Screenplay by Edmund Beloin and Nathaniel Curtiso. Produced by Arthur Freed and Roger Edens. *With Judy Garland, John Hodiak, Ray Bolger, Angela Lansbury, Cyd Charisse, Marjorie Main, Virginia O'Brien, Chill Wills, Selena Royle, Preston Foster, and others.*

Judy Garland in peak form, a glorious score by Harry Warren and Johnny Mercer, luscious Technicolor, and one of MGM's best plots distinguish this legendary musical. When the railroad moved west, the trains had to be fed and Fred Harvey drafted hundreds of beautiful waitresses to serve the passengers in Harvey Houses from New York to New Mexico. With the gangsters, gamblers, and honky-tonk girls on one side of the law and the wholesome, all-American Harvey Girls on the other, every boom-town where there was a train depot became a draw. The sparks really fly when Judy locks horns with saloon singer Angela Lansbury. This is the movie that made history with the Oscar-winning "Atchinson, Topeka, and the Santa Fe" number, shot from above the town with zoom lenses to include the train, the depot, the railroad yard, and everybody on the MGM lot. An absolutely vital addition to any home video musical library.

THE HAUNTING (1963)

★ ★ ½ Produced and directed by Robert Wise. Screenplay by Nelson Gidding, based on Shirley Jackson's The Haunting of Hill House. With Julie Harris, Claire Bloom, Richard Johnson, Russ Tamblyn, Lois Maxwell, and Fay Compton.

In 1963's The Haunting, the spooks scare the living daylights out of Julie Harris and Claire Bloom, huddling together and paralyzed with terror while listening to thuds, screams, and gunfire outside.

It's a study in psychic phenomena, with the scariest chills heard and implied rather than seen. There isn't much logic here, but by the time it's over, you may never turn the lights out again.

HEART BEAT (1980)

★ ★ ★ Directed and written by John Byrum. Produced by Alan Greisman and Michael Shamberg. With John Heard, Sissy Spacek, Nick Nolte, Ray Sharkey, Anne Dusenberry, Kent Williams, Tony Bill, and Steve Allen.

Heart Beat is a powerful, strangely affecting movie about Jack Kerouac, his best friend and literary prototype Neal Cassady, and the girl they both loved and shared, Carolyn Cassady. John Heard plays Jack, the shy, introverted writer trying to shake his Columbia University intellectualism, dodge the tenacious hold of his domineering mother, and establish his own, authentic identity. Nick Nolte is Neal, the ex-convict son of a wino who provides the material for Kerouac's typewriter. Together they worked, hitchhiked, talked, chased girls, drank, and smoked pot from New York to San Francisco.

Sissy Spacek is the society girl who took one look at them and got hooked. Everything they did and said was either a compliment or an insult. She didn't know the difference or care. To her, they were new and wonderful, and their beat generation had a heartbeat all its own.

John Byrum, who wrote and directed *Heart Beat*, captures all of that and more. The movie is about friendship, love, romantic ideals, adventure, and the growing pains of a young, rebellious nation moving into the modern age. Kerouac's *On the Road*, his homage to Neal Cassady, became the bible for the beatniks because it conveyed the awe these people felt at the sheer expanse of America, and at the possibilities of a life without rules. At a time when everyone came home from the war to get married and buy TV sets and look-alike suburban houses on the installment plan, Neal and Jack and their crazy poet friend Ira (based on Allen Ginsberg and played with slobby intensity by Ray Sharkey) would have none of it.

When Carolyn runs off with Neal and later marries him because she's pregnant, the ideals behind the good times are seriously challenged. Nick Nolte is wonderfully ill at ease as he tries to adapt to the suburban life style of respectability to the tune of Les Paul and Mary Ford records. But his train conductor's uniform is choking him and he becomes even more churlish when he has to talk to the squares next door. Sissy Spacek brings Carolyn to throbbing life as the intelligent woman accepting her responsibilities to Neal, Jack, and her kids.

Heart Beat is based on Carolyn's memoirs, and Spacek provides the perspective and the patience necessary for her appropriately central role. When she and Neal escort Jack to the Greyhound bus because *On the Road* has finally been published, you know that for them the dream, the rebellion, and the values are over. They struggle for words but don't hear what the others are saying, and you can feel an era, *their* era, dying. A friendship that weathered failure, mutual lovers, jealousy, and the stagnant air of the suburbs could not stand up to commercial, media-drenched success.

Neither could Neal and Jack continue happily without that friendship. Carolyn, once and for all, was left holding the fort. Older and wiser, she says: "Neal was sentenced to prison on a marijuana rap; Jack was sentenced to posterity. Something had ended. We used to call it innocence.''

Byrum is a director of great vision and sensitivity. From the actors, he has distilled performances that sizzle with joy, humor and pathos. Cinematographer Lazslo Kovacs has captured a beautiful, touching sense of unrestricted energy which will always be a part of America, even through the most repressive times. That particular struggle to survive and remain loyal to ideals, as experienced in three very different people, is a theme that stirred me deeply.

Everything about *Heart Beat*, from the Shorty Rogers jazz music, to the venetian blinds, to the coffeehouse bongos, is authentic, but styled with artistry. To miss it is to pass up a lasting experience, a chance to reflect on who we are, where we've been, and where we're going.

HEATHERS (1989)
★ ★ Directed by Michael Lehmann. Screenplay by Daniel Waters. Produced by Denis Di Novi. With Winona Ryder, Christian Slater, and Shannon Doherty.

Heathers is a takeoff (send-up?) of noisy, repulsive teenage flicks from the John Hughes school, in which first-time director Michael Lehmann and first-time writer Daniel Waters come up with a Bush-era satire of Reagan-era teen politics. The Heathers are three pompous, pretentious prom queens from an Ohio high school who set the social standards for power and popularity among the other students. Winona Ryder is their new protégée, Veronica. She's also rich, arrogant, and beautiful—but she's a rebel. After falling for the school outlaw J.D., played by scruffy weirdo Christian Slater, she decides the cruel and abusive Heathers and the dumb jocks they hang out with are expendable. So they feed one girl a bottle of liquid Drāno, blast the football heroes with bullets, and justify each murder with "Well, football season is over—they had nothing else to offer." By the time Veronica realizes you can't kill people just because they're creeps, J.D. has become a real psycho hell-bent on blowing up the entire school. In the end, what begins as a neat satire on moronic teenage movies ends as another horror flick grossout. The black comedy backfires, but taking on the geeky plague of movies about kids who seem to come from the planet Mars is a start in the right direction.

HEAVEN'S GATE (1980)
½★ Directed and written by Michael Cimino. Produced by Joann Carelli. With Kris Kristofferson, Christopher Walken, Isabelle Huppert, John Hurt, Sam Waterston, Joseph Cotten, and Jeff Bridges.

When I first saw *Heaven's Gate* in a movie theater, it was so incoherent throughout that when the screen finally turned to a complete blur, half of the audience started yelling "Focus!" and throwing popcorn boxes at the projection booth while the other half yelled "Shut up! It's supposed to look that way!" Any way you cut it, nothing makes a bit of sense. Harvard is really Oxford, Wyoming is really Montana, and the plot, dialogue, story, action, cinematography and editing are really stupefying. It's no worse than Robert Altman's *McCabe and Mrs. Miller*, a film it plagiarizes shamelessly, but it's still bad enough to be the worst movie of 1980.

Not five minutes into this empty epic, John Hurt delivers a speech to Harvard's graduating class of 1870 that bores even the people on screen. Then there's a waltz sequence on the lawn that has nothing to do with anything that follows. Then we get railroad cars, peasants pulling wagons through the dust, boxcars filled with refugees, and all kinds of pioneer poetics, and it's twenty years later.

Kris Kristofferson, one of the Harvard grads, is a marshal in Wyoming and his friends are planning to murder 125 immigrant farmers who have been stealing cattle from the local cattle barons for food. (Just one of the thousands of questions that result from Michael Cimino's demented screenplay is how all those Harvard lads ended up on the uncivilized frontier in the first place, instead of in nice government jobs in Washington.)

For three hours and forty-five minutes, it's Kris Kristofferson against the cutthroat villains, one of whom (Chris Walken) has become an enforcer for the cattle barons. Both are in love with Isabelle Huppert, who plays a bordello madam named Ella. This movie looks even worse when you try to explain it than it does on screen.

Scene after scene unfolds without a clue to the time, the year, the place, or the relationships of the people on the screen. Men fiddle while the whole town roller skates, and Vilmos Zsigmond captures it all with camera lenses that appear to have been sprayed with sherry. But banjos, cockfights, blazing Winchesters and thousands of extras running into each other in mass panic do not a movie make. By the time Kristofferson finally gets around to the big shootout at the end, like John Wayne in *The Alamo*, the movie may have you dozing.

You know who the villains are because they all wear gray coats and carry rifles. You know who the victims are because they all speak with subtitles. But what the hell are they doing and who the hell are all the other people who mumble incoherently behind clouds of dust and filters? All John Hurt does is drink and make cynical noises. All Sam Waterston does is squint his rodent eyes and wear fur hats. All Isabelle Huppert does is disrobe for the entire cast whenever she has to speak more than a paragraph in a single shot.

The now-familiar Western scenery is pretty when we can see it through all the Vaseline, and Kristofferson toils valiantly in a role that makes about as much sense as the Book of Deuteronomy printed backwards. The rest of *Heaven's Gate* is pretentious bilge.

HENRY V (1989)

★ ★ ★ ★ Directed by Kenneth Branagh. Produced by Bruce Sharman. *With Kenneth Branagh, Paul Scofield, Derek Jacobi, Ian Holm, Judi Dench, and others.*

Laurence Olivier's triumphant performance in this Shakespearean play transferred to film was a 1944 highlight, but in this brawling, handsome new version, twenty-eight-year-old Irish actor Kenneth Branagh gives the old war-horse a modern view that almost makes you forget the past. Where Olivier used poetic lyricism to convey the young king's anguish, Branagh uses brawn and passion. At times he resembles James Cagney playing a boxer. He's tougher and shrewder and wilder than Olivier, and the film—which he audaciously directed as well—has thrilling, mud-splattering war scenes of epic proportions. War is shown here not as glorified honor, but as tragic, hopeless, and blood-soaked realism. A grand, sprawling movie debut by a multi-talented actor-director who deservedly got an Oscar nomination.

**THE HISTORY OF THE
WORLD—PART I (1981)**
★ ½ Directed, written, and
produced by Mel Brooks. With Mel
Brooks, Sid Caesar, Madeline
Kahn, Dom DeLuise, Harvey
Korman, Cloris Leachman, and
Ron Cary.

Here's good advice to anyone planning to investigate Mel
Brooks's *The History of the
World—Part I*. Since there is
only a five-minute stretch of
this grotesque stupidity that
won't cause permanent brain
damage, I suggest you time it
perfectly. The five minutes I'm
talking about is devoted to the
Spanish Inquisition. It comes
exactly one hour after the film
begins and it is wonderful. So
let a word to the wise be suffi-
cient guidance. Fast forward
one hour into the movie, hang
around until the number is over,
and rewind. You'll see the only
thing worth seeing in this otherwise insufferable assault on the
senses, and you can leave with
your faith in Mel Brooks un-
shaken.

If the rest of the film were up
to the hilarious sophistication of
the "Inquisition" number, *The
History of the World* might have
added up to something more
than a massive Excedrin headache. Some of it is so filthy it
goes beyond vulgar Catskills

amateurism. Most of it is so flat
and predictable that the audience was saying the next line
before the comics on the screen
could get it out.

First, there's the "Stone
Age," in which Sid Caesar
plays a caveman who discovers
fire and does the first painting.
With Orson Welles's heavy-
handed narration, I just knew
somebody would come along
and urinate on the art, thus giving the world its first critic.
Sure enough, that's exactly
what happens. In the "Old Testament" segment, the audience
found the ten Commandments
before Moses did.

The "Roman Empire," which
went on forever without wit or
a fresh idea in sight, featured
Hugh Hefner presiding over a
Temple of Eros and discussing
centerfolds; gladiators who
couldn't get unemployment insurance unless they killed somebody; Mel Brooks as a stand-up
philosopher who plays Caesar's
Palace; Ron Cary as his agent,
Swiftus Lazarus; and Madeline
Kahn, wasted again in one of her
snorting nymphomaniac routines. The dialogue goes something like this: "What are you
looking for?" "A pack of Tro-
jans." "Gee, I just ran out."

It's not even up to the lowest
Mel Brooks standards. More

like something from the Marty Feldman–Three Stooges school of schlock. There must be something about the history of the world worth satirizing besides the size of people's genitals, or put-downs of women, homosexuals, and Jews.

At last, after a first hour that seems like three days, we get to the previously mentioned "Inquisition." Here, in only five minutes, Brooks achieves what the rest of the film fails to do. He captures our imagination with music, timing, editing, and a truly creative idea by staging the entire Inquisition like an MGM musical number.

In a song written by Brooks and Ronny Graham and orchestrated superbly by Ralph Burns, set in a torture chamber, even the heads in the stocks and the victims being revolved on racks and other medieval dungeon appliances sing along. "Hey, Torquemada, whaddya say?" sing the inquisitioners, while Brooks, dancing down a flight of stone stairs, rhymes with, "I just got back from the auto-da-fe." It's like a nonstop Kay Thompson number as Brooks sings, "We've broken their fingers, we've flattened their buns. Nothing is working, so send in the nuns!"

Here, a chorus line of nuns descend like Ziegfeld girls, strip to bathing suits beneath their habits, and precision dive into a giant swimming pool in a spectacular pastiche of Esther Williams production numbers, replete with sparklers rising from underwater to the full accompaniment of a swing band. This is the kind of syncopated rhythm the rest of the film sorely lacks. It is probably the single most amusing thing Brooks has come up with since his "Springtime for Hitler" number in *The Producers*. It also shows what a clever, inventive talent he is when some time and effort are invested in producing a comic idea and getting it right.

Unfortunately, the film sinks again without a trace after this terrific interlude. We are suffering through a stale French Revolution. "The peasants are revolting!" someone screams. "You said it!" says Brooks, as a white-wigged Louis XVI. "They stink on ice!" So does the movie.

HOLIDAY INN (1942)
★ ★ ★ ★ Directed and produced by Mark Sandrich. Screenplay by Claude Binyon, adapted by Elmer Rice from an original idea by Irving Berlin. *With Bing Crosby, Fred Astaire, Marjorie*

Reynolds, Virginia Dale, Walter Abel and Louise Beavers.

One of the all-time great movie musicals despite the absence of color, this successful Irving Berlin package introduced the timelessly popular "White Christmas," grossed a fortune and even had a chain of motels named after it. Bing Crosby and Fred Astaire teamed as a song-and-dance team that breaks up when Crosby retires to the Connecticut countryside to lead a life of rest and relaxation and opens an inn that is open only on holidays. Each of the eight holidays celebrated was accompanied by a special production number, making *Holiday Inn* a perennial classic throughout the year. You will never tire of this one. I always play it on Thanksgiving.

THE HOMECOMING—A CHRISTMAS STORY (TV, 1971)

★ ★ ★ Directed by Fielder Cook. Screenplay by Earl Hamner, Jr. With Patricia Neal, Richard Thomas, Ellen Corby, Edgar Bergen, William Windom, Andrew Duggan, Dorothy Stickney, Josephine Hutchinson and Cleavon Little.

A distinguished CBS-TV special that inspired the long-running, prize-winning series *The Waltons*, this gripping drama is set on a Depression Christmas Eve in 1933 as a poor rural family prepares to celebrate Christmas together. Times are tough, but the Waltons seek the truer meanings of the Yuletide season through togetherness and sharing, although their faith and courage are sorely tested while waiting for their father to return home in a treacherous snowstorm. Patricia Neal is a pioneer mother who must mask her own fears to be the pillar of maternal strength her family needs. Richard Thomas gives an indelible performance as the oldest Walton son, John Boy, and the remarkable supporting cast includes Ellen Corby, William Windom, Andrew Duggan, and Dorothy Stickney. An all-American experience as enduring as a homemade patchwork quilt.

HONEY, I SHRUNK THE KIDS (1989)

★ ★ ½ Directed by Joe Johnston. Screenplay by Ed Naha and Tom Schulman. Produced by Stuart Gordon, Brian Yuzna, and Jon Landau. With Rick Moranis, Matt Frewer, Marcia Strassman, Kristine Sutherland, Thomas Brown, Jared Rushton, Amy O'Neill, and Robert Oliveri.

Despite all the critical and audience hoopla that greeted *Honey, I Shrunk the Kids* when it hit the big screen, to my mind it's just harmless fluff that often seems little more than an excuse for the Disney special-effects team to work overtime. Still, it's fun to see Rick Moranis as a wimpy Rube Goldberg–type inventor whose shrinking machine accidentally reduces his two kids to the size of picnic gnats. "They're probably just at the mall," says Mom, when nobody comes home for supper. But actually they're being attacked by a swarm of backyard bees the size of helicopters and discovering how terrifying the spray from a garden hose can be. There's a lot of papier-mâché grass and even a sentimental Disney touch involving a sacrificial ant the size of a camel that saves the kids from a mean scorpion. I guess the point is to teach the audience tolerance for (1) small creatures the size of slugs and mollusks and (2) wacko inventors who play with laser beams on their patios. Some of the gimmicks were put to better use in *The Incredible Shrinking Man*, but it's an amusing enough way to kill ninety minutes.

HOOK (1991)
★ **Directed by Steven Spielberg. Screenplay by Jim V. Hart and Malia Marmo. Produced by Kathleen Kennedy, Frank Marshall, and Gerald R. Molen. *With Robin Williams, Dustin Hoffman, Julia Roberts, Bob Hoskins, and Maggie Smith.***

J. M. Barrie must be turning over in his grave with fury. This boring, overproduced, ugly, incoherent waste of $80 million is Steven Spielberg's pretentious attempt to tell us all what happened to Peter Pan. He grew up to be Robin Williams, a middle-aged lawyer from the Ivan Boesky school of ruthlessness who has a fear of flying. On a trip to London to visit Granny Wendy (Maggie Smith in latex) his own kids are kidnapped by Captain Hook (Dustin Hoffman) and you can imagine the surprise when, in revelations that are never too clear, this stuffy, bloated, and overweight slug (it doesn't look like padding) discovers he is really Peter Pan and the only way to save the children is to travel back in time to Never-Never Land. Julia Roberts, woefully miscast as Tinker Bell, instructs him to pass "the second star on the right" (everything sounds like a song cue) and he wakes up on a pirate ship that looks like the

Pirates of the Caribbean ride at Disneyland, falls off the mast, gets French-kissed by mermaids in Day-Glo and Dynel wigs, and ends up in a food fight with the Lost Boys throwing what appears to be lizard vomit—but to go on, I'd have to travel back in time myself: to the age of three. Never has a children's classic been so bastardized. The cacophonous John Williams music crushes whatever charm the story warrants, the special effects are cheesy, the color processing gummy, and the acting is embarrassingly awful. Dustin Hoffman has a few moments of hammy scenery-chewing glee, but there's nothing to relish from Robin Williams. Clumping heavily about with his hairy body shaved, he looks like a boiled pork butt. Bring back Mary Martin. This isn't Peter Pan; it's marzipan.

HOPE AND GLORY (1987)

★ ★ ★ ★ Directed, written and produced by John Boorman. With Sarah Miles, Sebastian Rice Edwards, David Hayman, Derrick O'Connor, Susan Wooldridge, Sammi Davis, Ian Bannen, Jean-Marc Barr, Annie Leon, and Charley Boorman.

In aerial attacks during World War II, sixty-one thousand British civilians died and it's no wonder the nostalgia of that period retains such powerful memories for that country. This is the subject of John Boorman's truthful, beautifully crafted Best Film nominee, Hope and Glory—an autobiographical diary of the experiences of his family and friends in a single London street as seen through the eyes of Boorman at age nine. It begins with a shot of the family's prized radio and cuts to a matinee full of rowdy youngsters ignoring a newsreel on air-raid safety precautions before giving full attention to a Hopalong Cassidy Western. The peril of war looms over London, but to the children it all became a great adventure.

The gas masks, the air-raid shelters, Dad joining up as a hero determined it would all be over by Christmas—these were magical events in the eyes of kids whose lives were about to be changed. And they didn't want to miss it, even when Mom tried to evacuate them to Australia. Sarah Miles, giving her sanest performance in years, is the family matriarch torn by confusion and love, and nine-year-old Sebastian Rice Edwards, as the boy for whom Hitler's bombs were more exciting than any movie, has an unaffected naturalism that is awesome.

Hope and Glory is a British *Radio Days*. It's episodic, but within the fragments of life on the home front a tapestry of courage and humanity emerges: mom playing Chopin in the ruins of her bombed-out house; a gang of rowdy kids collecting shrapnel led by a pint-sized James Cagney; the tension that mounts as the family opens a can of German jam, fearing it's poison; the spectacle of a German flier parachuting into the middle of a victory garden while a neighbor shouts "Mind the brussels sprouts!" These scenes are powerful and unforgettable.

There is a strength in remembrance, and what Boorman shares is a feast of nostalgia that expands and enriches our own experience. *Hope and Glory* is the work of a true artist—for out of Boorman's own family memoirs he has generated a marvelous sense of our common inheritance as friends across the sea.

THE HOTEL NEW HAMPSHIRE (1984)

★ ½ Directed by Tony Richardson. *With Beau Bridges, Lisa Banes, Rob Lowe, Jodie Foster, Paul McCrane, Jennie Dundas, and Natassja Kinski.*

The total disaster Tony (*Tom Jones*) Richardson has perpetrated from John Irving's *The Hotel New Hampshire* should be a lesson to filmmakers everywhere. Rarely have so many elements combined so diabolically in one movie to decimate the reputations of so many otherwise creative professionals. Don't say I didn't warn you.

The first of endless problems that plague this revolting exercise in cinematic diarrhea is the rambling, plotless, eccentricity of the book.

The demented Berry family Irving created is so bizarre you need five hours to explain them. Father (Beau Bridges) is a dreamer who keeps losing his shirt chasing a fruitless desire to be a great hotel magnate. Mother (Lisa Banes) just endures the insanity around her, like a coffee pot, characterless but reliable.

There are five mentally unbalanced children. Franny (Jodie Foster) is restless, bored, malicious, and a nymphomaniac. John (Rob Lowe) is the sensitive brother who loves her passionately and spends his life lusting after his sister's body. Frank (Paul McCrane) is a homosexual. Lilly (Jennie Dundas) is a dwarf. Last and definitely least, there's a baby brother named Egg because "he began as an egg and he's still an egg."

I kept thinking how things have changed since *Meet Me In St. Louis.* There were five kids in that MGM musical family, too, and everything happened to them in seasons. In *The Hotel New Hampshire* the Berry kids celebrate holidays in the American family tradition, too, but what a difference!

On Halloween, Franny gets gang-raped by the entire high-school preppie football team. On Christmas, the crazy grandfather drops dead lifting weights. On New Year's Eve, the kids end up in a wild bed scene, only John's girl turns him off when she spits out her dentures to swallow his tongue. Disgusting? We've got years left of this depraved saga.

In pursuit of a new hotel, the whole screwed-up family moves to Vienna. Mother and the little brother blow up in a plane crash with the mangy dog left to float in the sea with other debris. The rest are left, stranded and broke, in a foreign country to run a condemned hotel full of maniacs.

Upstairs are the prostitutes, a sadistic pornographer, and a lesbian in a bear suit. Downstairs are the radicals and terrorists who are building bombs to blow up the Vienna Opera.

Franny ends up having sex with all of them.

The dwarf becomes a rich, famous, best-selling novelist before committing suicide by leaping from the top of a New York hotel. John and Franny finally discover the glories of incest by fornicating non-stop for 24 hours.

Franny becomes a movie star who marries a black athlete. John ends up with the lesbian dropout from Sarah Lawrence. Father ends up blind, roaming the grounds of a brand new hotel that never attracts a single guest. None of this makes one bit of sense.

It's sick, nauseating, humorless, and utterly pointless. Director Tony Richardson heaps perverted people in our laps and expects us to think they're cute. He shows us the mad things they do, but he never analyses their motivations for doing them. The result is that everyone in *The Hotel New Hampshire* looks retarded, perverse, or stupid.

Worse still, every actor is hopelessly miscast. Beau Bridges looks like a brother, not a father. As the family femme fatale, Jodie Foster is pasty, pudgy and too asexual to attract gnats, must less half of the cast list. Natassja Kinski has proven countless times before that she can't act, but only a fool would cast her as a raving psychotic who hides her face in a bear costume because she's ugly.

Rob Lowe, as the son around whom most of the action revolves, is more beautiful than any of the women in the film—a miscalculation that wrecks the credibility of the relationships.

Nothing about *The Hotel New Hampshire* works on any level. It has no wit or shape.

It's just jabberwocky, out of control and looking for something to smash into. Many more movies like this, and critics will be writing reviews from padded cells at Bellevue.

HOW TO MARRY A MILLIONAIRE (1953)

★ ★ ★ Directed by Jean Negulesco. Produced and written by Nunnally Johnson. *With Marilyn Monroe, Lauren Bacall, Betty Grable, William Powell, Rory Calhoun, David Wayne, Fred Clark, and Cameron Mitchell.*

How to Marry a Millionaire teamed Marilyn Monroe with Lauren Bacall and the great Betty Grable as three gorgeous gold diggers with a playgirl penthouse and a plan to trap three millionaires to pay the rent. The combination was a box-office blockbuster that seems dated in the harsh realities of women's lib, but there is

no doubt the curvaceous stars can still command attention. Grable is the funniest of the ladies as she pursues skittish Fred Clark to a ski lodge in Maine, naively thinking she's on her way to an Elks convention. Bacall, as the caustic "brain" who plunges after William Powell, is a bit too cold and biting for her own good. But Marilyn, as a nearsighted confection constantly walking into walls without her eyeglasses, has the spirit of farce perfectly in focus. Not much substance, but lots of style.

THE HUCKSTERS (1947)

★ ★ ★ ½ Directed by Jack Conway. Screenplay by Luther Davis, based on Frederic Wakeman's best-seller. Produced by Arthur Hornblow, Jr. *With Clark Gable, Deborah Kerr, Sidney Greenstreet, Ava Gardner, Edward Arnold, Keenan Wynn, Adolphe Menjou and Frank Albertson.*

Clark Gable wasn't the king of Hollywood for nothing, and this 1947 satire about the greed, cynicism and phony manipulation of Madison Avenue advertising agencies is one of his most powerful and charming vehicles. The subject was radio, but the same lies, insincerity, and banalities that rule the airwaves still exist in TV. The brilliant script was—and still is—ahead of its time. Gable is the smooth heel who can sell anything; Sidney Greenstreet is the monstrous soap tycoon whose advertising dollars control the agency Gable works for; Deborah Kerr and Ava Gardner are the poles-apart women in his life; Edward Arnold is a talent agent who will stop at nothing to get his clients on the radio. A seedy business is burlesqued with wit, intelligence, and sarcasm. Definitely a thinking person's picture.

HUDSON HAWK (1991)

0 ★ Directed by Michael Lehmann. Screenplay by Steven DeSouza and Daniel Waters. Produced by Joel Silver and Bruce Willis. *With Bruce Willis, Andie Macdowell, Sandra Bernhard, Richard Grant, and Danny Aiello.*

Now I know that it doesn't matter how many Ninja turtles, Schwarzenegger terminators, or Madonna promos I have to suffer through; nothing will ever be as bad as *Hudson Hawk*. This movie is so rotten it's stupefying. I know I have used that word before, but until I saw *Hudson Hawk*, I didn't really know its full meaning. After the critics' screening, every important film reviewer in New York stood around in small circles, as if to seek safety in numbers, asking: "Did that really happen?" and "Did we really just see what I think we just saw?" All I know is that this movie cost $45 million. For that kind of spectacular waste of money in the middle of a recession, there should be a Senate investigating committee.

It would be easier to describe how to build a rocket ship out of paper clips than the plot of this brainless idiocy. I can't afford three extra sessions with my shrink just to prove I am not insane, so you'll have to take my word for it. Bruce Willis, in the worst movie of his career (it's the worst movie of *anyone's* career), plays a cat burglar just out of Sing Sing who wants to go straight but cannot adjust to the real world. Even his old saloon hangout is now a yuppie bar serving brandied goat cheese pizza. Somehow he gets framed into stealing three long-lost artifacts by Leonardo da Vinci commissioned by the Duke of Milan in 1481 by the CIA, the Vatican, and a gang of arch fiends who count frequent-flier mileage points like blue-chip stocks. Willis performs the task with the aid of his old pal Danny Aiello while they sing and dance to Frank Sinatra's big-band arrangement of "Swingin' on a Star." Then he gets stuck in a runaway ambulance careening across the

Triborough Bridge, and when his stretcher lands in a box full of styrofoam he wakes up in Rome tortured by crooks named after diseases and is seduced by Andie Macdowell, who (let me get this straight) may or may not be a nun doing undercover work for the pope, who watches Francis the Talking Mule movies on closed-circuit Vatican TV. Sometimes she's in a nun's habit, sometimes she's French kissing and showing her G-spots. Nothing is clear except that the master criminals are Darwin and Minerva Mayflower, played by wimpy Richard Grant, who looks like a submental Halston, and the revolting Sandra Bernhard, who wiggles her tongue and wears outrageous intergalactic fashions she must have retrieved from Grace Jones's garbage can. People get burned, stabbed, skewered in the eyes with hypodermic needles, blown to bits in explosions, and they all come back to life at the script's convenience. There's a dog who munches Bruce Willis's privates. And when all else fails, the movie returns to 1481 for a look at Da Vinci's medieval Mel Brooks iron factory where metal is transformed into gold. The dialogue is so confusing and senseless that you can't even write it down. Mr. Willis,

with a butch Marine drill sergeant flattop like "Major Dad" and four earrings, looks as stupid and confused as his character, but he produced this wretched horror, so he can't blame it on bad advice. I have no idea what anybody had in mind (not to mention where the $45 million went) but I call it "The Three Stooges Meet Die Hard." Call it what you will. *Hudson Hawk* is to movies what the stink of rotting sardines is to Cannery Row.

THE HUMAN COMEDY (1943)
★ ★ ★ ★ Directed and produced by Clarence Brown. Screenplay by Howard Estabrook, based on William Saroyan's novel. With Mickey Rooney, Frank Morgan, James Craig, Marsha Hunt, Fay Bainter, Butch Jenkins, Van Johnson, Donna Reed and Robert Mitchum.

A great MGM classic from 1943, *The Human Comedy* is a heartbreaking study of the effects of World War II on an all-American family in small-town California and is said to have been Louis B. Mayer's favorite film. It is certainly one of mine. Based on the novel by William Saroyan, it achieves a fine balance between literary expressionism and cinematic reality, with a beautiful texture seldom seen in movies. Mickey Rooney delivers the finest performance of his young career as Homer Macauley, who works in the telegraph office, and he is ably supported by Frank Morgan, James Craig, Marsha Hunt, Fay Bainter, Butch Jenkins, Van Johnson, Donna Reed, Robert Mitchum, and an illustrious roster of talents. Through its sensitive, dignified vignettes of small-town life, *The Human Comedy* communicates a comforting theme—that people are essentially good and faith and love can elevate men's hearts even in times of grief and sorrow. A timeless, life-affirming experience that will leave a glow in your heart, long after the final credits.

HUSH, HUSH, SWEET CHARLOTTE (1965)

★ ★ ½ Directed and produced by Robert Aldrich. Screenplay by Lukas Heller and Henry Farrell. *With Bette Davis, Olivia de Havilland, Joseph Cotten, Mary Astor, Agnes Moorehead, Cecil Kellaway, Bruce Dern, and Victor Buono.*

Bette Davis on a crumblin' ol' Louisiana plantation, honey. Years ago, a grisly hatchet murder took place under her scuppernong arbor. Now the state wants to construct a new highway right through the magnolia trees. When Bette says "Over mah dead body, y'all," she means it. Rolling her eyes like she's flipping flapjacks, she takes her bloody old hatchet to Olivia de Havilland, Joseph Cotten, Agnes Moorehead, and Mary Astor, and lawsy mercy, 'fore she's through, she's chewed up so much scenery the po' thing's headed for a terminal case of asbestos poisoning. Pure corn from the campy cotton-pickin' Hall of Fame, but some of the old Grand Guignol still works, and it's always a hoot to see Queen Bette tearing up the screen with her bare fingernails. When she hams it up, there's not much you can do except get out of the way.

THE HUSTLER (1961)

★ ★ ★ ½ Directed and produced by Robert Rossen. Screenplay by Rossen and Sidney Carroll, based on the novel by Walter Tevis. *With Paul Newman, Jackie Gleason, George C. Scott, Piper Laurie, Myron McCormick, and Murray Hamilton.*

Robert Rossen's tough, sardonic 1961 classic about an amoral pool shark is electrifying stuff, with Paul Newman giving one of his tautest performances as the arrogant poolroom hustler who fleeces everyone dumb enough to challenge him until he takes on Minnesota Fats (Jackie Gleason), the legendary pool champ who will stop at nothing to defend his title. George C. Scott is great as a predatory gambler determined to destroy Newman, and Piper Laurie is piercing as a lonely loser who makes the fatal mistake of falling in love with a man who is more in love with billiards. Riveting drama that crackles with cinematic tension. (A sequel, *The Color of Money*, was made by Martin Scorsese in 1986 with Paul Newman re-creating his original role and winning an Oscar for his efforts.)

I AM A CAMERA (1955)

★ ★ ★ ★ Directed by Henry Cornelius. Produced by Jack Clayton. Screenplay by John Collier, based on the play by John Van Druten. *With Julie Harris, Laurence Harvey, Shelley Winters, Ron Randell, Patrick McGoohan, and Peter Prowse.*

Long before Liza Minnelli sang her way to an Oscar in *Cabaret*, old chums, the wonderful "Berlin Stories" by Christopher Isherwood had made Sally Bowles a legendary character in the theater thanks to the historic performance by the great Julie Harris. The straight play was filmed in 1955. The movie was a big commercial flop, but on home video it's an obscure but heav-

en-sent treasure. Julie Harris literally burns a hole through the film she's printed on. As a glib, amoral playgirl trying to strike gold in decadent Berlin before Hitler's rise to power, this great actress puffs her foot-long Auntie Mame cigarette holder, downs her own hideous beverage called a "prairie oyster," and survives every near fatality with men you can think of by making life a never ending cabaret. Laurence Harvey and Shelley Winters contribute memorable support, but this is essentially a one-woman show and if you thrill to the passion and bravado of great acting, you will never forget Julie Harris, the definitive Sally Bowles to end them all.

I COULD GO ON SINGING (1963)

★ ★ ½ Directed by Ronald Neame. Screenplay by Mayo Simon. Produced by Stuart Millar and Lawrence Turman. *With Judy Garland, Dirk Bogarde, Jack Klugman, Aline MacMahon, and Gregory Phillips.*

Judy Garland's final film, tailored to fit her like a glove, ended up sagging like baggy overalls. Originally titled *The Lonely Stage*, which says it all, the movie was renamed to accommodate a title song by Harold Arlen, which the star belted out for the tear-soaked finale. It's a sappy, sentimental story about a lonely American singing star, played by Judy with a great deal of soulful agonizing, who arrives in London to play the Palladium and decides to look up a long-suffering ex-lover, now a distinguished British nose-and-throat doctor (Dirk Bogarde), and their illegitimate son she abandoned years ago. Showering the child with luxury and attention, she only manages to confuse and traumatize everybody until that predictable final resolution, the show must go on. The ravages of pills, booze, and life in the fast lane were alarmingly evident, the camera couldn't hide the puffy eyes or pudgy waistline, and the old timing and bounce were sadly missing. Despite the film's flaws, there is still a rowdy, funny drunk scene in which the old Garland sense of self-effacing humor rises triumphantly to the surface, and some of the actual concert footage is electrifying. A less than memorable swan song for the screen's greatest musical star, but it has a certain archival value for Judy fans of every vintage.

IDIOT'S DELIGHT (1939)

★ ★ ★ ½ Directed by Clarence Brown. Screenplay by Robert E. Sherwood. Produced by Hunt Stromberg. *With Clark Gable, Norma Shearer, Edward Arnold, Charles Coburn, Burgess Meredith, Laura Hope Crews, Joseph Schildkraut, and Virginia Grey.*

Norma Shearer is a gorgeous Russian countess stranded in the Alps on the eve of World War II, who may or may not be a former chorus girl from Omaha, Nebraska, and Clark Gable is the baggy-pants vaudeville hoofer who saves her from the Nazis. A bright, breezy entertainment with high-style performances, it also features Gable's only song-and-dance number ever filmed at MGM. Watching him thump through "Puttin' on the Ritz" with two left feet and a tuxedo so big you could hide the munchkins in the trousers, it's easy to see why Gable went into *Gone with the Wind* and left the top hat and tails to Astaire.

I'LL CRY TOMORROW (1955)

★ ★ ½ Directed by Daniel Mann. Screenplay by Helen Deutsch, based on the book by Lillian Roth, Mike Connolly, and Gerold Frank. Produced by Lawrence Weingarten. *With Susan Hayward, Richard Conte, Jo Van*

Fleet, Ray Danton, Eddie Albert, and Margo.

Susan Hayward, who made a career out of playing tough girls on the skids, won another Oscar nomination for depicting vaudeville singer Lillian Roth's sixteen-year battle with the bottle in this flawed but poignant "biopic." Clearly and ruthlessly explored without glamorizing, the subject of alcoholism is properly seedy and shocking, thanks to the star's relentless honesty. The big flaw is that the film fails to properly explain the psychological motivation for her downfall. A monstrous mother (played with vicious fury by Jo Van Fleet) and a few lousy marriages to heels and losers seem like contrived reasons for such a woeful slide from the heights of show business to the spidery depths of Skid Row and the brink of suicide. The leap to salvation through Alcoholics Anonymous seems equally brisk. But for sheer guts, there's nothing quite like Susan Hayward when she's in her cups. With quivering lips and flaring nostrils, she's too big for the TV screen.

I LOVE YOU TO DEATH (1990)

★ ★ ★ Directed by Lawrence Kasdan. Screenplay by John Kostmayer. Produced by Jeffrey Lurie and Ron Moler. *With Kevin Kline, Tracey Ullman, Joan Plowright, William Hurt, River Phoenix, and Keanu Reeves.*

I Love You to Death is an offbeat comedy that is black, earthy, lusty, and hilarious. An all-star cast assembles to knock off a two-timing, hot-blooded Italian pizza maker, played with vulgar, sexy, and delightful relish by the marvelous Kevin Kline. He's Joey Boca, a man of such insatiable lusts he just can't keep his hands off women, a chauvinist pig whose excesses are obvious to everyone but his loyal Yugoslavian wife, Rosalie, played with great honesty and no shtick by Tracey Ullman. When Rosalie finds out the truth, she enlists her wacky mother, sensationally played by the great British actress Joan Plowright, and two moronic hit men named Harlan and Marlon (William Hurt and Keanu Reeves) to do him in. These guys are so stupid they take a taxi to the murder site. But you don't want a man as funny as Kevin Kline to die, and not to worry. Poison in the spaghetti sauce gives him a tummy ache. A bullet in the head only gives him a headache. It's side-splitting to watch Kline staggering around half dead, saying "This virus is killing me." Great acting and a funny premise brighten up this screwball farce and make *I Love You to Death* (a true story, by the way) more laughable than lethal.

IMPROMPTU (1991)
★ Directed by James Lapine. Screenplay by Sarah Kernochan. Produced by Stuart Oken and Daniel A. Sherow. With Judy Davis, Hugh Grant, Mandy Patinkin, Julian Sands, and Bernadette Peters.

If you need a good rest, *Impromptu* will put you to sleep better than a Nembutol. James Lapine, author of the book for *Sunday in the Park with George* on Broadway, may be a protégé of Stephen Sondheim and an ex-roommate of Frank Rich, but he is no movie director, and this stillborn horror about George Sand, Frédéric Chopin, Alfred de Musset, and Franz Liszt is worse than any of the old MGM composer bios we now laugh off the screen. (I still wince when I think of Kate Hepburn and Robert Walker as Clara Schumann and Brahms in *Song of Love*.) *Impromptu* is scarcely a cut above the old "Ah, here comes Beethoven!" school of Hollywood schmaltz, only it's duller.

Australian Judy Davis swaggers about as George Sand, smoking cigars and wearing men's cutaways (ah, where is Merle Oberon, now that we need her?). Staring at a painting of a woman being eaten by a lion, she says: "I suppose it's better to feel something than nothing." (Took the words right out of my mouth, my girl.) This gum-chewer should be shown on a double bill with *Henry and June*. For deadly tedium, Ms. Davis is the deadliest screen literary creep since Anaïs Nin. So it's off to the country for a fortnight, where George Sand; her ex-lover Alfred de Musset (Mandy Patinkin); her best friend, social outcast and Paris scandal Marie d'Agoult (Bernadette Peters); and her lover, the mad pianist Franz Liszt (Julian Sands), await the arrival of Frédéric Chopin. It's the same plot as *A Little Night Music*. While the children amuse themselves by tying each other to trees and sentencing each other to the guillotine, the grown-ups prattle endlessly, challenge each other to duels, and ride horses through the house. As the country guests of gullible, foolish aristocrats, they end up staging a play which impertinently ridicules their hosts—a play about Noah and the flood, which is only slightly sillier than the real play around it. Hugh Grant makes a pale, pretty, and consumptive Chopin. Everyone else seems to be drugged. Mr. Lapine's appalling direction is understandable, since there is nothing in Sarah Kernochan's screenplay worth directing, but whoever let Bernadette Peters nurse a baby on screen should be tied to a hill of red ants.

THE INCIDENT (1967)
★ ★ ★   Directed by Larry Peerce. Screenplay by Nicholas Baehr. Produced by Monroe Sachson and Edward Meadow. *With Tony Musante, Martin Sheen, Beau Bridges, Jack Gilford, Thelma Ritter, Gary Merrill, Brock Peters, Ruby Dee, Jan Sterling, Ed McMahon, Mike Kellin, Donna Mills and Robert Field.*

The Incident, a powerful and shocking exercise in terror about two vicious hoods bullying and mugging a dozen helpless New Yorkers on an un-patrolled subway, was skeptically received in 1967 by critics who said, "This couldn't happen." (Years later, Bernard Goetz made world headlines for defending himself in a similar situation, and he's still paying the price for fighting back.) This can happen, and it often does. This movie, twenty-five years later, is as grim and staggering as ever. Tony Musante and Martin Sheen are the slimiest pair of drunken thugs you could ever hope not to meet on

a late-hour subway, and there are superb performances by the great Thelma Ritter and Jack Gilford as a cowering Jewish couple; Gary Merrill, as an aging alcoholic on the mend; Brock Peters and Ruby Dee, as a couple of militant racists who hate whites; Jan Sterling, Ed McMahon, Mike Kellin, and Robert Field, as various social and ethnic victims; and especially Beau Bridges, as a young soldier who pays the supreme price for his courage. This is not a public relations booster for an "I Love New York" campaign, but it is a brilliantly effective piece of filmmaking.

IN COUNTRY (1989)
★ ★ ★   Directed by Norman Jewison. Screenplay by Frank Pierson and Cynthia Cidre. Produced by Jewison and Richard Roth. *With Bruce Willis, Emily Lloyd, Joan Allen, and Kevin Anderson.*

I'm up to my eyeballs with movies about Vietnam aftershock, but as a needlepoint canvas of grass roots America, this one is honest, thought-provoking, and very moving. Emily Lloyd, the delightful British actress from *Wish You Were Here* and *Cookie*, is a small-town girl in Kentucky whose father was killed in Nam. She lives with her Uncle Emmett (unrecognizable Bruce Willis, giving one of the best and least appreciated performances of his career), a man so traumatized by war he has become a loony recluse. As their relationship develops, director Norman Jewison shows the frustrations of the younger generation trying to find out about a war they don't remember, from an older generation trying to forget. The atmosphere, the actors, and the sensitive script add up to an emotionally wrenching experience. Its vision of a fractured, post-Nam rural America is overwhelming.

INDIANA JONES AND THE LAST CRUSADE (1989)

★ ★ ★ Directed by Steven Spielberg. Screenplay by Willard Huyck and Gloria Katz, story by George Lucas. Produced by George Lucas and Robert Watts. With Harrison Ford, Sean Connery, Denholm Elliott, Alison Doody, John Rhys-Davies, Julian Glover, River Phoenix, Michael Byrne, and Alex Hyde-White.

Indiana Jones and the Last Crusade, according to creators Steven Spielberg and George Lucas, is the third and last walk around the block for the world's most beloved archaeologist and soldier of fortune. It's not the best, but it's still full of Saturday matinee escapism. This time you get not only Harrison

Ford as the unstoppable Indy, but Sean Connery, as the crotchety, troublemaking dad he grudgingly adores. They're on a mission to find the Holy Grail that takes them through rat-infested underground tombs, a castle in Austria crawling with Nazis, exploding sewers, snake pits, and even a face-to-face encounter with Hitler himself. Slick, expensive hokum that defies logic, but one heck of an entertainment.

INDIANA JONES AND THE TEMPLE OF DOOM (1984)

★ ★ ★ ★ Directed by Steven Spielberg. Screenplay by Willard Huyck and Gloria Katz. Produced by George Lucas. With Harrison Ford, Kate Capshaw, Ke Huy Quan, Amrish Puri, Philip Stone, and Roshan Seth.

Indiana Jones and the Temple of Doom, the sequel to *Raiders of the Lost Ark,* is a blockbuster, a lollapalooza, a classic. Call it twenty years of Saturday afternoon serial cliffhangers all rolled into one action-crammed adventure epic. Is this a rave? You got it. And if you pass this one by, you don't give a hoot in hell about the magic of movies.

This is that rare bird practically unheard of in movie history—a sequel that is even better than the original. It's unpretentious and totally entertaining. It even has the courage to poke fun at itself and at all of the adventure sagas and hammy heroes it parodies, from Jack Armstrong to James Bond to *King Solomon's Mines*.

From the first minute this movie hits the screen it grabs you by your lapels and never lets go. The setting is Shanghai, 1935. A wild Busby Berkeley tap-dancing musical extravaganza lights up the stage of a sinister nightclub, where Dr. Indiana Jones (Harrison Ford), world-celebrated archaeologist, has come to trade in priceless artifacts.

Before you can say "Spielberg's done it again" the floor is jumping with stolen diamonds, poison, gunshots, and a knife through the heart with a flaming shish kebab.

Indiana makes a daring and narrow escape through the jaws of death with a sexy, bewildered, and perpetually harassed American nightclub singer, Willie Scott (Kate Capshaw) on one arm, and a very young Chinese bodyguard, Short Round (Ke Huy Quan), on the other.

Dodging machine guns, this hapless trio makes a getaway from China on a cargo plane full of live chickens. When they come to, they realize the plane has no fuel, no parachutes, and no pilots. Seconds before it crashes they miraculously escape again in an inflatable rubber raft, sledding across the Himalayas, scaling the rapids, and landing in the middle of India.

This all happens in the first twenty minutes and the movie hasn't really begun. Thereafter, you'll find more breathless chills and nail-chewing close calls in any ten minutes of *Indiana Jones* than in the entire running time of most other action epics.

The plot (there is one, someplace in all the clutter and dazzling effects) has something to do with Indy's promise to return to his starving native rescuers a sacred stone with magic powers stolen by a child maharajah and hidden in a secret temple deep within the dark bowels of his fabulous palace. The adventure moves through a jungle of giant vampire bats and poisonous reptiles to the splendors of the palace, where poor Willie has to deal with eyeball soup and feasts of live bugs and chilled monkey brains, and finally to the Temple of Doom where Indy is forced to drink sacred blood that turns him into a zombie as Willie herself is lowered deeper into a bottomless pit of fire.

Just when you think it's curtains, they're on to another escape. Indy ends up on a conveyor belt in an underground rock quarry leading to a powerful rock crusher, his back paralyzed by a knife stuck in a voodoo doll. But wait. There's still a wooden bridge to cross over a river of man-eating crocodiles, with hostile natives closing in on both sides . . . .

Punctuated by a thunderous John Williams score, the movie is a nonstop roller coaster ride from start to finish, and the Spielberg magic still works. No physical stunt seems too difficult for him to stage, no mind-blowing effect too complex to master.

The technical credits on *Indiana Jones* list hundreds of artists and roll across the screen for what seems like an eternity. No wonder. An army was needed to assemble this movie.

Under the circumstances, it's pretty amazing that the actors weren't hospitalized. Capshaw is a spunky, captivating leading lady. Beautiful, too. And very funny, hiking through endless horrors in silver high-heeled shoes, battling a horny elephant who takes a fancy to her, complaining all the way. And Harrison Ford, with hard muscle replacing the white-bread flab of *Star Wars*, hits a bull's-eye. Gone is the tentative uncertainty about how to read a simple declarative sentence with conviction. He has real star charisma in this movie, forceful charm, and a scruffy vulnerability that makes him appealing to both sexes and all ages. *Indiana Jones* really makes his career as a rugged leading man in the Gary Cooper tradition.

Everything about this movie milestone is an affectionate salute to the good old days when life was less complicated, people were more innocent and fun-loving, and Saturday matinees were worth waiting for. I loathe the term *movie-movie*, but *Indiana Jones* gives it new definition.

INDISCREET (1958)
★ ★ ★ ½ Directed and produced by Stanley Donen. Screenplay by Norman Krasna. *With Cary Grant, Ingrid Bergman, Cecil Parker, Phyllis Calvert, David Kossoff, and Megs Jenkins.*

The impish sophistication of Cary Grant and the undiminished charm of Ingrid Bergman add up to timeless entertainment in *Indiscreet*. Cary's a "married" American banker-diplomat in London and Ingrid's a famous actress who becomes his devoted slave, understanding of his position and willing to risk her reputation anyway. But when she discovers he's been lying to protect himself from Cupid's slings and arrows, she has a field day getting even. Watching these two captivating pros go at each other with irreverent dialogue and lifted eyebrows makes for enchanting viewing and the carefree direction by Stanley Donen is a delight. Airy as a soufflé, but pounds of fun.

I NEVER SANG FOR MY FATHER (1971)
★ ★ ★ ½ Directed and produced by Gilbert Cates. Screenplay by Robert Anderson. With Melvyn Douglas, Gene Hackman, Dorothy Stickney, Estelle Parsons, and Elizabeth Hubbard.

I Never Sang for My Father, a heart-wrenching, beautifully written film version of Robert Anderson's Broadway play, explores the turbulent relationship between a widower (Gene Hackman), with a chance for a new life, a new marriage, and a new home with his bride-to-be, and his father (Melvyn Douglas), a selfish, demanding old curmudgeon afraid to be left alone in his old age. Love, hate, guilt, and the inability to communicate fill the family home with tension, with the son trapped between the desire to leave and make his own life and the responsibility he feels toward the people he must leave behind. The writing is so human and shattering it cannot fail to evoke tears of compassion and self-recognition in any adult viewer who has been through similar experiences that do not depend on macho clichés. Great roles are seldom written for men these days, but the humanity and sensitivity in the roles of the father and son, and the way they're played by Hackman and Douglas, restore faith in movie greatness. A wonderful film.

INTO THE NIGHT (1985)
★ ★ Directed by John Landis. Screenplay by Ron Koslow. Produced by George Folsey and Koslow. With Jeff Goldblum, Michelle Pfeiffer, Richard Farnsworth, Irene Papas, David Bowie, Roger Vadim, Vera Miles, Paul Mazursky, and Dan Aykroyd.

John (*Animal House*, *Trading Places*) Landis tours the Hollywood underworld after midnight in this comedy thriller about a bored space engineer with insomnia and a dangerous blonde with a fortune in smuggled emeralds on the lam from cops, assassins, and psychos. A screwy idea, divertingly acted by a stellar cast of stars and film directors in guest appearances, nocturnally photographed, and briskly paced. It's sort of like "Walter Mitty Meets the Maltese Falcon." Fresh and fun, despite the occasional sadistic violence.

IRMA LA DOUCE (1963)

★ ★ ★ ½ Directed and produced by Billy Wilder. Written by Wilder and I. A. L. Diamond. With Jack Lemmon, Shirley MacLaine, Lou Jacobi, Herschel Bernardi, Joan Shawlee, Hope Holiday, and Bill Bixby.

The songs are gone, but the Broadway musical about the life of a French whore in Pigalle retains the color, the wit, and the exposure of French hypocrisy, and the writing and direction by Billy Wilder add an extra dimension. Shirley MacLaine has a ball as the streetwalker with the heart of gold and Jack Lemmon is his usual befuddled self as the cop who raids her brothel and loses his job in the process. This is the 1963 film that Shirley MacLaine says changed her life. I wouldn't touch that one with a ski pole.

IT'S A WONDERFUL LIFE (1946)

★ ★ ★ ★ Directed and produced by Frank Capra. Screenplay by Frances Goodrich, Albert Hackett, Jo Swerling and Capra, based on the story "The Greatest Gift" by Philip Van Doren Stem. With James Stewart, Donna Reed, Henry Travers, Lionel Barrymore, Thomas Mitchell, Beulah Bondi, Frank Faylen, Ward Bond, H. B. Warner, Frank Albertson, and Gloria Grahame.

Frank Capra's durable cornucopia of small-town life has been an inspiration for generations of filmgoers who discover new magic with every showing. It has now been "colorized"—a process by which black-and-white movies are unnaturally turned into pallid color, like the phony dyes injected into processed cheese. I deplore this bastardizing of movie classics, but with Christmas trees, holiday spirit, and snow, *It's a Wonderful Life* is one of the rare examples of a film that may be enhanced by color. James Stewart is the hero who faces despair through a series of setbacks, only to be shown the true meaning of Christmas through a guardian angel. It's a performance—and a movie—to treasure.

I WANT TO LIVE! (1958)

★ ★ ★ Directed by Robert Wise. Screenplay by Nelson Gidding and Don Mankiewicz. Produced by Walter Wanger. With Susan Hayward, Simon Oakland, Virginia Vincent, and Theodore Bikel.

Susan Hayward, queen of the bad girls, gnashed her way to an Oscar in 1958 as hard-living, foul-mouthed party girl Barbara Graham, framed for murder and sent to the San Quentin gas chamber in 1955, screaming her innocence all the way to the harrowing zero hour. The movie is grim, brutal, and nasty, but our gal Susan throws herself into the role with nostrils flaring, pupils dilated, and fists flying. A bit hysterical, but never boring.

JACKNIFE (1989)

★ ★ ★ Directed by David Jones. Screenplay by Stephen Metcalfe, based on his play *Strange Snow*. Produced by Robert Schaffel and Carol Baum. *With Robert De Niro, Ed Harris, and Kathy Baker.*

A slow, meandering study of the psychological impact of Vietnam on two survivors trying to cope with life on the home front. Fifteen years later, Ed Harris is the haunted veteran who has become a tragic drunk, living with his sister Martha (Kathy Baker) in a shuttered house. Robert De Niro is the war buddy who tries to free them all from the pain of the past and the futility of the future. This is a talky film, short on action, but big on inner emotions and ideas. The actors are marvelous, but as the tortured, emasculated victim of guilt and terror, Ed Harris steals the picture.

THE JEWEL OF THE NILE (1985)

★ ★ ½ Directed by Lewis Teague. Screenplay by Mark Rosenthal and Lawrence Konner. Produced by Michael Douglas. *With Michael Douglas, Kathleen Turner, Danny DeVito, Avner Eisenberg, and Spiros Focas.*

The spirited sequel to 1984's surprise hit *Romancing the Stone* picks up the action six months later, with romance novelist Joan Wilder (Kathleen Turner) and her playboy lover Jack Colton (Michael Douglas) braving heat, dust, camels, machine guns and homicidal tribes in North Africa to save a holy man from the clutches of an evil potentate. Cornier and less thrilling than its predecessor, this romp is nevertheless harmless escapist fun, with the mesmerizing Kathleen Turner, dangling from speeding trains and flinging herself into sexy Nubian fertility dances with wild abandon, and every inch a star.

JFK (1991)

★ ★ ★ ½ Directed by Oliver Stone. Screenplay by Oliver Stone and Zachary Sklar. Produced by Oliver Stone, A. Kitman Ho, and Amon Milchan. *With Kevin Costner,*

Sissy Spacek, Kevin Bacon, Joe Pesci, Tommy Lee Jones, Laurie Metcalf, Gary Oldman, Michael Rooker, with guest appearances by Jack Lemmon, Walter Matthau, Sally Kirkland, Lolita Davidovitch, Donald Sutherland, and John Candy.

The dissidence and controversy—from both sides of the political fence—over Oliver Stone's massive, three-hour *JFK* was inevitable. So what? The Warren Commission report has already been labeled a fiction and there is nothing new about the conspiracy theory, so it doesn't much matter what side you're on. We'll never know the truth until the records are unsealed in the year 2029. The big question is: How good is the movie? In my opinion, it's powerful, compelling, brilliantly written and directed, superbly acted by a stellar cast of luminaries with courage and conviction, and one of the most important history lessons the cinema has ever told.

Mr. Stone has compiled a massive dossier to support his belief that Lee Harvey Oswald was just a naive pawn in a much deadlier government plot involving defense contractors, oil bankers, big business conglomerates, and the military—all of whom wanted the war in Vietnam, which JFK opposed, in order to pump $80 million into the sagging economy. What we have here, he says, will go down in history as a right-wing military coup d'état. Compiling the evidence (much of it awesomely convincing) is a painstaking effort that makes for quite an exhausting film. Still, you will not go away with your thumb in your mouth. The film pulses like an oncoming migraine.

Weaving actual footage with dramatization, *JFK* is not the story of an assassinated American President (although it is observed that he was set upon by assassins like Julius Caesar), but the story of New Orleans district attorney Jim Garrison (played with verve, intensity, and honest inspiration by Kevin Costner in a performance that will amaze you), a man worth making a movie about because he was the only man in the country who wouldn't put the assassination to bed. Beginning with Eisenhower's farewell address in January 1961 and moving through the Bay of Pigs, the film deals with Khrushchev, the family album (nothing, of course, on Marilyn Monroe), right up to the fatal Dallas motorcade in 1963. *JFK* chronicles the life of the man in documentary style, then spends the rest of the three hours unveiling the plot that killed the President and toppled Camelot, parading a cast of characters so bizarre no potboiler could make them up—including eyewitnesses who identified suspects and heard shots from different directions, then found their testimonies falsified and their signatures forged in the Warren Report. Mr. Stone seems to agree with Senator Russell Long (Walter Matthau), who says: "This dog don't hunt." And that's where Jim Garrison comes in. Described as a "mouse fighting a gorilla," he took on the homosexual underworld, the Mafia, the CIA, and anti-Castro forces, pimps, government informers from the Pentagon—everything that served his purposes in court, incurring the wrath of taxpayers, endangering his own life, and finding himself labeled "a threat to the national security structure" in the process. The fact that he failed to convict sleazy New Orleans subversive Clay Shaw (played with oily, reptilian grace by Tommy Lee Jones) as a co-conspirator doesn't make the story less conclusive, only doubly shrouded in mystery. Garrison's end-of-the-trial courtroom plea for American justice is a moving speech and Costner's marathon monologue is worth the price of admission by itself.

Meanwhile, there is the joy of watching some superb actors do their stuff, including Ed Asner, Donald Sutherland, Sissy Spacek, Joe Pesci, Lolita Davidovitch, Jack Lemmon, Sally Kirkland, and John Candy. Kevin Bacon is especially fine as a gay hustler, and Gary Oldman makes a very convincing Oswald. Oliver Stone redeems himself after the dismal *The Doors*. His *JFK* is more in the same vein as *Born on the Fourth of July*. It's preachy, but here is surely a subject about which we could all stand to be preached to more often.

JOHNNY BELINDA (1948)

★ ★ ★ ★ Directed by Jean Negulesco. Screenplay by Irmgard Von Cube and Allen Vincent, based on the play by Elmer Harris. Produced by Jerry Wald. *With Jane Wyman, Lew Ayres, Agnes Moorehead, Charles Bickford, Stephen McNally, and Jan Sterling.*

After a lifetime of playing wisecracking chorus girls, Jane Wyman won the Academy Award in 1948 for her magnificent portrayal of a drab and pathetic deaf-mute farm girl in Maine called "the Dummy," jeered at by the town, raped by a local villain, and forced to prove her fitness as a mother in a custody suit over the baby. Without speaking a word of dialogue, she brought superior insight and tenderness to the role, won the hearts of American moviegoers, and established a major film career. Ironically, 1948 was also the year she dissolved her marriage to Ronald Reagan. It's just as well. She would have hated living in Washington, D.C.

JUDGMENT AT NUREMBERG (1961)

★ ★ ★ ★ Directed and produced by Stanley Kramer. Screenplay by Abby Mann. With Spencer Tracy, Maximilian Schell, Richard Widmark, Burt Lancaster, Marlene Dietrich, Montgomery Clift, and Judy Garland.

A gigantic 1961 hit, an all-time classic, and the recipient of twelve Oscar nominations, Stanley Kramer's masterpiece re-creates the postwar Nazi trial of four German judges accused of crimes against humanity. Spencer Tracy is the wise, baffled, but rock-solid American judge presiding over the trial. Maximilian Schell won an Oscar as the German defense attorney. Richard Widmark, in an impassioned performance that speaks for the outraged free world, is the prosecuting attor-

ney. Burt Lancaster is one of the Nazis on trial; and Marlene Dietrich is the aristocratic widow of a Third Reich general. Among the star witnesses: Montgomery Clift, as a Jewish victim of sterilization, and an overweight, overwrought Judy Garland, making a "comeback" after a seven-year absence from the screen, as a survivor of the Nazi death camps. Abby Mann's Oscar-winning screenplay is talky, but it's also powerful in the way it attempts to analyze one of the great issues of the twentieth century. Positively overwhelming, Judgment at Nuremberg is one of the greatest courtroom dramas of all time.

THE KARATE KID (1984)

★ ★ ★ Directed by John G. Avildsen. Screenplay by Robert Mark Kamen. Produced by Jerry Weintraub. With Ralph Macchio, Noriyuki "Pat" Morita, and Elisabeth Shue.

The Karate Kid is a teenage Rocky with the same flaws and the same uplifting underdog-hero values. It's corny, but the values outweigh the flaws. It leaves you cheering.

John G. Avildsen, who directed Rocky, is again behind the camera, so if nothing else, you can expect the same pacing, the same energy, and the same action-packed buildup to the final showdown between the good guys and the bad guys.

Avildsen knows the territory and it doesn't much matter if it's been traveled before by audiences of all ages. Kids will love it, and there's nothing harmful or degenerate in it for them. What a relief it is to encounter an entertainment for youngsters in which their own age group doesn't spout filthy dialogue, take dope, or kill anybody. The violence in *The Karate Kid* is controlled, supervised, and legal.

The good guy is an Italian kid named Daniel Larusso (Ralph Macchio) who is forced to leave his friends and school in Newark and move to California when his mom takes a new job there in a rocket computer company. Every time Daniel turns around he gets totaled by a gang of local bullies called the Cobras, who work out in a karate school.

Tired of being victimized, Daniel becomes determined to learn self-defense in the martial arts. Aiding him in this goal are his two new friends: a pretty girl named Ali (Elisabeth Shue), who is not only the most popular girl in the new high school, but also the ex-steady of the karate team's aggressive head honcho; and a kindly old Japa-

nese handyman who dispenses philosophy between instructions in spiritual enlightenment.

To Mr. Myagi (Noriyuki "Pat" Morita), karate is a way of life that comes from the mind and the heart, not from the fists and the feet. Through his expert coaching, the boy learns balance, touch, control, and spiritual as well as physical maturity, while the other boys in the karate school only learn kicks and punches as a way of pulverizing their opponents.

Much of the film is devoted to this growing friendship between the kid, who sticks out like a sore thumb among the spoiled, rich California preppies, and the old man, who lost his wife and newborn child in a wartime detention camp for Japanese. Daniel eventually brings the movie to a climax after the hard work and grueling training leads him to the karate tournament, where he must use his new skills to defeat the evil Cobras. The Cobras fight dirty, of course, and Mr. Myagi has to step in with some Oriental magic of his own to get Daniel out of the ring in one piece before the Cobras pulverize him, but it's all in the line of duty. As the skinny nerd from Newark gains self-confidence, the audience gains faith, understanding, and love.

The Karate Kid has a simplistic message about how even the puniest kid can turn into a Charles Atlas through discipline, self-respect, and determination, to win despite the odds, and it's not above stretching credibility to achieve its goal.

I find it difficult to buy the all-American, privileged dream girl's passionate interest in this scrawny little twerp over all of the suntanned campus Adonises, but I guess if the kid was a young John Travolta or a young Sly Stallone the film wouldn't have the same heart-tugging impact.

Avildsen has a way with kids that pays off. Although it is the old Japanese man who steals the film as Daniel's surrogate father, the young, inexperienced actors (all unknowns) have been encouraged to relate, mingle, and connect in naturalistic ways that are engaging and believable.

The Karate Kid starts out as kid's stuff and turns into a work of such charm and sincerity that it grows on you, like a lichen.

KARATE KID—PART II (1986)
★ ★ ★ Directed by John V. Avildsen. Screenplay by Robert Mark Kamen, based on characters created by Kamen. Produced by Jerry Weintraub. *With Pat Morita,* *Ralph Macchio, Nobu McCarthy, Danny Kamekona, Tamlyn Tomita, Yuji Okumoto, and Charlie Tanimoto.*

The original *Karate Kid* was a *Rocky* for the bubble-gum set. There is no cogent reason for *The Karate Kid—Part II* except to microwave old ideas for the same audience, with the hope that maybe there's still some bubble gum left in the same wrapper. Happily, the taste is not bad.

The sequel picks up where the first movie left off. Myagi, the kindly, wisdom-dispensing old Japanese karate teacher (still played by Pat Morita), still eschews the violence and macho bull that reduces karate from an art to early arthritis, catching flies with chopsticks to show discipline and Oriental stamina.

His trophy-winning pupil Daniel (still played by Ralph Macchio) is still learning fair play with both karate and girls. When Daniel's mother's job transfers her to Fresno, the kid moves in with his mentor and we're off on a second adventure.

The plot shifts to Okinawa, where the old man must visit his dying father and face a decades-old reputation of dishonor and disgrace showered on him by his former best friend, who challenged Myagi to a karate-chopping duel to the death over the love of an old girlfriend, Yukie (played by the still-lovely Japanese film star Nobu McCarthy.)

Myagi's old opponent Sato (Danny Kamekona) has become a real estate tycoon, a feudal landlord who cheats and abuses the people of his ancient fishing village, and something of a heel.

Most of the film this time is thrown to Pat Morita (after all, he got an Oscar nomination for the first one), who rekindles his old romance with Yukie and displays courage and character by trying to make peace with his old enemy.

"Best way to avoid a punch," he tells confused Daniel, "is not to be there."

Ralph Macchio has nothing to do for the first half of the picture except tag along by his teacher's side, flirt with Yukie's pretty niece Kumiko (Tamlyn Tomita), and conduct the audience on a guided tour of Okinawa.

The tour would be approved by American Express. We see incredible sunsets, a touching funeral procession of floating lanterns on a moonlit river, rock cliff castles, a hurricane, and a big Japanese production number featuring jumping-jack acrobats.

But most of *The Karate Kid—Part II* just passes the time amiably until the inevitable showdown between good guys and villains. Nobody will be left disappointed.

John Avildsen directed both the first *Karate Kid* picture as well as *Rocky*, so he's an expert handling the action stuff. But most people tend to forget he also directed the deeply sensitive *Save the Tiger*, so he has an uncommonly human feeling for character development. And he moves both Ralph Macchio and Pat Morita through their now familiar roles with startling freshness.

I hate sequels, but this one is several cuts above most. It's an old-fashioned story with solid virtues and a teenage hero most kids can value. It has violence and compassion, heroism and villainy, and decency overcoming obstacles of misunderstanding. It's a sentimental picture, but a thoughtful one, not given to excess, and surprisingly entertaining.

THE KILLING FIELDS (1984)
★ ★ ★ ½ Directed by Roland Joffe. Screenplay by Bruce Robinson. Produced by David Puttnam. *With Sam Waterston, Dr. Haing S. Ngor, John Malkovich,*

Craig T. Nelson, Julian Sands, Bill Paterson, Athol Fugard, and Spalding Gray.

We've had "war is hell" movies. We've had movies about the horrors of Southeast Asia. We've had even more than our share of movies glorifying or excoriating the U.S. involvement in Vietnam. But no film in my memory has more harrowingly telegraphed the ravages of war than *The Killing Fields*.

This powerful, devastating and deeply moving film about Cambodia is an exhausting but memorable experience. There is greatness in it—in the shattering true story it tells of human struggle and sacrifice, in the rich cinematography, in the massive scenes of carnage and destruction, and in the honest, dedicated, and unforgettable performance by Dr. Haing S. Ngor, a real-life survivor of the Cambodian holocaust.

This man is no actor, but he delivers one of the most haunting performances ever captured on film (and won an Oscar for it). Everything about his work informs and elevates the material far beyond the perimeters of filmmaking and gives *The Killing Fields* lasting value.

Filmed in Thailand by producer David (*Chariots of Fire*) Puttnam and director Roland Joffe, *The Killing Fields* is a vast and sprawling story about the friendship Pulitzer Prize-winning journalist Sydney Schanberg developed with his Cambodian guide-interpreter Dith Pran, a man who influenced his life and even saved his neck before almost losing his own.

The film begins in 1973, when Schanberg (played by Sam Waterston) arrives in Cambodia as a correspondent for the *New York Times*. The first part of the movie is about the guts and hard times of a journalist trying to get news out of hell.

News is suppressed, the press is controlled, phones and telex wires are at a premium. Somehow Schanberg gets his stories back to America by defying all rules, taking chances, getting himself arrested, and risking his life.

At his side, his faithful partner and comrade, Dith Pran, makes all things possible, ignoring the danger to his own welfare.

After the fall of Phnom Penh in 1975, when the monstrous Khmer Rouge began its reign of terror, Schanberg managed to escape while the American troops were evacuated, taking the airlift with them. Pran was left behind to face tortures and inhumanities most civilized people never dream of.

The rest of the movie catalogues the four years in Pran's life under the unspeakable new Cambodian regime that reduced a once-beautiful and proud country to a death camp of insanity, brutality and unendurable hardship.

While Schanberg tried in vain to locate his friend, Pran disappeared into the interior, where seven million people were massacred. Brainwashed teenagers turned into zombies murder their elders without guilt or feeling. Men risk their lives to steal live lizards for food. The smallest human kindness becomes a death warrant.

So massive and filled with observation and detail is this canvas of chaos and suffering that you sit there watching the screen, helpless and outraged, as you feel the terror of the homeless, the diminished pride, the desperation to survive no matter what. And always there are children—lost, tortured, bewildered, dripping with blood, and screaming. Always screaming.

While Nixon was busy lying to the American people about how no U.S. troops would ever invade Cambodia, the reality was something quite different indeed.

Except for *The Boat People*, which made a gallant but clumsy attempt to tell and show what happened after the U.S. troops deserted the people to their own fates, no other movie in my memory has had the guts to deal head-on with the facts. *The Killing Fields* will leave you shaking and furious.

Waterston is splendid as Schanberg, and there is an excellent contribution from John Malkovich as a hippie photographer who does everything in his power to save Dith Pran by forging a phony passport.

But it is really Dr. Haing S. Ngor who illuminates this sad and wrenching human document. A real Cambodian refugee who watched his own family die of disease and starvation after the Khmer Rouge takeover, Ngor fuses every scene with a conscience and a spirit that gives *The Killing Fields* eloquence and sensibility. I cannot imagine a better technical adviser. The film benefits immeasurably from his presence, and so does the audience.

Amazing. Riveting. This is not just another movie. It's a profoundly heartbreaking, yet greatly edifying experience.

THE KING OF COMEDY (1983)

★ ★ ★ Directed by Martin Scorsese. Produced by Amon Milchan. Screenplay by Paul Zimmerman. *With Robert De Niro, Jerry Lewis, Diahnne Abbott, Sandra Bernhard, and Ed Herlihy.*

Every show-business success knows a Rupert Pupkin—those harmless but irritating pests who collect autographs, hang around stage doors, and day-dream of being "somebody."

In Martin Scorsese's *The King of Comedy*, Robert De Niro adds another repulsive portrait of anti-social American flotsam to his overcrowded gallery of freaks. His Rupert Pupkin is a seedy creep who feeds off the existence of stars, fertilized by the heat in the spillover from their spotlights, sweating with ambition.

He is the worst kind of leech, because he is firmly convinced he's got talent. All he needs to become the next media-incubated supercomic is a chance on network TV to prove it.

The star he chooses to father his career is Jerry Langford (Jerry Lewis, in an astonishingly freak departure that doesn't contain one laugh)—a Johnny Carson–styled TV talk-show host who makes the mistake of being nice to the poor cretin in a moment of weakness. Rupert sees this as a breakthrough.

He prepares his audition by practicing on a cardboard cut-out of Liza Minnelli in his mother's basement. Every day he marches into the network for his personal interview with Jerry, his idol, and every day he gets rejected by a brisk talent coordinator (crisply and intelligently played by Shelley Hack).

Humiliated by underlings, ejected by security guards, finally physically thrown out of the star's country house by the star himself, Rupert cracks. With the aid of a rich, brash, and pathetic crackpot groupie named Marsha (played by hammer-faced comic Sandra Bernhard), Rupert launches his most ambitious plan ever. He kidnaps Jerry with a cap pistol, ties and gags him, and holds him for ransom in exchange for a guest appearance on the show.

This is not a comedy. Up to a point, it's funny watching De Niro boil in his own juice and chase his own tail until he turns into butter. It's even funny when he talks like a series of *Photoplay* bios, dropping names and dreaming of getting married on network TV while Victor Borge plays the piano. But the humor wears off fast when it becomes obvious that Scorsese is out for nastier results than a few cheap laughs at the expense of autograph hounds.

The kidnappers build up so much fantasy in their minds that they finally reach the point of no return. They can't tell fantasy from reality. Paranoid obsession becomes dangerous. You can't dissuade these people, you can't avoid them, and you can't insult them. Worse, you can't get rid of them. They begin with chutzpah, then work their way into revenge.

In this nut's case, the network gives in. About eighty-seven million people see him, and—given the American taste for vulgarity—turn his stupid comedy routine into a media sensation. At thirty-seven, after serving only two years of a six-year prison sentence, Rupert Pupkin is released as a major star. In goes a wacko, out comes a living legend. And what we end up with is a mean-spirited polemic on the subject of America's obsession with instant celebrity, cloaked in the reminder that crime not only pays, but has lasting benefits and annuities, like movie deals, book contracts, and magazine covers. But don't take Martin Scorsese's word for it. Just ask Patty Hearst, Jean Harris, and the Son of Sam.

The King of Comedy gives De Niro a lot of laborious monologues, and provides Jerry Lewis with a fine opportunity to show his serious side and reveal a few harrowing truths about the loneliness and misery of life at the top. Looking made up for an open casket viewing throughout, he has never seemed more morose. Just to make sure everybody gets the point that this is really the *Tonight* show he's talking about, Scorsese even has Johnny's producer, Fred De Cordova, playing Jerry's producer. The scriptwriter, Paul Zimmerman, is a former movie critic (for *Newsweek*) who seems to hate them all.

There is no denying the film's lacerating impact as it peels away another layer of the ugliness of American life, but it is too lurid and mean-spirited to ever want to see twice. Its chief persuasion, I'd guess, is to make Johnny Carson hire bodyguards. The rest is crudely rhetorical, well acted, and clever—but, as they used to say, you won't respect it afterward.

THE KISS OF THE SPIDER WOMAN (1985)

★ ★ ★ ★ Directed by Hector Babenco. Screenplay by Leonard Schrader, from the novel by Manuel Puig. Produced by David

Weidman. *With William Hurt, Raul Julia, Sonia Braga, and Jose Lewgoy.*

Don't be turned off by the title. *Kiss of the Spider Woman* is neither a campy takeoff on the old Hollywood horror flicks with Gale Sondergaard nor a weird sci-fi potboiler for teenagers.

It's an exotic, sobering film about politics and sex, set in a Brazilian prison cell, with a titanic performance by William Hurt as a drag queen imprisoned for corrupting the morals of a minor. It's strictly for grown-ups.

Kiss of the Spider Woman is a Brazilian film with American actors, directed by Hector Babenco, the gifted South American whose film *Pixote* was a controversial sensation. Based on a book by the daring Argentine left-wing political dissident Manuel Puig, it tells the odd story of two prisoners who form an extraordinary bond of friendship in a horrifying confinement.

Hurt is a gay window-dresser thrown into a rotting jail in Rio, where he is forced to share a cell with a left-wing journalist (Raul Julia) imprisoned for supporting a revolutionary movement. In the outside world, neither man would befriend the other, but despite the revolutionary's initial revulsion, he is drawn to the homosexual through fate and circumstance.

"Without power in this country, no man is a real man," says the macho revolutionary, warming to his tragic comical cell mate, and the film follows the dramatic development of their relationship, questioning what constitutes real manhood, as each of them discovers nobility in the other and a different kind of self-respect.

The title, *Kiss of the Spider Woman*, comes from the fanciful plots of old movies the drag queen has either seen or imagined. As he passes the time between interrogations and tortures telling and retelling bizarre and romantic movie fantasies, the scenes from the movies themselves come alive with the erotic Sonia Braga as the glamorous Spider Woman.

As it switches hypnotically between fear and pride, day and night, fantasy and fatalism, Babenco forms cunning parallels between the B-movie plots and the intrigue-and-betrayal tale that is gradually unspooling in the prison cell.

Gradually, with irony and tenderness, the two men take a step into each other's worlds, and the weak man is the one who ends up with power over the strong man in a stirring psychological twist that leaves the audience dazed. The relationship culminates in a brief, touching love affair, directed and acted with wonderful discretion.

Everything about *Kiss of the Spider Woman* is original and powerful, but the one smashing impact that towers above everything else is William Hurt's magnificent, three-dimensional Oscar-winning performance as the pathetic homosexual with the heart of a woman trapped in the body of a man.

Creeping about the slimy perimeters of his black cell with his hair in a towel turban, his face aflame with red lipstick and blue mascara, and his big, bony feet protruding daintily from his rubber thongs, he minces, sighs, and flutters like a drunken butterfly on the verge of collapse.

This could have been a campy, hysterical parody, but Hurt has the creative genius to make you hurt, laugh, and feel repulsed at the same time. For an actor who is basically miscast, he elevates the art of make-believe to greatness.

KRAMER VS. KRAMER (1979)

★ ★ ★ ★   Directed and written by Robert Benton. Produced by Stanley Jaffe. With Dustin Hoffman, Meryl Streep, Jane Alexander, Justin Henry, Howard Duff, George Coe, and JoBeth Williams.

Kramer vs. Kramer is a rare and exemplary film about marriage, divorce, child custody, the changing sex roles in a confused society, and the complexities of love. It's a very fine film indeed, winner of five Oscars to prove it.

Dustin Hoffman plays Ted Kramer—aggressive, ambitious, going places fast in advertising while his marriage has been quietly collapsing. His wife Joanna (Meryl Streep) has been so busy supporting him in his meteoric career thrust, taking care of their seven-year-old son, and stifling her own needs as a person, that he's been too cozy and preoccupied to notice the turbulence inside her.

One day after eight years of marriage, she turns over her credit cards, her apartment keys, and her child, and walks out to find her own identity. Hoffman throws away her photos, destroys her sewing machine, and clears the apartment of her memories, but he can't ignore his new responsibility toward the kid he hardly knows.

In a few heroic attempts to be a mother, father, and pal to the boy, he burns the French toast, arrives at a birthday party after all the other children have left, and generally makes an awful mess of things. Only through patience and hard work and being there does he learn there is more to being a parent than yelling "Sit up straight" and "Drink your milk."

By the time father and son fall in love, the wife returns and demands her child back. This leads to guerrilla warfare in family court, and in the process, the viewer gets to know the Kramers so well that it becomes impossible to take sides.

He proves there's no law that says a woman is better qualified to be a parent because of gender. On the other hand, she's not a villain, either—merely a human being with needs, with pride, with self-esteem, who made a mistake and doesn't feel she should be punished for the rest of her life.

Thanks to the performances of Hoffman and Streep, the Kramers are three-dimensional people instead of soap opera clichés. There are no easy solutions to their dilemma and writer-director Bob Benton doesn't provide any. *Kramer vs. Kramer* becomes a film about feelings and people who aren't afraid to express them.

Dustin Hoffman is absolutely marvelous. Stumbling through the demands of child-rearing, he's funny and touching, frantic, irritating, and always im-

mensely believable in his desperation to hold on to his child even if it costs him his career and the last nickel in his checking account.

Meryl Streep is equally winning as Joanna Kramer—intelligent, convinced she's right, trembling with nervous determination, and eventually heart-rending in her humanity. She's also something of a writer, too. The courtroom scene—full of emotion, electricity, and tension—in which she pleads for custody of her son walks away with the picture, and she wrote it herself.

Bob Benton has a keen ear for the way people think and feel and talk to each other, but some of the best scenes in *Kramer vs. Kramer* are the ones where nobody says anything and we share the intimacy of the child and his daddy living their lives, puttering in the kitchen, or roaming around the apartment at dawn in their underwear.

The kid, a saffron-haired dumpling named Justin Henry, is one of the few child actors I've seen on the screen who seems to have real intelligence, honest instincts, and doesn't look like he's doing a Raisin Bran commercial.

The music is Purcell and Vivaldi, not rock and roll, and I

can't tell you how gratifying *that* is. In an age of blockbuster epics and overbloated sci-fi fantasies, it's wonderful to see the human race back on the screen.

LADY AND THE TRAMP (1955; 1987 rerelease)

★ ★ ★ Directed by Hamilton Luske, Clyde Geronimi, Wilfred Jackson. Screenplay based on the book by Ward Greene. Produced by Walt Disney. *With the voices of Peggy Lee, Barbara Luddy, Bill Thompson, Bill Baucon, Stan Freberg, Verna Felton, Alan Reed, George Givot, Dallas McKennon, and Lee Millar.*

Walt Disney's first full-length cartoon in Cinemascope is a triumph for all ages. The story of a romance between a dainty, well-bred cocker spaniel named Lady and a mutt named Tramp whom she meets during a brave clash with the outside world, it's one of Disney's most appealing, imaginatively illustrated cartoon classics, and honey-dripping Peggy Lee singing the voice of Lady gives it special musical savvy. You can never grow too old to love this one.

LASSIE COME HOME (1943)

★ ★ ★ Directed by Fred Wilcox. Produced by Samuel Marx. Screenplay by Hugo Butler, based on the novel by Eric Knight. *With Roddy McDowall, Elizabeth Taylor, Lassie ("Pal"), Donald Crisp, Elsa Lanchester, Nigel Bruce, Dame May Whitty, Ben Webster, Edmund Gwenn, and Alan Napier.*

For years, people have been taping this classic from faded prints on late shows for generations of kids to savor, but now a flawless, beautifully color-corrected home video is available. The first installment of the legendary Lassie movies is still the best and it hasn't aged a day since 1943. Roddy McDowall, a refugee from wartime England, and Elizabeth Taylor, already a classic beauty at age eleven, are the child stars, and Lassie (really a male collie named Pal) had such human qualities the wags called her "the only star who could play a bitch better than Bette Davis." I don't care how old you are. If you don't love *Lassie, Come Home* you need a pacemaker.

THE LAST EMPEROR (1987)

★ ★ ★ ★ Directed by Bernardo Bertolucci. Screenplay by Bertolucci and Mark Peploe. Produced by Jeremy Thomas. *With John Lone, Joan Chen, Peter O'Toole, Ying Ruocheng, Victor Wong, Dennis Dun, Ryuichi Sakamoto, Maggie Han, and Ric Young.*

The great Italian director Bernardo Bertolucci is our guide through this lavish history lesson about Pu Yi, the last emperor of China, and what an imaginative, massive journey it is. Imagine. Pu Yi, taken from his mother's arms at the age of three, carried through the night to the Forbidden City and crowned ruler of half the world's population. Pu Yi grew up the loneliest boy on earth, surrounded by eunuchs and ladies in waiting, but no friends except his Scottish tutor, a Mr. Chips type played beautifully by Peter O'Toole. He was a sad prisoner in his own palace, knowing nothing of the political revolution raging outside the walls until the age of eighteen, when a corrupt warlord captured Peking and forced the ex-emperor into exile. Pu Yi lived through decades of Communist turmoil and died in 1967 a humble and forgotten gardener.

The Last Emperor is a true story so remarkable it almost defies belief, but Bertolucci makes it vibrant, exciting, and real. From bewildered teenager to international playboy to a puppet ruler under the Japanese to suicidal war criminal, the multitalented John Lone gives a sensational performance as the tragic Pu Yi, turning each chapter in his life into a movie unto itself. From the windswept plains to the gilt-edged splendor of the Forbidden City, you see China the way no tourist ever will. This is a staggering accomplishment in world cinema that won three Oscars including Best Film, and it retains all of its pageantry, spectacle, and drama on home video. Don't even think about missing this one. Years from now, it will still be a genuine classic you'll want to see again.

LAST EXIT TO BROOKLYN (1990)
★ ★ Directed by Uli Edel. Screenplay by Desmond Nakano. Produced by Bernd Eichinger. *With Jennifer Jason-Leigh, Stephen Lang, Peter Dobson, Ricki Lake, and Jerry Orbach.*

Another harrowing detour to hell, not for the squeamish or prudish, this blistering adaptation of Hubert Selby's shocking short-story collection about violence and suffering in the Brooklyn slums of the early 1950s is like watching a gang rape. You are horrified, but unable to do anything about what you're seeing. Here are frank and explicit themes of homosexuality, prostitution, drug addiction, gang warfare, and union corruption that will make even the toughest viewer wince. But the acting is superb—especially Jennifer Jason-Leigh as a burned-out whore, and Stephen Lang as a gruff, two-fisted dockworker who discovers his true sexual identity with a fickle drag queen—and the bleak mosaic of Brooklyn's lower depths has a weird beauty, like a canvas by Brueghel. Senator Jesse Helms should see this one. It would give him cardiac arrest.

LEGAL EAGLES (1986)

★ ★ ★ Produced and directed by Ivan Reitman. Screenplay by Jim Cash and Jack Epps, Jr. With Robert Redford, Debra Winger, Daryl Hannah, Brian Dennehy, Terence Stamp, Steven Hill, David Clennon, John McMartin, Jennie Dundas, Roscoe Lee Browne, Christine Baranski, and Sara Botsford.

Legal Eagles begins and ends with blazing four-alarm fires, and there are plenty of sparks in between.

It's a thrill-packed humdinger of a movie all the way— a crisp love story, a superior murder mystery, as well as a keen and incisive look at the legal and art worlds of New York City.

The "legal eagles" are Robert Redford and Debra Winger, and neither has ever been better, bouncier, looser, or more attractive on film.

Redford is Tom Logan, an assistant district attorney with a brilliant reputation as a public prosecutor and a solid future in politics. Winger is Laura Kelly, a frisky defense attorney who will stop at nothing in court to win a case. She once even put a "talking dog" on the witness stand.

Initially they clash in court on opposite sides of the legal system, but his fairness, decency, and cocky attitude intrigue her.

Then there's Daryl Hannah, the gorgeous mermaid from *Splash*, a strange, seductive Winger client whose father, a famous painter, was killed in a terrible fire when Daryl was eight years old. Now twenty-six, she's arrested and charged with a felony for trying to steal one of her father's valuable paintings.

The painting turns out to be part of a $20 million cache of stolen artworks. It falls into the hands of a slimy art gallery owner played by Terence Stamp, but the charges are dropped and the plot thickens.

As it turns out, the girl's father did not die accidentally eighteen years earlier. He was murdered. Now a maniac is stalking the gorgeous damsel in distress. Winger convinces Redford they can defend Hannah if they team up.

An innocent attempt to see justice prevail results in Redford's firing when the cops break into his pad and find him in bed with the suspect herself!

If this sounds confusing, think of it as an updated Katharine Hepburn–Spencer Tracy movie with attitude. The result is arson, fraud, murder, and mayhem.

It's a complex case, and Redford's defense brief is further complicated by the fact that both his new law partner and his sexy client are in love with him. But the real fun is the wonderful way the scriptwriters Jim Cash and Jack Epps, Jr., develop the two lawyers' personalities.

After his colorless, indifferent performance in *Out of Africa*, Redford returned to the screen in this one with his old charming tricks, displaying comic talents never before revealed. He burns toast, drops groceries, bumps into things, and locks his keys in his car at pivotal moments.

Winger is his perfect right arm—and a very pretty arm it is, too. With her crisp demeanor, luminous eyes, and sleek page-boy hairdo, she's a whole new screen personality. Hand this girl a briefcase and she becomes uncommonly beautiful.

Together, these glamorous protagonists play detective, stealing confidential files, hoodwinking people all over town, and getting locked in a warehouse with a bomb and catapulted into the Hudson River by the explosion.

Like Nick and Nora Charles, they have their humorous moments, too. One of the film's most delightful touches is the scene in which both legal eagles fight insomnia in their respective apartments while raiding the fridge and watching *Singin' in the Rain*. Until you see Robert Redford in a blue bathrobe tap-dancing with Gene Kelly while wolfing down a quart of ice cream, you haven't lived.

With *Legal Eagles*, you can prepare to be knocked right out of your yuppie jogging shoes. From Elmer Bernstein's sparkling musical score to Laszlo Kovacs's shiny, sophisticated cinematography, Ivan (*Ghostbusters*) Reitman has filled the screen with elements that put a smile on your face.

He gets excellent performances not only from the three stars but from a batch of supporters like Brian Dennehy, Steven Hill, John McMartin, Christine Baranski, and Terence Stamp.

Legal Eagles is merely marvelous.

THE LEMON DROP KID (1951)
★ ★ ★   Directed by Sidney Lanfield. Screenplay by Edmund Hartmann and Robert O'Brien, from the story by Damon Runyon. Produced by Robert L. Welch. With Bob Hope, Marilyn Maxwell, Jane Darwell, Lloyd Nolan, and William Frawley.

Bob Hope in one of his classiest films, playing a Damon Runyon mug who hangs out at the racetrack, trying to pay off a betting error by dispatching phony Santa Clauses to solicit donations for an imaginary old folks home. Marilyn Maxwell, Jane Darwell, William (*I Love Lucy*) Frawley, Lloyd Nolan, and the zaniest crooks this side of *Guys and Dolls* follow in hot pursuit as Bob tries to escape the cops, the mob, and the gag writers in one hilarious escapade after another. A slapstick Christmas farce that's funny all year long, this is the movie that introduced the song hit "Silver Bells," performed by Ski Nose and the luscious Marilyn Maxwell.

LENNY (1974)
★ ★ ★   Directed by Bob Fosse. Screenplay by Julian Barry. Produced by Marvin Worth. With Dustin Hoffman, Valerie Perrine, Jan Miner, Stanley Beck, and Gary Morton.

Filthy-mouthed, heroin-addicted sociopath Lenny Bruce is not the kind of heroic biographical subject that draws crowds, but Bob Fosse's tight direction and Dustin Hoffman's mesmerizing central performance as the self-destructive comic make *Lenny* a controversial film worth serious study. Drug addiction, continual arrests for obscenity, and a desperate struggle to open the world's eyes to the ugliness of life through comedy led to a tragic downfall. Hoffman manages the miracle of making you see a thoroughly unpleasant creep in a new light. Not for the squeamish.

LES MISÉRABLES (1935)
★ ★ ★ ★   Directed by Richard Boleslawski. Screenplay by W. P. Lipscombe. Produced by Darryl Zanuck. With Fredric March, Charles Laughton, Sir Cedric Hardwicke, Rochelle Hudson, Frances Drake, John Beal, Florence Eldridge, Jessie Ralph, and John Carradine.

The classic novel by Victor Hugo has been the basis of a Broadway musical, and there's another television remake currently on the shelves of video stores, but stick to the real thing. The 1935 original is unsurpassed. You'll be amazed at how fresh it looks, and the performances are brilliant. Fredric March is an impassioned Jean Valjean, imprisoned and tortured merely for stealing a loaf of bread to feed his starving family, and Charles Laughton is the ultimate villain as the relentless police inspector Javert who hounds his victim even after he escapes and begins a new life. The massive crowd scenes, the looming shadow of the guillotine, and the excellent sets and costumes all add up to a sweeping canvas of the French Revolution. This is a movie even Marie Antoinette would dig.

LETHAL WEAPON (1987)

★ ★ ★   Directed by Richard Donner. Screenplay by Shane Black. Produced by Donner and Joel Silver. With Mel Gibson, Danny Glover, Tom Atkins, Mitchell Ryan, and Gary Busey.

Lethal Weapon is a superior two-cop thriller with real star performances from Australian heartthrob Mel Gibson as the reckless, suicidal cop, and Danny Glover as his cautious black partner, a happily married family man. Both are Vietnam veterans and the case they're working on one Los Angeles Christmas season turns out to be a legacy of that nightmarish war on the home front. Investigating the murder of a teenage cocaine addict, the pair uncover a vicious gang of ex-soldiers commanded by a former general, continuing in peacetime drug trafficking the same kind of ruthless business they conducted as CIA commandos in Southeast Asia. There's more hideous violence than usual, and the mayhem is nonstop, so I wouldn't recommend *Lethal Weapon* for children (one monstrous torture sequence isn't for fainthearted adults, either). Still, this exciting movie gives depth to the characters, and the settings are very unusual, especially a drug bust in a lot full of Christmas trees and a shoot-out in a posh Beverly Hills garden where a victim finds an instant shroud in the plastic winter cover of his swimming pool. Excessive and implausible, but never boring.

LETHAL WEAPON 2 (1989)

★ ★ ½   Directed by Richard Donner. Screenplay by Jeffrey Boam. Produced by Donner and Joel Silver. With Mel Gibson, Danny Glover, and Joe Pesci.

Mel Gibson, as Riggs, and Danny Glover, as Murtaugh, are back with the same unbeatable formula that made *Lethal Weapon* the most popular cop-buddy flick of all time. These guys are now so familiar they seem like old friends. By now we know how they live, feel and think. Riggs is the wild man with the collie, the passion for chili, and the rage. Murtaugh is the solid family man, the reliable cop who keeps his partner straight. This time they're up to their badges kicking butt, battling a new gang of murderous psychos, and baby-sitting a wimpy mob accountant (Joe Pesci) who becomes a reluctant third member of the team. The homicidal maniacs are South African fascists with diplomatic immunity, but that doesn't stop this team from breaking every law in Los Angeles to smash them. It lacks credibility, but who cares? This sequel's got great performances, a terrific mix of Three Stooges humor, creative violence, and enough breathless nonstop carnage for two movies—or at least a *Lethal Weapon 3*. Take a Valium.

LICENCE TO KILL (1989)
★ ★ Directed by John Glen. Screenplay by Richard Maibaum and Michael G. Wilson. Produced by Albert R. Broccoli and Wilson. *With Timothy Dalton, Carey Lowell, Robert Davi, Talisa Soto, Anthony Zerbe, Frank McRae, Everett McGill, Wayne Newton, Benicio Del Toro, Desmond Llewellyn, David Hedison, and Priscilla Barnes.*

Licence to Kill, the sixteenth chapter in the twenty-seventh year of the series, may also be the dumbest, but who cares? The formula still works. Plenty of toys, tootsies, and stunts. This time 007 battles a sadistic drug lord with bad skin and an even uglier personality who feeds his enemies to man-eating sharks for kicks. Bond enlists the aid of two new tomatoes in a plot so complicated I doubt if any of them know what they're doing. The problem is this 007 takes himself too seriously. Bond is no more believable than Batman. Sean Connery and Roger Moore understood that and let us in on the joke. Timothy Dalton, in his second outing as 007, has no humor. He's cool, suave, and well-groomed. But he's like an ad for After Six tuxedos posed by a model whose jockey shorts are too tight. For toys, you get exploding toothpaste. For sex, you get sly smiles and a pat on the rear. Is 007 getting soft? Is the series suffering from varicose veins? I think so, but die-hard 007 fans won't mind. The action never stops long enough for you to worry about it. Although like a Chinese fortune cookie, you may not remember it the next day.

LITTLE GLORIA, HAPPY AT LAST (TV, 1982)

★ ★ ★ Directed by Waris Hussein. Screenplay by William Hanley, based on the book by Barbara Goldsmith. Produced by David Nicksay and Justine Heroux. *With Bette Davis, Angela Lansbury, Christopher Plummer, Maureen Stapleton, Martin Balsam, Glynis Johns, Barnard Hughes, Michael Gross, John Hillerman, Lucy Gutteridge, and Jennifer Dundas.*

A compelling three-hour miniseries about the scandalous 1934 custody battle over poor little ten-year-old rich girl Gloria Vanderbilt (wonder whatever happened to *her*!), *Little Gloria, Happy at Last* makes for hypnotic viewing. The flawless cast includes Angela Lansbury as Gloria's aunt, Bette Davis as the patriarchal grandmother, and Maureen Stapleton as the nanny. A true story, impeccably dramatized, and shot on location in the breathtaking mansions of Newport, Rhode Island. Definitely superior to most television movies, and worth a second look without annoying commercial inserts.

LITTLE MAN TATE (1991)

★ ★ ★ ½ Directed by Jodie Foster. Screenplay by Scott Frank. Produced by Scott Rudin and Peggy Rajski. *With Jodie Foster, Dianne Wiest, Harry Connick, Jr., and Adam Hann-Byrd.*

Such are the times we live in that a critic praising a movie must cautiously avoid the word *nice*. *Nice* is the kiss of death. To also add that any film it the kind of warm and ingratiating experience you can share with the whole family without trepidation of brain damage is to guarantee no family will see it, including your own. This is the dilemma I face in trying to tell you how special, how rare, and how rewarding *Little Man Tate* really is without scaring you away. I will simply say this movie is honest, sincere, and heart-meltingly wonderful. The rest is up to you.

Marking the directorial debut of Jodie Foster, who also stars in it, *Little Man Tate* is about a year in the life of a lonely, sensitive seven-year-old child prodigy named Fred Tate. Fred's father is unknown; his mother is a gum-chewing, good-hearted waitress (played with great working-class wisdom by Ms. Foster herself) named Dede, who is torn between the need to further the intellectual experience of her extraordinary child and the knowledge that if she broadens his world she might also lose him. As Fred himself says, in voice-over narration of his own unique story, ''By the time I was in first grade, it was pretty obvious I was not like anybody else." He could talk at one, read the labels on china plates at two, paint murals in oils and play the piano at competition levels at four. By the age of seven, he plays jazz piano, does experimental art, writes poetry even his second-grade teacher doesn't understand, and is a genius in math and physics. Fred also worries about everything from bad music (he prefers Ella Fitzgerald singing Cole Porter to Mutant Ninja Turtles) to atomic meltdown and the defoliation of the Brazilian rain forest. Fred is a kid so brilliant the other kids hate him. The reward for genius in the world of children is isolation and loneliness. Fred has an ulcer.

Dianne Wiest plays Jane Grierson, a teacher and child psychologist who was once a prodigy herself, and now runs a school for gifted children. Instead of a summer at Disney World, Jane sends the child to college, where he drinks macrobiotic blender concoctions instead of Coca-Colas, studies neoclassic architecture, and excels in a competition called "Odyssey of the Mind," a sort of think tank for tots who know everything from history to double-digit calculus. For a re-

ward, Jane suggests that Fred rent "a nice documentary" before bedtime.

As the audience is plunged into the awesome world of this little renaissance man, director Foster keeps the human focus centered on the boy's struggle between the two women in his life. Jane, his surrogate mother and mentor, opens a new world of learning. A model of authority and academic control on the outside, she is a mess inside— a woman who has no idea how to be a real mother. Dede, on the other hand, walks the tightrope between holding on and letting go. She's a struggling single parent who makes the child her partner in life and then expects too much of him. And that leaves Fred in the middle— a little man who is still a child inside, living in an internal world yet desperate for the hugs and discipline only a mom can provide. Finding seven-year-old newcomer Adam Hann-Byrd to play Fred is one of the film's miracles. There is nothing pretty or show-bizzy about him; his eyes are big gumdrops in an odd face covered with freckles, like crushed cornflakes in a white bowl. Jodie Foster, who grew up in front of a camera and won an Oscar nomination at twelve for playing a child prostitute in *Taxi*

Driver, seems to have a special affinity for child actors. She has directed this one with a naturalism that never seems rehearsed. She pins him to the screen with an understanding that avoids stereotyping.

Ms. Foster and her scriptwriter, Scott Frank, artfully blend so many discordant vanities and frailties in these characters until they—and we—suddenly see a unity of purpose and hear a common heartbeat of achievement in the making of little Fred into a happy human being. Don't lean too hard on *Little Man Tate*. It's not a Spielberg spectacular. It has no sex, guns, runaway cop cars, or exploding helicopters. But within its self-imposed limits, it has plenty of intelligence and felicitous insights into human nature, and it generates enormous charm. Everybody goes away happy.

A LITTLE ROMANCE (1979)

★ ★ ★ Directed by George Roy Hill. Screenplay by Allan Burns. Produced by Yves Rousset-Rouard, and Robert L. Crawford. With Laurence Olivier, Sally Kellerman, Diane Lane, David Dukes, Thelonious Bernard, and Arthur Hill.

Movies about youth that you could send a youth to see without fear of insult are as rare as homemade pie crusts, but *A Little Romance* has an original and delightful script and the film George Roy Hill has made from it is uniquely intelligent.

A Little Romance is about two bright thirteen-year-olds in that sensitive transitional period between adolescence and maturity, when innocence and exuberance have not yet been replaced by cynicism. The boy is Daniel, a French youngster who has been weaned on American movies and can say "Let's mosey on down here a piece" just like John Wayne or "Here's lookin' at you, kid" just like Bogart, with equal relish.

The girl is Lauren, who is living in Paris with her mother, a thrice-married society dilettante (Sally Kellerman) whose current husband (Arthur Hill) is an ITT executive. Lauren has a 167 I.Q. and reads philosophy books for fun; Daniel is so bright he has devised an ingenious system of winning at the racetrack.

These are gifted children whose parents, from different cultural and economic backgrounds, are out of touch with their own offspring. Lauren's mother is too busy flirting with a candidate for Husband No. 4

(a conceited and ridiculous "auteur" film director who dresses in a boy scout uniform, played with delicious flamboyance by David Dukes); Daniel's father is a drunken taxi driver who fleeces American tourists. Here is a "case-closed" dossier on kids who don't deserve their parents, instead of the other way around.

But somehow, miraculously, Lauren and Daniel find each other, and a new best friend in an elderly boulevardier who tells them about the legend of the Bridge of Sighs in Venice— that to kiss in a gondola under this bridge at sunset when the bells toll, the way Robert and Elizabeth Barrett Browning did, means you will stay in love forever. The kids decide to try it. Together they invent a plan to win at the races with the aid of her stepfather's IIT computers and they run away to Venice with their elderly and eccentric chum as a chaperon.

Laurence Olivier, in his sixtieth motion picture, plays the old roué with appliquéd layers of wit, charm, and virtuoso artistry. Of course, he turns out to be someone quite different from the harmless old soldier he pretends to be, the parents think the children have been kidnaped, and there is a surprise

and a twist every few minutes of the journey, with a cordon of police and a few dismal American tourists in hot pursuit.

The acting is superb, and the children are exciting and mature discoveries who just happen to be trapped in teenage disguise for the moment. Wacky, anchovy-shaped Sally Kellerman gets her best and most comical role since *M.A.S.H.* as the girl's dizzy mother.

Olivier's battles with serious illness at the time were scarcely noticeable. He looks fit and feisty and even did some of his own stunt work in the film, including a strenuous uphill bike race. George Roy Hill once again displays a deft touch in his ability to handle children, recalling the touching, unique and underrated job he did on *The World of Henry Orient*.

This movie has the same magic. By the time the group gets to Venice, the bells start ringing, the old man is near the breaking point in police interrogation headquarters, and the kids are edging toward the bridge. I found myself rooting for them to find that gondola like I was at a Yale-Harvard game.

LITTLE WOMEN (1949)

★ ★ ★ Directed and produced by Mervyn LeRoy. Screenplay by Andrew Solt. With Elizabeth Taylor, June Allyson, Janet Leigh, Margaret O'Brien, Mary Astor, Peter Lawford, Lucile Watson, C. Aubrey Smith, Elizabeth Patterson, and Rossano Brazzi.

MGM's dreamy 1949 remake of the great Louisa May Alcott novel in Technicolor would make the perfect stocking stuffer for Christmas. There's even a Christmas sequence which depicts the poor March sisters struggling to find joy, happiness, and the true meaning of the holiday season in a glowing, snow-encrusted New England despite the fact that their father is away fighting the Civil War. June Allyson, in a radical departure from the musicals and sitcoms she graced during this period, gives the performance of her life as the throaty, independent tomboy, Jo. Elizabeth Taylor, Janet Leigh, and a meltingly radiant Margaret O'Brien are her sisters. Mary Astor (who, according to her memoirs, was going through menopause and was in a rotten mood with the four MGM starlets on her hands) plays Marmee. Peter Lawford, Lucile Watson, and most of the MGM stock company stalk richly through supporting roles to lend realism and poignancy to a grand piece of costumed period flavor. Keep plenty of Kleenex handy for this one—you'll be floating in tears. Purists often prefer the earlier version with Kate Hepburn, but the lush color, period charm, and impeccable sets and costumes make this remake my personal favorite. From the Concord snow to the sugary rainbow over the March home in the final fade, I'm a sucker for this kind of classy needlepoint corn.

THE LIVING DAYLIGHTS (1987)

★ ★ Directed by John Glen. Screenplay by Richard Maibaum and Michael G. Wilson. Produced by Wilson and Albert R. Broccoli. With Timothy Dalton, Maryam D'Abo, Jeroen Krabbe, Joe Don Baker, John Rhys-Davies, Art Malik, and Desmond Llewellyn.

The Living Daylights often makes no sense at all, but like most James Bond films, the reason its silliness doesn't much matter is that whenever it threatens to self-destruct, it drags in new sets, new countries, new perils, new escapes, new gadgets, new guns, and new girls! The plot has something to do with 007 assisting the escape of a prominent Russian defector from behind the Iron Curtain. In the process, he falls in love—with the glamorous KGB assassin he refuses to shoot. She turns out to be a Czech cellist and the lover of the defected spy and now it's up to 007 to help her escape, too. But let's face it. The fun is not watching Bond save the world, but the uncanny ways in which he eludes his enemies, his traps, and his killers, saving his strength—and wisecracks—for pillow talk. He scales walls, swims moats, escapes knife throwers, fleeing in the usual assortment of rockets, helicopters, and water-skiing airplanes. When his Aston-Martin hits the Swiss Alps, he grabs the girl and they flee the Czech border police by using her cello case as a high-speed toboggan. The movie flits from Austria to Tangier to Afghanistan to the Rock of Gibraltar, always in search of new locations to inflate the budget. All director John Glen does is organize the traffic so nobody gets hurt. But where is the old glamour? Maryam d'Abo, as 007's new girl, is a low-voltage Natassia Kinski, and Timothy Dalton, the new 007, looks like a model for Giorgio Armani. I miss the evil monsters, too—no Dr. No, Blofield, or Goldfinger here. Even the villains are working heavies in Johnny Carson suits. This Bond is definitely in bondage.

LOCAL HERO (1983)

★ ¹/₂ Directed and written by Bill Forsythe. Produced by David Puttnam. *With Burt Lancaster, Peter Riegert, Peter Capaldi, Fulton McKay, and Denis Lawson.*

Here's the situation: a bunch of hard-nosed Houston oil developers invade a remote fishing village in Scotland with one self-serving purpose in mind—to rip off the local citizens, buy up their sleepy picture-postcard hamlet, and turn it into an ugly oil refinery that will pollute the environment and blight mankind.

David Puttnam, who produced *Chariots of Fire*, and Bill Forsythe, who directed the sweet but inconsequential Scottish film *Gregory's Girl*, obviously see a situation here that is pregnant with comic possibilities. The result is *Local Hero*, a boring little movie that backfires loudly.

Local Hero is meant to be a wry comedy about a head-on collision between two cultures, in the style of those charming, eccentric little postwar films from Britain about country villages crashing into the twentieth century, generally starring Alec Guinness and Margaret Rutherford. But as a comedy, it's so lazily wry that it's only lazily amusing. As social commentary of the vulgar eighties, it's pretty treacly stuff. And as a movie entertainment, it vanishes without a trace before you can ever locate it on a radar screen.

Burt Lancaster is the board chairman of the Texas conglomerate, a gentleman obsessed with astronomy, money, power, and "abuse therapy," which serves as a contrivance to introduce a Don Rickles character who bursts out of closets and drops in from window ledges to scream insults at the demented old tycoon in what is supposed to be "comic thrust."

Peter Riegert is the dope from the acquisitions department sent to Scotland to firm up the deal because his name is MacIntyre (little does Lancaster know that the fellow is really Hungarian). Once ensconced in a quaint inn in the village of Ferness, the capitalists discover the charming locals are not such easy pushovers as presumed. Ferness is no Brigadoon, and the peasants are more than eager to get rich quick.

Among the less-than-colorful rustics there's an old hermit who, when asked what the coastline is worth, just roars with laughter. There's the greedy innkeeper, who cooks MacIntyre's pet rabbit for lunch. There's a Russian sailor who plays the stock market. And there's even a sexy marine biologist who wants to preserve the bay for a laboratory, and who may or may not be a mermaid.

The alleged "comedy" derives from the villagers' mistaken notion that they will soon be millionaires, and the American capitalists' slow initiation into the soothing way of life they're trying to buy, until all the Texans ultimately want to do is change places.

Subtlety is what Forsythe is going for, but there is such a thing as too much subtlety. Neither the people nor their motivations are ever totally believable, and it is never clear why either side would have the slightest interest in the other.

The "local color" shots are interminable; there's even a dance-social that is the most excruciating party sequence on film since the Ukrainian wedding in *The Deer Hunter*. The Texas honchos are so corny they wouldn't get past the bouncer at the Grand Ole Opry. The Scottish eccentrics are so pickled in atmospheric brine that they seem almost as rare and precious as the Loch Ness monster.

The acting is terrible, the actors are unappealing, the pace is slow enough to make a snail impatient.

Scotland is still an enchanted place, as the guidebooks say, but there is no enchantment in *Local Hero*. For a fairy tale of two cultures, I prefer *Brigadoon* where, if you don't like what you get, it just goes away.

LONG DAY'S JOURNEY INTO NIGHT (1962)

★ ★ ★ ★ Directed by Sidney Lumet, from the play by Eugene O'Neill. Produced by Ely Landau. With Katharine Hepburn, Ralph Richardson, Jason Robards, Jr., and Dean Stockwell.

The movie version of Eugene O'Neill's Pulitzer Prize-winning drama *Long Day's Journey into Night* is the only film in history for which all four stars received Best Acting Awards at the Cannes Film Festival. The autobiographical study of O'Neill's tortured family, called the Tyrones, brilliantly directed by Sidney Lumet, provides a quartet of artists with their most illustrious roles. Katharine Hepburn has never been more powerful as the morphine-addicted mother, a lovely and sensitive woman brought to emotional ruin by a divided family. Ralph Richardson, as the bombastic former matinee-idol father disillusioned by old age, is one of the most tragic figures ever captured on film. Jason Robards, Jr., as the alcoholic older son, and Dean Stockwell as his consumptive younger brother round out the impeccable cast in a film full of moods and shadows and emotional fireworks. Sticking to the O'Neill script without "opening up" the confines of the Tyrone house to accommodate the camera, Lumet gets great bursts of anguish from the actors, propelling voices and emotions into a claustrophobic maelstrom of human electricity. Really a staggering achievement.

THE LONG, HOT SUMMER (1958)

★ ★ ★ ★ Directed by Martin Ritt. Screenplay by Irving Ravetch and Harriet Frank, Jr. Produced by Jerry Wald. With Paul Newman, Joanne Woodward, Orson Welles, Angela Lansbury, Anthony Franciosa, and Lee Remick.

One of the screen's few distinguished forays into William Faulkner country, this steamy southern saga boasts one of the most illustrious casts from the 1950s, an excellent script, and actual location shooting in the Mississippi Delta. Paul Newman is the drifter suspected of barn burning; Joanne Woodward is the spinster he tames;

Orson Welles is the meanest, fattest, most mendacity-spoutin' plantation owner since Big Daddy; Angela Lansbury is his fleshy, flashy mistress; Lee Remick is his oversexed daughter; and a dozen or more able supporting players spin and buzz around the screen door like lightning bugs. Juicy, fascinating, and entertaining as a catfish rodeo.

THE LONG, LONG TRAILER (1953)

★ ★ ★ Directed by Vincente Minnelli. Screenplay by Frances Goodrich and Albert Hackett. Produced by Pandro S. Berman. With Lucille Ball, Desi Arnaz, Keenan Wynn, Marjorie Main, Gladys Hurlbut, and Moroni Olsen.

At the height of their fabulous fame, Lucille Ball and Desi Arnaz teamed up with veteran director Vincente Minnelli for this crisp, slick, and hilarious MGM Technicolor romp about life in a mobile home. The laughs are nonstop as Lucy hits the road on wheels and nearly wrecks everything in sight, including her marriage. The scene where she cooks her first meal while the contents of the kitchen fly through the door in a raging storm is pure *I Love Lucy*. This one is a must for the entire family.

LONGTIME COMPANION (1990)

★ ★ ★ ★ Directed by Norman Rene. Screenplay by Craig Lucas. Produced by Stan Wlodkowsky. With Bruce Davison, Campbell Scott, Patrick Cassidy, Mark Lamos, and Mary-Louise Parker.

Hollywood took twenty years after "bombing with honor" was over to discover Vietnam. I wondered how long it would take filmmakers to address themselves to the AIDS crisis. *Longtime Companion* is the answer. It is a brilliant, fascinating dramatization of the courage faced by people whose lives are affected by the No. 1 medical crisis of this era. Inspirational and humane, it's a vital work of monumental significance no person with a soul can afford to miss. I consider it as much a document of the world we live in today as *The Grapes of Wrath* was a mirror to the struggles of the Depression.

This is a ground-breaking film about a disease that touches us all, but while it tells a wonderful story cinematically, it also challenges our notions of how to get through periods of adversity, and explains how life's traumas can actually be turned into forces for positive change and growth. Playwright Craig Lucas and Broadway director Norman Rene make their film debuts, but the movie flows so naturally it's hard to believe they haven't been making films all their lives. The AIDS scene is so accurately observed and filmed it's sometimes embarrassing, and always shattering.

The story centers on the lives of eight friends, from their first knowledge of the disease reported in the *New York Times* in July 1981, to the devastating effects of AIDS on their relationships during the next nine years. George C. Scott's son, Campbell Scott, plays the historic witness; the film is observed by him, as each member of his circle of friends becomes profoundly affected by AIDS through the deaths of friends and lovers. Without sentimentality or emotional manipulation, the awareness level progresses as the film does. As the characters grow, the audience grows with them. From early stages of fear, ignorance, and confusion, through rage and denial, then the myriad of ways people play the cards they're dealt, everyone learns life is what you make of it, what you give of yourself in return. The performances are uniformly impeccable, from Patrick Cassidy's soap-opera hunk to Bruce Davison's sensitive, loyal friend. Mary-Louise Parker is wonderful as the good-hearted female pal. Award-winning actor Mark Lamos makes an outstanding movie debut as a TV writer whose career plummets as the disease takes over. *Longtime Companion* is one of the most powerful films I've ever seen about surviving defeat with dignity when life breaks your heart. Don't pass this one up just because you consider the subject of AIDS depressing. Experience it and learn something about how to be a better person in life. You'll be glad you did.

THE LORDS OF DISCIPLINE (1983)

★ ★ ★ ½ Directed by Franc Roddam. Screenplay by Thomas Pope and Lloyd Fonvielle. Produced by Herb Jaffe and Gabriel Katzka. *With David Keith, Robert Prosky, Mark Breland, G.D. Spradlin, Barbara Babcock, Michael Biehn, Mitchell Lichtenstein, and Rick Rossovich.*

Sadism, torture, cruelty, racism, and Gothic horror surface again in yet another southern military academy (Lordy Lou, aren't they always down in the cotton-pickin' Delta?) in *The Lords of Discipline*.

Under those honey-drippin' magnolias, there are still a few rocks to turn over. And you can bet your Confederate money that every time the moviemakers turn them over, the same old swamp rats crawl out. The slimy generals, pea-brained southern belles and bigoted cadets who populate the Charleston, South Carolina, military school in *The Lords of Discipline* seem to be left over from *The Strange One*, Jack Garfein's 1957 film version of Calder Willingham's novel and play, *End as a Man*.

This film is a variation on the same theme—how the brutalization and corruption of young men in southern military schools is often ironically fostered, approved and protected by a phony "code of honor."

Based on a popular novel by Pat Conroy, author of *The Great Santini*, the new movie deals with the same central problem of how a sensitive young man learns to cope within the inhuman value system imposed by militant authorities. Set in 1956, when times were crueler and codes were sterner than they are now, *The Lords of Discipline* stars that charismatic young actor David Keith as a senior cadet assigned by his commanding officer to look after the school's first black student (played intelligently by boxing champ Mark Breland). Keith doesn't have much stomach for the juvenile hazing of young recruits, or "knobs," on Hell Night. Using

these scared, humiliated newcomers as human piggy banks, shaving their heads, and abusing them mentally and physically is Keith's idea of kid stuff. But the worst is still to come.

There's a secret society called "The 10," made up of students who run the school with supernatural power, bending the rules their way and literally getting away with murder while the school authorities secretly approve of their vengeance. "The hole" is where they take you if you cross the institute in word, thought or deed. Needless to say, the black cadet is marked for demolition—first, there's just a nasty cut from a razor blade in his gym sneakers; later, electric shock treatments, the number 10 carved in his back with a knife in the shower, and worse. "If that's the honor of the institute," says Keith, "then the graduation ring is crap."

Tension mounts with unbelievable force as this heroic cadet conducts his own investigation with the aid of his three loyal roommates, risking his graduation and even his life in a private search for truth and justice.

The result is a much more adventurous and hypnotic film than a bare outline suggests. Some people will object to the violent atrocities; others will scoff at director Franc Roddam's obvious use of the academy as a microcosm of moral decay in America, and "The 10" as a mask for the Ku Klux Klan. But I must say this for *The Lords of Discipline*—it is never idle or boring for a single minute, and that's more than I can say for most movies.

It zings and zooms along with breathless speed, fleshing out real characters along the way instead of mush-mouthed southern clichés. David Keith's character might be too good to be true. Unaffected personally by the mendacity around him, he decides to clean up the school the way John Wayne cleaned up boom towns in the Old West, out of patriotic duty and an innate sense of decency. Still, how many genuine heroes does the screen have to offer anymore?

Keith, with his open-faced sincerity, is the perfect actor for the role. The way he discovers his own definition of manhood is one of the film's chief joys. In a forty-carat cast of exciting supporting players, I particularly like Robert Prosky, as a cigar-chomping officer who still believes in fair play; and Mitchell Lichtenstein, an offbeat newcomer who plays Keith's elegant, cultured, and complex roommate, whose preference for Mozart over football masks an even darker personality that is one of the film's more chilling revelations.

THE LOST WEEKEND (1945)

★ ★ ★ Directed by Billy Wilder. Screenplay by Wilder and Charles Brackett. Produced by Brackett. With Ray Milland, Jane Wyman, Philip Terry, Howard da Silva, Doris Dowling, Frank Faylen, and Mary Young.

The Oscar-winning Best Picture of 1945 was a gritty and uncompromising look at the degradation of an alcoholic that didn't whitewash the subject or spare the audience any ugly detail. Considered daring and controversial almost five decades ago, *The Lost Weekend* seems to have lost none of its venomous bite. That's a credit to the tough writing and direction of Billy Wilder and to Ray Milland's Oscar-winning performance as a man driven to the brink of ruin by the bottle. In a far cry from the conniving witch she later portrayed on TV's *Falcon Crest*, the young Jane Wyman lends sturdy support as the girl who never gives up on the guy she loves. Forget about seeing pink elephants. The scene in which Milland conjures bats through a hole in the wall is still so harrowing it might even make you give up frozen margaritas.

LOVE IN THE AFTERNOON (1957)

★ ★ ★ ½ Directed and produced by Billy Wilder. Screenplay by Wilder and I. A. L. Diamond. *With Audrey Hepburn, Gary Cooper, Maurice Chevalier, and John McGiver.*

A polished diamond from Billy Wilder, complete with romance, sophistication, wicked humor, and the beauty of Paris. Magical Audrey Hepburn is the innocent daughter of French detective Maurice Chevalier, who has been hired to spy on American playboy Gary Cooper. When Cooper and Hepburn meet, sparks fly. The result is one of the most hilarious seduction scenes in films. If you ever wondered why Gary Cooper has long been considered one of the most original and captivating screen legends of his time, examine this movie and ask no more questions. Hepburn is, as always, an angel from heaven who just happens to be trapped in the body of a movie star. An elegant, delicious farce.

LOVE ME OR LEAVE ME (1955)

★ ★ ★ ½ Directed by Charles Vidor. Screenplay by Daniel Fuchs and Isobel Lennart. Produced by Joe Pasternak. *With Doris Day, James Cagney, Cameron Mitchell, Robert Keith, and Tom Tully.*

Love Me or Leave Me is a powerful MGM musical that established Doris Day as a first-rate dramatic actress with an impressive emotional range. This scalding biography of Ruth Etting, nightclub singer and Follies star, was a front-runner in the Oscar race of 1955. Shedding the girl-next-door image, Doris shared acting honors with James Cagney, as the Chicago hoodlum Marty "The Gimp" Snyder, who dominated and wrecked the singer's life, then pumped a barrage of bullets into the piano player she really loved. Together they make an uncommonly interesting and dramatic couple for a musical film. Nobody gets lathered and shellacked for the sake of an MGM finale; the characters were honestly written and portrayed for the ruthless, ambitious, miserable lowlifes they really were, and Doris never sang better. A brittle gem.

LOVE STORY (1971)
★ ★ Directed by Arthur Hiller.
Screenplay by Erich Segal.
Produced by Howard G. Minsky.
With Ali MacGraw, Ryan O'Neal,
Ray Milland, and John Marley.

The overwhelming success
of *Love Story*, husbanded with
the bragging Erich Segal did
about it, is rather disheartening.
For writing a nonmovie outline
that was turned into a nonbook
that was then turned back into
an outline for a nonmovie that
was already presold, Segal has
no reason to be proud, even in
retrospect.

Love Story hit the screen with
the well-timed mechanics of
pre-packaged instant pudding.
Inflation is the father of *Love
Story* the way the Depression
was the mother of the Dead End
Kids. The smart-money boys
in Hollywood and Publishers
Row, with their Cyclops eyes
whirling in every profitable direction, are the men responsible
for *Love Story*. Erich Segal,
with his Yale professorship to
fall back on without losing too
much face, is merely their
pawn. Jointly, they've produced two students who would
make Spiro Agnew beam. They
never picket or march or demonstrate or voice any kind of
opinion stronger than the one
that going to Paris to pursue a

music career is unimportant if
one can find Truth and Beauty
carrying a briefcase through
Central Park to music by Francis Lai. These kids are about as
relevant to 1971 as "Ethel and
Albert" but they sure are cute.
They talk like Holden Caul-
field, they don't do nude
scenes, and the older generation
makes all the mistakes. Never
mind the fact that they are
selfish, arrogant, facetious, and
boring, or that they display the
same opportunistic values as
those of the boy's father, who
is supposed to be the villain, but
who (as played by Ray Milland)
looks more like *The Lost Weekend* never ended. They are
pretty to look at, even if they
are only caricatures of living
things, and besides, *she* has this
terminal disease, see, so who
in the poor audience which just
wants to come in from the traffic and have a good cry, is going to analyze? So everything
works. The youngsters have
their generation-gap theme and
the oldsters get their eyes wet
and it's suddenly 1945 again
and nobody suffers much, except the poor girl, of course,
who dies in the middle of a
blood transfusion looking so
beautiful you can almost taste
her lip frosting.

Okay. No harm in a little

computer-programmed emotionalism, as long as everyone knows how dopey and manufactured it all is, or how far removed from reality. But couldn't it have been a better movie? Segal's screenplay is still an outline. We never really know anything about these people. The music is so barren of ideas that it keeps stealing from Bach's Concerto No. 3 in D Major. The camerawork is banal and Arthur Hiller's direction is right out of a UCLA classroom. *Love Story* shines only through the radiant performances of Ryan O'Neal and Ali MacGraw, who hold the whole mess together admirably without benefit of helpful direction, camerawork, or dialogue. It is their charm and sincerity—helping to make the audience forget it's being had—that turns *Love Story* into a life story.

Otherwise, it's just *Apartment for Peggy* with cancer.

LUCAS (1985)
★ ★ ★ Directed and written by David Seltzer. Produced by Lawrence Gordon and David Nicksay. *With Corey Haim, Charlie Sheen, Kerri Green, Courtney Thorne-Smith, and Guy Bond.*

A refreshing look at teenagers who are not freaks, drug addicts or destroyers of public property, *Lucas* is a film that centers on a brilliant fourteen-year-old with a passion for insects and classical music instead of football games and rock and roll. Lucas is small for his age and something of an object of ridicule among the high school jocks. But he's one helluva guy who learns the hard way that it's okay to be who and what you are instead of seeking peer approval through compromise. Corey Haim makes Lucas a teenager anyone would want to know better. As the star athlete who befriends him, Charlie Sheen acts and sounds a lot like his father, Martin Sheen, and his brother, Emilio Estevez, but has more star appeal. As the girl Lucas loves but never gets, Kerri Green is sensitive and offbeat. Thanks to writer-director David Seltzer, they all seem to be living their roles instead of playing some wacked-out grown-up's idea of what kids are really like. You don't have to be a child psychologist to understand the kids in this movie. All you need is compassion.

MADAME SOUSATZKA (1988)
★ ★ ★ Directed by John Schlesinger. Screenplay by Ruth Prawer Jhabvala and Schlesinger. Produced by Robin Dalton. *With Shirley MacLaine, Navin Chowdhry, Peggy Ashcroft,*

Twiggy, Shabana Azmi, Leigh Lawson, Geoffrey Bayldon, and Lee Montague.

Shirley MacLaine has always been a character actress. It's just that the characters are getting older. Here, she triumphs as a tough, demanding old Russian dragon who teaches piano technique to gifted young pupils in a run-down flat in London. She doesn't stop with Beethoven sonatas. She takes over every aspect of her students' lives. Committed to her prodigies with an obsession bordering on madness, she gives of herself totally and expects the same in return.

This is not a big film full of action and events. It's a richly textured but very personal story of the emotional tug-of-war between a brilliant young Indian boy, his domineering teacher, and his struggling working-class mother. John Schlesinger's direction is so meticulous you know everything about Madame S. by the contents of her room. You also learn a lot from Shirley MacLaine's gutsy performance. Proud, stubborn, slightly pretentious, her mouth pursed in a hard, thin slice of lacquered citrus, her carrot hair a curly mass, rings on every finger, bracelets and earrings dangling, she's the kind of loony you see hanging around

the tea rooms near Carnegie Hall. Behind the gruesome makeup, a mercurial actress creates magic. The clash between her classical world of the past and the cruel, imperfect world of urban developers tearing her house down around her gives the film its rhythm, but it's MacLaine's sensational performance that gives *Madame Sousatzka* its music—and its life.

MAD MAX BEYOND THUNDERDOME (1985)

★ ★ Directed and produced by George Miller. Screenplay by Miller and Terry Hayes. With Mel Gibson, Tina Turner, Frank Thring, Angelo Rossitto, and Paul Larsson.

Mel Gibson returns in *Mad Max Beyond Thunderdome*, third in the Australian trilogy about a futuristic cop wandering through what's left of a world destroyed by nuclear war. Whatever the intentions of *Mad Max Beyond Thunderdome* might have been, all is lost now. What's left is hardware and sci-fi surrealism from heavy metal comic books.

Do not expect logic, coherence, or purpose. Just enjoy the zonked-out images, surrender all reason, or pass it up.

Civilization is burned out, and so is Mad Max. Looking like a long-haired beggar in a

Cecil B. DeMille Biblical epic, he wanders into Bartertown looking for his stolen camel train.

Bartertown is a medieval jumble of pipes and tunnels in an old strip mine run by Tina Turner, a kind of jive-ass priestess of camp who rules her slaves in a tight gown made of chicken wire and dog muzzles. When filming ended, I assume she used her wardrobe in Vegas.

The town gets its energy from distilled pig manure. To get his possessions back, Max must exchange twenty-four hours of his life and survive not only a dunk in the pig manure, but a visit to Thunderdome.

This is a caged circus arena in which two men settle their disputes and avoid wars by meeting in hand-to-hand combat with spikes, chain saws, and no rules, emceed by an Australian Howard Cosell who shouts to the bloodthirsty crowd: "Ladies and gentlemen, boys and girls, dyin' time is here!"

Narrowly escaping death at the four hands of something called the "Master Blaster," Mad Max is next rescued from a place of sandstorms and earthquakes called "The Crack in the Earth" by a desert tribe of feral warrior children descended from the survivors of an airplane crash.

They all end up in a post-apocalyptic demolition derby, pursued by Tina Turner and the tattooed freaks of Bartertown, smashing planes, locomotives, motorcycles, and jeeps made of scrap metal and buggy wheels.

None of this makes one lick of sense, so after a while I gave up and concentrated on looking at the pictures. Imagination is all that counts in *Mad Max Beyond Thunderdome*, and there is plenty of it.

It's a world unto itself, with its own laws ("Bust the deal, face the wheel!!") and its own philosophy ("Remember—no matter where you go, there you are!"). The violence and horror and carnage are abundant (it's pretty noisy, too) but it all finally becomes funny.

In the end the crazy images and unthinkable brutality create and communicate a unique, crude poetry that is both primitive and beautiful. Acting is the last thing on anybody's mind, but Mel Gibson gets through it without smiling, and Tina Turner, as the barbaric queen of Bartertown, is Grace Jones with soul food.

MAID TO ORDER (1987)
★ ★ Directed by Amy Jones. Screenplay by Jones and Perry and Randy Howze. Produced by Herb Jaffe and Mort Engelberg. *With Ally Sheedy, Beverly*

D'Angelo, Tom Skerritt, Valerie Perrine, Dick Shawn, and Michael Ontkean.

Maid to Order is a high-tech fairy tale with an irreverent contemporary slant—a Cinderella story in reverse. Ally Sheedy is a rich, spoiled Beverly Hills brat who doesn't know the value of a dollar. Tom Skerritt is her long-suffering father who wishes he never had a daughter at all. Shazam! After a drug bust, the brat gets bailed out by a chain-smoking Fairy Godmother who's a bit of a flake herself. There's one catch. Nobody recognizes the girl anymore. Even her dog tries to bite her. With no past, no credit cards, and no identity, she's on her own. "Get a job—then we'll talk," says the Fairy Godmother (wittily played by Beverly D'Angelo). Homeless and hungry, she takes a job as a maid to Valerie Perrine and Dick Shawn, two vulgar, outrageous lunkheads who make the Bette Midler-Richard Dreyfuss team in *Down and Out in Beverly Hills* seem like models of conservatism. Prince Charming composes rock songs. How a poor little rich girl learns money can't buy everything, but finds true love and helps others in the process, is what *Maid to Order* is about. It's got plenty of gags, some vicious pokes at Holly-wood social climbers, and a big heart. It also furnishes proof that fairy tales can still come true—at the movies.

MAKING LOVE (1982)

★ ★ ★ ½ **Directed by Arthur Hiller. Screenplay by Barry Sandler. Produced by Allen Adler and Daniel Melnick. With Michael Ontkean, Kate Jackson, Harry Hamlin, and Wendy Hiller.**

The unfair critical drubbing received by *Making Love*, an intelligent film that tries to show homosexuals as normal, responsible human beings for a change, is no different from the critical reaction to *A Raisin in the Sun* when critics were too discreet to reveal their own prejudices against black families moving into white neighborhoods, so they ended up dismissing the film as black soap opera. Critics mask their homophobia by calling *Making Love* "trite" or attacking it for its rosy ending.

Barry Sandler, who wrote the screenplay, says: "My intention was to show homosexuals from a diametrically opposed view from the one in that German film *Taxi Zum Klo*, which critics liked. In my opinion, movies like that one only reinforce gay stereotypes while distancing them from society, making it easy for nervous people to support because they know there's no danger of ever knowing those freaks personally.

"*Making Love* is more threatening because it shows that gays are just like your brother, your husband, your doctor, your son, your next-door neighbor, or the guy who changes next to you at the gym. It's not compromising, and people can't accept that. Their safe image of gays is of people who are self-loathing, pitiful, grotesque, and degenerate.

"Some people hate the ending because it's slick. The young doctor played by Michael Ontkean leaves his wife after eight years of marriage and ends up with a lawyer.

"That pushes a lot of buttons and some people react with panic. They have been taught to expect gays to be relegated to slums and back alleys, or to live their lives in VD clinics waiting for the latest cure. But the ending shows that gays are no longer victims. Ontkean comes to terms and Kate Jackson learns to accept him and respect him for what he is. That doesn't mean that they can't still be friends. And she learns to go on with her life, too. I never meant it to be a movie about homosexuality and nothing else. It's about self-discovery, accepting your own value for what you are, and learning to live proudly with that identity."

Making Love is, to this observer, also a movie about pain, loss, and the ultimate sense of recovery—all basic universal issues. The circuitous and tortuous route that some lives (most lives?) must take to find freedom is not a subject that should be dismissed so patly.

The film is acted with sincerity by its principals—Michael Ontkean, as the doctor who confronts his own sexuality; Harry Hamlin, as the young writer who cannot share his need for commitment but who learns that such a thing is possible; and Kate Jackson, as the loving wife who feels betrayed and devastated but who learns it's better to let other people be human than to idealize them.

I found it honest and touching in the end when, years later, the once-happy couple are reunited at a friend's funeral only to realize that they would always share a special affection for each other as friends.

I think life is like that. No matter what paths life forces you to take, don't you always reserve a deeply rooted feeling for the person you've loved the most? If that's soap opera, then there's nothing wrong with soap opera. Barry Sandler has written *Making Love* with integrity and compassion, and Arthur Hiller has directed with love and care and attention to detail. The film does not ring false, the people are worth caring about, and if some think of it as a squeaky clean approach to a controversial subject, so what?

Why should pre-AIDS gays be portrayed as diseased maniacs waving meat cleavers any more than blacks who used to be stereotyped as watermelon-munching pickaninnies in the old days? It's a refreshing change to see homosexuals who no longer have to conform to an outdated Production Code by committing suicide.

THE MANCHURIAN CANDIDATE (1962)

★ ★ ★ ★ Directed by John Frankenheimer. Screenplay by George Axelrod. Produced by Howard Koch. *With Frank Sinatra, Laurence Harvey, Janet Leigh, and Angela Lansbury.*

The Manchurian Candidate, the granddaddy of political thrillers, is living proof that old movies in the chiaroscuro of black and white are better and more riveting than ever. This cult classic about a brainwashed political assassin, the rights to which are owned by Frank Sinatra, shocked and thrilled the world when it was first released in 1962. Its biggest fan was President John F. Kennedy. One year later, Kennedy himself was assassinated and Sinatra withdrew the film for twenty-five years. Now, by public demand, he has released it for a whole new generation of movie lovers to discover on home video. He must have preserved it in a drawer with his old bobby sox, for it looks sharper and fresher than ever.

Sinatra, in his coolest performance, plays an Army major who returns from Korea with nightmares about his commanding officer (Laurence Harvey)—a decorated hero with the Congressional Medal of Honor. The truth is, he's no hero, but a psychotic robot trained by the Soviets to kill without guilt, fear, or remorse. A game of solitaire is the gun and the Queen of Hearts is the trigger, in a diabolical Communist plot masterminded by his evil ambitious monster of a mother, to kill the President and gain control of the White House. In one of the most galvanizing performances of her career, Angela Lansbury plays this bitch-fiend like a modern-day Lady Macbeth. If you only know her as that nice lady on *Murder She Wrote,* you better take a Valium.

As this great thriller builds to a brilliant finale at the Republican Convention in Madison Square Garden, I'll wager there won't be a single member of your household with a fingernail left intact. The racy dialogue by George Axelrod is sharp as a razor. John Frankenheimer's suspenseful direction is in the imaginative tradition of Orson Welles. *The Manchurian Candidate* is not only a work of consummate artistry, but two hours of original cinematic dynamite. Happy proof that great movies are like great love affairs—they get better the second time around.

MANHATTAN (1979)

★ ★ ★ Directed by Woody Allen. Screenplay by Woody Allen and Marshall Brickman. Produced by Charles H. Joffe. With Woody Allen, Diane Keaton, Michael Murphy, Meryl Streep, Mariel Hemingway, Anne Byrne, Karen Ludwig, and Michael O'Donoghue.

The thing about New York that always defeats and trivializes attempts to analyze it is its elusive quality. It's a city that becomes whatever it is you want it to be, and the metaphor is always changing. In a sense, it's like a Woody Allen movie. Ten different people might see *Manhattan* and see ten different movies, the way ten different

visitors might leave New York with ten different impressions. All of which makes it difficult to write about Woody Allen movies, the way it is almost impossible to describe New York for someone who has never been there. As soon as you get the words on paper, they've become obsolete.

To get the immediate impressions out of the way, let me say that *Manhattan* is not Woody's best film, the final half hour is tedious and vague, and the entire territory was explored better in *Annie Hall* with more sophisticated results. Still, with its flaws and its missed opportunities, it is nevertheless more endearing and entertaining than nine out of ten movies. It is certainly not a movie you should pass up.

Woody plays Isaac, the kind of anxiety-ridden "everything happens to me" schmo who gets followed around by life's plagues the way a terminal cougher and militant non-smoker always end up in the smoking section on a ten-hour flight, complaining all the way. "When it comes to relationships," he moans, "I'm the winner of the August Strindberg Award." With two alimonies, child support, and no job, his insecurity increases.

One ex-wife has ended up

working for the William Morris office. The other ex-wife (Meryl Streep) has left him for another woman and is publishing a book about the horrors of her marriage to Woody for all of his friends to read. His current amour (Mariel Hemingway) is a seventeen-year-old student at the Dalton School who has to leave Elaine's early to do her homework. Clearly, Woody is not the kind of loser who needs the burden of another affair, but when his best friend (Michael Murphy) introduces him to his own mistress (Diane Keaton), a hostile, neurotic journalist, it's hate—and love—at first sight.

Keaton has an instant opinion on everything. She hates Ingmar Bergman and Norman Mailer, whom Woody considers "achievers," and all they do is fight, while some negative energy keeps them going. But not for long. Murphy leaves his wife, Keaton goes back to feed her self-destructive needs, Woody returns to the woman-child who really understands him (she left a message that *Grand Illusion* was playing at the Bleecker Street Cinema on his answering service), but she's grown and moved to London. Like all Manhattan survivors, Woody will wait, like the city itself, until another neurotic attachment comes along.

The characters pretend to have old-fashioned virtues. Keaton keeps talking about how bright, beautiful, and lucky she is to come from a stable Philadelphia family in which marriage is an institution, yet she lives with a dachshund named Waffles who serves as a "penis substitute" and gets involved with men who don't deserve her. Woody pretends he believes in monogamy ("People should mate for life, like pigeons—or Catholics.") yet he gives up the one girl who worships him to seek more challenging thrills with women who torture his frail psyche. Streep sees nothing wrong with exposing her ex-husband to ridicule because in her book she has told the truth.

These are the people of Woody's world—not the leeches and drug-crazed dropouts in the discos, but the battered intellectuals who hang out in revival houses, concert halls, and the Russian Tea Room. To reiterate and emphasize the point, Woody has set his characters and action in a romantic soft-focus Manhattan orchestrated by Gershwin music and photographed in mellow, beautiful black-and-white images by Gordon Willis that make New York look like a modern photography exhibit at the Museum of Modern Art.

Woody grew up on romantic movie images of New York as the backdrop for illusion the way I grew up on the notion that the day I arrived in town I'd hear taxicab music on the city streets. (In my childhood moviegoing obsession, all shots of the Manhattan skyline were accompanied by soundtrack piano concertos.) But the irony—and it is an intentional zinger—is that when you juxtapose romantic shots of Manhattan with contemporary New Yorkers you get a delicious bedlam.

Woody believes Manhattan can still work as a faithful metaphor for survival, but it is an explosive comic effect when his characters waft through the landscapes of the moon at the Planetarium or watch the sun rise gracefully at dawn over the 59th Street Bridge, while chattering incessantly about Freud, self-delusion, and Bella Abzug.

There is no welfare, crime, violence, racial unrest, or garbage in Woody's *Manhattan* and while I felt alternately puzzled and comforted by the unthreatening aspects of the city the way Woody sees it, I kept thinking "It's the New York of my dreams" and "It's nothing like the New York I know" all at the same time. Woody Allen

is probably the only filmmaker who can show contemporary Manhattan and play "Rhapsody in Blue" at the same time and make everyone else wish they had thought of it first. You don't have to love Manhattan to like *Manhattan* but it helps.

THE MAN WHO LOVED WOMEN (1983)

★ ★ ½ Directed by Blake Edwards. Screenplay by Milton Wexler and Jeffrey Edwards. Produced by Blake Edwards and Tony Adams. *With Burt Reynolds, Julie Andrews, Kim Basinger*

Burt Reynolds often seems like a Dali nightmare in his films, swimming through a sea of mammary glands in pursuit of the ultimate orgasm. In this respect, *The Man Who Loved Women* vaguely resembles other Burt Reynolds movies in format, though its texture and impact are much different.

The Man Who Loved Women just very well might be the first Reynolds movie that gives his fans what they want while elevating the star's reputation from commercial commodity to class-act status.

For starters, it opens with his funeral. Crowding around the casket, the mourners are women—maybe even the whole damn Miss Universe pageant in black veils. They've come to pay their last respects to one of the world's most gifted sexual athletes, a hunk with a heart who loved them all.

The rest of the film describes, in flashbacks, how he got that way. The narrator is his analyst—a cool, compassionate observer who has special understanding for the huddled, weeping masses of foxy females whose bodies he bedded and whose hearts he broke along the way. She was one of them and Julie Andrews plays her beautifully.

This is the story of David Fowler, a successful California sculptor driven into psychoanalysis because he cannot make choices. A Chinese menu sends him reeling with anxiety, so deciding among the women who march through his king-size bed like Grant invading Richmond is really driving him bananas. He's lust crazy for all the women he's never going to know, and already destroyed by the image of all the women he's just left behind.

What results from his fetal-position visits to the shrink is not just the analysis of another macho stud. He's not really a womanizer. He's not a male chauvinist pig, either. This guy genuinely loves women. He loves them all—equally, indiscriminately, and utterly unfaithfully.

There's the hooker he rehabilitates but never sleeps with, the devoted live-in friend who cooks him elaborate chocolate surprises, the girl with sexy legs whom he follows down the street, denting his fender, and most hilarious of all, the oversexed wife of a Texas tycoon who works him over at the racetrack, in her husband's office, while he's getting a ticket from a traffic cop, even in a car wash.

These women are all unique, striking and perfectly cast—especially the gorgeous, talented Kim Basinger as the Texas tootsie who almost lands him in jail.

Some of these vignettes are touching, others are hysterically funny—the best of which can only be experienced instead of described, as it involves some elaborate silliness with Burt trying to sneak out of a cuckolded husband's bedroom with Krazy Glue stuck to his tongue, white shag bathroom rugs stuck to his boots, and a small dog stuck to his arm. This classic scene alone is worth the price of admission.

Acting out so many varied emotions, feelings and tempos, Burt gives one of his best and most consistently solid performances in years. Julie Andrews does some of her nicest work, too—filling the role of the professional but human lady shrink with a warmth and vulnerability that is pretty surprising considering her glacial reputation.

Most gratifying of all is the firm, stylish direction of Blake Edwards—a director whose middle name is often vulgarity itself. Not here. *The Man Who Loved Women* is not just another bawdy sex comedy. Edwards has fused carnal knowledge with wisdom and insight, sacrificing his usual cynicism and smart-alecky egotism.

The result is a portrait of a contemporary sexual icon that is both tender and elegant, although it doesn't hold up as well as the François Truffaut original it's based on.

MARIE (1985)
★ ★ ★   Directed by Roger Donaldson. Screenplay by John Briley, from the book by Peter Maas. Produced by Dino de Laurentiis. *With Sissy Spacek, Jeff Daniels, Keith Szarabajka, Morgan Freeman, Collin Wilcox, and John Cullum.*

The amazing, true story of Marie Ragghianti, the young mother who exposed political corruption in the Tennessee state government and sent the governor to prison in the process, is a profile in courage that would be worth seeing under any circumstances. But with luminous Sissy Spacek in the title role, *Marie* takes on an extra dimension. It radiates sincerity and leaves you with a lifted spirit. This is basically another issue-oriented movie about how one little insignificant person stands up in the face of adversity, but when Sissy Spacek beats the corrupt system she makes it a triumph for every person in the audience. She's one of those rare actresses who is as wonderful in the small scenes as she is in the big monologues. She could bake an apple pie on screen and move me to tears.

MARJORIE MORNINGSTAR (1958)
★ ★   Directed by Irving Rapper. Produced by Milton Sperling. Screenplay based on Herman Wouk's novel. *With Natalie Wood, Gene Kelly, Claire Trevor, Ed Wynn, Everett Sloane, Carolyn Jones, and Martin Milner.*

Hopelessly miscast, Natalie Wood and Gene Kelly are star-crossed Jewish lovers in a Catskills summer resort in this lush, sudsy adaptation of the Herman Wouk best-seller. The book was a careful examination of upper middle class Jews who make the transition from the Bronx to Central Park West.

The movie makes the same trek, but sketchily, following star-struck, teenage Marjorie from Hunter College to the borscht belt, where she meets a failed song-and-dance man who becomes the tortured love of her life, causing endless ulcers for all. Natalie Wood works well but without inspiration. Gene Kelly looks like he's suffering from jock itch. The actual Adirondacks lake locations are prettier in the the movie than they really are. Preposterous fluff, but the furs, jewels, and canoes go great with popcorn.

MASK (1985)

★ ★ ★ Directed by Peter Bogdanovich. Screenplay by Anna Hamilton Phelan. Produced by Martin Starger. With Cher, Eric Stoltz, Sam Elliott, Laura Dern, and Estelle Getty.

Rocky is a bright, good-natured fifteen-year-old ninth grader who seems normal in every way. He digs baseball cards and cheeseburgers and rock bands and girls.

But Rocky is not normal. He suffers from a terminal disease called ''craniodiaphyseal dysplasia'' that turns his face and head into a humongous grotesque mask. Rocky is a junior-league ''Elephant Man'' and when he turns his face to the camera for the first time, you'll know instantly why the movie about him is called *Mask*.

From behind this hideously deformed Halloween mask that is really Rocky's face, everything about this remarkable boy and his world evolves. The plot of this film bio (the story is true) is thin as a membrane, but as the horror and revulsion quickly dissolve, you see how Rocky perceives the world and how the world perceives Rocky.

It's a sad, wrenching story of human dignity and courage in the face of adversity, but out of it comes a lesson that is inspiring in its humanity. Everyone who meets Rocky goes away elevated.

This is something of a miracle, for Rocky's home life is something less than utopian. In fact, it's positively demented. The problem is Rocky's mother Rusty, played with ferocious trashiness by the indomitable Cher. Rusty is a raunchy slattern who snorts cocaine, smokes angel dust, and sleeps around with the Hell's Angels. Every night Rocky's house is turned into an orgy of bike chains and beer cans. In this weird, offbeat environment, it doesn't take long for Rocky to win your heart through sympathy.

But Peter Bogdanovich isn't easily reduced to tears. He's not after sympathy and he's not going into the Kleenex business. He has a generous, clear-eyed affection for these quirky, hungry characters that he obviously wants to share. Rocky and his mom are real and they are played that way by Eric Stoltz, and especially by Cher, with a feel for the taut, obsessive fiber it takes to rebel against her middle-class Jewish background and gum up her personal life along the way.

Cher doesn't call attention to her virtuosity: her no-fuss acting style matches Rusty's passionate life style. The portrait she paints is of a woman who thinks of herself as one of the boys, but has a strong maternal instinct in spite of herself.

Bogdanovich's direction locates the speed demon in her unconventional but adoring relationship with her son and the film very subtly weaves in and out of its Oedipal themes, leaving the viewer free to draw conclusions about her failed marriage, her stormy affair with a tough but loyal biker (Sam Elliott) and her enduring relationship with Rocky. You get to like her, even when she does everything wrong. You get to like the bikers, too—especially when they chip in to buy a blue suit for Rocky's junior-high graduation.

One subtheme, when Rocky finally makes his escape to a summer camp where he counsels blind kids, gets cloying. Rocky finds himself by being useful to others who are equally unfortunate, and even falls in love with a beautiful blind girl (Laura Dern) who can't see his deformity.

The pieces to his tortured soul fit a bit too neatly in order to prepare us for a tragic but unavoidable finish, and I'm not sure I care for the way the script manipulates our emotions in the end. Still, there is much of value and sincerity here that add up to a very decent metaphor for survival. *Mask* is a film that instructs and uplifts the spirit; through Rocky's amazing personality, it celebrates life the way good movies should.

MASS APPEAL (1984)

★ ★ ★ Directed by Glenn Jordan. Screenplay by Bill C. Davis. Produced by Lawrence Turman and David Foster. *With Jack Lemmon, Zeljko Ivanek, Charles Durning, Louise Latham, Lois de Banzie, James Ray, Talia Balsam, and Gloria Stuart.*

Jack Lemmon is one of America's finest character actors. In *Mass Appeal*, he portrays Father Farley, a beloved middle-aged Roman Catholic priest who tells Bette Davis jokes in the pulpit, drives a Mercedes, wears Lacoste shirts, and stashes booze in his filing cabinet. His parishioners love him, and so do the alligators on his Polo shirt.

Along comes a troubled young seminary student, Mark Dolson (Zeljko Ivanek), and the otherwise complacent priest suddenly learns the real meaning of the perils of Job.

Two fellow seminarians have been kicked out for homosexuality. Mark Dolson defends them. The conservative, fatuous, homophobic monsignor (Charles Durning) naturally begins to suspect Mark. When Father Farley is appointed as the boy's guidance counselor, the result is a head-on clash of ideals, philosophies, and inner truths that changes both of their lives forever.

Mass Appeal, adapted by Bill Davis from his successful Broadway play, is a little too slick, a little too smooth, a little too much Heavenly Hash to be completely digestible, but it opens for public referendum some important issues about Catholicism, neatly packaged in entertaining gift wrap.

Beneath the surface is a valid and touching mirror to the human heart about truth and pride and the sacrifice young men must make in order to be or-

dained priests in a modern, mixed-up society where the church is still supposed to be sanctified and holy.

Mark is inquisitive, honest to a fault, opinionated, modern. He has passion. The old priest has long surrendered his passion in exchange for popularity. The boy accuses him of preaching "song-and-dance theology." The older, wiser priest insists the only way to be a successful Catholic is to learn the importance of compromise.

Mark wants to deal with serious moral and social issues of the day in his sermons. Father Farley wants to give the congregation the pablum it wants to hear. "A priest is supposed to inspire, not irritate," he warns. To him, the size of the collection plate is like a Nielsen rating.

The central crisis on the boy's road to the priesthood occurs when he admits he has experienced sexual relations with both sexes before he took his vows of chastity. If he lies about his past, he will become a priest. But Mark doesn't want to sacrifice his principles.

The old priest grapples with his conscience and in the end, when he delivers the first honest sermon of his career to plead for his parishioners to defend the boy, we know he has learned the most valuable lesson a man of the cloth can learn: What he really feels deep down inside is more important than what his congregation thinks of him personally.

Lemmon segues from tears to comedy with utmost ease and conviction. Compassion, warmth, understanding, and courage are fluctuating emotions he displays with both words and deeds. Jack Lemmon is one of those rare actors who, like Spencer Tracy, can tell you more about what he's feeling inside with just a look or a glance than most other actors can with the aid of text.

And he is matched scene for scene by his talented young co-star. Zeljko Ivanek really must do something about that name. Nobody can spell it, pronounce it, or remember it. He's a fine, believable, emotionally direct performer, but how will he ever become the star he deserves to be if, after each impressive new appearance, the audience has to ask "Who?"

Glenn (*Only When I Laugh*) Jordan has opened up the play by taking the movie viewer out of the priest's office and onto the campus of the seminary, into the pulpit, and into the affluent homes of various members of the diocese. But *Mass*

Appeal is still very much a tight two-man religious debate between an old curate and a precocious free-thinking apostle of the New Order.

The appeal of the play was more massive than the audience response to the film, but it's still a thought-provoking work that stirs the emotions and pricks the conscience, raising valid questions about the roles of priests and their responsibility to the people who depend on them for spiritual guidance. It has universal significance.

MEETING VENUS (1991)
★ ★ ★ Directed, written, and produced by Istvan Szabo. *With Glenn Close, Niels Arestrup, and Macha Meril.*

Meeting Venus is a film of rich, funny, and beautiful excesses. Written and directed by the acclaimed Hungarian filmmaker Istvan (*Mephisto*) Szabo, it does for grand opera what Truffant's *Day For Night* did for movies. When Hungary's most celebrated conductor (Niels Arestrup) arrives in Paris for rehearsals of a gargantuan production of *Tannhauser* with an international cast, he is optimistic that world press attention will turn the assignment into a major career break. French customs officials make him feel like a vagrant entering a royal box with dog shit on his shoes. The musicians complain they are underpaid and overworked. The chorus union demands a change in rehearsal hours. The Swedish diva (Glenn Close) is cold and hostile everywhere except her bedroom. There are endless problems with the maestro's work permit and paycheck. The stagehands go on strike minutes before the opening night curtain rises. The theater is imperiled by bomb threats from an ecology group protesting the burning of the Brazilian rain forest. All the beleaguered conductor wants from this lavish production is a dedication to art, integrity, and Wagner, but he ends up misunderstood in six languages, with more political confusion than he ever experienced behind the Iron Curtain. There is comedy in the disorganized chaos, pathos in the love affair between the neurotic prima donna and the married maestro, and fun for all. Glenn Close has never looked more alluring or acted with less inhibition, and Szabo's script (based on his own experiences as a film director on foreign soil) is deftly, observantly hilarious.

MEET JOHN DOE (1941)

★ ★ ★ ★ Directed and produced by Frank Capra. Screenplay by Robert Riskin. *With Gary Cooper, Barbara Stanwyck, James Gleason, Edward Arnold, Walter Brennan, Spring Byington, and Gene Lockhart.*

Frank Capra's classic fable about honesty, apple pie, and the American way is so appealing and fresh it is almost impossible to believe it was made fifty years ago. Gary Cooper is the genial, aimless, shy, and gullible tramp tricked by a corrupt newspaper into playing the role of a cynical politician. Barbara Stanwyck is the tough ghostwriter behind his speeches who turns him into an accidental messiah. In the marvelously structured film that ensues, brotherly love and the courage to fight hard for democratic principles triumph over fascism and ruthlessness, with an inspirational message for all Americans that still works in this cross-purposed world of ours today.

MEET ME IN ST. LOUIS (1944)

★ ★ ★ ★ Directed by Vincente Minnelli. Screenplay by Irving Brecher and Fred Finklehoffe, based on stories by Sally Benson. *With Judy Garland, Lucille Bremer, Margaret O'Brien, Mary Astor, Leon*

Ames, Marjorie Main, Tom Drake, Harry Davenport, June Lockhart and Chill Wills.

Everybody's favorite, this Vincente Minnelli spectacular made MGM musical history. When Judy Garland sings "Have Yourself a Merry Little Christmas" to Margaret O'Brien, distraught after being informed the entire Smith family will have to leave their home in St. Louis and move to New York, I dare anyone to survive without an extra supply of Kleenex. An authentic American masterpiece.

THE MEMBER OF THE WEDDING (1952)

★ ★ ★ ★ Directed by Fred Zinnemann. Screenplay by Edna and Edward Anhalt, from the play by Carson McCullers. Produced by Stanley Kramer. With Ethel Waters, Julie Harris, and Brandon DeWilde.

As a novel (1946), a play (1950), and finally a motion picture two years later, Carson McCullers's poignant, heartbreaking study of growing up lonely and the end of daydreaming remains one of the most powerful and engrossing works about the pain of adolescence ever written. Fred Zinnemann was restricted by the subject matter and the thematic structure of the play to a very confining cinematic range—a

black cook and two children moving about in the claustrophobic atmosphere of a southern kitchen—yet the film gives a strong illusion of expansion and movement within that range, mainly because of the shrewd way in which Zinnemann makes the camera the fourth character.

The movie also features acting beyond compare. Please notice the performance of Julie Harris, for example, if you want to experience fluency, intensity, and wrenching sincerity that is rare by any artistic standards. Then remember that this miraculous actress was twenty-six years old at the time, playing a twelve-year-old tomboy. Here is a great danger in the transfer from stage to screen: On stage, she made theatrical history; would the cruel close-ups of the camera be a discouragement to illusion? For me, the transformation was complete without a hitch. Through the skill and virtuosity of her craft, I never doubt when I see this cherished film that I am living with a lonely, disturbed, restless twelve-year-old. Although the story seems to be about Frankie Addams, the child searching for "the we of me," and her growth into maturity, it is really held together by Berenice Sadie Brown, the understanding cook, who experiences the film's sadness more deeply than the children. *The Member of the Wedding* elevated Julie Harris to overnight stardom in the role of Frankie, but it is Ethel Waters's flawless portrayal as Berenice that today remains galvanizing—first, when she takes Frankie's cousin John Henry on her lap to sing "His Eye Is on the Sparrow," then again in the final scene as she sits alone in the empty house wearing hand-me-down, moth-eaten furs and sings the hymn to comfort herself at the loss of all the human companionship around her. Never on-screen has there been a more three-dimensional performance. Zinnemann says the actor he had the most trouble with was Miss Waters. Whenever he asked her to do something, she'd say, "I'll take my direction from God." No matter. She moves into your heart and owns squatter's rights.

There has always been a belief among filmmakers—unfounded, I believe, if the script is strong—that you cannot adapt a novel or play to the screen without taking liberties in opening up the work for the camera. It is to Zinnemann's everlasting credit that he resisted the pressures from his producer, Stanley Kramer, to take his characters to the picture show, to church, to a picnic social—or, worse still, on a trip to Niagara Falls. The only change from the play is the addition of a section from the original novel—a frightening nocturnal excursion into the cheap section of town when Frankie runs away from home. This scene does not intrude or break up the claustrophobic action, but rather intensifies the nightmare quality of the cruel world outside Frankie's own small frame of reference.

The physical design, flavorsome and realistic as the smells coming out of Berenice's stove, adds to the leisurely pace. This is a movie about writing as much as anything else. Today's movies are made by megalomaniacs berserk on ego trips to satisfy their own needs to make home movies at gargantuan expense. I sit through film after film saying, "The photography was beautiful, but what was it about?" Or "Why don't the characters ever talk to each other?" Here is a film that is almost all dialogue, a virtually one-set affair about people whose skins are on fire from the desire to burst out of their humdrum lives, and it is absorbing from start to finish—a movie from the soul, from the guts, and from the heart that glows with radiance. It doesn't matter whether it's a conventionally constructed film or not. It is art, and it endures.

MEMPHIS BELLE (1990)

★ ★ ★ ½ Directed by Michael Caton-Jones. Screenplay by Monte Merrick. Produced by David Puttnam. With Matthew Modine, John Lithgow, Eric Stoltz, Billy Zane, Sean Astin, D. B. Sweeney, and Harry Connick, Jr.

Memphis Belle is the name of the most famous B-17 in 1943, completing twenty-four missions without a scratch at a time when we lost more than fifty thousand fliers over enemy skies in World War II. This exciting movie, in the bombing-crew tradition of *Thirty Seconds Over Tokyo*, is about the *Belle*'s ten-man crew and its twenty-fifth mission. If you know your history, you know how it all works out, but that should not deter you from experiencing the fears, joys, friendships, rivalries, and male bonding in a polished, beautifully produced and action-packed war movie. Director Michael Caton-Jones has filled the picture with gut-wrenching aerial sequences, detailed 1940s ambience, and fine performances by an energetic ensemble of guys, any one of whom would be proud to fly twenty-five missions over June Allyson's organdy-curtained kitchen windows.

The always reliable Matthew Modine is the commander, and the rest of the talented crew includes Eric Stoltz, Billy Zane, D. B. Sweeney, and singer-pianist Harry Connick, Jr., making his acting debut. As the *Belle*'s tailgunner, he even gets to croon "Danny Boy" with sultry charm. The great cinematographer David Watkins creates a panic-inducing claustrophobia on board the B-17, and the excellent script, by Monte Merrick, creates unbearable tension. Far from just another whirring-propellers-and-fogged-up-goggles war flick, *Memphis Belle* evokes emotions while cataloguing an equally epic chapter in military history. It's riveting stuff.

MEN DON'T LEAVE (1990)

★ ★ ★ Directed and written by Paul Brickman. Produced by Jon Avnet. With Jessica Lange, Joan Cusack, Arliss Howard, and Tom Mason.

Single parents have been hot items at the box office in recent years. Following on the shapely heels of Bette Midler in *Stella* and Jane Fonda in *Stanley and Iris* came Jessica Lange in *Men Don't Leave*. At this rate, single mothers could replace cop buddies.

Jessica plays Beth Macauley, happily married with two sons, suddenly widowed with no life insurance and $63,000 in debt. So she sells the family house and moves her kids to Baltimore where things only get worse. Beth can't hold things together the way she used to. Her new job in a gourmet deli forces her to stay up nights baking bran muffins and leaves little time for romance, even with a handsome musician (Arliss Howard). Contact with men is nothing compared to her disintegrating relationship with her kids. Her oldest son takes up with a cradle-robbing nurse in a neighboring apartment played by that daffy weirdo Joan Cusack. And her younger son takes to stealing Milk Duds and works his way up to VCRs. Beth loses her job, has a breakdown, and takes to her bed in depression. The house is a mess, her life is a mess, her kids are a mess. The movie is An Unmarried Woman revisited, with elements of a sitcom, but director Paul Brickman, in his first film since Risky Business, makes it much warmer, subtler, and realistic than it sounds. It doesn't go for punch lines or gags. And a lot of what's good about it is Jessica Lange, who makes a stock character both moving and sympathetic while she grabs your attention and holds it. The way Beth takes command of her life is not always convincing, but the way Jessica Lange takes command of the movie is.

MEPHISTO (1981)
★ ★ ★ ★ Directed and produced by Istvan Szabo. Screenplay by Szabo and Peter Dobel. With Klaus Maria Brandauer, Krystyna Janda, Ildiko Bansagi, and Karin Boyd.

From Hungary, Mephisto is a gripping adaptation of Klaus Mann's 1936 novel about a ham actor from the German provinces who became the darling of the Nazis although he had no fascist leanings himself. A political naif who was obsessed with furthering his career, he wanted so much to be loved that he let himself become Hitler's puppet.

Called Mephisto because his portrayal of Mephistopheles was a Third Reich favorite, the character is based on the great German stage star Gustav Grundgens, a rascal who got by in an epoch of danger and madness by being ambitious, clever, and audacious. Watching his fellow artists banished into exile, standing idly by while the plays of Schiller were banned, forced to hire blond Aryan actors even when they had no talent, he eventually embraced the cause almost without knowing it. Director Istvan Szabo uses Grundgens as a metaphor for political complacency, a symbol of people who care so much about their careers and their personal success that they will do anything to get ahead.

The centerpiece of this fascinating film is the powerful Austrian stage actor, Klaus Maria Brandauer, who plays every aspect of the actor's rise and downfall with brilliance and panache. He is so good that he even makes his bad stage performances in the early part of the film sing with realism. As his prestige increases, his acting improves until the film progresses toward a shattering climax in the Olympic Stadium in Berlin where, caught in the spotlights, he protests to the world that he is only a poor actor; the sins of Germany are not his fault.

The point of the film, of course, is that nobody is just an actor or anything else in a political holocaust. Through Szabo's keen direction and the blazing truth of the actor's forceful impersonation, we realize that we are all political, in a sense, and to deny responsibility for our actions is itself a political act. *Mephisto* is a pro-vocative triumph, visionary and inquisitive, that still haunts after the projector stops rolling.

MIAMI BLUES (1990)
★ ★ ★ Directed and written by George Armitage. Produced by Jonathan Demme and Gary Goetzman. With Alec Baldwin, Jennifer Jason Leigh, and Fred Ward.

Miami Blues should have catapulted Alec Baldwin to stardom like a flaming torpedo. He's Junior, a pleasant, sweet-faced, clean-cut preppie psycho who kills people for the heck of it. Alluring Jennifer Jason Leigh is Susie, a college student who takes up hotel prostitution to save up for a Burger King franchise. Together they find the yuppie dream—plenty of money, a nice condo, and home cooking. Of course she has no idea Junior is doubling their assets on a daily diet of crime, robbing and looting his way through the malls and minimarts of Miami. She's so naive that when she asks what he does for a living, he tells her he's an "investor" and she turns over her own C.D.'s. The theme song for this wild movie should be "What I Did for Love."

The third element that keeps this black comedy bouncing is Fred Ward, superb as a broken-down cop who sleeps in a fleabag motel with his dentures in a whiskey glass. Junior steals his badge and gun, and now he's really in clover—beating, mugging, and robbing people while pretending to be a cop, while the real cop takes the blame. Susie's so innocent she meets the cop in a supermarket, trades recipes, and invites him home to dinner. What happens next is a quirky, fever-pitched comedy thriller that always manages to turn a corner and reveal a fresh surprise. It's violent but unique.

MIDNIGHT LACE (1960)
★ ★ Directed by David Miller. Screenplay by Ivan Goff and Ben Roberts. Produced by Ross Hunter and Martin Melcher. With Doris Day, Rex Harrison, Myrna Loy, Herbert Marshall, Roddy McDowall, and John Gavin.

Away from the bandstand, Doris Day proved she could scream her head off better than any dramatic actress on the block in this scary, classy Hitchcock-flavored thriller. Doris is a rich heiress being driven mad by an unseen killer in the London fog. Myrna Loy, Rex Harrison, Roddy McDowall, and John Gavin are all suspects, and there's a red herring a minute. The clothes, designed by the great Irene, made Doris look more glamorous than most of her spunky virgin roles of this period allowed. Slick hokum, with a strong supporting cast and a surprise unmasking of the villain at the end that leaves most viewers aghast.

MIDNIGHT RUN (1988)
★ ★ ★ Directed and produced by Martin Brest. Screenplay by George Gallo. With Robert De Niro, Charles Grodin, Yaphet Kotto, John Ashton, Dennis Farina, Joe Pantoliano, Wendy Phillips, and Richard Foronjy.

In Midnight Run Robert De Niro is lean and hard again, like an old Sean Penn, as a ruthless bounty hunter whose career as an honest cop was ruined years ago by a Chicago mobster. Charles Grodin is a Las Vegas accountant who has stolen $15 million from that same gangster, and jumped bail. De Niro is hired to make a "midnight run"—that's bounty-hunter talk for "easy job"—and bring the escaped accountant back from New York to L.A. in one night. He bags his man okay, but the trouble is just beginning. What should have been an easy five-hour trip turns into a five-day nightmare. Grodin is a whining wimp and neurotic hypochondriac who cannot fly. On planes, he's agoraphobic. On trains, he's claustrophobic.

The handcuffs hurt. And when he's not nagging De Niro about his smoking, he's lecturing him about cholesterol. Broke, dirty, and exhausted, De Niro will stop at nothing to collect his money—even while being chased by the Mafia, the FBI, and a rival bounty hunter.

Part of the fun in this movie is watching the diverse personalities connect at cockeyed angles. De Niro is full of life and zest—wolfing down junk food, picking locks, and tapping phones with glee while Grodin harasses, glowers, and groans with nagging disapproval. They're Abbott and Costello with machine guns. Martin Brest, director of *Beverly Hills Cop*, keeps everything breezy and fast-paced on biplanes, 747s, freight trains, Amtrak passenger trains, buses, automobiles, and pickup trucks, building laughs and investigating character at the same time. *Midnight Run* is funny, suspenseful and full of excitement. It's *Planes, Trains and Automobiles* with handcuffs and Magnums.

A MIDSUMMER NIGHT'S SEX COMEDY (1982)

★ ★ Directed and written by Woody Allen. Produced by Robert Greenhut. With Woody Allen, Mia Farrow, José Ferrer, Mary Steenburgen, Tony Roberts, and Julie Hagerty.

This is one of Woody's weakest and emptiest films. The final analysis is one of disappointment rather than elation, a work that borrows the best ideas of others and goes nowhere with them at all. *A Midsummer Night's Sex Comedy* is Woody Allen up a tree. It is never sexy, and only rarely wryly amusing.

Woody is a crackpot inventor, a Rube Goldberg whose mad ideas never work, and whose clogged but eager mind is fertile ground for plowing the mysteries of the universe without ever discovering any of the answers. Mary Steenburgen is his sexually frustrated wife. One idyllic weekend they are visited by José Ferrer, as a pompous philosophy professor, and his young fiancée (Mia Farrow), who turns out to be an old liaison of Woody's. The other houseguests are Tony Roberts, a raunchy doctor, and his nymphomaniac nurse, Julie Hagerty (of *Airplane* fame). The doctor and Woody both immediately lust after Mia, while the stuffy professor snorts after the dumb but sexy nurse. There are badminton games, fishing in brooks, communications with nature, walks among the fluttering butterflies in the excruciating heat, and a lot of gamboling on the green and howling at the moon. None of it comes to anything, and it is only vaguely less than boring. Gordon Willis's caramel-colored cinematography has the look of old Victorian sketches turning brown and there are one or two grins as Woody tries out his flying bicycle, looking like an old airborne cricket with orange hair. Unfortunately, there is precious little to remind anyone that this is a Woody Allen movie. Mostly, it just seems like a takeoff on *A Little Night Music*, with Mendelssohn instead of Sondheim providing the musical interludes.

Everyone salivates after someone other than the person he or she came with, and nothing quite ends up as it should. In this respect, it resembles Ingmar Bergman's *Smiles of a Summer Night* (from which *A Little Night Music* was borrowed in the first place) more than it resembles Shakespeare's *A Midsummer Night's Dream*. With its enchanted woods under the white moon that liberates the confused sexuality of the summer revelers, it does echo textures of Shakespeare, but with its dolorous pace, its gauzy filtered-lens camera work, and its people in linen frolicking in meadows, it also swipes a few

impressions from Renoir's *Picnic on the Grass*.

Mia Farrow, as the erotic sexpot who drives all three men wild with desire, is so hopelessly miscast that she wrecks whatever coherence the film might otherwise have. Mia Farrow is about as sexy as a can of tuna. The rest of the actors, with the exception of Ferrer, have been encouraged to squeak, mumble, and hesitate in the guise of naturalism until you wonder if they have all been forced by Woody to attend the Diane Keaton School of Delayed Timing. Woody himself isn't a very sensual Puck.

It's all very pretty, like grass seed catalogues photographed through gas fumes, but ultimately arch, superficial, and boring. Psychoanalysis is probably the worst thing that ever happened to Woody Allen. It taught him to wear cinematic hair shirts, X-ray his id on film, and make home movies out of his friends' group therapy. The disastrous reaction to *Stardust Memories* led him into a different direction this time around, and the result is the sweet, graceful little *A Midsummer Night's Sex Comedy* with an old-fashioned foreign-film texture that isn't much of an improvement.

THE MIRACLE OF MORGAN'S CREEK (1944)

★ ★ ★ Directed, written, and produced by Preston Sturges. *With Betty Hutton, Eddie Bracken, William Demarest, Diana Lynn, Brian Donlevy, Akim Tamiroff, and Porter Hall.*

Another frantic movie favorite from genius Preston Sturges, circa 1944. The legendary Betty Hutton plays a small-town girl who goes overboard with patriotic gusto, marries a soldier who disappears after the wedding night, and discovers she's pregnant. Trouble is, she can't remember the father's name. If they ever discover a way to bottle what critic James Agee once called Betty Hutton's own special brand of comic violence, they'll have the first woman on the moon.

THE MIRACLE WORKER (1962)

★ ★ ★ ★ Directed by Arthur Penn. Screenplay by William Gibson. Produced by Fred Coe. *With Anne Bancroft, Patty Duke, Victor Jory, Inga Swenson and Andrew Prine.*

1962 Oscars went to young Patty Duke (Supporting Actress) as Helen Keller and Anne Bancroft (Best Actress) as Annie Sullivan, the tough, unconventional teacher who taught her to communicate in a world of darkness and ignorance, molding her into one of the most remarkable women in American history. This is a great film, true to the Broadway play, tightly directed by Arthur Penn without a trace of sentimentality. The acting is miraculous, too. You may think you've had all you can take of the Helen Keller story, but this is a film of such inspiration it could renew your faith in the human race.

MISERY (1990)

★ ★ ★ Directed by Rob Reiner. Screenplay by William Goldman, based on the novel by Stephen King. Produced by Andrew Scheinman and Rob Reiner. *With Kathy Bates, James Caan, Lauren Bacall, Frances Sternhagen, and Richard Farnsworth.*

Misery is a horror flick in which the only monster is human, and not all that scary at first glance, either. In fact, Kathy Bates plays the predatory female almost like a normal, everyday person. She is Annie Wilkes, a registered nurse who lives on a secluded farm in the rugged Colorado mountains— a plain-Jane, mousy-haired, overweight cow of a woman who loves meatloaf, Liberace records, *The Dating Game* on TV, and the glitzy pulp fiction of best-selling romance novelist Paul Sheldon (James Caan).

Everybody, it seems, loves his books about fictional heroine Misery Chastain except the author himself. Even his tough New York literary agent, played with no-nonsense brio by Lauren Bacall, begs him for another Misery book. But Paul has other ideas. He packs himself off to a mountain lodge, kills off the Misery character in a final episode, and writes the serious book of his dreams. During a raging blizzard, he gets saved from an icy death in a car wreck by Annie, a "number one fan," who turns out to be a wacko. Locked in a room with both legs broken, the writer finds himself living every author's wildest nightmare. He becomes Annie's prisoner. Bandaged and splinted, drugged on painkillers, and miles from the nearest phone, the poor man's Harold Robbins finds his safety and survival jeopardized by an obsessed admirer who forces him to write a new book restoring Misery to life for literary posterity. Just about the worst thing that can happen to any writer happens when he watches not one but two unpublished novels burned with charcoal lighter fluid on a barbecue grill. *Misery* turns into a psychological thriller that matches wills between the killer nurse and her helpless patient while director Rob Reiner and star Kathy Bates pull out all the stops. While the camera moves in for graphic close-ups of a lady gargoyle in action, Miss Bates makes hypodermic-wielding lunacy positively genuine. No wonder she won an Oscar for doing it so well.

THE MISFITS (1961)
★ ★ ★ ★ Directed by John Huston. Screenplay by Arthur Miller. Produced by Frank E. Taylor. *With Clark Gable, Marilyn Monroe, Montgomery Clift, Thelma Ritter, and Eli Wallach.*

No Marilyn Monroe video collection would be complete without *The Misfits*, a brilliant, controversial, and much-misunderstood tribute to the star at a turbulent period in her life, penned as a valentine by her then husband, Arthur Miller. *The Misfits* is slow and arty, with long pauses and a lot of odd poetic metaphors, but it's the one film in her illustrious career that provided Monroe with a role closest to her own troubled, sensitive personality. Clark Gable (in his last film) and Montgomery Clift are the broken-down cowboys reduced to roping horses for dog food and Marilyn is the bruised, animal-loving child-woman who tames them in this John Huston movie immortal. Of all the

Marilyn Monroe films, *The Misfits* is the one that will survive the ages as a work of distinguished and lasting artistic value.

MISS FIRECRACKER (1989)

★ ★ ★ Directed by Thomas Schlamme. Screenplay by Beth Henley. Produced by Fred Berner. *With Holly Hunter, Tim Robbins, Mary Steenburgen, and Alfre Woodard.*

Bring along an off-the-wall sense of humor for this goofy trip to cornpone country and you'll have more fun than a wild skunk at a D.A.R. meeting. Wonderful Holly Hunter stars as a fish factory worker and small-town Mississippi misfit determined to win a wacky beauty contest full of screwballs with a spirited but horrifying tap dance routine to the "Star Spangled Banner." Tim Robbins and Mary Steenburgen are just two of the loonies who try to help in a gang of Beth Henley characters that include an aunt with monkey glands, and a bug-eyed seamstress named Popeye who sews doll's clothes on bullfrogs. They're hopeless, funny, and heartwarming. The writing is superb, the actors are captivating, and the small-town atmosphere is as mad as a convention of cuckoo clocks.

MOMMIE DEAREST (1981)

★ ★ ★ Directed by Frank Perry. Screenplay by Frank Yablans, Perry, Tracy Hotchner, and Robert Getchell. Produced by Yablans. *With Faye Dunaway, Diana Scarwid, Mara Hobel, Steve Forrest, Howard Da Silva.*

Forget everything you've read about *Mommie Dearest* and just prepare yourself for a dramatic earthquake of unparalleled emotional turbulence. It is a sensational motion picture that had me hypnotized from beginning to end. I believed every word of Christina Crawford's harrowing book about life as the adopted daughter of one of Hollywood's reigning sadists, and although the movie takes some liberties with the order in which she opened up the scar tissue, most of the facts have been retained and dramatized with artistry. But this is not a one-sided "let's get a dead movie star" piece of easy sensationalism. Frank Perry, a sensitive and intelligent filmmaker, has gone to great lengths to help explain the complex reasons behind Crawford's obsessive behavior and harrowing rages. *Mommie Dearest* examines thirty-nine years in the life of a schizophrenic star and while it does not whitewash the tigress it grabs by the tail, it at least helps us all to understand her multiple personalities better. It is a colossal achievement.

The opening title sequence, showing the brutal predawn routine of a legend preparing for a hard day's work before the cameras, is one of the most exciting preludes to a film about the picture business since the studio came to life in the darkness of morning in *Harlow*.

It is some time before we see Faye Dunaway's face, but when we do, the breath stops. The transformation is so eerily complete it is staggering. But more about her amazing performance later. From the beginning, we are plunged without delay into the golden era of movies—the lavish homes, the closed-door contractual negotiations by which a star lived or perished, the kidney-shaped pools that offered little comfort to a star who didn't know how they would be paid for, the glamorous clothes, the fighting and clawing for roles, the desperation to remain a box-office draw.

Crawford was the best in the business at maintaining her star status, even when she was box-office poison, but she was a lousy mother and her private life was a mess. Christina and her brother Christopher were both adopted for publicity pur-

poses at low ebbs in Crawford's popularity. She got a lot of mileage out of them, but the real tragedy was that after the photographers went home, the children stayed and Joan just didn't know what to do with them.

If she couldn't achieve the perfection she demanded in her own life, no children could ever achieve it for her. And so a horrifying war began between the star's nerves and the children's needs for affection and security, as Mommie Dearest descended into a nightmare world of self-made illusion, alcoholism, and child abuse.

The film is more than a gory study of Freudian torment in the homes of the rich and privileged; it is a story with a wider scope—the ever-changing horizons of love between children and parents and the terrible things people do to each other in the ambivalent name of love.

The key scenes are all intact: the famous wire coat-hanger scene, the way Joan forced Christina to eat blood-raw meat that had been left out for days, tying Christopher to his bed with straps, pounding discipline into their tiny heads, turning Christmas into a nightmare, bursting into the kids' room in the middle of the night to ransack their closets and beat them senseless, shipping Christina off to boarding schools and convents to ensure more privacy with her lovers, depriving Christina of all privileges, and eventually trying to murder her in the presence of witnesses.

The film follows this stormy love-hate relationship to the end, when Crawford got the final hammerlock hold by cutting the children out of her will for reasons they do not understand to this day. When the film fades to black, illuminating the shine of pain in Christina's eyes, you know the final irony will not be Crawford's but the best-seller Christina would later write. Judgment Day is still to come for Mildred Pierce, but this scalding, powerful, immaculately detailed film version of *Mommie Dearest* will surely contain damaging evidence in those ledger books in the sky.

The production details are dazzling: Irene Sharaff has designed costumes that are sumptuously accurate right down to the ankle-strap wedgies; the script by Perry, co-producer Frank Yablans, and others didn't miss a beat in re-creating a fascinating era of long-lost glamour; and the actors are impeccably cast.

A tiny miracle named Mara Hobel plays Christina as a child with the kind of amazing honesty we haven't had since Margaret O'Brien took her pension plan and walked out of MGM forever. Diana Scarwid, who looks exactly like a grown-up version of Mara Hobel, gives a deeply touching portrayal as the confused, tormented adult Christina, Howard Da Silva is a chilling Louis B. Mayer, and Steve Forrest uncovers many layers of injured manhood as one of Crawford's more sympathetic lovers.

But at the center of this holocaust is the howling, lacerating, three-dimensional performance of Faye Dunaway. It is a piece of acting that can only be called pyrotechnic!

"Nobody ever said life was fair," she says, growling, clawing, competing, and conniving to remain a star, and your heart melts for her. Later, when she confronts the Pepsi-Cola moguls who are trying to cheat her out of her controlling interest in the conglomerate stock, she levels those John L. Lewis eyebrows and hisses, "Don't fuck with me, fellas! This ain't my first time at the rodeo!" and you get the magnum force this formidable serpent was capable of.

In between, she plays a thousand moods and textures—sentimental elation, phony Good Samaritan, capable of blinding rages, desperation, and evil rolled into one gift-wrapped eight-by-ten glossy. With that tired crack in her voice, those pursed lips, the raised eyebrows, the cleanliness fetish that forced her to rub her hands like Lady Macbeth, the toss of her defiant head, the sideways glances that let everyone know she didn't miss a trick, Dunaway is Crawford, Crawford is Dunaway, and you can't tell them apart. If her performance is bigger than life, it's because Crawford was bigger than life.

If there is never anything warm or real or benign about her, it's because to her children she never appeared as anything but an immaculately coiffed star playing one of a thousand roles and the poor kids never knew when the roles would change.

This is the greatest work Dunaway has ever done on screen and it more than charges *Mommie Dearest* with hydroelectric shock. She is eerie, and so is the movie.

MONA LISA (1986)

★ ★ ★ Directed by Neil Jordan. Screenplay by Jordan and David Leland. Produced by Stephen Wooley and Patrick Cassavetti. *With Bob Hoskins, Michael Caine, Cathy Tyson, Clarke Peters, Kate Hardie, and Robbie Coltrane.*

This strange, disturbing film presents a squalid view of the London underworld that will hypnotize discerning audiences and leave even the most jaded viewer breathless. Bob Hoskins, a gruff, ugly toad of a man, literally knocked critics off their feet by the range and skill of his work. As a small-time punk dispatched by a gang boss to "escort" a black prostitute through the neon hell of London after midnight, Hoskins gives a galvanizing performance that moves caustically from rage to love as he falls under the spell of the mysterious whore. Michael Caine is the evil gang lord, newcomer Cathy Tyson is the satin-clad vixen who lures Hoskins to his downfall, and they are both brilliant and sardonic. This brooding, mean-spirited movie is not everyone's cup of poison, but its impact is original and unforgettable. For his performance, Hoskins won the Best Actor award from the New York Film Critics.

THE MONEY PIT (1986)

★ ★ ★ Directed by Richard Benjamin. Screenplay by David Giler. Produced by Frank Marshall, Kathleen Kennedy, and Art Levinson. *With Shelley Long, Tom Hanks, Alexander Godunov, Philip Bosco, Maureen Stapleton, Joe*

Mantegna, Josh Mostel, and Yakov Smirnoff.

Owning your own house may be part of the American dream, but buying an old house in the country can quickly turn into an American nightmare.

From *Mr. Blandings Builds His Dream House* to *George Washington Slept Here* and *The Egg and I* the trials and tribulations of naive city slickers who invade the countryside without knowing a hammer from a screwdriver have always provided profitable fodder for movies. *The Money Pit* brings new freshness to the genre, with contemporary insights, updated characters and viewpoints, and technical virtuosity.

The Money Pit is about a girl, a boy, and a house.

The girl is Anna, a classical violinist. The boy is Walter, a lawyer who handles the finances for various demented rock and roll groups. Anna and Walter are nice, attractive preppies, played by those nice, attractive real-life preppies, Shelley Long and Tom Hanks. They are madly in love, deeply devoted, and happily unmarried but living together in the apartment of Anna's ex-husband, a raving, over-sexed egomaniac symphony conductor named Max (played with great brio by

ballet star Alexander Godunov).

To make a long story short, Max returns unexpectedly, Anna and Walter are evicted, an offer they can't refuse leads to a mansion on Long Island with a ridiculously low selling price, and before the mortgage dries, they are up to their pointed little ears in homeowner horrors that are sidesplittingly hilarious.

The stairs collapse. The plumbing belches rust. The ceiling caves in. The electrical wiring is so faulty even the blender is on fire. Two hundred thousand dollars later, with no end in sight, they're facing financial ruin. Board by board, nail by nail, the house begins slowly to demolish itself. And as these lovable innocents fall victim to building inspectors, scheming permit dispensers, and insane demolition crews on motorcycles, I found myself sympathizing and laughing at the same time.

The point of the movie is that relationships are like houses. Through trial and error, with aching hearts and empty wallets, Anna and Walter discover their own relationship is very much like their exploding dream house—a mess, but the foundation is good. With a good foundation, everything else can be fixed.

As a homeowner for whom nothing in an old house is ever fixed, I didn't believe a word of it, but I had a wonderful time living through the real estate nightmare that became their way of life. The pitfalls and rip-offs they survive are neatly and humorously catalogued by director Richard Benjamin, crisply photographed by Woody Allen's cameraman Gordon Willis, and engagingly written by David Giler.

The actors are superb. Although her movie career since TV's *Cheers* has not been a cause for rejoicing, Shelley Long is an appealing actress with Carole Lombard qualities. She lights up the screen and makes all the turmoil livable, almost desirable. A man could go through anything with Shelley Long holding the coffeepot, but Tom Hanks is tested beyond endurance. He's a ruffled, teddy-bear actor with a wide-open eagerness that is contagious. Both stars have a field day in *The Money Pit*.

Philip Bosco is garrulously greedy as Curly the contractor, Alexander Godunov has a fine time as the pompous, self-centered Max, and Maureen Stapleton is a Long Island Madwoman of Chaillot as the previous owner of the Colonial-style lemon the kids buy. She must sell fast to get her husband out of the country before he's extradited by Israeli intelligence for Nazi war crimes. The performances are inspired lunacy, the situations brimming with imagination.

There is one elaborate sequence in *The Money Pit* in which Hanks falls blindly into a vat of paint, falls off the roof, and takes the scaffolding with him as the entire house collapses like Tinker Toys. It is so brilliantly choreographed it deserves an Oscar nomination for special effects. (It didn't get one.)

The punishing physical abuse in this section is so magnificently executed by Tom Hanks's stuntman-double that he deserves a special encomium all his own. His name is Scott Wilder, and I hope his SAG insurance is paid and up to date.

If you've ever owned a home, if you are even crazy enough to consider such a fate, this movie is going to make you scream and squirm. For me it's pure, undiluted fun from start to finish—although I must confess this is a minority opinion.

MONSIEUR VERDOUX (1947)

★ ★ ★ ★ Directed, produced and written by Charles Chaplin. With Charlie Chaplin, Martha Raye, Isobel Elsom, Marilyn Nash, Irving Bacon and William Frawley.

The most relentlessly fascinating of Charlie Chaplin's movie masterpieces, this 1947 comedy thriller is also one of his most controversial. He plays a timid bank clerk tenderly devoted to his invalid wife and child who, after losing his job in the Depression, discovers a new way to take care of them: by murdering a series of stupid, wealthy women for their money. Critics compared the film's message—good and evil are inextricably mingled—to Hitler's doctrines in World War II and the film was savaged. Fortunately, it has been salvaged and acclaimed as a work of pure genius. No matter what you feel about its morality, you can't help but roar at Chaplin's numerous but failed attempts to eradicate the rambunctious, indestructible Martha Raye. A comic milestone.

MOONLIGHTING (1982)

★ ★ ★ Directed and written by Jerzy Skolimowski. Produced by Mark Shivas and Skolimowski. With Jeremy Irons, Eugene Lipinski, Jiri Stanislave, and Eugeniusz Haczkiewicz.

High on my list of personal favorites of movies made in 1982 is *Moonlighting*, a fascinating, sharply observant, wryly sad, quirkily eccentric film shot in England by Poland's Jerzy Skolimowski, about four Polish laborers who arrive in London to work illegally on the cut-rate restoration of a carriage house owned by a rich fellow countryman from Warsaw.

During their stay, the events of December 1981 result in the declaration of martial law in Poland and the workers find themselves stranded in a foreign country, without funds, their visas expired, and all return flights canceled.

Jeremy Irons is the group leader, and the only one who speaks English. Taking the cowardly way out of the dilemma, he elects to keep the bad news from the others, and the film that revolves around his attempts to make ends meet by stealing from London shopkeepers is an expert and polished study of the comic problems of survival in an alien society.

On any level, *Moonlighting* is a very funny Polish joke about the plight of foreigners who devise elaborate systems for cheating on their hosts to survive. On a deeper level, it's a sober reflection on the betrayal of leadership.

"Don't trust your leaders!" seems to be the message, both in the streets of London—where life is observed by the Poles in that peculiar way that makes familiar strangers out of delivery boys and supermarket cashiers—as well as back home in the streets of Warsaw.

On both levels, *Moonlighting* proves it is possible to tell simple stories with passionate artistry on a shoestring budget when real craftsmen control the camera.

MOUNTAINS OF THE MOON (1990)

★ ★ ★ Directed by Bob Rafelson. Screenplay by William Harrison and Rafelson, based on Harrison's book *Burton and Speke*. Produced by Daniel Melnick. With Patrick Bergin and Iain Glen.

This is the amazing true story of the perilous adventures of Richard Burton and John Speke, the nineteenth-century explorers who set out in 1845 to search for the mysterious, unknown source of the Nile River in an uncharted wilderness called the "mountains of the moon." For three long years, they walked through the interiors of darkest Africa no white man had ever seen, experiencing hostile tribes, man-eating lions, and watering holes infected with small pox, even a bug that burrows its way into Speke's ear on its way to his brain. There's enough violence and horror to keep you feasting on your fingernails. Drought, famine, dysentery, malaria, monsoons, broken legs, human sacrifices—you get it all. Trouble is, you don't really discover much about the men themselves. The film hints at Speke's homosexual infatuation with Burton as well as Burton's own anti-Victorian views, but it doesn't go far enough to explore them. The last part, about the nasty rivalry that develops back home in England when their ordeal is over, seems anticlimactic. *Mountains of the Moon* can't make up its mind if it wants to be a sweeping African saga like *King Solomon's Mines*, a lavish biography like *Lawrence of Arabia*, or a coffee-table travelogue like *Out of Africa*. It tries to be all three and never quite makes it, but there's enough splendor and action to satisfy the armchair adventurer in everyone.

MR. AND MRS. BRIDGE (1990)

★ ★ ★ ★ Directed by James Ivory. Screenplay by Ruth Prawer Jhabvala. Produced by Ishmail Merchant and James Ivory. With

Paul Newman, Joanne Woodward, and Blythe Danner.

Paul Newman looks alarmingly like Ralph Bellamy playing Franklin D. Roosevelt. Joanne Woodward looks depressingly like Ma Perkins. But I doubt if you will ever see two more flawless performances than in *Mr. and Mrs. Bridge*. This is a perfect movie, with twin performances by the Newmans that shine like pure gold.

Based on two highly successful novels by Evan Connell, *Mr. and Mrs. Bridge* follows, like pieces in a patchwork quilt hand sewn by somebody's beloved grandmother, the story of an affluent family in Kansas City in a series of linked vignettes spanning several years before and during World War II. James Ivory, the director, is famous for his ponderous literary adaptations of historic novels on film, but although there is no real plot to speak of, there is also nothing Proustian about *Mr. and Mrs. Bridge*. It invites you into an American home and allows you to live with and observe the members of a family, much the same way David Selznick made the audience a part of *Since You Went Away*. Things happen to every member of the family and their friends, but at the same time, Mr. Ivory and his excellent scriptwriter, Ruth Prawer Jhabvala, investigate the attitudes, beliefs, prejudices, and dreams of that invincible fortress called the American family. It is quite an accomplishment, always involving, as real as Christmas, and it never lulls.

Walter Bridge (Mr. Newman) is a stuffy, conservative lawyer with a strict, acerbic outlook on life, while his wife India (Ms. Woodward) sees everything through rose-colored glasses, trying desperately to bring joy and peace to her home, ending up a second-class citizen to both her husband and her three children. As the film quietly and lucidly spans the years, we see Mrs. Bridge attempt various liberations, from art classes to psychoanalysis, always frowned on by the pompous and annoyingly self-assured Walter. We watch all three of the children's hormones rage while the war in Europe escalates. The loyal family cook (a role Hattie McDaniel was born to play) lands in jail, victimized by a no-good boyfriend, and Walter has to bail her out. Walter's secretary for twenty years announces her own pent-up resentment over her unrequited love for her boss and quits her job. India's best friend Grace (neurotically and delectably played to perfection by Blythe Danner) descends from kook to tragic, unstable suicide statistic. Son Douglas grows from Eagle Scout to Air Force pilot, while daughter Ruth goes to New York to become an actress. Giddy, romantic, silly, and easily frustrated, Joanne Woodward radiates such honesty it takes your breath away as she lives through every family episode with clear-eyed wonder. When she is alone, trapped in the family automobile in a snowstorm, she makes you understand how much she has needed the people in her life to define her existence. She rubs a hole in the fogged-up windshield, peers helplessly into the darkening night, and says in a voice small as a mouse's squeak, "Hello? Anybody out there?" It is one of the great moments of acting in movies.

This is a film about memories, about time and place, when things were easier and less complicated, when we fought wars because we knew what we had to lose if we didn't, when young people held each other close dancing to big bands, and there was always chicken every Sunday. From the terrible flowered dresses and marcelled bobs to the old Vuitton steamer trunks in the attic, every detail in the lives of

the Bridges is impeccably assembled. Paul Newman fans will be shocked to see a man so dedicated to liberal causes playing a snobby, stiff-necked conservative, but his integrity and dedication to getting it right is every bit as affecting as Joanne Woodward's delicate, fragile performance as Mrs. Bridge.

MR. NORTH (1988)
★ ★ ★ Directed by Danny Huston. Screenplay by John Huston and James Costigan, based on *Theophilus North* by Thornton Wilder. Produced by Steven Haft and Skip Steloff. *With Anthony Edwards, Robert Mitchum, Anjelica Huston, Lauren Bacall, Harry Dean Stanton, Mary Stuart Masterson, Tammy Grimes, Virginia Madsen, David Warner, Christopher Durang, Katherine Houghton, Mark Metcalf, and Hunter Carson.*

It's a source of both mystery and concern to me that we live in an age so cynical the term *old-fashioned* is a dirty word. Some of my favorite movies are old-fashioned—sweet, good-natured films with positive values and happy endings. *Mr. North* is all of those things. It's a gentle fable, a period piece set among the "Great Gatsby" mansions of Newport, Rhode Island. The year is 1926, and Anthony Edwards stars as

Theophilus North, a most unusual gentleman who bicycles into town looking for part-time jobs. Sometimes he teaches tennis to rich children, sometimes he reads to the elderly and sick. And always he amazes old and young alike with the extraordinary amount of electricity he stores up in his body—so much that he literally shocks people when he shakes their hands. It's just a parlor trick, but before long the people of Newport decide he's got a magic healing power and every loony in town invades his room at the YMCA.

Sure enough, his touch does seem to cure the migraine headaches of socialite Mary Stuart Masterson, and the bladder problems of the eccentric millionaire Robert Mitchum. But good deeds lead to trouble; Mr. North ends up in court accused of practicing medicine without a license, and one of the townspeople who comes to his defense turns out to be none other than Lauren Bacall. How it all ends is the cherry on top of a sundae that is guaranteed to entertain you.

Quaint, charming, and refreshingly old-fashioned, *Mr. North* is a small film but thoroughly enjoyable. Directed by John Huston's son Danny, it's chock-full of funny, quirky performances by Tammy Grimes,

Anjelica Huston, Harry Dean Stanton, Virginia Madsen and others. Best of all, it transports you to a voguish social world of the 1920s that is gone forever, with a Frank Capra quality of innocence that is always welcome.

MR. SKEFFINGTON (1944)
★ ★ ★ Directed by Vincent Sherman. Written and produced by Julius and Philip Epstein. *With Bette Davis, Claude Rains, Walter Abel, Richard Waring, Jerome Cowan, Charles Drake and Gigi Perreau.*

In *Mr. Skeffington*, Bette Davis plays a vain, egocentric socialite who ruins her long-suffering stockbroker husband (Claude Rains) only to discover, thirty years later, after he returns blind from a Nazi concentration camp, and she's been disfigured by a horrible disease, that "a woman is beautiful only when she is loved." One of Bette's all-time wettest tearjerkers, and the grotesque makeup created by Perc Westmore to show the ravages of diphtheria proved she was unafraid of physical surrealism two decades before *Whatever Happened to Baby Jane*.

MRS. MINIVER (1942)

★ ★ ★ ★ Directed by William Wyler. Screenplay by Arthur Wimperis, George Froeschel, James Hilton and Claudine West. Produced by Sidney Franklin. *With Greer Garson, Walter Pidgeon, Teresa Wright, Dame May Whitty, Lionel Barrymore, Reginald Owen, Henry Travers, Richard Ney, Tom Conway, Helmut Dantine, Henry Wilcoxon, Clare Sanders, and Rhys Williams.*

The best and most popular of the World War II movies about England under siege, this 1942 classic won the Oscar as Best Picture and was acclaimed by Winston Churchill as doing more for the morale of war-torn Britain than a flotilla of destroyers. Greer Garson also won a Best Actress Oscar for her portrayal of a brave and noble small-town housewife struggling to keep her family's faith together in a time of terror. Walter Pidgeon, Teresa Wright, Dame May Whitty, and Lionel Barrymore head a magnificent cast. Winner of seven Oscars and topping every wartime box-office poll, *Mrs. Miniver* seems a bit sentimental now, but its distinguished period artistry is timeless.

MRS. SOFFEL (1984)

★ ★ ★ Directed by Gillian Armstrong. Screenplay by Ron Nyswaner. Produced by Edgar J. Sherick, Scott Rudin, and David A. Nicksay. *With Diane Keaton, Mel Gibson, Matthew Modine, Edward Herrmann, Trini Alvarado, Jennie Dundas, and Danny Corkill.*

A bleak story, filmed in muted tones of chiaroscuro. It doesn't burst forth in prisms of red and yellow. It glowers and pouts from the midnight shadows, evoking gloom.

The story is true, which makes it all the more disturbing, and powerfully acted by Diane Keaton and the dynamic Mel Gibson, which makes it all the more convincing. It is still pretty shocking, although it happened more than ninety years ago, which makes it all the more timely.

Pittsburgh, 1901. Mrs. Soffel (Keaton) is the wife of a boring, proper prison warden (Edward Herrmann), and the mother of four children. She lives within the dark and oppressive walls of the Pittsburgh jail. A woman who is many things—frail, tough, substantial, and spunky—Mrs. Soffel passes among the cells of Death Row, passing out Bibles and warm blankets, reading from the Scriptures, and dispensing whatever kindness she can muster to the desperate inmates.

Mel Gibson is Ed Biddle, who, with his brother Jack (Matthew Modine), has been convicted and sentenced to hang for the murder of a local grocer during a holdup. "They had to pick the grocer's brains off the wall," says Mrs. Soffel's imaginative daughter. But Mrs. Soffel is not entirely convinced. "Nobody is completely innocent," she says. "We all sin."

The warmth of her visits has a profound effect on Ed Biddle. He prays. He write poems and slips them to her secretly. Her sympathy turns to love, but it's a pitiful affair, conducted on opposite sides of prison bars.

Then Mrs. Soffel makes a strange and sudden decision that scandalizes a nation and changes her life forever. While her children are home decorating their Christmas tree, Mrs. Soffel smuggles a saw into the prison. When the killers escape in the middle of the night, Mrs. Soffel leaves with them.

Heading north toward Canada in a horse-drawn sleigh with the fugitives, she realizes that the excitement on the run, pursued by vigilantes, bounty hunters, and bloodthirsty posses, has its limits. But there is no turning back. Her love is stronger than fear, than her social position, than even her life.

The ultimate tragedy, the final irony, is not that the lovers both die in a violent climax, but that Mrs. Soffel survives. In the end the prison cell that once housed the Biddles has a brand-new occupant.

The story, pieced together through prison records and love letters, is far from complete. It's more obscure than *Bonnie and Clyde*, which had the same reckless passion. But it's vital. It's the stuff of tales and legends.

The film breathes authenticity and reality into even the most sensational aspects of the case. The characters are not likable, honorable, or even sympathetic. Mrs. Soffel follows her heart, hurting people who loved her, destroying her husband's career. And Ed Biddle is scarcely more than a romantic dream.

But thanks to Keaton and Gibson, they come alive. They breathe fire. They have guts and courage. They are mortal without mortality.

Gillian Armstrong, the young Australian who created a sensation with her first feature, *My Brilliant Career*, directed with skill and control, capturing the bleak and solemn mood of the times, and the film is enhanced and enriched by the sharp, haunting cinematography of the great Australian cameraman Russell Boyd.

MOSCOW ON THE HUDSON (1984)

★ ★ ★ ½ Directed and produced by Paul Mazursky. Screenplay by Mazursky and Leon Capetanos. With Robin Williams, Maria Conchita Alonso, Cleavant Derricks, and Alejandro Rey.

Limousine liberal, arch-conservative, Abbie Hoffman or Jerry Falwell. It doesn't much matter what your politics are. You cannot help but love Paul Mazursky's wacky, wonderful comedy with political overtones, *Moscow on the Hudson*.

Its gleeful spirit, its unabashed patriotism and its big fat heart of milk and honey will make you send up three cheers for the red, white and blue while you're holding your sides laughing at the same time.

Robin Williams, in one of his greatest roles and one of his most brilliantly conceived characterizations, plays Vladimir Ivanov, a poor, good-natured musician who, while visiting New York with the rag-bag Moscow Circus, defects in the middle of Bloomingdale's. That, in essence, is all you really need to know. But *Moscow*

on the Hudson is about much, much more.

The opening scenes in Russia are hysterically funny, if you can imagine such a thing as humor within spitting distance of the Kremlin, as Vladimir practices his English ("Hello, mister, do you have a lamb chop?") while his girlfriend dreams, during sex, of exotic jeans by Jordache and Calvin Klein. But there's a serious side, too, as Mazursky shows the long lines for food that is inedible and shoes that never fit, the endless rain and cold endured in cloth coats, the oppression of the spirit.

Then, when the bedraggled circus troupe hits New York, what they get is a head-on collision with culture shock. Vladimir takes to capitalism like a robin takes to spring.

Once he defects, what he discovers is that all of New York is really made up of people defecting from somewhere else. He finds himself boarding in Harlem with a black family who fled Alabama. The lawyer who represents his case for immigration and citizenship is a Cuban who fled Castro. He even finds a new girlfriend, an Italian fleeing Abruzzi.

Chief among the lessons Vladimir learns is that there is no longer such a thing as

America—especially in New York. It's really a melting pot of ethnic polka dots.

Selling Chicken McNuggets at McDonald's, driving a taxi, or discovering the joy of free enterprise (a hot-dog stand on a street corner), Vladimir articulates his own new-found definition of freedom ("If all Russians could eat moo-shoo pork, they wouldn't be afraid of the Chinese!")

The movie turns corny when Vladimir, disillusioned after his first mugging, is confronted by what seems like one representative of every nationality in town, all reciting lines from the Declaration of Independence in a greasy-spoon coffee shop. But this is only a small reservation, and it drowns in all the wit and good-will around it.

What Mazursky is saying is that we are all essentially immigrants, and all of us are in it together. What a pleasure and thrill it is to see a pro-American movie that does not insult the intelligence for a change.

Robin Williams gives the film its heart and its soul, and he never stumbles for a second. From his broken, funny accent to his childlike radiance as he discovers everything from porno movies to chocolate chip cookies, he is simply dazzling. And he is supported admirably by a perfect group of sidekicks— Maria Conchita Alonso, Cleavant Derricks and Alejandro Rey in particular.

Moscow on the Hudson is a bountiful, big-hearted melting pot of a movie, uplifting and life-affirming, and filled to overflow with humanity. It should be applauded, then saluted daily, like the flag.

THE MUMMY (1932)

★ ★ Directed by Karl Freund. Screenplay by John Balderston. Produced by Stanley Bergerman. With Boris Karloff, David Manners, Zita Johann, Arthur Byron, Edward Van Sloan, Bramwell Fletcher, and Noble Johnson.

Forget about all those Egyptian partygoers hobbling along in Ace bandages and mustard plasters. There's only one creep from the crypt that matters— Boris Karloff! This original 1932 horror has inspired many imitations and rip-offs, but Uncle Boris is the only mummy who really looks buried alive for three thousand years. As Im Ho Tep, king of the dummies— er, *mummies*—Karloff wraps himself up in the part. When a British archaeologist on an expedition to the ancient tombs makes the big mistake of quoting from the forbidden Book of Thoth, something stirs from deep within the sarcophagus.

Before you can say "Mummy Dearest," hell breaks loose all over downtown Cairo. It's a perfect Halloween treasure, unearthed for home viewing. No tricks, just a true cinematic treat.

THE MUPPET MOVIE (1979)

★ ★ ★ Directed by James Frawley. Screenplay by Jerry Juhl and Jack Burns. Produced by Jim Henson. With Dom DeLuise, Orson Welles, Cloris Leachman, Charles Durning, Austin Pendleton, and the Muppets (Jim Henson, Frank Oz, Jerry Nelson, Richard Hunt, and Dave Goelz).

Neither animal, vegetable nor mineral, this adorable Technicolor musical is a delicious combination of all three, and uniquely original.

Children and adults, too, are in for a treat, for as the goony Lilliputians meet and match wits with real-life guests like Orson Welles, Bob Hope, Mel Brooks, and even Edgar Bergen and Charlie McCarthy along the way, the whole thing takes on the aura of one of the old Crosby-Hope-Lamour "road" movies.

Needless to say, the rag-and-styrofoam Muppets created by Jim Henson seem more human (and humane) than some of the flesh-and-blood humanoids they encounter on their journey to Hollywood.

The Muppet Movie begins in a screening room where all of the creatures are assembled to view their big film debut. Through flashbacks, we get the story of how it all came about, with Kermit the Frog being lured from his log in a lazy southern swamp by talent scout Dom DeLuise via an ad in *Variety* for frog auditions.

On his way to Tinsel Town, he picks up other Muppets as they all try to escape the clutches of Doc Hopper (Charles Durning), a quick-food entrepreneur who wants Kermit to do TV commercials for deep-fried frog legs.

At a gala where Bob Hope sells ice cream, Kermit meets Miss Piggy, whose porcine splendor is judged the star of the talent contest by none other than the father of puppetry, Edgar Bergen, who died shortly after his scene was completed and to whom the movie is fondly dedicated.

Miss Piggy, in her outrageous costumes with her Mae West purr and her Streisand cackle, is the sex kitten of the film, a barnyard Sue Mengers ("Hi there, short, green, and handsome," she snorts at Kermit, winking her sequined eyelashes and licking her snout suggestively) who must have that man (and a career besides). There's even a wicked parody of Claude Lelouch's *A Man and a Woman* as she and Kermit fall in love in a soft-focus haze of lush romantic music. In fact, discerning moviegoers will detect and relish a number of "in" jokes and cheeky parodies if they look sharp. There's a thrill around every corner.

Though *The Muppet Movie* is scarcely more than an elongated thirty-minute TV show, most of the gang is on hand to provide entertainment for every Muppet fan: Rowlf the dog philosopher bangs the ivories and howls about the pain of love; Sweetums the eight-foot lion is already halfway toward becoming a bathroom rug; and the Great Gonza, Monster, and Dr. Bunsen Honeydew, who is the spitting image of the film's financial savior, Lord Lew Grade, make notable contributions.

Statler and Waldorf, the New York tycoons, are cynical throughout ("Private screening, eh? Must be afraid to show it publicly!") and at the end Monster growls hysterically at the audience and screams, "Go home!"

But my favorite moment comes when the group is chugging toward Hollywood in a wooden station wagon. Big Bird, hitchhiking in the opposite direction, refuses a free ride, gurgling, "I'm on my way to New York City to break into educational television!"

Invading the Hollywood studios of Lew Lord (Orson Welles) the unruly group demands to be made "rich and famous," so he orders his aide (Cloris Leachman, who is allergic to the Muppets' shedding feathers and fur coats) to "get out the standard rich and famous contract" and the Muppet movie goes into production.

Rich and famous they are, too, and if there's any doubt, *The Muppet Movie* will make believers and fans out of the worst pessimists. These lovable characters are so real and endearing that I was never aware of the human hands making them work from mysterious hiding places. The Muppets made a wide-eyed child out of me, and I hope they continue to do so until I'm in my wheelchair.

MURPHY'S ROMANCE (1985)

★ ★ ★ Directed by Martin Ritt. Screenplay by Harriet Frank, Jr., and Irving Ravetch. Produced by Laura Ziskin. With Sally Field, James Garner, Brian Kerwin, and Corey Haim.

Longing for an old-fashioned romantic comedy with real people, honest values and home-spun homilies? Examine *Murphy's Romance*, a tailored vehicle for the considerable charms of Sally Field and James Garner that fits them like old dungarees. It's as down home as macaroni and cheese.

Miss Field, one of the screen's most natural and engaging actresses, plays Emma Moriarity, a thirty-three-year-old divorcee who arrives in a rural Arizona town with her twelve-year-old son Jake (Corey Haim) to make a new start boarding and training horses on a small ranch. It's another "spunky gal" role, but this time there's humor in the true grit, too. James Garner is Murphy, the local pharmacist who espouses liberal causes, takes French lessons by mail, campaigns for nuclear disarmament and the ERA, and worships an antique red Rolls with etched-glass windows and an eight-day clock. In his spare time, he's writing a chili cookbook.

It's not exactly love at first sight, but Murphy believes in Emma's spirit and determination enough to get her a bank loan and pretty soon he's a fixture at the ranch. When Emma's sexy, likable, but im-mature and irresponsible ex-husband Bobby (Brian Kerwin) arrives, the relationship turns into a friendly but tension-charged threesome, until Emma is forced to pick up the tab for her own life and choose the kind of future that will give her security and peace.

Murphy's Romance is a lovely movie about the quality of life, sensitively directed by Martin Ritt and intelligently written by the talented husband-wife team Harriet Frank, Jr., and Irving Ravetch, the triumvirate responsible for creating Sally Field's Oscar-winning *Norma Rae*. They know the American Southwest. From the old-fashioned *Saturday Evening Post* feeling of Murphy's drugstore soda fountain to the square dances and barbecues, everything in *Murphy's Romance* has a fresh, flavorful, and realistic authority. James Garner is a major surprise. Ditching his usual self-serving middle-aged macho act, he plays a sixty-year-old grandfather with a paunch and twinkle. He is superb. This is one film that leaves you with a warm, happy glow instead of the hives.

MUSIC BOX (1989)

★ ★ ★ ½ Directed by Costa-Gavras. Screenplay by Joe Esterhazy. Produced by Irwin Winkler. *With Jessica Lange, Armin Mueller-Stahl, Frederic Forrest, and Lukas Haas.*

Music Box is a riveting, suspenseful domestic thriller by Costa-Gravas about a Chicago family torn apart when the kindly and respected father is accused of Nazi war crimes. Hungarian immigrant Michael Lazlo has been an American citizen for thirty-seven years. His employees love him. His son fought in Vietnam. His daughter is a respected attorney. Suddenly he must stand trial for Nazi atrocities so monstrous nobody can believe them. Jessica Lange is his daughter, his lawyer, and his alibi. And the great German actor Armin Mueller-Stahl is the victim. Is this a case of mistaken identity? Is this kindly pillar of the community an innocent person unjustly accused? Or is he a fiend who has lived a lie, hiding behind the American flag for thirty-seven years? What do we really know about the events of fifty years ago? You'll ask these questions—and more—as each loose end unravels. The courtroom scenes are among the best since *Judgment at Nuremberg*. Jessica Lange is sincere, believable, and captivating. Mr. Stahl is so committed in his denial of the charges he'll keep you guessing. And another character is the music box of the title where all the facts have been concealed for decades. Part political thriller, part domestic tragedy, and nail-biting mystery all rolled into one, *Music Box* addresses a controversial issue with admirable style.

MY BEAUTIFUL LAUNDERETTE (1986)

★ ★ ★ ★ Directed by Stephen Frears. Screenplay by Hanif Kureishi. Produced by Sarah Radclyffe and Tim Bevan. *With Daniel Day Lewis, Saeed Jaffrey, Roshan Seth, Gordon Warnecke, Shirley Anne Field, and Rita Wolf.*

My Beautiful Launderette, a delightful, surprising, original, engrossing, and comical film from England, really took Margaret Thatcher's Britain to the wash—in more ways than one.

In England it opened to the most lavish set of rave reviews to come out of Britain since *A Passage to India*, and the fact that it has a gay love affair at the center of its action should not deter you for a single moment.

It's a marvelous, genuine, often funny sendup of Asians taking over London that should have everyone applauding.

My Beautiful Launderette is difficult to describe. It's not a gay movie, yet the two lovers who survive its continual pitfalls are the most charming and likable pair of screen romantics anyone has come across in ages, and they both happen to be men.

Their story is played out against a turbulent backdrop set in London's seedy, violent, racially mixed East End. The film talks about class, race, sex, ambition, business, and contemporary life in England, swinging a wrecker's ball at the shaky moral edifice of Mrs. Thatcher's New Enterprise culture.

At the center of the story is Omar (Gordon Warnecke), a good looking enterprising Pakistani immigrant who lives with his drunken, disillusioned, burned-out, bedridden father, a Bombay-born journalist who has never found the key to making a success in London, but who still believes in the value of a good education.

Omar is sent to his rich Uncle Nasser (played by the great Indian actor Saeed Jaffrey) for instruction. Uncle Nasser has made it. Like most Pakistanis originally brought to England as servants and blue-collar workers, he's been forced to cheat and slave his way into a position of authority and now he owns a series of small businesses and apartment buildings.

"There's no question of race in the enterprise culture," says Uncle, as he forcibly dispossesses an English poet from his flat for non-payment of rent.

Oman is a quick and eager pupil. He takes on a run-down failure of a launderette called, symbolically, the Churchill, finances its overhaul with money from the sale of porno films and heroin, and turns the place into a raving, kitschy hit with the help of his friend Johnny, a sensitive punk who is trying to break away from the gang of hooligans he's been running around with and start a new life.

Johnny, a white boy with a bleached white strip down his black hair clipped sharp as an upholstery brush, becomes Omar's employee and lover.

This complicates the web of racial violence in the neighborhood, just as the launderette separates both boys from their miserable backgrounds and draws them together.

The theme is that racial and political differences can be resolved through love. I'm not sure I believe it, but the direction by Stephen (*The Hit*) Frears and the brilliant script by the half-British, half-Pakistani writer

Hanif Kureishi makes everything very convincing.

The acting is juicy, especially the performance by Daniel Day Lewis as Johnny. It is hard to believe that this amazing young man—who looks like a well-groomed skunk on stilts here—can be the same slick-haired, bespectacled, pompous ninny who almost gets the girl in A Room with a View or the Oscar-winning poet in My Left Foot.

He is certainly a young actor of many faces and a wide variety of mood shifts whose range is awesome.

What the people responsible for this refreshingly different film have done is take us behind the closed doors of the Asian community in London. We see modern Britain through their eyes, and although the view is fascinating, it's not exactly a sight to be proud of.

MY BODYGUARD (1980)
★ ★ ★ Directed by Tony Bill. Screenplay by Alan Ormsby. Produced by Don Devlin. With Chris Makepeace, Adam Baldwin, Matt Dillon, Ruth Gordon, Martin Mull, John Houseman, Paul Quandt, and Craig Nelson.

My Bodyguard is a tidy affair, picturing kids as real people for a change and showing their problems and feelings without insulting their intelligence. Most movies about today's teenagers denigrate them by satirizing them as one-dimensional clones spouting filthy jargon in clouds of angel dust.

Like Breaking Away, this movie ferrets out their insecurities and complex personalities in ways that are touching and sometimes very funny indeed. Martin Mull is a hotel manager who moves to Chicago to take on a prestigious new job at the posh Ambassador East.

The problems with his eccentric mother (Ruth Gordon) who tries to pick up guys in the cocktail lounge seem minimal compared with the real problems faced at school by his fifteen-year-old son Clifford (disarmingly played by Chris Makepeace).

At home, Clifford is a precocious kid, wise beyond his years, who lives a charmed life in a luxury-hotel atmosphere that would have turned Eloise green with envy. But adjusting to the battle-scarred front lines in Chicago's public school system requires more than brains.

The local hood demands Clifford's lunch money as extortion in return for his life, the other kids live in mortal terror of the school bullies, and the teachers are too submerged in blackboard jungle red tape to be much help (to get the kids' attention, the English teacher discusses *Romeo and Juliet* as a play about "two kids who were hot for each other.")

Clifford uses his noggin and employs the biggest boy in the school to protect him. The irony is that the incredible hulk the kids think they're being protected by turns out to be more sensitive than they are.

Clifford's bodyguard is a coward when an even bigger bully destroys his motorcycle and the film's sweet mystery is why he got that way. There's honesty and depth in the sparse dialogue, no scenes are wasted, there's no wafting around while the movie tries to make up its mind about its characters or the direction it's headed.

Director Tony Bill has distilled from his young cast performances of great candor and truth. Makepeace is a delight, and I was particularly impressed by Adam Baldwin, a real Chicago high school student who makes a formidable debut as the bogus bodyguard with problems of his own. *My Bodyguard* is a sincere, exhilarating film that uses its modest budget wisely and well.

MY BRILLIANT CAREER (1980)

★ ★ ★ ★ Directed by Gillian Armstrong. Screenplay by Eleanor Witcombe. Produced by Margaret Fink. *With Judy Davis, Sam Neill, Wendy Hughes, Robert Grubb, Max Cullen, and Pat Kennedy.*

My Brilliant Career, an Australian import, is a movie produced, directed, scripted, and designed by women, based on a novel written by a 16-year-old girl in the Australian bush country before the turn of the century. But before anyone tries to categorize *My Brilliant Career* as a "women's lib picture," it should be noted that through sheer vitality, talent, and originality it soars above the mere intent of making a blunt point.

In this autobiographical account of the author's early life, Sybylla Franklin, the oldest daughter of a dirt-poor homesteader, is determined to have a career of some kind in the arts, despite her washed-out mother's discouragement.

Nobody can make sense of this headstrong, ambitious girl who will not settle for marriage and a dull routine. She escapes the dreary life of the outback and moves to her wealthy grandmother's estate only to find the refined Victorian way of life even more confining. There's a marriageable landowner next door and a chance for a civilized future, but Sybylla refuses to settle for a domestic life before she's tried her own wings, so she sits down and does the only thing she knows how to do—she writes a book.

The film ends when she puts the book in the mailbox and hangs on the country gate at the end of the road, waiting. *My Brilliant Career* is the book that was published in 1901, and they've made a very distinguished film of it indeed.

Judy Davis, the freckled, auburn-haired actress who won Australia's Academy Award for her performance, infused Sybylla with enough fire and pathos to both charm and confuse the dandies who court her, the maiden aunts who counsel her, even the servants who tend her.

She is funny, sweet, and smart as a whip. She can love without surrendering her convictions. In one scene she channels her sexual frustration into a beautifully filmed pillow fight with her beau that goes from the hall to the garden and out into the fields. With her stubbornness and sincerity, she reminded me of a young Katharine Hepburn.

The other characters are three-dimensional, too—especially the women around her. All of them—aunt, grandmother, mother—have capitulated to the insane laws of gender and are simultaneously captivated and threatened by Sybylla's solitary crusade. Nobody comes to her rescue. She provides her own compass through writing and her brilliant "career" costs her plenty, but in the end, you leave the film applauding her courage, strength, and hope.

Everything works for this film—looks, feelings, landscapes that look like paintings. Gillian Armstrong's direction, Eleanor Witcombe's script, and Don McAlpine's lavish photography conspire to translate Miss Franklin's novel to the screen with enough passion and loyalty to match the central character's zest for life.

The result is a film of extraordinary appeal that put Australia—and producer Margaret Fink—near the top of the ladder in world attention.

MY FAVORITE YEAR (1982)
★ ★ ★ Directed by Richard Benjamin. Screenplay by Norman Steinberg and Dennis Palumbo. Produced by Michael Gruskoff. *With Peter O'Toole, Mark Linn-Baker, Joseph Bologna, Jessica Harper, Lainie Kazan, and Lou Jacoby.*

Old-fashioned show-biz know-how returns intact, thanks to actor-turned-director Richard Benjamin. *My Favorite Year* is what they call a "sleeper" in the business—a little picture that creeps in on stealthy fingers, without the usual blare of press agents' trumpets, and finds its way into the hearts and funnybones of audiences starved for laughs without the usual insulting brain damage that goes along with them.

Maybe I love this endearing comedy about the "golden age" of "live" TV more than it deserves to be loved, but I find the nostalgia-drenched ambience of the Stork Club, Radio City, and the maze of corridors, rehearsal halls, studios, and control rooms backstage at NBC's 30 Rockefeller Center headquarters—all wonderfully re-created, just as they looked in the foolish '50s—completely irresistible.

The story covers a week in the life of a bright, impressionable Jewish boy from Brooklyn, Benjamin Stone, who works as a junior writer on a weekly variety show called *Comedy Cavalcade*. Benjy is Mel Brooks at twenty-two, the show is *Your Show of Shows*, and the star (an egomaniac played with unbridled hysteria by Joe Bologna) is a takeoff on Sid Caesar.

The action revolves around the week Benjy is assigned to watch over the show's guest star, a flamboyant, swashbuckling matinee idol named Alan Swann, who is Errol Flynn cross-pollinated with John Barrymore. Peter O'Toole is wildly wonderful as the living legend so pickled in scotch he has to be carried in and out of his Waldorf suite tied to a luggage carrier.

With an ego bigger than the Chrysler Building, he's a boozy comic vamp as he whisks through popping flashbulbs with his cashmere polo coat flapping about his shoulders one day, then the next wrecks the studio and the show fighting off gangsters while the cheering studio audience thinks it's all part of a live skit.

In between, there's time for a hilarious trip home to Brooklyn where Benjy introduces the star to his football-shouldered Jewish mother (Lainie Kazan, looking more like Fanny Brice every day). Mama has a new husband, an Oriental bantamweight has-been named Rookie Carocca, and there is even a mad aunt who shows up for dinner in her wedding dress.

Throughout this craziness, actor-turned-director Richard

Benjamin builds an achingly comic rhythm while letting us all in on what it was like to be part of a hit show in the days when television really meant something.

Best of all, O'Toole and newcomer Mark Linn-Baker, as Benjy, fuse their roles with a special radiance that really gives us the feeling of what it's like to be a star on the way down and a kid on the way up.

My Favorite Year has energy, style, and joy, proving that the knack for comedy in the grand Hollywood tradition is not dead. We've just been trusting the wrong people to keep it alive. Welcome, Mr. Benjamin.

MY LEFT FOOT (1989)

★ ★ ★ ★ Directed by Jim Sheridan. Screenplay by Sheridan and Shane Connaughton. Produced by Noel Pearson. *With Daniel Day-Lewis, Ray McNally, Brenda Fricker, Fiona Shaw, Cyril Cusack, Hugh O'Connor, Adrian Dunbar, Ruth McCabe, and Alison Whelan.*

From disease and despair, true greatness is sometimes born. This is the human and inspiring message in *My Left Foot* a film of such joy and resonance I doubt if it will leave anyone who sees it untouched. It's the amazing true story of Irish painter-poet-novelist Christy Brown, born in 1932 to a poor Dublin bricklayer, one of twenty-two children of whom thirteen survived. Life was hard, but for Christy it was intolerable. Born with cerebral palsy, disfigured and paralyzed, he was dismissed as a tragic half-wit, able to communicate only with his left foot, the sole part of his body his damaged brain could control. But Christy had one thing few healthy children can boast about—a wonderful mother who was a pillar of strength and support. Through his mother's unflagging belief in his intelligence, Christy learned to use that foot to hold a paintbrush, type his memoirs, and even flirt with girls, eventually marrying and becoming an international celebrity.

Considering the verbal and physical limitations of his role, it's miraculous how much passion Daniel Day-Lewis gets out of it. Without once playing for sympathy, he re-creates Christy Brown's affliction and his zest for life—and he does it with so little fuss that the character—cussed, exasperating, egotistical, aggressive, temperamental, and childlike—comes across with real power and fire. In England, he's considered the princely young actor most likely to inherit Sir Laurence

Olivier's crown. With *My Left Foot* you'll see why. You'll also understand why this titanic performance won him the 1989 Best Actor Oscar. Brenda Fricker, his fellow Oscar winner for Supporting Actress, is wonderful, too, as his long-suffering mother. This is not a sentimental Disease of the Month movie. It's a work of art.

MYSTIC PIZZA (1988)

★ ★ ★ Directed by Donald Petrie. Screenplay by Amy Jones, Perry Howze, Randy Howze, and Alfred Uhry. Produced by Mark Levinson and Scott Rosenfelt. With Annabeth Gish, Julia Roberts, Lili Taylor, Vincent Philip D'Onofrio, William R. Moses, and Adam Storke.

Encouraging proof that small budgets and unknown actors can sometimes produce big hits through word of mouth, this is a warm and inviting look into the lives of three appealing young women who work as waitresses in a pizza parlor in Mystic, Connecticut. Too old for dolls and too young for marriage, they're all on the threshold of leaving behind their teenage girlhood and on the verge of responsibility, commitment, and leaving home. Julia Roberts is the gorgeous, sexy one—on the verge of becoming the town tramp until she meets a rich preppie. Annabeth Gish is her brainy sister—on her way to Yale until she falls for a married architect. But it is really pint-sized Lili Taylor who will steal your heart. Funny, exuberant *Mystic Pizza* is thin as a pizza crust, but so fresh and tasty you can't resist it.

NADINE (1987)

★ ★ ★ Directed and written by Robert Benton. Produced by Arlene Donovan. With Jeff Bridges, Kim Basinger, Rip Torn, Gwen Verdon, and Jerry Stiller.

Tired of sophomoric farces that slap your face instead of your funnybone? *Nadine* is the girl to visit and the movie to see. It was written and directed by Robert Benton, the talented man who brought us *Kramer vs. Kramer* and *Places in the Heart*. His forte is people—especially Texans—the kind you know or wouldn't mind getting to know better. And in *Nadine* he creates two more. Kim Basinger and Jeff Bridges are Nadine and Vernon Hightower, two likable bumpkins who are a bit like a chicken-fried Blondie and Dagwood. They're nice folks, but there's not much going on in their upstairs window. Nadine's a manicurist who majored in beautiful. She's also pregnant by the good-for-nothing Vernon, her soon-to-be ex-husband, whom she enlists to help her retrieve some nude photos she posed for in Austin. The guy with the photos has been murdered and what Nadine and Vernon get in the wrong envelope are the blueprints for the new Texas State Highway. Now the Hightowers are up to their necks in cops and killers, dodging everything from guns to rattlesnakes.

Nadine is a funny, touching portrait of people who do their courting at the Dairy Queen and live in trailers. They're not sophisticated, but they're spunky and resourceful and they know how to survive. It's not so much what it's about, but the quality and texture of Benton's writing and the actors' honesty that gives *Nadine* its charm. Bridges plays a shiftless loser with a big goofy grin. As for Kim Basinger, just picture the quintessential Texas prom queen going to seed. Wearing her high school football jacket, with a Coke in one hand and a shotgun in the other, she's the prettiest cowgirl since Calamity Jane—a brainy Marilyn Monroe.

NAPOLEON (1927; reissue, 1981)

★ ★ ★ ★ Directed, produced, and written by Abel Gance. Musical score by Carmine Coppola. Produced by W. Wengoroff and Hugo Stinnes. *With Albert Dieudonné, Gina Manes, Antonin Artaud, and Abel Gance.*

Napoleon, the four-hour silent-film classic by the ninety-one-year-old French innovator Abel Gance, rescued and restored by British historian Kevin Brownlow, so revolutionized the cinema that watching it now is like a crash course in film technique. Lighting, movement, the use of crowds, the poetry that emerged from the camera, and the flow of plot and action and theme are so fluent and so imaginative that you can see where almost every great director got his ideas in the decades since *Napoleon* was made.

Beginning with Napoleon's childhood wars, using snowballs as weapons, moving into his first military successes at Toulon, advancing into the dark and steamy terrors of the French Revolution and ending in the massive Battle of Italy, the film chronicles the life of this heroic madman with a poetry that is as mystifying as it is beautiful. Gance's Napoleon is a heady mixture of revolutionary fire and giddy goofball (especially in the presence of Josephine de Beauharnais, who conquered him while he conquered Europe) and the scope of his life and times is so poetic it seems to have been filmed in poetic structure, like stanzas.

The film is so vast in its scope, so brilliant in its conception, and so overwhelming in its visual magnitude that you are not likely to miss the sound at all. Only in the conference table scenes where war strategy is being planned and in the Revolutionary Congress scenes where the manifestos of such legends as Robespierre, Saint-Just, Danton, and Marat are being debated with fury, did I miss the kind of dialogue that, in contemporary films, would explain the climate of the times. Most of the time you know everything you need to know from the way the cameras move. My favorite scene, in which the pitching of Napoleon's boat at sea is juxtaposed with the rhythmic obsession of revolutionary fever in Paris, is so exciting that the camera literally does all the talking.

The final three-camera triptych that opens up the Battle of Italy while simultaneously superimposing images of the French flag, the face of Napoleon, and his symbolic childhood eagle is a good example of film technique ahead of its time. At four hours, it is still too long and there are numerous indications that the film could be shortened to an equally effective length, but the purpose of this version is to show as much footage the way Gance shot it as one could edit together from existing archives.

I'm not sure I'd want to see it again, but I'm forever grateful for the opportunity to see it once. It is a cinematic experience that makes just about everything else look like children's recess activities by comparison, and its reissue was an event that can truthfully be called historic.

NARROW MARGIN (1990)

★ ★ ★ Directed and written by Peter Hyams. Produced by Jonathan A. Zimbert. With Anne Archer, Gene Hackman, M. Emmet Walsh, and James B. Sikking.

Narrow Margin is a wonderfully old-fashioned movie for fans who love the fast-moving train thrillers of the Forties. Anne Archer, a nice girl on an innocent blind date, witnesses a murder and flees the country. Gene Hackman, terrific as always, has to find her and bring her back from the Canadian wilderness to testify against the mob. For the next twenty hours, on a train speeding through the Canadian Rockies, hired assassins, red herrings, and corpses fill the club car, the sleeping compartments and even the depots along the way. Danger waits at every whistle stop while the audience is breathless. They can't get off the train. They can't phone for help. Nobody is what he (or she) appears to be. Now *this* is a real movie.

NATIONAL VELVET (1944)

★ ★ ★ ★ Directed by Clarence Brown. Produced by Pandro S. Berman. Screenplay by Theodore Reeves and Helen Deutsch, based on Enid Bagnold's novel. *With Elizabeth Taylor, Mickey Rooney, Anne Revere, Donald Crisp, Angela Lansbury, Reginald Owen, Arthur Treacher, and Terry Kilburn.*

The best girl-meets-horse movie ever made. For kids of any age with big hearts this has got to be the most touching and affectionate story of youngsters and animals since *Lassie Come Home*. Elizabeth Taylor became a star as the butcher's daughter who falls in love with a gelding and, with the aid of a vagabond orphan (Mickey Rooney), trains the horse to run in the Grand National Steeplechase. MGM pulled out all the stops, bathing the vivid story in breathtaking color and lush scenery, and the supporting cast is sublime. Anne Revere won an Oscar as the heartfelt mother, Donald Crisp is the father, Angela Lansbury is the pouty older

sister. And the section of the film showing the racecourse and the big meet at Ainstree is spectacular. Genial, refreshing, a movie that lives forever in the hearts of all who see it.

THE NATURAL (1984)

★ ★ ★ Directed by Barry Levinson. Screenplay by Roger Towne and Phil Dusenberry (based on the novel by Bernard Malamud). Produced by Mark Johnson. *With Robert Redford, Kim Basinger, Glenn Close, Robert Duvall, Wilford Brimley, Richard Farnsworth, Robert Prosky, and Barbara Hershey.*

It's the last game of the season between the Pittsburgh Pirates and a mythical team of losers and screw-ups called the New York Knights. This is the game that will determine the outcome of the World Series, but time is running out. For eight innings the Knights are scoreless. The bases are loaded. Two strikes and a foul ball. It's all up to Robert Redford.

This should give you some idea how corny *The Natural* is, but no idea at all of what a satisfying entertainment it turns out to be despite itself. There's a lyric in the song "Sunnyside Up" that goes something like this: "If you have nine sons in a row, baseball teams make money you know." Baseball movies do not make money as a rule, but if even one of the sons turns out to be Robert Redford, you've got it made in the shade.

The Natural is a macho fairy tale, based on an allegorical book by Bernard Malamud, written and directed by Barry (*Diner*) Levinson, and starring the all-American movie idol in his return to the screen after a four-year hiatus. It's a great tribute to Redford's overwhelming talent and charisma that *The Natural* succeeds, because the movie itself is often sentimental, pretentious and bulging at the seams with every cornball baseball-movie cliché ever invented.

The divinely inspired heroics (yes, Virginia, there are even angels in the outfield) would make Gary Cooper blush.

Redford plays Roy Hobbs, a pitcher whose only wish is to "break every record in the book." When we first meet him, he's twenty years old and a scout for the Chicago Cubs is taking him to Chicago for a chance at the majors. Redford looks like he did in *The Sting*— wool caps, argyle sweaters, suspenders, and an air of cocky, eternal optimism. He's so idealistic he even carries his own crude, homemade baseball bat, a lucky treasure he whittled from the oak tree that killed his father in a lightning storm. With his penknife, he has carved "Wonder Boy" and a bolt of lightning into the handle.

On the train, Hobbs meets a mysterious *femme fatale* (Barbara Hershey), who disappears in the dining car. Is she a messenger from the devil? Or is she just a rich psycho who lusts after baseball players? The movie never bothers to explain, but minutes later she invites him to her hotel room in Chicago, pumps him full of bullets, then plunges to her death.

There are weird and laughable references to *Camelot* throughout, so we think we're watching the death of Sir Lancelot, but this is a Robert Redford movie, so you ain't seen nothin' yet.

Cut to sixteen years later. Hobbs, now thirty-five, emerges from the dugout dressed like Indiana Jones in *Raiders of the Lost Ark* and announces himself as "the new right fielder" for the New York Knights. Is he an angel, back from heaven on a miracle mission? Where has he been for sixteen years? The movie never bothers to explain.

No matter. From his first chance at bat, it's home runs all the way. The cover of *LIFE*.

The idol of millions of American kids. The new Babe Ruth. The fans go wild and so will you.

But wait. There are problems too complex for *As the World Turns* to tackle. An evil judge, the majority stockholder of the Knights, wants the team to lose. Hobbs is subjected to blackmail, larceny, and the lurid lure of a sexy blonde named Memo Paris, who may or may not be poisoning him in the preplayoff cocktail parties.

Suddenly Hobbs has a fatal illness. A mysterious woman in white (Guinevere?) who hangs out in ice-cream parlors sipping lemonade appears from his past and rises majestically in the stands to give him luck. Will America's hero throw the game and lose the pennant? Will the crooks take over the team? Will he drop dead on the diamond? Only a cad would reveal the outcome, but I was rooting for Redford all the way.

As good as he is, the star does not perform solo. He is supported by an illustrious cast of unimpeachable pros who give the film a dignity and coherence that is not always provided by the script.

Robert Duvall brings toughness and humor to the role of a pushy, cigar-smoking sports columnist named Max Mercy who is hell-bent on scooping the true story behind the mystery man of baseball. Wilford Brimley is a wonderfully crotchety team manager, and Richard Farnsworth, as the kindly coach who believes in Redford before anyone else, is solid as a cypress.

The women are equally memorable. Glenn Close manages to find something three-dimensional in the role of Iris, the good-luck saint from Redford's past. But it is really Kim Basinger who steals the movie as Memo Paris, the bad-luck blonde who nearly ruins him. In sleek gowns and a peroxide page boy, she combines the sultry goofiness of Marilyn Monroe with the corn-fed sweetness of Carroll Baker.

What reservations I have about *The Natural* concern the movie, not the actors. It's a simple story, shamelessly old-fashioned, that deserves a simple telling. Director Levinson imposes an arty style on this light material that robs the film of a lot of fun. Every "Play ball!" fills the stadium with portentous urgency. Every pitcher's ball hits every catcher's mitt in slow motion to the blare of trumpets.

I liked *The Natural* despite its flaws, but c'mon, fellas. It's just another baseball movie, not *King Lear!*

NEVER SAY NEVER AGAIN (1983)

★ ★ ★ Directed by Irvin Kershner. Screenplay by Lorenzo Semple Jr. Produced by Jack Schwartzman. *With Sean Connery, Klaus-Maria Brandauer, Max Von Sydow, Barbara Carrera, Kim Basinger, and Bernie Casey.*

James Bond is back. I mean the *real* James Bond. We're talking Sean Connery, not some pretty boy in an After Six.

As far as I'm concerned, 007 has been on vacation ever since Connery threw in the towel after the six original and best Bond pictures wore him out. He went on to other, more high-minded enterprises, leaving 007 and his "license to kill" soaking in a bottle of Moet. As likable and debonair as Roger Moore was there was always something missing.

Bringing Sean Connery back in 1983 was just what the doctor ordered—a Bond who's older, hairier, grittier and greater than ever. This James Bond even has tattoos! When he socks the bad guys, they stay socked.

Taking into consideration Connery's age and girth, Lorenzo Semple, Jr., tailored a script to his specifications. This time 007 is declared over the hill by his superiors and sent to a fat farm where he is subjected to a punishing regimen of diets, exercises, and herbal enemas.

In the process of getting overhauled, of course, he uncovers a dastardly scheme to destroy the world and before you can tip your hat to Miss Moneypenny or wait for the inevitable distress telegram from M, our man is back in business, while his old cohorts at Secret Service headquarters welcome him back, longing for some of the good old "gratuitous sex and violence." They get it, in the sky and under water, and jaded moviegoers will have a wonderful time tagging along for the ride.

Like all Bond flicks, *Never Say Never Again* has a wild plot that makes no sense, evil schemes hatched by imaginative villains, exotic Technicolor locales in which Bond is always interrupted while in bed with a voluptuous female, narrowly escaping death in the process, as well as the usual bumbling British bureaucrats and sexy, lethal centerfolds creating mayhem in as few clothes as possible. But this time, the old formula has new sparkle.

In the Bahamas, Connery battles hungry sharks. In Monte Carlo, he's nearly electrocuted by a deadly computer game. In

North Africa, he's almost turned into buzzard bait by white slave traders. Always, he is captured, tortured, seduced, and forced to sit down to a sumptuous dinner with his enemies. Always, he escapes. But this time, the evil plot to dominate the world picks up steam and the heinous villains seem more glamorous and mysterious than ever.

The archfiend is played by Klaus-Maria Brandauer, the marvelous Austrian actor who starred in *Mephisto*. No weirdo from central casting, Brandauer brings freshness and irony to the role of Largo, a charming and spirited madman. Nicaraguan beauty Barbara Carrera is a gorgeous but deadly Venus flytrap as Fatima Blush, the villain's amoral sidekick, who drives her lovers recklessly to their deaths with live boa constrictors wrapped around her pretty neck.

Among the ingenious devices is a recorded voice that sends nuclear warheads to wipe out their targets with the impact of a hydrogen bomb and says, "Have a nice day!".

And it's nice to see Max Von Sydow back again, so far from Ingmar Bergman country, as Bond's brilliant cat-stroking enemy Ernst Blofield, whose specialties are "terrorism, extortion and revenge."

And it wouldn't be a bondable Bond without a new collection of gadgets—fountain pens that blow up buildings, laser beam watches, flying motorcycles, supersonic machine guns, poison darts, garrotes, and knives that do everything but phone the Pentagon. As for the distaff appeal, there is Kim Basinger in one of her earlier roles. The sex jokes are less smutty than usual, the sexpots more three-dimensional.

A lot of care has gone into the scripting, and the direction by Irvin (*The Empire Strikes Back*) Kershner is several cuts above the usual James Bond sleepwalking.

As for Sean Connery, he is the real thing because he seems to take Bond seriously instead of laughing him off as a comic strip buffoon. There can be no other James Bond for me. When it comes to 007, I'm still hoping he never says *Never Again* again.

A NEW LEAF (1971)

★ ★ ★ ½ Directed and written by Elaine May. Produced by Joe Manduke. With Elaine May, Walter Matthau, Jack Weston, George Rose, William Redfield, and James Coco.

As writer, director, and co-star of this witty, crisp, and sadly underrated comedy, Elaine May plays a frumpy botany teacher who looks like an unmade bed even though she happens to be the heiress to a gigantic fortune. Walter Matthau is a middle-aged playboy, suddenly and embarrassingly dead broke, who decides to marry her for her money. What she doesn't know is that he then plans to murder her for the inheritance. That's where the fun begins. Have you ever tried to murder Elaine May? She turns the tables by murdering the audience—with laughter. The scene in which she gets trapped in her wedding dress on her wedding night is a high point in screen comedy. If you want to giggle yourself silly, don't miss *A New Leaf*.

NEW YORK STORIES (1989)
★ ★ ★ Directed by Woody Allen/Francis Ford Coppola/Martin Scorsese. Screenplay by Woody Allen/Francis Ford Coppola and Sophia Coppola/Richard Price. Produced by Jack Rollins and Charles H. Joffe. *With Woody Allen, Rosanna Arquette, Mia Farrow, Giancarlo Giannini, Julie Kavner, Heather McComb, Nick Nolte, Don Novello, Patrick O'Neal, Mae Questel, and Talia Shire.*

They say there are a million stories in the naked city. This triple header only tries to tell three—a trio of short movies by three great directors for the price of one. I wish I could say you get three home runs, but two out of three's not bad. First up at bat is Martin Scorsese and it's Nick Nolte disguised as a neurotic painter struggling through the pretentious art scene in Soho. A big man with big passions—for his art, his independence, and his obsession for his nutty apprentice and roommate, Rosanna Arquette. He humiliates, compromises and sacrifices himself, and finally learns the New York "lesson"—if one girl exits through one door, another girl will always enter through the next.

Part Two, by Francis Ford Coppola, is a minor trifle about a precocious little rich girl growing up in the posh Sherry-Netherland Hotel. Patching up her parents' broken marriage, returning a diamond tiara to an Arab princess, dining at the Russian Tea Room, charging plane tickets to Paris for the Chanel show, and delivering Hershey's kisses to the homeless, she's like Eloise. Only Coppola displays no real knowledge or understanding of how actual New York kids behave, and the whole thing is so glossy and superficial it seems photographed through orange juice.

Last, there's Woody Allen, exploring his favorite New York theme—the neurotic guilt of a fifty-year-old with an Oedipus complex, still dominated and terrorized by his Jewish mother. Mama Sadie, played by the great Mae Questel, could drive you off the Brooklyn Bridge. When she disappears in a magic show, Woody's sex life gets better, but then she starts floating over the Empire State Building, embarrassing him from the sky, and the fairy tale gets silly. But this is New York—and New Yorkers will take anything in stride. Including Woody Allen movies.

NIJINSKY (1980)
★ ★ ★ Directed by Herbert Ross.
Screenplay by Hugh Wheeler.
Produced by Harry Saltzman and
Nora Kaye. With Alan Bates,
George de la Pena, Leslie Browne,
Ronald Pickup, Alan Badel, Colin
Blakely, Ronald Lacey, Carla
Fracci, Jeremy Irons, Janet
Suzman, and Sian Philips.

They said it couldn't be done, but *Nijinsky* finally made it to the screen. For thirty years, the life story of one of the world's greatest ballet dancer has baffled filmmakers. Ken Russell, Jerome Robbins, Tony

Richardson, and Franco Zefferelli are but four of the directors who gave up on it. Scripts were written by Edward Albee, Harold Pinter and British playwright Edward Bond. They were all discarded. Playing Nijinsky was the dream of every dancer from Nureyev to Baryshnikov. They all got too old for the part.

Nijinsky finally became a motion picture in 1980, thanks to Herbert Ross and his wife, ex-ballerina Nora Kaye, who proved with *The Turning Point* that ballet and drama do mix at the box office. I assure you that *Nijinsky* is a film of beauty, quality and excitement.

The film begins with a shot of the ravaged, yet youthful face of Nijinsky: eyes blazing like burning coals, arms pinned into a straitjacket on the cement floor of a madhouse. As the camera pulls away, we see that his legs are spread wide, like a doll whose limbs have been broken by a child and tossed in a toy box. This is a startling, yet perfect image to begin *Nijinsky* for the man was a broken harlequin onstage and off, and the opulent, disturbing tapestry Herbert Ross has embroidered from the remnants of his life shows how he got that way.

You are plunged into the exotic ballet world of 1912, where

Nijinsky was revolutionizing the dance at the Ballets Russes. You are part of the scandal when Nijinsky premiered *Afternoon of a Faun*, by masturbating onstage before all of Paris to the music of Debussy. You are hurled into his tempestuous love affair with Sergei Diaghilev, the powerful Russian impresario who dominated him and ruled his life.

You see painstakingly accurate re-creations of the original Fokine choreography for historic ballets like *Scheherezade*, *Petrouchka*, and *Le Spectre de la Rose*. You see the tortured life of Nijinsky unravel as he embarks on a course of fame and decadence. This is a ballet film in the best sense, but it is also the story of a love triangle built on the turbulent relationships of three people: the emotional, childlike genius Nijinsky; the paternal, selfish influence of his lover, Diaghilev; and the overprotective obsession of Romola de Pulsky, a Hungarian socialite who thought she could cure Nijinsky's homosexuality after they married.

An era of artistic experiment and energy that changed the dance world comes alive and forms the backdrop for a homosexual love story that seems amazingly contemporary today. Torn between the brutality of Diaghilev and the naive selfishness of his wife, Nijinsky found himself polarized by two controlling forces.

The diabolical Diaghilev terminated his contract with the Ballets Russes, ruthlessly threw him out of the dance world in a jealous rage, found a new protégé-lover, and left Nijinsky to meet his own fate, spending the last thirty-three years of his life in an insane asylum.

For such a complex story, you need great actors who can dance and great dancers who can act. Here, unfortunately, the film does not perform miracles; Alan Bates is so authoritative as the acerbic, aristocratic, arrogant Diaghilev that nobody else in the film matches his artistry, and a lot of people have wondered (rightfully so) why they didn't call it *Diaghilev* instead.

The twenty-two-year-old dancer George de la Pena works very hard as Nijinsky, acting and dancing with great determination, and although Baryshnikov would probably have provided more charisma, de la Pena certainly gives a more accurate impersonation. (The really perfect actor for the role, believe it or not, would have been Richard Thomas, who looks exactly like the young Nijinsky, but who would not have been able to do the dance sequences.) Leslie Browne, the American dancer who got an Oscar nomination for *The Turning Point* is too inexperienced to meet the complicated psychological demands of Romola, but she has a genuine honesty and emotional directness I found appealing.

There are other flaws: Hugh Wheeler's screenplay is too contemporary for comfort; the lush decor, fresh lilacs, candy violets, and carved ivory beds often upstage the dramatic conflict; the ballets are too short for enjoyment; and the whole thing is so pristine that I sometimes found myself wondering what a madman like Ken Russell might have done with the same material. I hate to say it, but a little perversion might have spiced it up a bit.

Still, these are minor grumbles, far outweighed by the significance of what the Rosses have done when everybody else said "Don't!" *Nijinsky* attempts to be something at a time when most movies don't even try. From sets to costumes to lighting to camera work, it utilizes every aspect of the filmmaker's art in a film that staggers the senses.

9 ½ WEEKS (1986)
★ ★ Directed by Adrian Lyne. Screenplay by Patricia Knop, Zalman King and Sarah Kernochan. Produced by Anthony Rufus Isaacs and Zalman King. *With Kim Basinger, Mickey Rourke, Margaret Whitton, David Margulies, Christine Baranski, and Karen Young.*

The movie *9 ½ Weeks* is a scummy S&M love story in which a nice girl willingly becomes the sexual slave of a real wacko who leads her, begging and squirming, into a life of degradation and madness. It's not supposed to be a comedy, but I haven't had so many laughs in years.

The weirdos in this movie must have been living in a time warp. Their idea of an instrument of sexual torture is a box of Birdseye frozen strawberries.

9 ½ Weeks is both the title and the amount of time it takes before the girl grabs her garter belt and what's left of her sanity and goes back to Bloomingdale's. The film seems to take 9 ½ months to sit through. You'll get the message in 9 ½ minutes.

Kim Basinger—luscious, sensual, but no ordinary tomato, a real woman instead of a nymphet—plays a smart, divorced career girl who works in a Soho gallery. Like a lot of on-the-move New York women, her biggest problem is she doesn't know any interesting men. In the New York art circuit, she's not likely to meet any.

One day in a flea market, she meets Mickey Rourke, with his now trademarked unshaved punk look. He takes her to a houseboat and plays "Strange Fruit" by Billie Holiday.

Cautious and apprehensive, she soon succumbs to his boyish grin and dates him again. Never mind the fact that he looks like a derelict or strands her on top of a Ferris wheel at Coney Island to scream her head off. Even when he blindfolds her with a silk scarf, she goes along with it.

But there's trouble brewing in this guy's id. In no time, he's driving her berserk with ice cubes in her navel and cough syrup on her stretch marks. There's a lot of puffing and writhing in this movie, but nothing much happens. Despite a lot of noisy publicity about the film's steamy eroticism, none of it is warranted. It's pretty tame stuff by porno standards.

It is also empty, pointless, and dumb, the kind of giggle flick that will only appeal to people who get turned on by honey on their kneecaps.

She becomes a victim of her own sexual masochism. He cooks her meals, feeds her, bathes her, dresses her, and allows her to see her friends from the outside only during the day. At night, she's his sexual prisoner, while the soundtrack plays "Slave to Love."

The whole movie looks like a string of music videos on MTV.

Meanwhile, director Adrian Lyne never bothers to explain any of it psychologically. He's too busy showing artsy-craftsy close ups of electric can openers.

Three scriptwriters—Patricia Knop, Zalman King, and Sarah Kernochan—have run out of sex manuals trying to think up new ways to have sex and new places to have it uncomfortably. He dresses up like Charlie Chaplin and takes her to Café des Artistes. They go at each other in sewers, alleys, even in the bedding department of a fashionable department store with the mortified sales clerk looking on.

By the time he forces her to watch him make love to a Puerto Rican prostitute and give herself to strangers in a Times Square porno peep show, you begin to wonder how she's managed to stay out of Bellevue so long.

9 1/2 Weeks is a morbid waste of Kim Basinger and Mickey Rourke. She wiggles her tongue and undulates. He never speaks above an inaudible whisper so that it is impossible to decipher ninety percent of his dialogue.

For two gifted people, it's a crime they keep getting trapped in rotten scripts. For two sexy people, it's even more bewildering that they do so much moaning and salivating without even taking their clothes off.

In the end, he's in tears, she looks like hell, and the audience is kicking itself for not sticking to a Bette Davis classic. None of this movie makes the slightest bit of sense. Just because a girl digs whips and chains and crawls through a gutter with defrosted strawberries in her navel doesn't mean she can't take time to have her hair done.

NINE TO FIVE (1980)
★ ★ Directed by Colin Higgins. Screenplay by Higgins and Patricia Resnick. Produced by Bruce Gilbert. *With Lily Tomlin, Jane Fonda, Dolly Parton, and Dabney Coleman.*

Everybody flocked to see *Nine to Five*, but aside from the delicious teaming of Jane Fonda, Lily Tomlin, and Dolly Parton—all pros, all lovable,

and all at sea in a comedy that whimpers when it should bark—there isn't much to knock your socks off here. I expected a biting satire on three secretaries who get even with their boss, but the film is less of a comedy about office politics than it is a demented farce of TV sitcom quality. There's a clever montage sequence in which the girls fantasize about how they'd kill off their lecherous boss, but the movie takes a serious detour into witless and outrageous buffoonery when Lily thinks she really has accidentally murdered him by pouring rat poison into his coffee and ends up in the hospital morgue, where she steals the wrong corpse.

In a movie that celebrates the various attributes of three such appealing ladies, the real irony is that Dabney Coleman gives the best performance as the horny, sexist, hypocritical, lying, egotistical, chauvinist bigot boss to end all bosses. He's a sexy, funny, likable, and very gifted performer who makes more out of the flimsy material than the script indicated. The girls do finally kidnap him and outwit him by using his own blackmail methods in the war of the sexes, turning the office from a pink-collar ghetto into a manicured battlefield, but it's a long time coming. Colin Higgins directed, gingerly.

1918 (1984)
★ ★ ★ Directed by Ken Harrison. Screenplay by Horton Foote. *With William Converse-Roberts, Hallie Foote, Matthew Broderick, Rochelle Oliver, Michael Higgins, Jeannie McCarthy, Bill McGhee, and Horton Foote, Jr.*

Horton Foote, the Oscar-winning writer of *To Kill a Mocking Bird* and *Tender Mercies*, has created poetry in motion with this wise, human film about life in a small Texas town during World War I. More like a Chekov play than a movie, it's not likely to attract the audience that lines up for *Rambo* or *Beverly Hills Cop*. But *1918* is Foote's *Places in the Heart*—a slow, literary film that embraces a time when people had values and dreams and life made sense, flowing at an even pace instead of a neurotic tempo. These are ordinary people living in a time of liberty bond rallies, church suppers, and two-bit picture shows starring Mary Pickford. Each character is diverse in his own self-absorbed concerns, yet united through a love of God and country and family. In their mundane but beautifully natural stories, the viewer gets a sense of life's continuity, what it was like in time of war on the American home front. Filled with sincerity, charm, and heartfelt compassion for the American fabric, *1918* is an exemplary film for demanding tastes . . . artistic, yet down-home as a buttermilk biscuit.

1941 (1979)
½★ Directed by Steven Spielberg. Screenplay by Robert Zemeckis and Bob Gale. Produced by John Milius. *With John Belushi, Dan Ackroyd, Tim Matheson, Ned Beatty, Lorraine Gary, Treat Williams, Robert Stack, and Toshiro Mifune.*

1941 is a stupid farce based on a stupid idea: What would have happened if, after bombing Pearl Harbor, the Japanese had gone on to attack Hollywood? It is the dumb premise of this idiotic picture that the Americans would have been so moronic that they would have done the enemy's job for them.

The Americans in this film knock each other out and destroy the California coast before the Japs ever get to Hollywood Boulevard. Since it never rises above the silliness of old Abbott and Costello, Three Stooges, and Martin & Lewis comedies—with an unhealthy dose of *It's A Mad, Mad, Mad, Mad World* thrown in for no good reason—the movie will only, at best, appeal to the *Animal House* audience. There's a lot of cruelty and violence in it that isn't the least bit funny.

I did enjoy the opening sequence, however. A nubile Lolita (the same one in *Jaws*, unless I'm mistaken) leaps from a car on a California beach in the quiet fog of December dawn, sheds her robe from the Polar Bear Club, and plunges naked into the freezing surf. As the John Williams music signals approaching danger in the watery horror, the girl is impaled on the phallic snout of a black monster and hoisted high above the waves, screaming her head off.

It's not a shark this time, but the periscope of a Japanese submarine commanded by Toshiro Mifune. The scene is short, but one of the few genuinely funny interludes in a movie that seems anchored in lead. Later, there's an exciting musical production number that involves a takeoff on both the Andrews Sisters and a Xavier Cugat–type bandleader, who keeps a white mouse on his shoulder instead of a Mexican chihuahua, in which a riot breaks out and the doughboys demolish a USO center in the middle of a jitterbug contest.

This kind of clever send-up of forties movies indicates real insight, and there's no doubt that Spielberg has seen *Hollywood Canteen* instead of just *Animal House*. Unfortunately, the movie slides quickly downhill from there, landing in a farrago of flying vegetables, broken plates, wooden situations, and imbecilic sight gags.

John Belushi is something that crawled out of a roach motel. Ned Beatty and Lorraine Gary, as a Dagwood and Blondie couple who get an anti-aircraft tank planted in their front yard, get lost in the confusion. Slim Pickens is nauseating in a scatological bit involving a swallowed compass from a Cracker Jack box and a lot of prune juice.

Robert Stack is a general who cries at *Dumbo*. Tim Matheson seems merely baffled as a pilot who crashes into the La Brea Tar Pits. Treat Williams is wasted as a bully. The cast is vast and unimportant. Mifune even says, "rotsa ruck." Actors will obviously do anything for Spielberg, even if it means sullying their reputations.

Farce is never effective unless it is played with deadly seriousness. Two hours of noise and custard pies are not enough. *1941* seems to have been made with the philosophy that if anyone stands still too long he gets his head shoved into a tank, a fist, a toilet, or a chocolate cake. The result is an overdose of high school humor that left this viewer with a massive migraine.

NORMA RAE (1979)

★ ★ ★ ★ Directed by Martin Ritt. Screenplay by Irving Ravetch and Harriet Frank, Jr. Produced by Tamara Asseyev. *With Sally Field, Ron Liebman, Beau Bridges, Pat Hingle, and Barbara Baxley.*

Sally Field must have tired of Flying Nun jokes even before the rest of us tired of making them, but after *Norma Rae* the references became as redundant as the old jibes at Richard Chamberlain for playing Dr. Kildare. When she turned in her habit, Sally Field learned how to act, polished her craft by dropping in occasionally to brighten up other people's bad movies, and in *Norma Rae* became a real star with a real vehicle that deserved and respected her abilities in a rewarding fashion. The lady arrived.

Norma Rae is thirty-one and the blackboard of her life looks messed up by a giant with a dirty eraser. Underpaid and overworked in the textile mill of a dreary southern town, she has accepted Christ since she was six and she's got two kids

and a dead husband, killed in a bar brawl, to show for it. She's got a mother going deaf from a lifetime in the factory, a father whose heart was worn out from being worked like a donkey, and a big afternoon is buying a white cotton brassiere at J. C. Penney and *Cosmopolitan* at a local drugstore, and if she's lucky, some sexual release with a traveling salesman in a local motel.

Norma Rae is going nowhere and this is the summer of her conversion to reality. The first Jew she's ever seen arrives from New York City to organize a union at the textile mill and Norma Rae sees her chance to contribute to her dilapidated society by bringing the blacks and whites and all the faiths together against overwhelming obstacles in a unifying love. This is the summer Norma Rae becomes a woman, and nothing else will ever be the same again.

Martin Ritt, the director, and Irving Ravetch and Harriet Frank, Jr., the writers, were the same folks responsible for *Hud*. They know the South, they've felt the oppression, they've catalogued the heat and boredom and the frustration before. The groundwork was laid for *Norma Rae* not only in *Hud* but in the team's other southern films,

The Long Hot Summer, The Sound and the Fury, and *Conrack*. There's something to be said about the maturity and vision of experience.

The result is a film of dignity and quality that should be an uplifting experience for all who see it, a valiant look at a certain kind of working-class woman that derives its strengths from closely observed details and emotions instead of the obvious movie clichés of action, sex, and violence. It grabs your heart through sensitivity to the human condition, not aggression.

The Alabama locations are perfect (you just can't find hound dogs in the middle of the road or peeling Dr. Pepper signs anywhere else, no matter how many Hollywood set designers you employ) and the pacing and laconic rhythm of the film are beautifully synthesized. But it's a film that depends largely on acting, and on Sally Field's triumphant performance in the title role.

From her downtrodden introduction to her final assertiveness, Oscar-winner Field demonstrates every nuance, every frailty, every exhaustion, and every hope of a poorly educated but deeply sensitive type of southern woman. From the slope of her shoulders to the proud lift of her chin, she has moved into the persona and spirit of Norma Rae. It's a memorable and touching portrayal of a different kind of southern woman—one who is vulnerable but vital and determined instead of neurotic and victimized.

Ron Liebman as the union organizer seems less mannered and quirky than usual, or perhaps it's just that his role is a refreshing counterpart to the lazy southern locals by whom he's surrounded. At any rate, he's a hardworking optimist who demonstrates the possibility of developing love, respect and genuine regard for a woman without ravaging her between the sheets, and that's a rare and admirable thing to see.

Barbara Baxley and Pat Hingle are wonderfully restrained, too, as Norma Rae's parents, and a special encomium must go to Beau Bridges, who in a quiet, unobtrusive and heroic way, takes the thankless role of Norma Rae's loyal and loving new husband and invests it with sweetness and strength.

Without hogging the show or making more of his role than necessary, Bridges ignites the screen even when he is silent. There is a scene in a local tavern, where he just listens to Norma Rae discuss the murder of her husband, that tells more about the unspoken feelings in his own heart than three pages of dialogue could reveal. Bridges delivers a solid, affecting portrayal of a "good old boy" that will destroy you, if you know or care anything about acting.

Throughout the film, I kept thinking about James Taylor's song "Working," about a woman who gives her youth and her life to a textile mill, with nothing to show for her toil but a bunch of hungry children to feed and an abyss of broken dreams. It would have been a much better musical illustration for *Norma Rae* than the drippy David Shire theme song they've incorporated into the opening and closing titles. This silly romantic ballad only weakens the strong and unsentimental film everyone has worked so hard to produce. Still, everything else is so letter-perfect that I'm willing to forgive one small transgression. Most of *Norma Rae* is pretty much something of a miracle.

NOTHING IN COMMON (1986)
★ ★ ★ Directed by Garry Marshall. Screenplay by Rick Podell. Produced by Alexandra Rose. *With Tom Hanks, Jackie Gleason, Eva Marie Saint, Hector Elizondo, Barry Corbin, Bess Armstrong, and Sela Ward.*

Nothing in Common is about father-son conflict, but with more comedy than tears. Tom Hanks, a gifted clown with excellent comic timing, plays a yuppie creative director in a Chicago advertising agency who makes his living selling products with immature gimmicks, now suddenly forced to take on adult responsibilities when his parents separate after thirty-five years together and his father (Jackie Gleason, in his last screen role), an insensitive philanderer, loses his job and falls seriously ill. A nice, rewarding mixture of funny jokes about television commercials and humane ideas about family relationships. Gleason is a gruff, sentimental Pooh Bear of a papa. In his swan song, he proved underneath that big windbag was a gentle breeze trying to get out. He'll be missed.

NO WAY OUT (1987)

★ ★ ★ Directed by Roger Donaldson. Screenplay by Robert Garland. Produced by Laura Ziskin and Robert Garland. *With Kevin Costner, Gene Hackman, Sean Young, Will Patton, and Howard Duff.*

Under oath, I would not be cad enough to reveal the surprise ending to this thriller in the Alfred Hitchcock mold, but I will tell you that it doesn't make much sense. That should not deter you, because you'll be mesmerized up to the final few minutes, and if you say "Duh—how's that again?" and rewind the finale, you will not be alone. The ending doesn't ruin the film. Slick camera work, fast-paced action, and wonderful acting more than make up for that final cop out. Kevin Costner is a handsome young naval officer assigned to the Secretary of Defense in Washington who becomes involved with a beautiful young prostitute. The tootsie turns out to be the mistress of the defense secretary (Gene Hackman), who murders her in a jealous rage. Now the poor hero finds himself in the middle of a whirlpool of intrigue. He is ordered to pin the murder on an unknown boyfriend who is really himself, and at the same time locate a Soviet spy long rumored to be on the Pentagon staff. There are more twists than you'll find on a roller coaster, but after the ride is over you may be scratching your head instead of rubbing your back.

THE NUN'S STORY (1959)

★ ★ ★ ★ Directed by Fred Zinnemann. Produced by Henry Blanke. Screenplay by Robert Anderson. *With Audrey Hepburn, Peter Finch, Dame Edith Evans, Mildred Dunnock, Peggy Ashcroft, Colleen Dewhurst, Beatrice Straight, and Dean Jagger.*

Audrey Hepburn, radiant as a fresh peony, won the New York Film Critics Award for Best Actress of 1959 in this distinguished, superbly acted, and brilliantly directed American masterpiece by the great Fred Zinnemann. From the stark rituals a postulant must pass before taking her final vows, to the harrowing and traumatic adventures the young nun encounters in the Belgian Congo, to the final spiritual tug-of-war between the vows of chastity, obedience, and silence and the demands of real life, you get every stage of a nun's life, touchingly and tastefully depicted. Luminous Audrey Hepburn gives one of the most fully realized performances of her illustrious career, and the impeccable supporting cast includes Dame Edith Evans, as the mother superior; Peter Finch, as the irreverent physician in the Congo who tests her faith; and such sterling actresses as Mildred Dunnock, Peggy Ashcroft, Colleen Dewhurst, and Beatrice Straight. Robert Anderson's fluid, articulate script and Zinnemann's refusal to insert any music in the astonishing final scene add great feeling and artistry to an immaculately constructed work of art.

NUTS (1987)

★ ★ ★ Directed by Martin Ritt. Screenplay by Tom Topor, Darryl Ponicsan, and Alvin Sargent. Produced by Barbra Streisand. With Barbra Streisand, Richard Dreyfuss, Maureen Stapleton, Karl Malden, Eli Wallach, and James Whitmore.

Nuts is a scalding courtroom drama with Barbra Streisand giving an electrifying performance in a real departure from her usual screen image. Barbra's a tough New York prostitute who murders one of her violent clients and gets locked up in a psycho ward. The result is not a trial—it's a competency hearing to determine whether she's sane enough to stand trial. Richard Dreyfuss, as the bewildered public defender appointed by the court to help her, matches the star in fireworks.

Nuts is a grim meal to swallow, raising some provocative questions: Can a prostitute be raped? Does a prostitute have any rights? The girl Barbra plays is not easy to like—she's arrogant, opinionated, hostile. But she's also human. You have to admire her refusal to play nuts just to placate everybody else. And as she stubbornly proves her innocence, we see through testimony and flashbacks how the pieces of the complex jigsaw puzzle form an emotional profile of a very complicated woman. It's a real tour de force for Streisand. Brilliantly acted by a cast that includes Maureen Stapleton, Karl Malden, Eli Wallach, and James Whitmore, beautifully photographed and tightly directed by the great Martin Ritt, *Nuts* is strictly for grown-ups.

OCTOPUSSY (1983)

★ ★ ★ Directed by John Glen. Screenplay by George MacDonald Fraser and Richard Maibaum. Produced by Albert R. Broccoli. With Roger Moore, Maud Adams, Louis Jourdan, Kristina Wayborn, Kabir Bedi, Steven Berkoff, Desmond Llewellyn, Vijay Amritraj, and Lois Maxwell.

It has been a long time since I could tell one James Bond movie from another. *Octopussy*, the thirteenth concoction in the batch, is no sillier than the others, and in some scenes, it is a great deal more amusing.

Roger Moore looked pretty long in the snout in *For Your Eyes Only*, the previous entry in the series. Miraculously, he looks younger than ever in this one. It can't be clean living. It probably has more to do with taking it easier than usual. In *Octopussy* the stunts provide punishing work for Moore's usual doubles and stand-ins, all of whom look much more obvious in the long shots than ever before.

No matter. This James Bond provides enough escapist nonsense to keep kids off the streets. Trying to piece together its ridiculous plot threads is as pointless as Christmas shopping on December 26. But when *Octopussy* threatens to get dull, it drags in new sets, new countries, new perils, new escapes, new gadgets, new guns and new girls.

Especially new girls. Octopussy herself is Maud Adams, who plays the queen of the jewel smugglers, a torrid tomato living on an island surrounded by man-eating crocodiles and populated by man-eating females.

Bond gets mixed up with this lethal beauty while investigating the murder of agent 009, who dies in Berlin in a clown costume, clutching a priceless Fabergé egg stolen from the Hermitage museum in Leningrad.

It takes the entire movie before the connection is explained, and even then you won't understand it, so let's skip the plot mechanics and get to the toys.

All that matters are the stunts, hardware, special effects, and gimmicks, and *Octopussy* doesn't skimp in any of these areas. The pre-title opening—which has nothing to do with anything else in the film—places 007 in Cuba, dodging nuclear rockets and destroying a missile base in a jet while the fuel tank is on empty.

The scene switches instantly to East Germany, to the Kremlin, to a Sotheby's auction in London, to the Taj Mahal in Agra, to the Indian hideout of exiled Afghan prince Louis Jourdan, who plots the end of the world in a heavily guarded monsoon palace, to the final showdown in a circus tent in Germany, where an atom bomb is set to explode and kill thousands of innocent people and force NATO to withdraw its nuclear weapons from Europe.

Did you get all that?

Not to worry. The fun is not watching 007 save the world, but the uncanny ways in which he manages to elude his enemies, his traps, and his would-be assassins. The wild situations and the bizarre characters are plentiful.

There's a hair-raising chase through the crowded Casbahs of India in three-wheel mopeds, and in one scene Bond encounters cobras, tigers, tarantulas, crocodiles, and blood-sucking leeches in the space of a few minutes. Scaling walls, swimming moats, and escaping knife throwers, blowtorches, and machine gun bullets, 007 is indestructible, as he flees in the usual obligatory assortment of helicopters, rocket ships, and water-skiing airplanes.

The directors of James Bond flicks are nothing more than traffic cops. In that capacity, John Glen was one of the best. The result is a harmless escapist picnic, diverting but inconsequential. When it's over, there are only the ants.

AN OFFICER AND A GENTLEMAN (1982)

★ ★ ★ ★ Directed by Taylor Hackford. Screenplay by Douglas Day Stewart. Produced by Martin Elfand. With Richard Gere, Debra Winger, David Keith, Louis Gossett, Jr., Robert Loggia, Lisa Blount, and Lisa Eilbacher.

Just when I thought everyone had forgotten how to make old-fashioned movies with beginnings, middles, and ends—movies that grip their audience from the first frame and hold their attention to the end, leaving everyone satisfied and deeply affected in some positive way—along came this shining gem to restore my faith in movies and the artists who make them. It is not a movie for children, but it is in many ways as tender, rare, and fulfilling as E.T., as fresh and honest as Diner and I can't praise anything more than that.

This is essentially the story of a punk who discovers his own value and self-respect through the military. But, thanks to a richly textured script that examines the lives of everyone around him, economical direction that takes mundane subject matter and gives it a unique feel, and especially a group of intelligently detailed performances that build even the most minor moments into throbbing portraits of character analysis, An Officer and a Gentleman stretches its theme across a wider canvas of human experience.

Richard Gere plays a street-tough Navy brat whose mother

committed suicide when he was thirteen, and whose alcoholic sailor father raised him above a whorehouse in the Philippines. Zack Mayo has been on his own most of his life, and he has the tattoos to prove it, along with the scars, both visible and internal. The only chance he has left is to make it through officers training school in Seattle. If he isn't ridiculed or beaten to death by the meanest drill sergeant you never want to meet (wonderful, lean, teeth-grinding performance by Louis Gossett, Jr., who won the Oscar), or distracted by the social-climbing, desperate local girls from the paper mill, Mayo (or Mayonnaise, as he comes to be known by the thirty-four other classmates being whipped into shape with him) just might become a jet pilot and find his own identity.

During the thirteen weeks of hell that follow, some of the officer candidates are weeded out through physical and mental breakdowns, but Mayo has the intelligence, the discipline, and the hard muscle to take whatever the Navy dishes out. Coming to grips with his own inner turmoil is a slower process, and one of the film's most endearing qualities is the way it develops character, stretches Mayo from a violent, smug, hostile loner

into a man who can love unselfishly and be a friend without compromise to his fellow recruits. The film gives an ugly, unsympathetic picture of Navy life from every angle. Mayo brings with him his survival techniques from the back alleys of the ports where he graduated from the school of hard knocks—cheating and bartering with his fellow trainees, trading polished brass buckles and boots for help on the aerodynamics quiz. He gets away with nothing. But there are times when the going is so rough that you really almost want him to cheat if it will make things easier. Kicked around by life, abused by the drill instructor, attacked by the locals who have an aversion to "flyboys," Mayo wants no attachments. Then he meets Paula (Debra Winger), who pretends she just wants to have a good time until he gets shipped off somewhere, knowing she runs the risk of being deserted just as her own mother was left behind pregnant years earlier by her own father.

There is nothing extraordinary about what happens to Mayo, Paula or their best friend, Sid (David Keith), or how they learn to face the future with optimism and courage despite all the terrible things they go through emotionally. However, the way every element comes together seamlessly makes *An Officer and a Gentleman* a gripping, suspenseful, and thoroughly moving film.

Richard Gere is perfect. His sidewalk smarts and his inner sensitivity blend in an explosive combination. After the rough deal she got in *Cannery Row* Debra Winger more than lives up to the potential she showed in *Urban Cowboy* in a full-bodied role that gives her a real person to play instead of a caricature. As the Polish factory worker who gets her romantic ideals from *Cosmopolitan* magazine, bravely meeting life's challenges in a head-on collision, she is heartbreaking, three-dimensional, seedily lyrical.

The best performance is by David Keith, who plays the Oklahoma hayseed with a built-in code of ethics with an intimacy and a charm that is infectious and ultimately haunting. He is the actor who was so wonderful as both the redneck bully in *The Great Santini* and the cocky, ill-fated prisoner in *Brubaker*. What a treat it is to see him in an even meatier assignment, stealing whole scenes from the demanding pros around him. The character he creates here has tragic dimensions that come from the actor's own charisma.

Taylor Hackford's superb direction gives everyone time to breathe and move at his own pace, and the script by Douglas Day Stewart has a real feeling for the way real people talk and hurt and survive. Considering the obstacle courses and physical endurance tests everyone goes through in *An Officer and a Gentleman* I'd say they were all underpaid. The result, however, pays off handsomely.

THE OLD MAID (1939)

★ ★ ★   Directed by Edmund Goulding. Screenplay by Casey Robinson, based on a novel by Edith Wharton. Produced by Hal B. Wallis and Henry Blanke. *With Bette Davis, Miriam Hopkins, George Brent, Louise Fazenda, Jane Bryan, Donald Crisp, and Jerome Cowan.*

In *The Old Maid*, a Civil War soap opera of epic dimensions, Bette Davis is a disgraced unwed mother who runs a nursery school for orphans and trades some of the most deliciously bitchy barbs of her career with lifelong rival Miriam Hopkins. Defiant or defeated, Bette always suffered for a good cause. This time she ages sixty years as a woman who allows her daughter to be raised by her vain, frivolous, self-centered cousin (played with waspish, brainless fury by Hopkins). The two stars' off-camera feuds were the talk of the Warner's back lot, but they manage to give solid performances on-screen and the film was a solid hit.

OLIVER! (1968)
★ ★ ★ Directed by Carol Reed. Screenplay by Vernon Harris. Produced by John Woolf. With Ron Moody, Oliver Reed, Shani Wallis, Mark Lester, Jack Wild, Harry Secombe, and Hugh Griffith.

I didn't much care for all the lumpy Dickens charm or the cotton candy Lionel Bart score when I first saw this musical (even though it won the Best Picture Oscar), but on second viewing, and by comparison with most of what I've suffered through in recent years, it's rather nice, homey family entertainment. John Box, who designed *Lawrence of Arabia* and *Doctor Zhivago*, has literally reconstructed nineteenth-century London in a dazzling array of architectural splendor, with such an eye for detail you can almost smell the cabbage leaves and horse dung under the carriage wheels. The workhouse where Oliver Twist and the other orphans are abused, the steaming docks and sweaty smoke-filled pubs, the whirling

vendors, the marching Queen's Guards, the shimmering green parks full of girls in bright pinafores, and the white birthday-cake splendor of Bloomsbury are really marvels of movie excess. Mark Lester, a dumpling with sky-blue eyes, is a photogenic Oliver; Shani Wallis is a show-stopping Nancy; Ron Moody is a scene-chewing Fagin, and Oliver Reed is just about the most evil villain you could conjure from a witch's cauldron. There is also a battered old curmudgeon of a dog named Bullseye, who steals the picture with the damnedest performance by anything with four legs since Flicka played a neurotic colt in love with Roddy McDowall.

ON GOLDEN POND (1981)
★ ★ ★ ★ Directed by Mark Rydell. Screenplay by Ernest Thompson. Produced by Bruce Gilbert. With Katharine Hepburn, Henry Fonda, Jane Fonda, Dabney Coleman, and Doug McKeon.

Katharine Hepburn at seventy-four years old; Henry Fonda at seventy-seven. Combine their ages and experience and you get what adds up to a century and a half of everything that is distinguished and first-class about American acting through the years. *On Golden Pond*, the first film they ever appeared in together, proves they still have a few surprises left. Kate the Great will probably be around to bury us all, but *On Golden Pond* was the final chapter in Fonda's illustrious career, and I can't think of a better way to sign off. His rich and all-encompassing portrayal of eighty-year-old Norman Thayer is the sum total of everything that has gone before. It is his finest work on-screen and I was thankful he lived long enough to get the Oscar he so deserved. (Hepburn also won.)

On Golden Pond is a warm, engaging, easygoing, sometimes funny, often deeply touching look at the mysteries and adventures of two people in the autumn of their years. For forty-eight summers, Norman and Ethel Thayer have retired to their lakeside cottage "on Golden Pond" to fish, relax, and look at life through rose-colored binoculars in slow, measured glances. This peaceful summer of Norman's eightieth birthday, the bucolic serenity of their country landscape is invaded by their daughter, Chelsea, her new dentist fiancé, and the man's tough, defensive, unhappy kid with all the baggage of heavy duty jargon and permissive psychology in tow. Leaving behind the unwanted, thirteen-year-old Billy

in the old folks' care, the lovers fly to Europe, and it's up to Norman and Ethel to teach the boy what real life is like on Golden Pond.

Like all great human dramas, this remarkably unclouded work explores with wisdom and subtlety a wide spectrum of intensely felt relationships—the conflict between father and daughter who have been estranged for years, between the confused young brat and the two old turkeys, and between the two old people, on the verge of their last days together and not wanting to see the green of summer end for fear it might be their last. None of these complex relationships—nor the ways in which they are comfortably resolved—are ever maudlin or sentimental, and there isn't a cliché in sight. Every time the movie almost reduces the audience to sobbing, there's a clever laugh to ease the tension and bring everyone back to reality. It's a marvelous triumph.

When I first saw Ernest Thompson's play on Broadway, I kept thinking what a tragedy of bad timing it was that Spencer Tracy was no longer around to make the inevitable movie version with Kate Hepburn. I kept seeing Tracy in the part of Norman, breathing life into each scene, like the one in which the old man is convinced he's living on borrowed time, ranting cantankerously as he reads the want ads aloud, muttering to himself, "I think I'll read a book—see if I can finish it before I'm finished. Maybe a novelette."

Henry Fonda fills his shoes brilliantly. Norman is a perfect role for him because it's about strength of mind when the apple won't bite. And Ethel is a perfect role for Hepburn because it's full of courage and spunk and indomitable human spirit. I'll wager there won't be a dry eye in the vicinity of your VCR when Fonda has a heart attack and Hepburn rages pathetically in her futile attempts to cradle him in her arms while trying vainly to rouse the sleepy country telephone operator.

These two majestic stars work vigorously but with restraint, starchy good sense, and riveting honesty. Just watching the two of them together, under Mark Rydell's generous, careful direction, is one of the most magical experiences the contemporary motion picture screen can offer.

The supporting players are all perfect, too. Jane Fonda, who raised the money to make the film as a tribute to her father, has a small role, but she fills it with luminous moments of her own as the troubled daughter, and when she fights to win her father's love, looking at these two generation-gap Fondas together is like peeking through somebody's keyhole. Dabney Coleman adds a spark of manly strength as the fiancé who will not be intimidated by the eccentric senior citizens, and youngster Doug McKeon displays a sensitivity and intelligence beyond his tender years as the surrogate grandson. All of them contribute to the feeling of small nuances and keenly-observed intimacies that make this an unusual film experience. By working homogeneously, they give the film depth, life, dimension.

There is balance, companionship, and mutual respect in every shadowy corner of this movie, and the result looks very much like love. Hepburn's voice comes and goes like static on a radio tuned to a distant station, and Fonda has never seemed more physically frail, yet they support each other in more ways than I thought possible—touching, watching each other, sharing the camera unselfishly, never hogging the spotlight, always knowing when to give the other one center stage. Finally, they teach us all something valuable about the joy of living and the dignity of growing old. The result is time well spent with people well observed.

THE OPPOSITE SEX (1956)

★ ★ ★   Directed by David Miller. Produced by Joe Pasternak. Screenplay by Fay and Michael Kanin. *With June Allyson, Dolores Gray, Joan Collins, Ann Miller, Joan Blondell, Agnes Moorehead, Ann Sheridan, Charlotte Greenwood, Leslie Nielsen, Sam Levene, Jeff Richards, Alice Pearce, Carolyn Jones, Dick Shawn, and Jim Backus.*

The Opposite Sex is the MGM musical remake of ·*The Women*, with songs, fashions, furs, and fire-engine red fingernails mauling every gal who crosses the screen. June Allyson is the wronged wife, Dolores Gray and Joan Collins are the bitches, Ann Miller is the tap-dancing fly in the beauty cream, with Joan Blondell, Agnes Moorehead, Ann Sheridan, and Charlotte Greenwood punching it out from ringside. For extra oomph, Miss Allyson re-creates her famous "Young Man with a Horn" number from 1944's *Two Girls and a Sailor*, with the entire Harry James band. A stellar cat fight from start to finish.

ORDINARY PEOPLE (1980)

★ ★ ★ ★   Directed by Robert Redford. Screenplay by Alvin Sargent. Produced by Ronald L. Schwary. *With Mary Tyler Moore, Donald Sutherland, Timothy Hutton, Judd Hirsch, Elizabeth McGovern, Dinah Manoff, and M. Emmet Walsh.*

Robert Redford makes an awesome directorial debut with *Ordinary People*, the adaptation of a best seller written by Minneapolis housewife Judith Guest, and winner of the Best Picture Oscar for 1980. I didn't read the book, so I don't know if the film is faithful, but it doesn't really matter because as a film, *Ordinary People* is astonishing enough to be embraced on its own terms. It's a rare bird among films because it's strong and sensitive and visual and filled with extraordinary human values that are foreign to most air-conditioned studio packages.

We should all hail Robert Redford for making it. If he wasn't Hollywood's golden boy, if he hadn't used his power and intelligence to make a meaningful film for his directorial debut instead of something easy with holdups and car chases and gimmicky camera work, if he hadn't bought the property with his own money, if he hadn't forced it down the throats of the dimwits who run the movie business, this marvelous film would probably have never been made. It is not the kind of personal movie Hollywood knows how to make, and God knows it is not the kind of movie Hollywood ever knows how to sell. Happily for Redford and all of us, it proved that good movies do have "legs."

Ordinary People owes more to *The Great Santini* than an open-door policy for quality filmmaking. It resembles *Santini* in theme and emotional content, too. The underlying force is family conflict and the meaning of various shades of concealed love as seen through the eyes of a disturbed teenager. I identified more readily with *Santini* because of its personal parallels to my own life, so I won't say *Ordinary People* is as good a movie. It didn't involve me emotionally in the same way. But it is one hell of a fine film and I can't imagine audiences going away without experiencing some kind of emotional catharsis. If you are among the legions who love *The Great Santini* you'll rejoice in your own discovery of *Ordinary People*.

This is the story of the Jarrett family, an upper-middle-class pillar of midwestern suburban society. The Jarretts have got it made: French toast for breakfast, designer sheets, a microwave kitchen, a garage full of cars, and soft sun filtering through shutters on autumn afternoons in rooms from the pages of *Better Homes and Gardens*. Calvin Jarrett (Donald Sutherland) is a good provider, a thoughtful husband, and an understanding father who commutes daily to his well-paying job as a tax attorney. Beth Jarrett (Mary Tyler Moore) is an enviable wife and mother, cool, calmly collected, chic, a fine figure on the golf course and in her own living room. Conrad (Tim Hutton) is a perfect teenage son—a straight-A high school student, the pride of the swimming team, a "nice" boy who doesn't take drugs or embarrass anybody. Then tragedy strikes.

An older brother is killed in a boating accident, Conrad assumes a hidden guilt and feels he can't take his brother's place in his parents' eyes, a schism grows between the parents and the boy attempts suicide. After four months in a mental hospital, he returns to discover a deep silence growing in his once-friendly home.

Redford holds his characters up to the light like X-rays in a research lab and one by one their inner roots are exposed down to the nerves. Beth's quirks reveal dark subliminal character traits we didn't see before. She prepares linen napkins in their holders the night before they're going to be used so they'll be ready for the next table setting. She centers vases in the middle of conversations. She fires maids because they don't dust right. Behind her coolness is an inability to communicate her real feelings. Calvin is torn between the needs of his son and the growing calcification of his wife until he can't talk to either of them. The boy turns first to a girl, who kills herself, then to his psychiatrist (Judd Hirsch), and learns finally, through the pain of self-discovery and therapy, a vital lesson: You can't expect more love than a parent has the capacity to give.

This is the toughest kind of film, because its issues are internal. It doesn't depend on action, controversy, or even big themes to reach the heart. Its concerns are small ones— which, of course, are actually big ones in matters of human survival. It's a film about feelings and people who don't know how to communicate them. Donald Sutherland works out his confusion and guilt by jogging. Mary Tyler Moore works hers out to a point by running away. And Oscar-winner Tim Hutton, in the most demanding and persuasive performance in the film, learns to face his own strengths and flaws by defining himself in his own eyes instead of on other people's terms.

The way Alvin Sargent's script and Redford's careful, gently modulated direction (both Oscar winners, too) unravel the clues that provide the keys to the locks that open the doors in this complicated, suffocating maze of relationships is like a great psychological mystery movie. The actors are brilliant, the design and pace of the scenes will fascinate you, and the result is three-dimensional. People function on all kinds of protective, safe levels for others to see, but strip away the veneer and you get beneath-the-surface truths that are harrowing. *Ordinary People* delves deeply and courageously for those truths, and enriches the fabric of human experience. You may be wiped out by it, but you won't forget it easily. Quite an achievement, really, for a director on his first date with a camera.

THE OSTERMAN WEEKEND (1983)

1/2★ Directed by Sam Peckinpah. Screenplay based on the novel by Robert Ludlum. Produced by Peter S. Davis and William N. Panger. *With Burt Lancaster, Rutger Hauer, John Hurt, Dennis Hopper, Craig T. Nelson, Chris Sarandon, Meg Foster, Helen Shaver and Cassie Yates.*

For a while, I thought we were rid of Sam Peckinpah, the king of sadistic gore and violence whose greatest claim to fame is showing blood spurting from eyes and mouths in slow motion.

His 1978 film *Convoy* was a fiasco that almost destroyed the career of Kris Kristofferson. After that, Peckinpah packed it in, left the movie business, and moved to Montana. I thought he had finally taken pity on people who had suffered through his two-fisted macho junk like *The Getaway* and *The Wild Bunch*.

Then came *The Osterman Weekend*, a junk movie from Peckinpah's frontline trenches. Like all Peckinpah movies, it is dedicated to the destruction of as many material things as possible—not to mention human lives, which seem secondary.

It begins with masked invaders jamming a giant hypodermic needle filled with poison through a naked girl's nose until it hits her brain. Peckinpah loves this ghoulish scene so much that he repeats it three times during the picture.

The last thing anybody cares about in a Peckinpah action epic is the plot, but this one is more ludicrous than usual.

Four friends who went to Berkeley are getting together for a reunion. Three of them are Russian spies. The fourth is a TV personality, played by Dutch actor Rutger Hauer as a cross between William F. Buckley and Dick Cavett. He'll do anything for a scoop.

Burt Lancaster, the slimy head of the CIA, agrees to be a guest on the TV show if this gullible innocent will betray his friends. All of which paves the way for a lot of gratuitous violence that is more laughable than repellent.

The first hour of *The Osterman Weekend* drones along setting up relationships that never make any sense, piling up motivations so scrambled they defy logic, and dispensing dialogue so undecipherable it borders on idiocy.

The second hour concentrates on the seemingly endless novel ways these various spies and double agents manage to kill each other.

By the end, they've managed

to dispatch men, women and children with gasoline, guns, swords, explosives, laser beams, even a bow and arrow. It all ends up on network television, where a mass execution gets a bigger rating than the last episode of *Dallas*.

John Hurt, as an anemic-looking CIA agent who controls everything on closed-circuit TV to seek revenge for the murder of his sexy wife, phones in his performance from a computer terminal.

Dennis Hopper, Craig T. Nelson, and Chris Sarandon are the KGB agents searching for a script in the chaos.

Meg Foster, Helen Shaver, and Cassie Yates are the women who look as glazed as campfire girls suddenly set upon by visiting peapods from Mars.

Burt Lancaster dashes off his sour-faced performance between martinis at the Polo Lounge. And Rutger Hauer seems bewildered and hopelessly miscast as he grapples unsuccessfully with both a zonked-out role and a wayward American accent.

Don't say I didn't warn you.

OUT COLD (1989)
★ ★ ★   Directed by Malcolm Mowbray. Screenplay by Leonard Glasser and George Malko. Produced by George C. Braunstein and Ron Hamaday. *With John Lithgow, Bruce McGill, Teri Garr, and Randy Quaid.*

A neat, clever, unpretentious, and delightfully offbeat black satire on American greed about two guys, one gal, and a frozen corpse. The guys are Dave and Ernie, played by John Lithgow and Bruce McGill. They're business partners in a butcher shop. Dave's the shy, wimpy, workaholic fool who does all the slave labor while Ernie's a wife-beating, two-timing big mouth who pilfers the profits from the cash register. The only thing they've got in common is Ernie's tacky wife Sunny, played by kooky Teri Garr—a bored floozie with an ice cube for a heart. Sunny bumps off the obnoxious Ernie for his insurance by locking him in the meat freezer and poor old Dave thinks it's his fault. A lot of hilarious energy in *Out Cold* is devoted to the disposal of the frozen Ernie. Then the endlessly conniving Sunny bumps off the seedy, submental private eye (Randy Quaid) on her trail, and Dave's got two corpses to get rid of! The biggest surprise is the way everyone in the end gets what he—and she—deserves even when it's not what you expect they'll get. Lithgow is great as the poor, dazed slob who thinks he's the greatest serial killer since the Boston Strangler, Teri Garr is a terrific combo of adorable birdbrain and calculating cookie, and even McGill's convincingly droll corpse seems to have a life of its own. A comedy very much in the Hitchcock vein, *Out Cold* turns death by Frigidaire into an absurd but delicious half-baked Alaska.

OUT OF AFRICA (1985)
★ ★ ½ Directed and produced by Sydney Pollack. Screenplay by Kurt Luedtke. With Meryl Streep, Robert Redford, and Klaus Maria Brandauer.

Meryl Streep and Robert Redford are giants in the big-screen movie-star sweepstakes. Sydney Pollack is a great director. Isak Dinesen's *Out of Africa* and other literary works are the bibles of book critics and readers alike. Africa speaks for itself. It is therefore curious that so many first-rate artists have combined their skills to come up with such a cold, passionless motion picture as *Out of Africa*.

It is big, beautiful to look at, impressive, and the kind of sweeping, aimless literary experience for which awards are given. (The Oscars this one got include Best Picture, Director, and Screenplay.) But it didn't involve me.

It's about a woman in love with a country, and that's a very difficult thing to film in the absence of dramatic human conflict. The result is a cross between *Masterpiece Theater* and the *National Geographic*. The lions and giraffes and herds of thundering buffalo are there. But where are the people?

Baroness Karen Blixen lived from 1913 to 1931 in Kenya, and then was forced through economic disaster to return to her native Denmark, where she was haunted the rest of her life by the images of the country she described as "a glimpse of the world through God's eye."

Her memoirs, written under her pen name, Isak Dinesen, form the material in *Out of Africa*, and director Pollack has been a faithful interpreter. The images are as luminous and evocative as the prose from the verdant valleys and dappled skies to the peaceful coexistence of man and game in a great country on the verge of destruction through progress.

Practically everybody connected with *Out of Africa* is British. They know how to light a scene. They know all about composition, movement, and cinematic form. The result is a film of extraordinary visual elegance in which every frame is suitable for eleven-by-fourteen framing.

But there comes a time when we grow restless of art-gallery exhibits and long for some real people to arrive. It's pretty, but I found myself looking at my watch more often than I cared to.

Meryl Streep is too damn aristocratic. She has the Danish accent down perfectly (would it be a Meryl Streep movie without a new accent?) and even manages to meld arrogance with humanity. But she never shows much vulnerability, even when her coffee farm reduces her to financial ruin. She never crumbles even when her rakish, good-for-nothing husband gives her syphilis and she's forced to return to Denmark for long and torturous arsenic treatments. She never cracks her porcelain exterior, even when she loses her dashing adventurer—aviator—big game safari hunter lover (Robert Redford). What's with this woman? Prick her veins and you get liquid mercury.

Isak Dinesen was a much more bizarre and fascinating character than the film implies. Meryl Streep marries a man she doesn't love in order to buy a title, moves to Africa with her books, antiques, and Limoges china, crosses the desert with only a compass, sleeps by a campfire beside the black na-tives, encounters rampaging lions and Masai warriors, and builds a reputation among the British colonials that is unconventional and controversial. But whether she is raising money to teach English to native children or watching a friend die of black-water fever, she is dispassionate, indifferent, reserved. And boring.

Klaus Maria Brandauer as her titled but irresponsible husband easily steals the film, while Robert Redford as the great white hunter who symbolizes the rugged, untamed Africa she loves only drops in from time to time to get his socks darned.

Although Redford gets top billing and piles of money, he has virtually nothing to do, and contributes only a minor presence while doing it. Rarely have I seen the golden boy of movies seem so detached or unfocused. This is a movie about feelings and ideas, not people, and Redford seems to be siding with the audience—trying to find out what the feelings and ideas are, and how to play them. He gives the impression of dropping in to visit the set and check the weather reports.

Out of Africa is too long, too slow, and too ponderous for its own welfare. It's a pleasure to see a film that is literate and tasteful, but it's a passive experience—a coffee-table movie you're happy to peruse before moving on to meatier things.

THE OUTSIDERS (1983)
★ ½ Directed by Francis Ford Coppola. Screenplay by Kathleen Rowell, based on the book by S. E. Hinton. With Matt Dillon, Rob Lowe, Diane Lane, and C. Thomas Howell.

A film director outlives his usefulness when he can no longer tell a simple story simply, in a style that is straightforward and coherent.

And so it is that Francis Ford Coppola has gone from Great White Hope to Small Change Disappointment through a series of bloated, pretentious calamities designed to appeal to nothing but his own mountainous ego. With The Outsiders he just about hit rock bottom.

The Outsiders is, like Tex, based on one of the adolescent novels by S. E. ("Susie") Hinton, who specializes in stories about youth and belonging and Oklahoma sunsets. Tex has universal appeal because it was transferred to film with an honest, no-nonsense sense of narrative style. It has a beginning, a middle, and an end. And it tells a story about kids with whom everyone can identify regardless of age or background, with an admirable absence of sentimentality and goo.

The Outsiders is a pretentious, disjointed tearjerker that takes a simple story (so basic it practically evaporates) and pumps it up to the size and status of Gone with the Wind while the kids read Gone with the Wind aloud to each other between tears and knifings.

Coppola must think this simple story of class barriers among teenagers in an Oklahoma high school is the equivalent of the Civil War, with West Side Story thrown in for portentous ideology. The poor story is practically choked to death in the ensuing noise and dust.

What's it all about, anyway? Well, it's about these sixties teenagers in Tulsa (no time is ever established, no location identified, but the book was published in 1967, and none of the kids resembles anyone you know today) trying to grow up before they all kill each other in gang rumbles.

The school is divided in half between the "greasers," a bunch of hoods with hearts of pure gold who torture girls at the drive-in, beat up little kids in vacant lots, and slash tires, and the "socs," made up of popular, affluent students with crew cuts, saddle oxfords and football jackets.

The "socs" drive Mustangs and date cheerleaders and make life pretty uncomfortable for the "greasers," although both gangs would probably convene for root-beer floats if Coppola and his dewy-eyed scriptwriter, Kathleen Rowell, would just leave them alone.

But before you can say *Rebel Without a Cause* the youngest greaser kills one of the clean-cut bullies in self-defense and runs away from home with his best friend, a sensitive greaser named Ponyboy.

Ponyboy has a brother named Sodapop, and he's the kind who sees beauty in clouds and sunsets, quotes Robert Frost, and reads *Gone With the Wind* aloud when he's not rescuing children from burning churches.

But society doesn't care. Lots of kids die before the end, and Coppola even steals a direct line from the Sal Mineo death scene in the aforementioned *Rebel* ("He's too young to die, he's only sixteen....") without a trace of shame.

The movie never stops proselytizing about how these kids are neither good nor bad, but a mixture of both, or romanticizing the theory that most kids have hearts as soft as peanut butter. Meanwhile, the kids kill and cry, kill and cry, while the sound track of syrupy, lugubrious strings (by First Father Carmine Coppola) saws away at fake emotions that are never present in the material. Stephen Burum's unbearably arty cinematography is busy blotting out the boys in mysterious gangster-movie shadows or cruelly exposing every zit in violent orange holocausts of blinding light like hospital X rays. Rarely have I seen so many elements conspire to demolish a good idea.

Everything works at cross-purposes with the story. The complex but easily identifiable emotional conflicts the boys experience—to causes, sexual explosion, a class bond—come across as arbitrary. A film that claims to be searching for love ends up only searching for both questions and answers.

Under these hellish circumstances, it's pretty amazing that Matt Dillon, Rob Lowe, Diane Lane, and C. Thomas Howell manage to turn in decent performances at all. They are often seduced and abandoned, and working on their own.

It is said that *The Outsiders* came to Coppola's attention through a school petition of seventh- and eighth-graders in Fresno who loved the book and considered it second in importance only to Clearasil. When they got a look at the giddy slush Coppola made of the movie, they probably returned to *Elsie Dinsmore*.

PACIFIC HEIGHTS (1990)

★ ★ ★ Directed by John Schlesinger. Screenplay by Daniel Pyne. Produced by Scott Rudin and William Sackheim. *With Matthew Modine, Melanie Griffith, Michael Keaton, Dorian Harewood, Carl Lumbley, Tippi Hedren, Mako, and Nobu McCarthy.*

Pacific Heights is another movie about yuppies in danger. This time, it's Matthew Modine and Melanie Griffith as a couple who purchase and restore a Victorian house in San Francisco, then rent the downstairs apartment to pay the bills. The new tenant is Michael Keaton, a psycho who never pays rent or security, refuses to leave, and turns his landlords' lives into a living hell. There are some genuinely scary and suspenseful sequences, thanks to the irony and polish of John Schlesinger's direction, but the real horror here is the insane laws protecting the rights of tenants, even when they are homicidal maniacs. This movie is the best reason I can think of for moving to the country.

THE PAJAMA GAME (1957)

★ ★ ★ Directed by George Abbott and Stanley Donen. Screenplay by Richard Bissell and Abbott. Produced by Abbott. *With Doris Day, John Raitt, Carol Haney, Eddie Foy, Jr., Barbara Nichols, and Reta Shaw.*

A delectable Doris Day stars as the prettiest, smartest female worker in a pajama factory whose feminist ideas turn management vs. labor topsy-turvy, in the first of two movie versions of Broadway smash hits by Richard Adler and Jerry Ross. (The second was *Damn Yankees*.) Skillfully transferred to the screen without many changes, *Pajama Game* has a rousing score, original cast members like Carol Haney (stopping the show again with "Steam Heat" and "Hernando's Hideaway") and a sexy Doris Day, who proved she could hold her own with the most seasoned Broadway pros. Best sequence: The once-a-year office picnic, featuring Bob Fosse's prancing, leaping choreography and some of the most athletic dancers this side of *Seven Brides for Seven Brothers*. Even the camera seems to do somersaults.

PARIS, TEXAS (1984)

★ ★ ★ Directed by Wim Wenders. Screenplay by Sam Shepard. Produced by Don Guest. *With Harry Dean Stanton, Nastassia Kinski, Hunter Carson, Dean Stockwell, Aurore Clement, and Bernhard Wicki.*

German director Wim Wenders has miraculously accomplished what most American directors never do—he has made an absorbing film about the landscape of the human soul that is haunting, beautifully shot, sensitively acted, and lyrically written by Sam Shepard. Harry Dean Stanton rises from the ranks of character actors to leading man with dignity and strength as the father trying to reunite his son with his whorish long-lost wife, played with amazing grace and naturalism by the usually nervous, kinky Nastassia Kinski. Dean Stockwell and Aurore Clement head a superior supporting cast. The film has a leisurely pace that takes getting used to, but give it a chance and you'll end up being greatly moved and uplifted.

A PASSAGE TO INDIA (1984)

★ ★ ★ ★ Directed by David Lean. Screenplay by Lean. Produced by John Brabourne and Richard Goodwin. *With Dame Peggy Ashcroft, Judy Davis, Victor Banerjee, Alec Guinness, James Fox, and Nigel Havers.*

For audiences and critics waiting for a movie to equal the greatness of *Gandhi* or *Chariots of Fire*, the suspense was over with the arrival of *A Passage to India*, an example of genuine movie greatness—the kind that endures for decades.

This is no real surprise, for *A Passage to India* was the first film in fourteen years by legendary David Lean, whose works of art include *Great Expectations*, *Lawrence of Arabia*, *The Bridge on the River Kwai*, and *Doctor Zhivago*.

This elder statesman worked slowly—from his first big job, the editing of *Pygmalion*, in 1938, until his death in 1991, he made fewer then twenty films—but he polished his products until they were perfect. *A Passage to India* is perfect.

Based on the novel by E. M. Forster, the film takes a deceptively simple story and transforms it into a priceless work of vision, beauty, and substance. It takes place in colonial India during the reign of the British Raj.

Mrs. Moore, a wise, courtly dowager, and her young, impressionable traveling companion, Miss Quested, book passage on an ocean liner to visit Mrs. Moore's son Ronny, a judge.

The younger woman plans to marry Ronny and stay on after the old lady's departure. But once they arrive in this strange, exotic land, odd things begin to happen.

Confronted immediately by the massive, squalid humanity that is India, they are appalled at the British superiority, power, Indian and snobbery. Warned by the high-minded Ronny not to socialize with Hindus and Muslims, they nevertheless accept the gracious invitation of a poor but generous local Indian, Dr. Aziz, to journey to the mysterious black caves of Marabar.

Chugging over the top of a waterfall by primitive train, then chugging up a mountainside on an elephant, the ladies get a feeling of India few tourists of their day ever experienced.

For Adela Quested, the trip has especially profound repercussions. Baffled, frightened, and intrigued, her repressed sexuality is awakened. With the echoes of the caves resounding in her ears, she runs and stumbles down a mountainside, away from Aziz.

In the confusion and crowds at the station, Dr. Aziz is arrested, charged with attempted rape, and imprisoned without bail.

Mrs. Moore and Richard Fielding, a British schoolteacher more sophisticated and humane than most of his countrymen, are the only two people who believe in Aziz's innocence because they judge only a man's character, not the color of his skin. They believe in justice.

The Indians believe in destiny—or karma. To them, the fate of Aziz is already sealed. At the noisy trial that ensues, only a miracle can save the poor, deluded Indian from British tyranny.

It is not so much the story that matters, but the way David Lean tells it. Like a masterly painter, he sees amazing truths in simple expressions, modest gestures, careful details. Then he shoots them leisurely, capturing moments and exchanged looks other directors miss completely.

"India frees you to discover things about yourself," says the old Brahmin philosopher Godbole (played mischievously by the great Alec Guinness), and while the exotic atmosphere does exactly that to all of the characters, Lean is doing the same thing to the audience. He doesn't spell out ideas in boldface. He allows you the luxury of making your own discoveries.

You get a breathtaking compilation of observations in this visual and sensual assault. The crooked bridge at Srinagar. The snow-capped Himalayas kissing the clouds. The houseboats of Kashmir. A crocodile turning over in the moonlit Ganges. The religious fertility ruins guarded by vicious baboons. And while the wildness of this mystifying country unfolds, the dark recesses of the human heart are bathed with light.

What a thrill it is to experience a film with old-fashioned respect for traditional storytelling values. *A Passage to India* is a tribute to artistry and self-discipline. Every scene is carefully composed, organized, and worked out in advance. Every shot is framed and edited with purpose. You get more out of one of David Lean's close-ups than you get in the whole two hours of *The Cotton Club*, yet he's always ready with the long shots, too, when they serve the material creatively.

And what a distinguished cast. Peggy Ashcroft, the Queen Mother of British actresses, is radiant and beautiful as Mrs. Moore. She gives the film its center of truth. Judy Davis, as the neurotic Miss Quested, gives her best performance since *My Brilliant Career*. Guinness, looking like a blue-lipped, spectacled walrus, is an amazing guru. Victor Banerjee, as Aziz, and James Fox, as Fielding, lend brilliant support.

But in the final analysis, *A Passage to India* is David Lean's masterpiece all the way. From Maurice Jarre's stirring, throbbing score to Ernest Day's stunning cinematography, every element has been chosen impeccably to contribute to the film's awesome madras fabric. Though nearly three hours in length, it is never boring for a moment and you will scarcely know the time has passed. This is a film that honors not only one of the greatest filmmakers, but revives my faith in the whole filmmaking process.

PATHS OF GLORY (1957)

★ ★ ★ ★ Directed by Stanley Kubrick. Produced by James B. Harris. Screenplay by Calder Willingham, Jim Thompson, and Kubrick, based on Humphrey Cobb's fact-based novel. *With Kirk Douglas, Adolphe Menjou, Ralph Meeker, George Macready,*

Wayne Morris, Richard Anderson, and Timothy Carey.

One of the most lacerating war pictures ever made, Stanley Kubrick's acclaimed 1957 study of injustice under fire tells the true story of a shameful World War I court-martial and execution. Three innocent French soldiers are brought up on charges of cowardice as a cover-up for a mad general's stupid mistakes. Kirk Douglas is an outraged colonel who tries vainly to intercede. The execution scene is a superbly vivid indictment of the abuse of military authority. One of the most controversial anti-war films ever. Unforgettable.

PEGGY SUE GOT MARRIED (1986)

★ ★ ★ ★ Directed by Francis Ford Coppola. Screenplay by Jerry Leichtling and Arlene Sarner. Produced by Paul Gurian. *With Kathleen Turner, Nicholas Cage, Barry Miller, Catherine Hicks, Joan Allen, Kevin J. O'Connor, Jim Carrey, Lisa Jane Persky, Wil Shriner, Barbara Harris, Don Murray, Sofia Coppola, Maureen O'Sullivan, Leon Ames, and John Carradine.*

Kathleen Turner is a good enough reason to see any movie. But *Peggy Sue Got Married* is doubly special. It's funny, wise, warm, adventur-

ous in spirit and tone, and it's Francis Ford Coppola's best film since *The Godfather*.

Peggy Sue is an all-American girl going haywire. She's a wife, a mother of two, and a businesswoman, facing a divorce and middle age with alarm. She's also facing her twenty-fifth high school reunion with dread. Urged on by her daughter, she dresses up "like a blast from the past" and reluctantly attends, groaning, "If I only knew then what I know now, I'd do it all differently—I wouldn't make the same mistakes." When the reunion committee crowns her queen of the prom, she's so mortified and overwrought that she passes out cold, and when Peggy Sue wakes up, it's 1960 and everyone is eighteen again. But what a difference! Peggy Sue knows about microwave ovens, women's lib, space travel, computers, and heart transplants, while her classmates are all twirling batons and mooning over Fabian!

The comic possibilities are limitless, and Coppola juices them for all they're worth. Seeing everything from a mature perspective, she tells her algebra teacher she won't be needing his course in the future and speaks from experience. When her father (Don Murray) buys an Edsel, only Peggy Sue knows it's a lemon. When her mother (Barbara Harris) asks her what she and her boyfriend Charlie fought about, Peggy Sue snaps, "House payments."

What a dilemma. She's a grown woman with a lifetime of experience and nobody believes her. "Get into microchips," she advises the school nerd, and he doesn't know what she's talking about. It's the best time of her life, but Peggy Sue knows how it all will change. Even a harmless date with Charlie (Nicholas Cage), the high school sweetheart she will later marry, takes a different slant when a girl's got twenty-five years of sexual experience and the boy doesn't know it. Things don't happen again the way they did when she was eighteen. This time they happen the way Peggy Sue wants them to. Using her knowledge of the future, she decides to change the events of her youth and alter history, confusing everyone in the process.

How Peggy Sue becomes dislodged in time and sent back home is like Judy Garland trying to get back to Kansas in *The Wizard of Oz*. It's one of the movie's most amazing secrets, and I won't divulge it here. The movie has magic and charm in

abundance, but what Coppola and his scriptwriters, Jerry Leichtling and Arlene Sarner, are saying is, "Be selective in life. Hold on to the things that matter—the experiences of lasting value." Peggy Sue learns the choices she made are not so bad after all. The message is deeply moving.

It starts out like *Back to the Future* and ends up like *Our Town*. Who wouldn't feel drawn to the idea of reliving the past? But through the range and emotional power of Kathleen Turner, it is immensely touching to see her visit her grandparents' farm again, watch Dick Clark's *American Bandstand* and feel the wallpaper in her old room once more. It's great to see classy veterans like Leon Ames and Maureen O'Sullivan as Peggy Sue's loving grandparents and even the younger actors seem regenerated by the material.

From the pastel birthday cake colors of Dean Tavoularis's production designs to the muted impressions of Jordan Cronenweth's camera work, Coppola has distilled the essence of a 1960s dream. As a person who often feels like he's living in the wrong period, I must admit the movie appealed to me enormously. 1960 was my high school period. What a thrill to see it again through fresh eyes. And I've also got a schoolboy crush on Kathleen Turner. Critics must be allowed their weaknesses, too.

To be honest, I'm not sure I can assess the impact of *Peggy Sue Got Married* rationally. At a time when I feel nothing about a lot of movies, that is gushing, but genuine, praise indeed.

PENNIES FROM HEAVEN (1981)

★ ★ ★ Directed by Herbert Ross. Screenplay by Dennis Potter. Produced by Herbert Ross and Nora Kaye. With Steve Martin, Bernadette Peters, Christopher Walken, Jessica Harper, and Vernel Bagneris.

Pennies from Heaven is about poverty, misery, hard luck, abortion, prostitution, rape, and murder. It's a musical.

If that sounds facetious, I apologize. *Pennies from Heaven* is actually a very unconventional musical, full of surprises, loaded with imagination and talent, and I liked it very much indeed. But although it contains gorgeously photographed production numbers as tuneful, exciting, and fun to experience as anything MGM turned out in its salad days, it would be misleading to imply that you're in for a frothy entertainment. That would be

nice, but *Pennies from Heaven* has a broken heart.

Herbert Ross and Nora Kaye, who knew more about how to construct musicals than just about any other two people working in films, made a courageous attempt to translate the silly musicals of the forties into the grim terminology of the cynical eighties, and with its black center, the result was as much of a commercial risk as their *Nijinsky* was.

Having nothing to do with the old Bing Crosby picture of the same title, *Pennies from Heaven* is based on the British TV series that was broadcast in the United States on PBS. The year is 1934, at the height of the Depression. Steve Martin plays a Chicago song plugger whose dream is to open a record store of his own. His mean-spirited wife won't give him a penny of her own money, the bank refuses his application for a loan, and for a while it looks like he'll have to settle for a meager living selling sheet music. All around him, spirits are low, people are desperate and poor, and the only escape from the bleak horrors of real life lies in the movies and popular songs of the period.

In truth, it was the sight of the chorus girls dancing on the wings of planes or forming kaleidoscopic montages in dopey Busby Berkeley numbers that kept people sane while they daydreamed of a silver lining. Herbert Ross has taken the actual recordings of the day and staged fabulous musical numbers around their optimistic beats. They act as bridges between the harsh realities of his characters' depressing lives. The result is unlike anything you've ever seen before.

When Steve Martin's bank loan is turned down, it's a sad blow, but in his mind the whole bank turns into a visual panacea of split screens and optical illusions as an army of chorus cuties tap dance across marble floors while coins rain down like pennies from heaven. When Bernadette Peters, a prim and innocent schoolteacher, enters the music store to buy some songs for a children's choir, their budding love affair is represented by silhouetted figures dancing romantically to Bing Crosby's "Did You Ever See a Dream Walking?" When she gets pregnant and fired in disgrace from her teaching job, her schoolroom turns magically into a Technicolor rhapsody of vanilla fudge as the children sing and dance in white tie and tails on top of school desks that have been transformed into miniature white grand pianos.

At their lowest ebb, the lovers scrape up enough money to see Fred Astaire and Ginger Rogers in *Follow the Fleet*. Suddenly they enter the screen while the picture is playing and dazzlingly re-create the original choreography for the famous "Let's Face the Music and Dance" sequence, filmed by genius cameraman Gordon Willis in glorious black and white. At the end, their canes form symbolic bars to show how life is closing in on them.

His job fails, she aborts the baby and drifts into a life of prostitution. He ends up getting convicted for raping and murdering a blind girl and is innocently sent to the gallows, while everything around them reeks of famine and death.

"There must be a place where the songs come true," he says hopefully, but the point is that life never quite ends the way the movies do. The butter and egg man never arrives, and director Ross forces us to the disturbing realization that life was not a bowl of cherries. In the end, Bernadette Peters has changed from a gullible, naive and prim little lady into a tough, raw-edged and thoroughly disillusioned whore. And still she says, "We've only got one life and we've made a mess of ours—it doesn't matter how it ends.''

But in pictures the ending does matter, and the magic of films was always that if the ending didn't work, you could order a rewrite. On a giant three-dimensional set that looks like an Edward Hopper painting brought to life, the finale paints a rosy hue as the lovers are reunited in that great big movie rainbow in the sky. The point, in retrospect, is no matter how lean and hard life is, there's still faith, hope and charity in 35-millimeter dreams.

Steve Martin worked for seven months to perfect the grueling dance routines staged by Danny Daniels, and the work pays off. He's as charming on his feet as Astaire, and as athletic as Gene Kelly. Another surprise is Christopher Walken, as a villainous Oil Can Harry who lures Bernadette Peters into a life of sordid sex with a spectacular striptease set in a speakeasy to Cole Porter's "Let's Misbehave." The magnificent sets by Ken Adam, the swinging musical arrangements by Billy May and Marvin Hamlisch, the razzle-dazzle costumes by Bob Mackie and the great original recordings by Crosby, Astaire, the Boswell Sisters, Helen Kane, Rudy Vallee, Guy Lombardo and others all add up to fireworks that haven't been seen since Arthur Freed cleaned out his office at MGM.

For all its taste and show-biz panache, *Pennies From Heaven* still has a tear in its Mondrian eye. Maybe the old musicals were phony as a three-dollar bill, and maybe they have gone the way of the nickel phone call, but they sent you out of the theater feeling rich as Rockefeller. Be forewarned. *Pennies From Heaven* leaves you with the feeling that the whole world is lining up for food stamps.

PHANTOM OF THE OPERA (1943)
★ ★ ★ Directed by Arthur Lubin. Screenplay by Eric Taylor and Samuel Hoffenstein. Produced by George Waggner. With Claude Rains, Nelson Eddy, and Susanna Foster.

Several film versions and a Broadway smash musical cannot diminish the popularity of this horror classic in its most definitive treatment. It's the 1943 Technicolor version, with the magnificent Claude Rains as the mad composer who lives in the sewers under the Paris Opera, and Nelson Eddy and Susanna Foster as the singers he haunts with demonic villainy. Opulent sets and costumes, lavish production numbers, and lush Technicolor add balance and dimension to the spine-tingling story of a lunatic terrorizing the music world of nineteenth-century France, and the marvelous concert sequences include excerpts from Tchaikovsky, Chopin and Liszt. A curious blending of monsters and music that has become something of a cult classic on the art-house circuit.

PICKUP ON SOUTH STREET (1953)

★ ★ ★ Directed and written by Samuel Fuller. Produced by Jules Schermer. *With Richard Widmark, Jean Peters, Thelma Ritter, Richard Kiley, and Murvyn Vye.*

One of the great gangster classics, this lurid Samuel Fuller gem stars Richard Widmark as a New York pickpocket who accidentally swipes the purse of a subway rider carrying priceless secrets on microfilm to Communist spies. Jean Peters, one of the screen's most alluring, talented, and underrated temptresses, is mesmerizing as the tramp who gets caught between opposing forces of crime. Thelma Ritter steals the picture as an aging stool pigeon whose violent and shocking demise is one of the most memorable scenes in film noir history.

PICNIC AT HANGING ROCK (1976)

★ ★ ★ Directed by Peter Weir. Screenplay by Cliff Green. Produced by James and Hal McElroy. *With Rachel Roberts, Dominic Guard, Helen Morse, Jacki Weaver, and Ann Lambert.*

Picnic at Hanging Rock, a beguiling mystery of mind over matter by the gifted Australian director Peter Weir, preceded his controversial and acclaimed *The Last Wave*, and in my opinion it is a far better film—remarkable work, chilling and hypnotic, and doubly disturbing because it is so delicately performed and sensitively directed, with camera work in the paintbrush style of *Elvira Madigan*.

On rare occasions, a film starts to roll and right away you know (the way you realize from hearing the first few notes of a concerto) that you're in for something new and wonderful and refreshingly different. That is the effect I got from this hypnotic excursion into another world, a reality far enough removed from our own to be pleasurable, yet one with which we feel an unsettling connection. It is St. Valentine's Day in Australia (February is summertime "Down Under"), the year is 1900, and a party of schoolgirls from an exclusive finishing school are giddily embarking on a picnic excursion to a strange, sloping, Neolithic monolith forty miles from Melbourne. Three students and one of the teachers disappear, with no trace. The subsequent search, interrogations of witnesses, amnesia of one of the girls who is later found, and the strange marks on the foreheads of the picnic survivors add eerie fascination to the story and its effect on the young ladies and their schoolmistress (brilliantly played by Rachel Roberts), resulting in a suicide and another disappearance.

An introductory caption informs us the story is true; any explanations for the mystery have receded into history and remain obscured by conjecture and superstition. It's a ghost story played in blazing sunshine and from the start it is clear that Peter Weir will provide no solution. Life is full of these unexplained mysteries (Judge Crater, Amelia Earhart, the JFK assassination) and what makes this one so special is that it allows viewers to fit their own pieces into the puzzle. A feeling of doom, of helplessness pervades the pristine sweetness of the girls in their gestures, in the deliberately laconic pace of their activity. What Peter Weir

conveys from first frame to last is the awful presence of the unknown. He denies us the comforting reassurance of speculation. There it is, he says— the inscrutable. Occasionally life's hidden power surfaces in the rosebud beauty of the girls in their white Victorian petticoats, in the sexual repression of the teachers, in the rock's connection to aboriginal magic. Still, we are denied easy answers. *Picnic at Hanging Rock* depends greatly on the imagination we can bring to it.

This presence of the unknown makes us share more palpably the tearing down of the lives of those who must face it. The school matriarch is hit the hardest. She is by no means a sympathetic character—unbudging pillar of vindictive principle, able to overcome anything in the normal, predictable course of events. Even the building she moves around in is one of classical symmetry and flawless order. Weeping for the loss of her best teacher, it's the mystery of what happened that is her final undoing, not the absence of the teacher. Weir has his finger on a human need, to have things explained tidily and filed away to be forgotten. What we get instead is apotheosis (the tragedy takes on the stature of mystical exaltation; Hanging Rock is still Australia's version of Stonehenge). The effect is cinematically stunning.

Picnic at Hanging Rock is a film about life in all its provocative lushness, with an intelligent ear to the rumble of the unknown forces beneath. What we know as life, Weir says, are only outward signs of those unknown forces that feed us energy, like volcanoes pushed up out of the sea.

That *Picnic at Hanging Rock* comes from Australia, a "new" frontier, one of evolutionary peculiarities and of practically no film heritage at all, seems most fitting. Peter Weir's movie is above all original—not a copy, not a descendant. We are blessedly spared those nagging reminders found in the works of so many "talented young directors"—reminders that this one loves Bergman, that one Hitchcock, another Capra, etc. Weir is as different and exciting as his homeland—a filmmaker who sees things with the feasting eyes a Peeping Tom must have, and a feeling of awe and wonder.

PINOCCHIO (1940; reissue, 1985)

★ ★ ★ ★ **Directed by Ben Sharpsteen and Hamilton Luske. Produced by Walt Disney.** *With voices of Dickie Jones, Cliff Edwards, Walter Catlett, and Evelyn Venable.*

Walt Disney's 1940 cartoon classic, three years in the making and never seen outside of theatrical engagements, hits the home video market with a hearty welcome. A pinnacle of movie animation, the story of the woodcarver's puppet who turns into a boy in search of a human conscience is peppered with memorable characters like the Blue Fairy, Jiminy Cricket, Figaro the Cat, and Monstro the Whale—all superbly drawn and brought to life by the finest craftsmen the Disney studios could hire. What child will not marvel at the fantastic marionette shop, the whale's belly, or the island where lemonade flows and popcorn grows on trees? Include the Oscar-winning song "When You Wish Upon a Star," throw in mouthwatering colors like cake frostings, and you've got the perfect package for anyone from six to sixty who is either young or young at heart.

PLACES IN THE HEART (1984)

★ ★ ★ ★ Directed and written by Robert Benton. Produced by Arlene Donovan. With Sally Field, Lindsay Crouse, Ed Harris, Amy Madigan, John Malkovich, Danny Glover, and Yankton Hatten.

Worldly achievement is only fleeting; true greatness can be found only in the deep recesses of the human heart. Translating this intangible spirit and love to the screen is an almost impossible task, but Robert Benton, one of the rare humanists among American film directors, achieves it brilliantly with *Places in the Heart*.

In the strong tradition of *The Grapes of Wrath* and *Days of Heaven*, Benton's lyrical and profoundly moving study of the Depression focuses on grass-roots people in the American heartland, this time the citizens of his—and his late grandmother's—hometown, Waxahachie, Texas.

Using the rich and compassionate feelings for people he displayed so knowledgeably in *Kramer vs. Kramer*, Benton observes these dirt-poor Texans keenly and wisely, without sticky sentimentality or self-serving nostalgic gimmickry.

There are period songs, period cars, and radios that play *Don McNeil and the Breakfast Club* to lend authenticity, but *Places in the Heart* is not a movie about nostalgia; it's a movie about love and strength and courage among the God-fearing country people who survived a shameful period of deprivation and hardship in American history with their pride intact, refusing to be victims while rising above life's hard knocks with heads held high in a celebration of the American spirit.

At the center of this patchwork quilt of thirties Americana is Sally Field, radiant and indomitable in her homespun gunnysack dresses with her stockings rolled down to her ankles, as Edna Spalding, wife of the local sheriff, mother of two children, widowed when her husband is accidentally killed in the line of duty by a Negro boy in his cups. The local rednecks lynch the poor creature, but that does not solve a thing.

Edna's problems are just beginning. Alone and terrified, with no skills to make a living and no means of support for her family; Edna doesn't even have enough money in the bank to pay the mortgage on her crumbling farmhouse. Arousing the skepticism and wrath of her neighbors, she turns to a homeless black sharecropper named

Moze (beautifully played with great dignity and humility by Danny Glover), who teaches her how to farm her acreage for cotton.

On the sidelines she is witness to the unhappy marriage of her sister Margaret (Lindsay Crouse), who ekes out a paltry income as a beautician, and brother-in-law Wayne (Ed Harris), who is having an affair with the local schoolteacher (Amy Madigan).

There are deaths, betrayals, visits from the Ku Klux Klan in the middle of the night, and even a Texas tornado that destroys most of the town, but *Places in the Heart* is not about things and events.

It's that rarefied movie experience that communicates feelings and emotions. Through true grit, determination, and dirt-hard work, Edna Spalding commits to life instead of defeat, and the audience miraculously shares the benefit of her strength. The movie makes you feel proud to be an American— this could be your grandmother or mine, no matter what your ethnic or demographic background. You leave uplifted and thrilled to be alive.

There are many beautiful and lyrical touches in the fabric of this fine film—from Nestor Almendros's gauzy, burnished camera work that rubs a patina of rural redolence on the canvas of country scenes, to Benton's extraordinary use of local extras from Waxahachie.

He moves people so smoothly and gracefully in front of the camera that the story fits them, instead of the other way around. Benton's screenplay gives everyone a chance to grow and develop naturally in small, revealing ways instead of big, noisy scenes or monologues. When Edna is forced to spank her son Frank for smoking in the schoolyard, we see how everyone in the house reacts without words. When the blind boarder comes out of his shell and pitches in by feeling his way through the kitchen to work the stove, we see how people reach out to each other for love in the strangest circumstances.

The actors are all so well-cast there isn't a hair out of place or a false note struck anywhere in the film, but no praise can be high enough for Sally Field. Accomplished as she is in the art of portraying spunky heroines, it would have been easy for her to fall back on her *Norma Rae* mannerisms. But this ever-searching, always surprising actress gives Edna astonishing dimensions. Her own grandmother came from Texas, so she knows the territory. But she wisely resists the obvious temptation to cloak a Depression feminist in contemporary terms. She is strong but vulnerable, tough in spirit but physically frail. A fountain of resources, she took home her second Oscar for this one.

In the end, the people who have occupied places in her heart are reunited in a country church during communion. The dead and the vanquished share a pew with the living survivors in a bold cinematic departure from the rest of the film's realism.

This is a startling climax to all that has gone before, and it might seem confusing to some viewers, but in this vision is Benton's message—that real love never ends, it transcends life's roughest kicks and punches and remains, undaunted, in those secret "places in the heart" where we store our values.

I did not leave *Places in the Heart* in tears because I never felt I had been manipulated in any phony way, but I did go away moved by a highly professional piece of work.

POCKETFUL OF MIRACLES (1961)

★ ★ ★ Directed and produced by Frank Capra. Screenplay by Hal Kanter and Harry Tugend. *With Bette Davis, Glenn Ford, Hope Lange, Thomas Mitchell, Peter Falk, Edward Everett Horton, Ann-Margret, Mickey Shaughnessy, David Brian, Sheldon Leonard, Barton MacLane, John Litel, Jerome Cowan, Fritz Feld, Jack Elam, and Ellen Corby.*

Hoods, tomatoes, and Damon Runyon land in Frank Capra's remake of his 1933 *Lady for a Day*, but it's Bette Davis's go-for-broke performance as Apple Annie, a bag lady with unforgettable class, that makes this comedy a pocketful of fun. Bette is Queen of the Broadway peddlers who has been supporting her daughter (Ann-Margret, in her film debut) in Europe while pretending to be a society matron named Mrs. E. Worthington Manville. When the girl comes home, engaged to a count, it's up to the molls, mobsters, and muscle men of New York nightlife to provide a penthouse, a husband, and a will for the old crone to carry off her charade while Dave the Dude (Glenn Ford) holds on to Annie's apples as his good-luck charms. The results are breezy and farfetched, but when Bette gets transformed from a Charles

Addams cartoon into the regal society duenna, you'll know why she was regarded as Queen of the Makeup Department.

POPEYE (1980)

★ ★ ½ Directed by Robert Altman. Screenplay by Jules Feiffer. Produced by Robert Evans. With Robin Williams, Shelley Duvall, Ray Walston, Paul Dooley, Paul L. Smith, and Richard Libertini.

Popeye is a flawed extravagance, but if you can survive its stumbling pace, its mumbling actors, and its dreadful songs, you will eventually experience a charming, unique comic-strip quite unlike anything you've seen before.

The film meanders stubbornly (a trademark of the director Robert Altman) until you get almost as "disgustipated" as Popeye. But there's a nice opening number, when the matchstick doors of the windblown shanties open and out pour the people of Popeye's island, Sweet Haven. And the primitive sets and the coarse but imaginative costumes add a comic dimension to Jules Feiffer's cartoon atmosphere the director and his stranded performers don't always seem capable of providing themselves.

But the characters do come to life—Robin Williams, with one eye closed, teeth sunk into a corncob pipe that makes much of his dialogue incoherent and beef-block arms that seem like woodcuttings, is a marvelous Popeye; Shelley Duvall looks exactly like Olive Oyl, although her flat, off-key singing will make you wince; and all of Popeye's other friends and enemies are here, too: Paul Dooley, as the hamburger-munching undertaker Wimpy; Paul Smith (the villainous prison sadist in *Midnight Express*) as the hog-growling, glass-eating Bluto; Ray Walston, as Poopdeck Pappy, the missing father Popeye's been searching for; Olive's blimp brother Castor Oyl; the gargantuan killer Oxblood Oxheart; and many others.

There's a great boxing match in which Oxblood almost pulverizes Popeye, and a marvelous finale in which Popeye finally eats his spinach in time to save baby Swee'pea from the revolting kidnapper Bluto. And best of all, there is a baby named Wesley Ivan Hurt, who is actually director Altman's grandchild in real life, but who gives a performance as the on-screen Swee'pea that is positively historic. This may just be the most gorgeously adorable baby ever photographed on a motion picture screen. He can predict the future and call the horse races, and nobody else is safe while sharing the camera with him. These are the good things about *Popeye*.

The bad news is that the songs, by Harry Nilsson, just lie there like dead smelts. Altman, as a director, has practically no talent for comedy; the simplest sight gag like a chair being jerked from under a customer in the Sweet Haven Café becomes deadly and slow as a traffic jam. What's missing is a consistent rhythm in the center of the film in which the characters just seem to be marking time. Sometimes crowds bump into each other aimlessly, breaking their necks to get some tempo going, while the entire thing begins to look like *Seven Brides for Seven Brothers* staged in a mental hospital.

Still, *Popeye* makes up for its dull stretches with wonderful imagery and enormous storybook style. And below its buffoon surface lies a morality tale about humanity and self-acceptance that is exemplified in Popeye's song "I Yam What I Yam," staged in the "house of ill repukes." Its individual lapses in judgment are more than made up for by the sum of its parts, and when all else fails, there's always Swee'pea, a baby even the most jaded of hearts will want to take home.

POSTCARDS FROM THE EDGE (1990)

★ ★ ½ Directed by Mike Nichols. Screenplay by Carrie Fisher, from her novel. Produced by Nichols and John Calley. *With Meryl Streep, Shirley MacLaine, Dennis Quaid, Richard Dreyfuss, Annette Bening, and Mary Wickes.*

When a middle-aged star strips away her wigs and makeup, baring baldness and liver spots for the cruelty of the camera, an Oscar nomination usually follows. And Shirley MacLaine received hers. In Mike Nichols's *Postcards From the Edge*, her guts and versatility literally explode in bursts of savage honesty as she strips away more than Max Factor. As the quintessential movie star mother, she opens her soul. It's all acting, of course. I've seen Shirley without her makeup, or much of anything else you could call a protective veneer, and she still looks terrific. But the scene in this talked-about (and much admired) comedy about the pressures of Hollywood in which she lies in a hospital bed after a drunken car crash, defenseless against the tabloid press outside the door, while her actress daughter (Meryl Streep) reconstructs her face, leaves no doubt that Miss MacLaine is a trooper who will try anything for her art. I haven't seen such honesty since Jan Sterling's makeup came off in *The High and the Mighty*.

Postcards From the Edge is, of course, the movie version of Carrie Fisher's book about her survival after drugs and depression while trying to cope as the daughter of Debbie Reynolds and Eddie Fisher. When the people in a book are alive, easily hurt, and often litigious, the term is "semi-autobiographical novel." But, as Richard Nixon says, make no mistake. The coke-snorting daughter is really Miss Fisher, and the fading alcoholic star from MGM musicals of the fifties and sixties is really Debbie. Daughter, when first seen, is nearly dead from an overdose of Demerol, Percodan, and cocaine. Mom, when first observed in a drug rehab clinic visiting her daughter, spends her time discussing her old production numbers with a drag queen who "does" her in his act. To work again, the daughter can only be insured if she lives in the custody of her famous mom. This means prison in a Beverly Hills mansion where she must listen to endless prattle about Mom's hysterectomy, fibroid tumors, and Louis B. Mayer. Both poi-

gnant and hilarious, Carrie Fisher's screenplay shows real people trying to survive in a surreal landscape.

Naturally it has elements of *Inside Daisy Clover* and *Terms of Endearment*, but if I have any problem with this movie, it's the excess. The movie is so flossy and air-conditioned that it looks more like *Stella*. But the same brittle humor, cockeyed way of looking at the absurdity of her life, and tart one-liners that made Carrie Fisher's book more than just another self-pitying *Mommie Dearest* memoir lift the picture out of its familiar "We've been here before" ambience and give it wings. The result is a shrill but touching look at a daughter trying to find her own uneasy identity in her mother's profession, and a mother who can't love her unconditionally without competing for the close-ups. Shirley is a vulnerable, tough, caring, but desperately frightened mother with growing pains of her own. How can we hate a gorgon so perky that she asks, "How would you like to have Joan Crawford for a mother—or Lana Turner?" She denies her alcoholism ("I just drink like an Irish person, that's all") and it's in her will that they can't bury her without her false eyelashes. When the daughter comes home from the drug clinic after detox and rehab, Mom throws a surprise party and insists the girl sing a song; when the daughter returns the request, Mom demurs for a few seconds, then, without missing a beat, barks at the piano player: " 'I'm Still Here' in D-flat." It's one of the funniest moments in the film.

The point of the picture is that it means nothing to live a privileged life everyone envies if everyone thinks it's wonderful but you. If you don't get the point from Carrie Fisher's book, then there is Debbie Reynolds's book . . . and Eddie Fisher's book . . . and . . . but yo! Enjoy this one for now. And there's plenty to enjoy. Meryl Streep is fine, although she's too old for the part (Mom almost always looks better and younger than she does), and Nichols has surrounded them with a star-studded Greek chorus of cameos: Richard Dreyfuss, as the doctor who pumps Meryl's stomach; Dennis Quaid, as a brief encounter more in love with his plumbing than people; and Mary Wickes, as the salty Texas grandmother who gave both her daughter and granddaughter their starch ("Cry all you want—you'll pee less!"). Rich and colorful and phony and universal in its gen-

eration-gap homilies, *Postcards From the Edge* is about show people coping, and provides MacLaine and Streep with two of the best roles of their careers. They may not break your heart in all the chaos, but they manage to scratch the aorta a little.

PRESENTING LILY MARS (1943)
★ ★ ★ Directed by Norman Taurog. Screenplay by Gladys Lehman and Richard Connell. Produced by Joe Pasternak. *With Judy Garland, Van Heflin, Spring Byington, Fay Bainter, Richard Carlson, Marta Eggerth, Marilyn Maxwell, Ray McDonald, Annabelle Logan, Bob Crosby, and Tommy Dorsey.*

Youthful, vibrant, kissed with the blush of good health and shining talent, Judy Garland never looked lovelier or sang better than in this breezy, tuneful MGM musical bonbon from 1943. Only nineteen, Judy stole the movie from such veterans as Van Heflin, Spring Byington, Bob Crosby, Tommy Dorsey, and Fay Bainter, playing a Booth Tarkington teenager who rises from small-town obscurity to big-time Broadway. Unlike MGM's more opulent, razzle-dazzle musicals of the forties, this one has a warm, human glow. Note to trivia buffs: Take a special look at

Judy's little sister, perky child star Annabelle Logan. She grew up to become jazz singer Annie Ross.

PRESUMED INNOCENT (1990)

★ ★ ★ Directed by Alan J. Pakula. Screenplay by Frank Pierson and Pakula. Produced by Sydney Pollack and Mark Rosenberg. *With Harrison Ford, Bonnie Bedelia, Raul Julia, Brian Dennehy, and Greta Scacchi.*

Anyone fascinated by courtroom dramas will be riveted to *Presumed Innocent*, Alan Pakula's blistering film about a prosecutor who suddenly finds himself accused of a murder. It was first a novel by Scott Turow—one of those books that refuses to be put down. Now, Harrison Ford stars as Rusty Sabitch, assistant D.A., family man, all-around good guy, and chief suspect in the rape and murder of an ex-mistress and colleague (gorgeous Greta Scacchi). Rusty has always been in the business of accusing, judging and punishing. Now he's in the hot seat, and nothing is going in his favor.

The forensics evidence points to Rusty, but with plenty of red herrings, scapegoats, a suspicious wife (Bonnie Bedelia) and a satanic defense attorney (Raul Julia), the screen bursts with shocks and surprises before the mystery gets solved. Harrison Ford has given livelier performances for my taste; he seems, at times, catatonic. But he once again proves to his detractors he's more than a pretty face with a scar on his chin. Audiences reliant on the fast pace of today's gut-wrenching thrillers may not appreciate the slowness of *Presumed Innocent* but the intricate plot and the meticulous building of clues add up to a gripping study of human interaction, law, and justice. A thriller for people who like puzzles.

PRETTY IN PINK (1986)

½★ Directed by Howard Deutch. Screenplay by John Hughes. Produced by Lauren Shuler. *With Molly Ringwald, Harry Dean Stanton, Jon Cryer, Andrew McCarthy, Annie Potts, and James Spader.*

Pretty in Pink wouldn't be pretty in any color. It looks hopelessly black to me.

The best description I've heard yet of this dismal, muddle-headed bore came from a real teenager who asked, "What country is this movie taking place in?" *Pretty in Pink* seems to occur on the moon.

Pretty in Pink was directed by newcomer Howard Deutch, a graduate of music videos, but that's just a formality. It's really in the frozen junk-food assembly line of demented teenage lunacies concocted by John Hughes, whose unsteady hand is obvious throughout.

Hughes is the king of tormented teenage flicks. He has polluted the environment with such dumpwaste landfills as *Sixteen Candles*, *The Breakfast Club*, and *Weird Science*. His films have certain distinguishing characteristics. None of them resemble real life. Most of them star Molly Ringwald. All of them are awful.

Pretty in Pink is not as genuinely nauseating as *Sixteen Candles*. After all, Hughes only wrote and executive produced it. But it's down there, jockeying for bottom position.

Like all teenage flicks by Hughes, this one takes place in a high school that makes *Grease* look like *Our Town*.

In these mythical high schools, anyone who wears pleated skirts, crewneck sweaters or penny loafers is a rich, pompous, self-serving, villainous snob, and anyone who looks and acts like a retarded freak is really a sensitive, misunderstood, saintly, iconoclastic nerd with the heart of a poet.

Despite the noise and smoke

of P.R. blitz proclaiming Molly Ringwald as the most beautiful reigning princess of the Hollywood Brat Pack, the films of John Hughes came close to destroying her.

In *Pretty in Pink* she is as beautiful as Gravel Gertie (her lips are bigger) and dresses like an eighty-year-old birdwatcher. She has a gap in her buck teeth wide enough to drive Lauren Hutton through, and her hair is the color of orange Jell-O. Oh, well. They can't all look like Candice Bergen.

She is Andie, a poor but good-hearted girl who lives with her father, a shiftless, unemployed bum (played by Harry Dean Stanton, who has made a career out of playing reprobates), in a tacky tract house on the wrong side of the Amtrak tracks.

In a school populated by dorks, Blane (Andrew McCarthy) is different. He's a senior. He's also rich, sophisticated, trendy, preppy, and drives a BMW.

He's also a bit weird. He saunters into the record shop where Andie works and buys a Steve Lawrence album. This is supposed to show what a character he is, despite his wrinkled linen sports jacket rolled up at the elbows.

Since buying a Steve Lawrence album is the only tasteful and intelligent thing anyone does in the entire movie, I missed the point of the whole scene. Nothing after that makes a bit of sense, so you figure it out. You'd have to be fifteen with zits to dig this movie anyway.

Should Andie cross the social barrier and let Blane take her to the prom even though she knows she'll look like Luba the Gypsy fortune-teller? And if she goes, should she wear pink? These are the burning questions here. It's a good movie in which to catch up on your sleep.

With submental dialogue like "Go for it!" and "I'm off, like a dirty shirt," there isn't much of a movie here to steal, but teenage clown Jon Cryer steals what there is with no difficulty. As a nerdy little twerp who dresses like a cross between a Harlem pimp and Jughead, Cryer is funny, outrageous, obnoxious and completely disarming. The rest of the movie is for cretins.

PRETTY WOMAN (1990)
★ ★ ★   Directed by Garry Marshall. Screenplay by J. F. Lawton. Produced by Arnon Milchan and Steven Reuther. With Richard Gere and Julia Roberts.

Julia Roberts may have worn the ugliest dress at the 1990 Oscar show and looked like a waif from a burning orphanage, but in *Pretty Woman* she has the body and beauty of a Rodeo Drive Aphrodite. If you've been longing for a rich, funny, beautifully photographed, old-fashioned yet modern romantic love story, this zinger is for you. Roberts plays a Hollywood hooker who shows lonely, rigid, self-made millionaire Richard Gere, a stranger in town, how to get back to Beverly Hills. Naturally, she stays for the weekend and what begins as just another business proposition turns to real fairy-tale affection. She loosens him up. He gives her a sense of value, self-confidence, and a limitless expense account. It's miraculous what an American Express card can do.

Director Garry Marshall borrows his ideas shamelessly from *Born Yesterday*, *The Prince and the Showgirl*, and even *Breakfast at Tiffany's*—but he has the wit and visual style to make it all seem fresh. Some of the dialogue is hilarious. When arguing whores on the sidewalk stars of Hollywood Boulevard establish territorial imperatives with lines like "I got the Ritz Brothers all the way to Carole

Lombard—you go work up by Esther Williams!" I gotta tell you, I laughed out loud. Gere is aging attractively, and despite her lip implants, Miss Roberts lights the screen with a torch. You won't go away from *Pretty Woman* humming "Who Cares?"

PRICK UP YOUR EARS (1987)

★ ★ ★ ★ Directed by Stephen Frears. Screenplay by Alan Bennett. Produced by Andrew Brown. *With Gary Oldman, Alfred Molina, Vanessa Redgrave, Wallace Shawn, Lindsay Duncan, Julie Walters, and James Grant.*

The scandalous murder of British playwright Joe Orton—hammered to death by his jealous lover Kenneth Halliwell in their squalid London flat—was as grotesquely macabre as anything in Orton's black comedies. It made headlines across the world and became the subject of a book by John Lahr and now a film that could easily be one of Orton's own gallows humor plots about sex, success, and homicide. It's grim stuff, but magnificently directed by Stephen (*My Beautiful Laundrette*) Frears, with remarkable tact and compassion. Gary Oldman, the actor who played Sid Vicious with such nauseating passion in *Sid and Nancy*, is positively brilliant as Joe. Alfred Molina, as the lover who lost his self-respect and eventually his marbles, is creepy. And Vanessa Redgrave, as Orton's eccentric agent, gives a deliciously pointed cameo. One of the most stunning British films of the 1980s, like a nightmare you still remember vividly the next morning.

THE PRIDE OF THE YANKEES (1942)

★ ★ ★ ★ Directed by Sam Wood. Screenplay by Jo Swerling and Herman J. Mankiewicz. Produced by Samuel Goldwyn. *With Gary Cooper, Teresa Wright, Walter Brennan, Dan Duryea, and Babe Ruth.*

This disarming sports film features Gary Cooper as legendary baseball star Lou Gehrig, an all-American slugger who rose from immigrant boy to the Baseball Hall of Fame, only to be rained out at the peak of his career by an incurable disease. Also starring Teresa Wright, Walter Brennan, and Babe Ruth himself. One of Cooper's finest performances, and one of Hollywood's all-time winners. Cooper, it must be admitted, is better in the dramatic scenes than on the baseball diamond, which may explain why the American League footage, with Lou at bat, seems sketchy. Baseball fans may grouse that there isn't enough baseball. But Babe Ruth and other old-time Yankees—Bill Dickey, Mark Koenig, and Bob Meusel, as well as famed sportscaster Bill Stern—lend credibility by playing themselves. It's less a baseball saga than a tapestry of American life—humorous, human, composed of patient details, never pretentious or sentimental (which were often Samuel Goldwyn trademarks). The result is one of the most moving tributes to a sports legend ever filmed. Since Lou Gehrig's valiant courage and exalted position in baseball history will never be dated, neither will this inspired film biography.

THE PRIME OF MISS JEAN BRODIE (1969)

★ ★ ★ ½ Directed by Ronald Neame. Screenplay by Jay Presson Allen. Produced by Robert Fryer. With Maggie Smith, Robert Stephens, Pamela Franklin, Gordon Jackson, Celia Johnson, and Jane Carr.

The Prime of Miss Jean Brodie won the fabulous Maggie Smith an Oscar in 1969 for her eccentric performance in the title role, and nothing about her work has diminished. This film is a must for lovers of great acting. Funny, noble, snooty, demanding, and opinionated,

Miss Brodie teaches young ladies in an exclusive school in Scotland, but some of the prize students she proudly molds go away learning some shocking things about sex and politics. Miss Brodie is idealistic and dedicated, but her passion for Mussolini lands her in hot water before her teaching job ends. Maggie Smith tears up a complex role like Kleenex. She is positively tremendous.

THE PRINCE OF TIDES (1991)

★ ★ ★ ½ Directed by Barbra Streisand. Screenplay by Pat Conroy and Becky Johnston, based on the novel by Pat Conroy. Produced by Barbra Streisand and Andrew Karsch. With Barbra Streisand, Nick Nolte, Blythe Danner, Kate Nelligan, Jason Gould, Jeroen Krabbe, and Melinda Dillon.

Fans of the cult novel by Pat Conroy may be disappointed that the director, in her capacity as star, has changed the focus to a Jewish psychiatrist who only played a peripheral role in the original story, but admirers of the star, in her capacity of director, will find much to applaud in her sensitive handling of actors and her cool, steady control of a complex plot. For Barbra Streisand, this film is a triumph.

It is really uncanny how she

literally turns the film over to Nick Nolte, nurturing and guiding him through the best performance of his career as Tom Wingo, the shrimper's son from the tides and marshes of South Carolina grappling with the harshness of New York and the ghosts of his past while trying to save his neurotic sister from suicide. The irony is that he has to travel to New York, where life is cheap and lacks value, to find his own, but Tom Wingo is no ordinary man. A victim of weakness, guilt, and insecurity, the son of warring parents who took their children as prisoners, he's trapped in his own misery, believing all women have betrayed him. The tension between Tom and his sister's doctor, Susan Lowenstein (played by Streisand with restraint and self-assurance) gradually eases into a working fabric which illuminates his own self-awareness, too. Learning to stop making jokes and start confronting his own pain, he also finds the key to love. The family secret that has plunged him into darkness, when finally revealed, is so horrible it's a miracle the whole family didn't self-destruct. As Nolte, in a flood of tears, lets his real feelings come out after months of sparring matches with the shrink, the emotional floodgate that

opens is deeply touching. In his most sympathetic and sensitive role, he is very fine indeed.

There is also excellent work by Blythe Danner, as his long-suffering wife; Kate Nelligan, as his cold, hardened, ambitious mother, festered with rage and guilt for the way her kids turned out; Ms. Streisand's real-life son Jason Gould, as a boy who needs some awareness lessons of his own; and Melinda Dillon, as the wounded sister. The director, as the shrink with a crumbling marriage of her own, does not have the juiciest role, despite its length, but she plays it without a shred of movie-star shtick.

The Prince of Tides is beautiful to look at, lush and willowy, but it gets ponderous in the middle sections and could benefit from sharper editing. Still, it's noble and sincere, intelligent and sophisticated, and warmly welcome to anyone longing for a movie about adult relationships instead of teenage twaddle.

A PRIVATE FUNCTION (1985)

★ ★ ★ Directed by Malcolm Mowbray. Produced by Mark Shivas. Screenplay by Alan Bennett. With Maggie Smith, Michael Palin, Denholm Elliott, Liz Smith, and Richard Griffiths.

Hilarious hijinks involving a group of crooked politicians in a small town in Yorkshire, an innocent chiropodist, his ruthlessly ambitious wife, and a black market pig named Betty. It all takes place during the royal wedding of Prince Philip to Princess Elizabeth in 1947; it makes some sharp moral comments on socialism and postwar food rationing, and is one of the funniest British films in decades. Maggie Smith, Monty Python's Michael Palin, and Denholm Elliott head the excellent cast, but the pig steals the picture.

PUNCHLINE (1988)
★ ★ ★ Directed and written by David Seltzer. Produced by Daniel Melnick and Michael Rachmil. With Tom Hanks, Sally Field, John Goodman and Mark Rydell.

In a world of ugliness and despair, the greatest gift one person can give another is laughter. Comedy is the hardest work in show business and getting started is the hardest part of all. *Punchline* is a fresh, inventive and surprisingly touching look at the world of stand-up comics and the sacrifices they endure to reach success.

Sally Field is a frumpy New Jersey housewife with three demanding kids, a furious husband, and a house that's falling apart, but she's driven to find her own identity through bad jokes she spends her cookie-jar money to buy. Tom Hanks, in the most colorful, complex, and fully realized performance of his career, flunks out of medical school not to *find* his identity but to *share* it, in routines that expose his inner pain and insecurity.

He's great because he's obsessed. She stinks because she doesn't know what comedy is. While her Polish jokes flop, he can get a laugh out of an anatomy chart. Drawn together at the same club where they work nights, he helps and she grows, milking humor from her own life.

But *Punchline* is not about one-liners. It's about the fact that gifted people who make us laugh are sometimes crying on the inside. It shows the seedy club world of stand-up comics where unfunny people sweat and fail. Writer-director David Seltzer invades this world and while people aren't always likable, they never sink to clichés. She doesn't leave home for him. He doesn't become the next David Letterman. But as they compete in the final contest that could lead to a spot on Johnny Carson, the results lead them to self-discoveries that will surprise you. Sally Field gives her usual no-nonsense "girl most likely to succeed" performance, but it is Tom Hanks who walks away with the picture. From wild and crazy to touching and tortured, he shows every vulnerable side of the clown he's playing without a trace of phony sentiment. He's miserable, angry, lonely, scared, ruthless and hilarious—but best of all, he makes us see in *Punchline* that comedy is sometimes no laughing matter.

PURPLE ROSE OF CAIRO (1985)

★ ★ ★ Directed and written by Woody Allen. Produced by Robert Greenhut. With Mia Farrow, Jeff Daniels, Danny Aiello, Stephanie Farrow, Ed Herrmann, John Wood, Van Johnson, Zoe Caldwell, and Karen Akers.

Every Woody Allen film is something of an event, and *The Purple Rose of Cairo* is no exception. It may not be a masterpiece like *Annie Hall* or *Zelig*, but even though it's a one-joke movie it never stubs its toe. I once wrote that even on an off day, Woody Allen is better than everybody else on Sunday, and *The Purple Rose of Cairo* is no reason to change my mind.

Only a mind as fresh, inventive, and quizzical as Woody Allen's could think up a movie like this. *The Purple Rose of Cairo* explores the mythic boundaries of make-believe the world of movies has taught most film fans to accept as gospel truth, and comes up with some illusion-shattering conclusions.

Woody does not appear in it, but his unique and witty observations on real life vs. reel life are the core of the movie and everything it professes. There's a black-and-white movie going on throughout *The Purple Rose of Cairo*, but it's Woody Allen's heart and soul that are unreeling.

The time is the Depression. The heroine is Cecilia (Mia Farrow), a hash-house waitress who is New Jersey's biggest movie buff. In reality, Cecilia's life is a clip from *Stella Dallas*. Nothing goes right for her. She's clumsy, underprivileged, and shopworn.

Her brutish husband (Danny Aiello) shoots craps, leches after girls and gives her grief. When Cecilia complains sweetly, she gets slugged.

In the darkness of the movie house where Cecilia escapes daily, things are different. Here she surrenders to illusion, and dreams come true. She can waltz with Fred Astaire, sail away to romantic places with

Clark Gable, and agonize with Garbo. At the movies, poor Cecilia comes alive.

One day, she's not alone. Watching her current matinee favorite, a romantic flick called *The Purple Rose of Cairo*, with a plot that careens from the mysterious mummy tombs of Egypt to the shimmering café society of Manhattan, Cecilia notices that the dashing young archaeologist in the movie seems to be watching *her*. Suddenly, pith helmet and all, he bolts from the screen and drags her off.

"How many times is a man so taken with a woman that he leaves the screen to get her?" gushes the unabashedly romantic character. The actors left on the screen lose their equilibrium and start insulting the audience. The public hates this miracle. It wants the movie to turn out the way it did the week before—"otherwise what is life all about, anyway?"

Alexander H. Cohen, the Hollywood producer of the movie within the movie, faces ruin unless he can reverse the miracle. The actor who created the role of the callow hero faces disaster unless he can capture the runaway character and get him back on the screen.

So you get a shy plain-Jane waitress being romanced beyond her wildest imagination by two men—a fictional character and the movie star who plays him, both breaking all the rules of make-believe.

Jeff Daniels, facing the difficult task of playing both parts, is charming, dexterous, and wonderful in a Herculean feat of duality.

Now Woody Allen's moral conscience takes over. In the style of Preston Sturges's *Sullivan's Travels*, Woody uses Cecilia as a guide for the movie character to explore the Depression. He finds poverty, Salvation Army soup kitchens, people who are not noble and brave and glamorous as they are on the screen.

There's no fadeout after the kiss. Play money doesn't buy a thing. Cars don't run automatically without a key. Life, he concludes, is safer on the screen.

Cecilia, too, realizes real life is all there is, that people are mean and they fight dirty and break their promises. In the end she learns how to deal with what she's got. Like the song says, it isn't so good it couldn't get better, but it isn't so rotten it couldn't get worse.

The Purple Rose of Cairo is not a laugh riot. It's not the kind of windmill-tilting comedy Woody Allen is famous for inventing for his fans. It's Pirandello on the loose, and once it establishes its conceit it doesn't go much farther. Nothing much happens to anyone on or off the screen. And the ending is less than what we want for Cecilia. But it's a delicate, thoughtful, and extremely wise film for audiences who want a bit more from their comedy than hokum.

Gordon Willis, the genius cameraman, and Susan Morse, the brilliant film editor—both of whom contributed so memorably to giving *Zelig* its fabulous period flavor—have united once more to balance the difficult equation of Technicolor reality and black-and-white movie-within-the-movie fantasy.

The cast is impeccable. Mia Farrow is a fetching and fawn-like victim of both harsh Depression-era life and Hollywood exploitation, and in the movie-movie about pyramids and Broadway, an illustrious group of people have been assembled to dish out the sophistication: Zoe Caldwell, Van Johnson, John Wood, Edward Herrmann, Milo O'Shea, and Karen Akers among them. They are all flawless, right down to their mascara.

At a time when most movies take hours to say nothing, Woody says it all in eighty-four minutes. For that alone, *The Purple Rose of Cairo* deserves a medal.

QUEEN CHRISTINA (1934)
★ ★ ★ Directed by Rouben Mamoulian. Screenplay by H. M. Harwood and Salka Viertel. Produced by Walter Wanger. With Greta Garbo, John Gilbert, Ian Keith, Lewis Stone, C. Aubrey Smith, Reginald Owen, and Elizabeth Young.

Queen Christina is widely considered to be the elusive Garbo's greatest achievement. This lavish historical vehicle is about the Swedish queen who shocked the world by abdicating her throne for love, beating the Duke of Windsor by three centuries. The famous close-up of her beautiful face sailing out to sea is one of the most enduring scenes in movie history. Director Rouben Mamoulian was the prewar Vincente Minnelli; his eye for luxurious detail and sumptuous lighting composition is very much in evidence here, and he gets from Garbo a performance full of angst and vibrance—a change from her usual Scandinavian stoicism.

QUICK CHANGE (1990)

★ ★ ½ Directed by Bill Murray and Howard Franklin. Screenplay by Franklin. Produced by Murray and Robert Greenhut. *With Bill Murray, Geena Davis, and Randy Quaid.*

New York, they say, is a place where anything can happen—and just about everything does when Bill Murray, his girlfriend Geena Davis, and his moronic pal Randy Quaid decide they're fed up with the city's filth, ugliness, and insanity, and plan to get out, taking a million dollars of the city's money with them. Ah, but this is New York—where it's easier to rob a bank than it is to get to the airport. They get lost when construction hard hats give them the wrong directions to the Long Island Expressway. They get mugged. The getaway car gets totaled. They take a taxi in desperation, but this is still New York—where the cab driver can't speak a word of English and doesn't know where Kennedy Airport is. Pursued by both cops and the Mafia, the daffy trio flags down a city bus. Ah, but this is *still* New York—where else do you have a city with passengers carrying oversized guitars and bus drivers who demand exact change? The moral of the screwball farce is if you're going to rob a bank,

don't do it in New York. This is a tailor-made vehicle for Bill Murray's dry deadpan wit, and Randy Quaid has just about perfected his grinning doofus routine. They don't go for easy laughs, predictable shtick, or corny sight gags. The real star is New York, but I wonder what the Chamber of Commerce will think. A movie like this could kill the tourist trade.

QUO VADIS (1951)

★ ★ ★ ½ Directed by Mervyn LeRoy. Screenplay by John Lee Mahin, S. N. Behrman, and Sonya Levien, based on Henryk Sienkiewicz's novel. Produced by Sam Zimbalist. *With Robert Taylor, Deborah Kerr, Peter Ustinov, Leo Genn, Patricia Laffan, and Finlay Currie.*

For pure spectacle, this 1951 MGM colossus is first cabin all the way. Robert Taylor and Deborah Kerr are two of the famous Christians thrown to the lions, and Peter Ustinov is the meanest, fattest, craziest Nero who ever terrorized a crowd of Roman peasants. Look closely and you might even spot a sultry Italian extra named Sophia Loren in the crown scenes. The visual splendors climax with the burning of Rome—probably the most elaborate sequence filmed at the greatest Hollywood studio since the burning of Atlanta in *Gone with the Wind*. The year is A.D. 64, but the story, like Rome itself, never wears out.

RAGGEDY MAN (1981)
★ ★ ★ ★ Directed by Jack Fisk. Screenplay by William D. Wittliff. Produced by Burt Weissbourd and Wittliff. With Sissy Spacek, Eric Roberts, Sam Shepard, Henry Thomas, Carey Hollis, Jr., and R. G. Armstrong.

For simple, unpretentious artistry, see *Raggedy Man*, a warm, moving, beautifully modulated little gem of a movie that stands out from its World War II Texas setting like a perfect emerald in a corncrib.

Sissy Spacek gives one of her miraculous performances as a hick-town telephone operator with two small boys to raise in an atmosphere of deprivation and bigotry. Her husband has deserted them and there isn't much chance of making a better life for the kids, but Nita Longley has gumption and spunk and the way she gets her brood out of Edna, Texas, on that bus to San Antonio charges the screen with the emotional intensity and deep-rooted heart of a meticulous short story by Flannery O'Connor, Eudora Welty or Carson McCullers.

There isn't a phony moment in this polished piece of cinematic art—from the Orange Crush machine to the kids' wide-eyed talk of Tojo to the hunger and need in Sissy Spacek's Raggedy Ann eyes. Eric Roberts is sensitive and touching as a sailor who drops in to steal her heart and open up new horizons for her boys before he moves on, and Sam Shepard makes an indelible impression as the silent sentinel who watches her house from a distance for mysterious reasons of his own that aren't explained until the film draws to a shattering climax.

Spacek's husband, Jack Fisk, makes a smashing directorial debut, and the script by Texas writer William Wittliff is the kind of marvelously detailed screenplay every movie should be so lucky to find. Special mention must be made of Henry Thomas and Carey Hollis, Jr., as the two children. I don't know where Sissy Spacek found them, but they are the two most adorable, engaging, talented, and heartbreaking little tykes I've seen on the screen in years.

Whatever you loved about the multifaceted Sissy Spacek in *Coal Miner's Daughter* or *Missing* you'll love even more here. There's not a trace of actressy dishonesty in anything she does, and *Raggedy Man* is the perfect vehicle for her homespun gingham personality. She takes the role of Nita Longley and lives in it, establishing squatter's rights. Her Sears Roebuck sincerity seems to have permeated every aspect of the film, because *Raggedy Man* turns a slice of cornbread into an emporium of delights.

RAGING BULL (1980)

★ ★ Directed by Martin Scorsese. Screenplay by Paul Schrader and Mardik Martin. Produced by Irwin Winkler and Robert Chartoff. With Robert De Niro, Cathy Moriarty, Joe Pesci, Frank Vincent, Nicholas Colasanto, and Theresa Saldana.

A heavy beating awaits anyone who sees Martin Scorsese's *Raging Bull*. It's based on a book by fighter Jake LaMotta, who also acted as technical adviser. That must mean that LaMotta approves of this sad, sleazy, humorless depiction of his cretinous life. The story Scorsese tells in this interminable assault on the senses is not a story worth telling in the first place, but the way he tells it leaves LaMotta without the slightest shred of decency.

Boxing movies must have some kind of heroism, some slight shard of humanity between knockouts to sustain in-

terest. This one has nothing but noise and bloodshed. Since fighters all end up the same way, on the scrap heap, the only thing that makes them remotely interesting is their souls. Without compassion, they remain big, dumb battering rams, and their fates have no tragic dimensions. Every good boxing movie—from *Body and Soul* to *Golden Boy* to *Somebody Up There Likes Me* to *Rocky*—has a hero to root for. The grim, one-dimensional picture Scorsese and screenwriters Paul Schrader and Mardik Martin paint of Jake LaMotta has no dramatic pulse, no structure, no suspense, no tragedy. It's supposed to be about the rise and fall of a self-destructive pugilist, but it isn't much of a rise, and the fall is no more interesting than a still shot of a Bowery bum fitfully ransacking a garbage can for a bottle of Muscatel.

It's a bleak and nasty film, shot in stark black and white, with personal milestones that might give clues to the character behind the fists—marriages, births, family barbecues—related in silent color home movies. The rest of the time, all we get is a relentlessly despairing look at an arrogant, inarticulate punching bag from an Italian neighborhood in the Bronx who lives a thoroughly loathsome life from first frame to last. I think I've been in that neighborhood before, in other Scorsese films, and I couldn't wait to get out.

The Italians are all from the "Hey, Goombah!" school of pizza-headed Italian clichés. The acting is so hammy and hysterical it makes Anna Magnani seem subtle. Amid the flying plates, filthy screaming curses, and Sinatra records, La-Motta leaves his wife for a pouty, peroxide blonde who is fifteen going on forty-five. The sound track shrieks of bones crunching, blood spattering from ruptured eye sockets, and slow-motion violence that would make Sam Peckinpah throw up.

Scorsese makes the atmosphere, but he hasn't made a movie. LaMotta emerges one of the most despicable characters ever revealed on film, despite Robert De Niro's Oscar-winning performance. Bashing Tony Janiro's face in because his wife thought he was "cute," throwing a fight to Billy Fox to please the mobsters, causing Boxing Commission scandals and investigations by the D.A., slapping his wife around, treating women like chattel, ending up in jail, working in the end as a broken-down comic without family or friends

in cheap strip joints, there is nothing to cheer about this man. The film ends with De Niro, bloated, beer-bellied, porcine and disgustingly vulgar, doing Brando's "I coulda been a contender" speech from *On the Waterfront* and you don't know if you're supposed to laugh or cry.

With cauliflower ears, a broken nose the size of a Coke bottle, Quasimodo face, and obesity bordering on the grotesque, Robert De Niro never elicits any sympathy, but he has an energy and magnetism worth watching. Cathy Moriarity, as his creepy wife, and Joe Pesci, as his equally crude brother Joey, are also memorable. But it's a heartless movie, cheerless and of somwhat mysterious purpose.

RAGTIME (1981)
★ ★ Directed by Milos Forman. Screenplay by Michael Weller. Produced by Dino De Laurentiis. *With Howard E. Rollins, Jr., James Cagney, Brad Dourif, Elizabeth McGovern, Mary Steenburgen, James Olson, Kenneth McMillan, Mandy Patinkin, Moses Gunn, and Pat O'Brien.*

Wasting money is something movie studios know how to do better than anything else. They wasted plenty of it on *Ragtime*, a big, expensive, lushly photographed, completely confusing, and totally inconsequential bore about turn-of-the-century New York, based on the jazzy literary newsreel by E. L. Doctorow.

The book was a movie unto itself the way it juxtaposed events in the lives of a family of fireworks manufacturers from New Rochelle with the headline-making celebrities in 1906. Along the way, a rich vein of Americana was mined, plunging the reader into a world of Model-T Fords, Gibson girls, silent pictures, and ragtime music. The movie tries hard, rambles interminably, employs thousands of actors, and goes nowhere. Its characters are sketched, not dramatized, and the result is rather like a Chinese banquet: The feast is impressive, but you won't remember a thing about it the following day. Thirty-two million dollars is too much to pay for heartburn.

Milos Forman's sprawling, gigantic mess of a movie takes you everywhere at once and nowhere at all. You are in the rooftop garden where millionaire Harry Thaw murders architect Stanford White (grumpily played by a tuxedoed Norman Mailer like a prizefighter in a straitjacket) in the middle of a Donald O'Connor number.

Then we're in the family dining room in New Rochelle where nobody ever gets beyond the soup course because a black baby is found in the vegetable garden. Then we're following google-eyed "Younger Brother" (Brad Dourif) as he follows chorus girl Evelyn Nesbit from her husband Harry Thaw's insanity trial through the Lower East Side where she meets a poor immigrant silhouette artist who later directs her in a silent movie in Atlantic City where "Mother" (Mary Steenburgen) falls in love with him and runs away from home with the black baby while the black baby's real father, a ragtime pianist named Coalhouse Walker, terrorizes New York by threatening to blow up the J. P. Morgan library while the police commissioner (James Cagney) mobilizes the entire New York City police force while . . . but why go on? I'm sinking into a coma just thinking about it.

Everyone works hard, to no avail, although James Cagney seems particularly stiff for a living legend. The best actors in the film are Elizabeth McGovern, who makes Evelyn Nesbit a very appealing cream puff indeed, and Howard E. Rollins, Jr., who makes Coalhouse Walker a firebrand with intelligence and purpose instead of just another hothead.

Ragtime is endless, and there doesn't seem to be any attempt on anyone's part to shorten it or make it any clearer. Some characters ride off into the sunset at the end; others just disappear from the screen into Technicolor oblivion. It is maddening.

If you want to see the most beautiful evocation of turn-of-the-century Americana ever filmed, have another look at Vincente Minnelli's *Meet Me in St. Louis*. If you want to see how to spend the equivalent of the national debt on potted palms, see *Ragtime*.

RAIDERS OF THE LOST ARK (1981)

★ ★ ★ ★ Directed by Steven Spielberg. Screenplay by Lawrence Kasdan, story by George Lucas and Phillip Kaufman. Produced by Frank Marshall. *With Harrison Ford, Karen Allen, Ronald Lacey, John Rhys-Davies, Denholm Elliott, Paul Freeman, and Wolf Kahler.*

An important part of growing up for me was Saturday afternoon at the movies. The best part of the whole day was always the serial. How I cringed over *The Purple Monster Strikes* and *Panther Girl of the Congo*. How I applauded *Don Winslow of the Coast Guard* and *The Adventures of Captain Midnight*, barely able to get through the next six days until I could continue the suspense for another week.

They were turning them out in their sleep at Republic and Universal, keeping the "scratch houses" filled with screaming kids, and enchanting scores of impressionable future filmmakers like Steven Spielberg, George Lucas and Philip Kaufman—all three of whom collaborated on *Raiders of the Lost Ark*, which brings back the Saturday afternoons of our youth for new generations of more sophisticated kids who don't know what they missed. This time the screen does not fade to black at the end of each cliff hanger and you don't have to come back again next week to see what happens. *Raiders of the Lost Ark* is two hours of nonstop thrills condensed into one fun-filled entertainment.

Movies, of course, have changed and tastes have become more sophisticated along the way. It took me a while to get into the rhythm of nonsensical escapism. I kept expecting logic, coherence, reality. Finally, I gave up on the archaeological mumbo-jumbo about the Ark of the Covenant containing the broken tablets of the original Ten Commandments, settled back, and just let the whole thing happen. I was rocked back and forth from South American jungles to Nazi excavations in Egypt, and it didn't really matter that I was looking at location sequences in a South America that was really Hawaii, or an Egyptian desert that was really Tunisia. I applauded the good guys, hissed the bad guys, and yelled when the horrors got too real (if you suffer from herpetophobia, do not risk your life—there are poisonous snakes all over the screen).

As the dangers become more diabolical and the escapes more preposterous, *Raiders of the Lost Ark* achieves its real intention—to blend the best qualities of fantasy and adventure from the old serials, employ the most sophisticated technical effects the screen can offer, and scare the living daylights out of everybody, with style and wit. There were times when I found myself laughing and hiding my eyes at the same time. There's a perfect balance of just the right mixture of realism to keep you believing in Indiana Jones and just enough campiness to keep you amused at your own suspension of disbelief. The imaginative horrors Spielberg has dreamed up include cracking

whips, poison arrows, bat-filled caves, plagues of tarantulas, booby traps with stone doors equipped with steel teeth that clash shut impaling their victims, catacombs containing hundreds of human skeletons, red-hot pokers, exploding submarines, fires, lost cities, mine shafts, and every kind of weapon ever conceived by the kinds of minds that create comic books.

There's even a monkey that gives a "Heil Hitler" before dying from poisoned dates, a Nazi Neanderthal who gets splattered to kingdom come by spinning airplane propellers, and the most horrible of the horrible—a dark pit into which the hero and his girl descend on ropes into a slithering mass of live cobras, asps, pythons, and boa constrictors.

And Harrison Ford is the perfect reincarnation of Saturday serial stars like Buster Crabbe, Don Terry, and Tom Tyler. A good actor would have slowed everything down worrying about continuity, motivation, characterization, and dialogue. Ford is so bad here that he gives derring-do the perfect tight-lipped crunchy-eyed woodenness of the old Republic contract players. With overwhelming John Williams music to telegraph every emotion, beautiful visual effects like the slave laborers raising pickaxes against the orange sunsets of the Sahara, and the kind of nerve-frying tension Spielberg displayed in *Jaws*, there isn't a wasted frame of film in view. He makes kids of us all.

RAIN MAN (1989)

★ ★ ★ ★ Directed by Barry Levinson. Screenplay by Ronald Bass and Barry Morrow. Produced by Mark Johnson. *With Dustin Hoffman, Tom Cruise, Valeria Golino, Jerry Molden, Jack Murdock, and Michael D. Roberts.*

Two top stars at the top of their form illuminate *Rain Man*. Dazzling tour de force performances by Tom Cruise and Dustin Hoffman make it doubly entrancing. Cruise is Charlie Babbitt, a vain, scheming Hollywood hustler whose father dies and leaves $3 million to his autistic brother Raymond—an institutionalized "idiot savant." Outraged, Charlie kidnaps his brother for ransom and hits the road to L.A., planning to fleece him out of his inheritance. In one of 1989's most awesome and vigorous performances, Dustin Hoffman plays the childlike Raymond. He will not wear underwear unless it comes from K Mart. If he misses his daily TV installments of *People's Court* he flies into a tantrum. Rigid and emo-tionally dead, Raymond does, however, have a genius for numbers. Drop a box of toothpicks on the floor and he can tell you the exact number with one glance. With Raymond's mathematical computer of a mind, Charlie drags him to Las Vegas in a scheme to cheat the blackjack dealers—and in the process learns to love unselfishly the brother who can never love back. By the time he racks up $85,000, Charlie has fallen for Raymond. A court battle ensues over custody and I won't tell you who wins, but you'll find laughter and a few tears before the end.

This is a tender, funny look at brotherly love. Despite its sweep at the 1989 Oscars (Best Picture, Director, Actor, and Screenplay), it's not a big movie, but it has big feelings. Hoffman makes every complex facet of an autistic believable without ever exploiting Raymond's mental disorder and Cruise really grows up as an actor of substance playing a greedy, self-centered jerk who learns how to feel and share his life with a brother who may never be able to love him back in the same way. Both actors give their finest performances, and director Barry Levinson finds the perfect balance between comedy and pathos. *Rain*

Man is not just another Disease of the Month weeper. It's a touching trip into the unexpected, without a single pothole along the way.

RAINTREE COUNTY (1957)

★ ★ ★ Directed by Edward Dmytryk. Screenplay by Millard Kaufman, based on the novel by Ross Lockridge. Produced by David Lewis. *With Elizabeth Taylor, Montgomery Clift, Eva Marie Saint, Lee Marvin, Agnes Moorehead, Walter Abel, and Tom Drake.*

It's not quite *Gone With the Wind*, but this Civil War saga runs a close second. Montgomery Clift is the hero of this sprawling costume drama—a naive Indiana boy with big dreams, destroyed by Elizabeth Taylor, the voluptuous and totally insane antebellum bitch who orchestrates his downfall. Eva Marie Saint, Lee Marvin, Agnes Moorehead, Walter Abel, and Tom Drake head the supporting cast. There are big action sequences, war scenes, and lots of madness and suicide before it ends. The plantations of Natchez, Mississippi, play themselves in location footage even MGM could never duplicate on the Culver City backlot.

RAISING ARIZONA (1987)

★ ★ ★ Directed by Joel Coen. Screenplay by Joel and Ethan Coen. Produced by Ethan Coen. *With Nicolas Cage, Holly Hunter, Trey Wilson, John Goodman, William Forsythe, Sam McMurray, and Frances McDormand.*

Raising Arizona is a wacky, offbeat action comedy by Ethan and Joel Coen, two brothers who popped out of nowhere with the low-budget murder mystery *Blood Simple* and later turned out the gangster epic *Miller's Crossing*. This surprising departure focuses on Hy and Ed, who meet in the Arizona state prison. Hy (Nicolas Cage) is a no-good antisocial crook who is in and out of the slammer so much he finally marries Ed (Holly Hunter), the lady cop who fingerprints him. His lawless days behind him, Hy dreams of being a father but biology keeps him childless. Hy and Ed decide to use their criminal know-how to steal one of the quintuplets born to a used car tycoon named—you got it—Arizona. It's not Ozzie and Harriet. It's more like Bonnie and Clyde doing a Pampers commercial, as the new parents shop for baby in a getaway car. It's cockeyed fun, with an amazing cast of characters that includes two escaped cons who get their inside tips from a cellmate who was once under-secretary to Richard Nixon, and a grenade-throwing, Harley-riding, fire-spraying bounty hunter called the "wart hog from Hell." The good-natured tot who plays Baby Arizona is so jolly he seems perfectly content regardless of who his kidnappers are. Not everyone's cup of tequila, but a comic slant on crime that is fresh and irreverent.

RAMBO: FIRST BLOOD, PART II (1985)

½★ Directed by George P. Cosmatos. Screenplay by Sylvester Stallone and James Cameron. Story by Kevin Jarre, based on characters created by David Morrell. Produced by Buzz Feitshans. With Sylvester Stallone, Richard Crenna, Charles Napier, Steven Berkhoff, Julia Nickson, Martin Kove, and George Kee Cheung.

I have nothing personal against Sylvester Stallone. For all I know, he's a fun guy who helps old ladies across the street and mixes a neat frozen margarita. But on the screen, he's to acting what Liberace is to pumping iron.

I can't tell one of this guy's movies from the next. Whether it's *Rocky IV* or *Rambo: First Blood, Part II*, I get them all confused. In all of them, he

wears three expressions—sullen, sour, and stupefied—and undergoes excruciating difficulty trying to say any word with more than two syllables.

Rambo: First Blood, Part II extends the mindless slaughter and retching carnage of *First Blood* with equally unnerving results. It begins with an explosion so loud it shakes the floor and threatens to dislodge the kidneys. This is to get your attention.

The rest of the movie follows John Rambo, the persecuted Green Beret, from the prison where he's serving time for smashing up most of the Pacific Northwest, back to the prison camp in Vietnam from which he escaped in 1971.

Sprung by the military and dispatched to the jungle behind Communist lines, he's ordered to track down American soldiers missing in action, determine whether they are prisoners of war, and take photos.

"Don't try the blood-and-guts routine," warns commander Richard Crenna—"Let technology do the work."

This is like telling Milton Berle to just stand there—while another comic tells the jokes.

There might be a presidential pardon if he completes the mission in thirty-six hours. What follows lasts only ninety minutes, but seems more like thirty-six days.

Deserted by the military and left to the mercy of the Viet Cong, Rambo is interrogated, brainwashed, tortured with electricity, and condemned to die as an enemy spy. No matter what inhuman horror he endures, he always emerges in the next shot with fresh ammunition. Like the cowboys in old Saturday matinees, he never runs out of bullets.

For someone who's been in prison, he's in fantastic shape (some prisoners use the library, others use the gym).

Why is Rambo betrayed by the U.S. Army? According to the movie, the American government agreed at the end of the war to pay the Viet Cong $4.5 billion in war reparations. They never paid the debt. The Vietnamese kept the POWs. Now the Pentagon doesn't want them freed, because it might cause a scandal.

Driven by ethics and a determination to get his fellow prisoners home, Rambo goes berserk, fights deadly odds, battles hundreds of guerrillas under artillery fire with only a bow and arrow, treks through rock slides and snake-infested jungles, and flies all his comrades to safety in a burning plane.

The premise is completely loco, and the derring-do fills the screen with noise, smoke, violence, and gore galore. Through it all, Sylvester Stallone stalks bravely, avoiding contact with anything that might be interpreted as acting, and looking like he's double-Valiumed himself into a stupor.

The direction, by George P. Cosmatos, consists mainly of close-ups of Stallone flexing his biceps, Stallone loading his artillery, Stallone crawling through mud, Stallone leaping from exploding gunboats, Stallone staring at his own armpits. He's Superman with helicopters.

"I always believed the mind is the best weapon," says Stallone, delivering the film's most comic line. *Rambo: First Blood, Part II* is utterly without humor, but that doesn't mean it's not funny.

RANDOM HARVEST (1942)
★ ★ ★ ½ Directed by Mervyn LeRoy. Screenplay by Claudine West, George Froeschel, Arthur Wimperis, and James Hilton, based on Hilton's novel. Produced by Sidney Franklin. *With Ronald Colman, Greer Garson, Philip Dorn, Susan Peters, Henry Travers, Reginald Owen, Bramwell Fletcher, Margaret Wycherly, and Ann Richards.*

A distinguished soap opera from MGM's golden era about amnesia, unrequited love, and box-office gold, this classic weeper catapulted Greer Garson to stardom, and it's still good for a bucket of suds fifty years later. Sensitive performances by a sterling cast, sumptuous sets, and first-rate production values elevate this woman's picture to classic status. As a studious account of personal anguish and frustrated emotions, this beautifully photographed and impeccably acted idyll has a perfumed poignancy that is oddly overpowering, and Greer Garson's charm and loveliness have never been better captured. Some stars have that indefinable "something special" that makes a lover of the camera. Greer Garson was one of them.

THE RAZOR'S EDGE (1946)

★ ★ ★ ★ Directed by Edmund Goulding. Screenplay by Lamar Trotti. Produced by Darryl F. Zanuck. *With Tyrone Power, Gene Tierney, Anne Baxter, John Payne, Clifton Webb, Herbert Marshall, Lucille Watson, Frank Latimore, and Elsa Lanchester.*

Forget about the sappy Bill Murray remake. This is the 1946 Somerset Maugham original, with Tyrone Power, Gene Tierney, Anne Baxter, and Clifton Webb as the doomed Americans finding degradation, death, and spiritual salvation in Paris. An intelligent, distinguished American classic with hypnotic texture, it's Hemingway with throw pillows. It's also long and sometimes tedious. But Tyrone Power, as the World War I fighter pilot looking for peace and spiritual morality in Tibet and Paris, gives the film an earnestness that often transcends its high-mindedness. Gene Tierney is also fine as the vain, vicious snob who wrecks his life, and Anne Baxter won a Supporting Actress Oscar as the doomed American in Paris who dies from syphilis, absinthe, and a slashed throat. Pretty elegant stuff by forties Hollywood standards.

THE RED BADGE OF COURAGE (1951)

★ ★ ★ ★ Directed and adapted from Stephen Crane's novel by John Huston. *With Audie Murphy, Bill Mauldin, Douglas Dick, John Dierkes, Royal Dano, Arthur Hunnicutt and Andy Devine. Narrated by James Whitmore.*

Somber, compelling Civil War saga of a young soldier (Audie Murphy, who was himself a decorated World War II soldier at the time) who progresses from boy to man through the horrors of the battlefield. Brilliantly directed by John Huston.

RED HEAT (1988)
★ Directed by Walter Hill. Screenplay by Harry Kleiner, Hill, and Troy Kennedy Martin. Produced by Hill and Gordon Carroll. With Arnold Schwarzenegger, James Belushi, Peter Boyle, and Ed O'Ross.

Thinking up movies for Arnold Schwarzenegger is like marrying Zsa Zsa Gabor—it's dirty work but somebody's gotta do it. *Red Heat* is no better than any other action thriller requiring this graduate from the Nautilus School of Dramatic Art to speak complete sentences, but at least it invents a neat ploy to explain his weird accent. This time he's a big, dopey Soviet cop who treks from Moscow to Chicago to round up a Russian drug dealer. The mindless balance of the film is just another dum-dum cop-buddy flick by Walter Hill, who directed *48 Hours*. It fact, it *is 48 Hours*, with stoic Arnold in the weary, straight-faced Nick Nolte role and Jim Belushi replacing Eddie Murphy as his wisecracking sidekick, who calls the Commie juggernaut "Gumby."

They run around breaking rules and wrecking the Chicago transit system, to the kind of sound track where every sock on the jaw is accompanied by what sounds like a ten-ton sack of cement thrown from a twenty-story window. You get the rhythm? Joke. Bones crack. Joke. Blood spurts. Joke. Glass shatters. Joke. A lot of people get maimed, chopped, machine gunned, and blown away before the fat lady sings.

For two-fisted philosophy, the incredible hulk from Red Square says he cleans up the mess back home by simply lining up all the drug dealers and junkies and shooting them in the back of the head. Mr. Belushi says it wouldn't work in America—the politicians wouldn't go for it. Mr. Schwarzenegger makes a small wrinkle in the meadow between his eyes that passes for acting and says: "Shoot *them* first!" Come to think of it, I'll take Zsa Zsa.

REDS (1981)
★ ★ Directed and produced by Warren Beatty. Screenplay by Beatty and Trevor Griffiths. With Warren Beatty, Diane Keaton, Edward Herrmann, Jerzy Kosinski, Jack Nicholson, Maureen Stapleton, Paul Sorvino and Gene Hackman. Cameo appearances by George Jessel, Henry Miller, and Adela Rogers St. Johns.

This nearly four-hour political saga about Communist journalist John Reed and his neurotic wife Louise Bryant has been so meticulously directed by Warren Beatty that it contains too many rich and valuable cinematic elements to dismiss easily. Still, I would be dishonest if I did not admit it bored me senseless.

Beatty is a sometimes capable and intelligent filmmaker with a real intuition for graphic design, and *Reds* has the sweep and splendor of a real movie-movie. Unfortunately, it rambles on and on in a structural mess, trying to tell the story of the Communist Revolution while feebly trying to make you care about its noisy lovers. In the end, you won't know much more about the enigmatic John Reed than you did before.

Beatty obviously has an obsession with this man—the only American to be buried in the Kremlin, as though that fact was some kind of honor instead of a disgrace—but his failure to communicate or share that obsession with the audience is the film's final defeat.

The film begins when Reed visits Portland, Oregon, in 1915, and meets Louise Bryant, feminist writer, nude photography model, dentist's wife, and dilettante. She follows him to Greenwich Village, where she finds herself thrown into the company of radicals, intellectuals, Bohemians, poets, and rebels in the days of Margaret Sanger and Isadora Duncan, when the weirder you were the better copy you made.

Reed's journalistic travels took him away from her most of the time, leaving her alone in the clutches of men like Eugene O'Neill (Jack Nicholson). In Nicholson's performance, the brooding playwright emerges as a sullen, moody, hard-drinking romantic who seduces her easily. Later, when she gets involved in communism, too, there's a kind of Clark Gable–Carole Lombard rivalry as John and Louise travel to Russia to file stories.

Behind the Iron Curtain, we are plunged into more talk of Trotsky politics, Leninism, strikes, and Bolsheviks, the purpose of which is only to irritate and baffle the audience. They seem to be the only Americans covering the Revolution, although it is never clear what papers they're working for. All the while, they yell and fight like Don Ameche and Frances Langford doing a skit from *The Bickersons*. She's abrasive, he's weak, and I was worn out before the intermission.

Later, as a representative of the American Communist party, he gets sent to Russia, wounded, and imprisoned. She searches for him on tramp steamers, on skis, and on snowshoes. You get something of the revolutionaries' sacrifice—forced to leave your country, live in exile, poverty, and misery, and maybe even die for your beliefs whether the rest of the world cares or not.

But Emma Goldman, beautifully played by Maureen Stapleton, is really the only revolutionary in the film who ever realizes that dream was a dying ideal. In Russia, nothing worked, human rights were squashed, and everything was drowning in chaos and bureaucratic red tape. Goldman is the only character who reveals the foolishness of this calling when she articulates her frustration at being persecuted in Russia for the same things she was persecuted for back home. John Reed never does come to such a moment of truth and dies in a charity ward in filthy and depressing conditions.

The point is that a man is a hero as long as he dies for what he believes, even if nobody else does. But why should we remember him? He changed nothing, made no impact, and influenced no succeeding generations. If truth was told, he was probably something of a nut.

I respect Warren Beatty for following his dream, but what good does it do if you end up talking to yourself?

RETURN OF THE JEDI (1983)
★ ★ ★ Directed by Richard Marquand. Screenplay by Lawrence Kasdan and George Lucas. Produced by Howard Kazanjian. With Mark Hamill, Harrison Ford, Carrie Fisher, Alec Guinness, Billy Dee Williams, Anthony Daniels, and David Prowse.

Enough is enough. When the final frame clicks into view at the end of *Return of the Jedi* it is the signal that George Lucas' *Star Wars* trilogy has at last come to the end of the stardust trail.

I loved *Star Wars*, a triumph of hardware and technical effects that appealed to the wide-eyed child in all of us. Next came *The Empire Strikes Back*, which proved the whole idea was still entertaining but running out of steam. The third and last installment, *Return of the Jedi*, with a $32.5 million price tag ties up a lot of loose ends, shows off 942 special effects, introduces a few new scaly monsters and furry heroes in a variety of shapes and sizes, and manages to sign off respectably, if somewhat sentimentally. I am not a bit sorry to have lived through the whole trilogy, but I was not a bit sorry to see it all end.

When *Jedi* begins, Luke Skywalker (Mark Hamill) is on his way to rescue Han Solo (Harrison Ford) from the claws of Jabba the Hutt, the slobbering, gelatinous, toadlike creature who rules the intergalactic underworld.

Return of the Jedi is full of shocks. Luke discovers Darth Vader is really his father (something we've suspected all along) and, worse still, that Princess Leia (Carrie Fisher) is really his twin sister.

Luke has a good heart; throughout the trilogy the prediction has been that his compassion will be his undoing.

The big question here is: Now that he knows Darth Vader is his father, what will happen when they finally clash? Will Luke kill his own father and save the universe? Or will Vader turn him over to the powerful emperor?

Will Luke's anger and fear seduce him into joining the dark side of the force, the way his father surrendered years ago?

All in good time, my pets. But first there's a visit to the land of the Ewoks, a ferocious tribe of tree creatures that look like cuddly koala bears. There's a dizzy chase through giant redwoods on supersonic air scooters. And there's a lot of talk about code clearances and moonshield generators that must be de-activated before Solo's Milennium Falcon can invade Death Star. There is also an incredible amount of earsplattering noise.

In the final tally, the special effects are neither as daring nor as innovative as they once were. It is quite a letdown to reach the inside of the forbidden Death Star, only to discover that it looks like a giant Con Edison plant. The bombs and explosions seem all too familiar. The miracles and last-minute reprieves from mutilations and death seem cornier than ever.

Hamill finally gets an opportunity to do some acting—especially in the final scenes with his father, when he pleads for the saving of a lost soul—but Miss Fisher still mutters goofy dialogue like "I gotta getcha outta here," most unfitting for a princess.

None of the humans have been well photographed. Fisher looks old, haggard, and tough. Hamill looks pale and emaciated. Ford looks bloated and sick. All of them go through the motions without much brio. They seem to be in it at this point for the money.

Who can blame them? Let's hear it for avarice and greed, and the security money can bring. But let's not pretend we're watching art. Richard Marquand, who directed under George Lucas's instructions, is certainly not pretending. He's given *Return of the Jedi* all of the style of a Saturday kiddie matinee serial. And Yoda is not pretending either.

Yes, folks, Yoda finally throws in the towel—not with a whimper, but with what sounds more like an enormous belch. I was kind of sorry to see Yoda go, but let's face it, kids—the poor old piece of elephant hide had bad teeth and at the age of nine hundred, had earned the rest. So have we all.

THE RETURN OF THE SECAUCUS SEVEN (1980)

★ Directed and written by John Sayles. Produced by William Aydelott and Jeffrey Nelson. With Mark Arnott, Gordon Clapp, Maggie Cousineau-Arndt, Adam Lefevre, Bruce MacDonald, Hean Passanante, John Sayles, and Maggie Renzi.

This boring, amateurish home movie about a group of sixties dropouts who meet ten years later and whose only claim to fame is that they were once detained by cops in Secaucus, New Jersey, on their way to a protest march is a waste of time I would recommend only to the kind of person who still plays Janis Joplin records and cares what happened to Abbie Hoffman. A more thoroughly unattractive or depressing group of retarded thirty-year-olds you aren't likely to meet. The guys go skinny-dipping, talk about girls, and play basketball. The girls talk about tampons and play "Clue." When they all get together, they play (can you stand it?) charades!

The film goes nowhere because it hasn't been anywhere and isn't likely to, and although the nonactors mumble and whisper the authentic-sounding dialogue incoherently, the way real people talk when they're dull, the film has no style, no rhythm, no sense of time and place. It was written, directed, and edited by John Sayles for $60,000. The same amount of money would make a nice down payment on an art-circuit revival house dedicated to showing the works of real artists—a project I'd advise Mr. Sayles to tackle immediately. Maybe he'll learn how to make a real movie. One misguided critic, an obvious sixties clone, compared the director to Billy Wilder. Wherever he is, the grand old man who gave us some real classics should come out fighting. (Sayles has made several equally low-budget films like *Lianna* and *City of Hope* since 1980, but has yet to impress me.)

REUNION IN FRANCE (1942)

★ ★ ½ Directed by Jules Dassin. Screenplay by Jan Lustig, Marc Connolly and Marvin Borowski. *With John Wayne, Joan Crawford, Philip Dorn, Reginald Owen, John Carradine, Henry Daniell, Moroni Olsen, Ann Ayars, Howard da Silva, and Albert Basserman.*

Reunion in France stars John Wayne as an American pilot hiding from Nazis in occupied Paris and saved by sultry fashion model Joan Crawford. One scene has two-fisted Duke punching out a German officer and saying, "See ya around, Bub."

REVERSAL OF FORTUNE (1990)

★ ★ ★ Directed by Barbet Schroeder. Screenplay by Nicholas Kazan. Produced by Alan M. Dershowitz. *With Jeremy Irons, Glenn Close, Ron Silver, and Uta Hagen.*

Reversal of Fortune, Barbet Schroeder's film about the sensationally sleazy conviction of Claus Von Bulow for the at-

tempted murder of his wife, Sunny, and his acquittal of the crime in a 1985 retrial, has the earmarks of a TV movie, but it is a great deal better. This time the director keeps the audience guessing. Did he inject his wife with a lethal dose of insulin, or didn't he? Was he a charming scoundrel or a venal monster? No one connected with the movie wanted to meet the real man for fear of obfuscating the creative process, but from the records and court testimony and from Von Bulow's own flamboyant, quirky behavior in and out of print during and after the trial, Schroeder and Jeremy Irons, who won an Oscar playing him, have created a riveting character, sinister and funny, who enjoys keeping alive the possibility of his guilt. Even at the close, you still aren't sure. There's a chilling moment when the end credits begin to roll showing Von Bulow in a London pharmacy where the shop girl recognizes him from the tabloid front pages. Her mouth falls open. He raises his eyebrow, obviously enjoying the notoriety and dubious celebrity of an acquitted killer. She asks if there will be anything else. "Yes," he says, "a container of insulin," adding ruefully, "Only kidding." It's that mixture of perversity and ambiguity that keeps the movie throbbing at a pace more exciting and unbelievable than the headlines.

In the opening shots, a plane sweeps slowly over the elegant mansions of the super-rich, gliding into the luxury of New Yorkers who sip and simmer away their lives in Newport and the Hamptons. From this peaceful perspective, Schroeder establishes, then invades, the cloistered, drug-clouded world of Sunny Von Bulow, who now lies brain-dead in an elegant hospital suite where she is bathed, powdered, made up, and coiffed daily, like a corpse being prepared by a cosmetologist for an open-casket viewing at Frank E. Campbell's. Played by Glenn Close with glazed perfection, Sunny astonishingly tells the story herself, in a narration from deep inside her coma.

The story is an amazing one. Hailed as one of the city's most dazzling couples, the Von Bulows' marriage was a comfortable arrangement, where he never criticized her pills and booze, and she tolerated his extramarital calisthenics. Life was spectacularly abundant for the morbid Dane until the day he asked for a divorce. The delicate balance that kept it together was gone, and their lives

spun out of control, while the children and staff looked on helplessly (fine work here by Uta Hagen, as Sunny's devoted maid). The house filled with paranoia, overdoses, and madness as Von Bulow's stepchildren Alex and Ala charged him with attempted murder, the tabloids went berserk, and Alan Dershowitz and his team of hotshot Harvard law students changed the course of legal history.

Ron Silver, as the passionate, aggressive Dershowitz, is a fine counterpart to the arrogant, bizarre Von Bulow—played by Irons in a haunted way that looks (and sounds) exactly like Boris Karloff. When they first meet, Dershowitz tells him "Everybody hates you" and Von Bulow retorts, without a beat, "Well, that's a start." America believed him guilty. Dershowitz's own students thought Von Bulow guilty. But this was the challenge—how to use the law to reverse a guilty verdict even if you don't trust your client. There's no question that Claus was a sick sister (he lived with his dead mother's body for five years before her death was reported, and any man who poses in leather and chains for Helmut Newton's photos in *Vanity Fair* at the height of his own infamy cannot be cooking on all four burners). He's even a bit of a card. "What's a fear of insulin called?" he quips. "Claus-tro-phobia."

Sunny, in her moments of lucidity, is funny, too. "First you marry me for my money," she screams, "then you want to go to work! You're the prince of perversion!" Fine acting, elegant sets, and a quicksilver script add up to a terrific movie that makes you feel like you're peeking through the keyhole at one of the strangest and most macabre scandals of the century. "When you're where I am," says Sunny from her living death coma, "you'll know what happened." I don't think I want to find out, but meanwhile, the unfinished story is a lot of fascinating fun to talk about, and one helluva movie.

REVOLUTION (1985)
No ★s Directed by Hugh Hudson. Screenplay by Robert Dillon. Produced by Irwin Winkler. With Al Pacino, Donald Sutherland, Joan Plowright, and Nastasia Kinski.

They saved the worst for last. *Revolution* was the last film to open in 1985; it was also the worst.

It is allegedly about the American Revolution, but except for one distant shot of General Cornwallis surrendering to George Washington, there is nothing in it remotely recognizable to anyone who knows anything about American history, and although I wasn't there in 1776, I doubt it took half as long to fight the War of Independence as it takes to sit through this movie.

Al Pacino, looking like Che Guevara and talking like something out of *The Godfather*, plays a fur trapper with a fourteen-year-old son. When they pull their boat into a Brooklyn harbor that looks like the QE2 dock at Southampton, a mob of patriots crying "Liberty or death!" and "No more king!" confiscates the boat, while the British Redcoats draft the kid into the army as a drummer boy.

When Donald Sutherland, as a sadistic torturer, straps the boy to a cannon and whips his bare feet into strips of rare sirloin, it's Pacino to the rescue. The rest of this eight-year saga equates the American Revolution with any modern insurrection in which agitators use liberty and justice as convenient excuses for rioting and looting. The result is cinematic chaos.

Revolution makes a half-hearted attempt to explore the courage of the revolutionaries, the sacrifices made by children who shed their blood "fighting tyranny,'' and the postwar disillusionment among the survivors who discovered they'd paid a high price for freedom when their land and money was confiscated by Congress to pay off the war debt.

The point of the movie, if there is one, seems to be that war is hell and the more things change the more they stay the same. Shades of Cuba, Russia, and Nicaragua here, in rather muddled doses.

No wonder *Revolution* was made by a British director. Even the most naive student of junior high American history would have laughed the script out of town before the recess bell.

But I expected more out of Hugh Hudson. He rose to international prominence with *Chariots of Fire*. His second film, *Greystoke: Legend of Tarzan*, wasn't very good, but it was no disgrace, either. *Revolution* is so idiotic it makes me wonder if it wasn't chewed to bits in the editing lab by a gang of mice (or studio executives, which is often the same thing, only worse). Kids staging a Fourth of July pageant couldn't come up with anything this hilariously bad.

You get scenes of how confused, unskilled, and unprepared the Yankees were. You

get the pomp, arrogance, and cruelty of the British, advancing with muskets and spears while scattering women and children in bloody profusion like rag dolls. You get a mock fox hunt with an effigy of George Washington as hound bait. You get cockfights. You get the Hudson River Valley, which looks like leftover jungle sets from *Greystoke*. You get Huron Indians who talk like Harlem pimps.

And you get the notoriously inept Nastasia Kinski, as a rebellious daughter of British Royalists who shows up in all the trouble spots and battle scenes like Madame LaFarge, cooing and gurgling and winking at the camera with bee-stung lips like a white-wigged Barbie doll. And you get Al Pacino, mumbling and scratching, with a Scottish accent that sounds like street-punk gibberish from the South Bronx.

What you don't get is a sense of cohesion, strategy, or historic chronology. The British locations don't resemble anything in America. How can you show a winter at Valley Forge without a single shot of Washington? How can you even mention the American Revolution without showing Washington crossing the Delaware? Where are Paul Revere and Betsy Ross? What happened to the Liberty Bell? For all the sense it makes, *Revolution* could be a movie about Napoleon at Waterloo.

As mind-boggling as it seems, there has never been one satisfying or successful motion picture about the most dramatic war in the history of America. *Revolution* not only fails to remedy that oversight, it sets back the cause two hundred years.

THE RIGHT STUFF (1983)

★ ★ ½ Directed by Philip Kaufman. Screenplay by Kaufman. Produced by Irwin Winkler. *With Sam Shepard, Ed Harris, Fred Ward, Dennis Quaid, Scott Glenn, Barbara Hershey, Mary Jo Deschanel, Pamela Reed, Charles Frank, and Kim Stanley.*

The Right Stuff is a three-hour twenty-minute history lesson about America's space program. It is expensive, exasperating, exhausting, exhilarating, overblown, overproduced, sometimes excruciatingly stuffy, often exciting, and always cinematic. It is entirely too long (what it needs more than anything else is a pair of scissors) and so filled with portentous sound effects, arty camera angles, and holy reverence that it might just as easily be a movie about the Dead Sea Scrolls.

Writer-director Philip (*Invasion of the Body Snatchers The Unbearable Lightness of Being*) Kaufman has always made messy movies. This one is no exception. How could it be otherwise? From beginning to end, it bites off more than it is possible to digest and still leaves something on the banquet table for the rest of us to gnaw on. It tries to tell all seven stories of all seven astronauts in the original Mercury space program, starting even before their involvement—back in 1947, to be exact, when Chuck Yeager became the first man to break the sound barrier in the X-1 rocket aircraft. In the thirty-odd years that comprise the rest of the movie, Kaufman cuts back and forth, from the astronauts who became celebrity heroes, to Yeager (played with wild stoicism by poker-faced Sam Shepard), who kept breaking new speed records without fanfare. The point of the movie seems to be that test pilots like Yeager, who did the dangerous dirty work without fame and adulation, are the real heroes with the real "right stuff," and the astronauts were merely doing the same thing any monkey could do. This thesis does not work because the astronauts are so much more lively and inter-esting than the sour, petulant Yeager that you don't care any-way.

The rhythm is inconsistent. The Yeager scenes strive for a sagebrush grandeur right out of *Duel in the Sun* (and come off just as awesomely pretentious) —with Sam Shepard swapping Madison Avenue double talk with his neurotic wife (Barbara Hershey) before riding off into the strawberry sunset, whip-ping his cowboy hat like Slim Pickens riding the bomb in *Dr. Strangelove*. By contrast, the scenes with the astronauts are plucky, comic, vaudevillian. Despite all the God-Mom-and-apple-pie they were supposed to represent, the film shows them as hell-raising heavy drinkers with an eye for the girls, and there's even a group masturba-tion scene that ought to take the wind out of Jerry Falwell's sails.

For domestic drama, there's an extraordinary file of infor-mation: Alan Shepard had to urinate in his space suit, and Gus Grissom's wife came un-hinged when, following Gris-som's capsule malfunction on his solo launch, he was given the short end of the stick and she did not get to meet Jackie Kennedy as planned. And for irreverent political sass, we get a picture of Lyndon B. Johnson that is not far removed from an orangutan wearing a Stetson.

The movie drones on— sometimes soaring, sometimes wafting—through the race with Russia, the embarrassment over Sputnik, the physical fitness regimens and punishing endur-ance tests, the construction of NASA's new space center in Houston, the ticker tape pa-rades, the new speed records, and John Glenn's triumphal earth orbit. All of this docu-mentation forms a collage of fuel gauges, goggles and cloud reefs that borders on mysticism. Every now and then, Kaufman introduces another human ele-ment to remind us it's people we're watching, not gods—but *The Right Stuff* is so fragmented that no scene gets enough de-velopment time to give you much of a grip on anything.

Having voiced these reserva-tions, however, it must be added that the high-mindedness is relieved by a fine set of hon-est, closely nurtured and elec-trically charged performances. I especially liked Dennis Quaid as the cocky, mischievous Gor-don Cooper, whose standard flip answer to "Who is the best?" was always "You're lookin' at him!" And Scott Glenn, as the mysterious, al-most smarmy-looking Alan

Shepard. The women are good, as far as functional roles go, but the presence of the great Kim Stanley is rather mystifying, to say the least. Ravaged beyond recognition (Is it makeup? Or life?) she plays a foul-mouthed, flea-bitten former Pasadena socialite named Pancho, who divorced her husband to run guns to Central America before becoming a movie stunt pilot and owner of the desert roadhouse where the test pilots hang out. Stanley appears in the early scenes, then disappears. In retrospect, she seems a gnarled apparition, rising in flames like the Phoenix.

Most of all, I think, I liked Ed Harris, whose grinning, self-righteous portrait of John Glenn comes off slightly dopey and terrifyingly accurate. He's a runty, muscular little tumbleweed of an actor who resembles a rodeo champ trying to tackle Bloomingdale's. He doesn't turn John Glenn into a widescreen saint, but instead gives you some indication that beneath that plastic Bible-thumping yahoo, there might be a bull ready to bust loose and gore somebody.

THE RIVER (1984)

★ ★ ★ 1/2 Directed by Mark Rydell. Screenplay by Robert Dillon and Julian Barry. Produced by Edward Lewis and Robert Cortes. *With Sissy Spacek, Mel Gibson, and Scott Glenn.*

The River begins with a drop of water falling on a lily pad where a boy is fishing. As the rain continues, it builds to a torrential downpour. Livestock are soaked, wooden shingles stretched. The river, swollen and bursting, overflows into a massive flood as farms, machinery, and cattle are drowned and crushed by falling trees. We know we are in for one of those serious films in which art imitates life. *The River* has more than its share of both.

Mark Rydell (*On Golden Pond, For the Boys*) has described *The River* as the most physically demanding film he's ever made. There are two gigantic flood sequences, scenes at steel mills and auctions requiring the services of hundreds of extras—plus sequences involving children, animals, mud, and storms. This is as it should be, for *The River* is very much a film about human endurance in the face of all sorts of detrimental elements, natural and otherwise.

Like *Places in the Heart* and

Country, it is about the grit and determination of small farmers trying to hold on to their land at a time when most American farms are being replaced by massive agricultural combines and business monopolies.

But it goes farther than those films to show the rape of the American heartland, and to share the dehumanization that is being experienced not only by farmers but by all laborers.

If there is a central political theme in *The River* it's the death of American individualism in a time of economic recession. Like the characters Jessica Lange and Sam Shepard played in *Country*, Tom and Mae Garvey (Mel Gibson and Sissy Spacek) are a young couple who have worked the soil all their lives. It's all they know.

Hard times have driven them to the brink of ruin. Their prime acreage is a target for greedy developers from the local feed and grain company, who want to buy up the farmland, build a hydroelectric dam, and flood the Garveys' cornfields. Scott Glenn, marvelously evil as the man who sets the grain prices and cheats the farmers, has an extra grudge against Tom, since he has always been in love with Mae himself. (Herein, a roman-

tic triangle for a subplot, adding more spice.)

Tom refuses to sell out, but he can't meet operating expenses without a loan and he owes the bank too much already. There's a tearful farm auction and liquidation sale, like the one in *Country* where everything from John Deere tractors to blackberry jam is surrendered in desperation. It barely keeps them going. When the Garveys' favorite cow is dying, they can't even call the vet because they owe him so much money already.

Tom is reduced through economic necessity and personal crisis to become a scab, stealing the jobs of union mill workers on strike, while Mae becomes mother *and* father to her children, running the heavy equipment to keep the farm going.

There are two horrifying scenes I will never forget that are perfect examples of how *The River* rises, through artistic vision and freshness, above its competitors.

Mae, her arm mangled and pinned beneath a tractor, is forced to anger a bull in a nearby cornfield into ramming the machinery hard enough with its horns to free her before she bleeds to death.

Meanwhile, in the strike-bound mill, where the scabs are starving to death in conditions that are inhumane, a frightened deer wanders into the furnaces. The men go wild, chasing the poor creature through smoke and hissing sparks, envisioning a barbecue. Cornered, the deer freezes. The men close in, stand in silence, and stare into the animal's eyes. In that terrifying moment of suspense, they realize how close they've come to being animals themselves.

The River is a shattering emotional experience that demonstrates how hard life has become for the little people. A woman's youth and femininity wear out early, and a man's pride is shredded daily.

But in the face of nature's ravages, grinding poverty and heartrending separation, the Garveys are a tribute to the courage and affirmative spirit that give Americans a special resilience.

Mark Rydell has brilliantly directed not only the big, turbulent scenes but the small, intimate personal interactions among people as well, bringing a wrenching universal catharsis to every frame.

Mel Gibson proves he's not just another pretty face. This guy is in the Gary Cooper tradition—vulnerable, strong, full of integrity and charisma. And Sissy Spacek becomes a mature, sexy woman for the first time. She's always been honest and real as breathing, but *The River* gives her a weathered patina, like a still-young girl aged by sacrifice and hard work. She is breathtakingly vital and alive.

From the helicopter shots of flooded land and stampeding cattle to the shadowy embrace of two grimy lovers in a seedy mill-town hotel silhouetted by a neon sign outside the window, *The River* has been photographed by the great Vilmos Zsigmond with artistry and beauty.

From that first raindrop to the final flood, the camera tells you everything you will ever need to know about these remarkable people and their fight for survival.

This is a great film, full of passion and decency, about real people whose love of the land is all but extinct. In a time of smashed hopes and trashed values, *The River* is something of a blessing.

ROAD TO RIO (1947)
★ ★ ★ Directed by Norman Z. McLeod. Screenplay by Edmund Beloin and Jack Rose. Songs by Johnny Burke and Jimmy Van

Heusen. Produced by Daniel Dare.
With Bing Crosby, Bob Hope,
Dorothy Lamour, Gale
Sondergaard, and Frank Faylen.

Bing Crosby, Bob Hope, and
perennial girlfriend Dorothy
Lamour in one of the merriest
"Road" pictures in the series.
Great songs, great sarongs, and
great gags make this one irresistible. This is what Warren
Beatty and Dustin Hoffman
tried to copy in *Ishtar* for fifty
times the budget and not one
fraction of the success. See
Bing and Bob do their stuff and
you'll see why nobody can ever
duplicate an original. In this
crazy quilt, the king-sized Sinatra and Ol' Ski Nose journey
to Brazil to rescue Dottie from
marrying a villainous swindler.
Bob does a high-wire bicycle
act that wrecks a carnival and
blows musical bubbles out of a
trumpet in a Rio nightclub with
the Andrew Sisters. Mayhem,
but the corn still pops.

ROBIN HOOD (1991)
★ ★ ½ Directed by Kevin
Reynolds. Screenplay by Pen
Densham and John Watson.
Produced by John Watson, Pen
Densham, and Richard B. Lewis.
With Kevin Costner, Mary Elizabeth
Mastrantonio, Morgan Freeman,
Christian Slater, and Alan
Rickman.

If there's one thing we probably don't need, it's another
movie about Robin Hood.
Kevin Costner doesn't agree.
So, in a ticker tape blizzard of
old-fashioned hoopla, his $45
million *Robin Hood* arrived on
the screen in 1991—a long, violent, colorful spree of epic
proportions and a rowdy, roaring, randy romp with something for everyone in the
audience (except maybe the
most discerning critics). Mr.
Costner doesn't have the stature
of Errol Flynn, but clumping
about in his chain mail and knee
boots, weighted down with
bows and arrows and rolling
around in the mossy glens of
Sherwood Forest like a Boy
Scout on vacation, he does
manage to be both brawny and
funny. Wrestling with plot maneuvers that include generation-
gap homilies, racial discrimina-
tion, sibling rivalry, and twelfth-
century women's lib, he just
might be the perfect "prince of
thieves" for the 1990s.

In this version, the legend begins in Jerusalem, where the
English nobleman who fought
in the Crusades escapes from a
dungeon and returns to the white
cliffs of Dover with a Moorish
sidekick named Azeem (Morgan
Freeman) to find his beloved
King Richard out of town, his

father murdered, his country in chaos, his land plundered, and his castle burned by the evil, ruthless Sheriff of Nottingham (Alan Rickman, giving his hammiest slanty-eyed, hissing scumbag performance to date). In an England that seems to be populated by goatherds and trolls, Robin finds comfort in the arms of a feisty tomboy, Maid Marian (Mary Elizabeth Mastrantonio) and companionship in the scruffy outlaws of Sherwood Forest who help him rob the rich and feed the poor. There's much bashing, slashing, and bleeding to be done before the good king returns from holiday, while director Kevin Reynolds does more than his predecessors to catalogue the intricacies of medieval life under duress. You'll learn more about how to find food, shelter, and the raw materials for archery in a natural environment than you ever wanted to know, which leaves little time for romance. This is an updated swashbuckler, as I told you, so there is a nude scene for Costner fans (he's getting a bit long in the tush) and nothing brings two people together like performing the first cesarian birth in the annals of surgery with a crude needle and thread.

For action, the fiery assault on Robin's camp is great stuff,

well filmed and choreographed. And for comedy, there's prissymouthed Mr. Rickman, no Basil Rathbone but pretty hilarious anyway, hissing like a radiator at his tax-poor serfs: "No more kitchen scraps, no more merciful beheadings—and cancel Christmas!" With lines like "Shut up, you twit!" it's never certain whether you're supposed to take any of this corn seriously, and the acting is half Shakespeare, half screwball. Since Mr. Costner, Mr. Freeman, and Christian Slater, as Robin's half-brother and would-be traitor Will Scarlett, don't bother to compete with all of the English actors in the cast, it's baffling to hear Ms. Mastrantonio struggle vainly with a muddled British accent which often renders her incoherent. As for the star, Mr. Costner makes a benign centerpiece. His Robin Hood is a cross between Batman and Gene Kelly's D'Artagnan. Depositing him in the middle of such noble company is rather like dropping Gary Cooper into the middle of the Old Vic in spurs.

ROCKY II (1979)

★ ★ ★ Directed and written by Sylvester Stallone. Produced by Irwin Winkler and Robert Chartoff. *With Sylvester Stallone, Talia Shire,*

Burgess Meredith, Carl Weathers, Burt Young, and Tony Burton.

Rocky II is better than *Rocky* because the boring character exposition has already been worked out and now we can sit back and enjoy the fully developed participants as old friends.

Both films end with fight sequences that reduce Rocky to bloody hamburger, but somewhere in-between he grew from a moron into a responsible husband, father and grownup and the reasons we want him to succeed seem manifold.

In *Rocky II*, the 200-pound Italian tractor marries the mouse from the pet shop, moves her from the Philadelphia slums into a neat new middle-class house in a respectable neighborhood, and settles down to become a regular guy. Alas, he has neither the education nor the experience to hold down an office job and even working in a meat-packing plant ends in unemployment.

Meanwhile the black champ Apollo Creed is having his own problems handling his hate mail from Rocky fans who insist he won the title at the end of *Rocky* through sheer luck and technicality.

Rocky gets smeared in a campaign to bring him back into the ring that labels him "The Italian Chicken," Talia Shire stops disapproving long enough to go into a coma after the premature birth of a new baby called "Rocky Jr.," everyone learns to pray, and when she recovers long enough to say "please win" the fans go wild.

Rocky is the eternal underdog. He fights because it's the only thing he knows how to do and Stallone keeps playing him because it's the only role he seems capable of playing. After five movies, Stallone still needs subtitles, but maybe I'm getting used to his acting style (he talks as though he's got four infected wisdom teeth) because I'm learning to decipher his mumbling.

Stallone's direction is solid, except for a few unnecessary slow-motion cliches, and the disco music by Bill Conti is inserted in just the right places to accent the mounting tension. Burgess Meredith is brilliant as the battered old pug who rants and pushes and insults Rocky until he gets those gloves on for the big re-match.

The other actors give the same performance they gave the first time around. The movie wallows in corn, to be sure, but it is so slickly assembled and edited and scored that it ends up winning new fans.

I don't think I care to see Rocky turn into the Andy Hardy

of the series flicks, but *Rocky II* is a sequel that soars.

ROCKY IV (1985)

★ ★ ½ Directed and Screenplay by Sylvester Stallone. Produced by Irwin Winkler and Robert Chartoff. *With Sylvester Stallone, Talia Shire, Burt Young, Carl Weathers, Brigitte Nielsen, Dolph Lungren, and James Brown.*

Among the very few things in life you can truly count on, it is comforting to know that winter turns to spring, taxes must be paid, and Rocky always wins. Knowing that going in, you may now proceed to *Rocky IV*, the latest installment in the life of America's punchiest and most popular pugilist.

After being bludgeoned by Mr. T., it's a miracle that Rocky Balboa can get through the streets of Philadelphia without a wheelchair. But, a right hook pays off. Rocky now has a magnificent mansion, sports cars, a happy nine-year marriage, a great son, and a fresh, contemporary haircut to go with his designer wardrobe. I know it's hard to swallow, but Rocky has turned into a class act.

Not to worry. Champs never rest. Along comes a 260-pound undefeated amateur heavyweight champion from the Soviet Union called the "Siberian Express" to shake Rocky out of the magnolias.

First, there's an exhibition match at the MGM Grand Hotel in Las Vegas between the Russian, Ivan Drago, and Rocky's best friend, fellow boxer Apollo Creed. The match begins as a joke, with sets, costumes and chorus girls. Hell, there's even a splashy rock and roll production number by James Brown. But the Russian bulldozer isn't laughing. Tragedy results when Drago kills Apollo Creed in the ring. Now it's up to good-hearted, loyal Rocky to avenge his buddy's murder by taking on the human jackhammer himself—in Moscow, on Christmas Day!

There's so little left to say about Rocky that Sylvester Stallone, who serves as star, writer, and director, has even resorted to padding Rocky with film clips from the three previous Rocky movies. The film is mercifully only 90 minutes long, but it isn't until the final half-hour that we get to the big fight.

The Russian is taller, bigger, heavier, and stronger. The entire country is cheering for his success. Poor Rocky is all alone, with his prayers and integrity. Who wouldn't root for the underdog?

Before the end of the first

round, we know Stallone has taken us with the smoothness of a professional con artist. He's not only written in a comparison between the championship match and the story of David and Goliath, but he's made it obvious that the fight symbolizes the whole political future of Russia vs. the free world. When Rocky takes on the Russian tank, it's hero vs. villain, man vs. robot, American patriotism vs. Communist tyranny. I almost gagged from the shameless sentimentality of it all.

Still, in fairness, I cannot help but like the old Rocky. I like Stallone in the role, too. It's the one character he knows and plays better than any other. I like the way he even pokes fun at his own shortcomings.

Rocky IV is manipulative, it holds no surprises and reveals nothing new, but a legion of Rocky fans grew up with the big lug, and it's now quite pleasant to grow old with him, too.

ROMANCE ON THE HIGH SEAS (1948)

★ ★ ★   **Directed by Michael Curtiz. Screenplay by Julius and Philip Epstein, and I. A. L. Diamond. Produced by Alex Gottlieb. With Doris Day, Jack Carson, Janis Paige, Don Defore, Oscar Levant, and S. Z. Sakall.**

Doris Day's very first film was a smash hit that rocketed the blond band singer from Cincinnati to international stardom and launched one of the most popular movie careers of the century. She is fresh, dewy-eyed, completely natural, and sings like an angel in it—all without a single acting lesson. Fresh from her first hit recording of "Sentimental Journey" with the Les Brown band, Dodo (as she was called in those days) found herself replacing an ailing Betty Hutton in this splashy, first-class Warner musical despite the original misgivings of Michael Curtiz, the legendary director who specialized in moody, nocturnal melodramas like *Casablanca* and *Mildred Pierce*. The gamble paid off. Doris was a sensation as a gum-chewing saloon singer without a dime who gets hired by a wealthy socialite (Janis Paige) to take her place on an ocean cruise to Rio so she can stay home in New York and spy on her cheating husband (Don Defore). Doris doesn't know it, but the husband has hired a detective (Jack Carson) to spy on *her* aboard the ship, and when the phony heiress and the bewildered gumshoe fall for each other, a hilarious mistaken-identity farce ensues, aided by a stellar cast of character actors, including Oscar Levant, S. Z. Sakall, Eric Blore, and Franklin Pangborn. Busby Berkeley staged the Rio carnival sequences, and the starry songs by Sammy Cahn and Jule Styne include the king-sized hit "It's Magic." The three-strip Technicolor is spectacular, and so is Doris.

ROMANCING THE STONE (1984)

★ ½ Directed by Robert Zemeckis. Screenplay by Diane Thomas. Produced by Michael Douglas. With Michael Douglas, Kathleen Turner, Danny Devito, Alfonso Arau, and Manuel Ojeda.

When a boat goes aground without a rudder, it's called a shipwreck. When a movie sinks without an idea, it's called *Romancing the Stone*.

This dumb comic-book adventure has no comedy, and I've had more harrowing adventures on the subway. It is awful.

Kathleen Turner, the sweaty sexpot from *Body Heat*, plays a writer of trashy best-selling romance novels. When her sister gets kidnapped in Cartegena, Colombia, the poor girl flies to South America to rescue her. Lost in the jungle when her bus is hijacked, she ends up hiking through banana trees with a parrot collector (Michael Douglas) named Jack T. Colton ("The *T* stands for Trustworthy").

For the first hour of this interminable bore, they glide down mud slides, fly across rapids on Tarzan vines, and dodge machine gun bullets while she hangs on for dear life to a crude map mailed to her in Manhattan by her murdered brother-in-law. It takes the rest of the movie to unravel the mystery of just what this is all about (something about a giant green emerald the size of a milk bottle) and even then it doesn't seem worth the effort.

Margot Kidder and Robert Hays hacked their way through the same threadbare plot in *Trenchcoat* with the same results: tedium. Poisonous snakes and guerrilla warfare are a far cry from the fragrance counter at Bloomingdale's, but you can just get so much mileage out of the old innocents abroad routine. And when you finally get to the emerald, buried inside a ceramic rabbit that looks like a myopic door prize at a Tupperware party, you're most likely going to wish you'd stayed in bed with a good book.

Diane Thomas's script hangs on the barest thread of a plot, no stronger or more durable than the spit of a spider, and there isn't a shred of wit in the direction by Robert Zemeckis. Michael Douglas, who also produced *Romancing the Stone*, looks greasy-haired, seedy, and ravaged beyond belief. Kathleen Turner is still quite a looker, even though she spends a dismayingly inordinate amount of time in the movie looking like she's just been released from an intensive care unit after being hit by a Madison Avenue bus.

A ROOM WITH A VIEW (1986)
★ ★ Directed by James Ivory. Screenplay by Ruth Prawer Jhabvala. Produced by Ishmail Merchant. With Helena Bonham-Carter, Maggie Smith, Denholm Elliott, Julian Sands, Daniel Day Lewis, Simon Callow, Judi Dench, and Rosemary Leach.

Before *Maurice*, *Mr. and Mrs. Bridge* and *Howard's End*, I considered director James Ivory, producer Ishmail Merchant and screenwriter Ruth Prawer Jhabvala a lumbersome trio who turned out one pretentious literary film after another regardless of how few people showed up at the box office.

They kept film festivals in business, fed the needs of pretentious critics who missed their calling as library custodians, and miraculously found financing where genuine cinematic geniuses light years ahead of them in talent and creative artistry were left to go begging for funds. It was all a major mystery to me. And yet the Ivory-Merchant-Jhabvala trio turned them out like procreating rabbits. I have since come to admire their more recent work, but I still don't care much for *A Room With a View*.

Prodded no doubt by the success of *A Passage to India*, they herein dusted off another work of E. M. Forster. *A Room With a View*, based on Forster's third book—by his own admission, one of his least successful works—dates back to 1908 and concerns a visit to Florence by an impressionable, proper, and rather dopey young woman named Lucy Honeychurch (Helena Bonham-Carter), who is in the charge of her stuffy, ridiculous old maiden aunt, Miss Charlotte Bartlett (Maggie Smith).

The ladies are chagrined to discover their room at the Pensione Bertolini has no view from the window. This admission over dinner prompts an act of chivalry from Emerson (Denholm Elliott), a particularly obnoxious tourist, and his son George (Julian Sands), a quiet, depressed young man with no singularity of personality.

What emerges are the manners and mores of people so stuffy and constipated that the mere idea of a man in his bath is profoundly unsettling. Lucy and her aunt exchange rooms, blushing profusely, and the rest of the visit to Florence is spent wandering among the frescoes and cathedrals but absorbing none of the city's grandeur—imposing instead a stupid vulgarity of their own.

Back in England, Lucy becomes engaged to a prissymouth jerk called Cecil Vyse (beautifully played by Daniel Day Lewis). At the garden party for their engagement, everyone talks of train schedules. The film moves to Surrey, where a series of *tableaux vivants* occur with little relevance. Cecil meets the Emersons in the National Gallery and brings them to the country, where they rent his cottage. Cecil wanders about with his spectacles on his nose, his patronizing pomposity lost in a book, while George proceeds to woo Lucy, to everyone's horror.

I spent a great deal of time looking at my watch and mentally tabulating the daily budget. The best part of the film takes place in the early scenes in Florence, where Ivory shows the hypocrisy of snobettes from a cold, miserable climate invading a warm, sensual climate to find new liberating experiences, where instead of extracting Latin flavors in Italy, they impose their own narrowminded sensibilities and Victorian morality, learning nothing.

The rest of the film disintegrates into a maze of babble at a long-winded tea party. None of the guests can remember who invited them or what they're doing there.

Like most early James Ivory films, *A Room With a View* is ponderous, beautiful to look at, and maddeningly inconsequential. This , I admit, is a minority opinion, but one which still holds.

THE ROSE (1979)
★★★ Directed by Mark Rydell. Screenplay by Bill Kerby and Bo Goldman. Produced by Martin Worth and Aaron Russo. *With Bette Midler, Alan Bates, Frederic Forrest, Harry Dean Stanton, Barry Primus, and David Keith.*

The Rose, Bette Midler's film debut, is not all that much to shout about as a movie, but Bette's blazing performance saves it from mediocrity, gives it pulse and glamour and heart. Thanks to the "divine Miss M," *The Rose* becomes everything Streisand's pea-brained remake of *A Star Is Born* tried to be but never was.

The story of a rock star's rise to fame and eventual self-destruction through rotgut whiskey and dirty hypodermic needles is nothing new, but Bette attacks the role of an ugly duckling from a backwoods hick town in Florida who glitters brightly in the acid-drenched galaxy of amplified noise and charges it with personal magnetism that sets the screen on fire.

Beyond exhaustion, desperately in need of some kind of escape from the vultures who make the money and refuse her even a vacation, shoving her—bone-tired and near starvation—into helicopters without any time to change from her sweat-soaked funky glitter to meet more mobs of cretinous fans elsewhere, Bette embraces and embodies every dreary, empty dream.

It is painful to watch her frail Petunia Pig body weave and twitch when they jam syringes of vitamin B-12 into her skinny behind.

It's heartbreaking to hear her frayed, worn-out voice grasping for notes that will not come as she hoarsely tries to scream her way through another mind-frying sold-out concert.

Her life is falling apart like the broken strings from a discarded electric guitar as she wanders through the Memphis traffic muttering, "I shoulda gone to college." Well, even if you've seen it all before, Bette makes you *feel* it for the first time. You've just got to *care*.

Based loosely on the Janis Joplin tragedy, *The Rose* uses bits of Janis's life (they call her "the Rose" instead of "Pearl," she's from Florida instead of Texas), mixes in some Grace Slick and utilizes a great deal of Bette Midler onstage and off.

When all the highs and lows, uppers and downers, trash and flash, straight sex and gay sex come out of the last cycle in the dryer, what's left is a harrowing portrait of life in the rock world that also mirrors the fantasy we all have of going back to whatever one-horse town it is we came from and rubbing their noses in it.

For Rose it's a rock concert in Florida. She never quite makes it, but *The Rose* shows her fighting all the way to get there.

She drives herself beyond fatigue, refueling with drugs and booze to stay awake, getting battered around by greedy promoters and managers, trying to find a moment of peace with a hillbilly chauffeur who can't keep up with the frenetic pace of her obsession to be somebody.

Eventually collapsing in the middle of a stadium from an overdose of heroin, Bette pulls out the stops, strips herself naked for all the world to see in a performance full of blood and guts and chutzpah.

Director Mark Rydell extracts from Frederic Forrest an immensely appealing performance as an AWOL soldier who picks her up as a chauffeur and teaches her the meaning of love when the noise dies down around her. Alan Bates is wasted in the unsympathetic role of her English manager, the Svengali who knocks her about and pulls her strings. But it's Bette who gives the film its centrifugal force.

The Rose is full of flaws, but Bette is so great you don't even care how illogical it is. The temptation to write it off as one of those "wasn't it sad about Janis Joplin" memoirs stretches from here to deadline, but the dynamic Bette sends it soaring into the stratosphere with her throbbing vitality. You can't call this acting debut "auspicious." Hell, she tears up the place.

RUMBLE FISH (1983)

No ★s Directed and produced by Francis Ford Coppola. Screenplay by Coppola, based on a novel by S.E. Hinton. *With Matt Dillon, Mickey Rourke, Dennis Hopper, Diane Lane, Diana Scarwid, Vincent Spano, Nicolas Cage, Christopher Penn, and Tom Waits.*

I recommend *Rumble Fish* only to those people who long to be present at lynchings and public executions. One of the worst movies ever made, it's a film of such stupefying insanity than it makes all other "worst movies" seem like masterpieces.

Rumble Fish runs ninety-four minutes. It seems like ninety-four days. Even kids who will sit through any brainless mush with Matt Dillon in it are going to retch when they see this monstrosity. *Rumble Fish* is not a movie; it's a mutation.

Twenty years after teenage gang pictures went out of style—and ignoring the fact that they are also out of date and out of fashion—Coppola decided to make one.

As perverse as his reasons are, they would be acceptable if *Rumble Fish* was a good movie. But this self-indulgent, pretentious, idiotic trash wallow makes *Rebel Without a Cause* look like Berkeley Square in bloomers.

Rumble Fish is like a long, dark, violent dream sequence— a Thorazine special.

There is no plot at all, only a series of vignettes involving a greasy, monosyllabic retard named Rusty James (with Matt Dillon in the role, it's type casting), his zonked-out older brother called "The Motorcycle Boy" (Mickey Rourke), and assorted goons, hoodlums, and adolescent cretins who seem to be invaders from Mars.

The boys have an alcoholic father, played by Dennis Hopper, who looks like Chico Marx. They all live in an alley where fire escapes move to a rock-and-roll rhythm and it always seems to be raining. The streets are always wet in this town, and on every street corner there are flames shooting out of burning barrels, sending clouds of smoke swirling through the alleys. The action all takes place in weather that seems to signify the end of the world.

It's a peculiar town, too, because everybody in it is either drunk or on heroin or carving each other up with switchblades. Is it New Year's Eve? Or Mardi Gras? You are never sure, but there *is* a party going on behind every window, with orgies and break-ins and bottles smashing through the windows, women screaming, and teenage punks breaking up the furniture. Most of the time the town looks like Sodom and Gomorrah when the bartender yelled: "Last call!"

This is not a comedy, but it is so full of unintentional howlers that it really becomes a laugh riot. After his skull is split open with a tire iron, Matt Dillon levitates toward heaven, puffing on a joint. There's a clock without hands, and billows of fog surround Diane Lane's front porch for no apparent reason. Maybe her icebox needs defrosting.

Then there's the heavy symbolism of the rumble fish. The whole movie is in black and white, but the fish in a pet store window are red and blue.

They're the martyred teenagers of America, and if Rusty James and The Motorcycle Boy can smash their tanks and throw them into the river, maybe they won't kill each other like American kids do. It's all as phony and mind-crunchingly juvenile as the speeded-up storm clouds rolling across the sail-cloth skies overhead.

The acting consists of little more than inaudible grunts and Neanderthal mumbles. The dialogue is unintelligible gibberish, which is probably a good thing, since it all comes off the walls of graffiti-stained public toilets.

Teen hunk Matt Dillon should never be permitted to appear in any film without subtitles. Mickey Rourke, who was so fine in *Diner*, is a catatonic zombie. Dennis Hopper seems to be on the verge of an epileptic fit.

Coppola makes no attempt to shape any of these people into anything that resembles a stable of unified performance. Everyone and everything seems to be floating in an advanced state of catalepsy.

In one of the more disgusting moments, after Matt Dillon's stomach is sliced open with a switchblade, his brother pours a bottle of vodka into the open wound. "He oughta see a doctor, man," slurps another comatose punk. It might not be such bad advice for Francis Ford Coppola, either. This is one of the saddest and most self-deluded examples of a director going downhill fast.

Three years later, Coppola's sagging career was revived with *Peggy Sue Got Married*, but he's been up and down ever since.

RUNNING ON EMPTY (1988)

★ ★ ★ Directed by Sidney Lumet. Screenplay by Naomi Foner. Produced by Amy Robinson and Griffin Dunne. With Judd Hirsch, Christine Lahti, River Phoenix, Martha Plimpton, Jonas Arby, Ed Crowley, L. M. Kit Carson, Steven Hill, and Augusta Dabney.

Sidney Lumet's *Running on Empty* grapples with the repercussions of the 1960s by addressing itself to a question many people are still asking: "What happened to the nice college kids who opposed the Vietnam War and ended up on the FBI's most-wanted list?" For Arthur and Annie Pope, intelligently played by Judd Hirsch and Christine Lahti, life did not turn out like "Leave it to Beaver." Twenty years ago, they bombed a government-funded napalm factory, accidentally killing a night watchman, and became fugitives. They've been on the run ever since. They've got a seventeen-year-old son, Danny (River Phoenix), who deserves a better life, and yet to give him a chance at a music scholarship at Juilliard means risking everything. Life underground demands sacrifices no child should make. The wrenching decision Danny's parents must make, endangering their security to provide a better future for their son, forms the central dilemma in this informed and sensitively made film.

Sidney Lumet has not made a political tract or a coming-of-age tearjerker, although *Run-*

ning on Empty has elements of both. With painstaking care and a keen observance of small details, he has turned out a searing emotional family drama about the enormous price idealists must pay for their own convictions. I like the way it refuses to pass easy moral judgments and I love the fact that the stars do not play the Popes as embittered hippie heroes or as criminals atoning for past sins. They're real as breathing. Regardless of your own political convictions, you'll take from this deeply moving film the knowledge that love is all that matters—and sometimes letting go is the only way to keep going.

RUTHLESS PEOPLE (1986)

★ ★ ★   Directed by Jim Abrahams, David Zucker, and Jerry Zucker. Screenplay by Dale Launer. Produced by Michael Peyser. With Danny DeVito, Bette Midler, Judge Reinhold, Helen Slater, Anita Morris, Bill Pullman, William G. Schilling, Art Evans, and Clarence Felder.

Ruthless People is a mad farce about murder, blackmail, kidnapping, and other assorted mayhem, in which each criminal is dumber and more naive than the next. The comic-strip characters who perpetrate the insanity that keeps the film rolling to its sidesplitting climax are so ruthless they even freak themselves out, while the audience has a ball.

If comedy is king, Bette Midler must be the crown princess. I miss her old Mae West send ups, but she's stretched so much she can now tackle a variety of characters with the same comic gusto.

This time she plays a miserable, overweight, vulgar, and thoroughly obnoxious heiress named Barbara Stone, stuffed into eight-inch spike heels and iridescent tube tops.

Fuming with rage until his runty little face turns purple, Danny DeVito is her husband Sam, a loathsome Spandex-miniskirt tycoon who spends every waking moment thinking of ways to murder his wife. The Stones are baby gargoyles—noisy, foul-mouthed, and mercenary. Nothing is safe in their presence—not even a parked car.

When the film begins, Sam is stalking Barbara in their ugly pink pop-art Bel Air mansion when fate steps in. Barbara has been kidnapped! The abductors are Ken and Sandy, a nice all-American couple new at the game of ruthlessness. Ken (Judge Reinhold), a salesman in a stereo shop, is so clumsy he chloroforms himself. Sandy

(Helen Slater) feels so guilty she redecorates the guest room for the victim.

Meanwhile, Sam's not-too-faithful bimbo mistress Carol (Anita Morris) plans to blackmail him for her share of Barbara's money by dispatching her idiot boyfriend Earl (Bill Pullman) to videotape the murder. Earl videotapes the police inspector by mistake. While Sam thwarts every ransom demand hoping the kidnappers will dispose of Barbara and make his day, Ken and Sandy remind each other to "think ruthless" and reduce Barbara's going rate to a bargain basement discount.

The victim is such a sadistic monster that she reduces Sandy to tears ("She won't eat a thing I cook!") and kicks Ken so hard in the groin he turns into a soprano. Chained up for self-protection, Barbara becomes an aerobic exercise nut watching TV, and loses twenty pounds in the process. Delirious with joy over her new figure, Barbara is transformed from an obscenity-yelling shrew into the sweetness of Shirley Temple and goes into business with her kidnappers to destroy Sam.

The directors of this lunacy are Jim Abrahams, David Zucker, and Jerry Zucker—the zany triumvirate responsible for *Airplane!*. This time they've produced a screwball comedy even the Marx Brothers couldn't follow, with a twist every five minutes. They can throw an infinitude of balls into the air at the same time and keep them all balanced and flying.

Plot threads get introduced and dropped. New characters enter and exit. Nothing is what it seems, and it's amazing how many venal people turn out to make greed and avarice pay off while never losing their charm.

There are some great gags in *Ruthless People*, most of them so filthy they cannot be repeated in print, but the directors know the value of farce as a contributing process. The emphasis is not on sick jokes, but on situations. Dale Launer's script is a roller-coaster ride, and the film never slows down long enough to let anyone off for air.

The cast works brilliantly. Bette Midler and Danny DeVito are Godzillas of bad taste. Judge Reinhold is immensely likable as a crook with butterfingers; Helen Slater has come a long way since *Supergirl*, and Anita Morris is the best foxy bimbo since Marie Wilson. The result is a raunchy, dirty-minded *Ransom of Red Chief* with a high-tech sheen that is very much a part of the irreverent eighties.

MEMOREX® HS
VIDEO CASSETTE

For best results, please follow these instructions and precautions:

• The cassette is designed with a safety tab so that you can protect a recording from accidental erasure. Simply break off the tab on the rear side of the cassette. To record again on a cassette that has the tab removed, cover the safety tab hole with tape.

• Allow the cassette to reach room temperature before use, if it has been moved from cold to warm surroundings. This will prevent damage caused by moisture condensation on the tape.

• Always rewind the tape when you have finished playing or recording. Then put the cassette in the protective case. Store it vertically in a cool dry place.

Safety Tab.

Taquet de sécurité.

To prevent accidental erasure, break the tab.

Pour empêcher un effaçage accidentel brisez le taquet.

To record again, cover the hole with vinyl tape.

Pour enregistrer de nouveau, couvrir le trou avec un morceau de vinyl.

Pour de meilleurs résultats, veuillez suivre ces instructions et précautions:

• La cassette possède un taquet de sécurité afin de protéger un enregistrement d'un effaçage accidentel. Brisez simplement le taquet à l'arrière de la cassette. Maintenant, lorsque vous insérez la cassette dans le lecteur de cassettes, il n'est pas possible d'enregistrer de nouveau.

• Pour enregistrer de nouveau sur une cassette dont le taquet est enlevé, il suffit de couvrir le trou du taquet de sécurité avec un petit morceau de cellophane ou de vinyl.

• Laissez la cassette atteindre la température ambiante avant de l'utiliser si elle a été déplacée d'un endroit froid à un endroit chaud. Ceci empêchera la bande de s'abimer à cause de la condensation de l'humidité.

• Rembobinez toujours la bande lorsque vous avez fini d'écouter ou d'enregistrer. Mettez ensuite la cassette dans sa boîte de protection. Rangez-la verticalement dans un endroit sec et frais.

Memorex Canada, Markham, Ont. L3R 3K5

MEMOREX
VIDEO
CASSETTE
HS
PROOF OF PURCHASE

| T-30 | T-60 | T-120 | T-160 |
| T-30 | T-60 | T-120 | T-160 |

MEMOREX HS ®

[VHS]

■ STEREO ■ MONO
■ SP ■ LP ■ SLP

SABOTEUR (1942)

★ ★1/2 Directed by Alfred
Hitchcock. Screenplay by Dorothy
Parker, Peter Viertel, and Joan
Harrison. Produced by Jack
Skirball and Frank Lloyd. *With
Robert Cummings, Priscilla Lane,
Norman Lloyd, Otto Kruger, Alan
Baxter, Alma Kruger, Dorothy
Peterson, and Vaughan Glaser.*

Saboteur is not one of Alfred
Hitchcock's classics for several
reasons—suave comedian Robert Cummings was hopelessly
miscast as a wartime factory
worker wrongly accused of being a Nazi spy, and the script
by Dorothy Parker was not always in the same suspenseful
tempo as the director's macabre
special effects. Nevertheless, it
is a briskly paced thriller that is
never boring. The train of circus freaks, the fire in New York
harbor, and the harrowing finale on top of the Statue of Liberty are classic Hitchcock, even
if some of the film's middle-
section ideas are not. Film buffs
love *Saboteur*, even if Hitchcock himself didn't.

SABRINA (1954)

★ ★ ★1/2 Directed and
produced by Billy Wilder.
Screenplay by Wilder, Ernest
Lehman, and Samuel Taylor,
based on Taylor's play *Sabrina
Fair*. *With Audrey Hepburn, William
Holden, Humphrey Bogart, Martha
Hyer, John Williams, Francis X.
Bushman, and Nancy Kulp.*

Sabrina stars delectable Audrey Hepburn as a chauffeur's
daughter who goes to Europe a
mouse and returns with so much
feline sophistication she makes
catnip of her father's two employers—Humphrey   Bogart
and William Holden. One of
Billy Wilder's most successful
comedies, with Audrey a witty
and beautiful delight.

SCANDAL (1989)

★ ★ ★1/2 Directed by Michael
Caton-Jones. Screenplay by
Michael Thomas. Produced by
Stephen Woolley. *With Ian
McKellen, Joanne Whalley, John
Hurt, Bridget Fonda, Britt Ekland,
and Jeroen Krabbe.*

Scandal is a terrific film version of the spicy John Profumo–Christine Keeler affair,
probably the most lurid political
sex scandal of the twentieth
century in England. Reexamining that sordid chapter, director
Michael Caton-Jones sweeps us
along in the grip of erotic tension and sexual intensity with
the blunt impact of a tabloid
headline. Joanne Whalley looks
exactly like the tacky tart who
destroyed the political career of
Queen Elizabeth's minister of
war, unbalanced the Conservative ruling power of Parliament,

and changed the course of British history. The great Ian McKellen, bald and palsied, is a pathetic Profumo, and John Hurt has never been better as the society pimp who brought them together and then ended up a scapegoat driven to suicide by the resulting scandal. Stylish, sexy, beautifully acted, one helluva good morality lesson.

SCARFACE (1983)
★ Directed by Brian DePalma.
Screenplay by Oliver Stone.
Produced by Martin Bregman.
With Al Pacino, Steven Bauer, Michelle Pfeiffer, Mary Elizabeth Mastrantonio, and Robert Loggia.

Brian DePalma's gut-busting remake of Howard Hawks' 1932 gangster melodrama *Scarface* sets out to accomplish only one thing—disgust, sicken and horrify the audience with a rampage of violence, bloodshed and carnage.

It accomplishes this dubious feat beyond debate, although Al Pacino's lip-licking, eye-rolling impersonation of a Cuban thug who rises from the bottom of the sewer to the top of the underworld sounds like Rita Moreno's Googie Gomez.

In a nutshell, *Scarface* is familiar stuff, noisy and grim, and ultimately rather pointless.

The 1932 *Scarface*, written by Ben Hecht and directed by

the aforementioned Hawks, to whom the new film is dedicated, was a tough, taut little action thriller about Chicago's murderous beer racketeers.

In the updated version, Chicago is Miami, beer is cocaine, and Tony Camonte, the Italian hood Paul Muni played so memorably, is now Tony Montana, a sleazebag refugee who floats in with the other 125,000 "Marielitos" who poured into Florida in May 1980 when Castro turned his slaves free.

Although the film is careful to point out that not all Cubans are pimps, killers, racketeers, and social leeches, it also points out that 25,000 of the 1980 refugees had criminal records.

This is the story of one of them. Like the other freeloaders who arrived with him, demanding political freedom and civil rights and giving nothing in return, Tony Montana throws himself on the mercy of the immigration officials, then carves up what's left of a troubled America with a switchblade.

The violence in *Scarface* begins immediately, with a riot in a detention center where Tony knifes his first victim. It's the beginning of a long and gruesome body count, in which the mustachioed extras drop faster than Comanches in a John Ford western.

The murder pays for Tony's green card and before you can say White Dust, this greasy hustler is making cocaine transactions while his best friend gets chained to a motel shower rod, his arms and legs buzzed off with a chainsaw, while the blood (or strawberry syrup) splashes all over Pacino's face—not to mention the bathroom wallpaper.

The rest of *Scarface*, which runs almost three hours, features more of the same. It doesn't take long for Tony to get a taste of the high life — $500 suits, vintage champagne, silver Porsches, blondes, and a Miami mansion surrounded by bodyguards that seems to have been interior decorated by Sabu the Elephant Boy.

Tony's goal: "To get what's coming to me—the world, and everything in it." He's learned the secret of the American dream—that money equals power, and drugs make money. Tony machine-guns everyone who gets in his way, and by the time he finally comes to his own grisly and predictable end, he's running a cocaine empire that takes in $100 billion a year. (And he still never heard of Brooks Brothers.)

Along the way, the flimsy and often unbelievable screenplay by Oliver Stone follows the original *Scarface* closely.

Tony corrupts his kid sister (Mary Elizabeth Mastrantonio) who adores him. He negotiates major drug deals in Colombia, muscles in on his own boss's connections (Robert Loggia is marvelous as the coke czar who addicts half of Florida from his Mercedes-Benz dealership), falls for the gang lord's sultry gun moll (Michelle Pfeiffer, looking like a Forties Lizabeth Scott), and ends up with a tax-evasion charge he must get out of by massacring what looks like most of the Gulf Coast.

Scarface provides one of the most nihilistic portraits of America I've yet seen on film. Not only are the Cuban gangsters reprehensible, but they are surrounded by crime on every level of social stratification: narcotics agents who protect drug imports with everything from money to first-class airline tickets, bankers who launder illegal money, cops who dig into the profits, lawyers who fix drug busts through connections that lead all the way to Washington.

(One fascinating shot reveals Loggia, the drug king Pacino bumps off, framed by personally autographed photos of everyone from Bobby Kennedy to Richard Nixon.)

The message here is that the whole world is corrupt, everybody has a price, and a sane and honest citizen hasn't got a chance. It's probably the worst public-relations black eye ever given to the city of Miami. Painted in garish, peeling pink, like toenail polish, the city looks like a running cesspool, and so many restaurants, hotels, and discos get riddled with machine-gun fire that I don't think I'd want to do anything there except stay in my room and watch television.

To be fair, *Scarface* does not condone or glamorize cocaine or crime. The people are so scummy that when Tony finally gets ripped apart by a thousand bullets and plunges into his swimming pool, only to float to the surface covered with blood, I regarded him with no more interest than a red lily pad.

But the paranoia, madness and wholesale massacre that forms the final half hour of the film is really almost laughable. The sight of Pacino, eyes rolling around in a junkie haze, his head almost obscured by a desk piled high with a mountain of cocaine, is almost comical. His head falls into the stuff (powdered sugar? baby laxative?) and comes up looking like a Fellini clown, while the supporting cast from *The Godfather* moves in with enough artillery to wipe Beirut off the face of the globe by sundown.

The controversy over the film's original "X" rating seems absurd. It's a sad thing to admit, but we've become so de-sensitized by movie violence, so anesthetized by the sight of bullet-ridden corpses, that *Scarface* doesn't seem any more repellent than any other movie, and a great deal less nauseating than any movie ever directed by Sam Peckinpah.

Still, what is the point? What are we supposed to take home from this bloodbath? Cocaine is bad for you? Crime doesn't pay? Never buy a Havana cigar from a man who looks like Al Pacino?

The violence is endless, the four-letter words take the place of English, the actors work vigorously, the decadence and perversion drown everything in a viscous grunge. When it's over, you feel mugged, debased, like you've eaten a bad clam.

Where is Jimmy Cagney now that we need him?

SCENES FROM A MALL (1991)
★ Directed, written and produced by Paul Mazursky. *With Woody Allen, Bette Midler, and Bill Irwin.*

Woody Allen, who rarely acts in other people's films, and Bette Midler, who is moving farther away from the campy combustion that made her a pop icon and more in the direction of serious acting, would seem to be a dream team on paper. It must have taken Paul Mazursky a year of phone bills to persuade them to co-star in *Scenes from a Mall*. I'm sorry to say the result is a long, tedious, whining kvetch from start to finish which reduces two of the most interesting personalities in the cinema to numbing bores.

They are the Fifers. He's a dreary sports promoter who signs teenage jocks to million-dollar endorsement deals for candy bars and underwear. She's a shrink with a best-selling book on "recommitment in marriage in the age of divorce." On the day of their sixteenth wedding anniversary they head for the Beverly Center, the Alphaville of science-fiction malls, to pick up the sushi for their dinner guests, after a quickie in the sheets conducted while he watches the Home Shopping Club on cable, she takes calls on her beeper phone from hysterical patients, and they both worry about nonbiodegradable plastic bags. I suppose Mr. Mazursky means to give us another look

at the cosmic absurdity of what passes for life in Los Angeles, but with the dual Saabs in the garage, the non-stress gum and the endless traffic jams, a viewer grows quickly weary and wonders why they don't just move.

After passing the parking lot test everyone must master to survive in an L.A. mall, the Fifers buy their sushi and move on to frozen yogurt, where Mr. Fifer confesses to Mrs. Fifer he's been have a six-month affair with a younger woman. The raging battle that takes up the rest of the movie is like an old script from *The Bickersons* with Don Ameche and Frances Langford, intermittently amusing but never really funny, and ultimately excruciatingly repetitive and pointless. A list of community property is made over margaritas and taco chips in the Mexican Cantina, witnessed by a noisy mariachi band from Central Casting.

They make up and work in another quickie during *Salaam Bombay* at the ten-screen cinema complex next to the Burger King. Then she announces she's been having an affair with another shrink (played in TV clips along the way by Mazursky himself, which must have reduced the budget considerably). Another walloping fight. She buys a bad dress, then passes out cold in front of the Stress Management Center. He loses his car. All the while, the ugly mall plays the Greek chorus to their bickering. It's the kind of horror set—more gruesome yet on the last shopping day before Christmas—where fake holiday trees and Shanghai acrobats compete for attention with junk-food bazaars and strolling barbershop quartets singing hideous carols. Bill Irwin, the only other recurring human in the cast, shows up from time to time as a rude mime who parodies the Fifers' various outbursts in white clown makeup. Lucky guy. He doesn't have to speak the atrocious dialogue.

With so much going on and so little content, Mr. Allen and Ms. Midler are like dervishes strapped into straitjackets. I've never seen either of them so listless. They're playing the characters as written, but are the characters worth playing? Eleven hundred dollars worth of sushi later, they're still in the mall, descending yet another escalator to nowhere, needling each other like one of those car commercials where the wife chews the husband to hamburger over a broken muffler. The point of the film, I guess,

it that every stage in the cycle of life can be experienced in one day—marriage, divorce, business deals, food, sex, and you name it—and you never have to leave the mall. The problem is, by the end of *Scenes from a Mall*, I never wanted to see, meet, or hear another word about these awful people for the rest of my life. That goes double for the mall.

SCROOGED (1988)

No ★s Directed by Richard Donner. Screenplay by Mitch Glazer and Michael O'Donoghue. Produced by Donner and Art Linson. *With Bill Murray, Karen Allen, Alfre Woodard, Lee Majors, Buddy Hackett, and Robert Mitchum.*

Bill Murray is about as funny in this film as a bandaged foot, but that only partially explains the paralyzing tedium of *Scrooged*. The immortal Charles Dickens classic *A Christmas Carol* has become as much a holiday tradition as jingle bells, plum pudding, and the lighting of the Rockefeller Center tree. There are already several solid versions on home video. Do we really need an idiot farce that roasts the story of Scrooge like a Boy Scout marshmallow?

Bill Murray thinks so, but it's a shame he didn't bring along Ivan (*Ghostbusters*) Reitman to pound a performance out of him instead of Richard (*Superman*) Donner, who only pulls strings. Instead of a coherent script, they get disjointed sketches out of Mitch Glazer and Michael O'Donoghue from *Saturday Night Live*, and the audience gets the turkey.

Murray plays Frank Cross, a contemporary, updated Ebeneezer Scrooge (which, to the *SNL* writers, means a TV executive). In fact, he's the youngest and meanest program executive in television—a raging, cruel, self-absorbed, opportunistic, greedy, and power-crazed curmudgeon who sees Christmas as just another way to rip people off, make money, and get ratings. His holiday specials include a violent "Movie of the Week" in which Santa Claus and his elves are rescued from rampaging psychos carrying machine guns by Lee Majors, and a trashy version of *A Christmas Carol* vulgarized by Buddy Hackett, scantily clad showgirls, and Mary Lou Retton as Tiny Tim. He's such a stingy S.O.B. he gives everyone ugly towels for Christmas bonuses, humiliates friends, relatives, and colleagues, and ends up alone and miserable in his glass network tower slugging down vodka.

Bob Cratchit is now a combination of moronic Bob Goldthwait, a yes-man who gets fired on Christmas Eve, and angelic Alfre Woodard, a long-suffering secretary whose son (Tiny Tim, of course) is a mute. Karen Allen is the saint who loves Mr. Murray despite the abuse he heaps on her pointed head, and Robert Mitchum huffs and puffs his way through a cameo as Murray's boss. The Ghost of Christmas Past is now a loudmouthed New York cab driver. The Ghost of Christmas Present is a sadistic sugarplum fairy (Carol Kane, overacting loudly) who bashes Murray in the face with a toaster. The Ghost of Christmas Future is a mechanical skeleton no scarier than a wall hanging in a Hallmark window. Add tacky sets, glitzy costumes, and guest appearances by everyone from Gerald Ford to the late John Houseman, and you get a big, weird, dreadful, uneven, and overproduced mess. You also get jokes like the waiter who goes up in flames while Bill Murray says, "Excuse me, I thought you were Richard Pryor!" Bah, humbug! That's not funny, just sick and embarrassing.

I guess I can't blame the star for looking and acting so dyspeptic throughout. He's not playing a part so much as smelling the garbage. This time his sometimes sullen, mean-spirited comic attitude backfires. It saps the film of a central energy from which it never recovers. Lumpy, leaden, and pockmarked, he's creepier than any of the ghosts who come to haunt him, and he's not even wearing makeup. The only reason to dump on *A Christmas Carol* is to turn it into an outrageous black comedy, and that's precisely what's missing from *Scrooged*. The result is, for the viewer, like being trapped at a depressing office party where the eggnog is sour and the tree's on fire.

SEA OF LOVE (1989)

★ ★ ★ Directed by Harold Becker. Screenplay by Richard Price. Produced by Martin Bregman and Louis A. Stroller. With Al Pacino, Ellen Barkin, John Goodman, Michael Rooker, and William Hickey.

Take a Valium before you settle down to watch this one. It's a steamy erotic thriller that seems to have been made by the Evelyn Wood school of speed shocks. There's a psycho on the loose in the New York night who stalks male victims through the personal ads and it looks like a female. Al Pacino gets his best role in years as the scruffy homicide cop on the trail of a lady serial killer and Ellen Barkin is his sexy suspect. But this time the cat falls for the mouse in sexy scenes guaranteed to short-circuit your pacemaker. Nothing happens the way you think it will, and the surprise twist at the end left me dazed. Pacino is great, Barkin has a body that could cause a traffic collision, and *Sea of Love* turns out to be taut, tense, terrifying, and terrific—the hottest thriller since *Fatal Attraction*.

THE SEDUCTION OF JOE TYNAN (1979)

★ ★ ★ Directed by Jerry Schatzberg. Screenplay by Alan Alda. Produced by Marty Bregman. With Alan Alda, Barbara Harris, Meryl Streep, Melvyn Douglas, Rip Torn, Charles Kimbrough, and Carrie Nye.

The Seduction of Joe Tynan is a brave, intelligent, beautifully crafted film, as contemporary as today's headlines, and just about everything you could want from a movie.

Alan Alda has always been one of those nice, dull actors for whom the word *adequate* was invented. But as Joe Tynan, a popular young liberal senator from New York who almost gets savaged in the Washington lion's den, he really shines with fresh energy and easy, relaxed charm.

Tynan is a new white hope in the cancer ward of political apathy and rot. He has integrity, sincerity, honesty, good looks and a loyal, helpful psychologist wife (Barbara Harris) who insists there is a difference between being a "good decent man in politics" and a "politician." She abhors the latter, which is the direction in which Joe Tynan finds himself heading when he opposes a racist demagogue with the aid of a sexy civil rights lawyer from Louisiana (Meryl Streep).

What emerges is a very skillful portrait of a horse in midstream—a fledgling Democrat on the verge of a big, sometimes cruel political career. The film is the stepchild of Robert Redford's memorable *The Candidate*, but in some ways more touching because it establishes the character of the man himself before it catalogues the changes he undergoes.

It's important because it reflects the enormous conflict in all people who strive for success and sharply focuses on the tough choices successful people must make between their professional and private lives.

Joe Tynan loves his family, but dinners at home become not only rare but disastrous. The kids hate fruit compote, he bores them talking about his idol, Roosevelt, and Mrs. Tynan finds herself struggling for her own identity in the middle of a phony media blitz.

Forcing her to sacrifice everything she believes in to create a public relations image that is safe and ambiguous, he almost loses her. He symbolizes justice and decency in government and his popularity gets him all the way to the nominating speech at the Democratic Convention, but the pressures take their toll on both his private persona and his own personal values.

One of the tragic consequences of the American success story is how little energy the demands of public life leave you, and how little time there is left to become a successful human being. These are some of the issues raised here, and they are raised with humor, directness, and believability.

Alan Alda wrote the script and it snaps, crackles, and moves with economic speed. Jerry Schatzberg's direction pays attention to small details and there is care in every frame. The acting is first-rate.

Barbara Harris has some lovely moments as the belabored wife; Melvyn Douglas is typically polished as a senile senior senator with a disintegrating political future; Rip Torn is wonderfully nauseating as a vulgar southern senator; and Carrie Nye claws her way through the Washington social scene with fire-engine-red fingernails as his alcoholic wife.

An ugly, arresting picture of Washington emerges from this film and it is as forceful in its examination of the differences between surface and reality as it is in its entertainment value. *The Seduction of Joe Tynan* is a film that tackles several levels of human consciousness, and illuminates them all.

SEE YOU IN THE MORNING (1989)

★ ★ ★½ Directed and written by Alan J. Pakula. Produced by Pakula and Susan Solt. With Jeff Bridges, Alice Krige, Farrah Fawcett, Linda Lavin, Drew Barrymore, Lukas Haas, David Dukes, Frances Sternhagen, and Theodore Bikel.

See You in the Morning got unjustly overlooked by critics and pretty much ignored by the public in its theatrical release, but take my word for it: It's an intelligent, mature, sensitively written, and impeccably acted love story about feelings and relationships. Alan (*Sophie's Choice*) Pakula has taken a look at the effect of death, divorce, and remarriage on two families that's as honest and truthful as a movie gets. Jeff Bridges, in one of his finest performances, is a New York psychiatrist whose wife (Farrah Fawcett) uproots their kids and moves to London, leaving him a lonely divorced man. Wonderful Alice Krige is a sensitive widow with two kids of her own. A friend plays Cupid. They date. They marry. And then the problems of adjustment begin. Old relationships still linger. The problems of stepchildren, ex-mates, and mutual friends are explored with equal perception. The script is insightful, the actors are brilliant, and Pakula's meticulous direction achieves an intimacy, especially in the love scenes, that will make you blush. *See You in the Morning* is about a lot of things mature viewers will have experienced—the tentative nature of love; the knowledge that real relationships don't end, they just change. I came away from this wise and often hilarious film convinced that life is not perfect and love is the only cure for pain. You'll feel you've been hugged.

THE SEVEN YEAR ITCH (1955)
★ ★ ★ Directed and produced by Billy Wilder. Screenplay by George Axelrod. *With Marilyn Monroe, Tom Ewell, Evelyn Keyes, Sonny Tufts, Victor Moore, Oscar Homolka, Carolyn Jones, and Doro Merande.*

The Seven Year Itch features Marilyn Monroe as the dumb blonde next door who drives bachelor-for-the-summer Tom Ewell bananas in the New York heat. This is the film that stopped traffic in Times Square and made headlines from Brooklyn to Bora Bora when Marilyn stood over a subway grate that was blowing air up the skirt of her pleated dress. She's remarkably and charmingly nimble, although the film sometimes slips on its own banana oil.

SHADOW OF A DOUBT (1943)
★ ★ ★ Directed by Alfred Hitchcock. Screenplay by Thornton Wilder and Sally Benson. Produced by Jack H. Skirball. *With Joseph Cotten, Teresa Wright, Macdonald Carey, Patricia Collinge, Henry Travers, Wallace Ford, and Hume Cronyn.*

Shadow of a Doubt is vintage Hitchcock with Joseph Cotten giving one of his most solid performances as a charming uncle visiting his relatives in the sleepy California town of Santa Rosa, and marvelous Teresa Wright as the niece who comes to suspect him of being a serial killer. Hitchcock builds horror in the most mundane small-town settings, leaving no shadow of a doubt why he was the greatest master of suspense. The film is best when it wrings tension out of the ringing of a phone or the tearing of a newspaper in the quiet of a suburban house. It is less successful when it moralizes about how the world is a horrible place (some of Teresa Wright's dialogue, as the disenchanted niece, is loaded with embarrassing bathos). But good acting, the flavor and ambience of small-town dullness, and riveting small details compensate for the film's occasional disappointments. Good psychological shivers.

SHAMPOO (1975)
★ ★ ★ Directed by Hal Ashby. Screenplay by Warren Beatty and Robert Towne. Produced by Beatty. *With Warren Beatty, Julie Christie, Goldie Hawn, Lee Grant, Jack Warden, Tony Bill, and Carrie Fisher.*

Shampoo is the crisp, bitchy story of a heterosexual Hollywood hairdresser (played with slimy charm by Warren Beatty in what some wags at the time labeled "type-casting") who destroys the lives of a number of foxy clients who all give him his comeuppance in the end. Sort of a Beverly Hills version of *Alfie*, it's fast-paced and cleverly written, with strong support from Goldie Hawn, Julie Christie, and Lee Grant. Although it's the hero who gets blow-dried in the end, some women in the audience will sigh and say "Send him over to me."

THE SHELTERING SKY (1990)
★ ★ ★ ★ Directed by Bernardo Bertolucci. Screenplay by Mark Peploe and Bertolucci. Produced by Jeremy Thomas. With Debra Winger, John Malkovich, and Campbell Scott.

Once, in Tangiers, I was a houseguest in Yves Vidal's famous York Castle, right next door to Barbara Hutton's house in the Casbah. One day I received a cable from my New York publishers, who didn't know how to reach me. There was a flurry of activity, a ringing bell, and the servants came to tell me a very famous man was waiting to see me by the swimming pool. When I descended the stone stairs and stepped into the light, blinded by the "sheltering sky" I had read about in the novels of Paul Bowles, I was greeted by Morocco's most celebrated citizen himself. My agent had wisely sent my telegram in care of Paul Bowles, figuring no matter where I was staying in this mysterious place, I was destined to meet its best-known author.

I will never forget that meeting. Brown and weathered, with a shock of sun-bleached hair and ice-blue eyes, Mr. Bowles stayed for dinner, smoking kif and talking into the firelight about his remarkable life, his harrowing journeys, the years spent with his wife Jane in this adopted land, and his hopes that someday his most famous novel, *The Sheltering Sky*, might be turned into a motion picture. Forty years after it first dazzled the literary world, *The Sheltering Sky* reached the screen. It took Bernardo Bertolucci, the world's greatest living film director, and his writing partner Mark Peploe, both fresh from winning nine Oscars for *The Last Emperor*, to do it. The result is not just another movie, but a masterpiece.

This is not an easy movie to describe. It has to sweep over you, like the changing formations of the Sahara. Whole sections of this delicate, beautiful film require no dialogue at all; it's about feelings and emotions and the intransigence of odd relationships, surrounded by a tapestry of arresting images. The story is of a civilized couple like Scott and Zelda Fitzgerald, or Dorothy Parker and Alan Campbell, or Paul and Jane Bowles since much of what happens is autobiographical, who wander so far from the civilization they know that they become lost to their own souls. Restless travelers after World War II in a strange and exotic place, they wander from the back alleys of the Casbah to the uncharted deserts of Algeria and Niger, where no camera has ever been. Kit and Port, played with enigmatic perfection by Debra Winger and John Malkovich, are, like the Bowleses, a writer and composer who desert the jazz, sophistication, and metropolitan fervor of Manhattan (brilliantly typified in the credits by black and white photographs of 1947 New York like the ones taken by their photographer friend Man Ray, accompanied by Lionel Hampton playing "Midnight Sun") in search of the unknown. The next two hours and seventeen minutes is about many things— the death of love, the loss of illusions—but mostly about the terrible consequences of what can happen when you wander too far away from the world you know with nothing but the sky for a compass.

Port succumbs to a raging fever, his passport stolen, ending up in a deserted Foreign Legion fort with no doctors, transportation, or even the possibility of a gin and tonic. Kit ends up locked in the mudroom of a camel caravan of nomads, where she becomes the sexual slave of a black camel driver, disintegrating daily into madness. In actuality, Jane Bowles died in a madhouse in 1973— blind, mute, and paralyzed— and lies to this day in an unmarked grave in Malaga. The one-way trip toward the territories of the sky and oblivion changes their lives tragically until it is obvious they will never be the same, and this is the precise quality Bertolucci imparts to the audience as well.

Revelations explode in every frame of this remarkable film. The lush camera work by the genius Vittorio Storaro exposes the viewer to images never experienced on film before. A train that stops in the middle of a desert rainstorm. Sex on a rocky precipice overlooking a dead valley. A black snowstorm of aggressive flies. Food so tainted every meal is accompanied by a can of DDT. A woman locked in a mudroom without light, her makeup kit the last vestige of the civilized world she came from. The shifting sands forming minarets and towers in the dunes, only to disappear with the next raging wind. This movie is more beautiful, primitive, scary, ugly, and haunting than *Lawrence of Arabia*.

The acting is impeccable. I don't usually care for John Malkovich, but his whiny dial-tone voice and straw-blond hair are perfect symbols of an intellectual aesthete pushing onward to his own self-destruction; while Debra Winger looks exactly like Jane Bowles, from what I've seen in photographs, down to the big olive eyes and butch hairdo. While some reviewers share my enthusiasm for them and the film, I have also heard words like *boring* applied to their characters. Kit and Port are not boring, but they are deeply committed people with a dual paranoia. They obviously love each other but are not in love. Yet together they form a bond that protects them, in their definition of love, against conventional society, much like the hot, blue-hard sheltering sky overhead. They have souls, but the Sahara buries them in pitiless sand. The film is about holding on to sanity in a merciless hell.

You could call *The Shelter-ing Sky* an art film. Certainly it is not everybody's cup of green tea. But it is so magnificent in its hidden emotions and physical splendor that it literally makes you feel that arid heat and bone-chilling cold and smell the rancid food and camel dung. The film is neither a road movie nor a travelogue, but if the mark of a great movie is the way it exposes the viewer to sights, sounds, and smells never before experienced, then it uses its vast backdrops almost as a benediction. It took forty years for Paul Bowles to see his literary oeuvre come to life on the screen. I doubt if even he expected the result to be what it is—one of the greatest films of all time.

THE SHINING (1980)

★ ★ Directed and produced by Stanley Kubrick. Screenplay by Kubrick and Diane Johnson. With Jack Nicholson, Shelley Duvall, Danny Lloyd, Scatman Crothers, Barry Nelson, Joe Turkel, and Anne Jackson.

The book *The Shining* by Stephen King didn't make much sense, and the film doesn't make much sense, either.

A Vermont writer named Jack Torrance moves his simpleminded wife and small son to a remote Colorado mountain resort called the Overlook Hotel to take a job as a winter caretaker while the place is closed off from the rest of the world under twenty-five feet of snow, then proceeds to go insane and starts chasing his family through the empty corridors with a meat cleaver.

Is it "cabin fever"? A claustrophobic reaction to isolation and loneliness? Or is it a case of demonic possession by spirits from beyond the grave?

There's talk of a former winter caretaker who went mad and murdered his entire family with an ax, and the minute Jack Torrance arrives he rolls his eyes like Bela Lugosi and says he feels like he's been there before.

Well, horror film buffs know what that clue means, and so, apparently, does Jack Nicholson, who telegraphs his insanity so early in the film that there's nothing for us to discover or for him to build a performance on.

Nicholson's work as Jack Torrance is the result of a childhood overdose of fright flicks as well as an early apprenticeship in movies like *The Raven* and *Psych-Out*.

By the time he crashes through Shelley Duvall's bathroom door with his hatchet, he's already narrowing his eyes into Wolf Man slits, crinkling his forehead, jutting out his unshaven chin, ripping his hair, flashing his molars, and cackling, "Here's Johnny!"

What he's giving is not a hair-raising portrait of a rational man possessed by homicidal mania, but a hammy impersonation of Paul Lynde on *Hollywood Squares*.

The child, played by wide-eyed moppet Danny Lloyd, is already flaky before he gets to the Overlook Hotel. He has conversations with his finger, a friend who lives in his mouth named Tony, and the supernatural ability to communicate without words the visions he sees, a trait shared by the hotel cook (Scatman Crothers) and called "shining."

Naturally, the last tourist isn't on the exit bus before he's already seeing the mutilated children and visualizing the hotel lobby filling with blood.

So what we have here is not a normal family in a haunted locale but a batch of loonies who would need psychiatric help on the corner of Forty-fifth and Broadway at high noon.

The fright value is considerably diminished as we wait patiently to see what they'll do to each other instead of ever learning why. The most effective horror films involve the audience in such a way that we are constantly identifying with the victims onscreen.

This time we're shouting for Shelley Duvall to get the hell out of there before she even moves in. By the time she finally clutches a butcher knife for self-protection, it's already too late. We just think she's stupid.

There are some silly nightmare sequences, and one haunted ballroom scene that looks like an outtake from *The Great Gatsby*. At one point, a rotting naked corpse rises from a bathtub and it isn't even remotely frightening, only repellent and senseless.

Near the end, when Nicholson finally gets around to chasing everybody through the halls, basements, and kitchens brandishing his hatchet, the movie picks up steam (this is what we came for), and there's a fine chase through a snowbound maze of hedges. But what little shock value *The Shining* musters comes too late, and the final shot of Nicholson's face in a 1921 crowd scene on the hotel wall still leaves me confused and angry.

Kubrick has taken a turkey and basted it with enough artsy-craftsy camouflage to make it seem like more than it is. The technique is evidently the work of a master chef, but the result is still a blue plate special.

The movie can't take the weight of so many gimmicks, long pauses, foreign-film camera angles, and classical music excerpts, and we end up with *The Texas Chain Saw Massacre* with delusions of grandeur.

Kubrick is like the pretentious hash slinger in a truck line café who gives French names to his greasy cuisine. Order *boeuf en croute* if you're gullible enough, but you'll still get meat pie.

SHIP OF FOOLS (1965)

★ ★ ★ Directed and produced by Stanley Kramer. Screenplay by Abby Mann, based on Katherine Anne Porter's novel. *With Vivien Leigh, Simone Signoret, Oskar Werner, Lee Marvin, Jose Ferrer, Jose Greco, Elizabeth Ashley, and George Segal.*

An all-star cast brings passion and poetry to Stanley Kramer's rather high-minded condensed version of Katherine Anne Porter's famous, exhaustingly overlong novel about a group of doomed passengers on a ship bound for Germany in 1933 who are intended as a microcosm of the pre-Nazi world. Sluggish and preachy in spots, but glorious performances by Vivien Leigh, Simone Signoret, Oskar Werner, Lee Marvin, Jose Ferrer and others. A bit dated, but worth watching for Vivien Leigh's Charleston number.

SHIRLEY VALENTINE (1989)
★ ★ ★ Directed and produced by Lewis Gilbert. Screenplay by Willy Russell. With Pauline Collins and Tom Conti.

Shirley Valentine has a heart as big as her girdle. Trouble is, she can't find it. It's been lost in a life so dreary she wonders aloud when the day, month, or year occurred that she became a missing person. Shirley's a bored middle-aged Liverpool housewife, mother of two grown, selfish kids who are jerks, an indentured servant to a dull drone of a husband. Plump and depressed, Shirley's days consist of grocery shopping, housecleaning and frying her husband's dinner. Sipping wine and talking to her kitchen wall, she tosses off witty one-liners about marriage, men, and sex with juicy wisdom, her potato peeler being a living tool of self-expression. Then something unexpected happens to jolt her out of her lethargy. Shirley tags along with a girlfriend to Greece and two weeks turn into a liberation that changes her life forever.

On Broadway, the magnificent Pauline Collins won the coveted Tony Award and her impeccable, funny, off-the-wall performance in the movie earned her an Oscar nomination. She doesn't lease the screen, she owns it. Director Lewis Gilbert has turned a one-woman stage vehicle into an enchanting movie full of romantic settings and rich, rewarding characters. But it is still the magical Ms. Collins who gives *Shirley Valentine* its ripe, earthy emotional center. She's fierce, proud, hilarious, and heartbreakingly real. The real message here is that we are not what others perceive in us, but we are what we make of ourselves, so we darn well better get it right. I'm afraid I've lost my heart to *Shirley Valentine*.

SHOAH (Documentary, 1986)
★ ★ ★ ★ Directed and produced by Claude Lanzmann.

After record-breaking business in selected art houses, unprecedented reviews from the grumpiest of critics, and tearful, heartfelt acclaim from audiences who have been moved beyond their expectations, *Shoah* finally made it to home video. It's not an easy experience. It requires time and commitment. But the rewards are inestimable. *Shoah*, of course, is the nine-and-a-half-hour epic documentary by French jour-

nalist Claude Lanzmann that re-
creates vividly and piercingly
the period of the Holocaust.
Don't expect grim footage of
concentration camps, blazing
ovens, Nazi swastikas, or the
mad ravings of Hitler. *Shoah*
relies exclusively on the filmed
testimonies of actual witnesses
and survivors to convey one of
the darkest chapters in the history of mankind, and the viewer
is led back in time through their
reminiscences. Eleven years in
the making, *Shoah* evokes shattering images through personal
recollections until a terrifying
view of the Nazis' final solution
emerges. It's not what I'd call
entertainment, but by watching
it the viewer gains access to history and learns one of life's
most devastating lessons—a
lesson that must never be repeated. Packaged in a boxed set
of five cassettes that includes an
informative booklet prepared
by the Simon Wiesenthal Center, *Shoah* is not for the frivolous collector of kung fu movies
and Sylvester Stallone junk. It's
simply monumental, in theme
and content and impact—one
of the most important films of
all time.

SHOOT THE MOON (1982)

★ ★ ★ ★ Directed by Alan
Parker. Screenplay by Bo
Goldman. Produced by Alan
Marshall. *With Albert Finney, Diane
Keaton, Karen Allen, Peter Weller,
Dana Hill, Tracey Gold, Viveka
Davis, and Tina Yothers.*

Alan Parker, who roared to
fame with *Midnight Express*
and *Fame*, and Bo Goldman,
the Oscar-winning screenwriter
responsible for *Melvin and
Howard*, collaborated on *Shoot
the Moon*, a lacerating, honest,
powerful and absolutely first-
rate look at an American marriage on the rocks. Don't miss
it.

Diane Keaton and Albert
Finney are Faith and George
Dunlap. He's a San Francisco
writer who has spent most of
his 15-year marriage struggling
to make a living and she's the
woman behind the man who
suddenly realizes, at the International Book Awards dinner at
the posh Fairmont Hotel where
George is finally being hon-
ored, that in the spillover from
George's spotlight she's no
longer the important force in his
life. Neglected, taken for
granted, she's become an embarrassing appendage. She's
aptly named Faith, but her own
is slowly running out.

This is the story of two

golden people who seem to have a perfect marriage. They are intelligent, they have a sprawling country house in Marin County, four frisky daughters with unique personalities of their own, and a promising future for health, wealth and happiness. But slowly, with keen observations and minute details, director Parker shatters the calm of this perfect facade and shows how stale and unconfident the inner lives can be of "folks who live on the hill."

There are silences, and rages, and pent-up emotional frustrations that pour forth violently, and through the directly emotional honesty and integrity of the actors and the moment-by-moment revelations of the script, the viewer is powerless to escape their personal tragedy. There are so many intimate details in the composition of this film that I often felt, while watching it, that I was spying on people in their most private moments when they were least expecting intrusion.

The Swedes can usually be counted on for this kind of disturbing invasion of privacy, and *Shoot the Moon* is the first American film I've seen that comes closest to Ingmar Bergman's *Scenes from a Marriage* in the way it compiles its intimate dossier on crumbling marital relations. The film is that powerful, yet without the coldness, or the plodding heaviness of Bergman. It has life, lunacy, imagination, gentleness, and lots of gray areas between the black-and-white values with which most film characters seeking "truth" lead their celluloid search.

From its theme music ("Don't Blame Me," played on a piano with one finger) to the way the children are always there as symbols of what collapsed in the marriage, never giving Diane Keaton any peace as she tries to make all of the pieces fit at home and in her head—these things are startling, full of imagery, as honest as peanut butter and jelly, yet so full of controlled and disciplined emotional contact that it never exploits the easy sentimentality often found in Hollywood films about divorce.

By showing the upheavals in the lives of both the adults and the children, Parker has achieved an unusual dimension through which we see every aspect of divorce. The ways of grownups can seem awfully odd to kids, but that bewildering, inquisitive and startlingly direct world inhabited by children can seem even stranger to adults. The multitude of ways all of these decent people affect and touch each other's hearts is one of the film's most gratifying surprises.

The children in this movie are so perfect that you cannot believe they are acting moppets. Dana Hill is one of the most amazing children since the young Margaret O'Brien squeezed tears out of Lionel Barrymore, and her three younger sisters—Viveka Davis, Tracey Gold, and Tina Yothers—are equally convincing and extraordinary. Parker makes them, as well as the adult performers, extensions of themselves, allowing them all the ease and introspection necessary (but rarely profited by in American films) to create a mood and ambiance of total reality.

Diane Keaton, for the first time since *Looking for Mr. Goodbar*, has been given the chance to examine and develop the nuances of a serious role, and she plays it with an impressive range of subtlety and circumspection. Albert Finney, who has been so glazed and boring in recent films that he's beginning to look like a robot experiencing mechanical failures, comes fully alive here for the first time since *Two for the Road*. His shaggy, rumpled,

unmade bed of a face shows strain, passion, confusion and rage as he tries to find out what went wrong with his marriage and with his life.

The ending bothered me—he returns after wishing her well with her new lover, wrecks her new tennis court and reduces the party she's giving to a blood bath of violence, and she realizes this is really the only psychotic way he can say "I love you." That's a tragedy we're unprepared for, and a lot of people will moan when the freeze-frame holds a look on her face that combines passion with pity. Will she take him back, or not? People are like that, and when they come out slugging, finally releasing all of their raw emotions, their newfound humanity can be painful and ugly. You may hate the ending, but you won't be able to say it's phony.

Shoot the Moon is a term in the card game of hearts when you want to signal your opponent it's time to go for broke. Relationships are like that; they change with each new shuffle of the deck. This is not a relaxing aperitif about breaking up. It's high-octane Texaco and it stings going down. But it says more about the impossibility of relationships in a neurotic age than any other film I've seen.

The aftertaste hangs on and you experience a hangover mixed with a new cinematic consciousness that may require oxygen.

THE SHOOTING PARTY (1985)

★ ★ ★ ★ Directed by Alan Bridges. Screenplay by Julian Bond, from the novel by Isabel Colgate. Produced by Mosfilm Studios. With James Mason, Dorothy Tutin, Sarah Badel, Robert Hardy, Rupert Frazer, Edward Fox, Sir John Gielgud, Gordon Jackson, and Judi Bowker.

The Shooting Party is a fresh, unexpected, and enormous delight. It radiates the same pleasure you get from curling up in a cozy bed with a juicy, well-written novel.

Directed with subtle richness by Alan Bridges, whose previous British films *The Hireling* and *Return of the Soldier* have been greeted with critical solidarity if not box-office cashola, *The Shooting Party* skillfully uses the weekend guests at a lavish country pheasant hunt as a microcosm of English society in 1913. George V was on the throne, but Edwardian values were still in evidence among the Elizabethan tapestries, Aubusson carpets, and freshly lit fires in the bedrooms. In this lush setting, a cross-section of aristocrats still living the carefree and privileged life reveal the decaying values that brought an end to the class distinctions that once ruled the British empire.

James Mason in his last screen role is the host of this elegantly turned piece of imitation Chippendale. Mason plays Sir Randolph Nettleby, a benign landowner with wealth and connections, who assembles a titled group of fellow aristocrats to shoot game for an autumn weekend. It's the perfect final role for this great actor, for it gives him sternness mixed with concern, compassion and gentility. His encounter with Sir John Gielgud, who plays a dotty animal rights campaigner, is a brief but enduring moment in British film history.

As we watch hypnotically, the film turns into a kind of *Upstairs, Downstairs* (Julian Bond, who wrote the screenplay, was a writer of that magnificent TV series) of country life, detailing brilliantly the thoughts and manners and mores of not only the stately lords and ladies of gentry, but the maids, valets, footmen, stable boys, and kitchen staff of the manor as well.

Everyone, both upstairs and downstairs, senses the imminence of war, that a way of life is about to end, that the slaughter of birds is soon to give way to the massacre of men. A distinguished cast presents the deceits, prejudices, and adulteries of the upper classes with dramatic glee, while never losing their grip on their characters' sympathetic qualities.

As ever, English actors seem more comfortable in period clothes, and Dorothy Tutin, Sarah Badel, Robert Hardy, Rupert Frazer, and Edward Fox portray the gentry to the manor born.

Chief among the gilded presences adding impeccable splendor to the period decor like Limoges place settings at an elegant dinner party is Judi Bowker, a radiant newcomer with porcelain skin, a rapturous smile, and a voice like warm cream, a youthful Dorothy McGuire.

Downstairs, there is equal polish and pluck from Gordon Jackson as a socially conscious poacher who, nevertheless, is still patriotic enough to whisper "God save the British Empire" with his dying breath. And Frank Windsor gives a very knowing interpretation in the part of the family retainer.

When the frivolous weekend ends in the tragic accidental shooting of a local peasant, thoughts of materialism and social form give way to guilts about the way "gentlemen of breeding" stop killing pheasants and start killing each other, as all the young men in the film prepare for the grim future that awaits them in the trenches.

In theme, content, and artistic achievement, *The Shooting Party* is one of the most provocative and compelling films to come out of England in years. It's not for audiences accustomed to popcorn and Twinkies, but for more discerning, sophisticated tastes, you can't find more solid fare.

SHY PEOPLE (1987)

No ★s   Directed by Andrei Koncholovsky. Screenplay by Koncholovsky, Marjorie David, and Gerard Brach. With Jill Clayburgh, Barbara Hershey, and Martha Plimpton.

Beware of Russian directors who move to Hollywood. Beware *especially* of Andrei Konchalovsky, whose films (*Maria's Lovers*, *Runaway Train*, *Duet for One*) are gloppy mixtures of numbing tedium and hilarious ineptitude. *Shy People*, a pretentious polyglot of Russian torpor and Actor's Studio mumbling, features hapless Jill Clayburgh as a reporter from New York who drags her nymphomaniacal, coke-sniffing teenage daughter to the Louisiana swamps to cover an anthropology story (!) for—get this—

Cosmopolitan! What happens to these two Cosmo girls in the bayou would embarrass Helen Gurley Brown.

They find some relatives living among the Cajuns in a clan run by Barbara Hershey, doing a rotten Ma Kettle impersonation as a toothless hag with four sons. One is retarded, the second is locked in a cage with the family goats, the third is waging war with poachers who tamper with his shrimp nets, and the fourth runs a strip joint near an oil rig. Stranded with her Vuitton luggage and no hair dryer, the daughter introduces the boys to the joys of cocaine and gets raped on the floor in an ooze of wild honey, while Mom gets chased by alligators the size of Volkswagens.

Part ghost story, part tone poem, and all ludicrous, *Shy People* is supposed to be arty stuff, accompanied by quotations from the Book of Revelations (Roger Ebert called it a "religious allegory," which was not only dumb but no help to the quote ads), but when Jill Clayburgh gets lost in the swamp in white high-heel shoes mouthing dialogue like "Ghosts! Alligators! Mosquitoes! You could go crazy in a place like this!" the sound track at the Cannes Film Festival, where I first saw it, got obliterated by the swell of derisive laughter. A real howler, and a resounding disaster.

THE SILENCE OF THE LAMBS (1991)

★ ★ ★ ★ Directed by Jonathan Demme. Screenplay by Ted Tally. Produced by Kenneth Utt, Edward Saxon, and Ron Bozman. *With Jodie Foster, Anthony Hopkins, Scott Glenn, Diane Baker, and Anthony Heald.*

Thomas Harris's best-seller paralyzed readers with emotions more profound than terror, and so does Jonathan Demme's faithful film adaptation, with an incredibly brilliant screenplay by Ted Tally. It's the scariest American movie since *Psycho*.

Jodie Foster is vivid and remarkably real as Clarice Starling, a rookie FBI trainee at Quantico, Virginia, who finds herself dispatched to a lunatic asylum to interview Dr. Hannibal Lecter (Hopkins). He is one of the world's most ingenious, demented, and inhuman psychos, a grisly maniac famous for devouring his victims' bodies, thus earning him the nickname Hannibal the Cannibal. The purpose of this routine assignment is to extract some criminal insights from the mad doctor which might lead to the identity of a serial killer called

Buffalo Bill, another monster who skins his female victims and then inserts bizarre cocoons of a rare death's head moth from Asia in their throats. What does all of this mean? It is Clarice's job to find out, and the insane but charismatic Dr. Lecter's acute perceptions and cryptic clues lead this smart, attractive, but inexperienced young agent into a nightmare world of death and horror every viewer will find hair-raising.

The first time I saw *The Silence of the Lambs* I sat next to a teenage girl who spent most of the film with her head buried in my raincoat. The second time, I sat next to a sophisticated critic who covered her face with her notebook, pleading "Tell me when it's safe to look." Be forewarned. It's not a movie for the squeamish or fainthearted. But while there are pathology reports, descriptions of murders, and sadistic mutilations so gruesome they require stomach emulsifiers, the scariest stuff in this movie is not so much what Mr. Demme shows, but what he implies. One of the film's best sequences is Dr. Lecter's escape from maximum security using a fountain pen. You shake through the aftermath of his carnage without actually watching it step by step. And the sensational edit-

ing—one of Mr. Demme's fortes—intercuts the ringing of two doorbells. Behind one of the doors, ghastly horror waits. But which one? The suspense is enough to guarantee heart palpitations. What could have been another slasher flick from the *Nightmare on Elm Street* school of schlock—graphic depictions of violence with soaring body counts and scenes of people bludgeoned, crushed, and blown to bits with nothing redeeming about he butchery from a cinematic or artistic point of view—has been studiously avoided. The violence in *The Silence of the Lambs* is never gratuitous and the more realism Clarice faces, the more her nightmare becomes our own.

Needless to say, Mr. Demme has been assisted with maximum dedication and sincerity by his cast: Jodie Foster builds her character in measured doses of courage and fright, while Anthony Hopkins is a case history of psychosis capable of both humor and menace, showing the weary boredom of an intellectual cannibal who has seen, read, observed, analyzed, and done—as well as eaten—everything. (Human liver, he remarks, goes especially will with fava beans.) The finale is unforgettable, and so is the film—black, hair-frying, a masterwork of unbearable maximum anxiety and tension that will leave you limp as a dead butterfly's wing. (It swept the Academy Awards for Best Actor, Actress, Director, Screenplay and Picture.)

SILENT MOVIE (1976)

★ ★ Directed by Mel Brooks. Screenplay by Mel Brooks, Ron Clark, Rudy de Luca, and Barry Levinson. Produced by Michael Hertzberg. With Mel Brooks, Bernadette Peters, Sid Caesar, Anne Bancroft, Burt Reynolds, Dom DeLuise, Liza Minnelli, Marty Feldman, Marcel Marceau and Paul Newman.

A madcap excursion through the world of silent films, conducted by maniac Mel Brooks, with Sid Caesar, Anne Bancroft, Liza Minnelli, Marty Feldman, Burt Reynolds, Paul Newman and a host of others. Slapstick goes berserk, and there's a running gag involving Dom DeLuise and a hostile Coke machine that is a comedy riot.

SILKWOOD (1983)

★ ★ ★ Directed by Mike Nichols. Screenplay by Nora Ephron and Alice Arlen. Produced by Nichols and Michael Hausman. With Meryl Streep, Cher, Kurt Russell, Diana Scarwid, and Craig T. Nelson.

Silkwood is powerful and honest, but it is also one of the bleakest, most depressing films I have seen. It is not the kind of movie I would recommend for any time when you feel like celebrating something.

On November 13, 1974, Karen Silkwood, a twenty-eight-year-old employee of the Kerr-McGee plutonium plant near Crescent, Oklahoma, died mysteriously in an automobile accident. She was on her way to a secret rendezvous with a newspaper reporter to spill the beans about safety violations at the plant, which had led to the radiation poisoning of several workers, including herself. The documentary evidence in her possession was never found, the case was never solved, and Karen Silkwood became a martyr—the Joan of Arc of the anti-nuclear movement.

Since Karen Silkwood has become a great heroine to feminists and liberals—a symbol of what an insignificant person with no money, power or education can accomplish in the face of adversity—it's only logical that the screenplay for *Silkwood* was written by the arch-feminists Nora Ephron and Alice Arlen. But in the final tally, it must be asked: What did she really accomplish after all? Wasn't she the ultimate victim—used by men, sabotaged by her co-workers, possibly even contaminated beyond all hope of normal recovery by plutonium placed in a factory sandwich, and eventually murdered for her bravery and commitment?

Like the ignorant mill worker Sally Field played in *Norma Rae*, Karen Silkwood learned the hard way about unions, management, and the rights of the individual. She wanted to change things. Posthumously, the Silkwood estate sued Kerr-McGee and the plant was eventually shut down. All nuclear power plants ordered since 1974 have been cancelled, and none have been ordered since 1978. So maybe Karen Silkwood's martyrdom has had an inadvertent effect on the nuclear industry. But that is not the story Mike Nichols and his screenwriters are interested in telling here.

Silkwood concerns itself with the personal side of the story—and everyone responsible must be congratulated on the restraint and honesty with which the details are processed. Not only is Karen Silkwood not romanticized as a saint, but the way Meryl Streep plays her, she's a rather trashy piece of work in the bargain. Like all Meryl Streep creations, the character

is a bit too calculatedly *studied* to be totally real (what a triumph Kim Stanley would have had with this role in her youth), but the portrait is a fascinating combination of southern bubble-brain, raw nerve, and true grit.

Streep's Silkwood is an ordinary Texas girl who leaves her three kids with her common-law husband to grow up in the shadow of pumping oil wells while she works in a factory in another state.

Blowing bubble gum while she handles plutonium oxide, oblivious to the dangers of radiation poisoning, driving home in the rain in her filthy little two-door Honda to the ramshackle house she shares with her boyfriend Drew (Kurt Russell) and her lesbian chum (Cher), Streep works hard to establish the unexceptional everydayness of Karen Silkwood. It's five-and-dime surface flash until the extraordinary circumstances begin to build and shape her consciousness. That's when Streep's emotional juices start flowing and *Silkwood* comes to life.

Eventually, she turns from a promiscuous working-class drone in mini skirts, pierced earrings, and cowboy boots to a mature woman—savvy, concerned, and alive. She reads up on the mental and physical defects plutonium radiation can cause, as well as the genetic damage and eventual cancer. She gets involved in union politics, flying to Washington for meetings with the Atomic Energy Commission.

Finally, she even spies on the plant and its employees for evidence of wrong doing in the area of job protection, health precautions, and safety measures, stealing X rays from the files and endangering her own life. At this point, I started wondering if maybe Karen Silkwood wasn't more than just a concerned citizen with a caring soul. Maybe she was lonely, tortured, driven, and dumb. Her lover left her. Her friends warned her. After she started getting poisoned by the people in her own plant, why didn't she see the writing on the wall?

There are many unanswered questions you will leave *Silkwood* muttering to yourself. But you will at least know you've seen a movie that tries to raise a few pertinent questions about the way we live now. And you will see some riveting performances. Lending firm support to Streep, Kurt Russell gives a sweetly flavored performance as the ape with the big heart who leaves Streep to find himself.

It's fun to see Cher stripped of her forty-pound eyelashes and Cher drag as the corny down-home lesbian who fills Streep's icebox with leftovers so mangy they've grown penicillin. And Diana Scarwid contributes her own deftly observed character concept as the peroxide floozie cosmetician from a local funeral parlor Cher falls in love with. They are all excellent.

Silkwood is an odd film—part social document, part feminist tract, part gum-chewing pulp fiction. In the end, most of all it's a mystery. Why was Karen Silkwood driven toward self-destruction? We'll never know, but in the power and beauty of Meryl Streep's last scene—driving to her fate singing "Amazing Grace"—there is recompense in the knowledge that it's not always the head honchos who make the difference. Sometimes it's the second-class citizens who count.

SILVERADO (1985)

½★ Directed and produced by Lawrence Kasdan. Screenplay by Lawrence and Mark Kasdan. *With Kevin Kline, Scott Glenn, Rosanna Arquette, John Cleese, Kevin Costner, Brian Dennehy, Danny*

Glover, Jeff Goldblum, and Linda Hunt.

Everybody looks fried in *Silverado*, the pretentious New Wave Western by Lawrence (*The Big Chill*) Kasdan. I don't blame them.

If you can buy Kevin Kline as a two-fisted gunslinger in the Old West, you can buy the Brooklyn Bridge.

If you believe Linda Hunt, the Oscar-winning dwarf who played an Oriental man in *The Year of Living Dangerously*, as a dance-hall queen, you still believe in unicorns.

If you believe Jeff Goldblum, the bug-eyed insomniac from *The Fly*, as a saloon gambler in a raccoon coat, or John Cleese, the zany comic from the Monty Python movies, as a mean sheriff, you can swallow weed killer without a stomachache.

Kasdan, whose screenplays for such comic-book fantasies as *Raiders of the Lost Ark*, *The Empire Strikes Back*, and *Return of the Jedi* made him rich and arrogant, obviously believes his audiences will accept anything. When audiences for *Silverado* laughed themselves silly, he passed the whole thing off as a comedy. This always happens when a movie turns out to be a bomb. The creators always turn indignant, claiming they intended to make people laugh in the first place.

Silverado is a riot, all right, but not because it's supposed to be funny. It's a Western that appears to have been a collaboration between Fyodor Dostoyevski and the Actor's Studio, with an assist from Sigmund Freud and Roy Rogers.

It's *The Big Chill* on horseback—a vast and tangled tale of greed, hate, and vengeance in cowboy boots, with nine stars lumbering their way through a plot so convoluted and preposterous that even while I was watching it I didn't know what was going on. Looking through my notes, I am more confused than ever. Just trying to keep the characters straight, you need a degree in calculus.

Battered, baked, and half dead, Kevin Kline opens his big gumdrop eyes in the middle of the desert and says, "Pleased to meetcha." He has been robbed and left there to die by villains. Scott Glenn, the astronaut from *The Right Stuff*, saves him. At the fort, they run into Glenn's younger brother, a daredevil cowboy played by Kevin Costner, who's been sentenced to hang by John Cleese, a comic sheriff who talks like Arthur Treacher.

The three guys escape with a

fourth sidekick, a black cowboy played by Danny Glover, the gifted actor who saved Sally Field's cotton crop in *Places in the Heart* before moving on to the *Lethal Weapon* pictures and real stardom. They all head for a town called Silverado with a wagon train and a hardy pioneer woman, played by Rosanna Arquette, the spirited star of *Desperately Seeking Susan*.

Silverado turns out to be a western town so spanking new and whistling clean it looks like Knott's Berry Farm. Glenn and his brother find their score with a murderous family called the McKendricks unsettled. Glover, who has been working in the Chicago stockyards, finds his farm burned, his family dead, his cattle stolen. The bloody McKendricks are the culprits. Now everyone is out for revenge. The movie is just beginning.

The McKendricks are in cahoots with Silverado's fat, mercenary sheriff, played by Brian Dennehy, the lovable alien in *Cocoon*. The sheriff also owns the town. Glover's sister works in the saloon. Kline leaves his three buddies and goes to work in the saloon, too. Glenn is his best friend. Now Kline is working for the McKendricks, who are Glenn's worst enemies. There are so many characters and stories going on at the same time—all of them boring, none of them related except by the thinnest thread possible—that the film can't keep them straight, either, so every ten minutes it keeps introducing new ones.

Wandering in and out of the confusion is Linda Hunt, a miniature saloon queen who has to stand on a box to serve a highball, and poor Rosanna Arquette, a nice pioneer virgin who tries to get the guys to settle down and raise chickens. You can count her lines on the fingers of your left hand. Considering what she has to say ("Nothin' wrong with this land, jes' some of the people in it") maybe you should forget the whole thing. I'm sure she has.

Silverado ends with an inevitable shootout on Main Street, but to get there it rambles. It wafts. It drags. And it piles up every cliché in the book: ambushes, kidnappings, burning homesteads, women and children terrorized, horses braying in the corral to signal the arrival of trouble, dance-hall girls reformed through the love of good men, bad men reformed through the love of good women. There's a horse stampede. Even a square dance. Everything but Gene Autry.

In the noisy finale, the four sidekicks ride again. They look like Hoot Gibson, Tom Mix, Ken Maynard, and Hopalong Cassidy. But they say things like "Let's get 'em!" and "Hi, guys!" Maybe it's an old script that was tailored for the four Marx Brothers and never used. Nobody has any clear definition of what's going on, so everybody appears to be making it up as they go along. Kasdan's direction doesn't help his idiotic screenplay. He must have directed the horse stampede by walkie-talkie from a hotel room in Santa Fe.

Silverado is a mess, but at least the noise keeps you awake.

SINCE YOU WENT AWAY (1944)

★ ★ ★ ★ Directed by John Cromwell. Written and produced by David O. Selznick. With Claudette Colbert, Shirley Temple, Jennifer Jones, Robert Walker, Joseph Cotten, Monty Woolley, Lionel Barrymore, Agnes Moorehead, Nazimova, Hattie McDaniel, Guy Madison, Keenan Wynn, and others.

Next to *Gone With the Wind*, this three-hour, star-spangled tribute to the American home front during World War II was David Selznick's greatest cinematic achievement. Finally on home video by popular demand, the 1944 classic still shimmers and shines with patriotic fervor and the American spirit in times of adversity. I have seen it countless times and discover something new and touching and wonderful every time I see it. It chronicles the lives of a typical American family coping with hardships under the abnormal stress of war, with a wealth of domestic details about midwestern small-town life. The people are so well drawn and perfectly acted they become neighbors by the time the movie ends. And what a staggering array of talent! Claudette Colbert, as the mother trying to keep home and family going while the man of the house is away on the front lines, is both gallant and human. Jennifer Jones and Shirley Temple as the daughters with growing pains, Robert Walker as the tragic young soldier who enters their lives, Monty Woolley as a curmudgeonly boarder, and the fabulous Hattie McDaniel as the strong-willed family maid, are just a few of the impeccably cast co-stars who give the film so much honesty, sincerity, and decency. Curl up with this one on a rainy Sunday afternoon and you will never be the same.

SIX WEEKS (1982)

★ ★   Directed by Tony Bill.
Screenplay by David Seltzer.
Produced by Jon Peters and Peter
Guber. With Mary Tyler Moore,
Dudley Moore, Katherine Healy,
Shannon Wilcox, Bill Calvert, and
Joe Regalbuto.

Except for the one about lost
collies, there is no movie theme
more time-worn, shock-absor-
bent, or annoyingly manipulative than a child who teaches its
cynical, sobbing elders how to
live the Brave Life before dropping dead from the Ali McGraw
Movie Disease.

Six Weeks is about a tough,
rich cosmetics tycoon, a sentimental politician, and a twelve-
year-old ballerina who doesn't
stand a chance in hell of making
it through the Christmas holidays.

The characters are about as
welcome as suspicious-looking
Tylenols and the movie is extravagant rubbish I thought
went out of style with Ross
Hunter.

Dudley Moore is the kind of
California politician who sends
singing telegrams to the governor and sings them himself.
Mary Tyler Moore is the Helene
Curtis of Beverly Hills. Im-
probably, they meet when he
accidentally befriends her precocious daughter. Mary insults
Dudley at a fund-raiser for try-

ing to get her money by using
the kid. Then she calls, apolo-
gizes, and donates some money
to his campaign for Congress.

"Isn't this an extraordinary
gesture to make on behalf of a
child?" he asks. "She's an extraordinary child," she replies.
I'll say. This kid is so extraordinary she would have made Margaret O'Brien retch. She wants
to be either Margot Fonteyn or
Walter Cronkite. Besides, she's
dying of leukemia, see, but is
she depressed? Not a bit of it.

"A butterfly's lucky if it
lives six weeks," she says
pluckily, explaining the title
while littering the aisles with
wet Kleenex. Her dream is to
see Dudley elected, Mary fixed
up with him, and herself dancing the lead in Lincoln Center's
The Nutcracker.

These are lavishly dressed,
powerfully extravagant, deeply
decent folks who never picket
or march or demonstrate or
smoke pot or voice any kind of
opinion stronger than the one
that growing to be thirteen is
unimportant if one can find
Truth and Beauty riding
through Central Park in a han-
som cab to a piano concerto
written for the sound track album by Dudley Moore.

They're about as relevant to
the eighties as Amos 'n' Andy,
but they sure are huggable in

air-conditioned studio-processed Technicolor. They talk like Ma Perkins running Union Carbide, they don't do nude scenes, they are so full of peace-on-earth-good-will-toward-men they make Hallmark greeting cards read like the collected works of the Marquis de Sade.

He leaves his wife and family to devote all his time to these strangers for reasons only the scriptwriter understands. In no time, they're fulfilling the child's list of last-rites day-dreams. By the time the child staged a mock wedding in a hotel suite the size of Gracie Mansion ("I now pronounce us man, child, and wife") I felt like I had a three-day-old chicken bone stuck in my esophagus. When the child replaces the star of the *Nutcracker* and dances the lead after one day's rehearsal, my jaw dropped. Then when this glamorous trio hit the subway in their $3,000 wardrobe, laughing at the graffiti, I knew in real life they'd be marked for death.

What the hell, it's only a movie. Even if they are only caricatures of living things drowning in an implausible Hollywood script, who, in a poor crowd that comes in out of the traffic and hysteria of the outside world to get off their feet and have a good cry, is going to analyze?

The grown-ups make all the mistakes, the kid teaches them how to live before it's too late, and it's suddenly 1945 again and nobody suffers very much—except the poor ballerina.

No harm in a little computer-programmed emotionalism, as long as we know how phony it is, but couldn't *Six Weeks* have been better? The screenplay is a bare outline. There are more holes in the characters and their motivations than you get in a sponge.

Both Moores try to hold the mess together with no help from the direction, camera work, or dialogue. The kid, a buck-toothed dancer named Katherine Healy, isn't going to make anyone long for adolescence again.

Six Weeks wants you to weep buckets and also have fun, but it's such a ridiculous downer that the audience does more laughing than crying—in all the wrong places.

SKOKIE (TV, 1981)

★ ★ ★ ★   Directed by Herbert Wise. Screenplay by Ernest Kinoy. *With Danny Kaye, John Rubenstein, Carl Reiner, Kim Hunter, Eli Wallach, Lee Strasberg, Brian Dennehy, Ed Flanders,*

George Dzundza, James Sutorius, and Ruth Nelson.

Skokie recreates the harrowing events of 1977 and 1978, when a band of Nazi storm troopers planned a demonstration march through the streets of Skokie, Illinois, complete with Hitler memorabilia and swastikas and uniforms of the Third Reich. Thirty thousand members of that community were Jews, many of them survivors of Hitler's death camps who watched the whole thing happen once before.

Danny Kaye plays Max Feldman, an immigrant who heard the pacifist pleas of "Go home, pull down the window shades, nothing will happen if you keep your mouth shut" decades earlier and vowed it would never happen again. Now he hears the same speeches from the mayor of Skokie, the local businessmen, and even his friends at synagogue: "Ignore them, don't give them the national exposure to spread their anti-Semitic garbage." This time he vows to stop them even if he has to resort to violence.

In a brilliant, analytical, yet down-to-earth screenplay by Ernest Kinoy, *Skokie* investigates every shadow in every corner of this modern dilemma. You see the kids of a new generation who don't understand any of it. You get the opinions of the militants in the Jewish Defense League. You get the moral and legal ramifications inherent in either protecting or opposing the First Amendment guarantees of free speech. In the process, you will be forced to reexamine your own values and your own feelings about the American system. In America, you cannot silence anyone's political ideas just because they're unpopular. If you support a presidential candidate's right to a platform, then you must by the same token support the constitutional rights of Nazis, Communists, and the Ku Klux Klan.

John Rubenstein gives a valid, sincere performance as the unlucky Jewish lawyer who must place his respect for the Constitution above his personal hatred of Nazis, defending them against the Skokie citizens' injunction against marching, in a controversial court case that brings him no personal pride.

As the senior legal adviser to the Civil Liberties Union, Lee Strasberg gives an equally impassioned performance in trying to draw the fine line between politics and common decency. And there are marvelous, full-bodied characterizations by Eli Wallach, as the town lawyer; Ed Flanders, as the bewildered and beleaguered mayor of Skokie; and Kim Hunter, as Kaye's terrified wife.

But it is still Danny Kaye who reduces the screen to the most palpable human denominator in a performance charged with sensitivity and emotional impact. They say behind the mask of every clown beats the heart of a great dramatic actor; I doubt if anyone really knew until *Skokie* just how wide-ranging and versatile this beloved clown's true talent really was.

Superbly directed in a semi-documentary style by Herbert Wise, the real power of this deeply moving television play lies not only in its relevance but in its complexity—in the way it makes its audience feel and understand all sides of every issue it explores. The events in Illinois remain a reminder of the high price we've paid for freedom. The way a small town stood up and fought also serves as a warning that the horrors of the past must never happen again.

SMALL TOWN GIRL (1952)

★ ★ ★ Directed by Leslie Kardos. Screenplay by Dorothy Cooper and Dorothy Kingsley. Produced by Joe Pasternak. With Jane Powell, Farley Granger, Ann Miller, Bobby Van, S. Z. Sakall, Robert Keith, Fay Wray, Billie Burke, Nat King Cole, Dean Miller, and William Campbell.

This is a delectable 1952 MGM musical about a rich, spoiled New York playboy (Farley Granger) who gets jailed for speeding in a Connecticut town and the judge's daughter (Jane Powell) who falls for him. Jane sings with her Baccarat crystal voice and Ann Miller heats up the screen with torrid production numbers, but it is really dancer Bobby Van who steals the movie in a Busby Berkeley number in which he literally jumps all over town, followed by citizens, babies, and even household pets. Solid entertainment from start to finish the way only MGM could provide it.

A SOLDIER'S STORY (1984)

★ ★ ★ Directed by Norman Jewison. Screenplay by Charles Fuller. Produced by Jewison, Ronald L. Schwary, and Patrick Palmer. With Howard E. Rollins, Jr., Adolph Caesar, Art Evans, David Alan Grier, Denzel Washington, David Harris, and Patti LaBelle.

It starts with a murder and ends, one hundred and two minutes later, with a proud black Army platoon marching to the swinging jazz beat of "St. Louis Blues." In the marvelous movie that goes between, the souls are splayed like fish fillets under a butcher's knife while the stunned viewer is riveted. The movie is Norman Jewison's production of *A Soldier's Story*.

Adapted by Charles Fuller from his Pulitzer Prize-winning off-Broadway play, the movie is savage and funny in the way it observes with an extraordinary eye the ordinary people in a Louisiana Army barracks in 1944.

The time is World War II, when everything was segregated, including the armed forces. Blacks could enlist, but to serve their country meant mopping latrines.

In a black military camp in the South, the sight of all those frustrated blacks in patriotic khakis on the drill field caused double trouble. When a tyrannical black sergeant is killed in the dead of night with a .45-caliber bullet, the case seems simple: It was either the Ku Klux Klan or local rednecks tanked up on moonshine.

Black soldiers were both feared and hated, but the worst thing of all—the thing more people resented than anything else—was when a soldier was black and Yankee to boot. Captain Davenport, a lawyer sent from Washington to investigate the case, is both.

To the white officers running the base, he's supposed to set an example for the black enlisted men, be a credit to his race, and still satisfy the Pentagon. To the awestruck black soldiers he must interrogate, he's looked up to as a calming influence, a prime example of a black man who made it to the top, a role model.

How can he complete his assignment honestly, soothe ruffled nerves, make peace, and avoid unnecessary friction among the white townspeople? This is clearly a job for Sidney Poitier, and if *A Soldier's Story* seems faintly reminiscent of *In the Heat of the Night*, you're not far off course. Same director, same basic premise (noble Negro from the North helps southern bigots solve a crime).

But *A Soldier's Story* is more than just a clever racial joke put to the test. Nothing is quite what it seems and as the cool lawyer uncovers layer after layer of piping-hot emotions, he finds black men who are more prejudiced than any Georgia cracker, as well as preconditioned, drawling bigots who turn out to be more decent than any black would ever suspect.

The film exposes not only military corruption among the

whites but inverted snobbism among the blacks. The ending does not pay off—the identity of the killer is less a revelation than the true nature of the victim's character—and as a tale of friction and violence in the confinement of an army camp, the story lacks the shock treatment of something like *Streamers*.

But in its examination of issues, in its unflashy imagery of time and place, and in its powerfully written characterizations, *A Soldier's Story* is exhilarating in a cautious way. It's a film that keeps you interested and awake.

Much of the interest centers on the fine ensemble playing. Howard Rollins, Jr., who walked away with *Ragtime* (he may be the only memorable thing about *that* film), has the Sidney Poitier role—the black Robert Redford—and he's good at it. He's in charge, he controls the tone, he has what contemporary black politicians call "controlled dignity."

In perfect contrast, Adolph Caesar as the murder victim is a tiny, gnarled little gnome of combustible TNT—an army sergeant driven mad by his hatred of his own skin color, fused by such a burning need to purify his race that he's willing to bully and destroy all black stereotypes. He'd happily kill any "Sambo" who liked cornbread or watermelon.

Ironically, he wants to be a real soldier and fight the Nazis, but what he turns into among his own men is the ultimate fascist.

It is one of the film's most bizarre pleasures that these two dynamic actors never meet in the course of the story, never share any scenes together, yet give the movie its contrasts and keep it moving. They dominate the screen from different time frames.

Both from a structural and thematic standpoint, *A Soldier's Story* is a difficult thing to pull off, but Norman Jewison has done a masterful job of blending so many diverse elements. He has been served by an impeccable cast, most impressively by Denzel Washington as a proud private who feels his race has been insulted by the neurotic sergeant, and by David Alan Grier as the corporal who has the courage to admit he's been wrong in his judgment of the investigator.

Patti LaBelle, the feisty and iron-lunged singer, makes a juicy debut as an entertainer who dispenses soul food and soul songs to the black recruits on the steamy side of town. And there is enormous energy and drive in the stirring, throbbing jazz score by Herbie Hancock.

A Soldier's Story is, above all, a literate film that honors the almost defunct tradition of the well-constructed script. It roots out a lot of horrible misunderstandings about racial prejudice in cinematic ways that result in a collision of temperaments and ideas. I came away from it not feeling distanced because I'm white, but charged with the conviction that there is black and white on both sides of the color barrier.

SOMEBODY UP THERE LIKES ME (1956)

★ ★ ★   Directed by Robert Wise. Screenplay by Ernest Lehman. Produced by Charles Schnee. *With Paul Newman, Pier Angeli, Eileen Heckart, Sal Mineo, and Robert Loggia.*

Paul Newman, in the role that made him a star, is wonderfully winning and believable as Rocky Graziano, the boxer from the slums who fought his way up from a life of street crime to become middleweight champion of the world. From reform school and penitentiary to the center ring, the story of how a hoodlum with nothing but courage and two fists gained respect in sports is every bit as inspiring as *Rocky* (this is the film that shaped Sly Stallone's passion for boxing films), and Newman could lick Stallone any day of the week in the acting competition. Pier Angeli, as Graziano's long-suffering girl, and the fabulous Eileen Heckart, as his consumptive, bedraggled mother, head a fine supporting cast, and the big fight between Graziano and Tony Zale is one of the best-staged slugfests in movie history. This one packs a whopping punch.

SOME CAME RUNNING (1959)

★ ★ ★   Directed by Vincente Minnelli. Screenplay by John Patrick and Arthur Sheekman, based on the novel by James Jones. Produced by Sol C. Siegel. *With Frank Sinatra, Dean Martin, Shirley MacLaine, Arthur Kennedy, Martha Hyer, Leora Dana, and Nancy Gates.*

James Jones wrote the definitive study of soldiers under stress in *From Here to Eternity*. This time he focuses on how they continued to agonize at home after World War II. Frank Sinatra is fine as a lonely and skeptical Army corporal adjusting to life after battle in his hometown in Indiana, and Dean Martin is a major surprise as the poker player who adopts the hero as a pal. But it is really Shirley MacLaine who steals the picture under Vincente Minnelli's sensitive direction, as a floozy with a heart of maple syrup who comes to a tragic end. Arthur Kennedy, Martha Hyer, and Leora Dana lend crisp support in this frank and explosive yarn.

SOMETHING FOR EVERYONE (1970)

★ ★ ★ Directed by Harold Prince. Screenplay by Hugh Wheeler and Harry Kressing. Produced by John P. Flaxman. With Angela Lansbury, Michael York, Anthony Corlan, Heidelinde Weis, Eva-Maria Meineke, and Jane Carr.

Angela Lansbury is magnificent as an aristocratic German countess after World War II whose Bavarian castle is falling on hard times. Her son is homosexual, her daughter is a fat wimp, and she owes on her caviar bill. Enter Michael York, a handsome young footman who corrupts, compromises, and cons everyone, rising to the top of the social ladder through both seduction and murder. A modern fairy tale, gorgeously photographed, brilliantly directed by Broadway's Harold Prince, and something of a cult classic.

SONG OF BERNADETTE (1943)

★ ★ Directed by Henry King. Produced by William Perlberg. Screenplay by George Seaton, based on Franz Werfel's novel. With Jennifer Jones, William Eythe, Charles Bickford, Vincent Price, Anne Revere, Lee J. Cobb, and Gladys Cooper.

The pious, heavy-handed story of the little girl who saw a miracle in Lourdes and changed religious history is a bit lumpy and overcooked, but you'll understand why Jennifer Jones won the Oscar in 1943. The luminous sincerity that pours out of her from beginning to end is the only miracle in this heavenly hash.

SOPHIE'S CHOICE (1982)

★ ★ ★½ Directed by Alan J. Pakula. Screenplay by Pakula, based on the novel by William Styron. Produced by Pakula and Keith Barish. With Meryl Streep, Kevin Kline, Peter MacNicol, Greta Turken, and Gunther Maria Halmer.

Before I saw Sophie's Choice, the alleged magic of Meryl Streep eluded me totally. I didn't understand what the fuss was all about.

At best, she seemed like a gifted, well-trained professional victimized by bad habits and irritating mannerisms. At worst, she seemed like a frozen, boring blonde with ice water in her veins, from the Grace Kelly–Tippi Hedren School of Dramatic Art. I simply didn't get the message. *Sophie's Choice* changed my mind.

As Sophie Zawistowska, the beautiful, tragic Polish immigrant who survived Auschwitz to be tortured by her memories in postwar Brooklyn, she is positively mesmerizing. Frankly, the film Alan J. Pakula has adapted and directed from the famous novel by William Styron is just as amazing as she is.

Sophie's Choice is a haunting, lyrical film of great emotional and intellectual stimulation that leaves the audience wasted and weak from excitement and grief. The book was a popular but lugubrious gumbo of overwritten literary pretentiousness, at the heart of which throbbed a frail but intensely vibrant story about three people whose lives are crossed by fate in an illogical time and place.

Except for its self-conscious voice-over narration, the movie prunes away the clutter and leaves the story where it belongs.

The time is 1947; Stingo, a twenty-two-year-old writer from rural Virginia, finds himself renting a room in a pink boarding house in Brooklyn.

Almost immediately, he is drawn to his exotic upstairs neighbors: Sophie, with her gossamer summer dresses, her sad, liquid eyes, and her trembling hands, wearing her doom like a string of pearls; and Nathan, her Jewish lover—a neurotic clown with a Jekyll-and-Hyde personality, sometimes charming and charismatic, other times violent and sadistic.

This unlikely trio becomes inseparable; despite the ominous warning cloud that hovers overhead, Stingo finds his new friends glamorous and fascinating.

He develops crushes on them both, the way young, impressionable southern boys who long to be great writers often find themselves infatuated with bizarre eccentrics who are so different from the folks back home.

And so begins a love story that changes Stingo's life forever.

The deeper he sinks into his new friends' lives, the more he learns about the mysteries and lies and secrets that enshroud them both.

In flashbacks that look like black-and-white newsreel footage, we learn the truth about Sophie—including her resistance work in Warsaw and the horrors of the concentration camp where she survived using her secretarial skills to work and flirt with Nazi commandant Rudolf Hess while her children were exterminated.

Nathan, who has rescued her after she passed out from anemia and hunger at The New York Public Library, has taken the place of Sophie's Nazi torturers, punishing her for her consuming guilt in a sadomasochistic love affair. And poor, shattered Stingo, who loves them both, is the only one who knows the truth.

Here are serious, sensitive, well-defined characters, played by real artists instead of Hollywood hacks.

Peter MacNicol astounded me, considering how bad he was in *Dragonslayer*. He is the observer, the camera. Sophie's story passes across the retina of his eye like a landscape seen from a train window. Yet he manages the swift changes of mood from joy to despair to youthful silliness to puppy love with admirable aplomb.

Kevin Kline, making his film debut, is a brooding, handsome clown as Nathan, filling the spaces with energetic rages and sunny sweetness in a complex performance rich with color and contrast.

But Meryl Streep is the swirling emotional vortex. Butchering the English language,

struggling to forget the past, trying to pull the jagged shards of her life together, her work is so natural and full of unexpected insights that she makes each scene a marvelous adventure.

It's hard enough for an all-American girl from New Jersey to play an ill-fated Blanche Du-Bois with the demons of World War II written all over her, but Streep does it in not one but *three* separate languages!

In the flashbacks, she works with the Polish actors in Polish and with the German actors in German.

At times, she actually seems to be thinking in the other languages and speaking in English, breaking up the sentences, making a shambles of the vocabulary, jumbling words and generally finding amusement in her faux pas. What she accomplishes is positively staggering.

If I may be allowed one tiny objection, she really does cry more than anyone since Margaret O'Brien.

Tears roll down her sculptured cheekbones in a constant flood, like the sap from maple trees. How can she expect the rest of us to cry for Sophie, if she's doing all the work for us?

Still, this is a very minor grouse. She is nearly flawless.

Alan J. Pakula's restrained direction is admirable.

Nestor Almendros, the great cameraman who is as much a screen presence as the stars he photographs, has given the film a burnished beauty, like the glow of old paintings.

I love the construction and shape and poetic tempo. And what a pleasure it is to encounter intelligent writing again.

Everything fuses to make *Sophie's Choice* a work of grace, sophistication, and substance. It lulled me into a trance, like the aroma of some powerful hallucinatory incense.

As for the Oscar-winning performance by Meryl Streep, I am happy to eat crow.

Not often—but sometimes—a critic is the last to know.

SORCERER (1977)
★ ★ Directed and produced by William Friedkin. Screenplay by Walon Green. With Roy Scheider, Bruno Cremer, Amidou, and Francisco Rabal.

William (*The Exorcist*) Friedkin's 1977 remake of Henri-Georges Clouzot's acclaimed 1953 French thriller *The Wages of Fear* was not well received by critics or ticket buyers, but on the home screen it seems more intimate and gripping, well worth a second look. The title is the name of a truck that drags four men through the muddy jungles of a banana republic carrying nitroglycerine to a burning oil derrick two hundred miles away. If they make it, the wages will be enough to buy their way out of this depraved hell and get them back home to civilization. They have nothing to lose but their lives. Roy Scheider is the New Jersey hood hiding from the Mafia; Bruno Cremer is the French banker wanted for criminal fraud; Francisco Rabal is a Mexican assassin, and Amidou is a Palestinian terrorist. All of them end up at the end of the world—broke, on the verge of mental collapse, victimized by crooked South American cops and immigration patrols, terrorized by local guerrillas, and desperate to escape. Defying the laws of man, nature, and gravity, they set out through the uncharted terrain of snakes, mud, rain, jungle, and precipitous mountain roads, and there is tragedy, heartbreak, and hysteria every inch of the way. The actors take a beating and so does the audience, but the camera work is awesomely poetic, the acting is first-rate, and the result is filled with tension, suspense, steamy atmosphere, and electrifying thrills. I won't give away the ironic ending, but I can't help but wonder where the lost souls of a poverty-stricken jungle outpost found a recording of Charlie Parker's "I'll Remember April."

SORROWFUL JONES (1949)

★ ★ ★ Directed by Sidney Lanfield. Screenplay by Melville Shavelson and Jack Rose. Produced by Robert L. Welch. *With Bob Hope, Lucille Ball, William Demarest, Mary Jane Saunders, and Bruce Cabot.*

Sorrowful Jones teamed Bob Hope and Lucille Ball for the first time in this Damon Runyon farce that is loaded with explosively funny gag lines and hilarious situations guaranteed to keep you laughing. Hope is a bookmaker who becomes the accidental guardian of an orphan girl and Lucy is the hard-boiled nightclub singer who mothers them both. This provides the stars with endless opportunities to clown and mug in their airiest style. The highlight is Hope's endeavors to bring a real horse from the racetrack into the hospital where the kid is dying, resulting in a Keystone Cops chase that will make you howl. Some folks prefer *Little Miss Marker*, the Shirley Temple original on which this film is based, but with the emphasis on the con man instead

of the child, the result is funnier.

SPLASH (1984)

★ ★ ★ Directed by Ron Howard. Screenplay by Lowell Ganz, Babaloo Mandel and Bruce Jay Friedman. Produced by Brian Grazer. With Tom Hanks, Daryl Hannah, John Candy, and Eugene Levy.

Splash is a whimsical piece of fluff that asks the burning question, "Can a mermaid from Cape Cod find happiness in dry dock with a wholesale grocery distributor from Manhattan?"

It is one of the more relentlessly silly farces you will ever see, but it's gentle, harmless and giddily romantic. And, after all, how many mermaid movies do you get in a lifetime?

Splash is the work of thirty-year-old Ron Howard. America will always know him first as little Opie on *The Andy Griffith Show*, then for years as Richie on *Happy Days*. Howard was always the freckle-faced redhead with the big gumdrop eyes who answered the eternal question of worried parents everywhere: "Do you know where your children are?"

Now that he's launched a successful new career as film director, it's probably safe to say there was some accuracy in his all-American clean-cut image. *Splash* is sexy and borderline raunchy (especially when funnyman John Candy is onscreen), but it's also wholesome and full of wide-eyed boy's book splendor and awe.

Howard is obviously a director with old-fashioned values. Still a pup, he couldn't have grown up on movies of the '30s and '40s, but *Splash* has the same sweetness, the same richness of spirit. And it is never boring.

What is it? Part farce, part love story, part male fantasy for girlie magazine subscribers, part underwater fable.

Tom Hanks, a likable, resilient actor, plays an industrious but unfulfilled urban achiever named Allen who runs a successful wholesale produce market, while his fat, preening and terminally horny older brother, Freddie (John Candy), gets the girls.

Allen has never been the same since he was eight years old, when he fell off a boat near Cape Cod and got rescued by a mermaid. Twenty years later, Allen is still hung up on that mermaid. No other girl measures up.

So one day he climbs into a New York cab, says "Cape Cod!" to the driver, and about $2000 later, he's back on the beach in Cape Cod, where the same mermaid rises from the sea and rescues him all over again.

Following him to the Big Apple to return his wallet, the mermaid emerges naked from the river and gets arrested at the foot of the Statue of Liberty for indecent exposure. Ensconced in Allen's apartment, her secret is safe as long as she's dry. But every once in a while, she almost blows her cover by pouring salt in the bath and growing a tailfin that looks like one of Marlene Dietrich's skintight beaded evening gowns from the Cafe de Paris.

As played by luscious Daryl Hannah, this mermaid is not just another beached brook trout. She's never been out of water before, but she knows enough to get to Bloomingdale's. She takes the name Madison from a street sign, learns English in one afternoon from watching TV, and in no time she's fallen in love with the joy credit cards can bring to a girl with no underwear.

The scenes that show her adjusting to a weird but wonderful new civilization are endearing and funny. There are no big laughs here, just mild chuckles. When a lobster arrives in a restaurant, she eats the whole thing, shell, claws and all, explaining that's how everybody does it back home.

There's a mirthfully malevolent mad scientist (Eugene Levy, from *SCTV* and a comic peer of John Candy's) who is on the case, following Madison's fishy scent with buckets, pails, seltzer bottles and garden hoses, eager to spray her with water and claim a scientific breakthrough. When he succeeds, the press has a field day ("Does she eat worms?" "Is it true she is also seeing Burt Reynolds?") and Allen even gets urgent messages on his answering machine from Mrs. Paul, manufacturer of frozen fish dinners.

Splash turns melancholy when the scientists torture and mutilate the once-beautiful Madison with lab tests and experiments, draining her of her independence and beauty.

But there's a daring escape yet to come from the fish tank at the Museum of Natural History, followed by the inevitable car chase through the New York traffic.

A number of people fall into the Hudson River, and if that is really Atlantis we see behind the end titles, then the people we see swimming toward it are very likely to arrive in need of a tetanus shot.

The script, by Lowell Ganz,

Babaloo Mandel and Bruce Jay Friedman, is never as clever as it should be, but *Splash* never swan dives into an empty pool. It dog paddles with amazing grace, thanks to Howard's visual and briskly paced direction, some poetic underwater camerawork, and a fine set of performances from the gifted cast.

Candy is one of the few screen slobs who is easy to take, Hanks combines the lanky good looks and flickering behind-the-eyes mischief of a young Henry Fonda, and as for the tasty Miss Hannah, I have only the highest praise. Wet or dry, she's a combination of Esther Williams and Charlie the Tuna.

STAND BY ME (1986)

★ ½ Directed by Rob Reiner. Screenplay by Raymond Gideon and Bruce A. Evans, based on "The Body" by Stephen King. Produced by Gideon, Evans, and Andrew Scheinman. With Wil Wheaton, River Phoenix, Corey Feldman, Jerry O'Connell, Kiefer Sutherland, John Cusack, and Richard Dreyfuss.

Rob Reiner's *Stand by Me* is about four twelve-year-olds on a perilous trek through the wilderness to view the corpse of another kid who has been killed by a speeding train. Rarely have ninety minutes of screen time been devoted to anything more trivial or pointless.

The year is 1959, a time of Hula Hoops and bubble-gum rock. The town of Castle Rock is so boring that the four younger kids who provide the center of the action hide out in a tree house smoking, cursing, talking jive, playing cards, and comparing the size of each other's sex organs.

The older boys in the town, who form a rival gang, amuse themselves by knocking people's mailboxes off their posts from car windows with baseball bats and terrorizing the younger kids.

Based on a short story by the prolific Stephen King, who publishes everything but his grocery list and calls it literature, *Stand by Me* is a "coming of age" movie. Everyone seems to come of age except the people who made it.

The kids are undaunted by moronic dialogue and no plot. "We know exactly who we were and where we were going," says the gooey-faced narrator, who grows up to be a writer played by Richard Dreyfuss. I wish somebody would tell me. I have no idea who any of these pubescent putzes are, and the movie—like the kids themselves—is clearly going nowhere.

One tough guy (River Phoenix) is considered a juvenile delinquent because he stole the school milk money. Another boy has a father in the nuthouse. A third boy is on the way to becoming the fat man in a circus sideshow. The central kid, who grows up to be the writer, has a father who hasn't paid any attention to him since the day he ate laundry bleach under the kitchen sink.

Although nothing of any consequence happens to anybody in *Stand by Me* the kid with the big imagination passes the time by telling the other kids stories. This gives Rob Reiner a chance to stage a fantasy scene that should win some kind of award for ultimate tastelessness. In the story, the fat kid swallows an entire bottle of castor oil before a blueberry pie-eating contest. The result is a "complete and total barf-o-rama" in which everyone on the screen vomits in a marathon that lasts too long for any sane purpose.

It is refreshing to see kids who don't wreck cars, break into houses, shoot up drugs, impregnate their school chums, or journey to an alien planet on school vacation. But if you're sensitive to filthy language, be forewarned: the kids in *Stand by*

Me (a title that makes no more sense than the rest of the movie) turn the air blue with idiot dialogue so blue it would shock a vessel of Merchant Marines.

The situations are dreary, the kids' adventures aren't particularly imaginative (they fall into a swamp and get covered with leeches), and in the last two reels Rob Reiner switches to some familiar teenage moralizing in which the characters are exhorted to believe in themselves.

The overriding impression is one of utter nihilism with no muted shades of pastel logic. The world is divided between the kids, who are bored and materialistic, and the older thugs, who are mercenary and without feeling. Somebody should have taken them to a Betty Grable movie.

STANLEY AND IRIS (1990)
★ ★ ★ Directed by Martin Ritt. Screenplay by Irving Ravetch and Harriet Frank, Jr. Produced by Alex Winitsky and Arlene Sellars. *With Jane Fonda and Robert De Niro*

Stanley and Iris is a love story with a social conscience. Statistics insist twenty percent of the United States is illiterate, and in an astounding performance of strength and courage, Robert De Niro plays one of the twenty-seven-million Americans over the age of seventeen who cannot read or write. He is Stanley Cox, a single man with an ailing father as a dependent, unable to write a check, read a newspaper, decipher a road sign, or drive a car. Still, he manages to hold down a job as a cook in the factory canteen of a bakery and keep his secret. Jane Fonda is fellow worker Iris King, a lonely widow with two kids to raise. When her purse is snatched and her paycheck stolen on her way home from work, Stanley comes to her aid and a friendship develops. When Stanley loses his job, Iris becomes his tutor and discovers the hidden intelligence and resourcefulness the learning disabled are capable of. She brings him out of his darkness. He brings her out of her paralyzing grief and frustration. It's a touching, sensitive look at working-class people, a territory traveled before by director Martin (*Norma Rae*) Ritt, but its heart sings loud and true. De Niro is wonderful, showing Stanley's pride, humiliation, and shame with affecting candor. Fonda is as real as breathing. It's about coping with drawbacks and making life work, about little people with small dreams and big feelings. *Stanley and Iris* certainly educated me.

STAR 80 (1983)

★ ★ ★ ½ Directed and written by Bob Fosse. Produced by Wolfgang Glattes and Kenneth Utt. With Mariel Hemingway, Eric Roberts, Cliff Robertson, Carroll Baker, and Roger Rees.

From *Playboy*'s Playmate of the Year to the supermarket tabloids' Scandal of the Year, the short, dazzled, and tragic life of Dorothy Stratten was the hairraising stuff cheap TV specials and dime-store paperbacks feed on.

It is something of a major surprise, then, to see *Star 80*, the powerful, harrowing, and deeply affecting movie Bob Fosse distilled from the journalistic facts in Dorothy's life. It is one bruising blockbuster of a motion picture.

A lesser director would almost certainly have gone for the lurid details, but in *Star 80* Fosse has tried to uncover something even more grievous than the story of a golden girl who died on her way to the top when her loser of a husband blew her head off with a shotgun, then committed suicide.

You can't really say Fosse has handled the gory details with tasteful discretion, eschewing sensationalism. *Star 80* spares nothing, and when it comes to the final confrontation between Dorothy, weak from pity and guilt, and Paul, the sleazy small-time promoter who built her career only to find himself discarded along the Yellow Brick Road, the film literally sprays blood and guts and brains all over walls in vibrant Technicolor.

No, *Star 80* doesn't mince daintily around the gruesome corners of this miserable story. But what Fosse does is make a strong, substantial attempt to explain the twists of fate that brought these two people to their destiny.

In the process, he not only makes Dorothy Stratten a three-dimensional all-American girl who wanted to be somebody, but strips away the flashy veneer of Paul Snider, a fast-talking punk who became the victim of his own stalled ambition.

By the time he's through, the viewer has experienced a roller-coaster ride through the high-tech world of fashion, glamour, photography, movies, and all the other Day Glo prisms of phony light where the American dream is trapped.

The camera plays a particularly valid role in *Star 80*. (The title, by the way, is the California license plate Dorothy used on her status-symbol Mercedes to advertise the merchandise behind the wheel.) From the day Paul Snider found her, ignorant and eighteen, working as a waitress in a Vancouver Dairy Queen, his camera started clicking, like the click of a gun trigger.

Brilliantly played by Eric Roberts, Paul is a small-potatoes, vaseline-domed hustler looking for a meal ticket. Sweeping Dorothy off her feet, he took her off malteds and introduced her to white wine. Instead of bobby sox and charm bracelets, he gave her angoras and topaz, promising her appointments with "agents, millionaires, the people who produce *Charlie's Angels* and read *Playboy*!"

Dorothy, played with wide-eyed innocence by the newly refurbished Mariel Hemingway, was a sweet, vulnerable girl who bought the success trip and paid for it with her life.

As Dorothy climbed toward Oz, scaling the hills of Beverly en route, the big shots with the money and power started to take their own pictures, and squeezed Paul out of the frame. As the ultimate "wizard," Cliff Robertson makes a rather slimy character out of Hugh Hefner—oozing through his vulgar parties in the Hollywood Playboy mansion in rainbow-colored satin pajamas like the contents of a lubricant that's been

stepped on by a high-heeled wedgie. But Dorothy was halfway there, and it was obvious she wasn't in Kansas (or Vancouver) anymore.

First, she felt guilty. She owed Paul something. Then she felt embarrassed. He was in the way. Then he got expensive, wasting her hard-earned money on cars, clothes and tramps. She was going places and he just could not keep up with her.

Her tragedy was loyalty. His tragedy was frustration. There is ultimately nobody more pathetic than the people who live on the sidelines, who cannot grow at the same speed as the people they started out with.

Paul's jealousy overcomes what little decency he had left; he first bullies Dorothy, then he shames her. Finally, when she moved in with the man who directed her in her first and only major film, Paul swallowed his pride and begged for her love. What came next is the stuff that turns ordinary girls with pretty faces and small talents into posthumous legends.

Fosse has forged these complex emotional materials into a film of sobering impact and substance. *Star 80* is shocking, disturbing, unforgettable. Fosse uses an almost documentary approach, bridging the fragments with the continuing click of metals, from the shutter snap that takes the first nude snapshots to the final click of the shotgun that completes the story.

The technical skill is awesome, the dark but revealing dialogue economical, the performances shattering.

In supporting roles, Carroll Baker is just right as Dorothy's skeptical mother, powerless to do anything more than stand by and watch her daughter change from a nice girl to sex kitten in pursuit of the elusive carousel ring; and Roger Rees is effective as the director-lover Aram Nicholas (a character based on Peter Bogdanovich.)

There is some indication that Miss Hemingway was learning how to act. As awkward, masculine, and unattractive as she was in the abysmal *Personal Best* she's soft, adorable, and genuine here.

But in the end, it is really Eric Roberts who gives this film its centrifugal force. Pumping his muscles for superiority, bellowing to hide his fear, sweating ambition, and drooling with insincere charm, he swallows the screen with the range and fluidity of his characterization. In certain scenes, he reminds me of a New Age Montgomery Clift; he has hungry eyes and heartbreaking charisma. His glazed, throbbing picture of a starving outsider driven mad by the scraps from somebody else's banquet turns *Star 80* into a personal triumph—an electrifying study of frustration as art.

A STAR IS BORN (1954; 1983, reissue)

★ ★ ★ ★ Directed by George Cukor. Produced by Sid Luft. Screenplay by Moss Hart. *With Judy Garland, James Mason, Jack Carson, Tommy Noonan, and Charles Bickford.*

The magic and majesty of Judy Garland lives on!

Liza Minnelli remembered her mother, depressed and distraught over the cutting of her beloved "Lose That Long Face" number from *A Star Is Born*, sitting on the edge of the nine-year-old Liza's bed saying: "They just don't care."

What the restoration of the uncut version of this 1954 movie classic proved, among other things, was that people *do* care. They care very much indeed.

But what about the movie? And what about the restored previously missing half hour? Was it worth the fuss?

In a word, yes. It seems redundant to review a film that is already acknowledged by everybody who knows anything about movies as the epitome of genuine motion-picture artistry.

But the contents of the footage that was unwisely excised help to solidify the relationships in Moss Hart's brilliantly crafted screenplay between Norman Maine, the fading film star played by James Mason, and Vicki Lester, the rising young starlet who loves him, played by Judy Garland.

In the cut version, Mason talks her into quitting her job with a swing band and taking a chance on Hollywood. She enters the studio for her screen test the very next morning, and the rest is history.

In the more subtle transitions director George Cukor intended, Mason forgets all about his promise and departs the following morning for a remote movie location, leaving the penniless Judy to shift for herself, in a variety of jobs, from singing the jingle for a coconut-oil shampoo commercial to working as a curb-service waitress selling nutburgers in a typical California drive-in. These vital scenes build a foundation for and are essential to an understanding of the intense relationship that follows.

But the real crime was the elimination of two of Harold Arlen and Ira Gershwin's musical numbers sung by Judy.

"Here's What I'm Here For" is sung in a studio recording session during which Mason proposes to Judy on a "live" mike and the mischievous studio technicians play it back, reducing the two stars to hysterical fits of laughter. Here, Judy reveals such a genius for comic timing and such a natural on-camera response to the requirements of a scene that it is inconceivable anyone could ever have thought of deleting the sequence from the film.

Finally there is the legendary "Lose That Long Face" production number, in which Judy—camouflaged as a freckle-faced newsboy—knocks herself out singing and dancing with a gang of street urchins although in reality her heart is breaking. First we see the number, one of those sparkling panaceas of Technicolor pizzazz, followed by a big dramatic confrontation between the star and studio chief Charles Bickford, culminating in a second ending to the song, in which the star is forced to pull herself together in the bravest show-must-go-on tradition.

Throughout, we are devastated by Garland's artistry, maturity, range, electricity, and emotional directness. This is one of the top ten first-ranking performances ever captured on film. No wonder the world fell in love with this amazing woman. No wonder her spirit and talent are still alive today through the magic of film. My hat is off to every person who pitched in to bring this lost footage back to the screen.

I only wish the whole world could see *A Star Is Born*. There will never be another Judy, and I doubt if I will ever see, in my lifetime, a better or more perfect film than *A Star Is Born*. It is imperative that we save, cherish, and preserve the one we've got.

STAR TREK—THE MOTION PICTURE (1979)

★ Directed by Robert Wise. Screenplay by Harold Livingston. Produced by Gene Roddenberry. With William Shatner, Leonard Nimoy, DeForest Kelley, Stephen Collins, James Doohan, George Takei, and Walter Koenig.

The fanatic following the *Star Trek* movies engender leaves me mystified. I never saw the TV series, so it was with total objectivity that I approached *Star Trek—The Motion Picture*, and it is with no axes to grind that I tell you I find it an excruciating bore. I could dismiss it as just another time-wasting rip-off movie initially aimed at trying to get couch potatoes back into the cinema, but this time-waster is also a money-waster, and with

$40 million down the drain, I feel angry, not bored. Instead of saying "So what?", Trekkies should yell, "How dare they?"

Star Trek—The Motion Picture isn't really a motion picture at all. There's not much motion in it, and the pictures look like they were drawn by blind cartoonists. A bit, in a way, like two weeks of Saturday morning kiddie shows on TV back-to-back.

It's an exhausting, interminable series of tacky old *Star Trek* shows glued together with $40 million worth of special effects that are as pointless as they are dull. The film is a perfect example of what happens when desperation and greed run the movies. Robert Wise, who has made some fine films, including science fiction films at a fraction of this elephantine budget, is not a stupid man. He might have made something of this mess if he had been given enough time to edit it into something more than a series of stares. But Paramount had the film locked into a premiere playdate and there was no time to preview it, test it on potential audiences, iron out the kinks and tighten up the loose screws. *Star Trek* opened cold, as they say at the Polo Lounge, and the result is like a funeral nobody has the heart to attend. *Star*

Trek should have addressed itself to people who have no idea what to expect. The rest of the audience, one assumes, will be "Trekkies," who will sit through anything.

As it is, the special effects are for the newcomers, who will have seen them all before in better films. The rest is for Trekkies, and everyone gets half a loaf. William Shatner and Leonard Nimoy have been reincarnated from the old TV show along with most of the lesser characters. They all look embalmed.

Among the new additions, there's a bald-headed Indian named Persis Khambatta who mutters a lot of clone talk about carbon monitors. If she possesses any acting ability, it's the only mystery in *Star Trek* that makes sense. Stephen Collins, a very fine actor, is reduced to a series of wide-eyed reactions that render him immobilized by the silliness of it all.

None of these actors has been given any fluidity, ease, pacing, tempo, or clarity of definition and purpose. They are like knobs on the spaceship control panel. Actors need as much editing as asteroids do.

I couldn't detect anything that even remotely suggests a plot, and for all the money wasted, the special effects observed through the Enterprise window as it zooms through time and space look like images you see inside a $2 kaleidoscope when you hold it up against a light bulb.

Imagination and suspense and originality are key issues upon which science fiction thrives. All are sadly missing here. Even if it did nothing but scare the living daylights out of me, like *Alien*, I could recommend it. *Close Encounters of the Third Kind*, *Star Wars*, and *Alien* were without insight, but they were real movies that charged the imagination and challenged the senses.

There is no denying the popularity of this phenomenon, but *Star Trek* is so ponderous and slow it just put me to sleep. The only people who could possibly benefit from seeing it now are spaced-out Trekkies and insomniacs. I call it "Star Drek."

STATE FAIR (1945)

★ ★ ★½ Directed by Walter Lang. Screenplay by Oscar Hammerstein II. Produced by William Perlberg. *With Jeanne Crain, Dana Andrews, Dick Haymes, Vivian Blaine, Charles Winninger, Fay Bainter, Donald Meek, and Frank McHugh.*

The video release of the original 1945 version of Rodgers and Hammerstein's only musical written directly for the screen, *State Fair*, was long overdue. This is the great one—not the tacky 1962 remake with Pat Boone—about an apple pie American family at the Iowa State Fair, with everything sung and strummed to a great score that includes "It Might as Well Be Spring" and "It's a Grand Night for Singing." Luscious Jeanne Crain is the farmer's daughter who finds first love with newspaperman Dana Andrews; Dick Haymes is the yokel who gets taken by showgirl Vivian Blaine, and the fabulous Fay Bainter is the mom with the prize-winning pickles and mincemeat. As all-American as a quilting bee and twice as colorful.

STEEL MAGNOLIAS (1989)
★ ★ ★ ½ Directed by Herbert Ross. Screenplay by Robert Harling. Produced by Ray Stark. With Shirley MacLaine, Sally Field, Dolly Parton, Darryl Hannah, Julia Roberts, and Olympia Dukakis.

Robert Harling adapted his hit play with so much southern fried hilarity you'll slap yourself frog-eyed from laughing so hard. It's about six dizzy modern-day southern belles who hang out in Truvy's Beauty Parlor down in Chinquapin, Louisiana—dishing dirt while dying their roots. Dolly Parton is Truvy, who believes "what separates us from the animals is our ability to accessorize." Shirley MacLaine is the town bitch who's been "in a bad mood for forty years." Darryl Hannah is a birdbrain beautician "first in her class in frostin' and streakin'." But they're not all zonked-out Scarlett O'Haras—there's also Sally Field, a devoted mother whose daughter, Julia Roberts, is young, beautiful, newlywed and a diabetic risking her life to have a baby. You'll laugh and cry and come to know these people like neighbors. The actresses work well as an ensemble, proving the true meaning of friendship through good times and rough hauls alike. And Harling's script captures the essence of today's South with a musical ear for dialogue. *Steel Magnolias* has a warmth that hugs your heart and a down-home humanity as real as grits.

ST. ELMO'S FIRE (1985)
★ ½ Directed by Joel Schumacher. Screenplay by Schumacher and Carl Kurlander. Produced by Lauren Shuler. With Rob Lowe, Demi Moore, Andrew

McCarthy, Judd Nelson, Ally Sheedy, Emilio Estevez, Mare Winningham, Martin Balsam, Jon Cutler, Joyce Van Patten.

Having established a new generation of stars nobody ever heard of, Hollywood is now risking a hernia trying to find suitable vehicles to star them in, beefing up the public's box office interest before they tire of the media hype. The best way to do this, Hollywood figures, is through a series of "psychological crisis" pictures—one, it seems, for every age group.

We've already seen young adults in crisis (*The Big Chill*, *Return of the Secaucus Seven*) and high-school kids in crisis (*The Breakfast Club*). The big questions are: How many of these soap operas can a public in crisis take? How many new actors can fickle moviegoers in crisis identify before throwing in the towel? Does anybody care?

It is doubtful that the answers to these intriguing questions will be provided by *St. Elmo's Fire*, a dull, talky little trifle. The film serves only one purpose—to showcase the talents of seven new stars labeled "Hollywood's Brat Pack."

Rarely have I seen seven more attractive, dissimilar, or thoroughly engaging performers atrophy in the skins of seven more boring, unimaginative, or thoroughly irritating characters. They are a noble, hard-working septet who deserve medals of valor.

Directed by Joel (*Carwash*, *D.C. Cab*) Schumacher, who co-wrote the enigmatic script with Carl Kurlander, *St. Elmo's Fire* is about the turmoil in the lives of a gang of friends who have just graduated from college in Washington, D.C., and are trying to adjust to the adult responsibilities of civilian life. The film seems to ask: "Is there Life After Sociology 101?" The answers can be found on daytime TV.

Rambling and unfocused, *St. Elmo's Fire* delivers snippets from the seven lives in annoying fragments. First, there is Billy (Rob Lowe), an irresponsible rock musician who wears an earring and who uses other guys' apartments and other guys' women—always without permission. Billy has a wife and baby of his own, but he's a cad, a free-loader and a womanizer, adored by Wendy (Mare Winningham), the daughter of a rich greeting-card tycoon.

Then there's Alex (Judd Nelson), a social-climbing snob with muddled political connections who works for a senator on Capitol Hill. Alex sleeps around, too, waiting for his painter girlfriend-roommate Leslie (Ally Sheedy) to marry him.

Leslie sees right through Alex's immaturity and beds down with Kevin (Andrew McCarthy), the single, unattached struggling journalist and group cynic.

Kirbo (Emilio Estevez) is a nerd with vague plans to become a lawyer who chases after an older woman.

Flitting in and out of their tangled lives like a doomed moth with singed wings is Jules (Demi Moore), who is strung out on cocaine and attracted to gang rapes and suicide attempts. She's the group swinger, but privately she voices what everyone feels inside: "I never thought I'd be so tired at twenty-two."

People who sit through *St. Elmo's Fire* will very likely know how she feels at any age. The movie is exhausting—and pointless.

College gave this trendy group a center, a focus, a safety net. St. Elmo's is the college bar in Georgetown where they sealed their friendship over endless draft beers; it's the place that draws them back to the good old times and keeps them young. The film attempts to examine what happens to the Ivy League when the ivy falls off. All it gave me was an allergy.

Meanwhile, there are some game performances worth catching. The four guys exemplify the self-serving, sexist hunger of immature American Yuppies who travel in packs for safety, while the three girls bring intensity and intelligence to the roles of their crazy, mixed-up women.

Most impressive of all in the high-voltage cast is Mare Winningham, a small symphony of aching repression in preppie skirts and penny loafers—a Raggedy Ann doll with heartbreaking eyes and vulnerable femininity who could easily live happily ever after in a Laura Ashley window.

Struggling vainly to jazz up a wooden film that stubbornly refuses to come to life, these seven "Brat Pack" members make lively, heroic paramedics, but their patient is dead on arrival.

STELLA DALLAS (1937)

★ ★ ★1/2 Directed by King Vidor. Screenplay by Victor Heerman and Sara Y. Mason, based on Olive Higgins Prouty's novel. Produced by Samuel Goldwyn. *With Barbara Stanwyck, John Boles, Anne Shirley, Barbara*

O'Neil, Alan Hale, Tim Holt and Marjorie Main.

Brave, long-suffering Barbara Stanwyck will empty your Kleenex supply in this 1937 tearjerker to end all tearjerkers that kept women of America standing in movie lines and glued to their radios for years after, following the tragic fate of Stella, a low-class woman with a heart of cotton candy who sacrifices her daughter to society so the girl can have a better life. Anyone who isn't reduced to salt water when Stella watches her long-lost daughter's wedding through a windowpane before a cop moves her on down the street must be made of tin foil. Remade with Bette Midler more than five decades later, the same story became a creepy, campy charade, but this one is still solid as Sears.

STEPPING OUT (1991)

★ ★ ★½ Directed by Lewis Gilbert. Screenplay by Richard Harris. Produced by Gilbert and John Dark. *With Liza Minnelli, Shelley Winters, Julie Walters, Ellen Greene, Carol Woods, Jane Krakowski, Sheila McCarthy, and Bill Irwin.*

Considering the pretentious junk that often overloads the circuits, it's both a thrill and a privilege to feel the genuine wattage surging from the screen to the viewer in *Stepping Out*. Though not a commercial success in theaters, it heats up the VCR as one of the warm, golden-hearted, feel-good movies of 1991.

Stepping Out is the story of ten people in Buffalo, New York, who polish their dreams for $10 a lesson in a tap-dancing class. Liza Minnelli, breaking new ground as a mature and multidimensional actress of depth and range, is the teacher—a former chorus hoofer in Broadway musicals named Mavis Turner who teaches amateurs in order to support herself. The closest she came to making it was an audition for Bob Fosse. ("I didn't get the job," she says ruefully, "but I got to touch his sleeve.") But as her class of awkward, uncoordinated, and hopeless students progresses, she gets her old self-confidence back through the team spirit she generates in others. And the class is magnificently cast and performed by a sterling group of wonderful people. Bill Irwin, as the only man in a class full of women, is a lonely klutz whose wife has deserted him, a shy insurance salesman who finds a new way to express himself through dancing. Sheila McCarthy is a bored housewife whose rich, stuffy husband abuses her. Carol Woods is a big, jolly, black homemaker who escapes through the class into a world where there is something more than dirty dishes and nagging children. Andrea Martin is an anxiety-ridden librarian who takes care of an aging invalid mother; dancing is her way of feeling attractive and feminine in a world that ignores her. Jane Krakowski (who lit up the stage on Broadway in *Grand Hotel*) is an idealistic nurse who dances to escape the sadness of her life in a hospital. Robyn Stevan is a fun-loving, gum-chewing working girl who flirts outrageously with everything in pants as an alternative to an unhappy marriage. Ellen Greene is the outspoken career woman from Brooklyn who dances to hide her inner vulnerability and insecurity. And the sensational Julie (*Educating Rita*) Walters is the British-born compulsive neatnik, obsessive about emptying ashtrays and insensitive about criticizing everyone else, trying to be perfect to mask the real pain she lives with at home, where her husband and teenage daughter from a pervious marriage are incestuously involved. And Shelley Winters is their grumpy, cantankerous senior citizen piano accompanist, the busybody and class pessimist who turns out to be human after all.

Lewis Gilbert, who directed *Educating Rita* and *Shirley Valentine*, is a modern-day George Cukor. He knows how to handle women. By the time he guides all of these disparate people to a level of pride and self-fulfillment, you know them as old friends. The movie is about how they not only come together as a class while working on a charity benefit for Save the Children, but change and improve their own lives in the process. Learning the value of self-worth through courage, camaraderie, and hard work, they also teach the audience a lesson—that little people with small dreams can make a difference. By the time they go on in the big show as the Mavis Turner Tappers, you'd have to be dead not to holler with joy and exhilaration.

Of course the big number is no surprise. This is what the movie has been leading to. But the movie retains its honesty even in triumphant choreography. The class members still retain their individual identities, with every imperfection intact, every fear showing. But friendship and group effort have taught them it is still possible in this cynical world to excel, to surpass even our most crippling self-doubts. By the time the postscript reveals the class one year later, back by popular demand, knocking their socks off in a dazzling MGM production number of the title tune by Kander & Ebb, the obstacles they've overcome will put a smile on your face and keep it there.

With synchronized intensity, a tony coordination, a svelte new body and an absence of girlish shtick, Liza Minnelli is certainly the centrifugal force that keeps this charming movie on its feet. She is a one-woman cause for celebration. But the incredibly real ensemble work, the sensitive direction, the fluid camera movements, and the lush musical underscoring by Peter Matz contribute in bountiful measure to the happy texture and resonance of this picture. The appetizers in this feast come in all the right places, and so does the dessert.

STILL OF THE NIGHT (1982)
★ ★ Directed and written by Robert Benton. With Meryl Streep, Roy Scheider, Jessica Tandy, Joe Grifasi, Sara Botsford, Josef Sommer, and Irving Metzman.

The direction and screenplay are by Robert Benton, the award-winning creator of *Kramer vs. Kramer*. The cinematography is by the award-

winning Nestor Almendros, who trained in the Eric Rohmer films before copping an Oscar for the gorgeous *Days of Heaven*. The stars are the award-winning Meryl Streep and the often-nominated Roy Scheider.

None of these are fools, all of them are gifted and accomplished, and their contributions should add up to the kind of movie that takes on "event" status.

Why then is their collaborative effort, *Still of the Night*, such a benign disappointment? Probably because it represents such a waste of their time, and ours. *Still of the Night* isn't likely to win awards for any of them. The audience goes away empty-handed, too.

The focus in this no-win situation is on the spine-tingling contemporary thriller genre. As such, it is just another in a long line of homage-cum-ripoff Hitchcock parodies. I expected so much more from the heavyweights responsible, and the film delivers so much less.

Scheider plays a cool, dull New York psychiatrist whose orderly life (we know it's orderly because he empties his ashtrays with a scowl on his face after each patient leaves) is disrupted by the savage throat-slashing murder of one of his patients. Retracing his steps, poring over notes taken during the patient's sessions, he finds a few clues that lead to a cool, dull blonde (Mèryl Streep) who works in an auction gallery.

The mystery unravels, like a case history, dropping bits of information here and there, as the corpses pile up. Slowly, the cool doctor finds himself breaking laws, obstructing justice, withholding evidence, and protecting the woman he suspects as a female Jack the Ripper.

The whole thing ends with everyone's life in jeopardy, a near-miss as the wrong suspect plunges from a balcony to the rocks below, and a neatly wrapped denouement that I found only slightly less believable than I would find the sudden announcement that Shirley Temple had become the new head of the KGB.

Along the way, there are more holes in the logic than there are in the West Side Highway. You get a lot of moods, tempos and even whole scenes from every chic thriller from *Spellbound* to *Dressed to Kill*. The principals work hard at looking cool, which means hardly working.

Scheider seems to have OD'd on Valium, while Miss Streep, in addition to her rather cool, detached mannerisms, also has

developed two annoying habits—tugging at her hair to keep it out of her eyes, and whispering her dialogue at a decibel level only a mouse can hear.

Wandering in and out is also Jessica Tandy, who lends dignity to the occasion but who seems utterly bewildered by her walk-on status. The insignificance to which she has been relegated in *Still of the Night* is as embarrassing as her brilliant performances on stage are exhilarating.

Everyone seems to be frittering away time between loftier assignments while inviting you along for the ride.

The ride is bumpy, but not much fun. *Still of the Night* is not only still; it's stillborn.

LA STRADA (1956)

★ ★ ★ ★   Directed by Federico Fellini. Screenplay by Fellini and Tullio Pinelli. Produced by Dino De Laurentiis and Carlo Ponti. *With Anthony Quinn, Giulietta Masina, Richard Basehart and Aldo Silvani.*

La Strada (*The Street*), the internationally acclaimed, Oscar-winning (Best Foreign Film) masterwork by Italian genius Federico Fellini, about a simple-minded waif (Giulietta Masina) who falls hopelessly in love with a circus strong man (Anthony Quinn), has a deeply moving power that must be seen and experienced. A genuine masterpiece.

STREAMERS (1983)

★ ★ ★ ★ Directed by Robert Altman. Screenplay by David Rabe. Produced by Altman and Nick H. Mileti. *With Mitchell Lichtenstein, Matthew Modine, Michael Wright, David Alan Grier, Guy Boyd, and George Dzundza.*

Streamers are parachutes falling from the sky that do not open. The young recruits in *Streamers*—the movie Robert Altman has made from David Rabe's shattering 1976 play—are waiting in an Army barracks for the orders that will send them to Vietnam, and also struggling with rip cords that will not open.

Their lives are threatened and altered by forces beyond their control, channeling them into a violent confrontation with themselves before they fully understand their moment of truth. The film is unsettling and powerful.

The year is 1965. The setting is a transit barracks in Virginia where tensions—sexual, racial and social—build into an increasingly bloody psychodrama between four young soldiers waiting for orders to be shipped to Vietnam.

In the maze of bunk beds that provide an impressive setting, three roommates share each other's longings and frustrations: Richie, a delicate lad who amuses, then disturbs the others with his fey, campy jokes; Billy, an all-American boy from Wisconsin trying to protect his masculine pride; and Roger, a street-smart black who rolls with the punches and doesn't make waves.

Into the unit comes a new arrival—Carlyle, a jiveass daddy whose aggressive jazz jargon and slick toughness brings with it a corrosive insinuation of sexuality and violence.

Hardly anything in the whole range of dramaturgy is more difficult than to write a play about feelings in the confined space of a room in which several lives must be explored simultaneously, but playwright Rabe has mastered the form and Altman has transcribed it beautifully to the film medium. By the end of the movie, I felt like I knew these men, had smelled their sweat and talcum, listened to their snores, touched their souls, and learned their secrets. Rabe has written a play and now a movie about feelings and the undercurrents of violence they produce, about the heat discharged by too many nerves frying in too tense a situation, too small a room. The setting becomes a rat's cage so claustrophobic that passion and murder are inevitable. By refusing to "open up" the play, Altman never dissipates the stage effects. This makes the carnage in the later passages all the more realistic and understandable.

The tensions build, at first through verbal articulation. We see the defensiveness, loneliness, anger, resentment, boredom and fear in all four boys. Then they explode as the characters are drawn into a vortex of swirling emotional intensity. It's a sobering, startling film that probes the stupid cruelty of how Army life strips the protective armor from people without their consent.

It is Richie, the prissy, sensitive one, whose homosexuality becomes the fuse that blows the other boys' masks to smithereens. The most intelligent and worldly member of the group, he flirts and teases, the way a woman tempts men in mining camps and boom towns. The others, in turn, use Richie as a symbol of their own masculine territorial imperative.

Altman's most convincing thesis is drawn from exposing the pain and rage that result when one human being ignores another's plea for sympathy. *Streamers* is his first film with a military theme since *M★A★S★H* in 1969, and one of his best.

The finely knit cast is an impeccable reminder of what accomplished screen acting is all about: Without this particular set of actors, *Streamers* would not have the same impact. Richie, the gay boy, grabs the audience instantly by the heart with his wit, knowledge, and suffering, but a lot of his charisma is due to the fascinating playing of Mitchell Lichtenstein, an actor who suggests defiled innocence masquerading as prep-school purity. Michael Wright, as the cocky, neurotic Carlyle, is like a scorpion poisoning everything in sight with his tail to hide his inner loneliness. Matthew Modine, as the kind and decent kid hiding behind macho arrogance, and David Alan Grier, as the black roomie who tries to hold the peace, have less showy roles, and are all the more compelling for their naturalistic ability to fuse their characters with deeply introspective insight without wrecking the balance.

I also admired George Dzundza, as a drunken sergeant dying of leukemia who learns there is something worse in life than being a "queer," and Guy Boyd, as his sidekick, already deranged by a career of gung-ho military mythology, who wanders innocently into the middle of violence.

Robert Altman interlocks all the pieces of this puzzle snugly and without strain. *Streamers* is talky and theatrical, like any good stage piece, but Altman relates his audience to the words with quiet, controlled bits of self-recognition. A masterful accomplishment.

SUMMER HOLIDAY (1948)

★ ★ ★ ½ Directed by Rouben Mamoulian, produced by Arthur Freed, written by Frances Goodrich, Albert Hackett, Irving Brecher and Jean Holloway. Starring Mickey Rooney, Gloria DeHaven, Walter Huston, Agnes Moorehead, Marilyn Maxwell, Frank Morgan, Jackie "Butch" Jenkins, Selena Royle.

Trying to duplicate the phenomenal, history-making success of *Meet Me in St. Louis*, veteran MGM musical producer Arthur Freed summoned to Hollywood the great Rouben Mamoulian, who had directed *Porgy and Bess*, *Oklahoma!* and *Carousel* on the Broadway stage, to tackle the monumental task of turning Eugene O'Neill's *Ah! Wilderness* into a big, splashy, red-white-and-blue piece of patchwork quilt Americana for Mickey Rooney, Walter Huston, and a glittering

cast. They dressed the package in Fourth of July fireworks, drenched it in lush three-strip technicolor, populated it with stars, and scored it with sparkling songs by Harry Warren and Ralph Blane. The result was an artistic triumph, but a commercial disaster that was, in 1948, way over the heads of the moviegoing public. Today it seems something of a creative milestone in movie musicals that departed radically from conventions of the day. Mamoulian, forced to make drastic cuts in the play to allow time for music, songs and dancing, decided to make this the first "musical play," with dialogue actually integrated into music. Songs were performed in cadence, like poetry. Actors, not singers, carried the score. In "Our Town," the first number in the first scene, every character musically articulates the ambience of life in a small Connecticut town. The glorious Fourth of July celebration begins with a firecracker and moves on to the picnic grounds, where the women sing about their pickles and pies and the men show their brawn in a beer-drinking contest, ending with the young people dancing through the park to prancing violinists. Later, to show the American fabric as the voices of the town's high school graduates drift through the acacia-lined streets and reach to the outskirts of town, Mamoulian duplicated famous paintings by Grant Wood and Thomas Hart Benton in living, human tableaux. The famous "Stanley Steamer" number, in which the entire Miller family tries out the new automobile on graduation day, is still the most rollicking number on a moving vehicle since "The Trolley Song." For the barroom sequence, in which young Richard becomes intoxicated in the hands of a New Haven trollop (played by luscious Marilyn Maxwell), the cheap hussy is transformed through the boy's eyes into a beautiful dream girl; even the room changes from a saloon into a palace. Then, as the illusion fades, everything returns to focus and becomes drab and shabby again. There was trouble from the start. Louis B. Mayer, a phony purist till the day he died, declared no prostitute could appear in an MGM musical and the whole thing was too "arty" for the average man anyway. Photography ended in 1946, Mickey Rooney's box-office appeal hit a slump, and the picture was shelved for two years. By the time it was finally released, some of the key sequences were missing and the search for the lost musical numbers (including an Arabian Nights dream sequence and Walter Huston's stirring ballad "Spring Isn't Everything") continues to this day, while *Summer Holiday* continues to build a reputation among movie buffs as a cult classic years ahead of its time. It's no *Meet Me in St. Louis*, but the gingerbread sets, hand-sewn applique gowns by Irene and Walter Plunkett, enchanting songs, magnificent period flavor of New England in summer, and warm, exceptional performances by every member of a stellar cast add up to a lot of warmth, wit and pizazz, and the experiments it made with Technicolor remain innovational.

SUMMER STOCK (1950)
★ ★ ★ Directed by Charles Walters. Screenplay by Sy Gomberg and George Wells. Produced by Joe Pasternak. With Judy Garland, Gene Kelly, Phil Silvers, Gloria De Haven, Marjorie Main, Ray Collins, Carleton Carpenter and Hans Conried.

In *Summer Stock*, Judy Garland plays a country girl whose farm is invaded by a madcap menagerie of New York thespians led by Gene Kelly and Phil Silvers, who wreck her tractor, frighten the chickens, and stage a summer musical in her barn. When Judy's kid sister, Gloria De Haven, runs off with the leading man, the terrified Judy takes over the lead, falls in love, and becomes an overnight sensation singing Harold Arlen's "Get Happy." Pure hokum, but warm and engaging, and chock-full of peppy numbers. Judy's opening number, "Happy Harvest," performed on a tractor, is a rousing and spirited winner, and Kelly does some of his most intricate dancing on a sheet of newspaper. As his feet shred and divide the paper into bits, the steps get smaller and more difficult, providing him with some fancy footwork indeed. The studio bosses, alarmed at Judy's weight problems, re-cut the film and added a new number after she underwent a strenuous weight loss, giving the movie an uneven look. The star wasn't happy with the result. It was her swan song at MGM after two historic decades.

SUMMER WISHES, WINTER DREAMS (1973)

★ ★ ★ Directed by Gilbert Cates. Screenplay by Stewart Stern. Produced by Jack Brodsky. With Joanne Woodward, Martin Balsam, Sylvia Sidney, Dori Brenner, and Ron Rickards.

Joanne Woodward gives a triumphant performance as a bored, middle-aged Park Avenue housewife whose ophthalmologist husband (Martin Balsam) is a nerd, whose daughter is a shrew, and whose son is gay. Her apartment looks like Dracula's tomb. Her mother (feisty Sylvia Sidney) drops dead in the middle of an Ingmar Bergman movie. How this woman learns to pull her life together and build a promising future despite her sour surroundings lifts the depressing subject matter beyond the level of soap opera, and how Joanne Woodward's unpretentious honesty and inner glow turn a tortured neurotic into a woman of substance and character— well, these are the elements that turn this drab material into a sensitive, touching, and beautiful movie. Highly recommended if you cherish great acting.

THE SUNDOWNERS (1960)

★ ★ ★ ½ Directed by Fred Zinnemann. Screenplay by Isobel Lennart. Produced by Gerry Blatner. With Robert Mitchum, Deborah Kerr, Peter Ustinov, Glynis Johns, Dina Merrill, Chips Rafferty, Michael Anderson, Jr., and Mervyn Johns.

Robert Mitchum and Deborah Kerr give generous, bountiful performances as a migrant sheep drover and his loyal, patient wife in this sprawling, lusty, beautifully photographed saga of the hard-knock life in the desolate country of the rugged Australian outback, directed with vitality and poignance by the great Fred Zinnemann. The human drama is as revealing as the vibrant action sequences are dynamic in this rarely seen, critically acclaimed little gem from 1960. Very highly recommended.

SUPERMAN—THE MOVIE (1978)
★ ★ ★ ★ Directed by Richard Donner. Written by Mario Puzo, Tom Mankiewicz, Robert Benton, and David Newman. Produced by Alexander and Ilya Salkind. With Christopher Reeve, Margot Kidder, Marlon Brando, Gene Hackman, Glenn Ford, Trevor Howard, Valerie Perrine, Terence Stamp, and others.

The first of four mega-movies about the comic book hero from the planet Krypton—and definitely the best—this 2½ hour entertainment is both the perfect fairy tale for grownups and an exciting enough cinematic marvel to bring out the child in every age group. Two years in the making, at a re-

ported cost of $35-million, *Superman* more than lived up to its promotional ballyhoo at the time of its release. It's the work of scores of dedicated artists and craftsmen (the end-title credits list more than 400 names belonging to everyone from process photographers to helicopter pilots, all of them invaluable contributors) whose combined efforts took comic-strip art to a movie zenith.

Director Richard Donner manages miraculously to contemporize and humanize the mythological Superman, shaping and sharpening every fantasy element to surpass mere science fiction and become part of a living dream. (Predicted newspaper headlines devoted to the untimely deaths of teenagers leaping off tall buildings in blue capes in a Superman frenzy did not come to pass.) Now, in retrospect, the only thing critics still grouse about is the silliness of the plot, but, hey, can we talk? Only a fool would pop *Superman* into the VCR expecting Eugene O'Neill. Donner went back to the source material for the Superman comics originally created by Jerry Siegel and Joe Schuster, and a flock of talented script writers fleshed out the story in dialogue that never patronizes. This is the saga of the baby, evacuated from his own planet Krypton before it explodes, and sent whirling through a myriad of galaxies on a flying star until he lands in the prairies and wheat fields of America to be discovered by a pair of Grant Wood farmers (Glenn Ford and Phyllis Thaxter) who raise him into manhood.

Deriving his strength, wisdom and power from another sun more dazzling than anything in our solar system, Superman heads for a big city called Metropolis, where he lands a job as mild-mannered reporter Clark Kent on the *Daily Planet*, falls head over biceps for dingbat city room doll Lois Lane, and uses his superior gifts to fight for "truth, justice and the American Way." Corny and somewhat campy, to be sure, but what style!

There are loose ends (a group of villains on Krypton led by Terence Stamp who threaten an eternal curse then never reappear, Superman's breaking of his father's rules forbidding him to tamper with human history) but they all fall into place in the sequel, *Superman II*. What we have to thrill to in the meantime are some of the most stupendous special effects ever seen on the silver screen: a dar-

ing helicopter rescue when Lois hangs precariously from the ledge of a skyscraper, air disasters, earthquakes, tidal waves, and a nest of screwy bad guys (Gene Hackman, Valerie Perrine, Ned Beatty) who live two hundred feet below Grand Central Terminal and aim a 500-megaton bomb at the heart of Los Angeles. The explosion of Krypton fills the screen with thousands of ice daggers that freeze the pulse as well as the landscape, and the flying sequences, in which the suspension wires have been individually brush-stroked out by hand, frame by frame, are pretty amazing, too. As special effects go, *Superman* is in a class by itself.

Marlon Brando is excellent as Superman's father (he earned $3.7 million for what looks like a cameo), Christopher Reeve is a likeable presence as both the Man of Steel and butter-fingered Clark Kent (I especially enjoyed the way he handles the humor of dashing into a New York phone booth to change clothes only to discover no door—even the superhuman magic wunderkind gets victimized by Ma Bell!), and Margot Kidder provides just the right confusion for Lois Lane—at times a relentless journalist out to get her story at all costs, and other times a kittenish nitwit, losing her cool over a guy in a Halloween costume. John Williams wrote a smashing score that wisely incorporates the Superman theme from the TV series, and real Superman buffs will get a charge out of a brief guest appearance by Noel Neill, the original Lois Lane, shown briefly on a speeding train looking properly befuddled. The cinematography by Geoffrey Unsworth, who died after the film's completion and to whom the whole thing has been generously dedicated, is work of such magnitude that I sometimes could not believe what I was seeing.

All told, an exciting and gleeful feat of stupendous filmmaking, a delight for the eyes and the nerves, and an extravaganza that zooms—sock! pow! shazam!—where other comic book fantasies often limp along like dwarfs with club feet.

SUPERMAN II (1981)

★ ★ ★ Directed by Richard Lester. Screenplay by Mario Puzo, David Newman, and Leslie Newman. Produced by Alexander and Ilya Salkind, and Pierre Spengler. With Christopher Reeve, Margot Kidder, Gene Hackman, Ned Beatty, Terence Stamp, Jackie Cooper, Sarah Douglas, Susannah York, and Valerie Perrine.

"Yeah, yeah," said the women of the world, "Superman's great—but what is he like in the sack?" Lois Lane finds out in Superman II, and it almost causes the end of civilization.

With madcap Richard Lester taking over the direction from Richard Donner, the sequel lacks the original film's structured lyricism and becomes more of an episodic James Bond orgy of mindless destruction. The flying sequences are less impressive, the metaphysical child-and-God gingerbread of the original is missing, and I longed for more of Donner's campiness. But there are still plenty of thrills, and the humor is relaxed.

Aided by about ten percent of the original footage shot for the 1978 Superman, the film opens with a prologue to catch you up on the past events. If further proof is needed of how fast the color processing fades in today's movies, these sequences are already turning brown. Nothing that is shown from the previous film has the same rich color contrasts as the scenes that follow.

The action begins anew with Superman foiling the attempts of terrorists to blow up the Eiffel Tower with a hydrogen bomb. Flying to Paris faster than the Concorde, he saves twenty hostages as well as Lois, who is climbing up the tower in heels and a lavender fashion ensemble muttering "Pulitzer Prize, Pulitzer Prize" to keep from freaking out before the Man of Steel plucks her to safety. Later, while he's retrieving a drowning child from Niagara Falls and lowering his defenses to Lois's female charms, Superman's alien enemies from Krypton are moving closer to earth, stopping on the moon to murder some U.S.-Soviet astronauts along the way.

Sneering at the Declaration of Independence and demolishing Mount Rushmore and replacing the faces with their own images en route, the villains are clearly a threat to mankind, not to mention the Moral Majority. Superman is the only other living creature who can fight them with their own Olympian power, but where is he, now that we need him?

He's in bed with Lois, *naturellement*, discovering the magic of post-coital bliss, junk food, rock music and probably Quaaludes (sex with Superman, Lois learns, is a psychedelic experience—she floats, as though stoned). Stripped of his powers after being reduced to saltwater taffy by the love of a woman, Superman is disgraced when he can't even protect her against a bully. (Are you ready for Superman being beaten up in a roadside diner by a redneck hillbilly truck driver?)

Meanwhile, a further threat is posed by the prison escape of earthly villain Lex Luthor (Gene Hackman) in a hot-air balloon. Superman's new sissy status is just what he's been waiting for and he's willing to join the sadists from outer space in return for a small favor—like being named the "king of Australia." There's only one thing to do: Superman must denounce Lois, give up women, get back into those blue long johns (no more need for phone booths, since his cover is blown anyway) and clean up the world.

The movie's most inventive sequence is the showdown in the middle of Times Square where Superman retrieves his powers long enough to pucker his cheeks and blow up a hurricane, freeze a flaming oil truck with his breath, hurl Terence Stamp through the Coca-Cola sign, and use the Empire State Building's radio control mast as a jousting lance.

None of this makes sense, of course. Nobody bothers to explain why he can't be Superman and marry Lois on the side. But don't let the filmmakers fool you with their explanation of why Margot Kidder didn't sign on for *Superman III*. They say it came down to money. The real reason, as any feminist can plainly see, is there is no longer any need for the services of a woman in Superman's life, since they've gone to careful lengths to explain why he can't afford one. Without the girls, folks, I've lost interest.

Christopher Reeve gives another of his charming Wheaties-after-Sunday-school performances, and although Valerie Perrine, Ned Beatty, and Gene Hackman are reduced to standby status, they're equally first-class. The special effects are fun and the music (Ken Thorne, replacing John Williams) is again thunderously corny.

Two more *Superman* installments followed, without success, proving a good vehicle can go just so far before it runs out of diesel.

SUPERMAN III (1983)
★ Directed by Richard Lester. Written by David and Leslie Newman. Produced by Ilya Salkind and Pierre Spengler. *With Christopher Reeve, Richard Pryor, Jackie Cooper, Annette O'Toole, Annie Ross, Pamela Stephenson, Robert Vaughn.*

Is it a bird? Is it a plane? No, it's Superdrek. For this third jog around the track, the comic strip ran out of steam and turned into a mindless farce, proving it was time to send Superman to the hangar where old flying objects go to rust.

Lois Lane flees this beached "threequel" early, heading for a Bermuda vacation with her string bikini, thus removing the ebullient Margot Kidder from the movie before it even gets started—the first in a series of tactical blunders from which *Superman III* never recovers. (A Superman movie without Lois in danger is like a Grand Prix without cars.) Worse, Clark Kent no longer changes in phone booths; he strips in police vans, passport photo machines, and even thin air. Considering what fun he started out to be, Superman certainly turned into quite a bore.

Gone, too, are Gene Hackman, Valerie Perrine and Ned Beatty, the old reliable villains. Here instead are Robert Vaughn, as an evil tycoon, and the great jazz singer Annie Ross, as his Vampira-vamped sister Vera. Together they devise an inexplicably complex plot to destroy Superman's power with the aid of computer technology. This is where Richard Pryor comes in, as an unemployed jerk who takes a computer programming course and reduces Superman to the status of a paraplegic bluejay.

Floating particles of Kryptonite do not kill the big flying drone; they just make him mean, greedy, avaricious and nasty—like everyone else in the movie. This plot-ploy also gives Christopher Reeve something to play for a change. It's rather nice to see Superman chasing blondes, drinking scotch and going to pot with a five o'clock shadow. This dark side of his personality is the only time Reeve is allowed the luxury of showing any expression other than a gooey, wooden grin.

But back to Richard Pryor. Whatever his talents (and in my opinion they remain locked in mystery) they are wasted here. It's as though the filmmakers decided, "We got Richard Pryor for two weeks—let's shoot something even if we don't have a concept or a script." Babbling incoherently about weather satellites and cosmic fallouts, he doesn't seem to know what movie he's in, or why.

Aside from one neat special effects sequence, in which Superman battles his malevolent alter ego in the pulverizing trash compactor of an automobile de-molition junkyard, there is nothing else in *Superman III* worth relating. None of the parts blend into any cohesive entity, the poor actor looks like they're counting percentage points instead of concentrating on their dialogue, and the high-tech sets look like they'd blow up within ten feet of a microwave oven.

THE SURVIVORS (1983)
★ Directed by Michael Ritchie. Screenplay by Michael Leeson. Produced by William Sackheim. With Robin Williams, Walter Matthau, Jerry Reed, and James Wainright.

The Survivors is a confusing, hysterical mess of a movie, with some funny New York dialogue and a couple of cheerful, irrelevant scenes of comic collapse administered by Robin Williams, but two-hours-plus is too much of a good thing, and this is not even a good thing.

The Survivors begins with a promising idea. A rude chorus sings Huey P. Long's political philosophy, "Every Man a King," as Robin Williams, a particularly insecure junior exec, gets fired from his job by the boss's parrot in an empty board room. When Williams complains to the secretary, she pulls an automatic pistol on him.

Embarrassed, humiliated, and hopping mad, he reluctantly heads for the unemployment bureau, where, after standing in long lines for hours, he finally gets to see an interviewer who doesn't speak English. We are clearly in for a comedy about urban chaos and the breakdown of society.

In another part of the city, Walter Matthau, a gas-station operator who is a genial product of the free-enterprise system, loses everything when his business blows up.

While Williams and Matthau are sitting in a greasy-spoon diner eating the most depressing chili dogs of their lives, a holdup artist enters, and in the ensuing fracas, Matthau recognizes the crook. Williams goes on TV, names his new friend, and now Matthau's life is in danger.

Through a series of dementedly contrived plot maneuvers too complicated to go into here, the pressures of a neurotic society persuade Williams to change his image from wimp to macho man, and he ends up in a snowbound survival camp for terrorists in the mountains of Vermont, where he takes a Green Beret-style course (for a $5000 fee) in how to be one of "the survivors" of everything from urban paranoia to Reaganomics. Director Michael Ritchie should have learned by now from other failed Hollywood comedies that nothing funny ever happens in Vermont.

Matthau looks mostly disgruntled, while Jerry Reed contributes a wooden bit as the professional killer with colitis who gets out of jail because the police computers are broken.

But it is really Robin Williams who survives *The Survivors*. There's one very amusing scene in which he demonstrates to his terrified girlfriend the grenades, knives, automatic rifles, and other weapons he's dragged home from a gleeful shopping spree. She is bewildered and appalled. He goes ape. "Whaddya gonna do if someone breaks in here?" he yells. "Stun them to death with your good taste?"

Still, the movie collapses in a clutter of missed opportunities and half-baked ideas.

It begins as a clever satire on how the frustrations of unemployment turn members of the middle class into urban guerrillas in a society where nothing works anymore. It ends up aiming its darts at polluted air, the collapsing economy, TV, U.S. presidents, America's obsession with guns—so many targets that the audience can't keep up.

Rarely have I seen a movie so desperately in need of scissors, or any script so badly in need of a red pencil.

One of the characters says that "society is going down for the big flush." If that's true, take the second half of *The Survivors* along with it.

SUSPICION (1941)

★ ★ ★ Directed by Alfred Hitchcock. Screenplay by Samson Raphaelson, Joan Harrison, and Alma Reville. *With Cary Grant, Joan Fontaine, Sir Cedric Hardwicke, Nigel Bruce, Dame May Whitty, Heather Angel, Isabel Jeans, and Leo G. Carroll.*

Vintage Hitchcock, with nail-biting tension and enough nervous stress to keep you up all night. Joan Fontaine won an Oscar as the shy, innocent girl who gradually realizes she's married to a charming liar, then begins to suspect him of trying to murder her. Nobody would ever believe Cary Grant as a killer, but watch for the scene with the poisoned milk and you'll be suspicious, too.

SWANN IN LOVE (1984)

★ ★ ★ Directed by Volker Schlondorff. Screenplay by Peter Brook, Jean-Claude Carriere, and Marie-Helene Estienne. Produced by Nicole Stephane. *With Jeremy Irons, Ornella Muti, Alain Delon, Fanny Ardant, and Marie-Christine Barrault.*

Long novels rarely make good films, and in the case of Marcel Proust infatuated directors have wisely stopped trying. More than one frustrated attempt to turn the great French writer's sprawling *Remembrance of Things Past* (the last translation ran more than thirty-six hundred pages) has been discarded through the years. Now, for the first time, we have Proust on film (or a reasonable facsimile, anyway). The result is *Swann in Love*, an intelligent, lavish, thoroughly captivating experience.

It is not, of course, the whole story. Volker Schlondorff, the German director who did an equally brilliant job of transporting Gunter Grass's *The Tin Drum* to the screen, knows how to extract cinematic lines from even the most literary of works, so instead of tackling Proust in its labyrinthine entirety, he has chosen to extrapolate one self-contained episode from the novel: the tormented love of Charles Swann, a dilettante connoisseur of the arts, for the alluring Odette de Crécy, a harlot beneath his station.

There are wickedly funny allusions to the broader panoramic backdrop of social change in fin de siècle Paris, but the enigmatic depths of Proust's writing—page after page of thoughts and memories that brought a whole society alive— remain on the library shelf. Instead, we get muted, romantic exploration of love beyond the physical, in an affair that becomes an obsession.

Jeremy Irons is marvelous as Swann—impeccably groomed, properly mannered, an arrogant neurotic who flirts with decadence beneath his refined demeanor. Torturing himself by imagining Odette in perversions with other women, driven mad by the need to possess her completely, he allows his infatuation to consume his life, his work, his dreams, wrecking his social reputation and his sanity in the process.

This is high-minded stuff, and Schlondorff handles it with rarefied taste and skill, making it all the easier to assimilate for people who know nothing of the novel. Proust lovers will carp, but film lovers will find a lot to marvel at.

Sven Nyqvist's lush cinematography gives the film a richly textured period look. All of Paris seems buttered, like a brioche.

From the gilt-drenched mansions of the super-rich to the extravagantly appointed brothels, to the sad, melancholy violin music, the film has been conceived and appointed with impeccable choices in decor, costumes, and details. Even the streets of Paris Proust wrote about have been miraculously duplicated.

The performances are superb. From Irons, speaking perfect French, to Ornella Muti, who fills the author's physical description of bruised beauty, everyone serves the project with utmost dedication.

Alain Delon, as the Baron de Charles, a flamboyant homosexual who masks his after-dark searches for young boys with an air of superiority, gives one of his most extraordinary performances. Rouged, puffed up, and prissy-mouthed, he's a remarkable study in loneliness and desperation. Marie-Christine Barrault brings a vulgar nouveau riche patroness of the arts to life with fine relish, contributing some dexterous comedy to the proceedings when she laughs so hard at dirty jokes during dinner that she dislocates her jaw.

The story ends with an epilogue some twenty years later, as a gray and dying Swann questions the waste he's made of his life, while a plumpish Odette, having achieved the status she longed for, takes the air and strolls through the boulevards of Paris, still catching the eye of her old beaux.

This is the essence of lost time Proust was trying to recapture on paper, and writer Peter Brook has managed a small miracle recapturing the feeling on film. Here is that exception among book-into-movie disasters: a film based on great literature that is literate but never self-consciously "literary," a study of artifice that is not artificial.

Swann in Love may not be a movie for all tastes, but at least it's a movie for everyone with *some* taste.

SWEET DREAMS (1985)

★ ★ ★ Directed by Karel Reisz. Screenplay by Robert Getchell. Produced by Bernard Schwartz. With Jessica Lange, Ed Harris, and Ann Wedgeworth.

Sweet Dreams is about the life and hard times of golden-voiced country singer Patsy Cline, who died at thirty in an airplane crash at the top of her career. Jessica Lange, who looks nothing at all like Patsy, manages to charge the character with resilience and heart, while Ed Harris, as her charming, brutal, and complex husband, steals the film with his acting virtuosity. Well directed by Karel Reisz, *Sweet Dreams* is a film that invests a small, famil-

iar rags-to-riches story with artistry and true grit, just as Patsy's voice charged her songs with emotional passion that transcended the country and western genre and expanded her popularity.

SWEET LIBERTY (1986)

★ ★ ★ Directed and written by Alan Alda. Produced by Martin Bregman. With Alan Alda, Michael Caine, Michelle Pfeiffer, Lise Hilboldt, Saul Rubinek, Lois Chiles, Bob Hoskins, and Lillian Gish.

Good movies about the insanity of Hollywood filmmaking are rare. Hollywood has never learned to poke fun at itself with any real wit. The rage and the madness that are Hollywood talismans to live by are easy, but the men who make the movies about the movies tell the jokes and miss the punch lines. Alan Alda's *Sweet Liberty* is a welcome exception.

Alda is not a jaded Hollywood hack like Blake Edwards. *Sweet Liberty* has the exasperation of Edwards' *S.O.B.* and some of the same vulgarity, too. But there's a big difference. *Sweet Liberty* also has intelligence and the frustrated sweetness of a man with an insider's view who remains wholesomely on the outside.

It's a refreshing, uplifting movie.

Alda plays Michael Burgess, a history professor in a small college in Sayeville, North Carolina. Michael has written a lively, well-researched best seller about the American Revolution that has been bought for the movies.

When the film company arrives in the campus town for location shooting, everyone reacts to the equipment trucks, honeywagons, and chartered buses as though the battle of 1776 were being staged all over again. The bells of sweet liberty have a resounding effect on the citizens of Sayeville like a cannon fired on Fort Sumter.

The male star, played by Michael Caine, is a wife-mauling egomaniac who kidnaps the dean's wife (Lois Chiles) in a helicopter during the welcoming ceremonies. The female star (Michelle Pfeiffer) is a tart who sleeps with anyone who can improve her dramatic scenes.

Saul Rubinek, as the lunatic lollipop-sucking director, has turned Michael's book, a serious study of the American Revolution, into a piece of typical Hollywood trash full of naked girls, gags, and historical inaccuracy. "The American Revolution was not a goddamn vaudeville show!" wails the wounded author. "We'll fix it!" is the Hollywood answer.

The Hollywood invaders, swooping down from the hills of Beverly to pin a Technicolor flag in every colonial doorframe, have introduced three elements into the historical script to make it conform to the box-office demands of movie going teenagers—"Defy authority, destroy property, and take people's clothes off!" yells the director. "These are the three things kids want to see on film. The American Revolution was full of all three!"

To Michael, there are only two things wrong with the movie—"the script and the dialogue." The comedy results from Michael's attempts to rewrite the script, with the aid of a demented Hollywood scriptwriter (amusingly played by the great Bob Hoskins).

Reshaping the star to fit the real-life role of the historical woman she's playing, Michael falls in love. This wreaks havoc on his own relationship with the college's prettiest embroidery expert (Lise Hilboldt), especially when the movie star hires his real-life girlfriend to give her needlepoint lessons.

In the end, by restaging the big battle scene, the extras take their own whack at correcting history and wreck the movie. The Hollywood nitwits get a lesson in American history and

Michael gets a lesson in studio politics.

Alan Alda's own screenplay generously mixes and matches the townspeople, who have been dressing up with muskets and wigs for two hundred years, with the phony stuntmen from La-La Land, whose cannons are provided by the prop department, with humor and psychology.

And Alda's direction does not go for the hysterical pun. Instead, he milks real comedy from the subtle interaction of people. Even dear old Lillian Gish is funnier than she's ever dreamed of being, as Alda's senile mother, who thinks there's poison in her food.

By the end of *Sweet Liberty* you get a real feeling of what it's like for a small town in America when it's turned into a movie set. Egos explode, weird things happen, people howl at the moon like werewolves, and you just know things will never be the same.

Sweet Liberty is a star-spangled entertainment.

SWEET SMELL OF SUCCESS (1957)

★ ★ ★ ★ Directed by Alexander Mackendrick. Screenplay by Clifford Odets and Ernest Lehman. Produced by James Hill. *With Burt Lancaster, Susan Harrison, Tony Curtis, Sam Levene, Martin Milner, and Barbara Nichols.*

A lacerating dissection of yellow journalism on Broadway, and one of the most acclaimed films of 1957. Burt Lancaster is the evil gossip columnist, J. J. Hunsecker, read by millions, who has the power to make careers or destroy lives with his acid typewriter (these were the days before computers); and Tony Curtis, in the best performance of his career, is the unprincipled hustler of a cheap, small-time press agent who will stop at nothing (including prostitution and blackmail) to achieve fifteen minutes of fame, not to mention a fast buck. Columnists no longer have the kind of paralyzing power they once had, but this film is set in the days of Walter Winchell, Dorothy Kilgallen, and Hedda and Louella, who dished the dirt and buried people under it. With pulsating dialogue by Clifford Odets, brisk direction, chilling performances, and the kind of stainless steel cinematography that captures the sights, sounds, and even the smells of New York after dark, *Sweet Smell of Success* has the perfect tempo to illuminate the sleazier, more sordid aspects of the Big Apple's night life. You might not love the hardened, immoral, and corrupt characters who make the scene come alive, but you will never forget them. Acrid, corrosive, and terrific.

SWING SHIFT (1984)
★ ★ ★ Directed by Jonathan Demme. Screenplay by Rob Morton. Produced by Jerry Bick. With Goldie Hawn, Kurt Russell, Christine Lahti, Ed Harris, Fred Ward, and Charles Napier.

Following on the well-polished heels of *Racing With the Moon*, Hollywood brought us *Swing Shift*, another movie about the American home front during World War II.

It's pretty, nostalgic, slickly professional and soft around the edges, like a melting Hershey bar. It is not without its problems, but when it's good, it's as good as American movies get. In times like these, this is good enough.

Swing Shift is about the women who stayed home while their men were off in godforsaken places with horrifying names like Guadalcanal and Corregidor—the women who did their part in the war effort by working in defense plants.

The film begins with the bombing of Pearl Harbor, works its way through D-Day, and ends with a victory dance while Jo Stafford sings "I'll Be Seeing You."

Within this time frame, we get the story of a California housewife named Kay, sweetly and bravely played by Goldie Hawn in one of the least flashy but most honestly conceived performances of her career.

Forty years ago, Claudette Colbert would have had the theater maintenance staff working overtime mopping the tears off the floor. Goldie plays it straight. You won't go for the Kleenex, but you will derive from her concept of the role some additional insight into what it was like for an oppressed housewife to discover her own self-value through independence and personal achievement. The Women's Lib angle is unmistakable. It is also one of the film's major strengths.

When Kay's husband Jack (nicely played with a mixture of charm and charisma by that fine actor, Ed Harris) ships off to the Navy to "protect the American way of life," she goes to work, toiling on the 4-to-midnight "swing shift" in a Santa Monica aircraft factory.

There are brief shades of *Pvt. Benjamin* in Goldie's adjustment to riveting guns and factory life, but the comedy never overrides the film's more serious issues: how women with no experience or training learned to overcome the prejudices and endure the practical jokes of their male co-workers, how they earned respect for keeping America on its feet when the guys were gone, and how they eventually found real dignity in achievement and friendship with other women.

Out of the sweat and labor and tenacity, Kay learns a new self-awareness, a sense of pride, and a lot of practical knowledge. By the time Jack returns on leave, she can even repair her own toaster. Naturally, she also falls in love with Lucky (Kurt Russell), a 4-F trumpet player who works as a mechanic.

There's a subplot involving Kay's best friend Hazel (Christine Lahti) and her romantic frustration with both Lucky and a dance-hall owner named Biscuits (Fred Ward) that would be superfluous pudding were it not for Miss Lahti's overwhelming performance. This is one of the rare examples of an actress in a secondary "best friend" role stealing the movie from the leading lady, and if I know Goldie Hawn, it won't happen again.

But Swing Shift is less concerned with plot mechanics than it is with needlepointing an entire canvas of period living. Jonathan Demme, the director, gets the details right—Eleanor Roosevelt pep talks on the radio, women in snoods dancing the jitterbug to Tommy Dorsey records, everyone who was still ambulatory joining in the scrap metal drives in a surge of patriotism. But the movie is too pristine and sedate for its own good. It seems to be living on Valiums.

Nothing much ever happens to anybody in Swing Shift, and the tone and pace often drag. For all of his attempts to be accurate, it is mystifying to think Demme could be led so far astray by the uneven musical score.

Most jarring of all is the insertion of a mushy contemporary pop song by Peter Allen, nasally screeched by the atonal Carly Simon, called "Someone Waits for You." This song has nothing whatsoever to do with World War II, the American home front, or much of anything else. I can't believe this was the director's idea. It reeks of studio interference.

Later, when Jo Stafford sings "I'll Be Seeing You," a wave of recognizable emotion hits the audience in the middle of the heart. This song does more to serve the needs of the film than anything else. For a theme song behind the credits, why didn't they just use Johnny Mercer's great defense plant song, "I Met My Baby on the Swing Shift"? The picture is full of missed opportunities.

Despite my reservations, I still recommend *Swing Shift* for its simplicity, its appealing performers, and its direct, clear-eyed look at nice people in times of stress. I'm just sorry that a picture this good could not have gone a bit farther in the direction of perfect.

TAKE ME OUT TO THE BALL GAME (1949)

★ ★ ½ Directed by Busby Berkeley. Screenplay by Harry Tugend and George Wells. Produced by Arhur Freed, with songs by Betty Comden, Adolph Green, and Roger Edens. *With Gene Kelly, Frank Sinatra, Esther Williams, Betty Garrett, Jules Munshin, and Edward Arnold.*

Take Me Out to the Ball Game reunited three of the stars of *On the Town*—Gene Kelly and Frank Sinatra and Jules Munshin—as baseball players who keep holding up the pennant doing vaudeville turns between innings. Although Esther Williams plays the team's owner, she has nothing much to do and only swims one time. Sinatra is so wimpy, it's a miracle he wasn't laughed off the

screen, giving girlfriend Betty Garrett an easy chance to steal the picture as a perky, aggressive, love struck fan who pursues him up and down the bleachers in a bombastic number called "It's Fate Baby, It's Fate." Legendary musical director Busby Berkeley gave it a lot of vitality. It was his last movie, and therefore a minor-league musical film of special interest to history buffs.

TALK RADIO (1988)

★ ★ ★ Directed by Oliver Stone. Screenplay by Stone and Eric Bogosian. Produced by Edward R. Pressman and A. Kitman Ho. *With Eric Bogosian, Ellen Greene, and Alec Baldwin.*

Eric Bogosian's titanic one-man show is turned into a powerful, fascinating, and repellent look at the country we live in by ace director Oliver (*Platoon*) Stone. After microwaving Vietnam and Wall Street, Stone takes on late-night blabbermouth radio, combining Bogosian's lacerating play with the real story of the murder of Denver's obnoxious radio host Alan Berg. The horrifying results may make you long for an MGM musical instead, but Bogosian's deranged monologues are inescapably hypnotic as he takes on the sick, perverted, and submental—invalids, bigots, religious zealots, brain-damaged shut-ins, rapists, child abusers, addicts, suicides and psychos. Like many of those late night dirges, his show is nothing more than a receptacle for America's trash. But Bogosian gives a galvanizing, turbulent performance—abrasive, cruel, and brilliant—as the "shock jock" whose ruthless quest for power, ratings and money harasses the lonely listeners who created him, and orchestrates his own downfall in the process. This is not a movie you'll want to take home to Mom, but you won't soon forget its paralyzing impact, either.

TAPS (1981)
½★ Directed by Harold Becker.
Screenplay by Darryl Ponicsan and Robert Mark Kamen.
Produced by Stanley R. Jaffe and Howard B. Jaffe. With Timothy Hutton, George C. Scott, Ronny Cox, Sean Penn, Tom Cruise, and Brendan Ward.

Taps pretends to examine a clash between the military, which gets its idealism from Patton and the Pentagon, and the new society, which gets its idealism from computers, home economists, real estate developers, and Erma Bombeck. The question it raises—"Do we need military schools any-more?"—is all but bludgeoned to death in a spray of gunfire as everything in the film gets annihilated in the crossfire of confused motives. Rarely have I seen a movie so at odds with its own purposes. You go away saddened and depressed without even knowing what you're supposed to be depressed about. What begins as food for thought ends up a big mess on the floor and you don't know how to clean it up.

George C. Scott, in an aging pastiche of his General Patton role, makes an all-too-brief appearance in the opening scenes, playing the general who runs a highly respected old school called the Bunker Hill Military Academy. "Man was meant to be a warrior—we're all sons of our Viking fathers" is the motto he delivers between old stories about long forgotten battles at the dinner table. Honor is the talisman by which he lives, and generations of cadets have adored him for it, looked up to him, tried to emulate him.

Timothy Hutton is the highest-ranking student, the boy with all of the best qualities of leadership, the cadet most likely to become a star at West Point. But there is bad news: After a century and a half, the board of trustees has decided to close down the school and turn the property into real estate blocks for condominiums. The outside world, with its capitalist greed and its disregard for the value and endurance of traditions, believes military schools are anachronistic and soldiers passé. The old general came here when he was twelve and spent the rest of his life in uniform. He has no intention of giving up his fight now. When a local punk agitator is accidentally killed in a brawl at the school dance, public opinion rises in a rage against the school. It is ordered closed immediately. Following his beloved general's philosophy, Hutton convinces the other cadets they are the real proprietors and must defend their home.

With military talent for organization, the boys take over the school, turning it into a fort against the outside world, confiscating the weapons in the school arsenal, and just like real life, an act of aggression turns into a full-scale war without anybody wanting one. This hypothetical situation turns into a microcosm of the world situation, as the boys imitate adults (a trace of *Lord of the Flies* here) in a cold war that turns the school into a battlefield. The most important thing they've learned from the old general is "Defeat and dishonor are worse things than death," but the old man has just died of a stroke (eliminating Scott from the film early and freeing him for other film commitments) and the boys are left to fight to their own devices.

The school turns into a trashy, sentimental metaphor for Vietnam with obvious factions representing the U.S. military and the Viet Cong. Practically everyone in the film is riddled with bullets and tear gas and by the end the cast has been reduced by half. Small boys lie in pools of blood and guts, and one of the hothead cadets who took his role too seriously even stages his own My Lai massacre. The helpless, horrified viewer who lasts this long will learn, like so many disillusioned soldiers do in battle, that honor doesn't mean much when you're holding a dead child or staring down the barrel of a National Guard rifle.

Some people have called *Taps* a fascist movie, but I don't think it even has the courage of that conviction. I'm not sure what we're supposed to take away from this grim, cynical experience. It is not sympathetic to the military and it doesn't show much humanity toward civilians, either. I guess its aim is to point out the dangers of infecting young minds with the kind of imbalanced military dogma that will turn them into terrorists. Instead of building character through manly codes of ethics many consider outdated, we're building reactionary right-wing nuts who masquerade their aggressions behind the flag and love of country. If that's the message, then I guess we need better and more responsible scripts than *Taps* to get it across.

The gung-ho cadets and even the cowards are played with honesty and fervor (look closely and you'll spot Tom Cruise and Sean Penn); the bewildered civilians are handled with just the right amount of moralistic confusion. But they're all on their own, fighting not for beliefs or issues but for close-ups. Director Harold Becker treats them all like clichés auditioning for body bags. It's "Best Foot Forward Meets Sam Peckinpah."

Taps is a most unfortunate disaster that further demonstrates how far afield good intentions can go in the Hollywood trenches.

TEA AND SYMPATHY (1956)
★ ★ ½ Directed by Vincente Minnelli. Screenplay by Robert Anderson, adapted from his Broadway play. Produced by Pandro S. Berman. *With Deborah Kerr, John Kerr, Leif Erickson, Edward Andrews, Darryl Hickman, Dean Jones, Norma Crane, Jacqueline de Wit, Richard Tyler, and Don Burnett.*

Vincente Minnelli's sensitively directed, softly photographed, and beautifully acted film version of the electrifying hit play by Robert Anderson is largely considered (by most critics) an act of 1956 Production Code butchery. It does seem dated in the 1990s, but the story of a prep school boy wrongly accused of homosexuality and the understanding housemaster's wife who saves him from suicide is still deeply affecting, despite a sudsy postscript tacked on to please the censors. Deborah Kerr and John Kerr, recreating their Broadway roles, are sublime. Not a masterpiece, but definitely worth a second look. Ms. Kerr's famous, oft-quoted last line, "Years from now, when you speak of this—and you will—*please* be kind," applies to the film itself.

TENDER MERCIES (1983)
★ ★ ★ ★ Directed by Bruce Beresford. Screenplay by Horton Foote. Produced by Philip S. Hobel. *With Robert Duvall, Tess Harper, Betty Buckley, Wilford Brimley, Ellen Barkin, and Allan Hubbard.*

Bruce Beresford's wonderful film *Tender Mercies* is about the intimate relationship between a down-and-out country singer and a shy widow who runs a weather-beaten motel-gas station in rural Texas.

That's about as far as you can get in theme, scope and content from the Australian director's previous film, *Breaker Morant*, which centered on a court martial during the Boer War.

But these diverse films have lots in common—both were made by a genuine artist instead of a hack-for hire, both have a stylish visual design that encompasses and frames the work, drenching it in reality. And both are dazzling gems.

Tender Mercies is a sensitive look at little people in the American heartland re-examining their priorities, learning to live with their own set of values, thanking God each night for his "tender mercies."

Robert Duvall is honest, real and down-home, unsophisticated as tobacco spit in the role of Mac Sledge, a battered icon in a Stetson hat who wanders out of the Texas panhandle mean as a horny toad and drunk as a Skid Row derelict.

Collapsing in a stupor in a deserted motel, he is nursed back to health by the owner, a young widow whose husband has died in Viet Nam, and her lonely little boy.

Their starchy American industriousness, hard work and Christian ethics inspire Mac to give up the bottle, go to church and seek new meaning to life with a built-in family that adores him.

But the new serenity he finds pumping gas and playing the new double role of husband and stepfather is shattered when a reporter tracks him down in his new hideout.

Now we learn that the man we've watched in this quiet, studied rehabilitation is not the saddle tramp we thought he was. Mac turns out to be a once-famous star on the Grand Ole Opry circuit with a turbulent past.

Mac has a bitter ex-wife named Dixie, who is now a major star in Nashville, and a wild, unhappy daughter on the verge of wrecking her own life.

Everyone moves in on Mac's new piece of mind like vultures.

Rosa Lee, his new wife, is more shocked than anyone by the revelation of Mac's true identity, but she's learned to endure. Now, in her prayers, she adds Mac to the "tender mercies" God has given her.

Mac is torn between his new beginning and the glitter of stardom he never got out of his system.

This is the subtle story of how he learns to be thankful for "tender mercies" of his own, be a man to the woman who loves him while defending his own dignity, and be the father to the boy who needs him without being a stand-in for somebody else.

Beresford has distilled from these emotional threads a story of real feelings, longings, fears and triumphs among simple people with complicated inner conflicts they cannot always articulate. The plot may seem tame in outline, but it is anything but ordinary inexecution.

Tender Mercies is not only the work of the immensely gifted Beresford. Horton Foote, author of the tight-to-the-skin and deeply moving screenplay, won an Oscar in 1963 for *To Kill a Mockingbird* and he knows how Southerners think, feel and talk.

Russell Boyd, the Australian cameraman whose magnificent cinematography on *Picnic at Hanging Rock*, *The Last Wave* and *Gallipoli* helped put Australian films on the map, has captured the blistered essence of Texas, with its peppermint highways and its cobalt skies.

From a first-rate group of actors, the feeling of rural isolation shines through with amazing perception.

Betty Buckley, the star of *Cats* on Broadway, plays the driven, passionate bundle of nerves that is Mac's ex-wife with piercing directness.

Ellen Barkin, so memorable as the frustrated wife who got her husband's record collection in a hopeless muddle in *Diner*, brings painful intimacy to the role of Mac's self-destructive daughter.

Tess Harper, a Dallas girl making her film debut, is as clear and without artifice as a mirror in the demanding role of Mac's new wife, Rosa Lee.

And as the centerpiece, there is Duvall—always leathered as a muddy boot, and as natural as breathing, who won an Oscar for this role. I salute them all.

Tender Mercies is a small, loving film about real people with whom everyone can identify. It might not change the course of cinema history, but it stands high among the corn Hollywood usually serves.

10 RILLINGTON PLACE (1971)
★ ★ ★ Directed by Richard Fleischer. Produced by Basil Appleby. Screenplay by Clive Exton, based on the book by Ludovic Kennedy. With Richard Attenborough, Judy Geeson, John

Hurt, Gabrielle Daye, and Andre Morell.

Somber, articulate, and chilling dramatization of the infamous Christie murders in London about a mild-mannered psychotic mass killer who murdered scores of women and buried them under the floorboards and inside the walls of his rooming house at 10 Rillington Place. After the wrong man was hanged the furor that surrounded the case was responsible for the abolition of the death penalty in England. Richard Attenborough (the now-famous director) gives one of the screen's finest and most subtle performances as the drab landlord who strikes again and again without suspicion and John Hurt is especially fine as the fall guy who goes to the gallows in his place. Eerie, creepy, and fascinating, with meticulous details and actual locations. Better than any fictitious murder mystery a screenwriter could dream up because it is amazingly true. The best thing about this film is Richard Fleischer's resistance to lurid sensationalism. The maniac responsible for these sordid events remains dull and unimaginative, just as he was in real life, the victims dim-witted and stupid. The result is scary, credible, and ultimately ironic, the impact gruesome yet hypnotic.

TEQUILA SUNRISE (1988)

★ ★ ★ Directed and written by Robert Towne. Produced by Thom Mount. *With Mel Gibson, Michelle Pfeiffer, Kurt Russell, and Raul Julia.*

Tequila Sunrise is the sexiest crime thriller since *Body Heat*. It's the kind of film noir Bogart and Bacall used to make, only with nudity, sex, and four-letter words. It scorches. It steams. It leaves you breathless. It may also leave you confused. The plot is contrived and illogical. Who cares? We're talking gorgeous movie stars here. We're talking Mel Gibson as Mac, a California drug dealer trying to go straight. We're talking Kurt Russell as his best buddy Nick, a narcotics cop who refuses to bust him. We're talking dropdead Michelle Pfeiffer as JoAnn, the delicious, sophisticated restaurant owner who warms up the sheets in both their beds. Mac and Nick fall for JoAnn. JoAnn beds them both, then gets kidnapped by a Mexican drug lord named Carlos (Raul Julia). Mac has to kill Carlos before Carlos kills JoAnn. JoAnn has to save Mac before Nick busts him. Take my advice: Don't try to figure it out. Just sit back, soak up the glamour, and concentrate on the erotic, sexy, sun-kissed stars. Nothing much matters as long as Michelle Pfeiffer keeps her clothes off, and she won't let you down. The result carries a warning for anyone with a pacemaker—*Tequila Sunrise* could wreck your blood pressure.

TERMS OF ENDEARMENT (1983)
★ ★ ★ ★ Directed, produced and written by James L. Brooks. Based on the novel by Larry McMurtry. With Shirley MacLaine, Debra Winger, Jack Nicholson, Jeff Daniels, Danny DeVito, and John Lithgow.

When I go to the movies, I usually arrive fully armed with pencils and notebooks into which I jot down impressions, lines of dialogue, credits, and other bits of useful information.

After *Terms of Endearment* I was astonished to discover I had not written one note to myself. This film is so absorbing and so powerful that I couldn't take my eyes off the screen for a single minute for fear of missing something.

There is no higher compliment that I can pay to any movie, but *Terms of Endearment* is not like any other movie. It's in a class by itself. Like most works of art, *Terms*

of Endearment is an almost impossible film to describe.

It simply has to be seen and felt. There's a triumphant purity about it—a silent tempo, like a throb in the temple, moving it quietly and subtly through thirty years in the lives of an extraordinary Texas mother and her equally unique daughter—that is almost always lacking in American movies.

Really, it is a film about the complex things they do to each other in the name of love. Nothing noisy or wild happens in terms of action or histrionics, but I'm willing to bet most people will be moved to tears before it's over, without feeling they've been manipulated in any way. That's a helluva lot for any movie to accomplish.

Larry McMurtry, the Texas writer who gave us *The Last Picture Show* and *Hud* and TV's *Lonesome Dove*, wrote the novel this movie is based on, and it has a sprawling literary quality that fills in the bones with marrow, mixing laughter with pain in an uncanny funny-sad style that is truly captivating. All the while, its characters are coming to life with a most comtemporary frankness and developing until we know them like neighbors and friends.

At the core there is a love-hate relationship between Aurora Greenway (Shirley Mac-Laine), a Cinemascope-sized gargoyle of a Houston mother, and her smart, full-hearted daughter Emma (Debra Winger). Aurora skips her daughter's wedding because she hates the bridegroom and feels her presence would be tantamount to hypocrisy, yet she doesn't feel the slightest guilt interrupting Emma by telephone at just the precise times she knows the newly-weds are in bed. Aurora is a mother trying to stay young, and Emma is a daughter trying to grow up. Mom drowns herself in mascara, platform heels and ruffles to trap a boyfriend, then flies into a rage at the thought of becoming a grand-mother. Daughter marries a good-natured mediocre school-teacher named Flap, with a daz-zling all-American smile, moves to Iowa and then Nebraska while he moves up the campus ladder, and bears three kids.

Back at home, Mom has an affair with the seedy, horny, potbellied astronaut next door (this is Houston, don't you know, so there's an astronaut on every block), while out in Des Moines, Emma commits adultery with a sad sack banker whose wife can't have sex be-cause of a back problem. Years pass and life is a series of moth-er-daughter combats, after which each side retreats to form new strategies. Things turn cloudy and tragic toward the end, when one of the characters gets cancer, and although I don't want to give away too much, it's fair to add that the passion both mother and daugh-ter have felt for each other throughout their lives does not desert them when the bad times come. They have learned, through patience and compas-sion, how to cope.

Terms of Endearment is ulti-mately heartbreaking, just like life. But it never loses its sense of humor, which is life's great-est lesson. It's about how peo-ple give each other strength in the strangest ways, when it is least expected.

A million details—ambigu-ous, outlined, embroidered, complicated—make up the tex-ture of its narrative fabric. Ev-ery scene is so honest and natural and emotionally direct the movie seems unwritten, un-rehearsed. Yet James Brooks, the director-writer, has an un-erring ear for the way real peo-ple talk and a savage eye for the way they act and feel.

As for the actors, there is re-ally no wonder they turned out to be that year's Oscar nomin-ees. Debra Winger's smoky, open-faced honesty gives Emma a simplicity mixed with wisdom that is admirable. Jeff Daniels has just the right definition of Flap, the aging preppie— charming and undependable and a cross between a campus Lothario and Dumbo.

Jack Nicholson gives his best performance since *Five Easy Pieces* (and won the Oscar) as the bloated, benignly macho space cadet who is spaced out in more ways than one. Horny and insulting one minute, disarmingly sweet the next, he builds a three-dimensional monument to the middle-age spread that is both brave and hilarious.

But for my money (and another Oscar), it is Shirley MacLaine who literally lights a match to the screen. First, with her terrible printed chiffon Neiman-Marcus dresses and her ghastly shopping mall hairdos, she's a frivolous flirt of a neurotic female.

By the end, the roots are showing in her hair and the real age is showing in the lines of her face and she no longer gives a damn. Watching her break down and say "I love you" to Nicholson in the Lincoln airport is a gut-wrenching experience. It's a great part, and MacLaine fills it with artistry and vision. *Terms of Endearment* is, quite simply, one of the few perfect and unforgettable motion pictures of the 1980s.

TESS (1980)

★ ★ ½ Directed by Roman Polanski. Screenplay by Gerard Brach, John Brownjohn, and Polanski. Produced by Claude Berri. With Nastasia Kinski, Peter Firth, Leigh Lawson, Rosemary Martin, Sylvia Coleridge, John Collin, Tony Church, and Brigid Erin Bates.

Roman Polanski's *Tess* is a sweeping romantic saga based on Thomas Hardy's *Tess of the D'Urbervilles* that should more than satisfy lovers of grandeur and plot. The book has always been perfect for filming, so it's a mystery why it took so long to get to the screen.

Teenage girls have wept buckets of tears over this sprawling costumed soap opera for decades and one of them must have been the young Sharon Tate. Polanski has attached a dedication in the opening credits: "To Sharon," in memory of his late wife. Too bad the murdered actress didn't live to play the role of Tess; something in the nature of sympathy and appeal are badly needed for the role to be a success, and these qualities are in limited supply from Nastasia Kinski.

Thomas Hardy's victimized

heroine Tess is a cross between Madame Bovary and Elsie Dinsmore: "everything," as Thelma Ritter observed waspishly in *All About Eve*, "but the bloodhounds snapping at her rear end." First dispatched by her drunken, poverty-stricken father to rich relatives in order to beg money, Tess learns that her name, Derbyfield, is really a derivative of a stately old name in England's historical archives, and that her ancestors were actually the proud but defunct D'Urbervilles. The rich relatives turn out to be bogus gentry who bought the name D'Urberville as the ultimate gesture in social climbing.

That doesn't stop Tess's cousin Alec from raping her, so she returns in shame to her grim family to have her baby in disgrace. When the baby dies, in misery and squalor, Tess baptizes it herself and buries it in the church cemetery without permission. Refusing all help from the wealthy D'Urbervilles, Tess returns to the rough life of a peasant, toiling miserably, first in the wheat fields, then as an apprentice to a dairy farmer. Here, she falls in love with Angel Clare, the university-educated parson's son who wants to become a laborer and reads Karl Marx with relish.

Tess confesses her guilty and shameful past in a letter that somehow never gets read, but she marries the boy of her dreams anyway, blurting out her sins on their wedding night. The husband turns out to be a boorish little self-righteous snob who turns her out to hike through mud, rain, and snow on her way to a life of insult, hardship, and worse misery than she's ever known.

Years later, when she finally does give in to her rich cousin and the father of her dead child in order to provide some relief for her widowed mother and her starving brothers and sisters, Tess at last lives in comfort and grandeur. But when the dairy farmer returns, tragedy ensues, as well as eternal damnation. It's the story of a girl with an obstinate pride, who elects uncompromising unhappiness over insincere prosperity.

The film, like the book, shakes an accusing finger at Victorian hypocrisy and injustice, and I suspect Polanski sees a metaphor in Tess's predicament and his own harsh treatment by what he considers an unfair, rigid, and repressive American society.

Unfortunately, such Victorian melodrama seems somewhat naive in the late twentieth century. As Alec D'Urberville says to Tess: "There's a point beyond which obstinacy becomes stupidity." It seems like the most logical line in the film. Tess seems to luxuriate in her despair. When the police come to drag her off from her hiding place in the ancient rock formations of Stonehenge, she says "I am ready!" as though she's been looking forward to the gallows. So much suffering seems unnecessary, especially when you consider the original rape as more of a seduction (she certainly seems willing enough) and especially when D'Urberville is played by the most charming and attractive actor in the piece—a dashing British performer named Leigh Lawson.

For some inexplicable reason, Nastasia Kinski plays Tess with an unyielding sullenness that distances her from the audience in a dismaying manner. There's no denying her beauty—at times she looks exactly like the young Ingrid Bergman in *Gaslight* and *Saratoga Trunk*—but she has practically no range at all, and no matter what contrasting emotions she's required to display, she seems transfixed, with a frozen expression as relentless as lead. Peter Firth, as the drippy, moralistic Angel Clare, is equally disappointing. Instead of dark, melancholy

pride, we get posing self-indulgence and a look of pained constipation throughout.

Tess was filmed in the rich farm country of Normandy, presumably because Polanski could not leave France to shoot actual locations. He's done a terrific job of making it look like England's Thomas Hardy country. The moors, the cottages, the farms, the peasants toiling in the mud, the swans on a lazy lagoon—right down to an amazingly accurate replica of the awesome Stonehenge, "the only thing older than the ages, older than the D'Urbervilles."

It's an interesting, straightforward departure for Polanski that shows him capable of much more ambitious projects on film than his past endeavors. I found myself sinking hypnotically into the projected atmosphere he creates with the aid of two great cameramen—Ghislain Cloquet and the late Geoffrey Unsworth—and for the most part, his *Tess* is an honorable piece of work, well worth investigating. Too bad about Kinski, though. The sound track is throbbing with portentous, lush music by Philippe Sarde and the London Symphony, while the star is doing a one-note samba.

TESTAMENT (1983)

★ ★ ★ ★ Directed by Lynne Littman. Screenplay by John Sacret Young. Produced by Jonathan Bernstein. *With Jane Alexander, William Devane, Ross Harris, Roxana Zal, Lukas Haas, Philip Anglim, Leon Ames, Lurene Tuttle, and Rebecca de Mornay.*

Films of real soul and substance are so rare that when one does come along I tend to come unglued with gratitude and joy. Such a film is *Testament*.

The danger in overpraising a film this true, this dedicated, and this inspired is that I might mislead its potential audience into expecting miracles it cannot deliver. But *Testament* is so unpretentious, so deeply moving and so filled with its own moral fervor that it really speaks for itself. All you have to do is experience it. It will do the rest.

Basically, it's the dramatic account of what happens to a small, uncomplicated, all-American community in the aftermath of a nuclear attack. It begins on a day like any other day. In an archetypal nuclear family, Mom (Jane Alexander) grapples with costumes for the school play and the torture of mastering the Jane Fonda workout. Dad (William Devane) bikes to keep trim before breakfast, competing in a friendly

spirit with his fourteen-year-old son, then dashes off to work with no time for taking out the garbage.

These are decent, churchgoing people for whom life's biggest problems are expanding waistlines and selecting the proper computer game for their three kids' birthdays.

Suddenly there's a blinding light. Sirens. The President is on TV. The electricity goes off in the middle of his State of the Union message. There's been a nuclear attack—the thing everybody dreads but ignores. People are in the streets, confused, clutching at their children. Chaos reigns, followed by looting and long lines at the gas pumps.

Elsewhere, there's been worse damage—actual blasts, radiation, contamination. But here, they are "luckier." Now they must learn to cope.

Some families head for survival camps in Canada. Others huddle in the church for warmth and friendship. Slowly, as the days drone by, town services diminish, the townspeople start dying from radiation poisoning, even the police surrender to fear.

At a time when humanity seems extinct, little things like vacation snapshots in old photograph albums take on an unprecedented importance. Flashlight batteries become talismans to live by.

One by one, the lights go out, the cemeteries run out of space, and even the bravest survivors must prepare for the ways in which they plan to leave behind some proof of their existence. And through it all, there is the heart-stopping desperation that comes when you know it's all over for the children.

This sounds like the ultimate downer among motion picture tearjerkers, but the big surprise is that *Testament* is a life-affirming work of great optimism and hope.

Lynne Littman, a marvelous young documentary filmmaker making her feature film debut with this exemplary gem of a movie, obviously wants to instruct us all. It is not her intention to drive anyone to suicide through despair.

Testament accomplishes a great deal without ever getting preachy or dragging its audience into a lot of confusing concerns about global politics. In fact, you never even see the violent destruction of a nuclear attack.

Instead, Littman focuses on the human aspects of such a tragedy and the instinct for survival. She is aided immeasur-

ably by a brilliant cast of luminous performers.

It is wonderful to see Leon Ames back on the screen. One of the staples of my childhood, this grand alumnus of scores of movie classics brings polish and dignity to the role of an old man with a young spirit, trying to keep in touch with the outside world on his ham radio equipment. Another member of Hollywood royalty, Lurene Tuttle, plays his spunky, devoted wife.

William Devane is the perfect Daddy; Philip Anglim demonstrates great strength as a priest who tries to console his friends and neighbors in the severest test of faith any man of God could ever face before finally giving in to his own humanity and suffering; Rebecca de Mornay (in a complete reversal from her sexy role in *Risky Business*) is sweetly touching as the mother of a dead baby.

The children—Ross Harris, Roxana Zal and Lukas Haas -- deserve special praise for their restraint, honesty, and total professionalism in playing roles that could easily have been mawkish and sentimental.

At the heart of it all is Jane Alexander—radiant, strong, proud, committed, heroic beyond the call of duty. Terrified, stubborn, refusing to give up on civilization, finally robotized by the truth, she never lets the candle of hope burn out of her eyes. In a performance that can truly be described as devastating, she shows, with her primal love for her children, the best reason of all why we must never allow a nuclear war to happen.

Poetic, profoundly disturbing, *Testament* is the most valid moral plea for disarmament ever seen on a movie screen. The fact that it was made for only $750,000 should give every money-wasting filmmaker cause for shame. It should be required viewing in Moscow, Laos, Baghdad and Washington, D.C.

THANK YOUR LUCKY STARS
(1943)

★ ★ ★ Directed by David Butler. Screenplay by Norman Panama, Melvin Frank, and James V. Kern. Produced by Mark Hellinger. *With Eddie Cantor, Joan Leslie, Dennis Morgan and Olivia de Havilland, Ida Lupino, Bette Davis, Ann Sheridan, Errol Flynn, John Garfield, Hattie McDaniel, Eddie "Rochester" Anderson, etc.*

Warner Brothers' star-spangled 1943 war effort was like many of the good-natured morale boosters for the boys overseas and the folks waiting at home—it was chock-full of songs, comedy routines, and patriotic cheers for anyone in uniform. But *Thank Your Lucky Stars* was different, too. It featured unusual performances by screen favorites not ordinarily associated with musicals, and reaped some surprising rewards. Eddie Cantor is the star, and his teacup eyes and moronic violence have not aged well. But if you can fast-forward through the dull Cantor ham, the trimmings are delicious: gorgeous Ann Sheridan singing "Love Isn't Born, It's Made"; Errol Flynn singing and dancing in a pub full of cockney sailors; Hattie McDaniel a far cry from Mammy in *Gone With the Wind* torching a rousing Harlem number called "Ice Cold Katy"; Ida Lupino and Olivia de Havilland as bobby-soxers; and the film's crowning achievement—Bette Davis creating screen history as she's thrown across a nightclub floor by whatever didn't get drafted in the hilarious Frank Loesser—Arthur Schwartz number, "They're Either Too Young or Too Old." Dated but classic stuff for movie buffs of all ages.

THAT CHAMPIONSHIP SEASON (1982)

★ ★ ½ Directed and written by Jason Miller, adapted from his play. Produced by Menahem Golan. *With Bruce Dern, Robert Mitchum, Martin Sheen, Paul Sorvino, and Stacy Keach*

Big guys also cry. That's the root of *That Championship Season*, the movie Jason Miller directed from his 1973 Broadway play. As a play, it was literate and worthy, but watching a bunch of aging ex-jocks and their dying coach crying in their beers and feeling sorry for themselves for two hours is not my idea of a fun way to spend an evening at the movies. The big guys Miller is writing about are staging a reunion in Scranton, Pennsylvania, on the twenty-fifth anniversary of the winning game that made them all-state basketball champs in 1958.

Amid the booze, the cigarette smoke, the locker room jokes, the bear hugs, and the old stories about long-lost teammates, the coach (Robert Mitchum) swells his potbelly with pride, surveys the guys he nurtured to glory, and brags: "I'm so proud of my boys—rising to the top of their professions."

But when the liquor loosens their tongues and blurs the tint in their rose-colored glasses, the "boys" begin to reveal their fears, failures, disappointments, jealousies, and inner truths. The champs from that season so long ago have turned out to be jerks.

Bruce Dern is a mayor so corrupt, incompetent, and despised that he's wrecked the city finances, given the building contracts and cushy jobs to his buddies while the city council takes the political blame for their screw-ups, and reduced the political fabric of Scranton to such a sick joke that everyone calls him "Sabu."

Stacy Keach, the smartest, the one with the most potential, is ten years behind everyone else because he's wasted his life taking care of a dying father who gave him no love in return for his sacrifice. Now he's so desperate for a piece of the action he's willing to destroy everyone to get it.

Martin Sheen is his brother, a once-promising athlete who never committed himself to anything and ended up a self-pitying alcoholic. Paul Sorvino is the flashy tycoon who has betrayed his best friend the mayor by sleeping with his wife.

These men are sad artifacts from bygone days, gifted boys who have trashed their lives through dissipation, greed, and compromise. All they've got left to remind them of the good old days is their old basketball jerseys, their old trophies, and their old gung-ho memories. As their nasty secrets pour out, the coach, who devoted his life to "excellence and superiority, like a priest," tries to hold them together.

As they all weep, wail, and punch each other bloody, the movie shows what happens to people weaned on the macho philosophy that winning is all that matters and losing is the only sin. These creeps have cheated, betrayed, and blackmailed each other and half of Scranton to win, and they've ended up losing anyway.

The most moving moment comes when the camera moves in on close-ups of their faces as they listen to a recording of their winning game in, "that championship season," when they had everything to live for and no idea how rotten it would all turn out.

There is powerful writing here, but it isn't movie writing. The film suffers from the suffocation of watching five miserable people in one setting—stripped down to their blackest feelings and forced to articulate their pitiful stories in a series of filibusters. The result is a two-fisted truth game that might have been electrifying onstage,

but not on the screen. We never see the wives, children, or local citizens they talk about. We just get the talk—endless reams of it—about people in the wings.

Fortunately, Miller's direction builds tension; he extracts fine, taut performances, especially from Dern, who sweats neurotic guilt and terror, and looks exactly like those obnoxious politicians you're always kicking yourself for voting into office, and Robert Mitchum, whose sagging jowls and swollen gut personify the eroded American dream.

But ultimately, you tire of the game and long to switch tapes. There is more to life than a gymnasium floor—and more to movies, too.

THAT'S DANCING! (1985)
★ ★ ★ ½ Written and directed by Jack Haley, Jr. Produced by David Niven, Jr., and Jack Haley, Jr. With Mikhail Baryshnikov, Ray Bolger, Sammy Davis, Jr., Gene Kelly, and Liza Minnelli.

All over the world, in every kind of life-enriching entertainment, it's always the dancing that turns people on. Imagination and fantasy combine through movement to create an emotional outburst of feeling that is the same in every language.

To that concept—and to the

magical dancers who make it happen—*That's Dancing!* is dedicated. It's a sparkling, vigorous, star-spangled movie that twirls and swirls and waltzes and pirouettes and taps its way into your heart, putting a smile on your face and a winkle in your toes. I loved it a lot.

Prompted by the enormous success of *That's Entertainment!* the folks who culled more than a thousand hours of dance numbers to come up with this two-hour extravaganza may think they've got another compilation on their hands—a selection of clips from movie musicals that concentrate on dance. But aside from its considerable entertainment value, *That's Dancing!* accomplishes more. It brings back the style of the lost elegance of a vanished era, while sadly reminding us all where movie musicals went wrong.

One reason why we no longer find flair in the movies is that nobody has any personal style. We can no longer look for guidance in the once-reliable source of all that was exemplary and worth emulating in the movies.

There aren't many movie musicals anymore, and all you have to do is watch *The Cotton Club* to realize that the wrong people are making them. The legendary dancers are gone or too old to dance, and we aren't developing any new stars to take their place. I like Travolta, but he's no Astaire.

In *That's Dancing!* it all comes alive again. Structured like a documentary, the film traces the origins of dance all the way back to the cave dwellers. Gene Kelly says "Dancing has always been with us," and shows how it evolved from primitive sources to the invention of the camera.

From rare footage of Anna Pavlova and Isadora Duncan, moving through Jazz Age Charlestons right up to break dancing, this movie creates its own history as it chronicles each decade. From the Lubitsch ball in the silent film *So This Is Paris* to the early sound musicals with clumsy choreography and pudgy showgirls to the goofy kaleidoscopic spectacles of Busby Berkeley, you get the development of dance on film.

But all this seems only a studious prologue for what's to come. There's so much more.

Fred Astaire always insisted his dance numbers be shown full-figure, from head to toe—something today's directors don't understand. Watch the Astaire and Ginger Rogers numbers that enthralled audiences in the thirties and you know instantly why today's musicals, with the dancer's feet missing and the self-serving directorial cross-cutting ruining the fluidity of movement, are so disappointing.

The late Sammy Davis, Jr., narrates the section that highlights the stars of early films—from Bill "Bojangles" Robinson and Shirley Temple to Eleanor Powell.

Ray Bolger's dance sequence with the young Judy Garland, cut from the final release print of *The Wizard of Oz*, is the only previously unreleased footage, and it's charming. But there are many other great numbers well worth a second look.

Bolger introduces the era of dance created by MGM that has never since been equaled, and the screen pulses with beauty, grace, color, and excitement as Ann Miller, Bobby Van, Bob Fosse, and Tommy Rall perform miracles with Hermes Pan's fabulous choreography in *Kiss Me Kate*.

Cyd Charisse, the greatest female dancer in the history of musicals, is a knockout doing Eugene Loring's dazzling "Red Blues" number from *Silk Stockings*—the perfect example of how a dance number *should* be photographed.

There are fluid and imaginative contributions from Jane Powell and Astaire, swirling through the fruity carnival colors of "I Left My Hat in Haiti," Gene Kelly and Donald O'Connor tapping through the deft and witty "Moses Supposes" number in *Singin' in the Rain*, Kelly with Dan Dailey and the great Michael Kidd flying through the streets of New York with garbage can lids on their feet in "It's Always Fair Weather."

Classical ballet is not overlooked, either. Mikhail Baryshnikov is the host for the section on toe shoes, with seldom-shown footage of Vera Zorina in the rarely revived *On Your Toes*, right up to Moira Shearer in 1948's cult film *The Red Shoes*.

But dance on film is nearing its hundredth anniversary, so what about the present and future? Here, the movie attempts to entice a younger audience with shots of Travolta, *Fame*, even a Michael Jackson video from MTV. This is the most depressing section of the movie, because what it proves is how far movie dancing has sunk.

Without the grace, charm, and elegance of dance, without the wonderful songs and the genius choreographers, if there are any stylistic lessons to be learned from an evening with MTV, we can lay the future of dance in a pauper's grave.

From the miles of film Jack

Haley, Jr., had to sift through as producer, writer, and director, one might quarrel with the selections (it makes me sick to know that the opulent "Coffee Time" number was deleted for time purposes), but not with the results.

That's Dancing! is a great tribute to all those stylists whose energy, dedication, and talent made movies the best thing in our lives for years. It's a ginger-peachy delight, and boy do we need it now.

THELMA AND LOUISE (1991)
★ ★ ★ ½ Directed by Ridley Scott. Written by Callie Khouri. Produced by Ridley Scott and Mimi Polk. With Susan Sarandon, Geena Davis, Harvey Keitel.

Thelma and Louise is the ultimate female fantasy trip—a road movie with the predictable elements of every on-the-lam flick every made, including aerial stunts, an FBI chase, a parking lot murder, motel confrontations, seedy diners and saloons, picture postcard views of the American landscape through rearview mirrors, and hot sex. The difference is that every action, every mood shift, every excitement, and every plot maneuver is instigated, conceived and played by women. The fact that the women are Geena Davis and

Susan Sarandon, giving two of the most dynamic performances of their careers, makes *Thelma and Louise* humorous, dramatic and mesmerizing—a film of kinetic intensity.

Thelma (Ms. Davis) is a bored housewife saddled to a demanding, vulgar, chauvinistic moron of a husband. Louise (Ms. Sarandon) is a bored short-order waitress in a greasy-spoon cafe. One day they decide to leave the men and the hassles in their dreary lives behind them and take a vacation together in Louise's '66 Thunderbird. It's supposed to be a liberating fishing trip, but on the way to the lake these two Arkansas bimbos stop off at a country and western roadhouse and Thelma gets a little bit too liberated on margaritas. A harmless flirtation with a cowboy leads to a brutal near-rape. Louise kills the creep in a blinding rage and the girls find themselves in an accelerating series of incidents from which there seems no turning back. The result is a survival course that turns into a crime spree, changing their lives forever.

For a while it seems like a vehicle for two extraordinarily spunky actresses to play varying stages of nerves, anxiety and panic. But the irony is that the more they try to run away from men, the more their lives become controlled by men. Bonding together emotionally is their only strength, and with each new turn on the highway, the two women experience truth through friendship and mutual trust they never knew with men. These are women who grew up buying the roles society expects them to play on assignment, only to discover that conformity leads to self-delusion. Suddenly they are forced to face the dark reality of independence. That discovery of the world within themselves takes a tremendous emotional toll. By the end, they have shared so much in their new identities as outlaws that they would rather die together than turn back.

Directed by Ridley (*Alien*) Scott, this is a refreshing departure from the usual gimmicks and mayhem in his movies. It's totally about character development, almost allegorical in concept; the women make all the moves, not spaceships. Observed from a female viewpoint, the men who constantly deceive, abuse and take advantage of Thelma and Louise—Thelma's gruesome husband (Christopher McDonald), Louise's quixotic boyfriend (Michael Madsen), a sexy con-man who rips off their life savings (Brad Pitt), even the detective who tries to save them (Harvey Keitel)—add valuable pieces to the mosaic, like fireflies banging against the ladies' screen door. But it is really the two stars who give the film its galvanizing force. Working together like two hands of the same body, they are tough, funny, vulnerable, dumb, articulate, and touching. By the end of the film they have explored and shared every key to their characters' substance. They roll along like the wide-open highway that stretches ahead of them, taking us all through a rite of passage that is unforgettable. There isn't a detour or a pothole in *Thelma and Louise*.

THEY GOT ME COVERED (1943)

★ ★ ½ **Directed by David Butler. Screenplay by Harry Kurnitz. Produced by Samuel Goldwyn. With Bob Hope, Dorothy Lamour, Otto Preminger, Lenore Aubert, Eduardo Cianelli, Marion Martin, Donald McBride, Walter Catlett, and Donald Meek.**

A pleasantly wacky Bob Hope farce from the 1943 Hollywood vaults, with Ski Nose as a disgraced newspaper clown and Dorothy Lamour as his favorite brunette sidekick, up to their gag writers' eyeballs in a frisky plot about murderous spies planning to blow up Washington, D.C. The villains include Otto Preminger, with hair, and Lenore Aubert, as a fetching Mata Hari. Some of it drags, but there are side-splitting moments before Bob winds up face-to-face with the killers. Good vintage laughs.

THE THIN MAN (1934)

★ ★ ★ Directed by W. S. Van Dyke. Screenplay by Frances Goodrich and Albert Hackett, based on the Dashiell Hammett novel. Produced by Hunt Stromberg. With William Powell, Myrna Loy, Maureen O'Sullivan, Nat Pendleton, Minna Gombell, Porter Hall, Henry Wadsworth, William Henry, Harold Huber, Cesar Romero.

William Powell and Myrna Loy are Nick and Nora Charles, the suave, sophisticated, wise-cracking husband-and-wife sleuths who turned mystery writer Dashiell Hammett's best-selling novel into a hit film in 1934, and launched an entire MGM series that continued to rake in box-office revenues for the decade that followed. A sublime mixture of screwball comedy and suspenseful thrills, this first entry in the "Thin Man" series never seems to age. The magic Powell-Loy combo, with their dog Asta, inspired dozens of similar husband-wife detective teams through the years, but none

could hold a candle to the originals.

THE THING (1982)

No ★s Directed by John Carpenter. Screenplay by Bill Lancaster. Produced by David Foster and Lawrence Turman. With Kurt Russell, Wilford Brimley, T. K. Carter, David Clennon, Keith David, and Richard Dysart.

Movie critics are like kids who cry wolf. We so often use words like *obscene* and *nauseating* to describe the violence and carnage pouring out of contemporary films that when a truly inhuman attack on human decency, such as John Carpenter's *The Thing*, comes along, there is the danger that nobody will take us seriously. Setting aside for the moment the fact that there was no reason to spend millions of dollars remaking an old horror movie that Howard Hawks produced much better in low-budget black and white back in 1951, there is the much more serious problem of how far a responsible filmmaker should be allowed to go for cheap thrills before he breaks every law of human decency. I'm no fraidy cat, and I love horror movies, but I closed my eyes and turned away from the screen during whole sections of *The Thing*, and not because the movie was scary.

The Thing has some tense moments, but it is so bloody and horrible that it is more disgusting and disgraceful than it is frightening. It's a thing, all right, but only cast-iron stomachs will survive it.

Carpenter isn't interested in plot or character development; he's too busy exploding guts and internal organs all over the camera lens in an attempt to make the audience throw up to bother with the kind of coherence and believability an audience might identify with. The "thing" is explained as a bloodsucking organism from outer space buried for a hundred thousand years in the frozen wastes of Antarctica. It can imitate life-forms by invading their body structures, which means it can presumably turn into dogs, men, or pepperoni pizzas.

The film opens promisingly enough when one of the pet huskies at an American space station on a frozen ice floe is chased by Norwegian scientists in a helicopter. The men are mad with schizophrenia, aiming at the dog with guns and even attacking the Americans before blowing up their own whirlybird in an act of explosive self-destruction. This is an eerie and mysterious beginning, but when the Americans investigate, they discover corpses with frozen blood hanging in red icicles from their slashed throats, surrounded by scaly, bloody, slimy ooze. The mystery that unfolds is fascinating up to a point, as the men use computers and the latest scientific equipment to put the pieces together. What they learn is that the "thing" has infected the dog, and now it is infecting the men one by one, until nobody trusts anybody else, and that is the end of the plot.

The rest of the film devotes itself to grisly special effects by makeup artist Rob Bottin in which the monstrous "thing" erupts from human bodies, spraying the screen with snaky tentacles, erupting kidneys, and four thousand tons of strawberry gelatin. The radio is dead, the generator is out, and there's an ice storm so fierce that nobody can dig out the survivors before spring, and in this frozen darkness the "thing" goes berserk until the serpent vomited forth by the astronaut in *Alien* seems like fishing for minnows by nasty comparison. The process by which the thing invades and infects the men of the ice station is never explained, but the process by which it splits open their anatomies—like cows being hacked open in a slaughterhouse or hogs being bled for bacon—is graphically and lovingly detailed in stomach-churning close-ups until you feel so mugged and beaten and humiliated that you go away numb.

The actors work hard to show fear, loathing, suspicion, and fury, but none of them is memorable because *The Thing* is not a movie about people. It's a movie about makeup and special effects and repulsive violence. The movie is never any fun—you couldn't remotely consider it entertainment—and the more I see of this expensive, egomaniacal, big-budgeted, big-studio, kick-their-intestines-out moviemaking, the more I admire unpretentious schlock like *The Texas Chainsaw Massacre*.

THREE LITTLE WORDS (1950)
★ ★ ★ ½ *Directed by Richard Thorpe. Screenplay by George Wells. Produced by Jack Cummings. With Fred Astaire, Red Skelton, Vera-Ellen, Arlene Dahl, Debbie Reynolds, Gloria De Haven, and Keenan Wynn.*

Fred Astaire and Red Skelton played the songwriting team Bert Kalmar and Harry Ruby in this tuneful, breezy, and delightful "biopic" from 1950. Relying more on plot than on production spectacles, it's an involving story of two separate showbiz careers. Fred is Kalmar, a vaudevillian whose hobby was magic, and Red is Ruby, a composer-pianist with a hankering to play baseball. When Fred's dancing career ends with a knee injury, the two mismatched personalities merge to write songs and take Broadway and Hollywood by storm, only to split up over a misunderstanding. Their wives, beautifully played by Vera-Ellen and Arlene Dahl, take it upon themselves to get the guys together again. The tuneful output of these two prolific tunesmiths provides a lot of opportunities for lavish song numbers, and a host of guest appearances by MGM stars. In only her third film, Debbie Reynolds emerged a star, playing "Boop-oop-a-Doop" girl Helen Kane. Gloria DeHaven played her own mother, singing star Mrs. Carter DeHaven, and sings a gorgeous, torchy "Who's Sorry Now." Arlene Dahl, in pink feathers, descends a white staircase against a purple backdrop better than any redhead on film, and Fred and Vera-Ellen dance with amazing grace. A total entertainment package that will make you twinkle.

THE THREE MUSKETEERS (1948)

★ ★ ★ Directed by George Sidney. Screenplay by Robert Ardrey. Produced by Pandro S. Berman. With Gene Kelly, Van Heflin, Gig Young, Lana Turner, Angela Lansbury, June Allyson, Vincent Price, Frank Morgan, Keenan Wynn, John Sutton, Reginald Owen, Ian Keith, Patricia Medina, and Richard Stapley.

A big, expensive risk was taken in 1948, when MGM cast Gene Kelly in one of his few nonmusical roles as the dashing acrobatic D'Artagnan in Alexandre Dumas's classic novel of seventeenth-century France. The results are surprisingly beautiful, fast-paced and graceful. Lana Turner is the evil Lady De Winter, Angela Lansbury is good Queen Anne, June Allyson is the ill-fated palace maid, and the supporting cast includes Van Heflin, Vincent Price, and Oz's favorite wizard, Frank Morgan. Gorgeous costumes, sets, and Technicolor.

A TIME TO LIVE (TV, 1985)

★ ★ ½ Directed by Rick Wallace. Screenplay by John McGreevey, based on the book Intensive Care by Mary-Lou Weisman. With Liza Minnelli, Jeffrey DeMunn, Swoosie Kurtz, Scott Schwartz, and Corey Haim.

Liza Minnelli won deserved raves for her nonsinging portrayal of a spunky mother who helps her son, suffering from deadly muscular dystrophy, through his ordeal. Forcing the kid to live as normal a life as possible, coping with the needs of her other family members, and finally facing the inevitable struggle in the tug-of-war between life and death, she is funny, brave, admirable, and deeply touching. The subject matter sounds depressing, but it is given surprising life and sweetness by this mesmerizing actress, utilizing aspects of her range and talent never before investigated.

THE TIN DRUM (1980)

★ ★ ★ ★ Directed by Volker Schlondorff. Screenplay by Schlondorff, Jean-Claude Carriere, Franz Seitz, and Gunter Grass. Produced by Frank Seitz and Anatole Dauman. With David Bennett, Mario Adorf, Angela Winkler, Daniel Olbrychski, Katherina Tahlback, and Charles Aznavour.

Every few years a movie comes along that is so unique, so gripping and so defiant in its immunity to clichés that it eludes conventional criticism. Such a movie is The Tin Drum, a German film of such magnitude and importance that I am at a loss to describe it properly. It won the Grand Prize at the 1979 Cannes Film Festival, an honor shared with *Apocalypse Now*. It is a genuine masterpiece.

The 493-page novel by Gunter Grass on which director Volker Schlondorff has based this amazing film is impossible to describe, too. It took sixteen years to get the book adapted for the screen, but Schlondorff has miraculously managed to capture its brilliant and biting satirical passages in a language that is completely and authentically cinematic.

It describes the harrowing misfortunes of the people of Danzig before, during, and after Hitler's seizure of the city, seen through the eyes of a dwarf who defiantly beats a toy drum as a symbol of protest. Born in 1924, he was a rebel from the start. There is a scene inside his mother's womb during childbirth, when Oskar peers out, refusing to enter the delivery room. When the family doctor attempts to examine him, fetuses, snakes, and salamanders explode from their jars of formaldehyde, splattering the room with acid and glass. It is evident from the beginning that Oskar is no ordinary child.

On his third birthday, he decides never to join the world of foolish grown-ups, so he takes his birthday present—a red-and-white snare drum—and throws himself down a flight of stairs. As the years pass, Oskar remains the size of a midget, banging his drum to acknowledge the events that pass across the retina of his eye and developing a scream so horrible and deafening that nobody dares to take his drum away. For the rest of the film, he never grows any larger.

When Poland falls and World War II begins, he beats his drum and the Nazi parades change tempo, forcing the stormtroopers and brownshirts to waltz to the "Blue Danube." His mother commits suicide eating raw fish because she doesn't want another child like this one. His father dies strangling on a swastika pin; his coffin is a bandage of grocery bags. Oskar survives them all because he is ageless. His eyes are the pages history is written on. He is indestructible.

Traveling through war-ravaged Europe with a circus troupe of performing gnomes, he makes his servant girl pregnant, is almost murdered by his own child (who may or may not have inherited his secret for remaining Lilliputian), and seems to be a wise man in a world gone insane.

There is an epic dimension to this film, in the style of a German fresco. The visions are shocking and strange, almost surrealistic in their impact. It is not something that can be told in a restricted amount of space, and it must have been an impossible film to make. At various times, Schlondorff considered filming it with midgets. Dustin Hoffman was also considered for the role of Oskar. But it is essentially the story of childhood wonder, of a sinister witness to the holocaust who remained locked in the body of a child.

The biggest miracle of all in bringing this off was in the casting of a young teenager named David Bennett in the role of Oskar. Bug-eyed and repellent, this bizarre child suffers in real life from the same physical malfunction as the dwarf in the story. But he doesn't rely merely on external weirdness. As the new-born infant, as a three-year-old, and as an old man, he seems haunted by the gallows humor of the role, like an elf from the *Tales of Hoffman*. Watching a Nazi rally through a hole in the wall or crawling through the attack on the Polish post office, using the frantic assaults on his drum as

both a link and a barrier between himself and reality, he gives a performance that left me speechless with awe.

The Tin Drum is a fantastic, piercing film that is unlike anything I've seen before. Like the novel, it has provoked argument and controversy, but it is a cinematic work of art that must be seen, savored and seen again. Its phantoms are tormenting me still.

TIN MEN (1987)

★ ★ ★ Directed and written by Barry Levinson. Produced by Mark Johnson. *With Richard Dreyfuss, Danny DeVito, Barbara Hershey, John Mahoney, and Jackie Gayle.*

Remember *Diner*, that surprise hit from 1982? It traced the roots of its talented young writer-director Barry Levinson to the Hilltop Diner in Baltimore, and was about a group of fifties buddies—jerks who had to decide about their jobs, their girls, and their futures. Here, Levinson is back in Baltimore with a look at the older guys on the other side of that diner—the fast-talking "tin men" who sell aluminum siding to hapless customers in elaborate scams for big commissions. *Tin Men* centers on two rivals—Richard Dreyfuss is B. B. Babowsky, a flashy, cocky little peacock whose brand-new Cadillac gets smashed, the minute he backs it out of the showroom, by Ernest Tilley, played to the hilt by Danny DeVito. It's hate at first sight and these two feuding banana heads spend the rest of this hilarious movie trying to humiliate each other with wacky results. Dreyfuss researches his enemy, hell-bent on the ultimate revenge, and seduces the other man's wife (Barbara Hershey). This leads to all kinds of comic complications. Like *Diner*, it's really a movie about male chauvinists unable to relate to women. They're more at home with each other, and the scams and frauds they dream up to cheat their blue-collar customers are beautifully observed. No wonder the two heels end up buddies. They talk the same language.

Richard Dreyfuss does what he does best, which means he's both obnoxious and sympathetic. Danny DeVito plays more of a human than just a comic caricature of a pint-sized loudmouth. The film is smart, solid, and freshly articulated. It's not slapstick, but it makes you laugh. The dialogue has rhythm and is well delivered by a superb cast. *Tin Men* is a nice change from the idiot Hollywood comedies we're used to.

TO BE OR NOT TO BE (1983)

★ ★ Directed by Alan Johnson. Screenplay by Thomas Meehan and Ronny Graham. Produced by Mel Brooks. With Mel Brooks, Anne Bancroft, Tim Matheson, Charles Durning, and Jose Ferrer.

In this remake of Ernst Lubitsch's 1942 *To Be or Not To Be*, Mel Brooks turns a classic comedy into a borscht-belt Polish joke.

For those who love the original with Jack Benny and Carole Lombard, Mel Brooks and Anne Bancroft are poor substitutes as the stars of a hammy acting troupe caught up in the real drama of World War II. Benny was droll, Lombard glamorous. Brooks and Bancroft make ham acting smell like pig's feet.

People who haven't been fortunate enough to see the original won't know what they're missing, but everyone will know they're missing *something*. This remake has holes in its pacing and comic rhythm you could drive bulldozers through.

The year is 1939. Europe is on the brink of war, but in Warsaw, at the Bronski Theatre, the Poles forget their troubles as the stars do "Sweet Georgia Brown" in Polish.

Bronski (Brooks) loves to do Shakespeare's "To be or not to

be'' speech so much that it takes him forever to deliver it. This is the perfect nightly cue for Mrs. Bronski (Bancroft) to rendezvous in her dressing room with the dashing, lovesick young lieutenant Sobinski (Tim Matheson).

The Nazis invade Poland before their affair can be consummated, but the handsome officer unwisely sends Mrs. Bronski a love note with "To be or not to be" and the Germans think it's a secret code. This understandably leads to trouble, as the theater is closed and its homosexuals, Jews and gypsies are persecuted.

Meanwhile, there's a Nazi spy (Jose Ferrer) who is taking the names of the Polish underground leaders to the Gestapo. He must be stopped. This gives the Bronskis a chance to drag out costumes, greasepaint and accents, and gives Mel Brooks the chance to impersonate the spy, the Gestapo chief, and, finally, the Fuhrer himself. The idea is still valid, but this movie is heavy as a two-ton bagel.

TO LIVE AND DIE IN L.A. (1985)
No ★s Directed by William Friedkin. Screenplay by Gerald Petievich and Friedkin. Produced by Irving H. Levin. With William L. Petersen, Willem Dafoe, John Pankow, Debra Feuer, John Turturro, Darlanne Fluegel, Dean Stockwell, and Robert Downey.

To Live and Die in L.A.? I can't imagine why anyone would want to do either. But if the title doesn't turn you off, there is always the movie itself.

This is a director whose entire career is based on two films, The French Connection and The Exorcist, a few glamorous marriages to famous women, and an ego the size of Trump Tower.

Having turned out one flop after another while failing at every other kind of movie, Friedkin has tried to make another French Connection—this time about the absurd and violent lengths to which subhuman secret agents go to catch a counterfeiter. The result is such an incoherent and stomach-churning disaster that I seriously wonder if Friedkin could direct campfire girls in a chorus of "Old Black Joe."

An Arab terrorist blows himself up on top of a hotel housing the President of the United States. A man runs across a rooftop. Cut to a helicopter shot of Los Angeles after dark. Somebody jumps off a bridge. Cut to close-ups of at least ten minutes of incomprehensible details in the printing of fake money. What is going on here? Nothing in this movie has anything to do with anything that precedes it.

You watch the showdowns, the deceptions, the intrigues, the ambushes, and none of them make the slightest bit of sense.

Characters enter and just when you think you know who they are, more characters enter and blow their heads off or rip their intestines to shreds.

There isn't a single person in the entire film with whom any sane member of the audience can identify. Everyone is a criminal. Everyone is scum. There is one terrific chase sequence while speeding in the wrong direction on the freeway. But the fun wears out when you realize Friedkin has destroyed enough vehicles to transport food and medical supplies to half the starving population of Ethiopia.

Friedkin doesn't bother to develop characters, explain their relationships, or move one scene to another with any logic. *To Live and Die in L.A.* has the dubious distinction of also being the worst-cast film ever made. More than a hundred actors are listed in the pretentious credits. With the exception of Dean Stockwell, I seriously doubt if I could ever bear to lay eyes on any of them again.

TOOTSIE (1982)

★ ★ ★ ★ Directed by Sydney Pollack. Screenplay by Larry Gelbart, Don McGuire and Murray Schisgal. Produced by Sydney Pollack and Dick Richards. *With Dustin Hoffman, Jessica Lange, Bill Murray, Teri Garr, Charles Durning, Dabney Coleman, Doris Belack, and Sydney Pollack.*

Dustin Hoffman in a dress? The idea is repulsive, but I'll be the next Orson Welles before I stop believing in the mysteries of movies and why the worst ideas sometimes turn out to be the best ones, on film.

Tootsie appears to have nothing going for it except the idea that everyone will find the sight of Hoffman in drag positively irresistible.

If the idea ended there, *Tootsie* would be a one-joke affair that would self-destruct before you can say *Victor/Victoria*.

But Hoffman is an industrious (and artistically hungry) performer who isn't much interested in easy catnip. He's going for a steak dinner.

The result is a comedy that is more than just another yarn about a man in Joan Crawford wedgies.

Tootsie is a lively look at the brain-atrophying world of day-time television soap operas, as well as a crisp and often heart-breaking comic mirror to the awful indignities actors suffer every day of their professional lives—the desperations, the rejections, and the overwhelming odds against survival.

And most importantly, it says something poignant about the way people define their identities in terms of role-playing, both on and off the stage.

If this sounds heavy, worry not. *Tootsie* will zap you with laughter. It is much more fun than real life, and Hoffman gives it so much more intelligence than you get in most dumb, sex-change films that you'll end up feeling terrific instead of embarassed.

Tootsie is about a frustrated actor named Michael Dorsey. He's thirty-nine and he's been steadily unemployed for twenty-four years.

Like the ragbag character James Coco played in *Only When I Laugh,* he's the kind of actor who can't even pass the audition for a hemorrhoid commercial.

He's played tomatoes, cucumbers, Strindberg in Central Park, even the Theater of the Blind.

But let's face it, Michael cannot get arrested. The only thing left is to become someone new. He dresses up like Polly Holliday's Flo character on *Alice,* changes his name to Dorothy Michaels, lands a role in a TV

hospital soap called *Southwest General,* and zooms to stardom. Suddenly, it's the life of a lady star for the ex-waiter who couldn't even hold down a job as a corpse Off-Broadway. He's up at 4:30 A.M., shaving the legs, applying the pancake, plucking the eyebrows, curling his lashes, combing out his wigs, and strapping on his falsies.

Suddenly, he's also noticing the height of mirrors, trying on his girlfriend's clothes when she's not looking, and getting a pretty good idea of what women go through as he gets pinched and used as a sex object, called "Honey" and "Tootsie" by the crew, and treated with disrespect.

This double life wrecks everything. His roommmate (Bill Murray) can't answer the phone because Dorothy doesn't want anyone to think she lives with a man. His hysterical girlfriend (Teri Garr) sees him entering his apartment in drag and thinks he's having an affair with another woman.

His sexy co-star on the show (Jessica Lange) treats him as the perfect gal to confide in. To make things worse, her father (Charles Durning) falls for Dorothy. And Dorothy changes the dialogue on the show, building a whole earth-grain woman viewers identify with, and becomes a national star. ("It's the woman in me coming out," quips Dustin. "Slut," sneers his mortified roommate.)

The things he detests in men around him are the same things he's done to other women himself. What happens, see, is that Michael develops a conscience as his consciousness is raised.

But that's just the beginning. Michael's girlfriend decides he's a gay man. Jessica Lange, the girl he really loves, thinks Dorothy is a lesbian. Durning is trying to slip an engagement ring on his finger.

An actor on the show tries to rape him. As confusion piles on chaos, he discovers he's a better man as a woman than he ever was as a man.

What we've got on our hands is another entry in the dragshow genre dedicated to the premise that all you've got to do to make people laugh is put a guy in a girdle and watch him squirm.

The movie is an absorbing, rollicking success because of all the things it makes you think about while Hoffman is squirming so shrewdly.

Like Julie Andrews in *Victor/Victoria*, he swaps sex roles to get ahead and then finds that nobody takes him seriously as himself.

But this film is one hundred times better than that smarmy, overrated Drag Queen Ball because it has vulnerability and humanity and intelligence.

Also, I don't think it is supposed to be taken seriously. Nobody would ever believe Hoffman's cuckoo drag for a minute.

His Streisand fingernails, his Bette Midler nose and his Scarlett O'Hara falsetto fool the girls and his agent (played with freaked-out frenzy by the film's director Sydney Pollack), but they wouldn't fool any streetsmart New Yorker who's ever been to the Christopher Street Halloween parade.

Tootsie becomes a fairy-tale for grownups that makes a point about the futility of contemporary sexual role playing.

It's an obvious point—made all the more entertaining and painless by Larry (*M*A*S*H*) Gelbart and Murray (*Luv*) Schisgal's wise script—but even if you miss the point entirely, you'll have such a good time watching *Tootsie* it really won't matter.

TOP GUN (1986)
★ Directed by Tony Scott. Screenplay by Jim Cash and Jack Epps, Jr. Produced by Don Simpson and Jerry Bruckheimer. With Tom Cruise, Anthony

Edwards, Kelly McGillis, Tom Skerritt, Val Kilmer, Michael Ironsides, Rick Rossovich, Barry Tub, Whip Hubley, Clarence Gilyard, Jr., and Tim Robbins.

If you survive the noise, the moronic script, the ego-trip smirking of the actors, and the nauseating sound track, you might just live long enough to discover that beneath the gloss and the beat and the posing for pinups, *Top Gun* has only one message—a bunch of illiterate kids are flying the U.S. government's $36 million defense planes, and they're doing it all to rock and roll.

Top Gun is nothing more than a lot of music videos strung together aimlessly as an expensive excuse to produce a hit album. Oh, sure. There's a halfhearted attempt to tell a cliche-riddled story swimming around among the jet blasts and the moog synthesizers. *Top Gun* is the nickname of the fighter-weapons school in San Diego, established by the U.S. Navy to train the top one percent of its fighter pilots. The guys have names like Cougar, Maverick, and Goose. You've met them all before, in countless flyboy movies that are far superior to *Top Gun*.

Tom Cruise is Maverick—a super-cool pilot with so much nerve he can guide another frightened pilot onto the aircraft carrier just by talking. Maverick is a wild card, unpredictable, flying "by the seat of his pants." "*I feel the need . . . for speed!*" cries Maverick. Maverick is very stupid.

At Top Gun, the fliers are thrust into competition for the big trophy. Maverick breaks the rules, poses risks for the other fliers, and arrogantly seduces his flight instructor, played by Kelly McGillis. Naturally, everybody hates him, except the drooling teenage girls in the audience, who don't know an F-14 from a Colt .45, and don't much care, as long as Tom Cruise keeps taking his clothes off.

That's about it. The rest of the film consists of a series of competitive flying sequences with an assortment of pretty boys in the cockpit who look like models for Calvin Klein underwear, facing different dangerous challenges each time out of the hangar. When they aren't blazing through the sky in their F-14s to eardrum-splattering Dolby stereo, they're visiting the base disco to eardrum-splattering Dolby stereo. There are endless lectures on negative-G pushovers and weight ratios, and a great deal of French kissing. To each his own jollies.

Finally, the moment of truth. When his best friend dies in a mechanical failure, Maverick feels responsible and loses his self-confidence. Will Maverick throw in the gym towel, or go for it? There's never any suspense about which option he'll choose. The dumb script, by Jim Cash and Jack Epps, telegraphs every emotion and every event before they happen. There's nothing for the audience to do but sit back and fight off the headaches.

Top Gun is a subject—and a film—of limited interest and practically no appeal to anyone over fourteen, except collectors of Tom Cruise beefcake calendar centerfolds and gullible teenage boys flocking to San Diego to enlist in flying school, praying their instructor from the Pentagon will look like Kelly McGillis.

TOUCH OF EVIL (1958)

★ ★ ½ Written and directed by Orson Welles. Produced by Albert Zugsmith. *With Charlton Heston, Orson Welles, Janet Leigh, Zsa Zsa Gabor, Joseph Cotten, Mercedes McCambridge, Keenan Wynn, Akim Tamiroff, Dennis Weaver, and Marlene Dietrich.*

Orson Welles, as a porcine, psychopathic, Texas-drawling cop, takes the viewer on a Peeping Tom's tour of a sleazy Mexican border town, clashing with honeymooners Charlton Heston and Janet Leigh, as well as a seedy assortment of whores, pimps, narcotics racketeers, and eye-rolling villains played by Zsa Zsa Gabor, Joseph Cotten, Mercedes McCambridge, Keenan Wynn, Akim Tamiroff, Dennis Weaver, and the one and only Marlene Dietrich, who, as the madam of a Mexican bordello, gets the film's best line when she gives the whale-sized Welles the once-over and sighs: "Better lay off the candy bars, honey— you're a mess!" The movie is a mess, too, but great campy fun.

TOUGH GUYS (1986)

★ ★ ★ ½ Directed by Jeff Kanew. Screenplay by James Orr and Jim Cruickshank. Produced by Joe Wizan. *With Burt Lancaster, Kirk Douglas, Charles Durning, Alexis Smith, Dana Carvey, Darlanne Fluegel, Eli Wallach, Monty Ash, and Billy Barty.*

The old pros are still the best, and in *Tough Guys*, two of the all-time greats give it all they've got. As the oldest train robbers in America, released from the slammer after thirty years, they light up the screen with pure entertainment, packing a lesson for today's undernourished filmmakers and restoring a good reputation to buddy-buddy movies at the same time. In jail Harry Doyle (Lancaster) and Archie Long (Douglas) ate three squares a day, lifted weights to stay in shape, and played Bing Crosby records. Now they're out on parole facing a changed society of punk rock, street muggers and computer technology worse than anything they encountered under J. Edgar Hoover. Harry, seventy-two, is sent to a retirement home to live on pureed spinach, and Archie, sixty-seven, heads for his first beer and accidentally finds himself in a gay bar. Abused by employers, harassed by cops, and patronized by welfare agencies and Boy Scouts, the old-timers discover it's no fun being senior citizens. Sick of trying to fit in, they go back to what they do best and hijack another train— the same one they got caught trying to hijack thirty years earlier. Only this time, they get it right.

Tough Guys is a cross between *Cocoon* and *Gunfight at the O.K. Corral*—fresh, funny, exciting, and filled with reliable and familiar faces like Charles Durning, as the cop who busted the public enemies thirty years ago, now relegated to the records division of the L.A. Police Department; Eli Wallach, as a myopic gunman who keeps falling into manholes; and Alexis Smith, more beautiful and desirable than most of today's junior sexpots half her age, as Lancaster's love interest—a sixty-year-old retired chorus girl who teaches aerobics in a nursing home. But it's mostly just great to see Douglas and Lancaster as a geriatric Butch and Sundance, flying high with the material and having a ball. When Lancaster shoots a withering look at Douglas and sneers "Shut up, or I'll put another hole in your chin," you feel the chemistry Burt Reynolds and Clint Eastwood failed to achieve in *City Heat*. These guys prove that senior citizens are not ready for the pasture just because the apple won't bite. The system robs them of their dignity, so they screw the system while the audience cheers. Today's movie moguls say nobody wants to see old stars anymore. *Tough Guys* made them eat their words in 1986 at the box office. The Brat Pack couldn't match their polish, energy, or ability to steal an audience's heart with four thousand retakes. If you think the movies are no longer any fun, you haven't seen *Tough Guys*.

TRADING PLACES (1983)
★ ★ ★ Directed by John Landis.
Screenplay by Timothy Harris and
Herschel Weingrod. Produced by
Aaron Russo. *With Dan Aykroyd,
Eddie Murphy, Don Ameche,
Ralph Bellamy, Denholm Elliott,
Jamie Lee Curtis, and Jim Belushi.*

Happy surprises at the movies often come in the most unexpected packages. Take *Trading Places*. I expected another trashy Dan Aykroyd farce. Instead, I got a film of real wit and imagination, populated by interesting and genuinely amusing characters and featuring the most consistently sustained piece of acting the former star of *Saturday Night Live* had yet managed in feature films. After *Neighbors* and *Doctor Detroit*, I threw in the towel on Aykroyd. Now my faith was restored. He is splendid.

First, the plot (or enough of it to give you the general idea without being accused of early senility): Ralph Bellamy and Don Ameche are septuagenarian sibling scions of a Philadelphia financial empire. Miserly, avaricious and utterly without regard for the rest of the human race, these bigoted bluebloods have nothing better to do than place bets on other people's lives the way normal folks would play the horses.

Dan Aykroyd is Louis Winthorpe III, a snobbish market analyst and financial wizard who is close to the top of the old goats' company. Winthorpe, with his WASP button-downs and upturned preppie nose, is a product of good education at Exeter and Harvard, good breeding on the Main Line, and good genes. Eddie Murphy, on the other hand, is Billy Ray Valentine, a jive-talking con man so vile he even pretends to be a blind, legless war veteran in order to fleece the crowds outside Winthorpe's private club.

This odd duo is as far apart on the social and economic scale as Margaret Thatcher is from Big Maybelle. In a one-dollar bet about heredity vs. environment, however, the two old millionaires decided to reverse the situation. Faster than a speeding Metroliner, they've got Billy Ray blissed out in an $80,000-a-year executive job replete with Winthorpe's luxury town house, mile-long limo and personal butler. Simultaneously, they strip Winthorpe of his elegant clothes, frame him for embezzlement, jail him for dealing drugs, freeze his bank accounts, and cancel his credit cards. Billy Ray turns out to be a smash selling pork bellies on the stock market, while poor Winthorpe sinks so low even mongrels relieve themselves on his leg, confusing him with a corroded fire hydrant.

For a while, the film hopscotches merrily between stories, but finally the hardworking, loyal executive-turned-bum and the hopeless psychopath-turned-Wall Street whiz kid both realize they're in the same boat—two puppets victimized by the bilious tycoons who are pulling their strings. Then it's full speed ahead as these two zanies pool their talents, their education in the school of hard knocks, and their thirst for revenge, and turn the tables on Bellamy and Ameche.

Aided by that grand British actor Denholm Elliott, as the bewildered but good-natured butler, and a sleek new Jamie Lee Curtis, in the best role of her career, as a tough whore with a pure heart, Aykroyd and Murphy learn who their real friends are and the audience cheers as they stage their final showdown on the floor of the New York Stock Exchange.

I won't spoil the fun and tell you how it all turns out, but I guarantee you more laughs than an invasion of white mice at a sorority house slumber party. *Trading Places* has many virtues, but chief among its delights is Dan Aykroyd's metamorphosis from arrogant, pretentious pain in the rear to humiliated slob so desperate and hungry he crashes a Christmas party and stuffs a whole smoked salmon into his filthy Santa Claus suit.

It's nice to see so many first-cabin talents, usually starved into mediocrity by bad scripts, playing real roles instead of cardboard clowns.

Much of what makes *Trading Places* superior to other comedies is a script in which humor does not come from idiot jokes or scatology, but from the essence of human nature. Director John Landis has come a long way since *Animal House* and *Blues Brothers*. His guidance honors structure and provides balance, giving the zany characters plenty of room to work in without jetting into the outer limits of stupidity just to milk the movie for laughs when there aren't any. I guess what I liked most is the kind of discipline that is so often missing in most Aykroyd comedies. And the movie is *about* something. It even has a moral.

Trading Places is updated Frank Capra with four-letter words, and I can think of no higher praise than that. Gentlemen, flowers for everybody.

LA TRAVIATA (1983)

★ ★ ★ Directed by Franco Zeffirelli. Produced by RAI-Radio Televisione, Italia and Accent Films. *With Placido Domingo, Teresa Stratas.*

Just when you thought movies had surrendered to mindlessness and schlock, Franco Zeffirelli comes up with a transposition of *La Traviata* from opera stage to movie screen that is positively miraculous.

In the film, musical drama and the true art of the cinema—moving pictures—have rarely been united with so much exquisite artistry. With uncommon dexterity and invention, the great Italian director has distilled from the Verdi opera a motion picture of enormous visual beauty and tragic impact, one that delights the ear and eye while simultaneously strumming on the heart strings.

Zeffirelli is famous for his sumptuous physical compositions, his lush landscapes, his opulent visual tapestries. This is perfect material for his kind of sensitivity. *La Traviata*'s luscious visions of Second Empire Paris resemble those of the French Impressionist painters, and its excursions into the neighboring countryside and forests suggest the brush strokes of Corot. The composition of every frame (Ennio Gu-

arnieri is responsible for the ravishing cinematography) sets the period to perfection. Piero Tosi, who did most of Visconti's elaborate films, has outdone himself with more than 150 Belle Epoque costumes that take the breath away. Gianni Quaranta's spectacular sets are accurately detailed right down to the authentic period books.

Zeffirelli is a master at all of this. But wizard of theatricality that he is, he knows a film does not live on looks alone. It must have thrust, meter, form, structure. All are evident in abundance. He has not altered the libretto, but has accorded it smooth cinematic fluency so that it has the aspect of a dreamy ballet. His version begins—as does the Alexandre Dumas novel that was the opera's inspiration—with the heroine, the 1840's courtesan who flees her lover to preserve his reputation, at death's door. The story unfolds in flashback.

(Some years ago, I was greatly impressed by a production of *La Dame aux Camelias* staged by Zeffirelli on Broadway; many of the haunting visual ideas from that production have been retained for the movie, such as the prelude, in which the dying heroine sees in a mirror all of the pageantry and glory of her past even as the auctioneers are stripping her house of its contents in preparation for her funeral.)

Such actresses as Sarah Bernhardt, Nazimova, Norma Talmadge, and Greta Garbo have played the part of Camille before the cameras of their day. And in several previously filmed versions of the opera, the lead has been sung by sopranos as varied as Nelly Corradi and Anna Moffo.

Never before, however, have the problems of welding opera and film been resolved with such visual harmony as in this picture. Zeffirelli has freshened the usual older-woman-younger man situation. In the person of Canadian-born Teresa Stratas, we have not the mature *diseuse* but the lost girl of the original, quick with the poignancy of doomed youth instead of the tired resignation of a dying consumptive.

Stratas is an enchanting singer, but she can also act. She effectively reflects the frail allure of the tragic moth who flitted through Paris night life a century ago and had one brief spell of ecstasy with a young admirer before his father burst into their country retreat and broke up the romance with cruelty. It is an interpretation full of grace and strength, vocally and histrionically a triumph.

Placido Domingo is strikingly handsome and somewhat thinner than usual as the disillusioned lover, and James Levine of the Metropolitan Opera conducts.

By moving the camera around freely and using it as the principal instrument for developing the drama while accommodating the music to the story, Zeffirelli has succeeded in giving considerable fluidity of movement to his film without losing the flavor of the opera. The result is spontaneous, illuminating, unforgettable. Even if you hate opera, you will go away from *La Traviata* dazzled right down to your socks.

A TREE GROWS IN BROOKLYN (1945)

★ ★ ★ ★ Directed by Elia Kazan. Screenplay by Tess Slesinger and Frank Davis, based on the book by Betty Smith. Produced by Louis D. Lighton. *With James Dunn, Dorothy McGuire, Peggy Ann Garner, Joan Blondell, Lloyd Nolan, and James Gleason.*

This 1945 classic, brilliantly directed by the great Elia Kazan (his first film), is one of the most trenchant tearjerkers ever made. The poignant and richly human story of a struggling family in the slums of Brooklyn at the turn of the century, it packs a tremendous emotional punch as it chronicles the lives of the Nolans. James Dunn and Peggy Ann Garner won Oscars for their warm, compassionate portrayals of Johnny Nolan, the poverty-stricken but cheerful loser of a father, and his daughter Francie, a sensitive and intelligent child whose dream is to attend a better school. Dorothy McGuire is luminous as always in the difficult role of the stern mother whose task is to keep the family together despite overwhelming hardships, and there's rewarding support from Joan Blondell and Lloyd Nolan, too. It's not the plot that counts, but the deep, sympathetic tenderness with which real people are shown that makes *A Tree Grows in Brooklyn* such a memorable experience. Elia Kazan's directorial debut paved the way for an illustrious career.

TRUE CONFESSIONS (1981)

1/2 ★ Directed by Ulu Grosbard. Screenplay by Joan Didion and John Gregory Dunne. Produced by Irwin Winkler and Robert Chartoff. With Robert De Niro, Robert Duvall, Charles Durning, Ed Flanders and Burgess Meredith.

I'm sure there will be those who disagree with me about Robert De Niro and Robert Duvall as mismatched brothers in *True Confessions*, but as good as both actors are, I felt while watching their mush-mouthed histrionics that I was listening to a shortwave radio broadcasting underwater. Still bloated and spongy from all the weight he gained for *Raging Bull*, De Niro plays a priest who uses saving souls as an excuse for attaining power within the already-powerful (and according to this film, totally corrupt) Catholic Church. Duvall is his brother, a jaded, cynical cop investigating the sex slaying of a prostitute.

The story is a simple one. One, a cop is looking for a killer. The other, a priest, is trying to cover things up. Why does *True Confessions* have to come off like a syllabus on income tax preparation? This movie is so unnecessarily confusing, so overbearingly hysterical, and so disturbingly incoherent that it took me nearly an hour to figure out what was going on. Not only is it hard to understand, but the actors are even less coherent than the plot. There's De Niro, whispering piously through his stoic double chins, with Duvall on the other side of the screen, swallowing his tongue and mumbling inaudibly, both of them overacting like crazy. Whatever happened to the actor's obligation to speak lines distinctly? Whatever happened to enunciation, diction, vocal projection? Kenneth McMillan, who plays one of Duvall's fellow cops, gurgles and gulps every line of dialogue with his mouth full of food. I couldn't understand one word he said in the entire film.

Some of this stupidity can be blamed on the self-indulgences of method actors who think what's good enough for an acting exercise in Lee Strasberg's class is good enough for the motion picture screen. But I also blame the director, Ulu Grosbard, for letting them get away with murder. The poor audience, fearing communal hearing disorders, ends up the victim.

Viewers who strain to hear are not the only ones likely to be offended by *True Confessions*. Catholics will be outraged, and rightfully so. This movie makes all priests, cardinals and monsignors look like pretentious thugs who use the church for their own personal gain. The police don't come off any better. Greed, avarice and total disregard for humanity are the talismans the cops and employees of the coroner's office seem to live by. Add to these slimy characters a bunch of whores going to the slammer, hookers at the end of their ropes, crooked politicians, fall guys,

bag men, and graphic details of lurid sex crimes mixed in with horrible stomach-churning closeups of fresh corpses being dismembered in autopsies while people look on munching on ham sandwiches, and you get the picture. *True Confessions* is quite the nastiest, most immoral presentation of humanity I've seen in a long time. Severed torsos, pornographic film clips, underworld construction contracts, corrupt lawyers and psychos on the loose are only part of the canvas Joan Didion and John Gregory Dunne present. Even more sour is the indication that priests don't make it to the top of the Catholic Church unless they join the reprobates of society and dirty their own ecclesiastical robes in the process. I've seen such scorching indictments in better films than this.

Charles Durning gave the best performance in the film as the vicious, evil Catholic Layman of the Year, a construction magnate who is one of De Niro's heaviest financial contributors. When he becomes Duvall's prime suspect in the murder case, De Niro tries to shield him from the investigation because he's building a new school for the archdiocese. The movie's point is that everyone is a criminal, some are just better protected than others. De Niro's career is ruined in the church because he isn't crooked enough, and although I don't know beans about how the Catholic Church is run from within, I find that assumption hard to swallow. In fact, I found just about everything in *True Confessions* difficult to believe. The two stars do enough swallowing for everybody. They've taken what is basically an old James Cagney-George Murphy idea and inflated it beyond all comprehension for no apparent purpose. Even the killer that Duvall pursues with such a vengeance, wrecking his brother's life along the way, turns out to be the wrong suspect. You need a slide rule to get through this one, and after you do, you'll hate yourself in the morning.

TUCKER: THE MAN AND HIS DREAM (1988)

★ ★ ★ Directed by Francis Ford Coppola. Screenplay by Arnold Schulman and David Seidler. Produced by Fred Roos and Fred Fuchs. *With Jeff Bridges, Joan Allen, Martin Landau, Frederic Forrest, Mako, and Dean Stockwell.*

Jeff Bridges is superb in the title role—dreamer, designer, inventor Preston Tucker, a Michigan industrialist who tried to revolutionize the automotive industry after World War II by introducing a brand-new car of tomorrow that was years ahead of General Motors. Smeared by the press, framed by corrupt politicians, and dragged through a sensational trial for fraud, Tucker built a better mousetrap and then became the mouse. In this big, brassy, entertaining film, Francis Ford Coppola finds a metaphor for the death of the American Dream and brings brilliantly to life the story of an original American hero.

TWELVE ANGRY MEN (1957)

★ ★ ★ ★ Directed by Sidney Lumet. Written and produced by Reginald Rose. *With Henry Fonda, Lee J. Cobb, Ed Begley, E.G. Marshall, Martin Balsam, Jack Klugman and Jack Warden.*

Twelve Angry Men is the most probing, incisive, and penetrating look into the hearts and minds of a jury that has ever been filmed. Sidney Lumet made his film directing debut with this sensitive and absorbing 1957 classic. Henry Fonda gave one of the most forceful performances of his distinguished career as the open-minded juror whose logical reasoning changes the verdict in a murder case. Lee J. Cobb, Ed Begley, E. G. Marshall, Martin

Balsam, Jack Klugman, and Jack Warden are just a few of the diverse jurors whose lives, prejudices, strengths, and weaknesses are revealed in the confines of the locked jury room. It's not as claustrophobic as it may sound; this movie has such powerful and perceptive acting, writing, direction and camera work, it will keep you as spellbound as the defendant on trial.

TWICE IN A LIFETIME (1985)
★ ★ ★ Directed and produced by Bud Yorkin. Screenplay by Colin Welland. With Gene Hackman, Ann-Margret, Ellen Burstyn, Amy Madigan, Ally Sheedy, Stephen Lang, Darrell Larson, and Brian Dennehy.

A piercing, heartfelt look at American divorce and the various ways every member of a decent family copes with the consequences. On his fiftieth birthday, Harry Mackenzie (Gene Hackman), a Seattle steelworker, steps out of his boring thirty-year marriage to a nice but dull wife (Ellen Burstyn) and falls into the arms of a ripe, mature, understanding waitress named Audrey (Ann-Margret). You'd have to be dead not to fall for Ann-Margret, but that's not the point. What the film is saying about divorce is that divorce is painful, divorce is horrible, divorce is often unplanned and blameless—but it's not the end of the world. The people in *Twice in a Lifetime* don't ask for the unpleasant things that happen to them, but they don't lie down and stop living, either. They survive. And they triumph. The film explores the anger, hurt, bitterness, resentment, and surprise experienced not only by Harry, but by his wife, friends, children and grandchildren. The results are wrenching, sad, always honest, and finally full of the hope and backbone that makes good people strong in the face of adversity.

As the central triangle, Hackman, Burstyn, and Ann-Margret bite into three juicy roles and find a feast. Amy Madigan lends sturdy support as Harry's anxiety-ridden eldest daughter, and Ally Sheedy is wonderful as the youngest daughter, on the verge of her own wedding, convinced she'll never make the same mistakes her parents did. Bud Yorkin's sensitive direction avoids clichés and distinguishes the rich material by Colin Welland, the Oscar-winning writer of *Chariots of Fire*. No hate, no violence, no rock and roll, no aliens from Mars. Just some valuable time spent with people worth knowing.

Twice in a Lifetime is the kind of marvelous movie they

mean when they say "They don't make movies like that anymore."

TWINS (1988)

★ ★ ★ Directed and produced by Ivan Reitman. Screenplay by William Davies, William Osborne, Timothy Harris, and Herschel Weingrod. With Danny DeVito, Arnold Schwarzenegger, Kelly Preston, Chloe Webb, Bonnie Bartlett, Marshall Bell, Trey Wilson, and Hugh O'Brian.

Far from the idiot farce its publicity suggested, this comedy by Ivan (*Ghostbusters*) Reitman is gentle, sweet, pleasant and highly agreeable. It also catapults Arnold Schwarzenegger into a new dimension as something other than a talking Mack truck. He's the result of a genetic experiment that backfires, producing mismatched twins. Arnold's the pure, virtuous Charles Atlas, and Danny DeVito is—oy vey!—"all the crap that was left over." Innocent and gullible, with an IQ as big as his biceps, Arnold uses his muscles to protect his brother, while DeVito, with the mind of a con man and the body of a toad, uses his twin's good-natured innocence with larceny in mind. Before the movie runs out of gas, there are some funny bits when Arnold nukes his dinner in a microwave and DeVito heads for Texas carrying stolen goods in his trunk, with Arnold and two sex kittens in tow. By the end, DeVito learns the value of self-respect and Arnold is no longer a 230-pound virgin. This is as unlikely a screen team as the movies will ever invent, but the casting is so inspired you get double the pleasure, double the fun.

TWILIGHT ZONE—THE MOVIE (1983)

★ Directed by Steven Spielberg, John Landis, Joe Dante, and George Miller. Screenplay by John Landis, George Johnson, Richard Matheson. Produced by Steven Spielberg. With Dan Aykroyd, Albert Brooks, Vic Morrow, Doug McGrath, Scatman Crothers, Kathleen Quinlan, Jeremy Licht, John Lithgow, and Abbe Lane.

Remaking old movies that worked better the first time around is a pointless waste of time; it makes even less sense to dig up old TV shows. *Twilight Zone—The Movie* is one of the few films I've ever seen that borrows old ideas from dead TV shows in such an uninspired way that it made me long for the old days of my black-and-white Magnavox. For a big, splashy, color movie with ear-splitting Dolby stereo, that isn't much of an accomplishment.

This four-part semi-anthology is the not-so-bright idea of Steven Spielberg and John Landis, who produced the movie and directed two of the segments.

The reason is obvious. Look at Spielberg's *E.T.* or Landis' *American Werewolf in London*, and you know automatically that they must have been fans of the old TV show and its creator, Rod Serling.

Twilight Zone—The Movie is therefore an affectionate "tribute" to the original series which ran for five years. (It is still popular in re-runs.) All of which might satisfy fans, just as the *Star Trek* movies thrilled Trekkies, but for anyone with more demanding tastes, it's pretty insipid stuff.

I loved the TV show, but on the big screen, with every flaw magnified, the material seems flat, the writing and direction mediocre, and the fantasy forced. It all adds up to an expensive but not very satisfying experiment on the *Creepshow* level.

Like the original series, the movie remains faithful in dramatic structure and style to Serling's concept of mood-drenched thirty-minute flights of fancy, each with an O'Henry twist.

There is even a prologue, in which two grownup kids of the '60s, played by Dan Aykroyd and Albert Brooks, ride through the night singing TV theme songs and talking about old *Twilight Zone* episodes.

The first segment of the film that follows is the tragic, controversial one Landis directed, during which actor Vic Morrow and two Vietnamese children died.

I will only say that neither the circumstances nor the plot—a muddled splash of heavy-handed symbolism about an unemployed bigot forced to change identities with the people he's maligned as he's pursued by Nazis and the KKK—seem worth the heavy price paid to get this segment on film. Morrow's death left a hole in the story that is painfully obvious.

The second segment, directed by Spielberg, uses syrupy music and a mushy, sentimental style to tell the flaccid tale of a group of senior citizens in a rest home who recapture their youth through a magic game of kick the can. Despite Spielberg's use of children, it has none of the charm of *E.T.*

Segment three features Kathleen Quinlan as a woman drawn into the bizarre world of a child with magic powers who tortures adults by forcing them to watch kiddie cartoons and eat hamburgers drenched in peanut butter. The animated special effects made me think of Walt Disney freaking out on hallucinogens, but the routine direction by Joe (*The Howling*) Dante is as dull as the story is pointless.

When the TV show was in full swing, the three directors just mentioned were American teens devouring each weekly installment with glee. The real irony, then, is that the fourth, final and best segment in the film is the work of George Miller, an Australian, who made the futuristic thrillers *Mad Max* and *Road Warrior*.

This segment also works splendidly because it is based on *Nightmare at 20,000 Feet*, an original episode that was actually broadcast to great acclaim on the old *Twilight Zone* show.

John Lithgow is wonderful as an hysterical passenger on a jet plane that is crashing through a turbulent storm, unable to convince anyone that he sees a hideous monster crawling on the wing. Miller has charged the story with maximum terror and unbearable tension. Too bad the

rest of the film doesn't meet the same standards.

One out of four makes for poor odds. Why not just bring back the old TV series for half the cost?

TWO-FACED WOMAN (1941)

★ ★ Directed by George Cukor. Screenplay by S. N. Behrman, Salka Viertel, and George Oppenheimer. Produced by Gottfried Reinhardt. With Greta Garbo, Melvyn Douglas, Constance Bennett, Ruth Gordon, Roland Young, and Robert Sterling.

Two-Faced Woman, a 1941 farce in which Greta Garbo starred as a ski instructor who poses as her own twin sister to win back her wayward husband, is her last movie. No wonder. It is awful. Featuring Melvyn Douglas, Constance Bennett, and Ruth Gordon, the film was a bomb, but as Garbo's swan song, it has a historic significance of its own. Garbo dances (dismally), laughs (gaudily), and postures (awkwardly) while draping herself (clumsily) across all sorts of upholstered chairs, sofas, and ski poles. She took one look at the final release print and left the screen forever.

UNCOMMON VALOR (1983)

★ ★ ½ Directed by Ted Kotcheff. Screenplay by Joe Gayton. Produced by John Milius and Buzz Feitshans. *With Gene Hackman, Robert Stack, Fred Ward, Reb Brown, Randall "Tex" Cobb, Patrick Swayze, Harold Sylvester, and Tim Thomerson.*

For action-packed thrills laced with suspense and real heroes to root for instead of cardboard facsimiles, you can't beat *Uncommon Valor.* Like most movies about the Vietnam experience, this one is more about guns and explosions than it is about people, but it's never dull and the massive battle sequences are among the best the screen has ever offered.

There are still twenty-five hundred American soldiers missing in action in Vietnam. For their families, the war will never end.

In *Uncommon Valor* Gene Hackman gives one of his toughest and most likable performances as a Marine colonel obsessed with the idea that his son is still alive in a prison camp in Laos. The Washington politicians who are aware of the numbers missing in action refuse to do much about rescue efforts because there's no financial gain. Hackman decides to take on the job himself, with the aid of the men who were his

son's five best Marine buddies at the time of his capture.

The guys Hackman recruits for the job have been wounded by more than bullets, and the psychological damage still shows. Trained in everything from karate to jungle survival techniques, they make the Green Berets look like a pep squad of pussy willows.

With the financial aid of a Texas oil tycoon (Robert Stack) whose own son is missing in action, the small band of two-fisted veterans builds a POW camp facsimile in Texas, endures a crash course in body building and basic training, and rehearses the rescue mission down to the last grenade.

It is clear from the start that director Ted Kotcheff is more concerned with stamina and courage under fire than with character development. *Uncommon Valor* really goes for broke after the men reach Laos (the Hawaiian island of Kauai, where *South Pacific* was filmed, provides amazingly similar terrain, and the locations are breathtaking contrasts to the horror and carnage that take place there).

Their weapons confiscated by the CIA in Bangkok, their sightseeing money spent for new artillery and equipment provided by black market gangsters, and their mission nearly destroyed by their fellow Americans, they remain undaunted.

Guided by an opium dealer and his two daughters, they crawl into Laos, drawing combat plans for their final battle. The resulting noise and fire levels hundreds of Hawaiian extras and gives the film a climax that will have you jumping, lurching, and yelping in your seat.

Uncommon Valor has the requisite amount of gut-busting action, on the ground and in the helicopters. The actors are all rough and believable and committed, and the stunts seem genuine. Not bad, really, for what is essentially a *Death Wish* with chopsticks.

THE UNTOUCHABLES (1987)
★ ★ ★ ★ Directed by Brian DePalma. Screenplay by David Mamet. Produced by Art Linson. With Kevin Costner, Sean Connery, Andy Garcia, Charles Martin Smith, and Robert De Niro.

One of 1987's surprise hits was *The Untouchables*. Instead of the tired rehash of the old TV series everyone expected, Brian DePalma took the true story of Eliot Ness, examined the facts in his autobiography, and illuminated the Prohibition Era in a style that was original and visually breathtaking. I expected

excitement—but I was unprepared for the scope and artistry in this picture. I also expected violence—and brace yourselves. Even on home video, it *is* violent! (It opens with a ten-year-old girl blown to bits by a bomb.) But the violence is not gratuitous. It's part of a violent era, and it belongs there.

The Untouchables is really a study in American corruption on an epic scale. From gangsters in $800 suits to period cars and Duke Ellington songs, the look and feel of Prohibition Chicago is a tapestry of perfection. And the performances are flawless. Sean Connery, as the only honest cop in Chicago, won an Oscar for his gutsy role as the man who teaches Ness his first lesson in street warfare. Andy Garcia, as a rough Italian cop with steel nerves, and Charles Martin Smith, as the nerdy accountant who hatches the scheme that finally sent America's Public Enemy No. 1 to the slammer for income tax evasion, are wonderfully vivid. Robert De Niro is a terrifically oily and toadlike Capone—a wily, cigar-chomping Edward G. Robinson kind of thug, and also a fat, sentimental slob who weeps over an aria from *Pagliacci* one minute and orchestrates a mob war the next. Kevin Costner is crime fighter

Ness—clean-cut, all-American, a bit square and corny, a dry, waspy combination of Robert Stack and Montgomery Clift.

Brian DePalma's colorful direction has the passion of grand opera. David Mamet's screenplay gives Ness's tireless crusade to clean up the underworld the riveting suspense of a great mystery story, separating truth from legend along the way. I'm always longing for the good old days of Cagney, Bogart, and the Warner Brothers gangster pictures. With *The Untouchables* the good old days are back—and better than ever. *The Untouchables* is an American classic.

URBAN COWBOY (1980)

★ ★ ★ *Directed and written by James Bridges. Based on an Esquire story by Aaron Latham. Produced by Robert Evans and Irving Azoff. With John Travolta, Debra Winger, Scott Glenn, Madolyn Smith, Barry Corbin, Brooke Alderson, Mickey Gilley, Bonnie Raitt, and the Charlie Daniels Band.*

Growing up in Texas prepared me for John Travolta's movie *Urban Cowboy* in ways most viewers won't even begin to understand. All I can tell you is that to me it's not an entertainment. It's a documentary.

This brawling, sprawling story about a country boy who finds his manhood in lusty Houston won't disappoint Travolta fans.

In *Urban Cowboy* Travolta reestablished himself as a most charismatic screen presence in the role of Buford "Bud" Davis, an ignorant hillbilly from Spur, Texas, who hits Houston like a confused tumbleweed. Bud is the new breed of Texas cowboy who gets no closer to roping a steer or busting a bronc than the Huntsville Prison Rodeo, but who carries on the tradition with pickup trucks, Lone Star beer, ten-gallon Stetsons, and lots of attitude. Most of these guys work on pipelines or oil rigs during the day, then head for Gilley's at night to act out their macho fantasies.

Gilley's is a real place in a Houston suburb called Pasadena—a noisy beer hall filled with three and a half acres of roughnecks and *Playboy* centerfolds where everybody does "cowboy dancin' " to endless country and western tunes until they get drunk enough to bash each other's heads in while the band plays "Mamas Don't Let Your Babies Grow Up to Be Cowboys" by Mickey Gilley and Johnny Lee. Whatever is left of the cowboy legend can be found in these sad, lost artifacts with chili on their chins and tattoos on their arms, slugging it out over honky-tonk angels.

Bud meets a gal named Sissy. He can't tame her so he marries her and they find temporary happiness in a mobile trailer home. Then trouble comes galloping along in the form of a mechanical bucking bull installed by Gilley's in the hope that it will rechannel some of the energy the customers spend punching each other.

Bud masters the bull quickly, but Sissy licks it too, with the aid of a mangy polecat ex-con named Wes, and the sexual competition in a male-dominated social structure wounds Bud's pride and wrecks his marriage. He drifts into the arms of a wealthy socialite from the skyscrapers of downtown Houston while Sissy piles in with Wes and learns about violence, infidelity, and male supremacy from the wrong side of the bed.

All of the above is interesting and very well acted, especially by Travolta and by Debra Winger as Sissy in a smoldering debut. The raw subterranean sexiness in her voice reminds me of a young, nubile Elizabeth Ashley. If it seems a bit old-fashioned, it is. The final showdown is so old-fashioned it's almost icky. Bud becomes a local hero, gets his wife back, and outgrows Gilley's in a five-minute span that is too good to be true.

Nobody rides off into the sunset on horseback, but when Bud puts Sissy's Texas license plate back into the rear window and drives her off through Gilley's parking lot in his pickup truck, you don't have to know your cowboy movie history to know the young lovers are heading off together for a life of chicken fried steak.

Aaron Latham originally wrote *Urban Cowboy* as an *Esquire* article about Gilley's, so there was no plot to begin with. Director James (*China Syndrome*) Bridges took a very thin slice of journalism about modern Texas and fleshed out a story. In doing so, he has drenched it with the same attention to detail and folksy Southern atmosphere he demonstrated with *September 30, 1955*.

What he didn't do was find a way to eliminate some of the cornball movie clichés along the way. But don't be deterred. There's enough romance, action, music, dancing (Travolta even does a production number in boots called "Cotton-Eye Joe" they soon started teaching at Roseland), and character analysis to make *Urban Cow-*

boy a jim-dandy treat big as Texas itself. More important, the film examines a microcosm of society in which masculinity is determined by how long a man can stay on a fake bull without falling off, how much Lone Star beer he can drink before his kidneys explode, and how much sexual power he can define with his fists instead of his brains.

At the same time, we get a good look at the kind of women who are attracted to this animal mentality in a sad, one-dimensional meat market of emotional energy where roles are established by exaggerated attitude instead of simple humanity.

The stupidity, the greasy food, the saloons, the refineries, the drawls, the nauseating whine of hillbilly music that permeates the air like decaying garbage, the know-nothingism are all reasons why I left Texas in the first place and never returned. These are the facts and the moods so perfectly created by Jim Bridges in *Urban Cowboy*.

Travolta is wonderful, making his role fit like a worn-out saddle, and he gets riveting support not only from Debra Winger, but also from Scott Glenn as the villain and Madolyn Smith as the social moth who goes slumming at Gilley's and hangs around long enough to get her wings burned. Everyone involved has documented a repellent but very real part of America I'm just as happy to leave on film. *Urban Cowboy* is a swell movie, but for me, it's like a trip back home. In chains.

THE VERDICT (1982)
★ ★ ★ ★   Directed by Sidney Lumet. Screenplay by David Mamet. Produced by Richard Zanuck and David Brown. *With Paul Newman, Charlotte Rampling, Jack Warden, James Mason, Milo O'Shea, Edward Binns, Julie Bovasso, and Lindsay Crouse.*

If Paul Newman searched for years for the right idea, then wrote it himself, he couldn't have come up with a more perfect character—or film—than Frank Galvin in *The Verdict*.

One of the screen's most durable and charismatic stars, Newman gets to play a real flesh-and-blood protagonist, a down-and-out lawyer who takes on the medical profession and the Catholic church to win a malpractice suit.

The movie has romance, humanity, suspense, issues that hit you between the eyes, and a built-in set of ethics that fit

Newman like a layer of new skin.

Strength and courage are in short supply these days, but Newman usually looks for these qualities in the roles he plays, which somewhat explains why he leaves an indelible impression.

As Frank Galvin, he begins as a washed-up drunk looking for clients in funeral parlors and on obituary pages. Throwing up in hallways, hanging out in saloons, covering up his desperate predicament with Visine and Binaca, he's a once-promising lawyer on the skids.

Personal tragedy and career setbacks have reduced him to the status of an ambulance chaser who takes on nuisance cases for small change.

A routine malpractice case leads Galvin to the discovery that two rich, powerful doctors at a famous Catholic hospital are at fault for administering the wrong anesthesia during an operation. Now the church owning the hospital wants to settle out of court without an embarrassing jury trial.

The defendants want to settle. Galvin's own client, the victim's sister, wants to settle. The old-guard Boston legal firm retained by the church offers to settle.

A check for $210,000 is placed in Galvin's hand. It's more money than he's ever earned. But stubbornly, idealistically, this broken, sour, cynical man near the end of his rope decides not to be bought, not to look the other way.

The case represents one last chance to redeem himself and find some value in his existence by defending his own sense of morality and justice in a court of law. It's all he's got left, so he's got nothing to lose—or everything.

The Verdict is a tough, fascinating, suspenseful, and gripping study of one small man with a big conscience going up against the system.

The Verdict's final quarter is quality courtroom stuff. Director Sidney Lumet's first claim to fame was *Twelve Angry Men*, one of the best trial dramas ever made, so he's on firm ground. He's always provided a running theme in his best films of little people with flaws and problems trying to do what's right, so he knows how to pinpoint dramatic highlights with slow, measured takes for maximum effect.

It's in Galvin's final summation—after a hostile judge has tried to destroy his case, after his chief witness has been bought off, after he has been all but annihilated by the overwhelming opposition of a major hospital, a prestigious law firm with limitless funds, and the archdiocese of Boston—that actor Newman and director Lumet make their most honest and revealing case for justice.

Here is brittle, terse writing by playwright David Mamet that makes valid points without being preachy. Here is clean, economical direction without frills. And here are beautifully modulated and deeply felt performances.

Charlotte Rampling is sultry and marvelous as the woman who provides the film with a shocking twist.

James Mason controls the screen like a chiropractor seizing a torn ligament in the role of the distinguished defense lawyer Newman must defeat to win his case. Milo O'Shea is juicily malevolent as the vicious, self-serving judge whose prejudice almost trashes the judicial system.

Lindsay Crouse makes a small but pivotal contribution as a nurse whose passionate testimony changes the outcome of the case.

The Verdict is uncommonly effective on many levels. It is unpretentious, it is valid, it is responsible, and it gives Newman one of his most spirited roles in years.

VICTOR/VICTORIA (1982)
★ ★ Directed and written by Blake Edwards. Produced by Edwards and Tony Adams. *With Julie Andrews, James Garner, Robert Preston, Lesley Ann Warren, Alex Karras, and John Rhys-Davies.*

Blake Edwards hasn't entertained an original thought in his head for decades, although he has been shameless about borrowing the ideas of others. He's the Otto Preminger of comedy—grabbing whatever sells in current social trends and newspaper headlines, then taking the credit himself. From the dreadful Pink Panther movies to the vastly overrated *10* to the "let's get Hollywood" impotence of *S.O.B.*, his movies reek of hack work and recycled staleness. The best that can be said of *Victor/Victoria* is that it is an improvement over *S.O.B.*, but that is not meant as an endorsement.

Based on a 1933 German film by Rheinhold Schuenzel called *Viktor und Viktoria*, this bloated farce cashes in on the transvestite popularity of *La Cage aux Folles* by dressing Julie Andrews in drag and trying desperately to milk some laughs out of stylized homosexuality. There is already something smarmy about Julie Andrews in drag (she looks neither male nor female—merely androgynous and sickly pale, like David Bowie playing a gay Martian), and although I applaud any filmmaker who tries to show the harm in sexual stereotyping, it has been done much better elsewhere.

Andrews plays a starving opera singer in 1934 Paris who is so hungry, she offers her body to the landlord for a meatball. Robert Preston plays an aging drag queen who has just been fired from his job at a gay cabaret, called Chez Lui, for insulting the customers and causing a riot. They meet in the rain, cheat a café out of dinner by pretending there are cockroaches in the food, and become friends, roommates, and business partners, in a fraudulent scheme to pass Mary Poppins off as a Polish count who sings and dances as a woman. Dressed in Preston's old lover's clothes, she becomes the transvestite rage of Paris, looking like a grotesque Berlin cartoon from the Nazi era.

Enter James Garner, a Chicago gangster so shocked at his attraction to a man that he goes out and beats a few waterfront toughs to pousse-café with his fists. What a mess. Here we have a swarm of clichés masquerading as comic perversion.

Andrews is a woman pretending to be a man impersonating a woman. Garner, playing his own stereotype, is a neanderthal who has to keep proving his manhood with violence to cover the truth that he's a macho man in love with a female impersonator, who is really a woman. Preston is a man who really wants to be a woman. To complicate things further, there is Garner's peroxide tramp of a girlfriend (Lesley Ann Warren) who thinks she can turn a gay man straight, and Garner's burly bodyguard (Alex Karras) who falls in love with Preston. The boys find they enjoy being girls, the girls find they enjoy being boys, and one expects a chorus from Rodgers and Hammerstein at any moment. Instead, we get abominable musical numbers by Henry Mancini and Leslie Bricusse, with chorus boys in boy-girl masks dripping with sequins and mascara, women impersonating men, men impersonating women, and not a shred of conviction from anybody.

Heavy-handed direction and boneheaded performances don't help, and there's no comic tension. Garner wears more makeup than Andrews, so the confusion is heightened beyond all intentions and for all the wrong reasons.

Instead of illuminating the

humor in sexual role reversals or pointing up the silliness of sexual stereotyping, Blake Edwards only succeeds in creating stereotypes of his own. The art deco bedroom Preston and Andrews share as platonic friends drowns in homosexual interior decorating, while Garner's room chokes on its own sterility. (Both in the same hotel? It's as though the manager looked over the reservation list and shrieked: "The queens are coming; get out the pink satin sheets!") You never know in this movie whether Edwards is being Noel Cowardly, or just plain cowardly. Every gender joke imaginable gushes forth, but there are few genuine laughs that come from anyone's heart. The best comic moment (in fact, the only comic moment) comes when Andrews grouses about strapping her bosom to look flat-chested in a man's suit. What bosom?

Poor Preston is relegated to bitch lines that must have been amusing to Edwards when he wrote them. "There's nothing more inconvenient than an old queen with a head cold," says Preston, and the line is not only unfunny—it doesn't even make sense. It's all very trashy and offensive, not to mention sophomoric.

A VIEW TO A KILL (1985)

★ Directed by John Glen. Written by Richard Maibaum and Michael Wilson. Produced by Albert Broccoli and Michael Wilson.

In the frozen wastes of Siberia, hundreds of Russian machine guns fire away at a familiar figure on skis. Yes, it's 007 again, leaping across a crevice to freedom, pursued by helicopters, snowmobiles, and Russian bombs. Nothing can stop him, not even an avalanche big and destructive enough to bury half the world's polar ice cap.

This is just the first in the series of challenges 007 must survive to complete his mission in a film titled, for no discernible reason, A View to a Kill. This Bond looks like a tired Xerox of an old Bond. Everything about it seems recycled, like a tin can made out of old bottle caps.

For most people looking for a couple of hours to kill, the James Bond formula still works. 007 fans don't care much about coherence; they like to check out the latest stunts, toys and tootsies. There are plenty to go around in A View to a Kill, but they all seem to have been around before.

In this installment, Bond battles two villains: Christopher Walken as a grinning baby-faced billionaire industrialist named Zorin, and Grace Jones as his karate-chopping sidekick, May Day.

Zorin was the creation of a mad Nazi doctor who had a talent for injecting steroids into pregnant women in concentration camps during World War II. Zorin is the result of one of those experiments—a leering madman with dead eyes who plans to control the world's supply of microchips.

May Day looks like the Queen of the Astroid Zombies and has a mean temper. When she gets a hate on for some guy, she pulls the lever on a trap door in the bottom of the Zorin Industries blimp and drops him through the sky without a parachute. This is not the kind of gal you want to meet at Studio 54.

It is instantly obvious that these dorks are up to no good, but it is never clear why. The plot has something to do with those bloody microchips--the parts of a computer that are impervious to nuclear damage. This means that if Russia attacks the world, the man who controls the microchips is the only man whose toaster will still function.

Zorin plans to load up on these babies by destroying the Silicon Valley with an earthquake that will wipe out the state of California.

This may or may not be a good idea, depending on how you feel about the state of California, but not to worry. The plot of every James Bond movie is like the weather in New York City—if you don't like it, just wait a few minutes and it will change.

For thrills, he gets trapped in a burning elevator shaft, braves a flood on the San Andreas fault, and climbs down the side of a flaming building with a curvacious cutie on his back. Pinned underwater in a locked Rolls-Royce, he survives by sucking the oxygen out of the tires.

For toys, there's a pair of sunglasses that dilates into telescopic lenses, a credit card that unlocks sealed windows with electronic beeps, and a desk computer that runs instant identity checks on everyone in the world.

Roger Moore is suave, cool and well-groomed even when he's hanging upside down from the Golden Gate Bridge. Grace Jones hisses like a radiator and always seems to be sniffing uncomfortably, as though she smells some part of her anatomy on fire. The men are all fearless, the women brave, strong, gorgeous, sexy, and wearing all the wrong clothes for narrow escapes.

Practically everyone in the cast ends up drowned, electrocuted, dynamited, machinegunned, poisoned and shredded beyond recognition.

Different strokes for different folks. Including, Roger Moore. This was his final appearance as 007, and not a moment too soon.

THE WAR OF THE ROSES (1988)
★ ★ ½ Directed by Danny DeVito. Screenplay by Michael Leeson. Produced by James L. Brooks and Arnon Milchan. *With Michael Douglas, Kathleen Turner, and Danny DeVito.*

The War of the Roses is a ferocious black comedy about divorce, both funny and cynical. Kathleen Turner and Michael Douglas are the perfect mates whose marriage turns to frog manure and Danny DeVito is the lawyer who watches while their dream house turns into a series of battle zones that make Beirut look like a trip to Knott's Berry Farm. Most people going through divorce hell kill each other in court. This couple decides to stay at home and do it. As the cold war over community property escalates into open artillery fire, the movie loses some of its comic brilliance and turns sick. By the time she serves his favorite pâté and tells him it's his dog, I began to lose my sense of humor. But the three stars are marvelous—especially Turner. As an all-American homemaker hellbent on all-American revenge, she's a cross between Betty Crocker and the Spider Woman.

THE WHALES OF AUGUST (1987)
★ ★ ★ ½ Directed by Lindsay Anderson. Screenplay by David Berry. Produced by Carolyn Pfeiffer and Mike Kaplan. *With Lillian Gish, Bette Davis, Ann Sothern, Vincent Price, Harry Carey, Jr., Margaret Ladd, Tisha Sterling, and Mary Steenburgen.*

"Legend" is a word thrown around so often it's losing its meaning, but this subtle, warm, and poetic sonnet to old age stars two ladies who really live up to the definition. Miss Lillian Gish, ninety-two, and Miss Bette Davis, eighty, are two sisters sharing their last days together in their ramshackle house on the coast of Maine. Ann Sothern and Vincent Price, as their oldest pals, complete this quartet of senior citizens who form a bond of friendship as a last defense against Father Time. Add up their ages and you get several centuries of what great acting is all about. It's *On Golden Pond* reworked by Chekhov, with four virtuosos at the top of their form. Radiant as scented lavender candles, they prove that talent is ageless.

WHISTLE DOWN THE WIND (1961)

★ ★ ★ ½ Directed by Bryan Forbes. Screenplay by Keith Waterhouse and Willis Hall, based on the novel by Mary Hayley Bell. Produced by Richard Attenborough. With Hayley Mills, Alan Bates, Bernard Lee, Norman Bird, and Elsie Wagstaffe.

A group of scruffy, adorable children, led by gumdrop-eyed Hayley Mills, discover an escaped convict (Alan Bates) in a country barn and think he's Christ. Hiding him from the town in a manger, they discover, through faith and compassion, the meaning of Christmas. This remarkable allegory by Bryan Forbes is the kind of thing the British do better than anyone else, and this is a rare, offbeat classic that deserves a wider audience than critics who are always praising it but who can never find it playing anywhere except film festivals. Now available for home viewing, it's a real heart-warmer, refreshingly devoid of sentimentality.

WHITE CHRISTMAS (1954)

★ ★ ★ Directed by Michael Curtiz. Screenplay by Norman Krasna, Norman Panama, and Melvin Frank. Produced by Robert Emmett Dolan. Music and lyrics by Irving Berlin. With Bing Crosby, Danny Kaye, Rosemary Clooney, and Vera-Ellen.

Inspired by the phenomenal hit status of *Holiday Inn*, Bing Crosby and Irving Berlin teamed up again to make this holiday sugarplum the top money-making film of 1954. In this tinseled Technicolor entertainment, Crosby and Danny Kaye are a song-and-dance team who travel to a New England ski resort to stage a mammoth Christmas benefit and save their old army general (Dean Jagger) from bankruptcy. The show is a hit, snow falls on Christmas Eve, Crosby revives "White Christmas" and the boys end up in the arms of Rosemary Clooney and Vera-Ellen. As easy to take as eggnog.

WHITE HUNTER, BLACK HEART (1990)

★ ★ ★ ★ Directed and produced by Clint Eastwood. Screenplay by Peter Viertel, James Bridges, and Burt Kennedy. With Clint Eastwood, Marisa Berenson, Jeff Fahey, Alun Armstrong, and George Dzundza.

White Hunter, Black Heart is Clint Eastwood's brilliant, witty and exciting film version of Peter Viertel's book about the making of the 1951 film classic *The African Queen*, in which Big Clint gives the finest performance of his career as a thinly disguised John Huston, a world-famous director who was reckless, unconventional, and ruthless. Life, for Huston, was an endless quest for self-destruction. He was a mad genius—arrogant, egocentric, driven, obsessed. Pessimistic and trusting nobody, he used *The African Queen* location as an elaborate excuse to travel thousands of miles from civilization just so he could kill an elephant, with no regard for his film, his crew, or his stars, Katharine Hepburn and Humphrey Bogart. This movie makes no attempt to whitewash this rather despicable man. In fact, Eastwood (who also directed) impersonates his every flaw with a characterization eerie enough to transcend tricks of voice and manner, offering a larger-than-life figure of Huston, an artist and a bully. This film not only gets inside the heart of the man, but explores the expatriate nastiness, anti-Semitism and white fascism among the posh safari clubs and jungle camps of Zimbabwe in the early fifties. Marisa Berenson's Kate Hepburn is mischievously accurate and the magnetic Jeff Fahey is a wonderful Viertel, but the standout is Clint Eastwood. He finally hangs up Dirty Harry's brass knuckles and, like a born Olivier, grafts the skin of a new talent onto himself. One of the best films of 1990.

WHITE MISCHIEF (1988)

★ ★ ★ Directed by Michael Radford. Screenplay based on James Fox's book. With Sarah Miles, Joss Ackland, John Hurt, Greta Scacchi, Charles Dance, Susan Fleetwood, Jacqueline Pearce, Murray Head, Geraldine Chaplin, and Trevor Howard.

A real-life murder and sex scandal forms the backdrop of this fascinating true story about decadent Britishers in post–World War II Africa. Add glamorous women, adultery, sexual perversion, and all manner of depravity in juicy, graphic Technicolor and you've got every ingredient for ripe, exotic movie material. It's the story of Josslyn Hay, the Earl of Erroll (played by tall, blond, elegantly groomed Charles Dance), who had already seduced every man's wife in Kenya when he took on Lady Diana Broughton (Greta Scacchi). Their doomed and torrid affair ended a year later when Erroll was found shot through the head in his Buick, and Lady Diana's elderly husband went to trial for murder. The lurid trial is dull, but the rest of the film is fascinating. Lushly photographed and full of beautifully observed period details, it's like an X-rated *Great Gatsby*. In this florid atrium of sexual excess, where women shoot drugs and walk pet leopards on leashes, men dress in pantyhose and lipstick, and everyone swaps mates like poker chips, a picture of a bored, privileged, and immoral social register emerges with a great cast wallowing in perversion, including Sarah Miles, Geraldine Chaplin, Trevor Howard, and John Hurt. Shocking but never boring, *White Mischief* is one you'll walk away from with your mouth wide open.

WHITE NIGHTS (1985)

★ ★ ★ ½ Directed by Taylor Hackford. Screenplay by James Goldman and Eric Hughes. Produced by William S. Gilmore and Hackford. With Mikhail Baryshnikov, Isabella Rossellini, Gregory Hines, Helen Mirren, Geraldine Page, and Jerzy Skolimowski.

It must be a recurring nightmare every defected Russian dancer experiences—from Baryshnikov to Nureyev to Godunov. A commercial airline carrying a great international ballet star catches fire and crash-lands in a Soviet military airfield in Siberia. It is certainly an opening scene of pulsating excitement with which every filmgoer can identify. And it gets *White Nights* off to a smashing start.

An electrifying explosion of ballet, tap-dancing, and international intrigue, *White Nights* is a high-water mark in cinema—a film of dazzling inventiveness, stylish concepts, and nail-biting suspense.

In a role so specially designed for Baryshnikov's talents and personality it fits him like a pair of dance tights, the legendary ballet megastar plays Kolya Rodchenko, a Russian who was sentenced to prison when he defected to the West to broaden his cultural and artistic opportunities.

He's an American citizen now, but to his Russian captors, he's just a criminal. To brainwash Kolya with party-line propaganda and entice him to return to the Kirov, the KGB enlists the aid of Raymond Greenwood, a black American tap dancer from Harlem (Gregory Hines) who defected to

Russia after the Vietnam war and is now relegated to appearing in seedy productions of *Porgy and Bess*.

While the free world anxiously waits for news of Kolya's condition and whereabouts behind the Iron Curtain, Raymond moves into the ballet star's former Leningrad apartment in a desperate attempt to persuade him to return to the Kirov. If he cooperates, life will also improve for Raymond and his Russian wife Darya (Isabella Rossellini), who is frightened and pregnant.

Here we have a fascinating contrast in political ideologies—the Russian's American patriotism vs. the American's bitterness and cynicism. There's one marvelous scene in which Raymond tells his life story while tapping furiously and ragingly to a sweat-soaked climax.

Hatred gradually turns to friendship—an unspoken connection only two dancers can share. When the two finally break down their defenses and meld their different styles on the dance floor, it's very exciting stuff indeed.

Finally, with the rehearsal hall as their prison, Kolya and Raymond work out more than dance steps. Kolya plans a daring escape with the aid of his former lover and dance partner at the Kirov (heartrendingly played by the great British actress Helen Mirren) and Raymond and his wife join him.

The final third of the film sometimes challenges credibility, but you'll be on the edge of a hot seat waiting to see if (and how) one (or all) will make it to freedom.

White Nights works on many levels. As a dance film with majestic choreography by Roland Petit, Twyla Tharp, and Baryshnikov himself, it ranks with the most artistic achievements the screen has yet offered. As a spider's web of political treachery, it's a work of dark and chilling terror.

And it presents a sobering view of Russian life under Soviet rule, in which even the children are suspicious pawns in a horrifying game of chess, where even the privileged are prisoners and only the sentences differ.

The film has been brilliantly directed by Taylor (*An Officer and a Gentleman*) Hackford, one of the boldest and most talented of America's young directors. The screenplay by James Goldman and Eric Hughes is strikingly original.

And the cast is merely fabulous, from Baryshnikov, whose magnetism is outshone only by his genius as a dancer (when he dances he defies the laws of gravity and yoga), and Hines, to the stunning supporting cast.

Geraldine Page is wonderful as Kolya's American manager, full of good old Reagan rage and naive American indignity. Isabella Rossellini, a bruised fawn with indomitable courage, looks like a young version of her mother, Ingrid Bergman, and even sounds like her in early films like *Intermezzo*.

And there is a delightful surprise in Jerzy Skolimowski, the director who turns actor as the cool, suave, well-traveled KGB villain who pulls their strings.

The surging music and awesome dancing are skillfully meshed with the turbulence of incidents and characters, with great sensitivity to background and location, the elements all blending into one impression— that dance is the greatest détente of all.

WHO FRAMED ROGER RABBIT? (1988)

★ ★ ★ ★ Directed by Robert Zemeckis. Screenplay by Jeffrey Price and Peter S. Seaman. Based on *Who Censored Roger Rabbit?* by Gary K. Wolf. Produced by Robert Watts and Frank Marshall. With Bob Hoskins, Christopher Lloyd, Joanna Cassidy, Stubby Kaye, Alan Tilvern, and the voices of Charles Fleischer (as Roger Rabbit), Lou Hirsch, Mel Blanc, Kathleen Turner, Mae Questel, Tony Anselmo, June Foray, and Wayne Allwine.

They say inside every grown-up, there's a small child trying to get out. I found mine at *Who Framed Roger Rabbit?* and neither of us will ever be the same. Produced by Steven Spielberg and directed by Robert (*Back to the Future*) Zemeckis, this instant motion picture classic cost $45 million and lists more than a thousand artists in its technical credits and I am here to tell you—never has so much money, talent, and state-of-the-art technology added up to such a bargain. This is the most dazzling, exciting, entertaining, and original movie in years. Brilliantly conceived and executed, it is guaranteed to thrill but impossible to explain. Spielberg calls it "a tale of greed, sex, and murder in Toontown"—but it's more! You get the Hollywood studios, moguls, bit players and superstars of the forties, mixed with animated characters called "Toons." Roger's a "wacky wabbit" like Bugs Bunny, and the great Bob Hoskins is a human detective who tries to save him from a frame-up that could lead to the electric carrot. It's a sendup of forties cartoons and a satirical swipe at forties private-eye flicks, complete with real period cars, costumes, music and sets, mixing real actors with animation in ways that will make you spill your popcorn. The big finale has not only Disney characters like Bambi, Mickey Mouse, Donald Duck, and the Seven Dwarfs, but guest stars from other studios like Tweety Bird, Sylvester, Woody Woodpecker, Bugs Bunny, and even black-and-white Betty Boop—all singing "Smile, Darn Ya, Smile"! This is an extravagant, sensational blockbuster for anyone seven to seventy who's in love with the magic of movies.

WILDCATS (1986)

★ ★ Directed by Michael Ritchie. Screenplay by Ezra Sacks. With Goldie Hawn, Swoosie Kurtz, Robyn Lively, Brandy Gold, James Keach, Jan Hooks, Bruce McGill, Nipsey Russell, Mykel T. Williamson, M. Emmet Walsh, and Woody Harrelson.

Goldie Hawn's fresh naturalism, intelligence, and charisma enrich this otherwise familiar tale of a spunky divorcee coaching an all-male football team in the Chicago ghetto. The film, directed by Michael Ritchie, would be a yawn without her, but even when the material fumbles, Goldie scores a personal touchdown. The camera likes her. So do I.

THE WILD ONE (1954)

★ ★ 1/2 Directed by Laslo Benedek. Screenplay by John Paxton. Produced by Stanley Kramer. With Marlon Brando, Mary Murphy, Robert Keith, Lee Marvin, Jay C. Flippen, Jerry Paris, and Alvy Moore.

A weird, hopped-up, neurotic cult classic, this is the original biker flick. The young Marlon Brando burned a hole through the screen as the leader of a vicious motorcycle gang that invades a sleepy California town and brings havoc to the lives of its citizens. Brando is the brooding, angry, violent, smoldering thug every woman longs to tame, and the dumb subplot about how he's saved from self-destruction by the love of a cop's daughter almost wrecks the film—but it quickened the pulses of female viewers and made Brando a star. This was before he discovered Indians, Tahiti, and junk food.

WISE BLOOD (1982)

★ ★ ★ Directed by John Huston. Screenplay by Benedict Fitzgerald. Produced by John Huston and Michael Fitzgerald. With Brad Dourif, Amy Wright, Harry Dean Stanton, Daniel Shor, and Ned Beatty.

Every now and then there are compensations for spending your life in a screening room, because among the muck and the yawners you never know when a film with the passion of its convictions will come along to make you sit up and marvel. John Huston's *Wise Blood* is such a film.

For discerning audiences who worry and fret about films as art, it's encouraging. You might be disturbed by it, even infuriated, but certainly nobody will doze off, or have nothing to think about when it's over. Of course, if you're looking for a melt-in-your-mouth moral or syrupy sentiment, you'll do better looking elsewhere.

The haunting visions in *Wise Blood* spring from the first novel by the late Southern Gothic writer, Flannery O'Connor. And John Huston, at seventy-three, proved himself once again to be an American director of imagination and talent. (Huston has always been fascinated by Southern writers; he once turned Carson McCullers' *Reflections in a Golden Eye* into a unique film when everybody said it couldn't be done.) *Wise Blood* is difficult to adapt, too. O'Connor wrote almost no dialogue, and her searing, apocalyptic visions of religious obsession among the freaks and

misfits of small-town Georgia have always been notable for their literary music, not their visual action. But Huston has filmed *Wise Blood* anyway, and the result is awesome.

The story is about Hazel Motes, a peculiar soldier with madness in his eyes, who returns to his backwoods hick town determined to get out of uniform, get to the city, and as he says to a passenger on the train, "do things I ain't never done before."

Brad Dourif, as Hazel, brilliantly portrays a country boy in a kind of spiritual torment. His eyes, his voice, even his posture suggest someone frying in a state of moral isolation. Flashbacks show the past he's trying to escape, and the fanatically religious upbringing that has molded him into a weirdo. As a boy he had been convinced he was "unclean," a sinner, and guilty enough to walk with cinders in his shoes.

The adult Hazel is incensed when the cab driver, taking him to a whorehouse, ironically mistakes him for a preacher. Although he does commence preaching the gospel from the hood of his car, his dogma is that there is no sin in his "Church Without Christ," where "the blind do not see, the lame do not walk, and the dead stay that way.''

Nobody buys it. All he stirs up is the antagonism of a phony blind street preacher, the flirtations of his daughter Sabbath Lilly, and offers of comradeship from another displaced outcast, a half-wit boy obsessed with apes.

The more Hazel flails and kicks and raves against religion, the more we see his hopeless entrapment. His is the sad desperation of a lover fighting the only thing he loves. His losing battle finally ends after life does appear unclean and he commits a murder.

The performances in *Wise Blood* are remarkable. Brad Dourif sizzles with anguish. Amy Wright plays Sabbath Lilly, Harry Dean Stanton her despicable father, and Daniel Shor is the retarded boy who claims the ''wise blood'' of the title. They are wonderful eccentrics for this bizarre world.

Huston's direction is fluid and dramatic, with the sustained suggestion of a dream journey. Here the grim side of life takes on a kind of flourishing beauty under overcast, foreboding skies. Factories, vacant lots, trestles, and modern office buildings form a perfectly nightmarish backdrop for

the story of a man at odds with the universe.

Wise Blood makes no bid for box-office sweepstakes. It looks like it was made by people with no idea what commercial gimmicks are. That's a strength, and that innocence and passion are the ingredients that make it so unusually welcome.

WISH YOU WERE HERE (1987)
★ ★ ★   Directed and written by David Leland. Produced by Sarah Radclyffe. *With Emily Lloyd, Tom Bell, Jesse Birdsall, Geoffrey Durham, and Pat Heywood.*

Thank God for the British. They seem to be making better movies than anyone else these days. In one of the best British films in years, the pain and confusion of growing up gets new focus and insight in *Wish You Were Here*, a moody, funny, and striking study of a working-class student's sexual awakening in postwar England. It's a real gem. The girl is fifteen-year-old Lynda—perky, unloved, and so bored with the dull, provincial life in her ugly coastal town that she learns to attract attention by doing outrageous things for shock value. Her widowed father, a former Navy man who works as a barber, is cold and unaffectionate. Embarrassed by Lynda's foul mouth and flaunting sexuality, he sends her to a shrink, but the girl prefers to dance to swing tunes, kiss the boys, and show her legs like her movie idol, Betty Grable. So she moons the neighbors, feeds a condom to the dog, and wanders the streets wearing a German gas mask. An affair with a heartless bookie leaves this foolish girl pregnant, abandoned, and more determined than ever to be somebody. The decisions she makes to live life to the hilt and survive make for a funny, wise, and deeply affectionate film that is all the more riveting because Lynda is a real person. The movie is, in fact, based on the early life of London's notorious brothel keeper, Cynthia Payne, whose later fame was the subject of another bawdy British hit, *Personal Services*.

David Leland, the brilliant screenwriter of *Mona Lisa*, makes his debut as a director, developing his film from the first half of Cynthia Payne's biography, *An English Madam*. *Wish You Were Here* is blessed with the radiance of sixteen-year-old Emily Lloyd, a spontaneous, self-assured newcomer who is positively adorable.

THE WITCHES (1990)
★ ★ ★ Directed by Nicholas Roeg. Screenplay by Allan Scott. Produced by Jim Henson and Mark Shivas. *With Anjelica Huston, Mai Zetterling, and Jason Fisher.*

I've always had a taste for witches, offbeat director Nicholas Roeg has a taste for the bizarre, and the late Muppet-master Jim Henson had a taste for charm. Combine these tastes and you get a delicious film about modern-day witches that should thrill and delight kids from six to sixty who have ever had a taste for Halloween. A little boy named Luke (Jason Fisher) has been fed a lot of folklore by his Norwegian grandmother, beautifully played by the great Swedish actress Mai Zetterling. Vacationing in a gloomy resort hotel on the rocky coast of England, they find themselves in the middle of a witch convention presided over by Anjelica Huston. With her Louise Brooks bangs and German accent, she looks and sounds like a vamp from Hollywood in the thirties. But when the rubber mask comes off, she's the Grand High Witch—the meanest hag on earth, who plans to use poison candy to turn all the children in England into mice. Luke and his fat friend Bruno are her first victims, and when the two mice decide to save the children of the world from extinction, the result is chaos, fun, and thrills. *The Witches* is great fun to look at. Roeg shoots with wide-angle lenses from dizzying heights and odd perspectives, achieving lots of strange effects, as though the story is being told through the eyes of both children and mice. Rasping and coughing like a diseased vulture who knows the heartbreak of psoriasis, Anjelica Huston has a campy field day as the bald and horrifying head witch. The special effects by Jim Henson's Muppet crew are wonderful. An enchanting cinematic experience, strange and scary enough to fascinate and entertain both parents and children alike.

WITNESS (1985)

★ ★ ★ Directed by Peter Weir. Screenplay by Earl W. Wallace and William Kelley. Story by Wallace, Kelley and Pamela Wallace. *With Harrison Ford, Kelly McGillis, Josef Sommer, Lukas Haas, Jan Rubes, and Alexander Godunov.*

The time is now. The place is another world: the quaint Amish countryside in rural Pennsylvania—fertile, picturesque, strange, mysterious, insulated against twentieth-century noise and progress. What a perfect setting for a different kind of contemporary thriller.

That's what the people responsible for making *Witness* thought. They were right. *Witness* is a suspenseful thriller and a love story. It's exciting, riveting, beautifully directed by Australia's Peter Weir, exquisitely photographed and tightly written. It provides Harrison Ford with a solid role as the tough, sardonic Philadelphia cop who invades the peaceful Pennsylvania Dutch country to hide out from a bunch of vicious killers and falls in love with the sweet Amish widow who saves his life.

I liked it a lot, but I'm sorry to admit I find it a great deal less original than some of the other critics do. Look beneath the surface trappings and you'll discover that *Witness* has been made before.

It's a retread of a 1947 John Wayne movie called *Angel and the Bad Man*. In that offbeat Western, Wayne was an outlaw who got wounded, nursed back to health by a Quaker maid (Gail Russell, with those gorgeous moo-cow eyes), and subtly won over and rejuvenated by the homespun philosophy of the Society of Friends. But when the villains arrived to attack the hero and his girl, it was time for

Big Duke to forget pacifism and again reach for his Colt.

Witness updates the plot, changes the Quakers to Amish, replaces John Wayne's renegade triggerman with Harrison Ford's renegade cop, and turns a sagebrush saga into a modern action-adventure. But the scenario is the same. It's *Angel and the Badman* with four-letter words.

But what the hell. *Witness* is still a more engaging thriller than most, even if its ballyhooed "freshness" is a bit smelly around the edges. And to give credit where it is due, they have forged some new twists to an old saw.

Witness begins placidly enough. An innocent young widow (played with enormous conviction and understated strength by the beautiful and talented Kelly McGillis, a dead ringer for the late Jean Seberg) takes her small son Samuel (Lucas Haas) on his first train trip to visit a relative in Baltimore. During a change of trains in Philadelphia, the boy goes to the bathroom and witnesses a brutal murder.

Unwittingly, these poor, simple people are plunged into a world of gruff and mean-spirited outsiders, subjected to their laws, and regarded as oddballs in a society that is ironically much screwier than they are.

Since the child is a material witness, he must be detained. The cop assigned to the case is Harrison Ford, who is surprisingly terrific—tough, tender, bemused by these strange characters, sympathetic to their desire to get back to their horse and buggy, yet determined to do whatever he has to do to keep them as long as they can help solve the case. And the case turns heavy when the kid identifies the killer as a highly regarded narcotics agent. Worse still, Ford discovers that two other powerful law enforcers are part of the gang, and the leader is the head of the police department himself.

Soon the roles reverse. Wounded and half-dead, the big-city cop must enter the Amish world to hide out. The widow nurses him back to health with strange brews, teas, and home remedies. The neighbors protect him in their sealed-off world without cars, electricity, TV, or telephones. He learns how to raise a barn, milk cows before dawn, and discover the peace simplicity brings.

He also finds out about the prejudices and cruelties directed at these non-violent people by tourists and other outsiders, and in one effective scene, by defending his new friends against some local punks, he even breaks their laws and invites trouble from the police.

In a thrilling climax, when the villains arrive, the newly re-generated cop uses the farm and its alien environment to give the killers more than they bargained for.

I like the way this movie resists cliches. Even the love scenes turn out differently than you expect them to. Nobody does anything out of character for the sake of jazzing up the movie.

The widow doesn't run away from home and open up a Pennsylvania Dutch restaurant in downtown Philly, selling shoo-fly pie. The child isn't warped beyond his comprehension by his exposure to the violent ways of strangers. The cop doesn't repent and plant pole beans with cow manure. The inevitable shoot-out is itself different from and a notch or two superior to your garden-variety confrontation between heroes and varmints. And your attention will never wane.

THE WIZARD OF OZ (1939)

★ ★ ★ ★ Directed by Victor Fleming. Screenplay by Noel Langley, Florence Ryerson, and Edgar Allan Woolf. Produced by Mervyn LeRoy. With Judy Garland, Ray Bolger, Jack Haley, Bert Lahr, Margaret Hamilton, Frank Morgan, Billie Burke, Charley Grapewin, Cora Witherspoon, and the Munchkins.

The Wizard of Oz is one of the handful of honest-to-goodness movie masterpieces in all of film history that truly deserves the label. No child from six to sixty should be without annual exposure to this joyous milestone in movie musicals. It's a film for all seasons. Judy Garland in her ruby-red slippers dancing down the Yellow Brick Road, Ray Bolger as the scarecrow, Frank Morgan as the befuddled wizard, Jack Haley as the heart-melting tin man, Bert Lahr as the cowardly lion looking for courage, and Margaret Hamilton as the wicked witch are the stuff Hollywood legends are made of. And the Harold Arlen–E. Y. Harburg score, with "Over the Rainbow" as its centerpiece, is as sparkling and fresh as it was more than fifty years ago. I have seen this magical relic more times than I can count, and I always find something new and wonderful with each viewing. The world has grown up with *The Wizard of Oz*. Now that it is on videocassette, you can grow old with it, too. Whole books have been written in praise of every aspect of its production. It would be redundant to add anything more—except to say it's all true.

WORDS AND MUSIC (1948)

★ ★ ½ Directed by Norman Taurog. Screenplay by Guy Bolton, Jean Holloway, and Fred Finklehoffe. Produced by Arthur Freed. With Mickey Rooney, Tom Drake, Janet Leigh, Betty Garrett, Ann Sothern, Perry Como, Cyd Charisse. Guest stars Judy Garland, June Allyson, Lena Horne, Mel Tormé, Gene Kelly, Vera-Ellen, Gower Champion, and others.

What a mess. The Lives of Richard Rodgers and Lorenz Hart, fictionalized and gift-wrapped in star-studded Technicolor, is lavish corn. A cut above one of those "Ah, here comes Beethoven now!" "biopics" (who could forget Cornel Wilde as Chopin or Kate Hepburn as Clara Schumann?) but no less of a howler. There wasn't much of a story to begin with—Dick Rodgers was a nice man with one wife and two daughters who went from one hit to the next without much

fanfare. And Larry Hart, who was Jewish, miserable, suicidal, and gay, was played by none other than Mickey Rooney, who was Irish, an egomaniac, and such a womanizer on the MGM lot that Louis B. Mayer ordered saltpeter for his noodle soup to control his raging hormones. The picture had twenty-two song hits, fourteen stars, and a plot that suffered from elephantiasis; the critics called it a tumultuous turkey. (Casting Rooney as the tragic Larry Hart was like casting Bette Midler as Josephine Baker.) All that remains of interest now are the numbers: June Allyson, singing and prancing "Thou Swell"; Lena Horne undulating her way through "Lady is a Tramp"; Mel Tormé crooning "Blue Moon"; Gene Kelly and Vera-Ellen re-creating a surreal "Slaughter on Tenth Avenue" ballet; Judy Garland belting out a show-stopping "Johnny One Note." One thing about the splashy MGM days—when the stars were called, they twinkled brightly, even when nobody bothered to read the script.

WORKING GIRL (1988)

★ ★ ★ Directed by Mike Nichols. Screenplay by Kevin Wade. Produced by Douglas Wick. With Melanie Griffith,

Sigourney Weaver, Harrison Ford, Alec Baldwin, Joan Cusack, Philip Bosco, Nora Dunn, Oliver Platt, James Lally, Kevin Spacey, Robert Easton, Olympia Dukakis, and Ricki Lake.

Working Girl is about an ambitious brokerage firm secretary who dreams about Wall Street stock options instead of Macy's lingerie sales. It's the kind of role Judy Holliday and Jean Arthur used to play in their sleep. With them, you didn't care if they sounded like Baby Snooks. You knew there was a bear trap inside their pretty blond heads. With Melanie Griffith, it's more like cotton balls. Never mind. Director Mike Nichols knows how to make a ding-a-ling look like a pink-collar E. F. Hutton. Before chic boss-from-hell Sigourney Weaver can recover from a ski accident, Melanie's borrowing her tailored suits, attending her cocktail parties, and stealing her business mergers. Then she pulls off a $68 million deal and steals her boss' boyfriend, too. Never mind that it's all illegal or that Melanie is scarcely more than a ruthless liar and larcenous criminal. This is a fairy tale, a charming fable, and a crisp delight. Harrison Ford shows a light touch at comedy as the goofy boyfriend that is a nice cross between Andy Hardy and Ivan Boesky. It's slick, contrived, and wobbly as a Dow Jones average, but *Working Girl* is feisty and engaging fluff. It's done wonders for the sale of designer briefcases.

THE WORLD ACCORDING TO GARP (1982)

★ ★ ★ Directed by George Roy Hill. Screenplay by Steve Tesich. Produced by Hill and Robert L. Crawford. *With Robin Williams, Mary Beth Hurt, Glenn Close, John Lithgow, Hume Cronyn, Jessica Tandy, Swoosie Kurtz, and Amanda Plummer.*

The World According to Garp defies description because it lives in its own selfish, demented world and that world exists only in the heads of its oddball creators. I didn't read the oddball novel by John Irving, but I don't know anybody who has ever been able to describe the book, either.

Naturally, any attempt to turn any book by John Irving into a coherent movie is like trying to build the World Trade Center out of popsicle sticks. Yet I consider this one of the most unusual, imaginative, and deeply touching movie experiences I've had in a long time. God knows it is not for everyone's taste, but I think discriminating filmgoers will find plenty to chew on in this overloaded, complicated, slightly insane movie. It is undeniably controversial. You will not come away saying "So what!" to this one.

Director George Roy Hill tries to capture the iconoclastic inebriation of the novel by exploding *Garp* into millions of tiny atoms, some of them as big as scenes, others as small as facial reactions. Somehow they add up to a heartbreaking look at a lovable wacko and the violent, horrifying circumstances that keep wrecking his life.

T. S. Garp (magnificently played by Robin Williams in an amalgam of emotions tinged with comic force but eventually moving and tearful as any great clown playing Pagliacci) is first shown in the credits floating in his diapers through clear, cobalt-blue air. This floating feeling remains throughout, as Garp walks through life a few feet off the ground at all times, never quite touching the same dull earth the rest of us drag ourselves across.

Named for the "technical sergeant" who impregnated his mother in 1944, Garp later interprets his initials as "terribly sexy." Raised by his ferociously liberated mother, who works as a nurse in a boys' school, Garp grows up accident

prone, always in trouble, but determined to live up to Mom's philosophy: "Everybody dies —the thing to do is have a life before we do. That can be a real adventure!"

Garp, like the book's author, John Irving, excels at wrestling and writing. (Irving even makes a guest appearance as a wrestling coach.) There's an endearing scene in which Garp tries to write about something that has happened to *him*, while his mother stops lecturing about lust and the world going to hell long enough to write about what happened to *her*.

The friendly competitive spirit that is to last his whole life through is established early, coupled with a compassionate closeness that makes for one of the most bizarre but indelible mother-son love scenes ever captured on film. (Not since Edna Ferber's *So Big* has there been such an Oedipal complex.) When he moves to New York to become a "real writer," Mom moves with him. But his writing doesn't sell.

Mom, meanwhile, writes a sexy best-seller without knowing anything about sex and becomes the Gloria Steinem of her day. It is just one of the ironies that keep intruding on Garp's peace of mind. He can't sell beans, while her book is acclaimed as a political feminist manifesto and gets translated into every language including Apache.

The day he finds the honeymoon house for his new bride and forthcoming family, a plane smashes through the roof as a symbol of doom. Meanwhile, there are dog bites, hideous mutilations, an assassination, and a freak car accident involving his wife, who is performing oral sex on one of her English students at the time.

There is also a linebacker for the Philadelphia Eagles who has a sex change, a society of women who cut out their tongues to protest the mutilation of a child rape victim, a feminist funeral that turns into a riot, and so many sex scenes you wonder where Irving dreamed up Garp—in a bookstore or a brothel.

Through it all, Robin Williams is absolutely wonderful. He's a great clown, but he sublimates his goony tendency to revert to bird calls when faced with a serious silence between laughs, and a three-dimensional portrait of a comic victim of life's neurotic tango emerges that is hypnotic.

When he discovers his wife is pregnant, he draws a smile-button of a baby face on her stomach with a child's crayon in a scene so intimate and full of joy it made me weep. Mostly he is called upon to react to the terrible things everyone else is doing around him—and this is the hardest, most demanding kind of acting he has ever done. I think he's sublimely wonderful. So are Glenn Close, as Garp's tough, daffy mother; Mary Beth Hurt, as the wife who remains the calming center of his life even though his goodness drives her into a marital infidelity that almost destroys their happiness; and John Lithgow, as the football-playing transsexual.

All of these variables are orchestrated by director Hill with a frenzy resembling inspired madness. There is horrible violence everywhere, mixed with sentimental, old-fashioned idealism. To many, the combination will not work.

The World According to Garp is not like any other movie I've ever seen, so I don't really think it can be judged so easily. It is not a moral tale, although the people are completely moral in character and tone. It conveys states of mind so unique that they always seem to verge on disappearing inside their trapped world before the rest of us can digest them. *Garp* ends up being a frustrating voyage, but one well worth taking.

WUTHERING HEIGHTS (1939)

★ ★ ★ Directed by William Wyler. Screenplay by Ben Hecht and Charles MacArthur. Produced by Samuel Goldwyn. *With Laurence Olivier, Merle Oberon, David Niven, Geraldine Fitzgerald, Donald Crisp, Flora Robson, Hugh Williams, Leo G. Carroll, and Cecil Kellaway.*

Heated passions on the foggy Yorkshire moors may seem a bit loony by today's standards, but nothing dates Laurence Olivier's charged performance as Heathcliff. Merle Oberon is a wax zombie. Wind, rain, ghosts and Victorian hysterics make this Samuel Goldwyn spectacular a golden oldie that is beginning to show its tarnish.

THE YEARLING (1946)

★ ★ ★ Directed by Clarence Brown. Screenplay by Paul Osborn. Produced by Sidney Franklin. *With Gregory Peck, Jane Wyman, Claude Jarman, Jr., Chill Wills, Margaret Wycherly, Clem Bevans, Forrest Tucker, Henry Travers, and June Lockhart.*

Marjorie Kinnan Rawlings, the writer whose life story was memorably filmed in *Cross Creek*, won a Pulitzer Prize for this heartbreaking story of a small boy's pet deer and the tragic results when the pet grew into a nuisance that destroyed the family crops in the Florida backwoods. Gregory Peck and Claude Jarman, Jr., give durable performances as the deprived father and son who must make the choice between survival and a family pet, that alters their lives forever. Clarence Brown, the director of *National Velvet*, had a way with animals. The deer seems more human than Jane Wyman, who played the hard, rawboned mother with the veneer of a cypress stump.

THE YEAR OF LIVING DANGEROUSLY (1983)

★ Directed by Peter Weir. Screenplay by David Williamson, Peter Weir, and C. J. Koch. Produced by Jim McElroy. *With Mel Gibson, Sigourney Weaver, Linda Hunt, Michael Murphy, Noel Ferrier, and Bill Kerr.*

The critics had a swell time trying to label *The Year of Living Dangerously*, calling it everything from "Our Man in Jakarta" to "Java Jive." Why not call it a boring, incoherent mess, and get it over with?

This demented gibberish is set in Indonesia in 1965, the year Sukarno's regime collapsed.

Civil war is breaking out everywhere, and there is endless talk about Communist guerrillas, military coups, and the death of colonialism.

To people who know nothing about Third World politics—and that includes just about everybody—approximately ninety percent of the dialogue sounds like Swahili.

There are stops along the way for high-minded philosophizing about moral disorder, poverty, and love, before we get to the love story between an ambitious but naive Australian radio reporter (Mel Gibson) and a frosty British military aide (Sigourney Weaver) who works for the British Embassy and is probably a spy.

As baffling and wooden as these characters are, I would have settled for the love story, but it never comes off.

Aussie director Peter Weir is not really interested in the mismatched lovers. He's more fascinated by a repulsive Chinese midget—a scar-faced man who drones on incessantly, quoting Tolstoy and spraying the screen with pretentious narration that sounds like a master's thesis in political ideology. This creepy troll turns out to be played by a woman (American actress Linda Hurt, who won an Oscar).

There is no explanation for this arrogant conceit. In my opinion, it wrecks what little there is left of an already unbearable

disaster. No wonder they called the director Peter Weird.

Everything goes wrong. First, the movie is about the wrong war. Does anybody know where Jakarta is? Does anybody remember Sukarno? Does anybody care?

Worse still, Weir has managed the impossible feat of making svelte, statuesque Sigourney Weaver look positively homely. It's not enough that she's hopelessly miscast in a role that lacks definition and credulity. She's so badly lit and photographed that in one scene she even looks cross-eyed. Mel Gibson seems to be suffering from either malnutrition or malaria.

The less said about the Chinese dwarf with her hoarse, high-pitched voice, butch hobble, Arthur Godfrey shirts, and sinister babbling, the better.

There are too many pointless shots of people staring into space and walking in the rain. There's plenty of humidity, plenty of atmosphere, and plenty of platitudinizing, but none of it adds up to anything.

The film drags along aimlessly, its characters spouting ambiguous information that leaves them as baffled as the audience.

Movies that have nowhere to go tend to turn upon themselves, covering the same ground over and over, beating it flat. *The Year of Living Dangerously* takes on the circular shape of a zero.

YENTL (1983)

★ ★ ★ ½ Directed and produced by Barbra Streisand. Screenplay by Jack Rosenthal and Streisand. With Barbra Streisand, Mandy Patinkin, Amy Irving, and Nehemiah Persoff.

Before I saw *Yentl*, if anyone had suggested I might find appeal in a movie about a Jewish girl in a turn-of-the-century Russian ghetto who disguises herself as a boy to get into Hebrew school—well, I would have sooner opened a charge account at Bellevue.

You can't be too hasty about such things. The movie Barbra Streisand spent fifteen years of her life trying to get on the screen—the movie every cynic in the film industry told her could not be done—is a movie that takes you by surprise with its calculated warmth.

I guess your reaction to *Yentl* is pretty much going to depend on what you think and feel about Barbra Streisand. She *is* the girl she plays, and you'd better love her a lot, for she is never off the screen for more than a few seconds at a time in more than two hours.

She co-wrote the film, she produced it with a great deal of her own personal financing, and—most wondrous feat of all—she directed it herself. I call this a passionate commitment, and at a time in history when passion is the key ingredient missing from just about everything in life, I bow sincerely to the lady for that, if nothing else.

Fortunately, there is much, much more. The movie is like rye bread; you don't have to be Jewish to like it.

The story of *Yentl* is deceptively simple. We are in Eastern Europe, 1904, a time when the world of study in the Jewish faith was restricted to men. Women read storybooks and picture books. Men read about religion, philosophy, and politics. Any woman who studied the Talmud was considered a demon.

But Yentl is not like the others. "Go on—turn the world upside down and inside out—you'll never be happy," says her long-suffering father (Nehemiah Persoff).

Of course, we know from his first tubercular cough that this kindly old father will die, leaving Yentl to face a life of servitude and latrine duty. But this mule-stubborn free spirit is full of surprises. At her papa's funeral, she shocks the whole village by saying the Kaddish herself.

This is only the beginning. There are 2,555 pages of the Talmud to learn, and Yentl walks for miles with dogged determination to Hebrew school with her identity masked forever to become a yeshiva boy.

Her capacity for knowledge is great, but in addition to maintaining her equality among the other students, she must now also grapple with her inner feelings as a woman when sexual emotions are awakened in her for the first time by her best friend and fellow student Avigdor (sensitively and forcefully played by Mandy Patinkin).

Yentl loves him so much that she even marries the girl Avigdor pines away for but cannot have, just to make him happy. The scenes in which Yentl cleverly manages to capitalize on the wife's innocence and postpone consummation of the marriage vows are tender, funny, and endearing.

But it is later, when Yentl, consumed by the fire inside, reveals her true gender to the gentle Avigdor, that the film packs its undeniable emotional wallop. At last they realize how much they've loved each other, but the terrible irony is that once stripped of the role-playing that goes with gender, Yentl can never be the same.

Yentl's final confrontation with her own conscience gives the film its emotional core, and the story of the girl who dared to be different its poignant appeal.

If I have my reservations about *Yentl*, they focus on the musical interludes. There are ten songs and they seem endless, probably because the intelligent lyrics by Marilyn and Alan Bergman are all but decimated by Michel Legrand's slushy, sentimental, and downright banal music.

If dreams are conversations with ourselves, then the pensive ballads in *Yentl* are Yentl's dreams. Although the songs are never actually "performed" visually, they form inner dialogues and comment on the action. I understand Barbra's artistic decision to use this musical "device" to articulate Yentl's feelings and thoughts while trapped by her disguise, but eventually the poetry wears thin and you want the star to burst forth with one teensy-weensy show-stopper, just to remind us we're still in show business.

The star remains undaunted throughout. She is vulnerable. She is appealing. It never rains on her parade. In her baggy pants, suspenders, granny glasses, and yarmulke, Barbra often looks like Disney's Jiminy Cricket, but the love and dedication positively glow from within, giving her performance an inner radiance that has often been missing from her less inspired work.

The Czechoslovakian locations, with their mud puddles, fish markets, and bearded old men in heavy wool caps, rub a burnished patina on the Jewish canvas that resembles museum prints of old masters. The rich wheat and coffee textures in the cinematography by the brilliant David Watkin, who photographed *Chariots of Fire*, give *Yentl* the period flavor of fading, yellowed old newspaper clippings. The film looks buttered.

From the casting (it's the first time I've cared for the myopic Amy Irving) to the scenic design, *Yentl* has been born and raised with an almost fanatic regard for detail. It is rare to see a film nurtured with so much care. But finally, it is more than just a fable of ethnic struggle.

Yentl is about love and sacrifice and learning to stand up for what you believe in, even if it's painful. It is therefore not only a deeply personal film for Barbra (she dedicates it to her fa-

ther), but a delicate, lyrical film everyone else in the world can identify with as well (she also dedicates it to "all our fathers").

Ignored at Oscar time, Barbra winced when her detractors called this one *Funny Boy* and *Fiddler on the Patio*. Barbra survived. So did *Yentl*, which seems even warmer on home video.

YOUNG SHERLOCK HOLMES (1985)

★ ★ ★ ½ Directed by Barry Levinson. Screenplay by Chris Columbus. Produced by Mark Johnson. Executive producer Steven Spielberg. With Nicholas Rowe, Alan Cox, Sophie Ward, Anthony Higgins, Susan Fleetwood, Freddie Jones, and Nigel Stock.

With movies, as in life, the nicest surprises often come when least expected. Such is the case with *Young Sherlock Holmes*, a pleasant, surprising sugarplum from the Steven Spielberg factory.

Sir Arthur Conan Doyle was explicit in his writings about the first meeting between Sherlock Holmes, the fictional detective of Victorian London, and his friend and associate in solving crimes, Dr. Watson. They didn't meet until both were grown men.

But Spielberg and his team

of wildly imaginative producers, writer Chris Columbus, and director Barry (*Diner*) Levinson have taken literary license to come up with an affectionate speculation on what might have happened if these two mismatched sleuths had actually met years earlier, when they were teenagers. The result is a wicked, mischievous, and thoroughly captivating adventure film, chock-full of thrills, romance, nightmares, terrorism, narrow escapes, danger, and schoolboy splendor.

The story is told by John Watson, a doctor's son from the north of England, transferred to a new school in the heart of London where he meets and befriends the tall, skinny, angular-faced young Sherlock Holmes, already a master of logic and deductive reasoning whose skills baffled even Scotland Yard.

In addition to strange and sometimes harrowing academic rituals, Watson is introduced to a life of unconventional adventure as his new pal draws him into a lurid murder case that is unfolding right under their noses.

A mysterious cloaked figure haunts the schoolyard and the shadowy cobblestoned streets, blowing poisoned thorns from a blowgun into the necks of innocent victims. Once shot in this way, the human targets are seized by nightmarish hallucinations and sudden, violent death. Inanimate objects turn into vampire bats, snakes, hideous monsters, flesh-eating serpents. The trail leads back to the boys' friend Elizabeth, a pretty orphan who lives on the school grounds with her dotty uncle, a retired schoolmaster and nutty inventor who wouldn't harm a fly.

Young Sherlock first demonstrates his skill at perception by locating the school's stolen fencing trophy in sixty minutes. Then he moves on to the real crimes, with Watson as his reluctant sidekick. When Elizabeth's uncle become the third murder victim, the boys' clues lead to the discovery of the murder weapon, an ancient Egyptian blow-gun, a secret cult of devil worshipers, a Pharaoh's curse that goes back to the days of Osiris, the god of death, and a pyramid under the streets of London where kidnapped girls are turned into mummies by being boiled alive in red-hot paraffin. The perpetrator of these monstrous crimes is not only more elusive than Jack the Ripper, but living right in the school!

Meanwhile, Victorian London comes alive with its dark, sinister alleys, steaming pubs, and fog-enshrouded cemeteries. The elaborate sets are more than matched by the imaginative, eye-popping special effects. The thrills are nonstop, resulting in encounters with fiends that are terrifying, spooky, and even hilarious (everyone else under the spell of the Egyptian blowgun sees indescribable horrors; Watson sees French pastries coming to life that lead to whopping belly-aches).

Barry Levinson keeps the action moving at breakneck pace. Just when you think the filmmakers have exhausted all of their creative ideas, new hair-frying thrills are introduced, stockpiling plot twists and cliff-hangers until you are breathless from the suspense and excitement.

The cast of coltish newcomers is perfect. Nicholas Rowe, as young Sherlock, and Alan Cox, as the clumsy but charming Watson, are so physically right for their roles that you can imagine them growing up to be Basil Rathbone and Nigel Bruce, while Anthony Higgins and Susan Fleetwood are as evil a pair of villains as you'd ever hope to avoid in a foggy London alley.

Young Sherlock Holmes is the kind of movie you want to snuggle up to on a snowy night, a movie that would amuse Sir Arthur Conan Doyle and even the master sleuth from Baker Street.

ZELIG (1983)

★ ★ ★ ★ Directed and written by Woody Allen. Produced by Robert Greenhut. With Woody Allen, Mia Farrow, and interviews with Bricktop, Saul Bellow, Bruno Bettelheim, Irving Howe, John Morton Blum, and Susan Sontag.

Who is Leonard Zelig, and why is everybody saying these terrible things about him?

The answers, to be found in Woody Allen's *Zelig*, will leave you screaming. For critics and public alike who are generally disenchanted with Woody's recent films, *Zelig* renews all faith and restores his mantle as America's most brilliant funnyman. *Zelig* is a work of originality, eccentricity, and genius.

There is no other movie in history like *Zelig*; it is in a class by itself. As such, it is quite understandably next door to impossible to describe. Tiny white letters against a black screen prepare you only for the fact that a documentary will follow, and one of the high marks I give this film is for making me believe it. For at least fifteen minutes I actually thought I was watching a documentary about a historical person. It was some time before I realized I was being had.

Here's the content: Leonard Zelig was an odd little nerd who first came to public attention in 1928, as he rubbed elbows at elegant parties with celebrities, politicians, and kitchen help alike. He showed up at the World Series, sharing the baseball diamond at Yankee Stadium with Lou Gehrig, then vanished in the ensuing limelight. Was he embarrassed to be caught and labeled an imposter? Not at all. He was just wafting into somebody else's persona.

The documentary traces his whereabouts to Chinatown, where he actually had turned into a member of an old Oriental tong, then to a twenties jazz band, where he became a black trumpet player. Taken into custody, Zelig was sent to a psychiatric hospital, where a dedicated staff psychiatrist named Dr. Eudora Fletcher (Mia Farrow) extracted from him a lot of amazing Freudian double-talk, delivered quite fluently. Zelig, in the company of eggheads and shrinks, had turned into one of them.

What emerges from this point on is the diabolically hilarious story of a human chameleon—privately antisocial, suffering from a low self-image, but capable of miraculously turning into a myriad of disguises, depending on whom he's with at the time. He can become black, Chinese, or Jewish ("but not women or chickens"). He can sing Caruso's arias. He can stand next to an Indian and grow feathers. In the presence of obesity, he even swells himself up to 250 pounds. Leonard Zelig is a human changeling.

Dr. Fletcher devotes her career to turning poor Leonard into a normal person, but before she makes much progress, Leonard's alcoholic half-sister and her greedy boyfriend remove the patient from the hospital and turn him into an exploited freak. Overnight, he becomes a curiosity, an attraction, a geek more outrageous than anything dreamed up by P. T. Barnum.

Bricktop, who owned a famous Paris bistro in the twenties, is interviewed, recalling how Cole Porter even tried to write a song about him (he couldn't think of anything to rhyme with "Zelig").

In magnificently coordinated period newsreel footage, intercut with visual tricks, Zelig is shown with Herbert Hoover, Calvin Coolidge, William Randolph Hearst, Al Jolson, Josephine Baker, and F. Scott Fitzgerald. Zelig becomes the idol of Billy Rose, Clara Bow, and Pope Pius XI.

He's the perfect international celebrity, because he's a symbol of everything. And herein lies the message. Nobody can be this perfect to so many people without confusing people in the end. And when people are confused, they come after you with moral outrage.

What Woody is saying is, it's tragic to be a marketable public commodity, worse still when everybody loves you. Today's fans are tomorrow's lynch mob.

Zelig goes from the perfect exponent of human détente to the perfect scapegoat. Showgirls come out of the woodwork, claiming Leonard fathered their babies. Creditors descend upon him, suing him for every transgression in the book—bigamy, adultery, property damages, polygamy, fraud, and "unnecessary dental work."

Public clamor for his punishment reaches fever pitch. On the eve of his sentencing, he vanishes.

I won't tell you how it all turns out, but Leonard's final act involves great heroism and an escape from Nazi Germany, featuring a wild impersonation of Adolf Hitler by Will Holt that has to be seen to be fully appreciated.

Zelig succeeds on so many levels simultaneously that it's tough to praise it for only one accomplishment. Woody has made a movie that is really about something. On the surface, he might be telling the story of a zany schlemiel ("It shows what you can do if you're a total psychotic," philosophizes Zelig in the film) who learns to find his true identity through the love of a good woman.

Woody is also digging deeper into the dark recesses of the inner psyche to make some piercing observations about the agony of celebrity, the need to be accepted no matter what the risk, and the loneliness of the iconoclast in a society that is unabashedly fickle in its affection and openly hostile to what it does not understand. Like all Woody Allen movies, it's a movie about Woody Allen.

But what ultimately makes Zelig the best movie Woody has ever made is its breathtaking display of technical expertise: the music by Dick Hyman, the stark lighting, the wonderful cars, the floppy Police Gazette clothes, Gordon Willis's grainy black-and-white cinematography —even the scratchy sound is astonishingly re-created from period films, stills, and nickelodeons.

Working himself into old Fox Movietone newsreels where he actually stands next to headliners of the day, he succeeds where Steve Martin failed in *Dead Men Don't Wear Plaid*. Integrating contemporary interviews with Susan Sontag, Saul Bellow and others on the cumulative effect of Leonard Zelig's career on American history, he accomplishes what Warren Beatty tried to do in *Reds*—without the slightest hint of pretentiousness. And special praise must go to Susan Morse, who has managed a colossal editing job that richly deserved an Oscar, but didn't win one.

From a technical point of view, *Zelig* represents a feat of such marvel, it's stupefying. From every other point of view, it's a swinging, syncopated, documentary-style movie of matters and morals that explores new ways to broaden the horizons of cinematic art. Bravo, Woody. *Zelig* is an absolutely smashing film of voluminous wit, skill, virtuosity, intelligence, and imagination.

It begins with a ticker-tape parade down Broadway for the fictional Leonard Zelig. Isn't it about time we staged the real thing for Woody Allen?